THE
AMERICAN INDIAN
Prehistory to the Present

D.C. HEATH AND COMPANY   Lexington, Massachusetts   Toronto

THE

AMERICAN INDIAN

Prehistory to the Present

ARRELL MORGAN GIBSON

The University of Oklahoma

Title page photograph courtesy of the Peabody Museum, Harvard University. Photograph by Edward Curtis, 1910.

Maps and charts by Norman Adams.

Poem on page 578 from the *South Dakota Review*, Volume 7, Number 2 (Summer 1969). Copyright 1969 by the University of South Dakota. Reprinted by permission.

International Standard Book Number: 0-669-04493-8

Library of Congress Catalog Card Number: 79–84501

To
Rosemary

PREFACE

My rationale for writing *The American Indian: Prehistory to the Present* is twofold: to present a resource for courses and studies in American Indian history and to provide timely information and useful interpretation to the general public.

As Americans have become increasingly pluralistic, they have also become less satisfied with selective, limited literature about America's past. They have sought the broader, and often richer, history of America's unlike peoples and cultures, which are no less a part of our heritage. And they expect to know the full, unvarnished story. They have become less interested in the material-technological and institutional sagas of American development and more concerned with the human elements—particularly the non-European—of their national culture.

It is essential, however, that historians respond cautiously to the demands of America's many voices. Expanding interest in ethnic Americans has produced an ever-enlarging body of writing. Some of this literature has been good, but too much of it has been hastily done and is as chauvinistic as the earlier writings on American history that so many people had found abhorrent. Much of the recent Hispanic-American, Black, and American Indian literature has unfortunately been disputatious, exaggerated, and polemical rather than illuminating, informative, and useful.

Traditionally, historians have concentrated on the colonial and national phases of American history (1492 to the present). Recently, however, considerable research has been focused on American Indians. Archeology, anthropology, sociology, and social psychology, fused with history, have yielded interdisciplinary perspectives. The result has been an increased understanding of and appreciation for the Native Americans' 50,000-year-old genetic and cultural residency in the Western Hemisphere. Isolated from the influences of peoples from other continents, Indians made significant material and non-material contributions to modern American and world culture. These contributions are demonstrated in Chapter Twenty-two, "The Native American Legacy."

Most historians have largely overlooked or simply ignored evidence to the contrary and have portrayed the Indian as a bit player in the American historical drama. They have failed to account for the fact that the preoccupation of the colonial era, 1492–1776, was largely with the interaction of the Indian tribes and the European imperial nations. Most of the attention of early national, state, and territorial governments was absorbed in relations with the Indian nations. Certainly the day-to-day concerns of white settlers were with Indians, ranging from seeking security from reprisals for invading tribal lands to obtaining title to these lands. The activities of the national government, the basis for most American history in the period after 1776, were largely devoted to Indian matters, at least until almost 1900. Most of the treaties concluded by federal officials and ratified by the United States Senate up to 1871 were with the Indian nations. Congress was always concerned with Indian questions, including the appropriation of funds for Indian lands, annuities, and claims from settlers for damages from Indian attacks. Some of the most important United States Supreme Court decisions involved Indians and tribal questions. Above all else, *The American Indian: Prehistory to the Present* seeks to show the Indian's proper and deserved place in American history.

A.M.G.

CONTENTS

MAPS

THE
AMERICAN INDIAN
Prehistory to the Present

CHAPTER 1

THE HUMAN PRESENCE

Life...rests on five successive periods. Its first was...self-born. That was the divine spirit, the first cause, the desire to be. Then came the creation; the creation of being, the bringing into being of material things—the stars of heaven, the elements of earth and atmosphere, life in its elemental form, the desire to live and survive....The first earth's environment was one of mists— immaterial, unformed. The second was of water, with land portions floating on it. During this period all sea life was conceived and developed. The third stage brought the coming of animals and bird life of many kinds along with elemental human types. The fourth stage was a time of earth wandering, a search by Navajo forebears for a durable home. This was found; the land of turquoise skies. The fifth has been of gradual advance...of the Navajo people.

Navajo Creation Account

♥

The story of the American Indians is among the most intriguing in history. Indian presence in the Western Hemisphere, their rich culture, great variety of languages, and interesting life-style have captivated scholars for centuries. Indians have been the subject of continuing investigation, study, and analysis, first by theologians and philosophers and more recently by scientists who apply increasingly sophisticated concepts and technology to understand Indian presence and the evolution of their culture and life-style.

One of the most persistent questions through the centuries has been the origin of Indians and their presence in the New World. A second question and, like the first, not yet answered to scholars' complete satisfaction, is how their culture evolved, isolated as Indians were from Euro-Asian-African developments. In earlier times the question of Indian status and worth was a subject of considerable concern. Christian newcomers scorned native religion, rejecting it as pagan heathenism. Christian theologians debated whether Indians were worthy of or even capable of salvation. Another major question has been "for how long" have the Indians lived in the Western Hemisphere. The first Europeans speculated that Indians had occupied the New World for only a few hundred years. This estimate was gradually increased to over 3,000

Chapter Opening Artifact: Male and female creation effigies on a ceramic bowl—New Mexico Indians. (Courtesy of Museum of the American Indian, Heye Foundation)

years and to 5,000 years around 1900. Since the 1940s, research based on archeological evidence has extended the time of the original presence of the ancestors of the American Indian in the Western Hemisphere to 50,000 B.C.

THEORIES OF INDIAN ORIGIN

Thus, American Indians may have lived in "splendid isolation" for as long as 50,000 years. Near the dawn of modern times Scandinavian mariners visited tribes along the North Atlantic coast, but they seemed to have no genetic or cultural effect upon the Indians. Then around 1500 Spaniards, followed by the French, English, Dutch, and Russians, established permanent settlements on the American continent. Their arrival dramatically changed the established Indian way of life and affected the fate of Native Americans into the twentieth century.

In 1492 Christopher Columbus, an Italian navigator in the service of Spain, sailed west across the Atlantic Ocean, searching for a direct water passage from Europe to India. Columbus anchored his three-ship squadron off an island he calculated to be near India. As a result, Columbus called the hospitable natives Indians. Cartographers later identified Columbus' landfall as Watling Island, part of an archipelago near a vast continent they named America. But Columbus' misnaming of the American natives became the European designation for them.

Monogenesis Versus Polygenesis

Tidings of Columbus' discovery—a new continent populated by exotic people—tantalized scholars in Spain, France, Portugal, and England. They engaged in a sustained debate, speculating on the origin of the native people Columbus called Indians. Most scholars accepted the *monogenesis* ("one-beginning") theory, which maintained that American Indians were connected with known human sources in Europe, Asia, and Africa, their cultures simply extensions of Old World civilizations. They contended that Indians were the result of the same single act of creation as all other people.

On the other hand, several scholars concluded that God had created a second Adam for the New World—that the biblical account of creation referred only to the Old World—and thus the native people of America were the result of a separate, local creation. This position on the origin of the American Indian is called the *polygenesis* ("many-beginning") theory.[1]

While monogenesis advocates held that American Indians were created in common with the people of Europe, Asia, and Africa, they held different views about the Indian's precise geographic origin. Some of these scholars believed the Indians were descended from Phoenician mariners who had ventured far off their familiar Mediterranean sea routes. Another group contended that the American natives were descendants of Welsh people led

3

by the legendary Prince Madog to the New World in an earlier age. Some speculated that ancestors of the American Indian were from Egypt, the Orient, the Lost Continent of Atlantis, or from Carthage.

Gregorio Garcia, a Spaniard who lived for several years in Peru and other New World colonies, contended that because of the cultural and physical differences he had observed among the Indian tribes, particularly the diversity of their languages, their ancestors must have come from many different places including Egypt, Carthage, the Orient, Atlantis, and probably many from Israel. José de Acosta, also a Spanish scholar, published a treatise in 1589 which stated that American Indians had originated in Asia. He speculated that at one time the continents of Asia and North America were connected by a land causeway. Ancestors of the American Indian, of Asian-Mongol stock, had migrated from northeastern Asia to the Western Hemisphere over this land bridge.

The Israelic Connection

In 1567 Lumnius published *De Extremo Dei Judico* in Antwerp. He exulted in answering one of the most mystifying questions of the ages: What happened to the Ten Lost Tribes of Israel? Lumnius concluded that Columbus' discovery of people in the New World provided the answer—the Lost Tribes had crossed the Atlantic Ocean to America. The Ten Lost Tribes theory became the most popular view of the origin of the Indians.

Between 1600 and 1800 many Europeans in America studied Indian culture and observed that numerous Indian tribes practiced what they believed were Jewish customs, such as first-fruit ceremonies, sacrifices, feasts, exorcisms, purification rites, fasting, and food taboos. These Indian practices, in their view, confirmed Lumnius' thesis that American Indians were descended from the Ten Lost Tribes of Israel. Cotton Mather, William Penn, and James Adair accepted Lumnius' view. Adair reinforced the popular acceptance of the Israelic connection with his book *The American Indians*, published in London in 1775. He recounted in this book his life among the tribes of the lower Mississippi Valley and found "conclusive evidence" to support the Ten Lost Tribes theory. During the nineteenth century the Irish nobleman Viscount Kingsborough spent many years and a fortune in a devoted attempt to prove that the Ten Lost Tribes of Israel and the Indians of Central America and Yucatán were related. The Israelic connection perseveres into the twentieth century in the doctrine of the Church of Jesus Christ of Latter Day Saints. The *Book of Mormon* explains that Indians are descended from the Lamanites, a "degenerate element" among the Jews.

Tribal Views of Indian Origins

Although none of the Indian tribes in the territory that later became the United States had developed a system of writing, each tribe had formed a traditional history passed down orally generation by generation. Most Euro-

DEI IVDICIO, ET
INDORVM VOCATIONE
L I B R I II.

Authore *IOAN. FREDERICO LVMNIO.*

DEVTERO. XXXII.
Iuxta eſt dies perditionis, & adeſſe feſtinant tempora.
MATTH. XXIIII.
Et niſi breuiati fuiſſent dies illi, non fieret ſalua omnis caro.
MARC. XIII.
Videte, & uigilate, & orate, neſcitis enim quando tempus ſit.

VENETIIS,
APVD DOMINICVM DE FARRIS. 1569.

Title page from Lumnius' *De Extremo*, which introduced
the Lost Tribes of Israel theory. (Permission of the
Houghton Library, Harvard University)

peans migrating to the New World had a strong sense of their own superiority
and held Indians and their culture in low esteem. Since the Indian viewpoint
was pagan and therefore unreliable, Europeans scorned and ignored it as a
source to explain tribal origins. And because Indian accounts of creation and
migration did not correspond with anything in the Christian tradition, they
were labeled as mere myths, legends, and folktales, even though many were
no less likely than many hallowed biblical accounts. Thus it rarely occurred to
any of the European immigrants to ask Indians for their views on their origins.

As a matter of fact, each tribe had, and many continue to preserve and
transmit, a rich tribal tradition including creation and migration stories.
Virtually every traditional tribal history includes an epic of creation from
earth—"the mother"—and other natural elements and an account of a flood
and a long migration. The migration is generally from the "land of the setting
sun," although some tribes claim to have come from the North or South, and
a few from the East.

5

RECONSTRUCTING THE PREHISTORIC CHRONICLE

In recent times the task of explaining the origin and development of the Indian tribes and their cultures has largely shifted from theologians and philosophers to scientists. Not having a written record, these scientists have turned to nonliterary sources to reconstruct the pre-Columbian past.

Scientists who study American Indian prehistory are professional archeologists or anthropologists. They start with several assumptions. One is that American natives had no system of writing before 1492. This year marks the end of their prehistoric and the beginning of their historic age because with the coming of Europeans there were written records (diaries, letters, journals, and reports) concerning America and the Indians. The pre-Columbian Age (before 1492), on the other hand, must be reconstructed through the study and analysis of archeological evidence. Besides the lack of an Indian written historical record, the archeologist or prehistorian faces the additional problem of destruction of important archeological evidence by people and by nature. Vandals ruthlessly loot archeological sites for personal artifact collections and for sale to dealers. Environmental conditions also progressively destroy archeological evidence. The generally mild, variable climate of North America, with alternating seasons of hot and freezing temperatures and precipitation in various forms, has destroyed much valuable archeological evidence in most of the United States except the dry Southwest.

A second assumption the scientists make is that human existence in the Americas did not begin as recently as was earlier assumed. Each year the discovery of new archeological evidence has extended human presence back from 3,500 or 5,000 years ago to 15,000 years ago—now a conservative view— to 25,000 to 40,000, or perhaps even 50,000 years ago.

An example of new evidence that challenged the conservative prehistorian's estimate is the 1973 report of an archeological excavation near Puebla, Mexico. Geologists found in a local stream bed

relatively sophisticated stone tools ... that they dated by several techniques as about 250,000 years old.... The main problem with that finding [that man may have lived in North America 250,000 years ago is that] the tools were considerably more advanced than the tools used in Europe and Asia 250,000 years ago.... The least sophisticated of the tools found at the Mexican site were of a type used in the Old World 35,000 to 40,000 years ago.... [They concluded] we are painfully aware that these results deepen the dilemma already recognized that so great an age for man in the New World is archeologically unreasonable, especially for artifacts of such sophisticated workmanship.[2]

Unlikely as it seemed to these geologists, the sophisticated, ancient tools were most likely used by the ancestors of the American Indian.

A third assumption is that ancestors of the American Indian migrated to the Western Hemisphere because evidence of subhuman types from which modern Indians could have evolved has not been found here. Yet another prehistorian's assumption is that the American natives lived in virtual isolation from

6

An inscription on Dighton Rock, believed to be an early pictograph done by Indian ancestors.

Europe, Asia, and Africa until 1492. Evidence includes the American Indian's high susceptibility to measles, the common cold, tuberculosis, and other diseases common to the other continents. All of these assumptions provide archeologists and anthropologists with a useful foundation for analyzing remains of Paleo-Indian (prehistoric) material culture.

Interdisciplinary Application

To find these remains, prehistorians search out pre-Columbian sites and excavate and retrieve tools, weapons, ceramics, textiles, and art pieces. They assign dates to the material and develop the archeological record through analysis, synthesis, and interpretation of the artifacts. Their informed judgment helps them understand the social, religious, and political aspects of life-styles during the Paleo-Indian, or Stone Age, period in America.

Increasingly, prehistorians use the resources of other disciplines to refine concepts and to cast additional light on the unrecorded past. They have turned to meteorologists, geologists, chemists, botanists, zoologists, physicists, linguists, ethnologists, and paleontologists for supporting information on prehistoric evidence. Paleontologists supply important data on extinct animals (such as the Columbian mammoth, mastodon, and primordial bison) that Paleo-Indians hunted. Geologists assist in dating archeological evidence by studying related glacial movements, site stratigraphy (rock layers), and layers of silt at the bottom of now-dry lakes. Ethnologists reconstruct ways of life of extinct cultures from their study of existing primitive cultures. Other scientists study seeds, plants, ceramics, and bones taken from prehistoric sites and the site environment, including soil and climate.

Techniques for Analyzing Paleo-Indian Material

From the interdisciplinary approach has come a wide range of techniques and methods that yield essential information, including dates, on material excavated from Paleo-Indian settlement sites. *Stratigraphy,* a geological dating

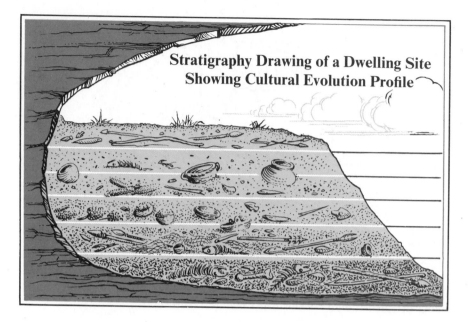

Stratigraphy Drawing of a Dwelling Site
Showing Cultural Evolution Profile

technique, is the study of the order and relative position of the strata or layers of the earth's crust. Its value to Indian prehistory is in the principle that layers of earth are laid down slowly through time, the earliest or oldest layers being the deepest and each successive layer relatively younger or more recent. Objects can be dated by noting the layer in which they are found. Stratigraphy provides relative rather than absolute dating. Using this simple principle, prehistorians have applied stratigraphy to the analysis of profiles of cultures exposed in cave and ledge floors, sometimes eight to ten feet deep. The record of each successive culture or habitation level is separated by a layer of soil.

Carbon 14 dating is a widely used method for determining the age of Paleo-Indian material. Carbon 14, a radioactive element or isotope, is present in all living plants and animals. When a plant or animal dies, carbon 14 decay begins and continues at a fixed rate that can be measured. Analysis of bone, wood (including charred wood in ancient campfires), horn, hair, and shell objects by the carbon 14 test measures the amount of carbon 14 isotope present and yields an approximate age with a possible error of two hundred years either way. The limit for measuring carbon 14 loss is 50,000 years; beyond that age, carbon 14 loss in an object is complete.

Dendrochronology, or tree-ring dating, is another widely used method for dating Paleo-Indian material, particularly in the arid American Southwest. This method uses a tree-ring calendar, formulated on the principle that each ring in the trunk of the tree represents one year's growth. Not all trees can be used for dendrochronological dating because some do not form a ring each year. Most pines, fir, spruce, red cedar, juniper, and sagebrush are reliable, but yellow pine is rated the best "time keeper." The tree-ring calendar is applied to charred pieces of wood from ancient campfires and wooden beams used in Paleo-Indian dwellings and ceremonial buildings. Some calendars permit dating back to nearly 3,000 years.

Archeomagnetism is another method used to date prehistoric material, particularly ceramics made from clays containing oxides of iron. Metallic particles in these clays, when heated to high temperatures in a pottery kiln, will, on cooling, freeze or set in a magnetic field keyed to magnetic north of the time of heating. Since the location of magnetic north is a known variable that can be charted through time and since the oxides of iron will acquire the current magnetic declination from true north when the clay is fired, the date of manufacture can be determined. Dates provided from archeomagnetic calculation generally agree with dates from carbon 14 tests.

Glottochronology is the technique used to determine the age of a particular culture from characteristics of its language. Linguists have found that languages go through predictable changes—they tend to lose words in what is called language erosion. The rate of change, about 19 percent of the original words lost each thousand years, has been calculated and is predictable. Glottochronological analysis of American Indian languages indicates that the many tongues spoken in 1500 required at least 15,000 to 20,000 years to evolve.

Other methods or techniques used by prehistorians to study Paleo-Indian cultures are *obsidian hydration* and *ethnology*. Obsidian, volcanic or natural glass, was a favorite material among the Indians for making sharp-edged tools and weapons. Scientists have found that obsidian absorbs water at a constant rate; thus one can determine the age of the tool or weapon by matching the measured amount of water absorbed with standard hydration tables. Ethnology is another useful technique for analyzing past cultures. Ethnologists reconstruct unknown past ways of life by using as a guide what is known of existing primitive cultures.

The Indian Viewpoint

Indians have assisted archeologists and anthropologists in reconstructing the prehistoric chronicle by relating tribal traditions. In preliterate times honored elders were expected to retain knowledge of the tribe's history and teach it orally to younger members of the tribe. In several of the surviving Indian nations, tribal elders continue to fulfill this special tribal function. Like the acknowledged talent for great oratory and debating, the Indians' ability to recall tribal history precisely and to transmit it accurately is a way of compensating for lack of a written language. French Jesuit missionaries working in the seventeenth century among the tribes of the Old Northwest were awed by the tenacious memories of Native Americans, noting their "marvelous faculty" for remembering events and places and their ability to relate this information to others. These clerics declared that Indians could recall matters that Europeans would have to write down to remember.

From earliest times a few European investigators respected Indian culture sufficiently to ask tribal spokesmen about the pre-Columbian past. James Adair interviewed Choctaw, Chickasaw, and Creek spokesmen in the 1760s and used their responses as the basis for his widely read *The American Indians.* Henry R. Schoolcraft and Lewis Henry Morgan continued this practice during the nineteenth century, using information from Indians as the basis for their writings. In the early part of this century James Mooney, John R. Swanton, and other Bureau of American Ethnology staff members interviewed tribal leaders and recorded their testimony in Reports and Bulletins published by the bureau. And in more recent times academic specialists from colleges and universities in states with large Indian populations have collected Native American oral traditions under the auspices of the Doris Duke Indian History Project.

From the application of advances in modern science and technology to prehistory combined with the Indian viewpoint, the facts about the prehistoric age are much clearer and more satisfying than even a decade ago. Some of the perplexing questions this integrated approach answers include, "From whence did the American Indians' ancestors come?" and, "How did they disperse over the American continent?"

PIONEER AMERICAN SETTLERS

Evidence presently available indicates that most ancestors of American Indians migrated to the American continent from northeastern Asia during the prehistoric age. At no time, however, was there a large-scale or sustained migration. For the most part the pioneer settlers of the New World came in small groups, families, and bands of hunting people. Some came by land, others by water. The migration extended over a period that began perhaps 50,000 years ago and concluded as recently as 2,000 years ago. The geological history of North America had important effects on the pioneers' experience in settling the new land.

The Exotic Environment

Before 8000 B.C. the North American environment was quite different from what it is today. The era from about 75,000 years ago to about 8000 B.C. is called the Pleistocene or Ice Age. Huge glaciers formed a deep ice cap that covered much of the northern half of the Northern Hemisphere. The Pleistocene Age had several far-reaching effects on the climate of North America, a major factor for the aboriginal pioneers settling the new land.

First, it interrupted the hydrologic or water cycle. The natural, cyclical moisture pattern for the northern latitudes begins over the oceans. Air currents pick up water vapor and transport it to land where it precipitates as rain, sleet and snow. The moisture on the land eventually drains into rivers and returns to the oceans to continue the cycle. The formation of glaciers in the northern latitudes during the Pleistocene Age broke this chain. Moisture vapor carried from the oceans and precipitated over the land was caught and locked into the glacial ice cap. Through the millenia the ice cap eventually reached an average height of one mile and in some places accumulated to a height of over 9,000 feet. Centered over Hudson Bay, the Pleistocene ice cap covered much of the northern latitudes, extending southward into the northern portions of the present United States.

The second effect was a result of the first. The Pleistocene ice cap created the means by which the pioneers could reach the new land. And it perhaps answers in part the perplexing question of aboriginal origin and confirms Acosta's theory that the Indian's forebears migrated from Asia by way of a land bridge from Asia to the Western Hemisphere. The basic shape of North America, including the Bering Strait, was formed eons before the Ice Age. The strait separates Alaska's Seward Peninsula from the eastern shore of Siberia by fifty-six miles of water, but it is broken by the two Diomede Islands, so that the longest stretch of water is only twenty-six miles. However the Indians' ancestors' of 25,000 to 50,000 years ago had not yet developed boats. At that time they were still carrying the simplest stone tools and clubs. The Pleistocene ice cap, by locking in vast quantities of water, eventually caused the level of the ocean to drop an estimated 250 to 300 feet. This exposed the land across Bering Strait, which is only 180 feet deep, and created a wide natural bridge, called Beringia, into Alaska. Hunter families from Asia could then easily cross Beringia into Alaska. Also, at that time much of the Bering Strait area and Alaska's interior were free of ice, and an ice-free corridor extended diagonally from the Arctic Circle into the American Southwest along the base of the Rocky Mountains.

The third major effect of this southward extension of the Pleistocene ice cap was to produce a very different type of climate in the rest of continental United States from that of today. Today's interior arid plains and deserts were, 50,000 years ago, a milder, cooler, and considerably wetter region of lush savannas, dense forests, and lakes, swamps, and bogs. The coarse savanna grasses sustained exotic wildlife—Columbian mammoths (elephantlike creatures with huge tusks), mastodons, giant primordial bison, and small horses and camels. This was the environment that greeted America's first settlers, the ancestors of the American Indian.

Populating the New Land

Ancestors of the American Indian may have reached the New World from several directions at various times in the past, but evidence mustered thus far strongly supports the thesis that the first important access into the Western Hemisphere was from Asia via Beringia. This archeological evidence from eastern Siberia, Alaska, and along the ice-free corridor into North Amer-

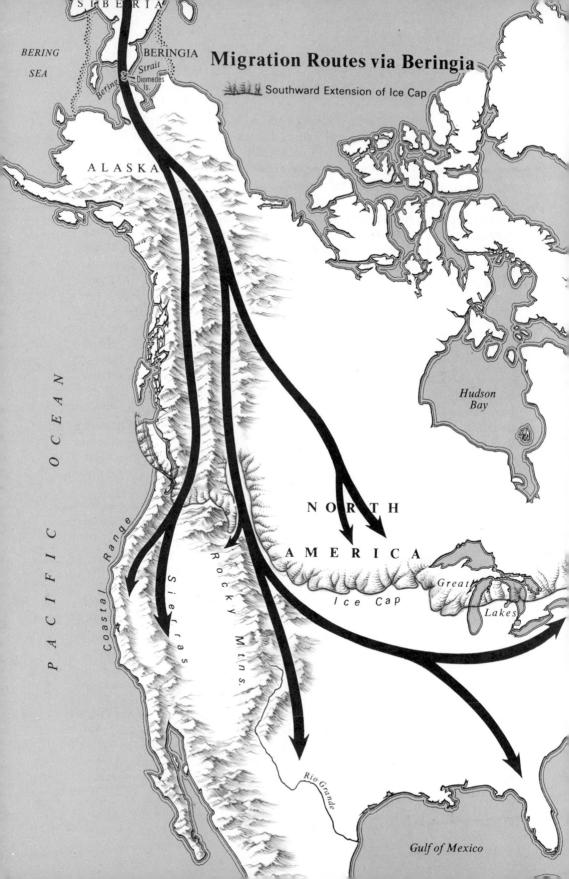

Migration Routes via Beringia

Southward Extension of Ice Cap

*BERING
SEA*

SIBERIA

BERINGIA

Bering Strait

Diomedes Is.

ALASKA

PACIFIC OCEAN

Coastal Range

Sierras

Rocky Mtns.

N O R T H

A M E R I C A

Ice Cap

Great
Lakes

*Hudson
Bay*

Rio Grande

Gulf of Mexico

ica's continental interior indicates that Beringia was the principal source of migration. Prehistorians also have traced migration routes south of the ice cap over which pioneer hunting families spread east to the Atlantic, west to the Pacific, south into the Mississippi Valley, and finally into Mexico and Central and South America.

The date of the first migration from Asia into America is not settled, but it has been progressively moved back as archeologists find and analyze new evidence of early human presence in the Western Hemisphere. The conservative documented view for first arrival is about 15,000 B.C. However, evidence found in caves in the Southwestern United States suggesting human occupation as early as 20,000 to 25,000 B.C. challenges that conclusion. Populating the Western Hemisphere from Beringia to the Straits of Magellan at the southern tip of South America, a distance of 11,000 miles, was a slow process extending over many thousands of years. Archeological findings in the ancient camps in Fells Cave in southern Chile confirm the slowness of this southern movement. The finds from Fells Cave have a carbon 14 date of 8000 B.C.

Migrations Away from America

The wanderlust of the ancestors of American Indians continues to amaze many historians. Having traced the migration chronicle, archeologists are now studying the possible Indian role in populating islands in the Atlantic and Pacific oceans. They have established that Indians settled the islands of the Caribbean quite early. Their role in populating the islands of the Pacific is less certain. Tribes on the Pacific Northwest coast in pre-Columbian times developed large, seaworthy double canoes, and scientists are now speculating on the possibility that Hawaiians might be a mix of Polynesians and mariner Indians. Most recently the Kon-Tiki epic, an Indian tradition linking Native Americans with Pacific island peoples, has been the specific object of investigation. The epic relates how, in prehistoric times, the Peruvian sun king Kon-Tiki and a band of followers were driven out of South America. The émigrés traveled on balsa rafts to Pacific islands. Archeologists believe that the stone figures in Peru and similar ones on Easter Island are of the same prehistoric technology. In 1947 Thor Heyerdahl, copying ancient Peruvian marine technology, constructed a balsa raft and sailed westward from the Peruvian coast, using trade winds and equatorial currents to proceed from island to island. He relates his adventures in tracing the Kon-Tiki story in the travel classic *Kon-Tiki: Across the Pacific by Raft*, published in 1950.[3]

Scientific techniques and reconstructions have illuminated ancient migration and settlement patterns. Archeologists and anthropologists also have applied these methods to the study of Native American material (artifacts) and non-material (institutions, values, religion) culture. Their investigations trace the progression of the Indian's ancestors from wandering hunters to settled tillers of the soil. This transition is the subject of Chapter Two.

Notes

1. Dwight W. Hoover, *The Red and the Black* (New York, 1976), p. 9.
2. *New York Times*, November 18, 1973.

3. Thor Heyerdahl, *Kon-Tiki: Across the Pacific by Raft* (Chicago, 1950).

Selected Sources

Survey works on North American prehistory that describe archeological technology and conceptualization and explain the migration and diffusion of American aborigines include Robert F. Spencer, Jesse D. Jennings, et al., *The Native Americans: Prehistory and Ethnology of the North American Indians* (New York, 1965); Jesse D. Jennings, *Prehistory of North America* (New York, 1974); C. W. Ceram, *The First Americans* (New York, 1971); Kenneth MacGowan and Joseph A. Hester, Jr., *Early Man in the New World* (New York, 1962); George E. and Gene S. Stuart, *Discovering Man's Past in the Americas* (New York, 1969), and Gordon R. Willey, *An Introduction to North American Archeology* (Englewood Cliffs, N.J., 1966), Vol. 1.

Analysis and interpretation of European viewpoints of Native Americans are presented in Dwight W. Hoover, *The Red and the Black* (New York, 1976); Peter Farb, *Man's Rise to Civilization* (New York, 1968); Edward H. Spicer, *Cycles of Conquest* (Tucson, Ariz., 1972); Lee E. Huddleston, *Origins of the American Indians: European Concepts, 1492–1729* (Austin, Tex., 1967); and Robert Wauchope, *Lost Tribes and Sunken Continents: Myth and Method in the Study of American Indians* (Chicago, 1962).

CHAPTER 2

NATIVE AMERICAN CULTURAL FOUNDATIONS

The Master of Life has given us hands for the support of our men, women, and children. He has given us fish, Deer, Buffaloe, and every kind of birds and animals for our use; they abound in our lands.

Ottawa statement at Drummond's Island Council, 1816

❦

Archaeological evidence indicates that during most of the prehistoric age ancestors of the American Indian had an almost uniform life-style. One example of their homogeneity, based on their common experience, was the universal use of the same types of weapons. Although tools for hunting might change from Clovis to Folsom-type points fitted into the spear and lance shafts, almost all hunter families from Alaska to Mexico and from the Atlantic to the Pacific would adopt each change.

About 5,000 years ago, however, this homogeneity began to break down as the Paleo-Indians of prehistory developed regional differences in their culture. By the time the Europeans arrived around 1500 A.D. cultural diversity was the rule. The community had fragmented into hundreds of tribes, each following its own life-style. Thus, from the beginning of the Indians' recorded history their identity has been with their tribes—they have been Cherokee, Seneca, Kickapoo, Pima. Not until the 1970s did Native American consciousness begin to shift from a narrow, parochial tribalism to a broader, more embracing "Indianness." And the Indians are discovering that their roots are deep and nourish an unquenchable ethnic pride; Native American homogeneity is being restored.

The Paleo-Indian epic readily divides into four eras or ages. The first age has been called *Pioneers in the American Wilderness* and includes the period from the first migration to the New World, perhaps 50,000 years ago, to the close of the Pleistocene Age, about 8000 B.C. Prehistorians designate the second era the *Archaic Age*. It lasted from the close of the Pleistocene Age to about 1200 B.C. The third age, the *Golden Age of American Prehistory*, is the period from 1200 B.C. to 1250 A.D. And the fourth, 1250 to 1500 A.D., is called *Prelude to Imperialism*.

Chapter Opening Artifact: Hopewell effigy pipe. (Courtesy of Field Museum of Natural History, Chicago)

16

PIONEERS IN THE AMERICAN WILDERNESS

Ancestors of the American Indian traveling over the great migration trail, from Eastern Asia across Beringia into Alaska and south along the ice-free corridor on the eastern flank of the Rocky Mountains, finally passed the southern edge of the glacial cap. They entered an ice-free territory along the present northern border of the United States. From that point to wherever they moved east, west, or south, they found throughout the continent a generally uniform climate, regulated by powerful influences of the huge glaciers. There was abundant annual rainfall; temperatures were mild; and there were no seasonal extremes. Such conditions created dense forests, savannas covered with tall, coarse grasses, and many lakes, springs, swamps, and bogs. This lush plant life supported a variety of animals dominated by large species such as Columbian mammoths and mastodons, elephantlike creatures with huge tusks, each weighing on the average six tons and standing

Columbian mammoth skeleton. (Stovall Museum, University of Oklahoma)

17

nearly fourteen feet high at the shoulder. Other now-extinct creatures that flourished in this environment were the huge early bison, tapir, ground sloth, and the camel and horse. There were also deer, elk, antelopes, rabbits, wolves, piglike peccaries, and many other species that survive today.

Early hunter migrants to the Americas subsisted on these creatures. Their stone weapons and tools are the principal remains of the ancient past, helping to identify and describe their users. Changes in tool and weapon styles by early hunters provide the basis for subdividing this Pioneer Age.

Pre-Projectile-Point Stage

The earliest stage of the Pioneer Age, covering the period up to about 25,000 B.C. has been named "Pre-Projectile Point" because the surviving weapons and tools are simply crafted pieces of stone. Projectile points on spears were not yet used. Large quantities of crudely chipped stone implements have been found throughout the Western Hemisphere, and they help to document the earliest period of human occupation.

Prehistorians believe that pioneer big-game hunters used clubs and wooden shafts with sharpened, fire-hardened tips. They used crude stones to skin the beasts and to dress the hides for clothing. Artifacts from this stage have been found at Lewisville, Texas, with the earliest documented human remains in North America. Finds there are estimated to be 38,000 years old and consist of charred plant and bone material in ancient hearths. At Tule Springs, Nevada, pre-projectile-point camp sites have yielded stone and bone artifacts calculated to be 28,000 to 32,000 years old. On Santa Rosa Island, California, camp sites have been found with burned mammoth bones estimated to be more than 30,000 years old.

Paleo-Indian Stage

This second period lasted from about 25,000 B.C. to 8000 B.C. During this time Indian ancestors began to improve their technology. They shifted from using simple stones to functional stone tools, knives, and projectile points for spears and darts. They were increasingly specialized and well crafted, most of them fashioned from a hard but easily shaped material called chert, or flint. Different phases during the Paleo-Indian Stage are identified by tools and weapons associated with sites and archeological analysis that assigns dates and uses descriptive interpretation. Several different periods or phases during the Paleo-Indian Stage are identified by the name applied to their principal weapons and tools—Sandia, Clovis, Folsom, and Cascade.

Evidence for the *Sandia Phase* was first discovered in the Sandia Mountains near Albuquerque, New Mexico. In Sandia Cave during 1936 prehistorians began cutting through a six-inch layer of the travertine mineral formed by water dripping from the cave roof when the New Mexico climate was under Pleistocene influence. Below the travertine layer archeologists found a Paleo-Indian cultural profile; that is, successive layers or levels yielding flint knives, scrapers, and points. In the lower levels they came upon large points, some of them six inches long, each with a distinctive rounded base, which they called Sandia points. In Sandia hearths workers found bones of extinct animals including the mammoth, mastodon, and early bison, and artifacts made from bone. More recently carbon 14 tests have been applied to the material in the lower Sandia cave levels and suggest a life of from 20,000 B.C. to 25,000 B.C. The Sandia people, among the earliest American Indian ancestors, were calculated to be active during the period from 25,000 B.C. to 15,000 B.C.

The next phase in the progression of the American Indian's forebears is the *Clovis Phase,* named for a type of weapon point first found near Clovis, New Mexico. The ancient hunting culture associated with the Clovis point is sometimes called Llano. Clovis points are carefully formed, lance-shaped projectiles, three to six inches long, made by pressure flaking; that is, pressing off stone flakes with a piece of pointed stone or bone. Each Clovis point is distinctive because of its beauty, slenderness, length, and fluting—the channels cut on either side of the projectile face. Clovis hunters also made stone scrapers, mauls, and knives as their methods became more refined. Besides weapon making their crafts included fashioning clothing from skins and making sandals from shredded sagebrush.

Clovis hunters used the *atlatl,* the spear thrower, a short stick two feet long with a pair of animal hide loops at the end to grasp it and a hook and a weight for balance and whip action. With the *atlatl,* the hunter could throw his spear with greater velocity and with more accuracy than with his arm only. Archeologists have concluded that ancient hunters fastened the slender fluted points into long spear shafts with thongs of animal skin or plant-fiber twine. A spear launched by an *atlatl* easily reached a target 300 feet away. Probably Clovis hunters used the *atlatl* to launch spears at deer, elk, horses, camels, and other game from a distance, but used the spear alone to jab mammoths and mastodons when the huge creatures became mired in the mud of swamps and bogs.

Search for food occupied most of the ancient hunter's day. If hunters bagged small animals, the family or band would feast for a day, then move on; killing a mammoth or a mastodon was a windfall for the hunting band because it provided food for several days. Clovis hunting people lived in scattered, temporary camps and built no shelters. Because of the generally temperate climate across North America, these peoples had little need for caves or ledges except for protection from human and animal predators. Their baggage was light; they had few possessions except what they could carry in their continual search for food. As could be expected, their social and political organizations were uncomplicated. Artifacts of Clovis hunters, rather than appearing in camps or settlements, are found in what prehistorians call "kill sites," clusters of ancient hearths around the bones of mastodons or mammoths. Clovis points have been found from Alaska to Mexico, from Massachusetts to Arizona, in the East associated with mastodon and in the West with mammoth remains.

The Clovis Phase of the American Indian's prehistory concluded around

11,000 B.C. and was succeeded by the *Folsom Phase*, again taking its name from the characteristic projectile point of the period. The Folsom point is named for Folsom, New Mexico, where in 1926 the first such projectile point was found in association with signs of human occupation. Folsom, which extended to sometime after 8000 B.C., is sometimes also called Lindenmeier Culture after an ancient kill site near Lindenmeier, Colorado.

Folsom people were wandering hunters like their Clovis predecessors, and their technology was quite similar. They continued the practice of fluting their flint projectile points. A principal difference, however, was that the average Folsom point was two inches long, considerably shorter than the Clovis point. Another difference was that the Folsom people's quest for food centered on the large early bison rather than the mammoth, mastodon, camel, and horse because, by 10,000 B.C., they were disappearing from the continental United States.

In the Folsom Phase there is evidence of cooperative group activity in the surround-and-jump kill, the technique of driving a herd of bison over a cliff for an easy food harvest. This technique required several hunters working in unison, and its practice indicates a shift to a larger functional social group even if only for specific situations, than the family or small hunting band of the Clovis Phase. As in the earlier Clovis culture, remains are found over a wide area from Alaska to Mexico and from the Atlantic Coast to the Colorado River. This wide dispersal of similar artifacts from both the Clovis and Folsom periods confirms the cultural homogeneity of the Paleo-Indian Stage.

However, artifacts from the late Paleo-Indian Stage indicate that there were two notable exceptions to the general cultural homogeneity. One regional deviation was called Cascade, the other, Desert Culture.

The *Cascade* or *Old Cordilleran Phase* flourished in the Pacific Northwest in the region now embraced by northern California, Washington, Oregon, and much of Alaska from 9000 B.C. to about 5000 B.C. The Cascade point, a distinctive willow-leaf-shaped stone projectile, identifies the period. Cascade culture seems to have evolved independently of the Clovis and Folsom big-game hunting traditions in the East. It provided the foundations for later cultures of northern California, the Northwest Coast, and portions of Alaska.

The other deviation from the continent-wide cultural homogeneity during the Paleo-Indian Stage was the *Desert Culture* that developed in the Utah portion of the Great Basin and in southern Arizona. At the same time that Folsom hunters, 600 miles to the East, were stalking early bison, Paleo-Indians in Utah and Arizona were developing a new life-style based on gathering and processing seeds. As we shall see, this practice eventually spread into other communities and provided the foundation for the Archaic Age and finally the adoption of agriculture.

Excavations at Danger Cave, Utah, yield grinding stones and woven containers that have been dated 9000 B.C., the oldest examples of basketry in North America. These Great Basin pioneers also made twine and small rope from plant fibers and animal fur and hair and fashioned snares, nets, and traps to capture rabbits, gophers, porcupines, and other small game. They hunted deer and antelope with spears and darts fitted with small points. Desert Culture people gathered seeds from wild plants, parched them, then ground them on milling stones. They wove fine baskets from dried cattails and other plant stems and used them to carry and store seeds. The baskets were woven so tightly that they held water; filled with water and hot stones, they were used for cooking. Little change occurred among the peoples of the Great Basin from 8500 B.C. to 1860 A.D. The modern Paiute and Shoshone tribes are descended from the peoples who formed the Desert tradition.

The Cochise people in southern Arizona joined with the Great Basin peoples to perfect a gathering economy. This area was once covered by the huge Lake Cochise; the Cochise people lived on its shore. On Whitewater Creek in southern Arizona archeologists have found prehistoric sites that yield mammoth, wolf, and horse bones; flint pieces; charcoal; and grinding stones. The hearths have been dated from 10,000 B.C. to 12,000 B.C. The Cochise peoples supported themselves by a mixed economy of hunting and gathering. They ground plant seeds on stones which evolved into the Southwestern *metates,* flat stone grinding basins, and the *manos,* hand-held grinding stones.

Transition to the Archaic Age

About 8000 B.C. the Pleistocene Age began to conclude. The glacial ice cap retreated northward. The weather over all of North America changed drastically as the climatic patterns we know today with regional variations began to emerge. Thus the great integrating force of rather constant, continent-wide, mild climate, which had produced a homogeneous Paleo-Indian culture, faded. While the eastern portion of North America remained humid and well watered, arid plains and deserts formed in the central and western sections. This evolving regional climatic variation produced ecological alterations. Swamps and bogs dried up. The coarse savanna grasses which had sustained the mammoth, mastodon, horse, camel, and sloth were replaced by shorter grasses that favored the smaller bison, antelope, deer, elk, and other species familiar today. Pleistocene creatures became extinct in the lower latitudes of the continent, and some ancient people followed them as they retreated toward the Arctic Circle. These groups maintained with little change their tradition of hunting large animals for another thousand years. However, most ancestors of the American Indian remained but were forced to change their ways. Obtaining food became increasingly difficult, and Paleo-Indians began to adopt the gathering techniques of the Desert Culture. They mixed hunting with collecting seeds, berries, nuts, and edible leaves and roots.

This dramatic environmental change and the Paleo-Indians' shift from near total reliance on hunting to a mixed economy of hunting and gathering ushered in the Archaic Age. Some archeologists identify the *Plano* or *Plainview Culture,* from about 7500 B.C. to about 4500 B.C., as a bridge connecting the Paleo-Indian and Archaic periods. The heaviest concentration of Plano activity was on the Great Plains, where they followed a mixed hunting and gathering economy. Their technology included use of unfluted points, some with notches characteristic of later projectile points, and grinding stones. Plano ancestors of the American Indian hunted surviving game—bison, elk, antelope and deer—and they achieved cultural advances of considerable importance. One was the discovery of processes for preserving food. While for the most part Plano peoples had a subsistence economy, they preserved meat for times of scarcity by drying it in the sun. They mixed this with animal fat and berries to produce a primitive pemmican, which they packed in cleaned gut containers, like sausage, or in skin bags. Plano ancestors of Native Americans also developed a more complex social organization than their predecessors as indicated by evidence that they made wide use of the jump-kill technique in hunting. Furthermore, in flat country where there were no bluffs, they constructed corrals to trap animals for slaughter.

The Plano attempted to maintain the characteristics of the Paleo-Indian hunting culture, although tempered with Desert Culture characteristics that came to dominate the Archaic Age. The Plano culture had faded by 4500 B.C., but in many respects it seemed to return during the eighteenth and nineteenth centuries in the buffalo-hunting culture of the Plains tribes.

THE ARCHAIC AGE

The Archaic Age of American prehistory lasted from about 8000 B.C. to about 1200 B.C. Certainly some Paleo-Indians adopted the Archaic pattern earlier than 8000 B.C., and many Archaic characteristics persisted among certain Indian tribes even well past 1850 A.D. Archaic Age technology and material culture became dominant across the North American continent and were the foundation upon which Indian tribes developed the life-styles that Europeans observed in 1500. Intensive hunting, gathering, and fishing were important in the period. Unlike the Paleo-Indian period when the people depended mainly on a single resource, meat, derived from hunting, in the Archaic Age they developed the means to exploit the total environment, drawing from it the full range of their increasing material needs.

The Archaic Age had a rich technology. Archaic people created many useful and special tools and utensils of stone, bone, horn, ivory, shell, wood, hide, fiber, and copper. Their inventions included techniques for preserving and storing food, allowing a relatively large population to exist at a level of sophistication generally thought possible only with an agriculturally based economy.

Substantive environmental change produced by the retreat of the Pleistocene ice cap caused the homogeneous Paleo-Indian hunting culture to break down into a variety of cultures, each determined by its natural environment. In the Archaic Age the physical environment eventually settled into the familiar contemporary landforms, regionally varying climate, vegetation, and wildlife. For example, the American bison or buffalo, an important food source for the ancestors of the American Indian during the Archaic Age, spread from the Atlantic to the Pacific, even occupying remote mesas and upland parks in mountain areas, although its major concentration was on the Great Plains. Adjusting to these differing environments and gaining increasing control over them, or at least learning to cope with them successfully, was the theme of Archaic life.

The Archaic Age may be divided into Eastern Archaic and Western Archaic. The Western Archaic is treated first because the Archaic life-style began in the Western portion of North America. The Desert Culture, where Paleo-Indian pioneers formulated an alternative to exclusive hunting, based on Great Basin and Cochise foundations, became the basis for Archaic culture, both East and West.

The Western Archaic

This culture, sometimes called the Desert Archaic, developed in a harsh environment with limited plant and animal resources. People of Western Archaic culture continued a migratory existence, but over less territory than the Paleo-Indian hunters. They moved in a circuit from one food source to another, from season to season, in small groups directed by a simple sociopolitical organization, perhaps led by the patriarch of an extended family. Searching for food still occupied most of everybody's waking hours. However, their skill in handicrafts continued to improve. They used the *metate* and *mano* for processing seeds and made fine baskets for collecting, storing, and cooking food. Western Archaic peoples made a wide range of stone and bone implements, tools, and weapons, including knives (now fitted with wooden

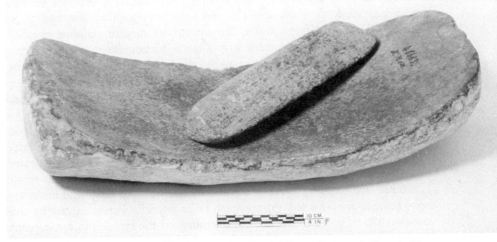

A mano and metate set, the household manual mill used by prehistoric Indians in New Mexico for grinding seeds and grains. (Smithsonian Institution, National Anthropological Archives)

handles), scrapers, hammers and mauls, stone axes, and spear points. They fashioned fiber twine and small rope into snares, nets, and traps to catch birds, small game, waterfowl, and fish. They regularly occupied caves and ledge shelters where they hid surplus food and valuables. During one season in the year they might be in the desert collecting yucca seeds, fiber and roots, and prickly pear fruit; the next season on the highland mesas gathering grass seeds, acorns, juniper berries, and piñon nuts; and the next in the pine and aspen forests extracting pitch to line water containers and trapping and spearing fish in the mountain streams and lakes. Their exploitation of the environment included hunting rabbits, antelope, deer, elk, and occasionally buffalo with the *atlatl* and lance, and gathering insects, snakes, and lizards. There were few creatures in their environment to domesticate. However, they did convert wolves to dogs which they used to guard their camps and to assist them in hunting.

Out of the Southwest's harsh, limited environment the Western Archaic people forged a social system receptive to innovations in agriculture and the manufacture of ceramics. These additions to their culture brought about the region's Golden Age of Prehistory, which reached its zenith in the Mogollon, Anasazi, Hohokam, and Patayan cultures.

The Eastern Archaic

The Eastern Archaic culture was like its western counterpart in its intensive exploitation of the environment and in some of its technology. However, the Eastern peoples had an easier task. They had a milder climate and a greater variety of animals and plant resources to draw upon. Western Archaic technology used by Eastern natives included weaving fibers into mats for wall and floor coverings and baskets and bags for gathering, transporting, and storing food. They used fiber twine and rope to make traps and nets for snaring birds, waterfowl, small animals, and fish. They adopted the *metate* and *mano,* the Western stone grinder, but developed another grinding device, a wooden cylinder hollowed from a tree-trunk section fitted with a wooden plunger-crusher, making a mortar-and-pestle-type unit. With a wider range of natural products to sustain them, Eastern Archaic craftsmen developed many stone, bone, copper, and wooden tools.

In addition to the natural environment, Eastern Archaic life differed from the Western Archaic in at least three important ways. One was population density. A richer natural region, the Eastern environment, with more intensive exploitation, could support more people; the population of the Eastern Archaic area was perhaps five times greater than that of the Western Archaic. The other two differences relate to technology: use of copper and ecosystem management. By 3000 B.C. groups near Lake Superior began extracting shallow deposits of natural copper. They hammered the metal into spear points, harpoon heads, knives, axes, fishhooks, and other tools, implements, weapons, and decorative pieces. Gradually use of copper spread along trade channels throughout the Eastern Archaic region and was used extensively as basic

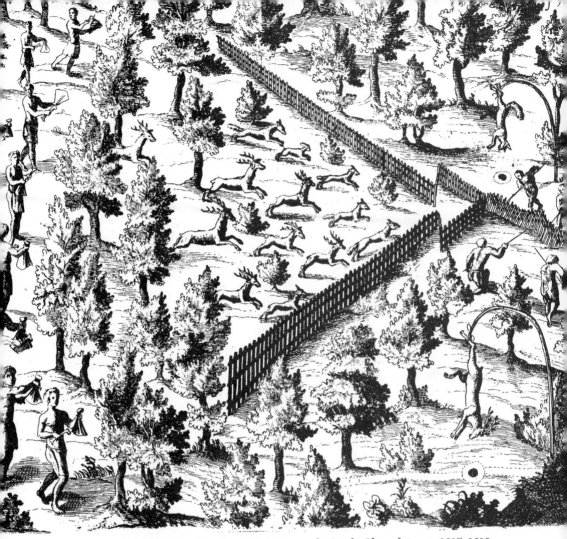

Indian method of hunting deer, from *Les Voyages du Sr. de Champlain*, ca. 1615–1618. (Houghton Library, Harvard University)

material for tools, weapons, and decoration.

Eastern Archaic people also learned that by controlled burning of forests in certain places, they produced a so-called climax growth. The new growth after a fire consisted of plants yielding berries, nuts, fruits, and edible roots and leaves, and small bushes which provided abundant food for animals, particularly the deer, which increased in numbers in burned-over tracts. Use of this technique meant less moving about in their search for food and permitted more permanent occupation of a region. By controlled burning of forest tracts, Eastern Archaic peoples maintained the environment best suited to their life-style by a simple form of ecosystem management.

The material culture of the Eastern Archaic peoples provided the economic base for the Hopewell, Adena, and Mississippian cultures. These cultures together made up the Golden Age of Prehistory for the Eastern Archaic.

THE GOLDEN AGE OF
AMERICAN PREHISTORY

Over a period of about 50,000 years, ancestors of the American Indian had pioneered a virgin continent, had learned to survive in two drastically different natural environments, and had achieved a slow but steady advance from a primitive life-style to a more sophisticated one. Paleo-Indians had achieved those essential landmarks common to the advance of primitive people throughout the earth. They had learned the uses of fire, developed weapons, tools, and other items required for a successful life in the prehistoric age. They had diversified their economy by adding gathering and had invented all kinds of useful ways to improve hunting through use of decoys, game calls, snares, traps, nets, weirs, and the surround-and-jump kill. They had learned to process foods with the stone *metate* and *mano* and the wooden mortar and pestle and invented food preservation and storage techniques. They had learned ecosystem management to increase the food supply and thus reduce the territory required to sustain the group.

Earlier primitive peoples in America had reached the limits of exploitation of the natural environment by hunting and gathering; their population had increased manyfold. Yet they still had to spend most of each day obtaining food. To this point their advances had largely been in the realm of material culture—things, processes, technology, the support of life. There had been little time for development of nonmaterial culture—enrichment through the creative self in art, the mind, and the spirit. However, during the Archaic Age many American Indian forebears had become saturated with the material culture of their age and were receptive to innovation. This innovation was agriculture—growing food as distinct from merely taking it from nature—which reached North America from Mexico.

Domestication of plants began in Mexico before 5000 B.C. Early farmers there domesticated corn (maize), beans, squash, cotton, and pumpkins. Widespread adoption of agriculture by Mexican Indians led to settled village life, the development of pottery, and other signs of maturing culture. Agriculture first reached New Mexico and Arizona between 3500 and 2500 B.C.; Eastern Archaic peoples began to adopt farming about 1000 B.C. Widespread adoption of agriculture, particularly the production of corn, produced those economic conditions that enabled the long-thwarted nonmaterial cultural development of the Archaic peoples to come to flower. The result was the Golden Age of American Prehistory.

Golden Age of Prehistory—The West

Agriculture was widely adopted by Desert Archaic peoples earlier than by those in the East largely because farming was much more attractive to the Western peoples. Their harsh environment with its limited resources, made the search for food very difficult. Agriculture provided an important and

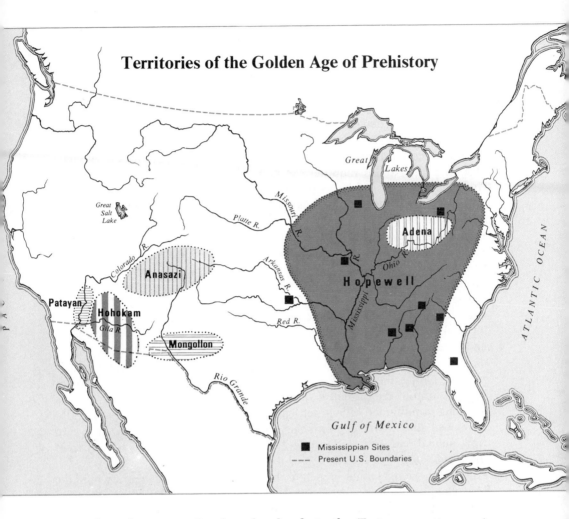

appealing alternative. On the other hand, in the East a more temperate climate and richer natural environment made it difficult to displace the Archaic way of life there.

The spread of agriculture across the Southwest gave rise to four different cultural communities, each descended from the Cochise-Desert Culture tradition—the Mogollon, Hohokam, Anasazi, and Patayan. In each case the adoption of farming expanded the material culture. Food gathering and hunting continued but became secondary enterprises, improved by the adoption of the bow and arrow. Domestication of wild creatures continued. The dog was widely used to guard households and to assist in hunting. The turkey was domesticated as a food source and a source of abundant and colorful feathers that were used for personal decoration, for making religious fetishes, and for creating elaborate feather blankets. Food containers became increasingly important with the adoption of farming. Basket making continued to be an important enterprise. Southwestern peoples also imported pottery making from Mexico. Weaving technology expanded to include production of textiles from cotton and animal fibers.

The agricultural foundations of these four cultural communities rested on growing corn. Other crops included beans, squash, pumpkins, and cotton. Successful farming in this arid land depended upon irrigation which required community management of labor and authority for allocation of water.

Just as farming expanded the material culture, it also produced those conditions which encouraged the development of nonmaterial culture. Baskets, ceramic pieces, and textiles became popular media for expressing creativity. And religion developed to assist in interpreting the universe and, they hoped, to provide the community with additional control over it, including bringing rain to parched fields.

Southwestern peoples traded with peoples in other regions of North America. Blankets, baskets, and pottery from the Southwestern settlements were carried over trails to the Pacific Coast to exchange for marine shells and other esteemed items.

The Mogollon people were desert dwellers in western New Mexico and eastern Arizona, the first people in present-day United States to adopt farming and pottery making. Mogollon farmers produced crops of corn, beans, and squash to sustain a growing population which by 300 B.C. lived in villages of pit-house dwellings. Each Mogollon community was built around a large public building, the kiva, also of pit-house construction. The Mogollon architectural form of the pit-house was widely used in the Southwest by peoples adopting farming and village settlement patterns. The Mogollon people also developed fine weaving, producing blankets of feathers, cotton, and yarn from animal fur. The modern Hopi and Zuñi peoples are descended from the Mogollon.

The Hohokam, another branch of the Cochise, were contemporary with the Mogollon. It is believed that about 100 A.D. the Hohokam shifted from hunting and gathering as an exclusive way of life and settled in the Salt and Gila River valleys of southern Arizona to pursue farming as their major economic base. Their settlements consisted of square pit-houses of jacal construction, that is, upright poles or sticks chinked or plastered with mud. Their crops were watered by irrigation although some farmers occasionally used the overflow from the annual flood of the Gila and Salt rivers. Hohokam irrigation works rank among the engineering wonders of prehistoric North America. They consisted of diversion dams on the rivers and a grid of canals for directing river water to the fields. Canals were six feet deep and thirty feet wide, some of them extending ten miles. Workmen controlled the flow and diverted water in the canals with woven mat valves. Their principal settlement of Snaketown, near present-day Phoenix, was occupied for 1,200 years. They raised corn, cotton, beans, squash, and pumpkins and made baskets, pottery, and cotton textiles. Hohokam craftsmen perfected the etching process 300 years before it was used by European artisans. Their method was to cover the

Hohokam stone palette, fashioned in impressionistic human figure, used for mixing vegetal and mineral pigments. (Arizona State Museum, University of Arizona/Helga Teiwes)

surface of a shell, or whatever object was being worked, with pitch, transfer the design with a stylus, then apply an acid solution made from saguaro cactus fruit which implanted the design. The modern Pimas and Papagos are descendants of the Hohokam.

The most advanced culture to develop in the Southwest during the Golden Age was the Anasazi. These people, also Cochise-descended, were preeminent as basketmakers, farmers, and designers and builders of new architectural forms. The Anasazi occupied the Four-Corners Area in the San Juan River drainage basin. Their settlements were situated on the well-known Mesa Verde in southwestern Colorado, and at Aztec and Chaco Canyon in northwestern New Mexico. Called the Basketmakers because of their skill in fashioning containers from yucca, straw, vines, and rushes, after 100 A.D. they turned to making pottery for which they also achieved renown. Anasazi settlements, some of them on mesas over a mile high, were agricultural. Anasazi farmers terraced the highland fields and trapped water in small reservoirs, releasing it through canals to irrigate fields. One canal at Mesa Verde was

Anasazi Ruins—Mesa Verde, Cliff Palace. (The Denver Public Library, Western History Department)

four miles long. Their settlements consisted of stone-walled, multifamily dwellings centering on the kiva. Around 1000 A.D. Anasazi builders began constructing high (five-story) apartment buildings, called terraced cliff dwellings, under protecting ledges. Pueblo Indians on the Rio Grande are descended from the Anasazi.

West of the Mogollon, Anasazi, and Hohokam in the lower Colorado River valley were the Patayan peoples, also descended from the Cochise. By 600 A.D. they were living in agricultural settlements in houses of jacal construction. Patayans made pottery and baskets and raised corn, beans, and squash. They relied less on irrigation and more upon seasonal flooding of lowland areas by the Colorado River for watering their crops. The Patayans are ancestors of modern Yuman-speaking peoples including Yumas, Cocopas, Maricopas, and Mohaves, who live in the valleys of the lower Colorado and Gila rivers.

Anasazi ceramic male effigy. (Peabody Museum, Harvard University/Photograph by Hillel Burger)

Golden Age of Prehistory—The East

In contrast with the Golden Age in the West, peoples in the territory of the Eastern Archaic did not diversify their culture so drastically to achieve their Golden Age. By around 1500 B.C., Eastern peoples had reached that stage of cultural maturity which prehistorians call Woodland, their ultimate adaptation to the environment. Their technology had advanced just a bit with adoption of the bow and arrow; slowly some Eastern peoples adopted pottery and a limited agriculture but, for the most part, their ways of living continued in the same patterns until Europeans arrived about 1500. Three local or regional exceptions to this model were the Adena, the Hopewell, and the Mississippian cultures.

The Adena, flourishing by 800 B.C., was concentrated in the upper Ohio Valley in present-day Ohio, West Virginia, and Kentucky. The name comes from the name of the estate near Chillicothe, Ohio, where a huge mound, built by the Adena people, was excavated in 1902. The Adena lived in large towns. Their dwellings were permanent, circular structures with pole frames anchored in the ground. The walls were covered with woven mats, and the roofs were made of heavy thatch. The Adena used pottery, cloth, and copper tools, but supported themselves by traditional Archaic methods of intensive hunting and gathering. Adena culture centered around a highly developed religion with complex rituals concerned with the afterlife. Death was the object of particular attention. The dead were buried with great care, and much public labor went into building huge burial mounds. The demands of their cult of the dead required that most of the wealth of the community be poured into grave goods which were buried with the deceased. The Adena culture ushered in a 1700-year period of mound building, a custom adopted by succeeding Hopewell and Mississippian cultures.

The people who developed the Hopewellian culture, which lasted from 200 B.C. to about 500 A.D., in many respects simply built upon the earlier Adena culture. Certainly they continued the mound-building tradition and persevered in the death-cult religious focus. They did add agriculture to their economic base, they had a richer technology, and they extended their mound building over a wider geographic area than that covered by Adena culture. Hopewell-type settlements were established all along the Ohio Valley, into the lower Mississippi Valley, and east along the Gulf of Mexico to Florida. Hopewellian traders ranged over a wide area. They brought to their eastern settlements great quantities of obsidian from the Yellowstone and Black Hills areas, alligator teeth from Florida, mica from the southern Appalachians, copper from the Lake Superior country, and conch shells from the Gulf of Mexico. Hopewellian craftsmen fashioned these materials into weapons, tools, implements, and ornaments including human and animal figures, ceremonial pieces and fetishes. Most of their production was magnificently executed and was buried as grave goods.

Last of the East's Golden Age trio was the Mississippian Culture, which lasted from about 500 A.D. to 1250 A.D. It continued to focus on the death cult of the Adena and Hopewell cultures with mound building its most conspicuous characteristic, but Mississippians used a different mound-building technique. Many of their mounds, rather than being hollow with burial chambers, were solid earthern pyramids to provide heights upon which were constructed shrines and temples for the priests. The largest is Monks Mound near Cahokia, Illinois, on the Mississippi River, begun in 900 A.D. and completed 250 years later. Monks Mound covers eighteen acres, its rectangular terraces reaching a height of one hundred feet about the ground. Technology of this culture was similar to that of the Hopewell, except that there was greater reliance on maize production. Geographically this life-style was largely confined to the lower Mississippi River and its tributaries.

Native America's Golden Age of prehistory concluded soon after 1250. By 1500 when Europeans began their conquests by claiming vast territories in the new land and integrating resident natives into their empires, they found

Cultural Stages of American Indian Ancestors

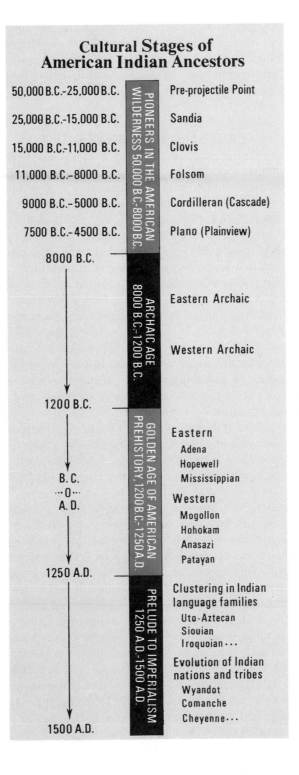

50,000 B.C.-25,000 B.C.	PIONEERS IN THE AMERICAN WILDERNESS 50,000 B.C.-8000 B.C.	Pre-projectile Point
25,000 B.C.-15,000 B.C.		Sandia
15,000 B.C.-11,000 B.C.		Clovis
11,000 B.C.-8000 B.C.		Folsom
9000 B.C.-5000 B.C.		Cordilleran (Cascade)
7500 B.C.-4500 B.C.		Plano (Plainview)
8000 B.C.	ARCHAIC AGE 8000 B.C.-1200 B.C.	Eastern Archaic

Western Archaic |
| 1200 B.C. | GOLDEN AGE OF AMERICAN PREHISTORY, 1200 B.C.-1250 A.D. | **Eastern**
Adena
Hopewell
Mississippian |
| B.C. ···0··· A.D. | | **Western**
Mogollon
Hohokam
Anasazi |
| 1250 A.D. | | Patayan |
| | PRELUDE TO IMPERIALISM 1250 A.D.-1500 A.D. | Clustering in Indian language families
Uto-Aztecan
Siouian
Iroquoian··· |
| | | Evolution of Indian nations and tribes
Wyandot
Comanche
Cheyenne··· |
| 1500 A.D. | | |

no advanced Anasazi or Hopewell civilizations. Rather they found North America north of Mexico occupied by several hundred different Indian communities, each nation or tribe occupying a particular territory, its people maintaining a life-style in many cases substantially below the level achieved by the Golden Age peoples.

PRELUDE TO IMPERIALISM

A greater leveling process had been at work during the period from 1250 to 1500, and while many Indian groups maintained a high cultural level, none could match the earlier brilliance of the Mogollon, Hohokam, and Anasazi or the Adena, Hopewell, and Mississippian. Some details of this period preceding European Contact in the West have been pieced together by prehistorians' analysis of archeological evidence and by tribal traditional histories. This evidence shows that two forces terminated high cultures there and forced the people to disperse. One was a blistering drought, documented by dendrochronology, from 1276 A.D. to 1293 A.D. In a land where water is scarce even under normal conditions, certainly a drought of any proportion would make life impossible in the Southwest. In addition, about this time fierce Athapascan raiders from the north, ancestors of the Navajos and Apaches, began to occupy territory near the desert people and to prey upon their settlements. Sustained drought and punishing military pressure by Athapascan intruders forced the peoples of the Golden Age to leave their home areas. The Mogollon scattered, then regrouped to form the modern Hopi and Zuñi peoples of northern Arizona; the Hohokam were the ancestors of the modern Pima and Papago tribes of southern Arizona; and the Anasazi divided, most of them settling on the Rio Grande and establishing foundations for the Pueblo tribes of modern times, while a few mixed with the Mogollon to form the Hopi and Zuñi peoples.

For Eastern aborigines, however, deciphering the immediate pre-Columbian past is a more difficult task, and as yet no satisfying chronicle for the period 1250 to 1500 has emerged. Prehistorians hesitate to speculate on this period. Certainly some Adena-Hopewell-Mississippian traits continued. Journals of the Hernando de Soto expedition, 1539–1541, in the Southeast contain descriptions of natives practicing Mississippian-Era ways. And Southeastern tribes continued this Golden Age culture's practice of first-fruits ceremony, centering on the Busk, the green corn rite, and preoccupation with death and burial into the nineteenth century. The theocratic Natchez, with their all-important death cult, were the lineal descendants of the Mississippian peoples.

However, for most of the tribes in the Eastern ethnic region in 1500, there is virtually no evident cultural connection with Golden Age peoples. For example, the western portion of the Hopewell-Mississippian region centered on Spiro, a huge and prosperous agricultural community in the Poteau and Arkansas River valleys near Fort Smith, Arkansas. The legacy of these technologically advanced people is evident in the abundant treasures excavated from the huge Spiro mound. Archeological analysis of Spiro material indicates these people were active as late as 1350. Yet no material culture remains or traditional history have survived to link the Spiro people with the Quapaws, Osages, and Caddoes who occupied Spiro territory at the time of European Contact, although the Caddoan agricultural orientation suggests some remote Spiro-Caddo connection. Likewise there is no apparent connection between Algonkian peoples of the lower Ohio River Valley and the Siouian and Algonkian peoples of the upper Mississippi Valley with earlier Adena-Hopewell-Mississippian peoples.

Among the explanations of what happened during this blank period, speculative possibilities include conquest and annihilation by vandal-type outsiders. Also, climatic deterioration like that which ended the Golden Age in the West could have had a similar devastating effect on the Hopewell-Mississippian cultures in the thirteenth century. In addition, the monumental mortuary projects, including burial mounds of the Eastern Golden Age centers, required a huge and continuous labor supply for construction and maintenance. Perhaps slaves or serfs were used as low-class workmen to construct the vast public works; possibly worker revolts so weakened the Eastern societies that they collapsed. Or disease may have brought them to an end. Eastern Golden Age communities carried on wide commercial contacts with distant peoples. Perhaps their traders carried epidemic disease from coastal tribes on the Atlantic and Gulf of Mexico which had occasional contact with European fishing and trading crews.

Whatever the explanation, on the eve of European Contact Native Americans had divided into hundreds of tribes. These tribes spoke many different languages and pursued a variety of life-styles. To the development of this type of sociopolitical organization we now turn.

Selected Sources

The Paleo-Indian period in North American prehistory is traced in H. M. Wormington, *Ancient Man in America* (Denver, 1957); Waldo R. Wedel, *Prehistoric Man on the Great Plains* (Norman, 1961); D. M. Hopkins (ed.), *The Bering Land Bridge* (Palo Alto, Calif., 1967); D. Jenness, *Archeological Investigations in the Bering Strait* (Ottawa, Canada, 1926); Jesse D. Jennings and E. Norbeck, *Prehistoric Man in the New World* (Chicago, 1964); and T. H. Patterson, *America's Past: A New World Archeology* (Glenview, Ill., 1973).

Transition of Paleo-Indians from wandering hunters to more settled Archaic peoples is detailed in Robert F. Spencer, Jesse D. Jennings, et al., *The Native Americans: Prehistory and Ethnology of the North American Indians* (New York, 1965); Jesse D. Jennings, *Prehistory of North America* (New York, 1974); P. S. Martin, et al., *Indians Before Columbus* (Chicago, 1947); and C. L. Redman (ed.), *Research and Theory in Current Archeology* (New York, 1973).

Alfred Tamarin and Shirley Glubok, *Ancient Indians of the Southwest* (New York, 1975); Elman R. Service, *Primitive Social Organization* (New York, 1962);

A. V. Kidder, *An Introduction to Southwestern Archeology* (New Haven, 1962); A. L. Kroeber, *Handbook of the Indians of California* (Washington, 1925); J. C. McGregor, *Southwestern Archeology* (Urbana, 1965); and J. H. Seward, *Theory of Cultural Change* (Urbana, 1955) explain specialization and internal group change under altering environmental conditions.

CHAPTER 3

GENESIS OF MODERN TRIBALISM

Where today is the Pequot? Where are the Narragansetts, the Mohawks, the Pokanoket, and many other once powerful tribes of our people? They have vanished before the avarice and the oppression of the White Man, as snow before a summer sun.

Tecumseh oration, 1811

Native Americans found that European nations, and later the United States, demonstrated a curious and unrelenting concern for the Indians' "heathen state," and they maintained an expensive and prolonged effort to "civilize" them. Europeans and Anglo-Americans made two broad assumptions about Indians: first, they were uncivilized pagans, heathens, even savages; and, second, because Indians appeared to be a standard type, a single "civilization" program would work for them all. Both assumptions were false and costly, for Indians and for their conquerors. Indians had well-established cultures, and there was no standard Indian. Rather, there were many different types of Indians, speaking various languages and following differing life-styles. By 1500 the ancient Paleo-Indian homogeneity had been replaced by a pervasive heterogeneity.

Certainly there was no typical Indian in physical appearance. None of the so-called Redmen were red. Virtually all Indians were darker than Europeans, ranging in skin color from mahogany to lighter shades of brown. Adult males averaged five feet eight inches, and were slender due to their vigorous existence. However, warriors over six feet in height were common among the Osages and Cheyennes. Indian women ranged from five feet to five feet two inches in height. But in each tribe one found the common range of appearance—some were tall and slender, some were short, others squat, and a few were obese. Indians as a rule had dark, straight hair although some, particularly along the Northwest Coast, had wavy to curly hair.

The diversity of Indian languages and the advanced political, economic, social and religious systems of many tribes proved that Indians had creatively enhanced their cultures. But the fact that their life-styles differed from that of Europeans, that their religions were not Christian, led many Europeans and

Chapter Opening Artifact: Spiro dancers etched on a conch shell gorget. (Woolaroc Museum)

Anglo-Americans to scorn and denounce Indian cultures and to seek to destroy their ways of life which had been evolving in North America for perhaps 50,000 years. Five hundred years of calculated, concentrated effort to erase Indianness has largely failed. Many aspects of Native American culture survive into the twentieth century. One of their most resilient traits has been language.

NATIVE AMERICAN LANGUAGES

Among the Indian tribes north of Mexico nearly 300 different languages were spoken at the time of European Contact in 1500. More than half are still live languages, that is, they are used by Indians today. No Indian tribe within the present United States had devised a system for writing its language although they had created some effective substitutes.

Language Classification

Several nineteenth-century linguistic pioneers including Albert Gallatin, Thomas Jefferson, Henry Rowe Schoolcraft, and Lewis Henry Morgan studied Indian languages and attempted to apply some orderly classification. Finally in 1891 John Wesley Powell, director of the Bureau of American Ethnology of the Smithsonian Institution, formulated a system for classifying the Indian tribes by language. Powell's system was widely used by anthropologists, archeologists, and linguists until the 1950s.

Powell identified fifty-six different linguistic families or stocks under which the languages of the hundreds of tribes were categorized. The principal language families or stocks in the Powell system, which would accommodate most of the leading tribes, were Algonkian, Caddoan, Shoshonean, Muskhogean, Iroquoian, Siouian, and Athapascan. More recently Edward Sapir, Morris Swadesh, D. F. Vogelin, F. M. Vogelin, Harold Driver, and other linguists and anthropologists have altered Powell's model and formulated the genetic system of classification, borrowing from biology the use of the concept of phylum and family for Indian language categories. The genetic-system stocks that embrace the principal tribes are Algonkian, Athapascan, Iroquoian, Muskhogean, Siouian, Uto-Aztecan, and Penutian.

Language and Culture

Many of the Indian tribes in 1500 were distributed in clusters of common culture that included language. Thus north of the Ohio River there were concentrations of Algonkian-speaking tribes with a common culture. Muskhogean-speaking tribes with a common culture lived in the lower Mississippi Valley, and Siouian-speaking peoples with a common culture were in the upper Mississippi Valley. However, there are so many exceptions to this pattern of

American Indian Language Families

Present Day Boundaries

regional linguistic homogeneity that it is impossible to establish the principle of common language and culture concentrations. For example, the Pueblo tribes live in close proximity to one another and have a fairly similar material culture, yet the tribes speak four different languages. In the Southeast, Cherokees were neighbors to the Muskhogean-speaking Creeks, Choctaws, Chickasaws, and Seminoles and practiced a similar way of life. Yet the Cherokees spoke a drastically different tongue. And there is great cultural diversity within a language family—witness that the sophisticated Aztecs of Mexico spoke the same Uto-Aztecan dialect as the seed-gathering Paiutes of Nevada.

Characteristics of language as they relate to culture provide insight into changes in life-style and thus tribal history. Linguists have concluded that language is subject to change from the influence of languages used by neighboring tribes, but a tribe's language is more stable—that is, its rate of change is slower—than the rest of its culture.

Genetic analysis of language classification reveals history of Native Americans. In the study of genetic classification to reconstruct the history of aborigines, the cultural anthropologist uses *glottochronology*, mentioned in Chapter one. Designed about 1950 by Morris Swadesh, glottochronology analyzes languages through time to determine when derivative languages emerged from parent tongues. Glottochronology holds that language changes at a regular rate; each "daughter" will shed about 19 percent of its basic

Selected Language Families and Member Tribes

Algonkian	**Uto-Aztecan**
Delaware	Comanche
Cheyenne	Pima
Kickapoo	Ute
Blackfeet	Hopi
Shawnee	Paiute
Iroquoian	**Athapascan**
Wyandot	Navajo
Oneida	Tanana
Mohawk	Hupa
Seneca	Chirichaua-Mescalero
Cherokee	Apache
	Jicarilla
Siouian	**Muskhogean**
Osage	Choctaw
Ponca	Chickasaw
Quapaw	Creek
Crow	Seminole
Dakota	Natchez
Caddoan	**Tanoan**
Wichita	Kiowa
Caddo	Taos
Pawnee	Isleta
Arikari	San Juan
	San Ildefonso

words every thousand years. These types of linguistic analysis yield information on tribal migrations and relations with other tribes. For example, all Eskimos, from Greenland to western Alaska, speak a language which is so similar that any Eskimo can converse with any other Eskimo, even if their homes are a thousand miles apart. The lack of regional differentiation in language leads anthropologists to conclude that Eskimos are recent arrivals in the American Arctic. They have not been dispersed over such a large area as they now are for long enough to develop regional differences in languages.

Substitutes for Written Language

No Indian tribe in pre-Columbian times had an alphabet or a written language. Indians compensated for the lack of written languages in various ways. The Plains tribes used pictographs and ideographic symbols to record important personal and tribal events including warrior deeds, battles, and buffalo hunts, as well as time counts or calendars on walls of cliffs and caves, buffalo skulls, and elk and buffalo hides. Other substitutes for written language included wampum belts, woven strings of colored shell beads used as

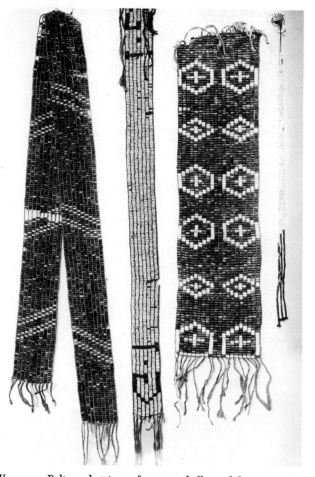

Wampum. Belts and strings of *sewant* shell, used for communication, adornment, and currency. (Courtesy of American Museum of Natural History)

mnemonic devices to record important events. Knots in strings, notches in sticks, and the long memory of the elders, the keepers of tribal tradition, were Indian responses to a lack of a written language.

Indian "Esperanto"

In spite of language diversity, Indians of different tribes communicated with one another. Sign language of conventional hand gestures, developed by the Plains tribes, became a widely used medium for overcoming language barriers. Theatrical gesture, pageantry, and traditional ritual and ceremony in Indian councils were important means of nonverbal communication. Tribes also circulated belts of wampum, red or black for war and white for peace, which conveyed specific, understandable messages. The regal calumet was an important means for communicating tribal intent in diplomacy. The calumet was a highly ornamented flat pipe stem, decorated with eagle feathers and quill work and fitted into a stone elbow pipe, which tribal leaders smoked ceremonially. The pipe head was carved from red catlinite, a stone quarried in southwestern Minnesota and in west central Wisconsin and in great demand as a trade item.

In certain regions the military power of a certain tribe might force nearby tribes to use its language or dialect in situations of international discourse. For example, on the Southern Plains from the Arkansas River to the Rio Grande, a region of considerable linguistic diversity, the Comanches were dominant. Other tribes acknowledged Comanche hegemony by using that tribe's language in discussing matters of trade and diplomacy; Comanche was the *lingua franca* of the Southern Plains.

The Indian calumet, the ceremonial pipe used to celebrate various occasions by many tribes. (Peabody Museum, Harvard University/Photograph by Hillel Burger)

Reducing Indian Dialects to Written Form

During the early nineteenth century, George Guess, better known as Sequoyah, a Cherokee genius, converted his tribe's spoken language to written form with a *syllabary* or, as it is sometimes called, the Cherokee alphabet, of eighty-six characters. The Sequoyah syllabary is still used by the Cherokees. The Cherokee language is taught in schools in the old Cherokee Nation of northeastern Oklahoma, and Cherokees publish books and newspapers in this language.

During the nineteenth century Christian missionaries also attempted to reduce some Indian languages to written form by assigning syllables composed of Roman alphabet characters to the basic sounds. In modern times, linguists have created an international system of symbols with which they can transform any spoken language to written form. This system is based upon the

Sequoyah (George Guess) created the Cherokee syllabary. (Library of Congress)

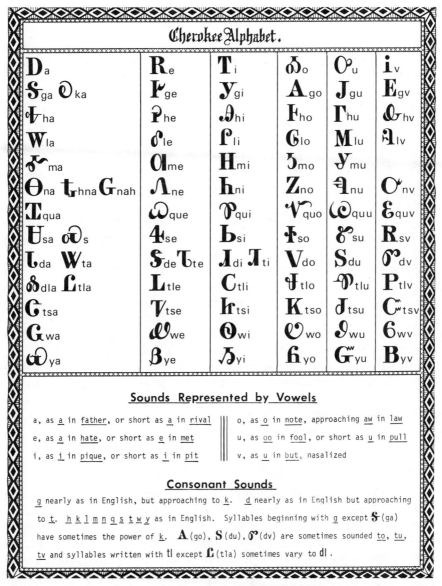

Cherokee syllabary—the so-called Cherokee alphabet, created by Sequoyah, consisting of 86 characters. (Courtesy of the Oklahoma Historical Society)

principle that any spoken language is composed of basic sound units called phonemes; each phoneme can be represented by a single letter in an alphabet. Linguists use the Roman alphabet with some Greek letters, special signs, and diacritical marks over, under, and on both sides of letters to form an international alphabet of about one hundred symbols.

NATIVE AMERICAN ECONOMY

That the area later embraced by the United States was in the seventeenth century a virgin land to be occupied by intrepid Anglo-American pioneers is a myth. Peoples from Asia had pioneered this land perhaps as many as 50,000 years earlier. By 1500 the descendants of these pioneers were distributed in tribal clusters from the Atlantic to the Pacific, from the Great Lakes to the Rio Grande. They had occupied the land, learned its secrets, and formulated techniques to exploit its abundant resources at a rate sufficient to support themselves at a level of at least minimum comfort.

The character of the Native American economy, the manner in which the Indians supported themselves, was strongly influenced by environmental conditions. And in turn, their particular economies determined the social models, religion, and political systems adopted by each tribe. Whenever environmental conditions permitted, Native Americans practiced agriculture, although they were never entirely dependent upon it for subsistence, mixing crop production with hunting, fishing, gathering, and trade. Where agriculture was impractical, they sustained themselves in the style of the Archaic—intensive exploitation of the environment through hunting, fishing and gathering. Certain staples dominated the economy of various tribal territories. In the humid, well-watered East corn was supreme. Tribes in the Great Lakes area gathered wild rice. For the Great Plains hunters the buffalo was the staple. Corn, produced by irrigated agriculture, sustained the economy of the desert Southwest. The acorn supported a surprisingly large population in California. Salmon was the mainstay for the tribes of the Pacific Northwest, both on the coast and in the interior plateau. And sea mammals and salmon were the principal staples of the Indians and Meso-Indians in Alaska.

Medicines from Nature

Many thousands of years of experience in the North American environment had by 1500 enabled the Indians to develop a rich and useful medical knowledge essential to the healing arts. Because many of the most cherished plants grew only in remote regions, they became valuable trade items. Aboriginal healers, women in the household, as well as shamans (tribal healers), used spice wood, ginseng, cottonwood, sarsaparilla, huckleberry, red willow, black locust, button snakeroot, skunk tree bark, mistletoe, yarrow, common dock, crushed melon seeds, ends of cedar limbs, elder, mint, and cusseena, as well as various herbs and berries. With these they compounded potions, teas, poultices, emetics, and drenches and used them to treat toothache, stomach disorders, snakebite, headache, dysentery, constipation, back and leg ache, cramps, fever, swelling, the itch, and eye trouble. They compounded remedies to treat female disorders and to prevent miscarriages. Women had secret herbs which were believed to prevent pregnancy, and they wore beaded strands of buffalo hair on their legs for ornaments and for protection from miscarriage, difficult childbirth, and other problems.[1]

Peyote, a plant of the cactus family which grows only in the arid Southwest, circulated widely over Native American trade routes. Indians used dried peyote buttons to assuage hunger, thirst, and fatigue during hard work, to detect the approach of an enemy, and to predict the outcome of a battle. They wore it to ward off disease and danger. Shamans used peyote in the curing process. Many tribes used peyote ritually to dispel anxiety and despair and to assist in the search for visions. In the twentieth century peyote became the focus of the Native American Church.[2]

Jimsonweed or *datura* was used extensively as a drug. Stems, leaves, and roots of this plant, soaked in water, yield a potion that reportedly produced visions, dreams, and clairvoyance. A person under its spell could see things hidden from ordinary view as well as events at a distance or in the future. Healers used it as an anesthetic to distract the patient from the pain of setting broken bones or surgery.[3]

The mescal bean, grown in West Texas and New Mexico, was consumed in ritual to transfix the group. And *Ilex Cassine* served as the basis for the black drink, an emetic used by many tribes in ritual purification before a war expedition, a council meeting, and the Busk, the green corn festival.

Native Americans used tobacco for both secular and religious purposes. Commonly they mixed it with dried sumac leaves or the inner bark of the dogwood and smoked the mixture or added it to the *datura* potion or to the black drink. In this form it was often used as a ceremonial emetic. Most shamans used tobacco to exorcise evil spirits and to hasten the healing process. Tobacco was also important to diplomacy. Tribal leaders smoked tobacco in the calumet to ratify agreements. And warrior medicine bundles, packets of fetishes containing sources of warrior power, included tobacco and a pipe.

A Case Study in Native American Economy

Aborigines in the lower Mississippi Valley best exemplify the Native American's talent for coordinating the ancient skills of hunting and gathering with agriculture to establish the economic foundations for one of North America's highest Indian civilizations. These Native Americans obtained food, shelter, clothing, and other needs from nature's bounty by hunting and gathering, agriculture, some trade with other tribes, and plunder from wars with neighbors.

There was a rather precise division of labor, based on sex, among these Indians. Men protected their households and communities, campaigned against enemy nations, provided meat for their households by hunting and fishing, performed tribal political and religious duties, and were artisans for certain crafts, particularly tools and weapons. Women managed households, provided meals and clothing for their families, gathered foods from nature, dominated certain crafts including weaving, and tended the crops.

The male was first and foremost a warrior and a hunter. He mixed his invocation of spirit power and supernatural approval for success on the game trails with the familiar skills of tracking, trapping, and using decoys and calls. The largest hunt occurred in the autumn. If successful, hunters turned most of their skins and smoked meat over to their households although they customarily set aside a portion for feasts and for food gifts to old people in the village. Young boys hunted wild turkeys and other small game near the villages as a part of their training.

The basic meat in the economy of the lower Mississippi tribes was the deer and bear, plus the bison when hunting parties went to the prairies. Deer was the favorite; its flesh was eaten fresh or dried and smoked for winter use. Its skin served as the principal material for clothing. Antler tips were often used as arrow points, and dried deer sinew and entrails were twisted and used for bowstrings and thread for sewing and weaving fishnets. Indian women used deer brains for softening and tanning skins. The bear ranked next in usefulness. Women fashioned heavy winter robes and bed coverings from bearskins. The rough hide was made into strong moccasins and hunting boots, and dried bear gut was a favorite with the warriors as bowstring material. They pierced bear claws for ornaments and necklaces. An important product from the bear was oil. Women took slabs of fat from the carcass and rendered them over fires, producing a clear oil which they mixed with sassafras and wild cinnamon and stored in large earthen jars. Indians used bear oil as cooking oil, as a hair dressing, and as a body rub for common complaints.

At certain seasons, fish was a popular food. Men made substances to drug fish from devil's shoestring, buckeye, and crushed green walnut hulls which they cast into deep holes in the rivers and creeks near their villages. When the drugged catfish, drum, and bass surfaced, the fishermen caught them by hand, speared them, or retrieved them with arrows fitted with a special barb and a hand line; they also placed creels, weirs, and nets on the edge of deep holes and in the shallows of rivers to trap fish.

In season, women and children gathered wild onions, grapes, plums, persimmons, mulberries, strawberries, and blackberries, as well as walnuts, chestnuts, pecans, acorns, and hickory nuts. They dried plums and grapes into primitive prunes and raisins and pressed dried persimmons into cakes. Boiled sassafras roots made a popular tea. The Indians gathered salt from local licks and springs, and robbed bee trees for honey which they used for sweetening. They felled the bee tree and placed the comb and thick, sweet liquid in a sewed deerskin container.

Agriculture matched hunting and gathering in importance in their economy. Public farms and household gardens were planted near the villages on meadow and prairie plots and cleared tracts in the timber. Workers cleared forest patches by deadening trees. They killed each tree by girdling, cutting a circle through the tree bark with notched stone axes; then they burned it, using saplings and undergrowth as fuel. Corn was the principal crop. Between the grain hills in the corn patches farmers planted melons, pumpkins, squash, sunflowers, beans, peas, and tobacco. Women served green corn as roasting ears and processed ripe corn into porridge, grits, gruel, hominy, and meal for

This illustration shows Indians using the weir to trap fish.

bread. They crushed dried corn kernels with a long-handled pestle in a mortar made from a chunk of hollowed hickory.

These peoples also used many other items in nature to meet their needs for clothing, decoration, household utensils, ceremonial tools, and shelter. Besides chipping stone pieces into projectile points, knives, and axes, they fashioned local clays into pottery vessels for cooking and for storing food and water. They spun thread and yarn for textiles out of the inner bark of the mulberry tree and animal fur. They converted eagle, hawk, and swan feathers into elegant decorative pieces, notably the warrior's mantle. They colored textiles and finely tanned deerskins with a bright yellow dye made from sassafras roots, and red, yellow, and black dyes from sumac. Walnut hulls yielded a rich dark dye used to color baskets and to mix with bear oil to color their hair.

The forests of the lower Mississippi Valley yielded many products useful in their crafts. Large logs were hollowed out by fire; when the charred insides were scraped with clam shells or sharpened stones, the result was river boats. From pine trees they took material for the framework for their houses and made pitch torches. Cane was another important plant for their crafts. They wove cane baskets and mats, used woven cane for house siding, constructed cane fish traps, sieves, and fences, and made blowguns from hollowed cane stems. The hickory tree had a number of uses. Besides using the nuts for food, they split hickory logs into strong, resilient withes or strips and wove house walls and heavy containers. Hickory was an important firewood, and its bark was used to cover shelters. Because of its strength, craftsmen used it to make arrow shafts and bows; in fact, white hickory ranked with black locust as the favorite bow wood. Red hickory was used for making mortars and pestles for grinding grain.

Economic life was enriched by commerce with other tribes. These Indians counted quantity by tens. Traders exchanged deerskins, Indian slaves, and bear oil sealed in clay urns with merchants from other tribes for special materials required in the construction of war implements; for conch shells, used as ceremonial chalices; and for pearls and sheet copper for making ornaments.

As indicated, women among these Indian nations did most of the household work and labor in the fields. Thus they prized the Indian slaves captured in their tribe's wars. And the women could be expected to urge their men to more fury, more raids, and the taking of more slaves, which changed their own status from laborers to overseers of slave laborers. To prevent escape from bondage, the captors mutilated their slaves' feet by cutting nerves or sinews just above the instep. Thus hobbled, the slaves could work but could not flee.

Warriors labored on the public farms and other civil works, constructed houses, and made tools and implements of war. They spent most of their time on the game trail and warpath or resting from their exertions and watching the women and slaves toil. Europeans condemned these men as slothful. They charged that a male bestirred himself only, as one of them put it, "when the devil is at his arse."[4]

Limitations of the Aboriginal Economy

Native Americans lacked several basic items that would have enhanced their technology, made their dominion over the land less fragile, and made them more of a match for the Europeans. First, they lacked the wheel. Second, Native Americans had no large domesticated animals such as the horse, ox, and cow. And third, they had no knowledge of metallurgy other than hammering sheet copper into tools and gold and silver into ornaments.

Lack of knowledge of the principle of the wheel restricted their technology, including land transportation. Dogs pulled sleds and the travois, and slaves acted as porters for moving goods overland. They used water transportation when available, ingeniously developing boats adapted to their environment. The northern tribes developed the bark-covered canoe, its joints and seams waterproofed with pitch. Indians in other parts of North America devised large rafts, dugouts, round hide-covered bull boats, and ocean-going, double-rigged craft with sails. Sea-mammal hunters in Alaskan waters fashioned sea-worthy bidarkas and kayaks. Lack of the wheel also limited their access to labor-saving devices like the pulley.

Native Americans domesticated the dog to guard their settlements, to hunt, to act as a burden bearer with travois poles or, in teams, to pull sleds over northern ice and snow. Some tribes used dogs for food. They also domesticated the turkey for food and feathers. Tribes of the Pacific Northwest approached domestication when they developed fish farming, stocking streams by depositing salmon eggs at favorable locations.

However, their lack of large domesticated animals and their failure to apply water power to grinding grain and other burdensome tasks made Indians unduly dependent upon human muscle power. And their limited metallurgical knowledge restricted weapon and tool materials to stone, wood, bone, antler, and hammered copper, no match for the iron tools, weapons and cooking utensils of the Europeans.

The Economy as a Cultural Determinant

As emphasized earlier, the manner in which Indians supported themselves had a great influence on their religion, social and political system, and life-style generally. Time spent obtaining food was a crucial factor in life-style quality. Those groups who spent most of each day searching for food could be expected to have an uncomplicated life-style. The search for food required that they travel great distances for meat, roots, berries, nuts, and fish to sustain themselves. Theirs was a hand-to-mouth existence. Casting over one part of their hunting territory one day, another the next, they developed no sense of specific place or fixed abode.

On the other hand, those tribes that practiced agriculture were sedentary. They occupied fixed territories, residing in villages. Farming was demanding; crops required regular care. Agriculture also generally supported more people than an exclusively hunting-gathering economy. With public management a surplus of grain and other essentials could be produced, collected, stored, and distributed in times of crop failure or other disaster. Specialization of labor, refinement of craft skills, and more intricate division of labor were also possible. More people living close together in each community required a more elaborate, complicated social system and control to regulate individual behavior, to protect the group interest, and to manage effectively the larger human group than were required in the simple hunting-gathering economy.

INDIAN SOCIAL SYSTEMS

The basic unit in Indian society was the family, although marriage customs and family structure varied in form from tribe to tribe. As the foundation for Indian society, each family provided the setting for legitimate sexual relations between husband and wife, the social setting for procreation and child rearing, and fulfillment of primary social needs of individual members. And in many tribes clusters of families comprised the building blocks for clans and moieties (clusters of clans), which in turn provided the basis for tribal political organization and religion.

Marriage Customs

The manner in which the family was formed and the direction it took varied among the tribes. The formulas for a couple joining in matrimony ranged from parental commitment of male and female infants to future marriage to bride capture by men in wars with neighboring tribes. Several tribes followed a system of purchase called "bride price" and "bride service" or "suitor service" where male or female youth lived with and worked for future parents-in-law for a year to prove one's worth as a homemaker or as a provider. Most tribes practiced exogamic marriage, that is the bride and groom were required to be from different clans.

Among the Southeastern tribes where courtship in the modern sense was permitted, a suitor might declare his matrimonial intentions by sending the hoped-for bride a small present, perhaps a trinket or a fine deerskin garment. Her acceptance meant that the couple was engaged. At the simple public marriage ceremony, the groom divided a choice ear of corn into two parts before witnesses, handing the bride one half and keeping the other half as a sign of his willingness to share, or giving her a deer's foot "as an emblem of the readiness with which she ought to serve him; in return, she presents him with some cakes of bread, thereby declaring her domestic care and gratitude.... When this short ceremony is ended they may go to bed like an honest couple."[5]

Native Americans practiced both monogamy and polygamy. Of the forms of plural marriage—polygyny, marriage of a male to more than one female, and polyandry, marriage of a female to more than one male—the latter was rare. Where it existed, it was a response to harsh economic conditions as found in the Great Basin or Arctic where supporting a wife and children might be too much of a burden for one man. In many polygynous marriages a man had chosen a woman with several sisters, and he wed them all. The advantage of this type of arrangement was that he needed to maintain only one household. Otherwise, for domestic peace, the polygamist established separate residences and visited his wives in rotation. An early European writer observed that Native Americans "were fond of variety, that they ridicule the white people as a tribe of narrow-hearted, and dull constitutioned animals, for having only one wife at a time; and being bound to live with and support her, though numberless circumstances might require a contrary conduct."[6]

The Native Americans matched simplicity in marriage with ease in ending the marital contract through divorce. Public declaration of intent and establishing separate residence generally accomplished this. Among the Iroquois where women were so powerful in public and private matters that their system comprised a matriarchate, disgruntled wives could divorce husbands simply by tossing their husbands' belongings out the door.[7]

Family Forms and Functions

An Indian family or household could be nuclear (father, mother, and children) or extended (father, mother, children, grandparents, and other kin by blood and marriage). The extended family predominated. In some instances it was maintained throughout the year, in others most of the year but split off into nuclear family groups during certain hunting and gathering seasons.

Some families were mother-centered, others father-centered. As a general rule families in agricultural tribes were mother-centered while father-centered families were more characteristic of hunting-gathering tribes. Anthropologists use various words to characterize the family forms, like matrilocal, matrilineal, patrilocal, and patrilineal. The prefix "matri" means female; "patri" means male. In the matrilineal family the husband-father's role was largely to sire children. The children were in the mother's clan, lived in her household, and they inherited personal property and land use rights from her. Associated with the matrilineal-matrilocal type of family was the avuncular system whereby the mother's brothers (the children's uncles) were responsible for bringing up her sons. Their biological father was responsible for bringing up his sister's male children. The opposite situation, where the father-husband was dominant, is called patrilineal.

There was precise division of responsibility by sex in the instruction of children. Boys between the ages of twelve and fifteen were assigned, depending upon their tribe's familial system, to their mother's brothers or to village elders to be taught the knowledge and skills considered necessary to make them successful hunters and warriors. Their curriculum included swimming, jumping, running, wrestling, and using weapons. Their warrior ordeal included plunging into water at the coldest season and eating special herbs to increase their strength and to extend their spiritual sensitivity as they sought visions. This elder-dominated educational process concluded with elaborate rites whereby each male protégè was transformed from youth to warrior.[8]

While girls' upbringing was less active and rigorous than that of the boys, it was no less demanding and essential for family and tribal well-being. Indian girls were taught household skills, cooking, and gardening by women in the family. They were also instructed in processing skins and hides, making clothing for family members, and gathering fruits, nuts, roots, berries, and useful plants. Among some tribes women formed guildlike groups in weaving and ceramics; each year they accepted certain girls as apprentices.

The Clan and the Moiety

The social models of the North American tribes ranged from simple associations of wandering hunting-gathering families, which anthropologists call *triblets*, to elaborately organized, complex associations called chiefdoms or nations. In the latter grouping, the families clustered into clans. Clans or *gens* were groups of blood-related families, the number in each tribe varying with the population. Tribes with small populations had perhaps seven, the more populous ones twelve to twenty or more. Each clan claimed a mythical origin and traced its genealogy to a common ancestor, a *totem* which served each clan member like a patron saint or special guardian and provided the name for the clan. Deer, eagle, raccoon, panther, wildcat, skunk, and buffalo were common clan names.

In the more populous tribes clans formed into two divisions called moieties. Clans were ranked by tradition and prestige in each moiety. The premier clan in each moiety provided the religious, military, and political leaders for the tribe. At the time of European discovery, some of the tribes had so increased in population that they were forming a third division. This was the case of the Choctaws, who had three grand divisions; a principal chief from each moiety functioning in unison comprised a sort of triumvirate executive for governing this populous Indian nation.

INDIAN RELIGION

Europeans brought with them a militant Christianity that rejected all non-conforming religions as pagan, all non-Christians as heathens. Native Americans, though far from being irreligious, were subjected to five hundred years of intensive evangelization by Christian imperial nations seeking to overthrow tribal deities and to coerce the Indians into Christianity. Ironically, an authority on Indian culture has observed, "In comparison with Whites in the United States today, the Indians were at least ten times as religious. [Their] every thought and act was hedged or bolstered by religion."[9]

Religion as a pervasive force in the Native Americans' daily life committed them not only to work out their status after death but, even more important, to develop the means to cope effectively with the supernatural each day. The universe was directed by an omnipotent creative-directive force, and the physical environment was alive with various spirits, good and bad, which had to be placated in order to succeed in various enterprises. One's clan association provided a supernatural link with an animal ancestor which related one to all living things; one could establish contact with one's deity and the multitudinous spirits through this intermediary. This in part explains the Indian reverence and awe for the earth—the mother—and all other elements of nature. Living so close to nature in a physical sense, Indians regarded harmony with nature and respect for its processes and its requirements to be essential. Disharmony would cause illness, pain, death, or other misfortunes.

Indian religion explained, interpreted, and provided answers for the mystifying aspects of the life processes—birth, puberty, marriage, and death—and natural phenomena. All things in the natural and social universe had religious overtones and spiritual causes. And aboriginal religion was both an individual and a group matter. Some tribes had a simple concept of the deity, others an elaborate, formal religion.

Individual Religion

In the West among hunting and gathering tribes, religion generally was less elaborate and more an individual than a group observance. Thus, an essential part of the rites which marked the transition from youth to adulthood was the search for a vision, where the youth meditated and contemplated the vital mysteries of the metaphysical. If fortunate in the vigil, the youth received a supernatural visitation and was assigned a spirit helper essential to success in love, war, and hunting.

Medicine to the Indian meant power derived from a supernatural source, a special gift Indians all across North America sought. A symbolic focus for the individual's power was the medicine bundle, a small skin-wrapped packet containing consecrated pieces of bone, small exotic stones, and sometimes a "shadow fighting knife" for use in "spiritual encounters." This weapon might be buried with the warrior to help him in fighting off enemies on his way to the world of spirits. The medicine bundle and certain charms worn by the warrior were calculated to counter various spirits, draw on supernatural power, and bring good fortune.

Group Religion

Rather elaborate public religious systems evolved among the agricultural tribes of the Southwest and the settled tribes of the East. Much of the doctrine, spiritual tradition, and form of worship of the Eastern religious establishment were derived from the Adena-Hopewell-Mississippian mound-building culture. Religion had many uses besides preparation of the mortal for the immortal state. It was used to benefit the group in many secular ways: to predict the future through divination; to provide a nonmaterialistic, nonscientific explanation for the natural universe and its phenomena (thunder, lightning, seasons, storms); to bring rain to parched corn fields; and assure victory in war or success on the hunting trail; or some other matter beyond human ken and capability.

Formal religious systems generally included a creation story, a migration epic, and an explanation of what the end of the world would be like. Priests instructed each generation about the long and difficult search for the home-land ordained for the tribe by the gods. Among agricultural tribes, as a re-flection of specialization of vocations and professions, a priesthood evolved to serve as links between the people and their gods. Priests were selected on the basis of their special talents for making supernatural contacts. They presided over religious ceremonies and rituals, performed sacrifices, enforced taboos, and performed the religious exercises required for placating and winning favor of the gods.

Several tribes had advanced in their mental exploration of the metaphys-ical to the point where they postulated an unseen but all-powerful creative-directive force that filled the universe. Its essence—called Orenda by the Iroquois, Manitou by the Algonkians, Wakan by the Sioux, and Ababinili by the Southeastern tribes—was the cumulative spirituality of the tribe. Thus each living person contributed to it. Many Native Americans had in their religious beliefs the story of a folk hero who in the dim past had taught the members of the tribe their way of life. Christians scorned these epics as myths and legends, but the exploits of the Iroquoian Deganawidah are no less credible than those of the Zoroastrian Mithras or the Hebrew Moses.

Because in the Indian view sickness was caused by invasion of the body by a spirit, clergy also served as healers. In this role they have been called shamans or medicine men. Indian healers used a mix of trickery, ritual, and practical medicines to cure the sick. In addition they applied exorcism, ex-tracting an illness-bearing spirit from the person by esoteric formula and transferring it to another animal.

NATIVE AMERICAN POLITICAL SYSTEMS

Indian political systems ranged from the most rudimentary wandering family triblet of the Great Basin, headed by a patriarch, to elaborate chiefdoms, theocracies, and matriarchies in the agricultural East and Southwest. With rare exceptions the component units, such as towns or bands, were supreme and self-governing. Many of the functions of government, including dis-ciplining or punishing tribal members, were taken care of in the clan or in the family.

Government and the Tribal Citizen

Many tribal governments of sedentary Indians were an extension of the clan system, particularly in the Southeast. These clans and towns were self-governing and confederated into a single political unit, the tribe, for purposes of promoting the general welfare and protecting the common interest. Officials in the tribal government, both local and national, held their positions because of clan status. Each clan or town was governed by a council of elders and a clan chief selected by the council. At the top of the political hierarchy was the principal chief, selected from the ranking clan of the supreme moiety of the tribe. Assisting him was the national council speaker. The national council, composed of clan chiefs and certain other respected and wise elders, shared the functions of tribal government at the national level. This group met on the call of the principal chief. Runners from the national "capital" stopped at each town to summon clan representatives to the national council house. The national council was less a law-making body than a consultative and policy-forming group for particular issues and situations of tribal concern.

The weight of authority rested lightly on tribal citizens. A European observer commented that they were "governed by the plain and honest law of nature, their whole constitution breathes nothing but liberty." He went on to point out that their languages "have no words to express despotic power, arbitrary kings, oppressed, or obedient subjects [and] they have exquisite pleasure in pursuing their own natural dictates." The basis for status and public acclaim was "by superior virtue, oratory, or prowess."[10]

The "plain and honest law of nature" was a direct and viable *corpus juris.* A basic precept was that the tribal domain was held in common ownership. Each town had its common fields, and local citizens were required to work together in sowing and cultivating the crops on these public farms. They stored the yield in public granaries for use in time of need. Private land use was permitted; families selected and farmed small plots of their own for household needs. The local council of elders served as an arbitration court, settling disputes arising from private land use. Citizens were required to assist in erecting public buildings, such as council houses and religious shrines, and in preparing town defenses.

Proscribed actions in law included homicide, theft, blasphemy, and adultery. The tribes practiced a mixed system of private and public punishment. The clan council of elders passed judgment on most crimes. Since retaliation and vengeance pervaded their legal customs, more often than not the council simply served as a detached tribunal to see that the aggrieved or their family did their duty in exacting proper retribution. In cases of theft, the local clan council supervised the punishment of offenders by public whipping. In homicide cases, where private action was a public duty, the relatives of the victim had a holy mandate to seek out and kill the slayer. If the slayer could not be found, a brother could be substituted as a sort of sacrifice to the law of retaliation.

Confederacies

While particularism predominated in Indian political systems, certain tribes, to serve broad mutual interests including military defense, formed larger political units called confederations. This trend was quite common among the

Eastern Algonkians. The Abenaki and other New England tribes associated at times for greater collective military strength. Central Atlantic Coast Algonkians, centering on the Delawares, confederated during the sixteenth century. And the Southern Algonkians joined to form the Powhatan Confederacy around 1600. The political wonders of aboriginal North America were the Iroquois, with their marvelous matriarchally based confederation, and the theocracy of the Natchez which will be considered in the next chapter.

Notes

1. James Adair, *The History of the American Indians* (London, 1775). Reprinted with an introduction by Samuel C. Williams (Johnson City, Tennessee, 1930), p. 448.
2. *Ibid.*, p. 178.
3. Harold E. Driver, *Indians of North America* (Chicago, 1969), pp. 111–113.
4. *Ibid.*, p. 114.
5. Adair, *American Indians*, p. 146.
6. *Ibid.*, p. 145.
7. Driver, *Indians of North America*, p. 231.
8. John R. Swanton, *The Indians of the Southeastern United States* (Washington, 1946), pp. 715–716.
9. Driver, *Indians of North America*, p. 396.
10. Adair, *American Indians*, pp. 406–407, 459.

Selected Sources

Useful surveys of Native American cultural evolution during the period from 1250 to 1500 include Ruth M. Underhill, *Red Man's America: A History of Indians in the United States* (Chicago, 1971); Robert F. Spencer, Jesse D. Jennings, et al., *The Native Americans: Prehistory and Ethnology of the North American Indians* (New York, 1965); Jesse D. Jennings, *Prehistory of North America* (New York, 1974); P. S. Martin, et al., *Indians before Columbus* (Chicago, 1947); H. M. Wormington, *Ancient Man in America* (Denver, 1957); and T. H. Patterson, *American Past: A New World Archeology* (Glenview, Ill., 1973).

Illuminating contemporary accounts of the state of Indian culture soon after European Contact include Edward G. Bourne (ed.), *Narratives of the Career of Hernando de Soto* (New York, 1922), Vols. 1 and 2. James Adair, *The History of the American Indians* (London, 1775), reprinted with an introduction by Samuel C. Williams (Johnson City, Tennessee, 1930); and P. F. X. de Charlevoix, *History and General Description of New France,* translated with notes by John G. Shea (Chicago, 1962), Vols. 1–6.

An essential reference source, containing descriptive sketches on early development of each Native American community, is Frederick W. Hodge (ed.), *Handbook of American Indians North of Mexico* (Washington, D.C., 1907–1910), 2 vols. Reprinted (New York, 1959), 2 vols. *Annual Reports and Bulletins* published by the Bureau of American Ethnology, Smithsonian Institution, contain archeological and anthropological studies of the Indian tribes. An example of this class of literature is John R. Swanton, *The Indians of the Southeastern United States* (Washington, 1946).

The most useful reference on the material and nonmaterial culture of the Indian tribes, arranged by cultural subject, is Harold E. Driver, *Indians of North America* (Chicago, 1969). A quite readable study of the Indian tribes on the eve of European Contact showing the differential in cultural progessions is Peter Farb, *Man's Rise to Civilization as Shown by the Indians of North America* (New York, 1969).

The rising public consciousness toward Native Americans and escalating interest in their culture, as could be expected, has generated a vast new literature on the aboriginal experience. A very popular bibliographical group centers on Indian supernaturalism. Carlos Castaneda has contributed several books to this category: *The Teachings of Don Juan; A Separate Reality;* and *Journey to Ixtlan: The Lessons of Don Juan* (New York, 1972).

CHAPTER 4

THE TRIBAL SETTING
IN 1500

*We do now crown you with the sacred emblem . . . of the sign of your lord-
ship. You shall now become a mentor of the people of the Five Nations. The
thickness of your skin will be seven spans, for you will be proof against anger,
offensive action, and criticism. With endless patience you shall carry out your
duty, and your firmness shall be tempered with compassion for your people.
Neither anger nor fear shall find lodgment in your mind, and all your words
and actions shall be tempered with calm deliberation. In all your official acts,
self-interest shall be cast aside. You shall look and listen to the welfare of the
whole people, and have always in view, not only the present but the coming
generations—the unborn of the future Nation.*

**Charge by Deganawidah, Iroquois folk hero, to leaders
of the Iroquois Confederation, 1564**

At the time of European exploration and settlement, Indians numbered an
estimated 1,500,000. They were fairly well distributed across the continent,
with some areas, such as present-day California with 150,000 people, more
populated than others. And although some Europeans and their Anglo-
American successors regarded Indians as subhuman shadows, a part of the
wilderness along with the deer, panthers, wolves, and bears, Indians had
established viable, functioning societies.

By 1500 all Native Americans had become associated with particular
groups which have come to be called tribes. In some cases the tribal name was
the designation a people had borne for several centuries, either the name a
particular group called itself or one that other tribes had given to it. Many
tribal names are derived from what administrators, traders, and missionaries
of European empires called certain groups.

Only in rare cases are modern-day Native Americans living on the lands
their ancestors occupied in 1500. Today many Indians live on reservations or
allotments far removed from their ancestral territory. Administrators, traders,
and missionaries of European empires moved tribes or bands of tribes here
and there across the continent to serve various purposes. Anglo-Americans
continued this relocation. This history of uprooting and relocating Native
Americans is recounted in the "Trail of Tears" sagas of several tribes including

Chapter Opening Artifact: Hohokam bird-effigy vessel. (Courtesy of Museum of the
American Indian, Heye Foundation)

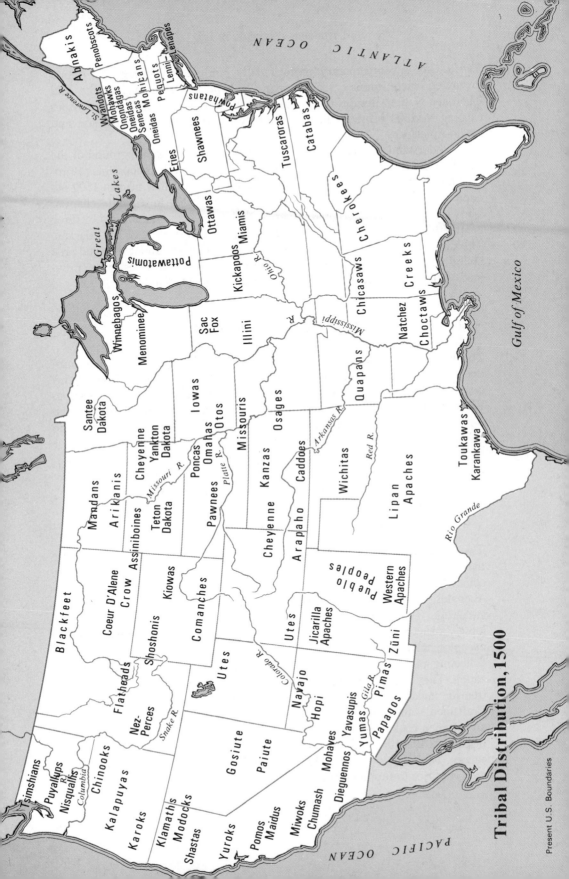

Tribal Distribution, 1500

Present U.S. Boundaries

ATLANTIC OCEAN

PACIFIC OCEAN

Gulf of Mexico

Great Lakes

St. Lawrence R.

Abnakis
Penobscots
Wyandots
Mohawks
Onondagas
Oneidas
Senecas
Oneidas
Mohicans
Pequots
Lenni-Lenapes
Eries
Powhatans
Shawnees
Tuscaroras
Catabas
Ottawas
Miamis
Cherokees
Pottawatomis
Kickapoos
Chicasaws
Creeks
Ohio R.
Winnebagos
Menominee
Sac Fox
Illini
Mississippi R.
Natchez
Choctaws
Quapans
Santee Dakota
Iowas
Missouris
Osages
Arkansas R.
Cheyenne
Omahas
Otos
Red R.
Yankton Dakota
Ponca
Platte R.
Kanzas
Caddoes
Wichitas
Toukawas
Karankawa
Mandans
Arikanis
Missouri R.
Pawnees
Cheyenne
Arapaho
Lipan Apaches
Rio Grande
Assiniboines
Teton Dakota
Blackfeet
Coeur D'Alene
Crow
Kiowas
Comanches
Utes
Jicarilla Apaches
Pueblo Peoples
Western Apaches
Zūni
Shoshonis
Flatheads
Nez-Perces
Snake R.
Utes
Colorado R.
Navajo
Hopi
Yavasupis
Yumas
Gila R.
Pimas
Papagos
Simshians
Puyallups
Nisquallis
Columbia R.
Chinooks
Kalapuyas
Karoks
Klamaths
Modocs
Shastas
Yuroks
Gosiute
Paiute
Pomos
Maidus
Miwoks
Chumash
Mohaves
Dieguennos

Tsa-La-Ghi, a contemporary professionally produced Cherokee folk drama presented each summer season near Tahlequah, Oklahoma, in the Old Cherokee Nation. Besides the groups that were moved around, several tribes existing in 1500 subsequently were nearly exterminated by Europeans and Anglo-Americans.

To understand that later history, we need to establish a background of the situation the Europeans found in 1500. Clearly it would be impossible to present a detailed description of each of the nearly 300 tribes who in 1500 occupied territory now embraced by the United States in a single chapter. Thus the survey of aboriginal America that follows is organized into three great ethnographic provinces—the Eastern, the Western, and the Alaskan. The discussion of each will consist of a general comment about the total area including the geographical extent, linguistic families, and tribes in the province, with brief highlights of common or comparative life-styles.

THE EASTERN PROVINCE

The Eastern province extends from the Atlantic Seaboard to the one hundredth meridian, where the humid prairies end and the semiarid Great Plains begin, and from the Great Lakes to the Gulf of Mexico. Today the Mississippi River is usually regarded as the boundary between East and West. But the same moisture and soil conditions and general environment found east of the Mississippi River extend west of it for nearly two hundred miles. Hence, for a discussion of Indian cultures, the one hundredth meridian is a more appropriate boundary. In the Eastern ethnographic province lived Indians of the Algonkian, Iroquoian, Muskhogean, and Siouian language families.

Algonkian

Two distinct life-styles were found among the Algonkians. The tribes along the north shore of the Great Lakes and eastward into Maine, where the cold climate made agriculture impractical, followed an Archaic-type life-style. The Abenakis, Penobscots, and Chippewas subsisted by hunting, fishing, and gathering. Their political organization of linguistically related bands was loosely structured; they followed a seminomadic life and had no permanently occupied villages. They moved on a circuit each year, following game and collecting plants. The northern Algonkians were patrilineal in social organization. They had not adopted pottery but used bark stripped from the birch tree for making household containers, storage vessels, and cooking utensils. Craftsmen waterproofed these containers by sealing the seams with pitch, and women cooked the family's food by dropping hot stones into water-filled birch-bark utensils. And on a larger scale, birch bark was also used to cover canoes. The Chippewas and Menominis along the western Great Lakes gathered wild rice to supplement their hunting and fishing.

The remainder of the Algonkians, living farther south in a warmer climate, were agricultural, mixing farming with hunting, gathering, and river and oceanic fishing. The Wampanoags, Narragansetts, and Pequots of New England fertilized hills of corn in their fields with alewives, small fish which swarmed in the estuaries near their villages.

The different tribes varied greatly in the kinds of houses they built. Algonkians used three types of dwellings—the conical shelter similar to the Plains tribes' tipi, a small circular wigwam, and a large multifamily lodge that looked like a quonset hut. Whatever the shape, the framework was poles, lashed with strips of bark or skin thongs, and the sides were covered with bark, woven mats, and skins. The agricultural Algonkians practiced a mixed matrilineal-patrilineal social system, made and used pottery, and occupied permanent village sites which they left for seasonal buffalo-hunting trips to the western prairies.

The Algonkians are noted for their confederations for mutual protection, a tradition that lasted from pre-Columbian times to the post-Contact period when Algonkian tribes created military confederations to resist the European and Anglo-American advance. In the 1760s the Ottawa chieftain Pontiac formed a confederation to resist British extension into the area between the Ohio and the Mississippi rivers. In 1808–1812 Tecumseh, the Shawnee, forged a powerful pan-Indian force to stop expansive American settlement in the same territory. Algonkian tribes also produced such orators and patriots as Pontiac, Tecumseh, and Black Hawk, the Sac and Fox chieftain. There were well-known Algonkian native religious prophets as well, such as Elskwatawa, a brother of Tecumseh, and Kennekuk, the Kickapoo prophet. Certain Algonkian tribes have shown a deep attachment to aboriginal ways and a determination to resist detribalization programs. For example, in the 1860s a large community of Kickapoos, who formerly lived on the Illinois prairies, moved to northern Mexico to escape the "civilization program" of the United States government and to pursue their ancient way of life.

Iroquoian

The Iroquoians were primarily sedentary agricultural peoples, who also did some hunting, fishing, gathering, and trading with other tribes. The tribes of the League of Five Nations, a confederation composed of Senecas, Cayugas, Onondagas, Oneidas and Mohawks, lived year round in large settlements enclosed by heavy log palisades. Dwellings were the famous longhouses, quonset-shaped structures covered with elm bark, each one fifty to one hundred feet long and accommodating eight to ten families. The northern Iroquois were as dependent upon elm bark as their Algonkian neighbors were upon birch bark as a basic material for crafts, canoe covering, and home building. They fashioned elm bark into vessels, containers, and utensils, although they also used pottery. They separated elm fiber and used it to make strong ropes and cordage for fish nets, game traps, rope ladders, and other items. The Iroquois were active traders, ranging over a wide territory to acquire exotic products from far-off places to enrich their lives.

The northern Iroquoian peoples were unsurpassed among the North American tribes for their warrior tradition, their military successes and the fear and dread their presence stirred among their neighbors. And their political confederation was unusual in pre-Contact America. Formed in pre-Columbian times and called the *Hodesaunee*, the League of Five Nations was a confederation of the Seneca, Oneida, Mohawk, Cayuga, and Onondaga tribes. In 1713 the Tuscaroras moved north and joined the confederation; thereafter it was known as the League of the Six Nations.

Iroquoian government, both tribal and league, was an extension of the Iroquoian social model, thoroughly female dominated and directed—matriarchal, matrilineal, matrilocal—the only matriarchate in North America. Family continuity and clan affiliation passed through the women. Children were under the complete control of the mothers of each clan; property and goods, including dwellings and the right to use agricultural tracts, belonged to the mothers and passed to heirs through them.

Each of the five nations was governed by a council of sachems or chiefs selected by the women from the family-clan-moiety divisions. Women had the power of review and veto over the tribal council actions and could remove men acting on their behalf. Each of the five member tribes of the League was proportionately represented on the league council of fifty male sachems. League council members also were chosen by the women who maintained review powers over league actions and could recall council members. While the tribal and league governments functioned as indirect matriarchies, the men ruling at the pleasure of the women, females sometimes participated directly in council proceedings as regents when a newly selected sachem was too young to take part. The council of the League of Five Nations had no voice in the affairs of the self-governing member tribes except that it could act as an arbiter in case of an irreconcilable internal dispute. The league government primarily occupied itself with matters of intertribal concern—diplomacy and war and peace with other nations.

The Cherokees were best-known for their sophisticated internal polity and their law and court system. However, their cultural orientation was closer to that of their southeastern neighbors, the Muskhogean peoples.

Muskhogean

In 1500 these groups, rather than being identifiable tribes, were associated in what appeared to be ethnic conglomerates which by 1750 would become consolidated tribes. The Creeks, Choctaws, Chickasaws, and the culturally close Natchez were expanding in population and territory through absorption of scores of smaller neighboring tribes. This ethnic expansion was less a voluntary, confederation-type association than a forced permanent biological, cultural, and territorial domination of the small and weak by the large and strong. The Creeks were the most variegated, an association of dozens of small tribes centering on the Muskogees, Hitchitis, Alabamas, and Euchees. The Seminoles, not identified until the early nineteenth century, are an example of this integrating trend. They withdrew from the Creek nation and joined with several tribal remnants on the Georgia-Florida border to form the Seminole nation.

Muskhogean territory was a rich land. Its bountiful resources in food plants, animals, fish, and other essentials for high-quality life and its mild climate even in winter made life easier there than in most of the other ethnographic regions. The economy was based on agriculture, some hunting, gathering, fishing, and trade. Their government structures, derived from tribal social models—matrilineal family, clan, and moiety—consisted of town and national councils of elders directing the affairs of the nations in conjunction with principal chiefs drawn from each of the grand moiety divisions of the tribes.

Each tribe had a special reputation. The Choctaws were renowned for economic excellence, particularly in agriculture and trade. The Creeks were

Choctaw eagle dancers, from a George Catlin painting. (Smithsonian Institution, National Anthropological Archives)

esteemed as peacemakers, council sponsors, and diplomats. The Chickasaws were first in the martial arts, the greatest warriors of the lower Mississippi Valley. And the Natchez were North America's only theocracy, or society ruled by religious leaders.

Nevertheless, all the Southeastern tribes were religious and shared common religious characteristics, including a professional priesthood—the *hopoye* or holy men—drawn from the leading clan of the primary moiety of each tribe. Their religious observances centered on the sun, the great holy fire above as a part of their compound god. The sun was represented in each national capital by a sacred temple fire. Guardian priests watched over this fire and dispensed coals for household fires, bringing the composite force into each home. Each tribe also observed the annual Busk festival, held at the beginning of the first new moon when the green corn was ripe. The *hopoye* and their attendants extinguished the old sacred fire, removed the ashes, and struck a new one. On this simple altar the priests offered a bit of tobacco, button snakeroot, and several ears of new corn to the fresh flames to symbolize annual renewal of the nation. As a part of the Busk, which was also a time of purification and thanksgiving, the people fasted for two days, then drank an emetic of boiled cusseena, the "black drink," which caused vomiting to symbolize purging of all evil from their bodies. Following purification, they feasted on roasting ears.

The Natchez exceeded all other Southeastern tribes in religious fervor and complexity. In other ways, too, the Natchez were an anomaly among the Southeastern tribes. Other tribes of the region for the most part were so free and democratic that they verged on license and anarchy. Not so the Natchez. They lived under a theocracy where the state, the people, and their resources were devoted to the edification of the religious establishment. The people were completely at the mercy of the head of state who was also the high priest—the Sun. Natchez were required to be devout worshipers of the sun. By worshiping the earthly Sun, their head of state, they also worshiped their heavenly Sun. They built high mounds on which they erected temples so the "earthly sun" could converse with his elder brother the "heavenly sun." No Oriental potentate had greater power over his subjects than the Sun over the Natchez. They were forbidden to show their backs to him when leaving his presence. His feet were never allowed to touch the earth. He was carried on a litter by eight men working in relays.

Natchez society was divided into four classes. At the top of the social pyramid were the Sun and his wives and children. Next were the nobles, then the honored people. At the bottom of Natchez society were the Stinkards; they performed menial tasks for the support and comfort of the upper classes. However, there was a compensating mobility in the Natchez social system. Every member of every class above the Stinkards had to marry a Stinkard, and each new Sun had to have a Sun mother and a Stinkard father. Thus Stinkards moved up, however slowly.

Siouian

On the eve of European Contact Siouian-speaking tribes occupied the Mississippi and Missouri valleys, but in earlier times they had lived in the Ohio Valley as agriculturalists. However, pressure from expanding Iroquoian and Algonkian tribes had forced some of them westward and others southward.

By 1500 the economy of these people was becoming mixed. In early times they had been predominantly agricultural; after 1500 several tribes altered their economies, particularly the Teton Sioux who were becoming largely nomadic buffalo hunters. The Santees and Winnebagos were somewhat agricultural, although they also depended upon hunting, fishing, and gathering wild rice for subsistence. The agricultural tribes included the Mandans, regarded as the first farmers on the Great Plains and extremely skilled agriculturalists; they are credited with developing a variety of corn adapted to the northland's shorter growing season. They also raised tobacco, squash, beans, and sunflowers. Sunflowers were a staple rivaling corn in importance. The women parched and ground the sunflower seeds and added the meal to vegetables and meat for thickening. Also they formed sunflower meal into balls, much like pemmican, which warriors carried as rations on hunts and military campaigns. Most of the Sioux also were fishermen. The northland rivers and lakes provided an abundance of fish which was an important food resource. They used nets and weirs to trap great quantities of whitefish which they dried for winter use. Also they speared huge sturgeon from boats. The nomadic hunting Sioux used the dog travois for land transportation. The many rivers of the north encouraged water travel, and the tribes used canoes, round hide-covered bull boats, and rafts. Their shelters varied from the Mandans' earth lodges to wigwam-type Osage dwellings to the skin-covered tipis of the Teton Sioux buffalo hunters.

Adjustment to new territory and in some cases changing economies caused several Siouian tribes to change their social models. When they had been agricultural, they had had a matrilineal-matrilocal organization, but by 1500 the picture was becoming mixed. Many tribes retained the old system but some, particularly those who were becoming nomadic hunters, were adopting the patrilineal-patrilocal system. Nearly all Siouian tribes were divided into clans, and most of them also had moieties, which the tribes retained. Their tribal governments were an extension of the social system; most sovereign powers were centered in the local group. Controls over the individual largely came from the family, the clan, and tribal religion. In most cases the principal governing agency was a national council composed of town chiefs, or if nomadic hunters, of band chiefs. Annual religious festivals tied the scattered Siouian villages and bands together.

Siouian religion required intensive individual and group commitment. All young men, besides observing the ordinances of the religious system, were expected as a part of their rite of adulthood to search for a vision wherein they would receive guardian spirits and guidance on their mission or purpose in life. Sioux religion included a great deal of ritual and use of personal and group sacred objects. Each warrior owned a sacred bundle which symbolized the sources of his medicine or power. Likewise there was the group fetish or ark which was the source of tribal power.

Wakan, a compound god consisting of the Sun, the Sky, and Earth (the Mother), was the great inscrutable power in the universe, so mysterious in its workings that people were unable to comprehend it. The principal links to Wakan and other Siouian deities were the shamans. They were also the healers, since illness was believed to have supernatural causes.

Two rituals express the character of Siouian religion—the Mandan Okipa ceremony and the Teton Sun Dance. The Mandans observed the Okipa each midsummer. Tribal welfare was believed to center on this four-day festival. Participants fasted, feasted, sang, and danced, and reenacted a folk drama of their creation and development as a people. During the Okipa certain young warriors offered to submit to the Mandan ordeal. Shamans cut slits with sharp tools in each one's back, breast, and legs. They passed wooden slivers through the slits and secured a thong to each sliver. To the leg thongs they tied buffalo skulls. By the thongs secured to the back and breast they raised the candidates off the floor of the ceremonial lodge and suspended them from the altar. Through their endurance of torture, the young warriors demonstrated the power of the spirit over the flesh. The Okipa revitalized the world for the Mandans and renewed the strength of their society.[1]

The Sun Dance, the most important Teton Sioux ritual, was held in early summer when the food plants and game animals, particularly the buffalo, were in prime condition. It was a time for giving thanks, for renewing national solidarity, and for gaining personal strength and status. Since the Teton Sioux were in the process of abandoning agriculture and becoming nomadic hunting people, the Sun Dance was also an important unifying experience for the Sioux nation. Bands gathered at a location previously agreed upon. Leaders selected a sacred tree; honored women chopped it down, trimmed the trunk, painted it with symbolic colors, and fashioned a bison deity figure at its top. When raised and placed in position, the decorated tree trunk became the Sun Dance altar.

The four-day festival consisted of fasting, feasting, singing, and performing mock battles against evil forces. The highlight of the festival was the consecration of young warrior candidates to the buffalo deity through self-torture. Each candidate was required to possess the four great Sioux virtues—bravery, generosity, fortitude, and integrity. Shamans spent much time with the candidates, purifying each one and instructing him in the performance of the ceremony and the significance of each action. Much like the Mandan Okipa, shamans slit the body of each candidate, but in the case of the Teton Sioux only in the back. They inserted skewers in each wound, attached a long leather thong to each skewer, and fastened heavy buffalo skulls to the trailing leather lines. The candidates pulled their burdens about the consecrated ground, their eyes fixed on the altar, dancing in cadence to drums and chants, the accompanying repertoire repeated in sequence throughout the day and into the night. At a climax point set by the shamans, each dancer jerked at his thongs, tearing the slits in his back to free himself. If he had not fainted or fallen out, if he had endured his ordeal to the end, the warrior received gaping wounds in his back. When healed into scars, these marks became badges of highest honor and a source of instant status as a revered warrior.

THE WESTERN PROVINCE

The Western ethnographic province embraces all the territory between the one hundredth meridian and the Pacific shore and from the Canadian border to Mexico. Characterizing this area in 1500 is more difficult than was the case for the Eastern ethnographic province, primarily because unlike the East, it contained no broad language patterns over equally broad geographic areas. The harsh environment offered only a limited number of really good places to live, around which Indians of differing linguistic and cultural backgrounds clustered. Thus in many cases tribes representing several language families occupied the same subregion of the Western ethnographic province. Because of this province's environmental differences and linguistic-cultural peculiarities, the presentation will be by subregion: the Great Plains tribes, the Southwest tribes, the Great Basin tribes, the Plateau tribes, the California tribes, and the Northwest Coast tribes.

The Great Plains Tribes

This vast geographic region, extending from Canada to the Rio Grande and from the one hundredth meridian to the Rocky Mountains, consists largely of grassland. In 1500 it was the range of vast herds of buffalo primarily, although deer, elk, antelope, and other game also flourished there. The Great Plains became more glamorous and more heavily populated after the reintroduction of the horse by Europeans which revolutionized life there. However, without the horse only a few tribes were permanent residents.

Tribes on its eastern border—basically agricultural, and on its western border—basically hunting-gathering, entered the Plains for annual buffalo hunts, returning to their peripheral habitats the rest of the year. The Teton Sioux, Cheyennes, and Arapahoes, primarily upper Mississippi Valley farmers, were around 1500 just beginning to move onto the Plains to follow a nomadic, buffalo-hunting existence. On the Great Plains' western margins Kiowas, Comanches, Blackfeet, and Crows lived in their mountain canyon and plateau coverts, entering the Plains only for the annual buffalo hunt. The permanent residents of the Northern Plains at this time were the Mandans, their farming villages scattered along the fertile lowlands of the upper Missouri River.

The Southern Great Plains in 1500 was the home of several tribes including the Athapascan-speaking Lipan Apaches. They were the most easterly of

71

several Athapascan groups then entering the Southwest. They roamed the southern Great Plains hunting the buffalo. The Spanish conquistador Francisco Vásquez de Coronado visited their camps in 1540 during his search for the Gran Quivira, a reportedly fabulously rich Indian settlement on the northern frontier of New Spain. The expedition's chroniclers commented on the Plains Apaches' dependence upon the buffalo for food, shelter, and clothing; in a land that was largely treeless, even the dried buffalo dung was used for fuel. The Spaniards described how the women tanned buffalo hides for garments and covers for their portable shelters, the tipis, which later became characteristic for most of the buffalo-hunting tribes. The Lipan Apaches used dogs hitched to travois poles to transport their shelters and other possessions from one hunting ground to another.

The Mandans were not the only agriculturalists on the Great Plains during the pre-Contact period. Occupying present-day western Nebraska and Kansas were the Pawnees. These Caddoan-speaking people maintained permanent

Wichita-Caddo (Taovaya) grass house. (Western History Collections, University of Oklahoma Library)

villages of large earth-covered lodges in the river valleys close to their fields of corn, squash, beans, and pumpkins. They also hunted the buffalo to supplement their basic vegetarian diet. Pawnee craftsmen produced quality pottery, baskets, and textiles. Their social model was matrilineal-matrilocal. Tribal government was village-centered, each community governed by a council of elders and leading men who occasionally came together as a national council to conduct the business of the entire tribe. Shamans presided over the Pawnees' complex maize-centered religion. Corn was regarded as a sacred gift from their creator and was called "mother"; seasonal religious ceremonies directed its planting, cultivating, and harvesting.

South of the Pawnees, on the Red, Arkansas, Canadian, and Brazos rivers, were the Caddoan-speakingWichitas, Caddoes, Tawakonis, and Wacos. They were agricultural people like their Pawnee relatives, living in large farming villages composed of dome-shaped dwellings, each thirty to fifty feet in diameter, framed with poles and covered with grass thatch. The Wichitas and Caddoes were particularly skilled farmers and traders. They regularly produced a surplus of corn and tobacco which they bartered to other tribes for hides, dried meat, and captives. Their talent for commerce made them strategically important when Europeans appropriated their territory. Their many religious ceremonies included a festival similar to the Green Corn Dance of the Eastern tribes' Busk ceremony. These Caddoans produced pottery and baskets. The Wichitas and Caddoes, also called Picts because of the elaborate tattooing both men and women applied to face and body, were the inhabitants of Quivira, Coronado's principal goal.

The Southwest Tribes

The Southwest, from the Pecos River to the Colorado River including most of present-day New Mexico and Arizona, accommodated many tribes speaking varying languages and following differing life-styles. They may be divided into the Pueblo Peoples, the Riparian Peoples, and the Intruder Peoples.

The Pueblo Peoples were identified by their house type—the pueblo—rather than by tribe. Although they spoke a number of different dialects and languages, they were much alike in material and nonmaterial culture, particularly economy and religion.

The Pueblo Peoples are believed to be the descendants of the Anasazis. In 1500 they lived in settlements scattered along the Rio Grande and its tributaries. The Zuñi and Hopi pueblos were on high, protective mesas in western New Mexico and eastern Arizona. The Pueblo Peoples were farmers, their principal crop corn although they also produced beans, squash, and tobacco. The men tended the fields assisted by the women at planting and harvest times; otherwise the women and children gathered piñon nuts and other natural fruits and plants from the highlands near their settlements.

The pueblo environment was desert, rarely receiving as much as ten inches of rainfall each year. Pueblo farmers attempted to overcome the problem of

Zuni Pueblo, New Mexico. (Library of Congress)

aridity by constructing irrigation works along the Rio Grande and its tributaries, developing varieties of corn that would withstand intense heat and drought, and by focusing their religious attention upon those supernatural forces which they believed controlled nature's rain-making apparatus. While Rio Grande pueblo farmers depended upon irrigation, Hopi and Zuñi agrarians were dry farmers. They planted small fields on alluvial fans formed by dry creeks or washes draining the canyons of their mesa country. Thus their crops benefited from runoff after rains. They were also expert at selecting locations with shallow subsurface moisture. Besides agrarian foods, Pueblo Peoples also produced fine pottery, baskets, cotton cloth, and blankets.

The pueblos were autonomous. Although not a theocracy in the sense of the Natchez government, the pueblo political system was heavily overlain with religion. Each pueblo was a maze of complex functional religious societies. The head of each society was a member of the pueblo council which directed the affairs of the community. One of the most important secular functions of pueblo government was water management. An elected commissioner was responsible for the annual community labor levy which required all men to repair irrigation works which conducted water from the creeks and rivers to the fields. This official also allocated water to each pueblo farmer.

The pueblo people were deeply religious. Each pueblo spent much public time each year observing ceremonies, rituals, pageants, and festivals. They all revolved around the two all-important sustainers of life: rain and corn. The annual opening of the irrigation ditches, the harvest, rain-making pageants—all were occasions for pueblo religious observance. It is estimated that pueblo men spent at least half of their time in religious activities. Some were private, covert, esoteric rites in the kivas; some were public ceremonies with colorful costumes, ritual, dancing, and chanting. The ultimate in holy observance was masked dancers impersonating *katchinas,* the ancestral spirits including rain makers.[2]

Southwest of the Pueblo Peoples were the settlements of the Riparian Peoples, farmers who occupied the territory along the Salt, Gila, San Pedro, Santa Cruz, and Colorado rivers. Toward the east, primarily on the Salt and the Gila, were the Pimas, Papagos, and Sobiapuris, descended from the Hohokam Peoples of late prehistoric times. They spoke a Uto-Aztecan dialect. The westerly Riparian tribes along the Colorado River, the Yavapais, Maricopas, Mohaves, and Yumas, were descended from the Patayan Peoples of late prehistoric times. They were a part of the Yuman linguistic family.

These Riparian Peoples were desert dwellers. Their settlements, later called rancherías, tended to be located in oasislike locations near streams where they practiced irrigation or flood-plain agriculture to produce crops of corn which, prepared in various ways, comprised 80 percent of their diet, and beans, squash, sunflower seeds, and cotton. Their crafts included exquisite baskets, textiles, and pottery, embellished with colorful art and design.

Each tribe's government consisted of a loosely organized association with no head chief. Each band or village was autonomous and was led by a head man with very limited authority. His most important function was calendar keeper for essential rites, particularly the rain dance, and manager of the irrigation works. He directed the annual labor levy to maintain the *acequias* or water ditches and managed the water allocation to family plots. He was assisted by a council consisting of all adult men in the village and, as with most of the tribes in council, all decisions required unanimous consent. The decision-making process was dominated by elders. Shamans presided over the religious observances and served as healers. Riparian tribal ceremonies centered on the tie between crops, particularly corn, and the need for favorable weather, especially rain. The summer rain-inducing effort included drinking wine made from fermented saguaro cactus juice. Riparian Peoples believed that ritual drunkenness brought a purification of mind and heart, which would bring rain.[3]

Living near the pueblo and riparian settlements and maintaining sustained

An Apache wickiup. (Smithsonian Institution, National Anthropological Archives)

pressure on these farmers were the Intruder Peoples, Athapascan-speaking raiders from the far north. It is believed that, along with extended droughts, the Athapascan vandals were responsible for uprooting and scattering the Anasazi, Mogollon, and Hohokam peoples during the late prehistoric age. The Athapascans, fierce predatory people, used the sinew-backed bow which propelled arrows at great speed with killing accuracy at considerable distance and which made them militarily superior to the peaceful agricultural Indians who had only limited defensive weapons of crude lances, hoes of bone, and stone axes. The vigorous Athapascans had vastly differing life-styles and value systems from the settled peoples of the Southwest.

Athapascans were more characteristic of the far northwest in Canada and Alaska, and these Intruder Peoples were the most southerly extension of this large language family. By 1500 they had differentiated into two large groups, one of which was Apache, and they were in the process of further dividing into subgroups. The Apache had included several smaller groups or bands which came to be called Jicarilla Apaches, Kiowa Apaches, Lipan Apaches,

Chiricahua Apaches, Mescalero Apaches, and San Carlos Apaches. The other large Athapascan division was Navajo. The Navajos did not proliferate into scattered bands as did the Apaches but maintained a closer association.

While all Athapascan intruders roamed over the Southwest and raided the agricultural tribes, they varied in their economy. Some imitated their pueblo neighbors more than others. Thus the Jicarilla Apaches were somewhat agricultural, as were some Navajos. However, both Apaches and Navajos were primarily hunters, gatherers, and raiders. And the Athapascans were just as dependent upon the Pueblos and Riparian settlements for grain and other foods as they were upon hunting and gathering. Through the centuries the raiders had worked out a parasitic type of relationship with the agricultural settlements, never completely destroying a pueblo during a raid but wisely leaving enough grain and other food so as not to discourage the settled tribes' efforts the next year.

The hunting, gathering, raiding life-style limited Athapascan material culture and technology. Some bands produced baskets, made pottery, and wove textiles although most of these industries were a later adaptation. Most Apache bands used the wickiup—a crude temporary shelter of sapling frame covered with grass and brush. Jicarilla and Mescalero Apaches used the Plains-type tipi. The typical Navajo shelter was the forked-support hogan.

Athapascans had no central tribal government. Both the Apaches and Navajos associated in autonomous bands, matrilineal and matrilocal in social organization. Bands consisted of clusters of extended families. Band leaders or head men won their positions by endurance and physical strength and their skill and daring as war leaders. In educating their youth, the Athapascans emphasized preparing the boys for the hardy, dangerous life of hunting and raiding. They stressed the need for the young warrior to accomplish feats of physical endurance, master military skills, and strive for personal achievement. Because of their glorious war tradition, the Navajos and Apaches in historic times became the most glamorous of the Southwestern tribes.

Both the Apaches and Navajos were deeply religious. Apache religion consisted of praying to gods for success in hunting, raiding, and rainmaking. While most tribes publicly stressed the upbringing and training of boys, the Apaches gave considerable public attention to girls. Their puberty rites were the most important of the tribe's religious festivals, a four-day ceremony for which the honored girl was secluded and prepared by the shamans through elaborate purification. As with the Pueblo Peoples, their public worship consisted of impersonating the gods with *katchina*-like paraphernalia. At the puberty festival, the Gans, representing the Apache Mountain Spirits and each wearing a black mask, skirt, wooden slat headdress, and carrying a wooden scepter, dominated the ceremony. A chorus of older women with drummers grouped about a huge fire supported the Gans dancers. On the fourth night following the concluding dance, shamans sang a sacred song over the honored girl and sprinkled her with pollen as a symbol of fertility and the hope of the Apache nation.

The Navajos regarded the universe as an entity of harmony and balance. People through inevitable human error created an occasional imbalance in the cosmos, resulting in misfortune, perhaps sickness or even death. Thus people had to work constantly at maintaining a balance with the universe and achieving harmony. Lay people and shamans used many sacred chants and sacred deity-ordained formulas to accomplish this and to win favor with the Navajo Holy People. This included mastery of a repertoire of more than 500 traditional dry paintings (sand paintings), which foretold the future for some situations or healed sickness.

Great Basin Tribes

The Great Basin subregion, lying between the Rocky Mountains and Sierra Nevadas, is flanked by the Plateau and the Southwest areas. It is perhaps North America's harshest natural region, containing the least resources to sustain human life. The various Great Basin tribes all spoke a single language—the Shoshonean branch of the Uto-Aztecan linguistic family—and followed a similar life-style. On the northeastern edge of the Great Basin lived the Shoshonean-speaking Comanches, who in later times became the all-powerful proud lords of the South Plains. However, in 1500 they were a humble hunting-gathering folk.

The Great Basin's austere environment required that its inhabitants make a complete adjustment to their surroundings, using the limited plants and animals, even insects, for food. They collected and ate mice, lizards, snakes, locusts, grasshoppers, caterpillars, crickets, and ants. They roasted grasshoppers alive and pounded the residue into a flour. Great Basin Indians collected seeds of weeds and grasses; they dug roots; and they trapped birds, ducks, geese, and rabbits. And they made a large number of useful items from grasses, sedges, twigs, saplings, bark, fiber, and fur including shelters, clothing, footwear, mats, nets, traps, receptacles, storage containers, and cooking utensils. Shoshonean artisans made the large amounts of rope and twine they needed by twisting long fibers of milkweed into strong line. Their crafts included making nets, some of them eight feet high and thirty feet long, to trap birds, ducks, geese, and rabbits. The rabbit was the most useful animal in the Shoshonean economy. Besides eating its meat, they made its fur into warm blankets and clothing.

The Great Basin tribes had no permanent villages. They were of necessity nomadic peoples, moving from one location to another, gathering seeds, berries, roots, piñon nuts; trapping birds and rabbits; occasionally bagging an antelope; and when in the highlands, catching fish in creeks and lakes. Their dwellings were crude, temporary wickiups, framed of saplings and covered with brush and grass.

Shoshonean social models were simple, ranging from a nuclear to extended family to an occasional group of several extended families. But scarcity of food made any prolonged social association impossible. The Great Basin tribes practiced monogamous, polygynous, and polyandrous marriages.

Tribal government was rudimentary, centering on a patriarch who dominated an extended family or group of families. He directed piñon-nut-gathering expeditions, assigning harvest areas to particular families, and managed the communal rabbit drives, serving as "rabbit boss."

Because they had little time to contemplate the metaphysical, the Great Basin tribes had the simplest religion. Their shamans presided over the few religious observances and served as healers. One of their most important functions was composing songs to confound the antelope and other game to make trapping them easier. The individual guardian spirit quest also was an important part of the Shoshonean religion.

The Great Basin life-style was forged over ten thousand years ago. These people invented gathering and processing of food plants and seeds and roots as substitutes for total reliance upon hunting during the period of large-game hunting. Their techniques were adopted by early peoples all across North America as a foundation to support the development of other life-styles. Yet, ironically, the Great Basin peoples held fast to this system of livelihood, changing little until near the middle of the last century.

The Plateau Tribes

The Plateau lies due north of the Great Basin subregion and east of the Cascades in the Snake and Columbia river drainage. The Plateau environment varies from sweeping mesas, so arid that, like the Great Basin, they support only sagebrush and salt grass, to narrow grassy valleys drained by salmon-filled tributaries of the Snake-Columbia system, thence to temperate highland forests. As a whole, the Plateau is less harsh than the Great Basin.

Twenty-five different tribes occupied the Plateau ethnographic subregion. The four principal languages spoken there were Penutian, Athapascan, Algonkian, and Salishan. Life in the Plateau was somewhat easier than in the Great Basin so that both population and ethnographic complexity were greater.

The Plateau's principal food resource was the salmon. Every year great numbers of these fish moved from the ocean into the Columbia-Snake river system seeking fresh water to spawn. Each of the Plateau tribes had access to one of the salmon waterways, which was often a part of the established tribal territory which also included a hunting and gathering reserve. Although the Plateau tribes practiced no argiculture, they lived in permanent villages, generally of multifamily earth lodges, ranging from these settlements to fish, hunt, or gather food. They collected food for winter use and returned to their villages during winter for protection from the Plateau's heavy snows and low temperatures. Most of the tribes primarily depended upon the salmon which they caught by spearing and by using dip nets, seines, and weirs. They dried salmon by smoking it on racks over slow-burning fires. Their crafts included making quality baskets, dugout canoes—used primarily for fishing with spears—and snowshoes.

The Plateau tribes had no elaborate social models of clans or moieties.

An old Cayuse woman weaving a decorated bag. (Smithsonian Institution, National Anthropological Archives)

Tribal life centered on the village, governed lightly by a headman and council which managed whatever matters might cause disputes including allocation of fishing stands on the rivers. Most of the Plateau peoples were wealth-oriented; an individual achieved status not by feats of bravery or physical endurance but by labor which accumulated material goods. In several of the Plateau tribes' languages the same word meant "chief" and "rich man"; poverty and sloth were scorned.

Religion permeated the lives of these tribes. Taboos and sacred formulas directed fishing, hunting, and gathering methods and scheduling. Shamans presided at the water-spirit fete, the appearance of the first salmon of the season, and other public ceremonies, but they were primarily healers. Religion was largely an individual concern which centered on the search for the personal guardian spirit on whom all success in life was believed to depend.[3]

With all their cultural homogeneity, certain Plateau tribes were sufficiently different to provide dramatic contrast. Thus the Klamaths were intensely

80

aggressive, always ready to wage war, taking scalps and captives as slaves in their campaigns. Their favorite public observances were scalp dances which celebrated victories over their neighbors. By contrast the Sanpoil were supreme pacifists. They avoided friction and conflict with one another and with their neighbors at all costs. In their search for peace the principle function of Sanpoil chiefs was the promotion of harmony.

The California Tribes

The California subregion contained one of the most favorable environments for aboriginal peoples in all North America. Its climate at lower elevations on the Sierra's western slope and on the seacoast was mild throughout the year, making the problem of clothing and shelter rather simple. This area was very rich in natural food resources: abundant wild plants; seashore foods, particularly shellfish; salmon in the rivers of northern California; hunting in the upland country; and vast oak forests from which came the acorn, the staple food for most California tribes.

This rich natural environment, which made human life easy, supported a vast population. It is puzzling that, with abundant food resources and mild climate, no advanced cultures developed there. This anomaly has been the subject of continuing speculation, some authorities believing that the reason was that, with mild climate, rich food resources, and easy life, there was no challenge for the California Indians, no environmental goad to drive them to high achievement. The rugged relief of this region probably contributed to this cultural inertia; it also produced extreme cultural and political particularism.

California Indians showed great diversity in physical type, language, and culture. One commentator has asserted that more different languages were spoken there than in any other single region of the world. Scores of dialects from dozens of parent languages were spoken by hundreds of different groups, which anthropologists call triblets rather than tribes. Each triblet consisted of from fifty to three hundred persons. The principal language families were Athapascan, Algonkian, Hokan, Uto-Aztecan, Shoshone, Penutian and Yukian.[4]

Material culture of the California Indians was simple. The triblets practiced no agriculture, their people subsisting upon seashore gathering of marine life and shellfish, collecting upland plants, some hunting of deer and other animals on the Sierra slopes, catching salmon in season on the rivers of northern California, and taking trout and other freshwater fish in the Sierra rivers and lakes. Virtually all California natives depended upon the acorn as their staple food. Women and children gathered and shelled the acorns, crushed the nuts with a stone pestle, and ground the coarse meal into fine flour. They spread the flour in large flat baskets and drenched the contents with water to leach out the bitter tannic acid. Generally acorn flour was eaten as mush cooked in baskets in water heated with hot stones or baked as flat bread on hot stones.

Native American dwellings in California ranged from temporary crude wickiup shelters in the south to the more elaborate cedar plank houses in the north. The California tribes had no pottery but excelled in making baskets which they used for wearing apparel, as hats, for food containers, and storage receptacles. Baskets were also used as cooking vessels. Hot stones dropped in baskets of water produced sufficient heat to cook their food. Their crafts included skillful cedar wood carving. An extension of their material culture was a strong wealth consciousness among most of the triblets. They used many items to represent prosperity and personal wealth, including elaborately decorated skin and feather garments and strings of dentalium shells which they used in a sense as money.

Social models of the California triblet were simple. Several families composed a village, and from one to three villages comprised a triblet. Each triblet was an autonomous community with an established territory, a common estate which all members had the privilege of using. Triblet government likewise was simple, managed by a community council of elders and a headman with limited authority. His primary duties were presiding over public matters and resolving internal disputes. Most of the triblets lived at peace and had no military tradition of consequence.

In their religion, the California Indians paid tribute to several gods, observed a number of religious festivals including a world renewal pageant and female puberty rites, and supported a clergy of shamans who presided over the religious establishment and served as healers. In their medical arts the California shamans practiced magic, pantomimed conversion of themselves to animals, and used sand paintings and datura (jimson weed). The individual's search for a spirit helper was an important religious duty, and datura was used to help the worshipper to achieve this sublime state. The Hupas, probably the most ostentatious of the California Indians, used religious festivals as times for displaying their wealth in the form of fine dress.

Northwest Coast Tribes

The Northwest Coast ethnographic subregion extended along the Pacific coast from northern California to the Alaska panhandle. Its exceptionally mild climate, temporized by the Japanese Current, produced rather stable, year-round, pleasant temperatures. The abundant rainfall created dense forests of redwood, cedar, pine, and fir, all softwoods and easily worked with primitive tools. The many different types of plants, shrubs, bushes, and trees yielded berries, nuts, fruits, and edible roots. The region's many streams teemed with fish, particularly salmon. And food was readily harvested from the sea—halibut, cod, shellfish, and deep-sea mammals including the sea otter and whale. The Northwest coast competed with California as the richest natural food resource region in North America. The Northwest Coast subregion supported a large population with many tribes representing three language stocks: the Na-Dene, Penutian, and Mosan.

Northwest coast plank house with totem carvings. (Library of Congress)

As in California, economic life was uncomplicated for the Northwest Coast tribes. But while the California tribes languished in the mild climate where food was easily obtained, the Northwest Coast tribes developed a spectacular culture. Anthropologists regard their life-style as a separate development, an "isolate," because it evolved with little or no influence from Mexico or from Asia. Anthropologists have described the Northwest Coast life-style as "highly distinctive" and "unique." One writer commented, "The vitality of the Northwest Coast, its dramatic organization and its inventive spirit, make it one of the most outstanding and at the same time most exciting of the New World culture areas."[5]

The economic life of the Northwest tribes was exceedingly complex, particularly in view of the fact that they were nonagricultural. They supported themselves by fishing, gathering, hunting, and trading. Yet they were the wealthiest Indians in North America. The basis of their wealth was the salmon.

What corn was to the Eastern tribes, rice to the Great Lakes tribes, buffalo to the Great Plains tribes, the acorn to the California tribes, salmon was to the Northwest Coast tribes. In a few months an Indian family could catch, dry, and store enough fish for a year. And from the ocean they took cod, halibut, and shellfish, and they hunted the sea otter, seal, and whale from canoes. Food was so easily obtained that a perpetual surplus was available. Thus they had time to devote to more elaborate economic as well as non-economic aspects of life.

Most of their travel was on rivers or along the seacoasts from island to island in large dugout canoes, some of them seventy feet long, made from red cedar logs. A single canoe, with its elaborate carved bow, could accommodate fifty oarsmen and three tons of cargo. There was much trading from island to island and at annual fairs at mainland settlements. Traders transported cargoes of foodstuffs, blankets, skins, baskets, and wooden utensils from one market to another in the huge watercraft.

Most of the tribal handicrafts centered on woodworking, especially red cedar. Logs of this softwood were floated to the village beach, cured out, then split into planks with hard wooden wedges driven by large stone hammers. Workmen used the planks for many purposes. Dwellings were large multi-family structures made of these planks. Craftsmen carved bowls, trenchers, tools, and decorative pieces, including tall totems, from this softwood. Woodworking tools included a stone adz and a beaver-tooth chisel. By steaming, bending, and sewing wooden pieces, craftsmen of some tribes fashioned wooden boxes of all sizes and shapes for many uses including storing food and cooking by the water-and-hot-stone method. Most tribes, however, made baskets and used them for most of these purposes including cooking. Women in some tribes wove exquisite blankets on looms. Their materials were mountain goat hair and milkweed fibers or dog wool. Many tribes had large numbers of slaves who performed menial and routine tasks, freeing the artisans for work on their special crafts.

Northwest Coast tribal social models were largely matrilineal-matrilocal. Several tribes practiced the moiety system for dividing the community to arrange marriage and to select leaders; there was very little sense of nation. Most of the tribes associated through language and culture rather than political commitment. Thus each community was largely autonomous. Local chiefs or leaders came from the highest-ranking clan or house in each moiety. Family association and identity were very important because of wealth distribution and social ranking through the family. The Northwest Coast tribes followed a system of social stratification nearly as rigid as the Natchez. Below the chiefly families in each community were the nobles, followed by commoners, and below them were the slaves. Some social mobility was permitted in that low commoners with skills for carving or some other valued talent could receive from the community chief a title and right to a crest with totem pole signifying noble status. Conflict among tribes of this region was frequent; the principal prize was revenge and captives who became slaves.

The religion of the Northwest Coast tribes required both individual and group attention. Each youth, as a part of his rites for adult status, was expected to undergo fasting and purification ritual to make himself worthy of the vision where he would receive his spirit helper or guardian. The public aspects of this region's religion centered on their clergy—the shamans—and their success in managing the supernatural world. The shamans were also healers. A major part of their religious activity was focused on placating animal spirits. Their way of life depended largely on fish and animals, and they believed that these creatures, existing for human benefit, had spirits which were released at death and would return repeatedly to serve people if they were not offended. Since material success was so important to the Northwest Coast tribes and since this material success depended in large measure on the annual fish and animal harvest, placating animals received special attention.

Because of abundant natural resources, it was relatively easy for one to accumulate the much-desired surplus of material goods, including blankets, baskets, skins, shells, curiously shaped copper plates, obsidian blades, albino deer skins, and strings of dentalium shells (Pacific Coast currency). The great wealth of these tribes was a source of continuing public display. Besides individual prosperity displayed in lavish personal adornment, it provided the basis for one of the hallmarks of the Northwest Coast tribes, their most conspicuous custom—the potlatch. The potlatch was a public sharing of one's goods, generally preceded by a feast sponsored by the host. Modest potlatches could be held, even by a commoner, to commemorate the birth of a son, a marriage, or some other event of great moment in a family. The biggest potlatches were those held by rich, high-ranking nobles or by the local chief himself, given to show his generosity and to shame his rival by distributing in a single day huge quantities of goods—bales of blankets, great numbers of valued copper plates, and other items of value. Then the only way for others to gain greater status was to throw a bigger potlatch and give away even more goods.

THE ALASKAN PROVINCE

Alaska, the most northerly portion of the United States, also was populated by peoples of contrasting life-styles. They may be divided into the Meso-Indians, who arrived more recently in North America from Asia, and the Alaskan Indians.

Alaskan Meso-Indians

Aleuts and Eskimos, the Alaskan Meso-Indians, were the last aboriginal peoples to migrate from Asia to the New World, perhaps as recently as 4,000 years ago. They are similar physically, with characteristics of their Asian kinsmen and speaking a virtually common language. The Aleuts' habitat is the island chain extending southwest from the Alaskan mainland. Eskimos occupy the area around the Arctic Circle between sixty and seventy-two degrees north latitude.

Most of the northward-dwelling peoples live in a frigid desert, so cold that the atmosphere can hold only enough moisture to produce about four inches of precipitation annually. They must cope with the problem of brief summers and very long winters, a short time of barely warm light and a long period of cold darkness. This environment is one of the most discouraging in the world; yet through resourcefulness and great energy and inventiveness these peoples adapted and were able to cope and to work out a successful and satisfying life-style.

Aleuts and Eskimos were primarily hunters and only minimally gatherers of plants and other nonanimal foods, in part because the tundra which comprised most of their environment, with its permafrost and short growing season, produced only a limited plant life. They were primarily meat eaters, consuming great quantities of meat per person per day. During the winter an extended family averaging twelve persons consumed an estimated one hundred pounds of meat each day; a like amount was required for the household's pack of dogs. Game animals also provided skins and hides for clothing, footwear, shelter covers, hunting line, and other uses. Caribou hides and wolf and fox as well as grizzly, brown, and polar bear pelts were particularly valued for making clothing.

Eskimos lived in fixed villages near a beach or estuary. Their dwellings, framed of driftwood, bone, and antler pieces, were covered with sod and skins. They used a temporary skin shelter during the summer when away from their village, and during the winter when on a hunt the men sometimes erected the igloo or ice house, more characteristic of the far north, as a temporary shelter.

Eskimos spent most of their time obtaining food, the period of most intensive activity occurring during the short summer. With the arrival of summer, as the frozen ground thawed a bit on the surface, vegetation grew, birds and animals began to move north, and salmon began their search for river spawning grounds. Warmer temperatures caused breaks in the ocean's ice cover, forming expanses of open water where sea mammals could be found. Eskimo families moved from their village; some traveled to the interior to hunt caribou and to fish for salmon; others took to the sea in large skin-covered boats called umiaks to hunt the whale and walrus. Every member of every family was engaged during the summer gathering food for winter. Eskimo values stressed the duty of work and scorned indolence. With the approach of winter and shorter days, Eskimos returned to their villages with the food, skins, and hides they had collected. They stored their large boats on the beach and made any necessary repairs to their houses. When ice formed on the ground, the men used dog-drawn sleds to carry them to hunting grounds near the villages where they sought game birds and seals. Techniques for preserving food included caching meat, packed in skin bags, in the permafrost, and drying, smoking, or fermenting it, and packing it in skin bags for winter use. They stored whale and seal oil in bladders and tightly sewed skins.

Eskimo crafts included weaving useful and attractive baskets from sedges and shrub stems and carving figures from bone, soft soap-stone, and sea-mammal ivory. Some Eskimo groups made crude pottery. Artisans carved colorful masks and other paraphernalia required in their religious ceremonies.

For transportation, besides the dogsled, the Meso-Indians used several types of skin-covered boats. The largest was the umiak, requiring a crew of eight to twelve oarsmen and used for hunting the whale and for moving goods in trade. The kayak was a widely used one- or two-passenger craft. The Aleuts, rated by some authorities as the greatest hunters of aboriginal America, hunted the ocean waters in the bidarka, a highly maneuverable, swift, skin-covered boat with cockpit for oarsman in the stern and the harpoon man in the forward cockpit.

Their social models were simple, consisting of the basic nuclear families which clustered into extended families during winter. During the summer food hunt, nuclear families—husbands, wives, children—scattered into the interior. In prehistoric times little political organization was apparent or required. The Eskimos and Aleuts associated in small subsistence units, and individual autonomy predominated. The only cooperative activity of consequence occurred during whale hunts when the owner of an umiak formed an expedition.

During winter men collected in the "men's house," a large community building. It served as a social, ceremonial, and recreational center. There Eskimo men wrestled, performed feats of strength, or entertained with singing and dancing. Shamans held religious observances in this building to placate supernatural forces and to perform healing.

The Eskimo's polytheistic religion centered on the raven, their creator who served as the great manager of the universe, and a sea goddess. Annual festivals included dancing and singing, the participants wearing masks representing gods. Most religious attention was directed to placating animals as was the case of the Northwest Coast tribes. Eskimo and Aleut hunters followed particular formulas and observed elaborate taboos in order not to offend the animal spirit. The hunter even opened the slain creature's skull to permit its spirit to move freely into the world which they believed pleased the animal. They hoped that reports of the care and good treatment would reach other animals and that they would cooperate and permit themselves to be easily taken. Eskimo shamans were specialists in managing the supernatural, presenting the formulas for hunting success, and were the community healers, using sorcery and magic in their treatment of the ill.

Alaskan Indians

Indians of Alaska fell into two cultural classes. The Haidas and Tlingits, dwelling on Alaska's coast and offshore islands, in their life-style were an extension of the Northwest Coast culture—advanced handicrafts, intense wealth commitment, and potlatch. In Alaska's interior lived the Athapascans. Their environment in the Yukon watershed, south of the Eskimo's tundra-type range, consisted of dense coniferous forests. Their homeland's climate of short summers and long, snow-filled winters was a strong determinant of their life-style. These tribes were wandering hunters of caribou, moose, deer, elk, and bear, and fishers in season, principally of salmon. The Athapascans were tied by language and culture into a large common-interest community, but they lived in bands in semipermanent villages of log structures, spending most of their time obtaining food which, besides game, involved considerable amounts of berries and edible plants. The Athapascans preserved meat for winter use by smoking it over slow-burning fires and drying it in the sun. Often they made the meat into pemmican. On hunts they used temporary shelters resembling the Plains tribes' tipis. Their primitive techniques extended to cooking. Meat was cooked on a spit or in a hole in the ground that was lined with a caribou paunch, filled with water, and heated with hot stones. Athapascans traveled on the water with canoes and rafts when the streams were open; when iced over they used snowshoes and dog-drawn sleds.

Northern Athapascan social models were very simple, consisting of hunting bands which were related nuclear families who hunted and worked together. The strongest in each band in personality and physical strength was the leader or band chief. His directive role was important for settling disputes over fishing or hunting rights in certain territories and directing the group in communal hunts.

Athapascan religion was primarily concerned with placating the spirits of the animals they hunted for food. In this their formulas and taboos were quite similar to those of the neighboring Eskimos. Their shamans, as with most other Western tribes, were not only intermediaries with the supernatural forces in the Athapascan universe but also central figures in curing illness.

These functioning societies with their adaptive economies had evolved in continental isolation over a period of perhaps 50,000 years. Around 1500 European nations began to establish colonial beachheads in North America. They appropriated the land and its great resources, generally ignoring any aboriginal rights. And their designs for exploitation frequently included a demeaning role for the Native Americans.

Notes

1. Robert F. Spencer, Jesse D. Jennings, et al., *The Native Americans: Prehistory and Ethnology of the North American Indians* (New York, 1965), p. 350.
2. Ruth M. Underhill, *Red Man's America: A History of Indians in the United States* (Chicago, 1971), p. 188.
3. Spencer and Jennings, *The Native Americans*, p. 301.
4. Harold E. Driver, *Indians of North America*, pp. 25–52.
5. Spencer and Jennings, *The Native Americans*, p. 168.

Selected Sources

Works which include surveys of the Native Americans and their life-styles on the eve of European contact include: Alvin M. Josephy, Jr., *The Indian Heritage of America* (New York, 1968); Angie Debo, *A History of the Indians of the United States* (Norman, Okla., 1970); Ruth M. Underhill, *Red Man's America: A History of Indians in the United States* (Chicago, 1971); and Robert F. Spencer, Jesse D. Jennings, et al., *The Native Americans: Pre-history and Ethnology of the North American Indians* (New York, 1965). Also useful for this period in aboriginal history is the *Handbook of American Indians North of Mexico* (Washington, D.C., 1907–1910), 2 vols. Reprinted (New York, 1959), 2 vols., edited by Frederick W. Hodge.

The University of Oklahoma Press, Norman, Oklahoma, publishes the best-known studies of the Indian tribes in its *Civilization of the American Indian* series, containing nearly 150 volumes, each devoted to the history of Native Americans. Most of the tribes discussed in this chapter, in all the ethnographic provinces, are included in these studies.

CHAPTER 5

SPAIN AND THE
NATIVE AMERICANS

They are artless and generous with what they have, to such a degree as no one would believe but him who had seen it. Of anything they have, if it be asked for, they never say no, but do rather invite the person to accept it, and show as much lovingness as though they would give their hearts.

Christopher Columbus' description of Native Americans

❦

Christopher Columbus' encounter with Native Americans on the beach at Watling Island in 1492 following his unexpected discovery of the New World was one of several turning points that marked the emergence of Europe from its somnolent, thousand-year-long Middle Ages. The catalyst that produced modern Europe was the Renaissance—a series of political, economic, and religious revolutions precipitating drastic change in every facet of life for Europeans, Asians, Africans—even by its impact for Native Americans. It produced a revolution in political form, the self-conscious nation state, an apparatus that improved on feudalism as a way to manage territorial, human, and material resources in the new order which was being born. Out of the Renaissance came mercantilism, a body of new economic thought that stressed, first, bullionism (that is, that the volume of gold and silver in a nation's vaults determined its wealth and its power), and second, national self-sufficiency with colonies as sites for gold and silver mines and sources of vital raw materials and markets for the expanding home economy. New versions of Christianity generated by the Reformation, another Renaissance-spawned revolution, challenged the Roman church's claim to universality and stirred intensive, competitive missionary efforts to evangelize the heathen in far-off lands. Meanwhile, inventions and new technology permitted advances in metallurgy, textiles, engineering, navigational techniques, and firearms.

Spain, Portugal, France, and England were committed in varying degrees to the new order of nation-states. Each, to fulfill mercantilist goals, lusted to conquer overseas colonies. As Christian communities these emergent imperial powers now had to find ways to justify appropriating land, resources, even humans as laborers. Their theologians went to work and gave each European nation a dogma of national mission. Public duty demanded con-

Chapter Opening Artifact: California Indian (Karok) basket. (Courtesy of Museum of the American Indian, Heye Foundation)

quest of overseas territories and their peoples in order to serve the higher goals, as they stated them, of civilizing savages and Christianizing pagans.

Spain and Portugal had been the most successful of the European nations in exploring Africa, Asia, and America. Each followed the rule that discovery was tantamount to ownership. On appeal, Pope Alexander VI quieted their competitiveness by dividing the world outside Europe between them in 1493–1494. Thus to Spain fell the entire Western Hemisphere except Brazil, which was assigned to Portugal. In partitioning the world outside Europe, Pope Alexander admonished Spain and Portugal that "the peaceful conversion of the native inhabitants should have primary consideration."[1]

THE INDIAN AND THE SPANISH EMPIRE

Supposedly to fulfill the papal commission, Spain expanded from bases on the Caribbean Islands onto the American mainland, in 1519 to Mexico, then into Central and South America, and northward into the present United States. Eventually Spain formed a chain of settlements from St. Augustine on the Atlantic Coast of Florida westward across the Gulf of Mexico into Texas, New Mexico, Arizona, and California. About twenty-five years of harsh, destructive experience for the Indians went into developing imperial Spain's system for ruling this vast territory and its native population. For many of the tribes of the United States the Spanish administration endured until 1821.

Spaniards differed in their view of Native Americans. Columbus, one of the first Europeans to have contact with Indians, said of them: "They are a loving people, without covetousness, and fit for anything. . . . They love their neighbors as themselves, and their speech is the sweetest and gentlest in the world." He added that the Indians were open in their dealings, innocently direct, and free of acquisitiveness—generous and hospitable to a fault. Spanish author López de Gómara, author of a biography of Hernando Cortés, conqueror of Mexico, and a history of the early Spanish empire in America, condemned Indians as "filthy devil-worshipers, sodomites, liars, public fornicators, naked cannibals," and because of their "depravity," "fit only to be slaves." Most Spaniards in the New World agreed that Indians were human beings, but with "inferior manners." As descendants of Noah they "were both rational and capable of being Christianized." Pope Paul III ruled that Indians were human and could own property and be baptized.[2]

Early Colonial Exploitation

In the early days of Spanish settlement in the New World colonists captured hundreds of Arawaks in the Caribbean Islands and sent them to Spain to be sold as slaves. They also impressed work gangs of Indians and forced them to labor in the islands' mines and on plantations. Disease, crowded, unsanitary conditions in the labor camps, and cruel working conditions killed thousands of island peoples.

Dominican priests working in the Caribbean were quick to protest. When colonists ignored their pleas for more temperate treatment of Indian workers, several churchmen went to Spain to lay the matter before the Spanish court. Dominican Friar Antonio de Montesinos, who had seen firsthand the terrible treatment Spanish colonists inflicted upon Indian workers, was the principal clerical spokesman. With him began the tradition of clergy regularly-interceding to the crown on behalf of Native Americans. Bartolomé de las Casas, also a Dominican who succeeded Montesinos as vigilant protector of Indian rights, for nearly half a century regularly inspected conditions among Indians in the colonies and reported abuses to the crown.

The Courtly Debate

Montesinos' revelations of conditions among Indians in the Spanish colonies stirred considerable discussion at the court, and the king's ministers began composing a body of policy and law to direct the orderly development of the Spanish empire. Survivals of medieval ideas influenced its foundations. The regal councillors proceeded from the position that the head of the Christian world was Christ's earthly vicar, the pope; the Spanish monarch was a secular or worldly arm of Christendom. Spanish Christian society consisted of the "feudatory, the *encomendero*, [who] was expected to bear arms; the cleric to preach and pray; the peasant . . . to work and to support the others by his work."[3]

By right of discovery and papal dispensation the land and people of the New World, excluding Brazil, were under Spanish dominion. Sixteenth-century law proclaimed that subject peoples,

whether subdued by violence or merely the threat of violence, had no rights save such as the conqueror might freely choose to concede to them . . . Indian nations were obliged to recognize the sovereignty of the Spanish sovereign, and, through this, the ultimate sovereignty of the Pope . . . the spiritual over-lord of the whole earth. The persons and the land of the Indians were . . . at the disposal [of the monarch] who might do with them what [he] wished, according to [his] own mercy, and, according to need and expediency."[4]

As papal agent, the Spanish monarch had the specific duty to disseminate Christian civilization throughout the New World and to integrate the pagan Indians into Spanish society by conversion to Christianity and instruction in civilization. Native Americans were subjects of the Spanish crown. To be worthy of this new and cherished status they were expected to submit to conversion to Christianity and to instruction in civilization. To the Spaniard being civilized meant becoming Hispanicized, including speaking Castilian Spanish, living in adobe and stone houses, wearing European dress, and adopting "political organization focused through loyalty and obedience to the King of Spain, and with the Roman Catholic form of Christianity." Thus missionary and empire officials were directed to "replace correspondingly features of Indian culture with these and other elements of Spanish culture."[5]

In their Christian zeal and Iberian shrewdness, the king's councillors concluded that the most efficient way to Christianize and civilize Indians, thus making them worthy Christian subjects, would be to require them to perform productive labor. This fitted well the mercantilist goals of the Spanish government and the labor needs of Spaniards involved in empire building. While royal policy for colonial development had to protect Indians and promote their welfare, it also had to consider the needs of its subjects who were building personal fortunes from mines and plantations in the New World, for the crown also had a large stake in the economic success of its colonies. Their prosperity yielded rich revenues which contributed substantially to national strength. More and more the crown came to depend upon the wealth of the colonies, produced largely by Indian labor, to sustain its role of premier nation in Europe.

In an age of limited technology and general lack of labor-saving devices, production was dependent largely on human and animal muscle power. Mining and plantation agriculture, both requiring large amounts of labor, were the most important economic activities. The labor-supply problem of the Spanish empire was futher complicated by the pattern of immigration from Spain. Most Spaniards coming to the New World scorned common labor. Eventually slaves from Africa were imported to the mines and plantations of the islands and the Caribbean coast of Mexico, Central America, and Colombia and Venezuela to replace Indian workers who died under the cruelty of labor exactions of early-day Spanish colonists.

However, for the time being Spaniards expected to use Indian labor. The ongoing court discussion on Indians in the empire produced laws and procedures for dealing with the Native Americans. The code distinguished between those Indians who submitted to Spanish rule and accepted civilization and conversion to Christianity, including labor for Spanish entrepreneurs, and those who resisted. The latter could be taken as slaves and also required to labor for Spaniards but under quite different circumstances. The councillors also adopted procedures that the *conquistador* must follow in opening a new land and contacting the native inhabitants.

The Requerimiento

The royal household was concerned that Indians residing in a territory newly opened by the Spaniards be aware of what the king expected of them so "if they refused these reasonable demands their blood should be upon their heads and not his." For this purpose, court councillors drafted a statement called the *Requerimiento* which the *conquistador* upon first making contact with an Indian tribe was required to read to their leaders. Each expedition would include at least one priest who would certify that he had witnessed the reading of the *Requerimiento* to the Indians and that they clearly understood its contents. Cynics claimed that to satisfy the king in far-away Spain *conquistadors* would "crawl up to an Indian village in the dead of night, read the document in a whisper among themselves," or "to the trees," properly inscribe the *Requerimiento* with a witness certificate, "then rush on to massacre with the cry 'Santiago!' "[6]

The *Requerimiento*, written of course in Spanish, stated,

We ask and require you that . . . you take the time that shall be necessary to understand and deliberate upon it, and that you acknowledge the Church as the ruler and superior of the whole world, and the high priest called the Pope and in his name the King [of Spain] as lords of . . . this terra-firma by virtue of the said donation. . . . [If you submit,] we . . . shall receive you in all love and charity, and shall leave you, your wives, and your children, and your lands, free without servitude. . . . But, if you do not do this, and maliciously make delay in it, I certify to you that with the help of God we shall powerfully enter into your country, and shall make war against you . . . and shall subject you to the yoke and obedience of the Church, [and the Spanish sovereign, and] we shall take you, and your wives, and your children, and shall make slaves of them, and as such shall sell and dispose of them . . . and we shall take away your goods and shall do you all the harm and damage we can, as to vassals who do not obey, and refuse to receive their lord, and resist and contradict him.[7]

Indians as Spanish Slaves

From earliest Spanish conquests in the Caribbean islands, colonists had taken Indians as slaves. The Spaniards claimed to own the Indians, directing their lives, using them in the mines or on plantations, or shipping them to Spain for sale as household servants. Indian slavery was a matter that received continuing attention in the royal household's discussions of colonial policy. Missionaries regularly protested enslavement of Indians by Spanish colonists. They claimed that the *Requerimiento* was abused because even those tribes who submitted peacefully were made slaves by colonials, under the guise that they resisted Spanish civilizing efforts, for the purpose of providing a larger labor supply. Mine operators and other colonial economic groups answered these charges before the Council of the Indies, the governing body for Spanish colonies in the New World, by denying that they enslaved Indians by unlawful means. They swore that they placed in bondage only those Indians who resisted Spanish rule and failed to abide by the terms of the *Requerimiento*. Their rationale was that slavery benefited recalcitrant Indians. By rejecting the opportunity to live under Hispanic patronage, they had demonstrated their "barbarous natures." Savages should "be brought under the guardianship of a Christian master who would teach them the arts of civilized life and lead them to Christian salvation."[8]

Accumulated reports by missionaries to the crown, recounting abuses and illegal enslavement of Native Americans, led to a spectacular debate in the Spanish court in 1550–1551 between Las Casas, the indefatigable protector of Indian rights and welfare, and Juan de Sepúlveda, a Spanish lawyer and defender of the mercantilist-businessman's view. Basically, Sepúlveda contended that Indian slavery was required to provide the labor essential to develop the resources of an empire to enhance private Spanish fortunes and build greater strength for the crown. The Spanish legalist declared that "inferior nations must serve their superiors." His basic defense was reference to Aristotle's position that persons whose customs were barbarous were natural slaves. Spaniards should enslave Native Americans "because of the rudeness [primitiveness] of Indians' natures, the need to spread the faith and to protect the weak among the natives, and the gravity of the Indians' sins—the chief of which was idolatry." Las Casas responded that Indians must be given a chance to accept civilization. The cleric admonished that only if they rejected this civilization was war which would result in their enslavement permissible.[9]

The missionaries eventually appeared to triumph. During the sixteenth century popes as well as Spanish monarchs on several occasions issued decrees banning enslavement of Native Americans under any conditions and requiring humane and fair treatment of them. However, great distances separated popes and monarchs from the New World colonies. In an era of slow communications the rough-and-ready colonists, to whom the finer points of fair treatment of Indians were of no great interest compared with the fortunes to be made from their labor, were able to ignore the well-intentioned royal regulations.

The Encomienda and Repartimiento Systems

Alternatives to enslavement of Native Americans for labor in Spanish colonial enterprises were the *encomienda* and *repartimiento* systems. Spanish law repeatedly stated that Indians were vassals of the crown and free persons if they followed the prescriptions of the *Requerimiento*. However, as pagan savages, Spanish officials held that they had to be civilized and Christianized before they could enjoy the full benefits of Spanish vassalage and status as subjects of the crown. It was assumed that although Indians were free, most of them were incapable of using their liberty. Productive labor, plus instruction in civilization and Christianity, were regarded as the means to accomplish their Hispanicization. The *encomienda* system was established for the Spanish colonies in the New World by the Laws of Burgos, issued in 1512. This code was framed by the crown to guard Indian welfare after Montesinos made his shocking revelations to the Spanish court of gross exploitation of Indians.[10]

Under the *encomienda* system, as prescribed by the Laws of Burgos, Spanish colonists received Indian workers to develop their properties. Every male Indian commended under the system was required to labor nine months of each year for the *encomendero* who, in return, paid a head tax to the crown for each Indian assigned to him and was to bear the expense of instructing his charges in Christianity, Spanish civilization, and vocational arts. This was believed to be the most effective method to achieve conversion and Hispanicization.

Under the Laws of Burgos a class called *Indios capaces* was regarded as able and willing to embrace Christianity and to adopt the European way of life, and within limits, capable of self-governing. *Indios capaces* were exempted from *encomienda* because their civilized state would lead them to become gainfully employed in the Spanish economic system.

The *encomienda* system was much criticized by vigilant missionaries. They claimed that it masked a system of servitude nearly as destructive of Indian vitality and life as slavery itself. And they denied that the *encomendero* paid much attention to civilizing and Christianizing their commended Indians; rather their only real interest was a supply of free and dependable labor, and the Hispanicization process was of little concern. Thus by 1600 the *encomienda* system was being replaced by a *repartimiento* system, a labor draft much like the European *corvée*. Under the *repartimiento* system, every settled Indian town through its headmen was obligated to furnish a fixed proportion of its male population for labor, for a stated number of weeks in rotation throughout the year, on various Spanish projects. A local Spanish official allocated Indian workers to road and bridge building, erection of public buildings, churches, and hospitals, and for labor in mines, and on plantations and ranches.

Thus Native Americans were integrated into the Spanish empire under the system of legal enslavement, the *encomienda,* and the *repartimiento.* Many Indian tribes within the present United States came under Spanish dominion, and their descendants bear the stamp today of the Spanish culture forced upon them.

THE SPANISH EMPIRE IN NORTH AMERICA

Spanish officials regarded the territory in the present United States as the northern frontier of New Spain. Between 1565 and 1769 they established settlements from Florida's Atlantic Coast westward across the Gulf of Mexico into Texas, New Mexico, Arizona, and California. At one time Spain also dominated the Mississippi Valley as far north as St. Louis, claiming dominion over the many tribes of that vast region.

The work of bringing portions of the territory north of Mexico City under effective Spanish dominion and administration was carried out by three agencies of expansion—the mission, the presidio, and the civilian settlement, the last consisting of miners, stock raisers, traders and trappers, and some farmers. The government of New Spain expected representatives of all three agencies as they occupied the wilderness north of Mexico City to transmit the by now familiar, standardized Iberian civilization and conversion program to resident pagan peoples.

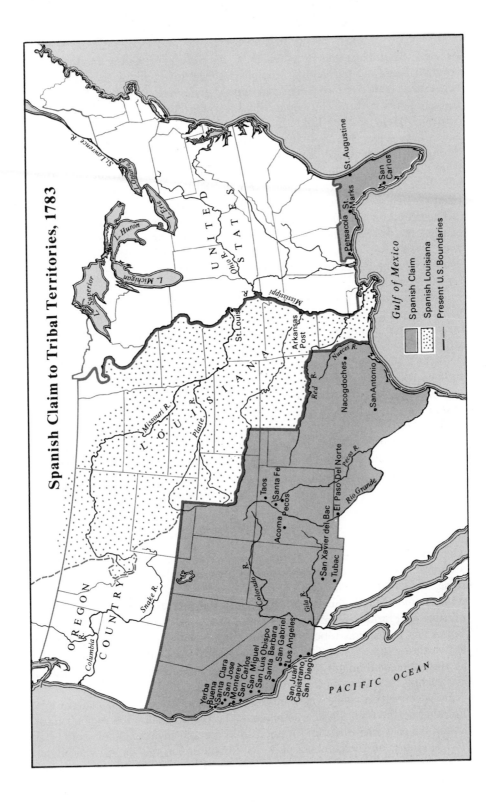

Spanish Claim to Tribal Territories, 1783

Spanish Claim

Spanish Louisiana

Present U.S. Boundaries

UNITED STATES

OREGON COUNTRY

LOUISIANA

Gulf of Mexico

PACIFIC OCEAN

St. Lawrence R.

L. Superior

L. Huron

L. Michigan

L. Erie

Ohio R.

Mississippi R.

St. Louis

Arkansas Post

Missouri R.

Platte R.

Snake R.

Columbia

Colorado R.

Gila R.

Rio Grande

Pecos R.

Red R.

Nueces R.

St. Augustine

San Carlos

St. Marks

Pensacola

Nacogdoches

San Antonio

Santa Fe

Taos

Pecos

Acoma

Del Norte

El Paso

San Xavier del Bac

Tubac

Yerba Buena

Santa Clara

San Jose

Monterey

San Carlos

San Miguel

San Luis Obispo

Santa Barbara

San Gabriel

Los Angeles

San Juan Capistrano

San Diego

Missionaries, mostly of the Franciscan, Jesuit, and Dominican orders, instructed the Indians and prepared them for conversion and trained them in vocational arts and husbandry. Missionaries introduced grains, notably wheat, vegetables, fruit trees, and livestock among the tribes. Frontier clerics were Indian agents with official commissions, serving both church and state. The Spanish system of close union of church and state made this dual role possible. Thus there was a continuity of authority, ecclesiastical and secular, through the bureaucratic hierarchy, with a mix of secular and spiritual power, from the missionary on the northern frontier in Florida, Texas, or New Mexico, through the viceroy in New Spain, to the Spanish monarch, who exercised the *real patronato* as defender of the faith.

The presidio was the frontier military post manned by a garrison consisting of from ten to two hundred royal troops. The function of this military force was to provide official protection for the frontier district, to scout the countryside, maintain order and control over the Indian tribes, and watch for intruders.

The mission and the presidio were the vanguard agencies in Spanish expansion among the Indian tribes across North America. These religious and military settlements, in turn, served as nuclei around which civilians subsequently established ranches, farms, mines, and settlements.

In the early years of Spanish penetration into the present United States, Indians who resisted the Spaniards were enslaved. Some were assigned to *encomiendas,* and after 1600 they were under the *repartimiento,* systems discussed earlier. Indians were required to donate a tithe portion of the fruits of their labor in grain and livestock to the mission and a tribute portion to the local Spanish government. Also, under Spanish law, after a frontier territory had been conquered and pacified by the mission and presidio and was open to civilian settlement, civilian pioneers—stockmen, farmers, mine operators—could request a levy of workers each month from the Indian towns.

Atlantic-Gulf-Texas Sector

The first Native Americans in the present United States to receive serious attention from the Spaniards were the Calusas, Apalaches, Yamasees, Mikasukis, and others in Florida and along the Gulf Coast. Pedro Menéndez de Aviles founded St. Augustine in 1565, and Jesuits and Franciscans established missions in Florida and among the tribes of coastal Georgia. In 1597 Native Americans in Florida rebelled against the missionaries to protest attempts to overthrow tribal gods. The beleaguered padres appealed to the presidio at St. Augustine, and Spanish troops defeated the Indians by burning their towns and seizing their granaries.

However, in the early years of colonial development Spanish interest in Florida and the Gulf Coast was minimal. To the Spaniards the region's most important role was guarding Mexico from foreign invasion; their rule of it was random, and their impact upon its inhabitants in this period was slight.

Then as a part of the grand diplomatic settlement for North America in 1763, Spain ceded Florida and the Gulf Coast to Great Britain. However, after the territory was restored to them in 1783, the Spaniards' interest and activity in Florida and the Gulf Coast area and the resident Indian tribes quickened noticeably.

The Texas Gulf Coast was also a part of Spain's defenses against French encroachment. Spain did not enter Texas in earnest until around 1700 following establishment of French rule in the lower Mississippi Valley and Louisiana. Then Spaniards penetrated Texas from bases in northern Mexico with missions and presidios but only limited civilian settlement.

In 1690, soon after a Spanish patrol found evidence of the La Salle expedition's presence on Matagorda Bay, officials in Mexico ordered extension of Spanish dominion into Texas. As a result, two missions were founded among the Asinai Indians on the Nueces River. In 1702 these Indians revolted and forced the Spaniards to evacuate Texas. However, in 1715 reports of French traders encroaching into eastern Texas from bases in nearby Louisiana brought the Spanish back in greater strength. Clerics restored their missions among the Asinai Indians and began trying to convert the Karankahuas, Tawakonis, Tonkawas, and other Texas tribes. Texas military settlements were established on the Louisiana-Texas border to check French traders. In 1718 Spanish officials founded San Antonio as a mission and presidio.

Texas was closer to Mexico (the center of action for Spaniards in North America because of its rich silver mines) than other portions of this sector. Thus the Texas tribes received more sustained imperial attention from Spanish colonial officials than did those Indians on the eastern Gulf Coast toward Florida. Dominican friars relocated the Karankahuas, Tawakonis, Pamayas, and other tribes at mission settlements, the largest at San Antonio de Valero, the famous Alamo, situated near the presidio of San Antonio. Indian families were required to abandon their native life-style of gathering, hunting, and limited agriculture for a sedentary life of labor at the missions constructing churches, schools, dwellings, roads, and irrigation works. At mission schools clerics taught Indian youth the Iberian language, religion, and vocational arts including agriculture by irrigation. Heavy labor demands imposed by the missionaries and labor levies drafted by the settlers up from Mexico, as well as imported European diseases, notably smallpox and measles, caused a drastic decline in native population of central and southern Texas during the late eighteenth century. Those who survived were thoroughly Hispanicized.

New Mexico Sector

During 1598 the Council of the Indies directed the viceroy of New Spain to occupy that portion of the northern frontier drained by the Rio Grande, an area which came to be called New Mexico. Spanish officials gave this order for two reasons. First, reports of great wealth in gold and silver in that region continued to circulate despite negative reports from Francisco Vásquez de

Coronado's extensive explorations of 1539–1541. Second, Spanish officials believed settlement and development of the interior of the northern frontier would be prudent to thwart anticipated moves by the English.

The Rio Grande expedition formed in Chihuahua, now in Mexico. Headed by Don Juan de Oñate, it consisted of 129 soldiers, plus women and children, and 10 Franciscan missionaries. The colonists reached the Rio Grande Indian settlements—the pueblos—during July 1598. Oñate at once sent small squads of troops to visit each of the sixty-six pueblos. His officers, in council with tribal leaders, were to inform the Indians that they were subjects of the Spanish crown; that their lands were now a part of the royal patrimony to be assigned, distributed, and disposed of as the Spanish monarch through his representative, the viceroy of New Spain, might direct; and the new Spanish vassals were expected to cast aside their pagan religions and submit to Spanish civilization and conversion to Christianity. Most of the pueblo peoples, curious and hospitable and totally ignorant of what was going on, acquiesced.

However, at Ácoma pueblo the Spaniards met with great resistance. Late in 1598 Indians at Ácoma contested the troops; thirteen Spaniards including three officers were slain. An army of Spaniards returned to Ácoma in January 1599. Royal troops scaled the steep, protective cliffs and captured the mesa after three days of fierce fighting, some of it bloody hand-to-hand combat. After the defenders capitulated, the soldiers proceeded to kill 800 Indians and capture 80 men and 500 women and children. At a trial, which Oñate deliberately made public to serve as an example to the other pueblo peoples, the Spanish tribunal passed harsh sentences upon the Ácoma survivors as punishment for resisting Spanish rule. Each male over twenty-five years of age was to have one foot amputated and to serve twenty years' servitude. Each male between the ages of twelve and twenty-five was to serve twenty years' servitude. Each woman over twelve years of age was to serve twenty years' servitude. Captives were to serve sentences as slaves to Spanish colonists in New Mexico. All Ácoma children under twelve were placed with missionaries. Two Hopi Indians, who were present at Ácoma during the battle and taken prisoner, were, in the words of Oñate, "to have the right hand cut off and to be set free in order that they may convey to their land the news of this punishment."[11]

The Ácoma Indians' fate augured ill for the other pueblos recently drawn into the Spanish empire. At the time of Oñate's *entrada* New Mexico's sixty-six pueblos had a combined population of over 40,000. In 1800, near the close of Spanish dominion in this area, their numbers had declined to less than 10,000. The principal officials directing the pueblo Indians' cultural metamorphosis from savage and pagan to Spanish subject and Christian were the royal governor of New Mexico and the *custos*, the Franciscan superior for New Mexico.

Various royal governors took such drastic steps as relocating Indians, moving their pueblos ostensibly to consolidate them to ease the problems of administration, defense, and education. Officials expected that Native Americans would more readily abandon their native tongues and learn Spanish in consolidated settlements, thus understanding instruction by their Franciscan missionary teachers. The pueblos occupied some of the most fertile land, well situated for irrigation from the Rio Grande or its tributaries. And royal governors had to grant land to colonists to induce them to venture to New Mexico. The colonists also expected Indian laborers for work in the fields, sowing, cultivating, and harvesting, tending cattle, sheep, and horses, working in blacksmith shops and at looms, erecting public buildings, and building roads. Indian women were assigned to colonial households as domestics under the New Mexico *repartimiento* system.

The *custos* directed the work of the Franciscan missionaries at the pueblos. Like the royal governor, the *custos* also drew on the Indian settlements for laborers. Pueblo Indians were impressed to build churches and chapels and to labor on church farms and orchards and to herd church livestock. Occasionally a *custos* or a leading missionary would show compassion toward the Indians and force a relaxation of both civil and ecclesiastical exploitation of the Native Americans in New Mexico. Thus Fray Alonso de Benevides, incensed at the callous appropriation of pueblo Indian labor by the colonists, appealed to the crown to help the Indians. His petition was instrumental in the royal household's legal abolition of the *encomienda* system in 1635 in New Mexico. However, the respite was brief. Soon, as a substitute for the *encomienda*, colonists were pressing the royal governor for additional *repartimiento* labor assignments. Thus Indians in the New Mexico pueblos under Spanish rule were little more than serfs serving colonists and missionaries.

While Franciscan padres often interceded on behalf of oppressed Native Americans, they brooked little deviation from the *régula*, the process which they had developed to convert the Indians from native religions. In most pueblos missionaries used threats of punishment to enforce conformity; civil officials carried out the punishment prescribed by the padres. Indians who "strayed" were punished in various ways. Some were hung by their arms from the public whipping post and lashed; others were required to stand in a small circle for hours at a time on public display; and a few recalcitrants were hung. One of the commonest punishments was to cut the religious rebel's hair. Hair was an important symbol of personal worth to pueblo Indian men; to escape the shame of the public haircut, many fled to some isolated spot to return, unmolested, to their own religious customs. Spaniards in New Mexico went through periods of intense religious zeal, condemning with great evangelical fury native religion as the curse of Satan and persecuting Native Americans for their determined attention to pagan ritual. During one such period in 1661, royal troops on orders from the padres raided the kivas, the pueblo ceremonial chambers, seized 1,600 katchina masks, the most sacred objects of the Indians' religious paraphernalia, and burned them.[12]

The pueblo Indians of New Mexico contributed greatly to the Native American tradition of resistance to Europeans and Anglo-Americans which was well established by 1800. Accumulated resentments and grievances against Spaniards—civil officials and colonists—for cruel and unlawful *repartimiento,* tax, and tribute exactions, and missionary padres for labor levies and suppression of cherished native religion—eventually sparked revolt.

In 1680, Popé, an Indian from San Juan pueblo, organized a secret resistance movement. Popé planned to integrate warriors from the pueblos into one grand army and drive the Spanish oppressors out of the Rio Grande Valley. Popé's runners readied the pueblos, even the Apache bands on the periphery of the Rio Grande settlements, for the outbreak. The revolt began on August 10 at Taos pueblo. Popé's army surged south, obliterating all sign of Spanish presence and rule. His troops laid siege to Santa Fe, the royal capital of New Mexico, defeated the Spanish defenders, and forced Governor Antonio de Otermin and other survivors to flee south. Every Spanish settlement north of El Paso was cleared of Spaniards; over four hundred died in the fighting. For several years after 1680, the New Mexico pueblos were free of Spanish officials, troops, colonists, and priests.

Almost at once the refugees made plans to reconquer New Mexico. In 1689 troops from El Paso marched north to Zia pueblo, captured and destroyed the settlement, killed 600 Indians, and captured 70 survivors who were later sold as slaves. Then in February 1691 Don Diego de Vargas became royal governor of New Mexico. The following year he led an expedition from El Paso which eventually reached Santa Fe. De Vargas mixed peaceful negotiations with military fury to restore Spanish rule along the river, culminating in a peaceful return to Santa Fe, the result of patient negotiation with its defenders. From there his troops continued the reconquest, steadily restoring Spanish dominion. With the return of peace 800 Spaniards returned to New Mexico. Those pueblos that resisted were destroyed, and the survivors were enslaved and divided among the colonists. The reconquest officially concluded on January 10, 1695, although sporadic resistance of little consequence continued among the pueblo peoples for several years. Eventually all Indian settlements in the Rio Grande Valley submitted.

Thereafter, until the close of Spanish rule in New Mexico in 1821, relations between European settlers and pueblo Indians were somewhat less tense. Staffing the pueblo missions was becoming increasingly difficult; by 1776 there were only twenty priests in all of New Mexico. The resulting decrease in religious pressure on the Indians allowed them gradually to return to their native religion. An even greater cause of relaxed Spanish rule on the pueblo Indians was the threat to both the pueblos and the Spanish colonists from Navajos and Apaches to the west, and Comanches and Kiowas to the east. By 1700 these tribes had adopted the horse and thus were increasingly mobile and deadly. They ranged over wider territories; they regularly raided Spanish settlements and Indian pueblos for grain, horses, and captives.

Spanish attempts to deal with the Navajos and Apaches, to settle bands from these tribes near the pueblos to become farmers and stock raisers, caused one Navajo leader to retort that his people had been "raised like deer" and that they "did not want to live in settlements like Christians."[12]

Comanches and Kiowas, from the northern Rocky Mountains, had also adopted the horse and recently carved out a vast territory that extended from the Arkansas River south to the Rio Grande. The horse revolutionized their life-style; mounted, they preyed upon the great buffalo herds in their hunting range for subsistence, and with their new mobility became the most deadly raiders in North America, regularly striking Spanish settlements in New Mexico and south of the Rio Grande in northern Mexico for horses, plunder, and captives. Most of the Spanish effort in New Mexico after 1700 concentrated on defenses against Comanches and Kiowas from the east as well as Apaches and Navajos from the west. Thus these Indian raiders relieved Spanish pressure on the pueblo tribes and, in that sense, made life easier for them.

Arizona Sector

The thrust of Spanish settlements northwestward from Mexico City led officials to establish the administrative province of Pimería Alta, extending from the Altar River in Sonora north to the Gila River in Arizona, and from the San Pedro River on the east to the Colorado River and Gulf of California on the west. The Jesuit order was assigned to the mission frontier in Pimería Alta. By the 1680s Jesuits had established a chain of missions in the southern half of Pimería Alta and were ready to open the northern portion under the leadership of Padre Eusebio Francisco Kino, an Italian. Kino's missions eventually extended from the San Miguel River in Sonora northward along the valley of the San Pedro and Santa Cruz rivers in southern Arizona and included San Xavier del Bac, Tumacacori, and Guebavi. As a carrier of Spanish civilization, Kino worked tirelessly to convert the peoples in the scattered agricultural settlements, most of them Pimas and Papagos, of Pimería Alta. He introduced to the region cattle, sheep, goats, horses, wheat and other seeds, and trees. One of Kino's associates estimated that the Bac rancherías contained 3,000 Indians but that the fertile, irrigated land of the creek and river valleys together with pastures on the uplands for herds of cattle and horses could support a mission of at least 30,000.

But the high hopes the founders had for upper Pimería Alta were dashed by seemingly insurmountable obstacles that eventually halted Spanish progress into Arizona. One was the continuing nativism and loyalty to their tribes among the Indians of Pimería Alta. The other was the threat of the awesome Apache.

The Riparian People were intensely independent. Although they had been gracious and hospitable to the early Jesuit fathers, they found conformity to the structured life in mission communities difficult. Each ranchería was autonomous and each resident proudly so. The pressure and structure of Spanish administration had antagonized the Piman peoples of the Altar Valley region. In 1695 they revolted, killed missionaries, burned public buildings, and drove off livestock. The insurrection was put down with great effort by presidio and Indian auxiliaries and heavy expense to the Spanish royal government of Sonora. The Pima uprising was a protest against the progression of the Spanish civil frontier and the growing exploitation of Indians through labor levies by the miners and stock raisers. The Pimas were also protesting the growing interference of the mission programs with their native life-style, including the overthrow of tribal deities and general tampering with Indian culture.

The continuing spread of mining and stock-raising settlements across Sonora placed even greater labor demands on the Pimas of lower Pimería Alta. Through the years, many Indians fled north and settled in the rancherías of the San Pedro and Santa Cruz region. They carried stories of the traumatic changes that missionaries, soldiers, and settlers made in their lives, and they warned their Arizona kinsmen that they soon would suffer a similar fate.

Kino attempted to reassure the people of upper Pimería Alta by showing them a *cédula* (document) from the viceroy which exempted them from forced labor and tribute for at least twenty years. Nonetheless, an undercurrent of anxiety persisted among the Arizona Indians, fed by the grim stories of migrating southern Pimas of gross exploitation.

By 1750 Jesuit missionaries intensified their efforts among the Riparian People of southern Arizona. Nine resident clerics labored in the rancherías of upper Pimería Alta. The accelerated Jesuit program to bring drastic changes in Indian life-style and religion, to substitute Spanish culture for Indian ways, and to replace the ancient Indian personal and group autonomy with submission to stern Spanish law and authority increased Piman discontent.

At this juncture there emerged an Indian leader, Luis Oacpicagigua, who had many characteristics we now associate with a nationalist. He was a persuasive orator, with keen native intelligence and consuming ambition. He had associated with Spanish officials in Sonora and once led a Pima army to help the governor of Sonora put down a revolt among the Seris. From these contacts with provincial leaders and from his military experience, Luis had observed the workings of administrative organization and the power that came from concentrated group action. He conceived a plan to fuse the scattered rancherías of upper Pimería Alta into a unified nation. With such a group he could expel the oppressive Spaniards and free his people from the increasingly objectionable daily impositions of the Europeans, and remove the threat to the cherished native way of life. Luis based his appeal to the Riparian People for unified action on charges of Jesuit exploitation and harsh treatment in their Indian missions. And he exploited the Pimas' fear of impressment, warning the Indians that the mission stage was but the prelude to civilian communities, with miners and stock raisers, who would require Indian labor in mines and on ranches.

In 1751, after secret meetings at Saric, a settlement southwest of Bac, Luis collected a small Pima army and swiftly struck the scattered settlements and missions of upper Pimería Alta. The rebels killed eighteen Spaniards and a number of converted Indians whom Luis's Pima followers distrusted. Unrest and some disorder appeared in the San Pedro and Santa Cruz rancherías, but most of the Pimas shunned direct participation in the raids. Massed Spanish forces crushed the outbreak and captured and executed several rebels.

This revolt had several consequences. It undoubtedly helped to bring about the expulsion of the Jesuits from the Spanish empire in 1767. After the Jesuits left Pimería Alta, their place was taken by the Franciscan order. The new missionaries continued to complain that the independent Pimas had returned to what the padres called "their ancient barbarism."

Another result was extension of the Spanish military frontier into southern Arizona. In 1752 officials in New Spain directed the founding of Presidio San Ignacio del Tubac to support the reoccupation of missions and to provide the Spanish with a nearby military force to maintain surveillance over the incorrigible Pimas. A few settlers followed the troops up the Santa Cruz Valley to establish the pueblo of Tubac and the church of Santa Gertrudis de Tubac.

Certainly the Indian insurrection, the continuing Piman determination to preserve their independence and to maintain their ancient life-style and religion, contributed to the blunting of the Spanish advance into Arizona.

The other obstacle to Spanish ambitions in Arizona was the continuing Apache menace. The Apaches, latecomers to the Southwest, had by restless, predatory conquest, established a home territory in southern New Mexico and southeastern Arizona. During the latter part of the seventeenth century these people mounted a destructive, terrorizing series of banditti-type raids south into Chihuahua and Sonora and west into Arizona. This guerrilla warfare became a way of life for the Apaches which was not completely contained until 1886. Their quick, swooping raids on Spanish settlements and Indian rancherías netted an annual harvest of cattle, grain, horses, plunder, and captives. Besides raiding and terrorizing Spanish towns in Sonora, the Apaches preyed on Pima rancherías and mission settlements in the San Pedro and Santa Cruz valleys of southern Arizona. Then each year they followed the San Pedro Valley into Sonora. And the constant raids turned the stream of Spanish settlement away from the north, depopulating several European settlements in Sonora. In 1751 Apache invasion of Sonora forced Spaniards to abandon their capital at San Juan Bautista and move it to greater safety at Arizpe. Years of Apache use of the San Pedro Valley as their principal route into Sonora changed this region of Indian rancherías into a wasteland and forced the residents to join the Santa Cruz settlements, creating a compact enclave of Riparian People in Arizona.

Apache raider bands also occasionally swooped through the Santa Cruz Valley, even threatening the livestock herds of the mission at San Xavier del Bac. Pima warriors resisted these invasions of their territory and served as support troops with Spanish forces in extended campaigns against the elusive Apaches. But fighting the Apaches was like fighting phantoms because of the tactical skill and mobility of the enemy bands. Apaches rarely risked open combat with the Spanish-Indian armies.

Under a plan applied by the Spanish crown after 1763 to reform colonial administration, which included a scheme to tame the Apaches, Arizona and

New Mexico were integrated into an administrative jurisdiction called the *Provincias Internas;* it subsequently included Texas and California. The reform plan secularized Indian affairs by placing the Indians under the jurisdiction of presidio commanders. Three presidios were established in Arizona—Quiburi on the San Pedro River astride the route of Apache raids into Sonora, Fronteras in the San Bernardino Valley in southeastern Arizona, and San Augustin del Tucson at Tucson ranchería. These posts provided Spanish frontier commanders with forward stations to support offensive operations against Apaches in southeastern Arizona. Officials were to maintain continuing military pressure on the Apaches with regular Spanish and auxiliary forces and to contact the predatory bands and, wherever possible, to eliminate the justification for raiding by negotiating agreements with the leaders to settle their followers near missions and presidios where they would receive weekly rations of grain and other food. Frontier officials were permitted to issue Apaches firearms "of poor quality," effective for hunting but not for warfare. No effort was to be spared in making the Apaches dependent upon the Spanish. Local officials were to issue liquor as a part of the weekly ration in order to addict the Indians to strong drink, and to encourage trade with the relocated Indians, developing a taste and need for European goods and further increasing their dependency.

Between 1775 and 1790 Spanish regular and Indian auxiliary forces maintained great pressure on the Apaches. They found several Apache bases, defeated the Indian defenders, and resettled the captives near presidios. Several Apache bands voluntarily took up residence near Spanish settlements in southern Arizona. While some raiding continued throughout the Spanish period, after a few years of the pacification program raids decreased to a level where they were at most a nuisance, certainly not producing the devastation of the pre-1775 period, which had depopulated much of upper Sonora and forced the concentration of Arizona's Riparian People in the Santa Cruz Valley. Spanish miners and stock raisers returned to upper Sonora, and a number settled in southern Arizona to establish mines and ranches. An official report of 1800 from the frontier commented that raiding had virtually ceased and that many former guerrillas, now called Tame Apaches, had settled in the region between the San Pedro and Santa Cruz, at convenient locations for drawing their weekly rations.

Native Americans blunted the Spanish thrust into Arizona. The intensely independent Riparian Peoples' protectiveness toward their traditional ways of life and religion frustrated the Iberian civilization program. The Apaches must receive considerable credit for slowing the Spanish advance into Arizona and thereby conserving local Indian culture. In an oblique sense, for 150 years their awesome guerrilla activity checked the flow of Spanish settlement into Arizona. Paradoxically, while Apaches also preyed on the Riparian People, in the long run they protected their victims from Hispanicization by drawing Spanish attention to themselves.

California Sector

By 1750 Jesuit missionaries had established Spanish dominion over Baja California. About that time Russian fur hunters from bases in Alaska were moving south along the Pacific Coast. Alien activity on territory claimed by Spain spurred officials in Mexico to undertake the occupation of Alta California, roughly the area of the present state of California. This region of unusually dense Indian population was to be settled largely by expansion of missionary activity supported by presidial troops and a few settlers who would form civilian settlements.

Missionary work in Alta California was assigned to Franciscan padres headed by Junípero Serra. Spanish settlement there began in 1769 with the landing of missionaries and troops and founding of a mission and presidio at

This illustration shows Indians dancing at the mission at San Jose in 1806. Their body painting is red, black, and white. (Bancroft Library, University of California, Berkeley)

San Diego Bay. Additional missionaries, troops, and settlers from Sonora and southern Arizona came overland via the Gila River Valley with livestock to start herds at the mission. Eventually the Franciscans founded a chain of twenty wealthy missions between San Diego Bay and San Francisco Bay.

Indians of southern and central California for the most part submitted peacefully; the Franciscans found bringing them under their direction rather easy. Padres selected mission sites on the basis of location, soil quality, water availability, and pasturage, and gathered in Indians from their scattered settlements. The practice was to settle a small number of Native Americans at each mission, subject them to mission discipline, routine, and instruction, then send them back to their homes with instructions to bring in others. The Franciscan padres taught Christian doctrine and agriculture and vocational arts.[13]

Discipline at the California missions was stern. Refusal by an Indian to work resulted in his being deprived of food as well as other punishments. For tardiness to worship or work, absence from church, dilatory habits, or slowness in tasks the punishment was lashing on the bare back in public and then confinement.

The number of Indians at each mission varied from a few hundred to two or three thousand. Through the years the California missions with strict Franciscan oversight and productive Indian labor developed irrigated fields for grain and other crops and pastures supporting large herds of cattle and sheep. By both civil and ecclesiastical law these wealthy mission estates, with

This Chumash rock painting in Southern California's Santa Monica Mountains probably represents an early encounter with white people mounted on horseback. (*The Call to California*, a Copley book)

their riches in irrigated fields, crops, and livestock, were the property of the Indians, held in trust for them by the Franciscan padres.

Missions so dominated the lives of these Native Americans that they lost their tribal identity and came to be called "Mission Indians." The total number of baptisms of California Indians performed by Franciscan missionaries during the period of Spanish dominion in this region (1769–1822) amounted to about 90,000. But it should be borne in mind that, despite the nearly total Spanish impact upon the Mission Indians, many California tribes in the interior and to the north of San Francisco were never touched by Spanish missionary or secular influence. These Indians were not contacted until Anglo-American miners opened the northern California interior beginning in 1849.

Mississippi Valley Sector

In the twilight of the Spanish empire, Spain acquired new territory and dominion over several additional Indian tribes in North America. While Spanish dominion over these tribes—mostly in the lower Mississippi Valley—was so brief that no appreciable, lasting Iberian imprint was left, Spanish officials did exploit them intensively to support the final stage of Spain's imperial dream in North America. By the Treaty of Fontainebleau (1762) France ceded New Orleans and the vast trans-Mississippi province of Louisiana to Spain. The following year, by the Treaty of Paris, Spain lost Florida and the Gulf Coast to Great Britain, but this strategic territory returned to Spanish rule in 1783. Spain held Louisiana until 1800; Florida and portions of the Gulf Coast remained Spanish until 1819. Spain attempted to integrate the peoples of this new territory into a grand defense against the expansion by the newly formed United States into New Spain.

Spain used experienced French traders and the established commerce in furs and annual gifts rather than missions to control the Indian tribes of Louisiana. The important fur-trade centers of St. Louis, Arkansas Post, and Natchitoches became contact points for Spanish officials in dealing with the Native Americans of Louisiana and the lower Mississippi Valley. Chiefs of the Caddo, Wichita, Osage, Comanche, and Quapaw tribes came to these towns each year to receive gifts and medals and to meet with Spanish officials.

Many French traders from east of the Mississippi River moved into Spanish territory on the west bank and became a part of the Spanish frontier commerce-defense system. In several cases these traders brought bands of tribes from east of the Mississippi with them. These migrating Indians, including Kickapoos, Delawares, and Shawnees, established villages along the Missouri, Arkansas, and Red rivers and their tributaries and continued to hunt in the trans-Mississippi region for pelts to trade with their French sponsors, now under Spanish rule. Thus at Spanish invitation and the urging of French traders a voluntary migration of portions of several tribes was underway years before the United States government inflicted its forced removal program on the eastern tribes.

After 1783 the L-shaped territory of Spain boxed in the Americans on the south and west. Spanish agents forged the tribes of that area into a powerful defensive cordon to stem the American advance in that direction. Creek, Cherokee, and Choctaw leaders regularly met with Spanish representatives at Pensacola, Mobile, and New Orleans for directions. The southern Indians in the Spanish defensive community were led by Alexander McGillivray, a Creek mixed blood who was passionately attached to the land of his Indian ancestors. Spanish settlements, consisting in part of Indian mercenaries, extended from Florida along the Gulf Coast to the mouth of the Mississippi, then north along the east bank of the river. Spanish and Indian troops occupied military posts at Natchez and at Chickasaw Bluffs near the present site of Memphis. Spanish agents supplied their Indian allies with arms and at times sent them against American settlements.

In the 1790s Spain's power in the lower Mississippi Valley collapsed. McGillivray, the most important link between the Spanish and the southern Indians, died in 1793. American diplomatic negotiations with the Spanish government forced Spain to abandon those Mississippi Valley military posts that were on American soil. Finally in 1800 Spain returned Louisiana to France. Three years later the United States purchased this vast territory from France. This transfer made the United States the ruler over the Native Americans only recently used by Spain against that expanding young nation. American forays into Florida's Gulf Coast and later invasion of Florida to punish Indians for raids into the United States led in 1819 to cession of Florida and its peoples to the United States.

During its Age of Empire, Spain was regularly challenged in the New World for hegemony over the land, resources, and Indians by France and Great Britain and to a limited extent, by Holland and Russia. However, for most of the colonial period Spain was the dominant imperial power and exercised the greatest influence over the Native Americans, its imprint in ancestry, language, and culture surviving among certain Indian communities in some places today. Of all other contesting powers, France, until 1750, was Spain's most serious rival for preeminence in North America. In some respects the French empire even surpassed the Spanish in successful control of certain Indian tribes.

Notes

1. D'Arcy McNickle, *Native American Tribalism: Indian Survivals and Renewals* (New York, 1973), p. 27.
2. Dwight W. Hoover, *The Red and the Black* (Chicago, 1976), pp. 11, 15.
3. J. H. Parry, "Spanish Indian Policy in Colonial America: The Ordering of Society," in *Three American Empires*, edited by John J. TePaske (New York, 1967), p. 112.
4. William C. MacLeod, *The American Indian Frontier* (New York, 1928), pp. 69–71.
5. Edward H. Spicer, *Cycles of Conquest: The Impact of Spain, Mexico,*

and the United States on the Indians
of the Southwest, 1533–1960 (Tucson, Ariz., 1962), p. 5.

6. MacLeod, *American Indian Frontier*, pp. 72–76.
7. *Ibid.*
8. *Ibid.*, p. 121.
9. Hoover, *Red and the Black*, pp. 14–15.
10. Parry, "Spanish Indian Policy," p. 115.
11. Ward A. Minge, *Ácoma: Pueblo in the Sky* (Albuquerque, N.M., 1976), pp. 13–14.
12. *Ibid.*, p. 34.
13. "Mission Indians of California," in *Handbook of American Indians North of Mexico*, edited by Frederick W. Hodge (Washington, D.C., 1907), Vol. I, pp. 873–74.

Selected Sources

General works which contain information on the American Indian's role in the Spanish empire include Howard Peckham and Charles Gibson (eds.), *Attitudes of the Colonial Powers Towards the American Indians* (Salt Lake City, Utah, 1969); Charles Gibson, *Spain in America* (New York, 1966); Carl O. Sauer, *Sixteenth Century North America: The Land and the People as Seen by Europeans* (Berkeley, Calif., 1971); and Herbert E. Bolton and Thomas M. Marshall, *The Colonization of North America* (New York, 1935).

The progression of the Spanish empire across the southern rimland of the present United States and its engulfment of the Indian peoples are discussed in Herbert E. Bolton *The Spanish Borderlands*, (New Haven, Conn., 1921); Arthur P. Whitaker, *The Spanish-American Frontier, 1783–1795* (Boston, 1927); John W. Caughey, *McGillivray of the Creeks* (Norman, Okla., 1938); J. Leitch Wright, Jr., *Anglo-Spanish Rivalry in North America* (Athens, Ga., 1971); Elizabeth A. H. John, *Storms Brewed in Other Men's Worlds: the Confrontation of Indians, Spanish, and French in the Southwest, 1540–1795* (College Station, Texas, 1975); Herbert E. Bolton, *Texas in the Middle Eighteenth Century* (Berkeley, Calif., 1915); Hubert H. Bancroft, *History of the North Mexican States and Texas* (San Francisco, 1889), 2 vols.; Herbert E. Bolton (ed.), *Athanase de Mezieres and the Louisiana-Texas Frontier, 1768–1780* (Cleveland, Ohio, 1914), 2 vols.; S. D. Aberle, *The Pueblo Indians of New Mexico* (New York, 1948); C. W. Hackett and C. C. Shelby, *Revolt of the Pueblo Indians of New Mexico* (New York, 1948); Elsie Clews Parsons, *Pueblo Indian Religion* (Chicago, 1939), 2 vols.; France V. Scholes, *Troublous Times in New Mexico, 1659–1670* (Albuquerque, N. M., 1942); John F. Bannon, *The Mission Frontier in Sonora, 1620–1687* (New York, 1955); Herbert E. Bolton (ed. and trans.), *Eusebio F. Kino: Historical Memoir of Pimería Alta* (Berkeley, Calif., 1948); and by the same author, *Rim of Christendom: A Biography of Eusebio Francisco Kino* (New York, 1936); Charles E. Chapman, *The Founding of Spanish California: The Northwestward Expansion of New Spain, 1687–1783* (New York, 1916); Herbert E. Bolton (ed.), *Anza's California Expeditions* (Berkeley, 1930), 5 vols.; and Lewis Hanke, *The Spanish Struggle for Justice in the Conquest of America* (Philadelphia, 1949). Two additional works by the same author illuminate Spanish Indian policy—*Aristotle and the American Indians: A Study of Race and Prejudice in the Modern World* (London, 1959); and *The First Social Experiment in America: A Study in the Development of Spanish Indian Policy in the Sixteenth Century* (Cambridge, 1935).

CHAPTER 6

FRANCE AND THE
NATIVE AMERICANS

I have had frequent opportunities to observe moral dispositions in men we call savages, that would do such honour to the most civilized European.

Pierre Marie Francois de Pages' on Native Americans morals

▼

France, which became an imperial power in North America a century after Spain, was no less devoted to the new economic gospel of mercantilism, which maintained that the foundations of national power lay in overseas colonies providing the home country with vital raw materials, than the other major European nations. By the middle of the sixteenth century, France began to defy the pope's division of the world outside Europe between Spain and Portugal. Several French exploring and colonizing expeditions before 1600 sought a foothold in the New World, but they were unsuccessful. One, on the South Atlantic Coast, ended in disaster when a vigilant Spanish patrol discovered the Gallic intruders and executed them.

ORIGINS OF FRENCH COLONIAL ESTABLISHMENT

After nearly half a century of failure, France finally succeeded in founding a permanent colonial base in North America. Spain had entered the present United States from the south by way of Mexico and the Caribbean Islands. France, thwarted by Spanish power on the South Atlantic Coast and blocked along the northern Atlantic Seaboard by the emerging English and Dutch colonies, penetrated the present United States from the northeast by way of the St. Lawrence River Valley to establish dominion over the resident Native Americans and their tribal territories.

In 1608 Samuel Champlain began the formation of the French empire in North America by founding settlements in the St. Lawrence River Valley centering on Quebec. This territory was populated by Algonkian- and Iroquoian-speaking peoples. Quite early in the formation of New France Champlain entered into an alliance with the Hurons and Montagnais against

Chapter Opening Artifact: Moundbuilder diorite bowl. (Courtesy of American Museum of Natural History)

116

French artist's views of Native Americans used to illustrate *Les Voyages de Sr. de Champlain*, ca. 1615–1618. (Houghton Library, Harvard University)

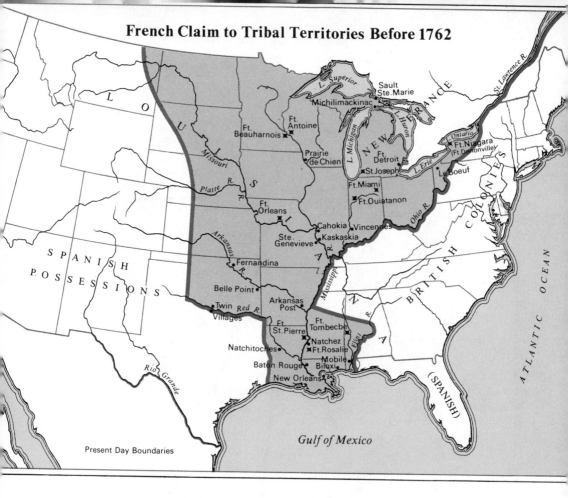

French Claim to Tribal Territories Before 1762

their ancient enemies, the tribes of the Iroquois Confederacy—Mohawk, Seneca, Onondaga, Oneida, and Cayuga—south of the St. Lawrence. This alliance with local Indians assured success for the first permanent French colony in the New World.

Pioneer French settlers traded tools, hatchets, knives, and cloth to their Indian neighbors for animal furs and skins. Bales of furs were the first French cargoes shipped from North America. Furs stimulated intense commercial interest in France and ultimately committed its leaders to the single-minded pursuit of trade with the Indians for pelts to provide hat and clothing manufacturers, shoe, boot and harness makers, and other home industries with essential raw materials.

In its feverish rush across great portions of the present United States in search of new fur-trading territories, the French empire came to assert dominion over tens of thousands of Native Americans and several thousand square miles of territory. The Iroquois Confederacy's great military power thwarted French expansion south of the St. Lawrence Valley, for during the pioneer period French officials were never able to muster a strong enough force from French regulars and Indian allies to destroy it. Thus French pioneers were deflected westward across the Great Lakes into the Mississippi Valley. Supported by Native American allies, the French came to dominate the territory between the Great Lakes and the Ohio River, the upper Mississippi Valley, the lands west along the Missouri River into the Rocky Mountains and, ultimately, the lower Mississippi Valley all the way to the Gulf of Mexico.

The Unfortunate adventures of Mons.r de la Salle.

LaSalle's unsuccessful attempt to establish French presence among the Gulf Coast tribes, 1684. (Permission of the Houghton Library, Harvard University)

Scattered French posts became tiny wilderness urban centers for maintaining the bonanza fur trade and for ruling the Indians and engulfing them in that trade. Each Indian in a sense became a worker in the service of the French empire.

In 1673 Louis Joliet and Jacques Marquette, with Indian guides and body-guard, set out from Green Bay to follow the Fox and Wisconsin rivers to the Mississippi. From there they continued downstream to the mouth of the Arkansas River before returning north. They speculated that the Mississippi emptied into the Gulf of Mexico. If true, they realized, they had found a water route through the continent—not the long-sought east-west passage, but a north-south route via the St. Lawrence River, Great Lakes, and Missis-sippi River to the Gulf of Mexico. This prospect created great excitement among New France pioneers.

Robert Cavelier, Sieur de la Salle, who had established the fur trade in the Ohio Valley, saw in the Joliet-Marquette discovery the means to drive a wedge through the heart of Spanish territory in North America. In 1682, with a large party of Indians and Frenchmen, he followed the Mississippi all the way to the Gulf of Mexico. On the basis of this exploration La Salle claimed the vast Mississippi Valley for France, naming its western segment Louisiana after the French king. Moreover, he devised a plan for founding fortified settlements at the mouth of the Mississippi River and for occupying and exploiting the rich resources of Louisiana. These fortifications would guard the strategic Mississippi Valley from foreign attack and would provide a base from which to contact and control the many Indian tribes and to settle the territory between French posts in the Old Northwest north of the Ohio River and the Gulf of Mexico. Because their climate was milder than that of the northern settlements, these southern posts would give French traders a year-round export depot. Finally, the military stations would give France an advantageous position to control Gulf shipping. La Salle's subsequent expedition to the mouth of the Mississippi via the Gulf of Mexico to establish a permanent settlement failed. However, in 1699 French persistence to carry out La Salle's plan was rewarded when Pierre LeMoyne d'Iberville estab-lished Biloxi and other fortified settlements on the Gulf Coast.

The French Imperial Management System

The expanding French empire in North America was populated by scores of different Indian tribes. The problem of integrating the many different tribes into the French imperial system and absorbing their divergent energies into useful service for the crown vexed French administrators for over a century. Their system for governing their North American empire and its native peoples evolved slowly. In the early years French officials were com-mitted to developing New France according to the mercantilist model. Frenchmen in the colonies were expected to establish a wide range of eco-nomic activities including agriculture. The colonies were to serve as markets for domestic manufactures, to assist the nation in becoming self-sufficient in food and other essentials, and to serve as a haven for France's surplus population.

For many years the king and his court, as the supreme proprietor of the colonial establishment, followed the practice of rewarding those who had gained the king's favor with economic grants and privileges including monopolies of certain colonial enterprises. Thus in 1627 the crown chartered the Company of One Hundred Associates, a business association similar to the Virginia Company of Jamestown. This nonspecialized company was to be the instrument for the colonization and development of New France by developing the land's resources, populating it with French farmers, and trading with the Indians. Its failure, particularly in attracting an appreciable number of settlers for New France, caused the crown to revoke its charter in 1633. French pioneers neglected the essential work of taming the New France wilderness for the easier and more exciting fur trade. In the following year the crown chartered the French West India Company with a similar mission to develop New France. Like the earlier company, the West India Company became so infatuated with the fur trade that it, too, neglected the basic needs of the colony including the necessity of bringing an adequate number of colonists. And in 1663 its charter was also revoked. Management of New France was thereupon transferred to direct royal control; in 1674 New France became a crown colony, its officials appointed by the king.

It was largely under royal management that French expansion into the Ohio Valley, the entire Mississippi Valley, and Louisiana was completed and that French rule was extended over many new Indian subjects. The pattern of government that evolved for the French empire in North America and remained in effect until the expulsion of France from North America in 1763 centered on the royal household. The minister of marine, a member of the Royal Council of State and directly responsible to the king, governed New France and Louisiana through his Department of the Marine. Canada, which included the upper Mississippi Valley and the Old Northwest (the area between the Mississippi and Ohio rivers), and Louisiana, which included the Gulf settlements, were considered provinces of France, the colonists and Indians as French subjects. A governor, usually a naval officer, appointed by the king and working under the Department of Marine, was the provincial chief executive. Another official of equal rank and power was the intendant. He shared management of the province or the colony with the governor; each served as a check on the other. Generally the intendant was in charge of the fur trade and the Indian tribes of the province.

Local government functioned at the military-trading posts scattered across the Western wilderness. Each post was situated at a strategic portage, on a water strait, or near the mouth of a river. Leading French fur posts included Miami portage, St. Joseph, Green Bay, Michilimackinac, Arkansas Post near the mouth of the Arkansas, and Natchitoches and Twin Villages on Red River. Detroit and New Orleans were the largest settlements in the United

States portion of New France, each with about 1,500 population in 1740.

Each military-trading settlement was surrounded by a log palisade with four bastions, the fortification equipped with two cannon and several mortars, and manned with a garrison of twenty to forty soldiers with two officers. All depended upon the fur trade; the commander and troops at each post were paid from the income generated by the local fur trade. Soldiers, traders, settled Indians, and families made up the population at each post. The post commandant's civilian duties included supervising the fur trade in his jurisdiction. He issued trading permits, regulated transportation of trade goods, and was responsible for maintaining law and order including settling disputes between Indian hunters and French traders.

The French attempted to make the New World wilderness society an extension of French society. They expected the traditional French respect for authority and the highly structured, regulated, authoritarian French socio-political system to function in New France. Thus, by royal decree, political institutions, the family, Indian affairs, the range of permissible trade and occupations, the amount of prestige associated with each status in society, were all carefully regulated. But such expectations were often incompatible with New World reality. Most French colonists were men. The enticing appeal of wilderness freedom snared many of them. Rather than conforming to royal expectation and becoming peasant farmers in New France, they became exiles in the forest, *coureurs de bois,* wilderness traders, adopting many elements of the Indian life-style, exulting in their new-found freedom. The tighter the control, the more appealing was the life of freedom in the forests. From the very beginning the *coureurs de bois* emerged as a distinct and somewhat romantic figure—and a continuing thorn in the side of both secular and ecclesiastical authorities. Life in the wilderness with Indians provided these Frenchmen an exciting alternative to the regulated existence which colonial administrators were attempting to establish in New France.[1]

Indian Policy

The French were the most successful of all Europeans in their relations with Native Americans. Spaniards dealt with as many tribes, and by Iberian standards their record of success in subduing them was creditable. But they consistently used coercion and cruelty, at times to the point of genocide, to achieve their goal of civilization and conversion. Frenchmen used coercion, in one case killing almost a whole tribe, but generally only as a last resort. Whereas most Indians feared, even hated Spaniards, they often found reason to respect Frenchmen and to accept them as partners in the great enterprise of the fur trade. There is marked contrast in the Indian reaction to the expulsion of the Spanish and of the French. When Spain was ejected by revolutionary overthrow in 1821, there was general rejoicing among Native Americans who had endured Spanish rule. On the other hand, when the French surrendered their empire in North America to the British in 1763, there was a widespread uprising among the tribes of the Old Northwest, protesting the loss of their French patron and their determination not to accept the new British ruler.

Indian policy in early New France was "Francisation," calling for a complete transformation of the Indian life-style and adoption of French civilization. It included conversion to the Christian faith and relocation of Indians close to French settlements where they could observe enlightened European Christian living as their model. In addition, Francisation encouraged intermarriage and education of the Indians in French ways in the hope that, made tractable by their reeducation, they would swell the labor force. The policy's failure was soon evident.[2]

Its failure was due, more than anything else, to the lure of wealth from the fur trade which distracted and diverted French administrative attention and the energy of French colonists. Missionaries working among the tribes attempted to force administrators to remain committed to the imperial policy goals, but their efforts were generally of no avail. Thus, the French departed rather quickly from rigid, structured Indian relations and cultural alteration, such as the Spaniards were applying to the tribes under their control, and moved instead toward a more permissive, *ad hoc* policy. They recognized tribal sovereignty and used diplomacy to keep the tribes friendly, loyal, and committed to the French cause. The thriving fur trade, which served to keep the Indians increasingly dependent upon the French, was the overpowering consideration, the foundation of the French-Indian relationship.

This permissive, *ad hoc* policy, which endured until the French were expelled from North America in 1763, was based on a shrewdly conceived and applied diplomacy. The fur trade, New France's economic staple, required Indian workers to hunt the fur-bearing animals, to process the pelts, and to pack them in bales for shipment to France. Hence, Indian cooperation and peace in the wilderness were essential, and French administrators placed primary reliance on diplomacy to maintain these conditions, resorting to military action and coercion only as a last resort. For purposes of dealing with the tribes of New France, officials divided the Native Americans into three classes: (1) Indians living near French settlements in the St. Lawrence Valley, (2) Indians who lived at trading posts in the West, and (3) "free Indians," those beyond the immediate control of traders and officials.

To maintain goodwill of the tribes, Frenchmen, rather than scorning Indian language and culture as Spanish, British, and later the Anglo-Americans did, developed a respect for them. Significantly, France was the only European power whose official policy recognized the many differences among Indian cultures. The French did not scorn the Indians' way of life, but rather came to respect it. Thus instead of naively assuming that all Indians were alike and attempting to force all tribes to adopt a common culture, the French followed a pluralistic approach. They early discerned the differences and what they called "peculiarities of the native character." Francis Parkman, a leading authority on France in the New World, has commented that Frenchmen "labored with eager diligence to conciliate the Indians, and win them to espouse" the French cause. French agents "were busy in every village, studying the language [of the Indians] complying with their usages."[3]

The governors of Canada and Louisiana spent at least three months every year traveling around their territories visiting the Indian tribes. They required the commandant at each of the fur trade-military settlements in the wilderness to be above all a diplomat and to work incessantly to cultivate and maintain harmonious relations with the tribes.

Each year during the month of May the governor of Canada met with leaders of the western tribes at Montreal, and the governor of Louisiana met with leaders of the southern tribes at Mobile. These conferences were the diplomatic highlight of the year, and French officials went to great effort to make the convocation impressive for the visiting tribesmen. During the sessions viewpoints were exchanged between tribal leaders and the governor. The governor's closing comments invariably admonished the tribesmen to remain loyal to France and to trade only with the French. Then he distributed gifts to tribal leaders. These councils were gala affairs attracting many rank-and-file warriors who brought packs of pelts to barter with local merchants.

The French style, contrasted with the stiff, formal, and structured Spanish and British conduct of relations with the tribes, was easy and sanguine and appealed to the Indians. Parkman stated that this relaxed style promoted genuine friendship between French officials and traders and Indians. "When a party of Indian chiefs visited a French fort, they were greeted with the firing of cannon and rolling of drums." Their hosts plied them with scarlet uniforms, French flags, and medals, and at the banquet tables whispered "friendly warnings in their ears against the wicked designs of the English." Parkman claimed that the French were

Far wiser than their rivals [the British; they] never ruffled the . . . dignity of their guests, never insulted their religious notions, nor ridiculed their ancient customs. [Count Louis de Frontenac, Governor of Canada,] himself plumed and painted like an Indian chief, danced the war-dance and yelled the war-song at the campfires of his delighted allies. [Frenchmen] copied their model with infamous fidelity.[4]

It was claimed that French success with Native Americans was in part the result of the "pliant and plastic temper" of Frenchmen which made them particularly suited to friendship with the Indians. From their earliest times in the New World the French had been particularly closely associated with the Indians. Some historians believe that, compared to the Spanish and the British, French character led them to see Indians as fellow human beings. One result was that the greatest intermarriage between Indians and Europeans north of Mexico is represented by the mixed bloods of Canada and the northwestern United States.[5]

The Indian policy of the French did include occasional relocation of tribes. Most removals consisted of traders moving groups of hunters and their families, attached to them by need for trade goods and by debt, from one hunting territory to another. French officials also occasionally resettled an entire tribe for security and commercial purposes. During the 1640s military pressure from the Iroquois Confederation forced the Hurons (Wyandots) to abandon Huronia, their territory in Ontario between Lake Simcoe and Georgian Bay. Many settled near Quebec and became successful middlemen for French interests in the Western fur trade. Later, to support their opening of the territory around the Great Lakes to the fur trade, French officials settled several Wyandots near Detroit. Then around 1725 they were moved to Sandusky on the south shore of Lake Erie. The plan was to settle the Shawnees in the territory near Detroit vacated by the Wyandots as a preventive step. British traders were luring the Shawnees from the French orbit.

French officials also punished certain tribes who failed to support the French cause or who resisted French rule. Thus as a penalty for failing to cooperate with the French the Fox tribe was forced to move from western Illinois and Wisconsin to a place near Detroit where officials could maintain closer surveillance.

Remnants of several eastern tribes, fleeing British colonial expansion on the Atlantic Coast, crossed the Appalachians into New France and placed themselves under French protection. Thus in 1749 French officials founded the Missikoui settlement near the north end of Lake Champlain for the Abenakis, Delawares, and other refugees from British settlements.

The French occasionally enslaved Native Americans during the early period of colonial development. But French interest was largely focused on the fur trade, they believed that the Indian, so essential to a continuing prosperous fur trade, would function more effectively in the economic service of New France as a free hunter. In a sense, however, Frenchmen indirectly enslaved Indians in this industry through a bondage of debt. During the later colonial period in the lower Mississippi Valley, enslavement of Indians became increasingly common. In a desperate attempt to destroy the recalcitrant Chickasaws and Natchez French officials sent captives from these tribes to labor on plantations in the West Indies.

Frenchmen occasionally punished northern Indians for resisting and thwarting French design, particularly for threatening the fur trade, by making them bondsmen in royal service. For many years the opposition of the Iroquois was the principal obstacle to French success in the North. Time and again French armies invaded the Iroquois domain in an attempt to conquer these fierce people and force them to demonstrate their loyalty to France. Rarely was a campaign successful. King Louis XIV in 1684 directed his royal agents in New France to use all dispatch in bringing the Iroquois to terms,

as it concerns the good of my service to diminish as much as possible the number of Iroquois, and, as these savages, who are stout and robust, will, moreover, serve with advantage in my galleys, I wish you to do everything in your power to make a great number of them prisoners of war, and that you have them shipped by every opportunity which will offer for their removal to France.

Iroquois warriors captured in these campaigns were shipped to France, placed in shackles, and consigned to a morbid half-life of rowing the king's ships. On one occasion, however, the Iroquois so battered French troops that tribal leaders were able to force the French to free some of the galley prisoners and return them to their people as a condition of peace.[6]

For the most part, however, French officials were sensitive to the Native American's attachment to the land and judiciously received approval for locating military and fur-trade posts in tribal territories. Until about 1720, the number of French settlers engaged in farming in French territory south of Canada was small. Thus, except in the lower Mississippi Valley, the French never faced the problem of intensive competition between colonists and Indians for land which faced the British on the Atlantic seaboard. The small tracts required by the few tiny agricultural settlements in the Old Northwest at Vincennes, Kaskaskia, and Cahokia were obtained by French officials through negotiations with tribal leaders. The land was also drawn from hunting range and not from the intensively used village sites. However, after 1720 in the lower Mississippi Valley when the French began large-scale agricultural operations in the rich bottomland belonging to the Natchez, a bloody contest with the Indians ensued.

Like the other European empires, France exploited Native Americans, but less so and with a certain style. As a result Indians did not feel so put upon as they did under the other powers. French exploitation largely concentrated on using Indians as hunters for the fur trade and as soldiers in the French army in North America. With a vast territory to defend and with only limited regular royal troops for assignment to New France, the Indian soldier was essential for the empire's security. Native American troops protected the French position against British and Spanish armies and their Indian allies and participated in four major wars to defend French interests in the New World.

Missions

In the early years of the French empire in the New World, a primary goal was to convert the Indian tribes to Christianity. The mission's purpose was, first, to fulfill an obligation France felt toward Native Americans, its duty as a Christian nation to carry the Gospel to the heathen, to convert pagans to Christianity. Royal advisers believed that through missions maintained by Roman Catholic clerics, Indians could also be instructed in French civilization and thus converted to loyal, productive French subjects much as Spanish missions were attempting to do. For this purpose the crown, particularly in the early days, gave substantial financial support to Indian missions.

The principal French religious orders working in the New World were the Recollects, Jesuits, Sulpicians, and Capuchins. Recollects established missions among the St. Lawrence Valley tribes in 1615. Nine years later they were joined by the Jesuits, the order which became the leader in French missions in North America. By 1630 French missionaries had converted the Wyandots (Hurons) who at the time lived in Ontario between Lake Simcoe and Georgian Bay.

The Iroquois Confederacy tribes were bitter enemies of the Wyandots and, after Champlain allied with the Wyandots, bitter enemies of the French as well. The French-Wyandot alliance complicated matters for the missionary frontier in New France. In the 1640s warriors from the Iroquois Confederacy tribes repeatedly attacked Montreal and the surrounding area. They burned Wyandot villages, killed hundreds of converted Indians, and scattered them in all directions. Jesuit missionaries venturing among the Iroquois Confederacy tribes were martyred. Thus French missionaries followed traders into the territory south of the Great Lakes where they attempted to convert the Algonkian-speaking tribes of the so-called Illinois country, the territory between the Great Lakes and the Ohio River. These Indians were being integrated into the fur trade, and missionaries had a difficult time fulfilling their assignment. It quickly became apparent to the Jesuit and Capuchin fathers that the "fur trade and the civilization of the Indian were incompatible. The fur trade unsettled the native life. It made him much more of a roamer and less of an agriculturalist."[7]

NATIVE AMERICANS AND THE FUR TRADE

As we have seen, French empire builders hoped to create in New France a balanced colonial establishment to include agriculture, mining, and lumbering and naval stores. However, most pioneers in New France were caught up in the fur trade bonanza; it provided to France quick wealth much as the Mexican silver mines enriched Spain.

The Wyandot Monopoly

During the first fifty years of the French fur trade, the Wyandots dominated. Frenchmen served simply as suppliers of trade goods to Indian entrepreneurs who ventured into the wilderness, visiting the western tribes and exchanging French manufactured goods for pelts they delivered to French merchants at Montreal. The Wyandots were great traders even before the French arrived. In pre-Contact times they maintained a far-flung network of commercial contacts with tribes as far west as the upper Mississippi Valley. Through the Ottawas, their allies and agents in the Old Northwest, the Wyandots controlled intertribal trade southward into the Ohio Valley. Wyandot merchants exchanged corn, corn meal, tobacco, and hemp (used in making rope, nets, and cordage) for furs and captives. Wyandot women were skilled corn growers. They carefully harvested and cured the ears of corn, then spent much time during the winter shelling and grinding the grain into fine meal.

Men carried the meal, as well as corn, tobacco, and hemp, in birch-bark canoes across the lakes and rivers to the western tribes.

The French simply continued this established commercial system, using Wyandot traders as middlemen. After all these Indian merchants had established profitable contacts with the western tribes, knew the routes of travel, and had trade talent and command of travel technology and skill. Soon after 1600 Wyandot traders included French trade goods in their westbound cargoes—knives, hatchets, brass kettles, awls, beads, textiles including blankets, and vermilion, a bright red cosmetic paint valued by many Indians. Each autumn flotillas of fifty to nearly 300 canoes returned to Montreal laden with buffalo robes, bear skins, and packs of beaver pelts. Wyandot agents for French trading houses at Montreal extended their orbit to include the Potawatomis in Michigan and the Winnebagoes at Green Bay. The Ottawas continued to provide the Wyandot with cargoes of furs for transfer to the French from the Illinois country. The Wyandot trading empire also included all the tribes of the north. From these hunters Wyandot merchants received furs which they "poured, as through a funnel" into Montreal.[8]

Wyandot power in the early years of the fur trade in New France derived from experience in intertribal commerce, French favoritism as designated middlemen—and French firearms. French policy permitted sale of firearms, much desired by Indians, only to Christian Indians, not to "infidels." Missionary officials quite early announced that 7,000 Wyandots were baptized; they were supplied with guns (arquebuses), which enabled them to awe less fortunate tribesmen.

Wyandot power declined by 1650. Tribes of the Iroquois Confederacy, under the commercial dominion of the Dutch at Fort Orange (Albany) on the upper Hudson River, had by the middle of the seventeeth century exhausted the beaver and other fur resources in their own lands. Driven by Dutch traders for more and more pelts, Iroquois hunters searched for a new hunting range in the West. There they confronted the French-supported Wyandot monopoly of commerce with the western tribes. Like the Wyandots, the Iroquois were armed. They attacked Wyandot settlements, ravaged their hunting territory, raided the towns of their tributary tribes, and intimidated them into providing an annual fur tribute to the Iroquois. Iroquois war parties ambushed fur convoys in the Ohio Country and as far west as the Mississippi River. This Iroquois pressure played havoc with the French fur industry. For the five years before 1653 not a single trading fleet of any size reached Montreal through the Iroquois blockade. On several occasions during the 1650s the Iroquois made peace with the French and their Indian allies and used the truce time to regroup and prepare for fresh attacks on the French fur establishment. Sporadic raiding, preying on trade lines, and attacks on Wyandot settlements continued throughout the 1670s. After 1684 the Iroquois resorted less to military force and more to diplomacy and business tact in their attempt to control the western fur trade. By then the Wyandots were prostrate, drastically reduced in population, and unable to supply the French with furs.

The Age of the Coureurs de Bois

To counter the growing Iroquois menace, in the 1670s Frenchmen spread out from their St. Lawrence Valley settlements and began to occupy strategic points around the Great Lakes and in the Ohio Country to rehabilitate the fur trade. LaSalle and other French pioneers established fur-trade posts in the wilderness among the Indian tribes and became directly involved in the fur trade. Frenchmen carried, besides the long-familiar trade goods, guns— now available to "infidels"—and brandy.

Missionaries objected to both the unlimited sale of firearms to Indians and the increasing use of brandy in the fur trade. After much pressure on the French government they succeeded in obtaining a royal ban on liquor as a trade item. Wilderness traders countered that Indian hunters could easily obtain alcohol from the British and Dutch, and they claimed that the ban encouraged their Indians to defect to British and Dutch traders. Business triumphed over religion. Threat of declining fur-trade income caused royal officials to lift the ban on use of liquor in commerce with Indian hunters, although they did direct colonial officials to guard against abuses.

After 1700 the fur trade became increasingly competitive and expansive. The effect on the Indian tribes was disastrous. Native Americans were torn loose from their home territories and scattered across the West as fur hunters in the employ of French traders. Many became soldiers in the service of France in wars with equally expansive British traders from seaboard towns and Spanish traders from the Rio Grande settlements.

As the fur-trade industry prospered and increased in power in the councils of New France, it also became increasingly opposed to agricultural settlement. Trading interests worked assiduously to prevent agricultural expansion in New France. They warned that French farmers would disturb the fur-bearing animals and crowd Indian hunters from the land. Except in the case of Louisiana they succeeded. As a result, by 1763 there were only about 80,000 Frenchmen in North America compared to about 1,200,000 British.

As French traders pressured Indian hunters for more and more pelts, fur resources in territory close to Indian settlements became depleted. New hunting range had to be found to meet the demands of the ever expanding industry. Thus the intensified fur trade became the impetus for expansion and exploration. French traders entered the trans-Mississippi region, which the French called Louisiana, and followed the Missouri River to the eastern edge of the Rocky Mountains, crossed the central Great Plains on the Platte River system, and explored the Southwest by way of Red River. They brought additional tribes into the French trading orbit, introducing many heretofore uninfluenced by Europeans, to trade goods, firearms, and brandy. French traders often took a score or so of Indian families from a tribe in the Old Northwest across the Mississippi River into new hunting areas. The men hunted pelts and protected the expanding French territorial interest; the women processed the furs and skins and prepared them for market.

Painting of the Indians in Florida in 1564 by Jacques Le Moyne. The Indian chief, Athore, is showing the marble column erected by Jean Riboult two years earlier. (New York Public Library)

As the fur trade expanded into Louisiana, new bases developed to serve the newly opened areas. From their stations on the Great Lakes traders entered Minnesota and the Dakotas. The Illinois Country settlements supported French penetration of the central Great Plains to the eastern edge of the Rocky Mountains. Their Gulf Coast settlements were their gateway to the southern portion of Louisiana. Traders from Biloxi and other Gulf stations established by the French around 1700 soon integrated the tribes of the lower Mississippi Valley, including the Choctaws and many Creek bands, into their trading scheme. Only the Chickasaws resisted, continuing to maintain an independent attitude toward the French.

From settlements on the Gulf Coast Frenchmen moved up the Mississippi and Red rivers into the West. New Orleans, founded in 1718, became the great center for the Louisiana fur trade. Restless, wide-ranging *coureurs de bois* swarmed over the territory drained by the Arkansas and Red rivers and established themselves among the Wichitas and Caddoes—Taovayas as they called them—who came to dominate the southwestern fur trade somewhat as the Wyandots had in an earlier age in the Old Northwest.

The French traders, adaptable to wilderness living and generally popular and well received by the tribes, married Indian women and lived in their villages. Habituating the Indians to French trade goods, notably guns, ammunition, knives, beads, axes, hatchets, hoes, cloth, blankets, mirrors, and body paint, the *coureurs de bois* encouraged the tribes to abandon their self-sufficient life-style and become dependent fur hunters. Each year the traders transported out of this southern segment of Lousiana countless bales of beaver, otter, mink, and muskrat furs and buffalo robes, all in great demand in Europe. These products were sent to Arkansas Post, Natchitoches, and New Orleans by flatboats and pirogues (Indian dugouts). The remotely situated traders used pack trains of horses to reach the river landings. In season the *coureurs de bois* returned to their Indian families on the Canadian, Arkansas, and Red rivers with a new supply of trade goods.

Devastating raids by Osage war parties from the north finally disrupted the easy village life in the Arkansas and Canadian valleys and forced the Taovayas and their French traders to resettle on the upper Red River where they formed the Twin Villages of San Bernardo and San Teodoro. By 1749 only a single Taovaya village, Ferdinandina, remained in the north, strategically located at the head of navigation on the Arkansas, on the eastern edge of Comanche territory.

Rather than venturing onto the Plains themselves, French traders used the Taovayas as middlemen to deal with the Comanches and other Plains tribes. By their trade with the Plains tribes through Taovaya middlemen, the French indirectly touched the Spanish settlements on the Rio Grande. Spanish devotion to mercantilism, which forbade trade with aliens, plus enduring hostility toward French traders for arming the Comanches and resentment to trespass on territory claimed by Spain caused Spanish officials to enforce

A Wichita man, descendant of the Taovayas. (Courtesy University of Oklahoma Library)

131

a ban on commerce with the French in Louisiana. Comanche raids on New Mexican ranches and towns netted plunder, captives, and horses and mules which the Taovayas obtained by providing the Comanches with guns and ammunition, and which they subsequently turned over to their French sponsors. Then Ferdinandina fell to the Osages in 1757, and the Taovayas and French traders there moved south to Red River and joined their kinsmen at Twin Villages.

Through the years this Indian settlement on the Red River came to exert a peculiar influence on the Spanish borderlands. The Taovayas prospered as middlemen for the French. With French assistance they constructed elaborate fortifications around their villages to protect themselves against Spanish and Apache raids. But their greatest strength lay in their enduring alliance with the most powerful Indian nation on the Southern Plains, the Comanches. In the late eighteenth century when the Kiowas entered this territory, they too became a part of this association.

As the key group in the trading economy of the southern Plains the Taovayas continued to harvest furs and buffalo robes and hides for French traders. At the peak of Twin Villages' prosperity during the 1750s the Taovayas required twelve French traders to supply their needs in manufactured goods. But the Taovayas were more than just fur traders; their economy was diversified. Some produced beans, corn, melons, and pumpkins, which were in demand as frontier trade items and were especially popular with the non-agricultural, buffalo-eating Comanches. The Taovayas also gathered salt and other local products. Each season Taovaya traders brought into San Bernardo and San Teodoro bales of furs, deer skins, soft tanned buffalo robes, stiff buffalo hides, and horses, mules, captives, and plunder from the Rio Grande settlements. At high water on the Red River flotillas of rafts and pirogues packed and stacked with bales of furs and hides and cargoes of corn and salt departed the landings at Twin Villages for Natchitoches and New Orleans. The Taovayas' populous, prosperous settlements on Red River comprised a sort of wealthy, well-managed city-state.

Clever traders and shrewd diplomats, the Taovayas used other tribes, particularly the Comanches, to protect their special role in the French trading system on the southern Plains. Although they were primarily a mercantile people, the Taovayas mustered fighting forces on occasion. During the 1750s, with their Comanche allies, they raided expanding Spanish settlements in Texas for plunder to trade at Twin Villages. Spanish officials in Texas were determined to end this threat. Diego Ortiz Parilla, Spanish presidio commander at San Luis de las Amarillas, organized an expedition from northern Mexican settlements to punish the *Norteños*, as they called the Taovayas and their Comanche allies.

During 1759 Parilla marched a force of over 300 Spanish regulars north to the Red River, arriving there in October. His Indian scouts found the Twin Villages, and he sent his troops in assault waves against the defenders' positions. Each time the Spaniards were driven back with heavy losses. Counterattacking Indians captured Parilla's artillery, and his men begged for mercy in retreat. All seemed hopeless, and Parilla gathered the remnants of his army and marched south.

Four years after Parilla's dismal failure, Spain received from France all of Louisiana without firing a shot. Although the French were ousted after 1763 from imperial power by the British and Spanish dominion extended over the Indians of Louisiana including the Taovayas, the French traders remained and continued to dominate the fur trade. The primary aim of Spanish officials was to abolish the traffic in guns and ammunition for which Twin Villages had long been a primary depot. The Taovayas had enjoyed free trade under the French flag. Their new masters established a restrictive, government-licensed system of frontier trade which included careful scrutiny of inventories of traders dealing with the Comanches and other resistive tribes. Taovaya middlemen continued to deal with their preferred French merchants, but Spanish surveillance of goods entering the country and restrictive commercial policies gradually dried up the long-standing prosperity of the Taovaya communities.

During the 1750s French power was on the decline; in 1763 the British ousted France from North America, and Great Britain and Spain succeeded to control of the territory and Indian nations formerly under French dominion. French power and capability to defend North American possessions had been progressively sapped by, among other factors, Indian insurgency. Sustained resistance to French rule by the Fox, Natchez, and Chickasaw nations diverted and weakened French military resources and contributed to the ultimate conquest of New France by the British. This insurgency admittedly contradicted the rule of traditional French friendliness with Native Americans. However, before this contradiction is examined, it would be well to note impact of the fur trade upon Indians and Frenchmen.

Human Effects of the Fur Trade

The Indian was a prime casualty of the fur trade. The disastrous physical and social effects of alcohol on Indians, the swath cut in tribal populations by trader-carried epidemic diseases to which Indians had virtually no resistance, and cultural destruction produced by the periodic uprooting of hunters, tearing them loose from bonds of clan and tribe, in the feverish rush for more and more furs—all contributed to the Indians' decline. The fur trade also caused pervasive "ecological disruption," and damage extended to all levels of aboriginal society, for once traders entered the villages and accustomed them to their goods, including brandy,

Indians changed from hunters for limited local needs to commercial gatherers of ever-increasing quantities of pelts and hides to meet their expanding tastes for trade goods. This growing dependence on trader goods disturbed, and at times destroyed, aboriginal self-sufficiency. In reverberating rings, this commerical intrusion corrupted the native lifestyle, encouraged neglect of essential family, clan, and tribal duties and observances, and caused pervasive personal and social disorientation and decay. If the Indian eschewed the blandishments of the trader, saturation trapping and hunting over his range soon destroyed the wild creatures that had provided him with food, shelter, and clothing. He and his tribe were reduced to a state of poverty not of his making.[9]

Wilderness living, in daily association with Native Americans, had equally pervasive effects on French fur traders. The view held by most Europeans and later by Anglo-Americans that in the contest between Indian and European life-styles the latter would always triumph, was challenged by many Frenchmen who adopted Indian ways. Through the years thousands of French *coureurs de bois* were drawn into the North American wilderness to participate in the fur trade. By 1700 the *coureur de bois* had emerged as a distinct social type, regarded by the genteel in Montreal and Quebec as a menace, a threat to colonial French society. French officials ordered them "quarantined so that their lawlessness could not contaminate what was hoped would be an obedient agricultural society." Intendant Talon declared that men who deserted farming to go off to the forests were "without Christianity, without sacraments, without religion, without priests, without laws, without magistrates, sole masters of their own actions and of the application of their wills."[10] Parkman observed,

At first, great hopes were entertained that, by the mingling of French and Indians, the latter would be won over to civilization and the church; but the effect was precisely the reverse, [because rather than Indians becoming French, Frenchmen became Indians.] These outflowings of French civilization were merged in the waste of barbarism, as a river is lost in the sands of the desert. The wandering Frenchman chose a wife or a concubine among his Indian friends, and, in a few generations, scarcely a tribe of the west was free from an infusion of Celtic blood. . . . The fur trade engendered a peculiar class of men known by the appropriate name of bushrangers, or coureurs de bois *. . . shaking loose every tie of blood and kindred, identified themselves with the Indians. [Throughout the wilderness,] the traveler would have encountered men owning the blood and speaking the language of France, yet, in their wild and swarthy visages and barbarous costume, seeming more akin to those with whom they had cast their lot. The renegade of civilization caught the habits and imbibed the prejudices of his chosen associates. He loved to decorate his long hair with eagle feathers, to make his face hideous with vermilion, ochre, and soot. [In his wilderness dwelling] he lounged on a bearskin [while his wife] boiled his venison and lighted his pipe. In hunting, in dancing, in singing, in taking a scalp, he rivalled the genuine Indian. His mind was tinctured with the superstitions of the forest. . . . He placed implicit trust in the prophetic truth of his dreams.*[11]

INDIAN RECALCITRANCE

The French succeeded in maintaining harmonious relations with most Indian tribes. However, there were notable exceptions: besides the Iroquois Confederacy, the Fox, the Natchez, and the Chickasaw tribes refused to submit to French rule.

The Fox Rebellion

The Fox lived in western Wisconsin and Illinois. Spirited, restless, and war-like, they were the only Algonkians against whom the French waged war. In the early years of the fur trade, the Fox were powerful enough to force all French traders passing through their territory to pay them tribute. The French supplied arms to the Chippewas, their neighbors and long-standing enemies. Guns emboldened the Chippewas and made them more dangerous antagonists. The Fox increased their raids on both Chippewas and French-men, becoming a hazard to the French fur trade much like the Iroquois in an earlier age. Fox war parties blocked trade west of Lake Michigan and threatened several times to close the upper Mississippi to French shipping. During the 1720s French councils seriously considered proposals to extermi-nate them. Finally it was decided to resettle the Fox insurgents near Detroit where they could be watched. The Indians refused to move, and only after nearly a decade of campaigning by French and Indian troops did the Fox submit.[12]

Destruction of the Natchez

The Natchez, longtime residents of the lower Mississippi Valley, had de-veloped an advanced culture and an elegant life-style before European Con-tact. In disputes with colonial officials at Biloxi in 1716, the Natchez killed four Frenchmen. A French army from Mobile occupied Natchez territory; troops constructed Fort Rosalie on the bluffs at the river-port town of Natchez. The French military presence encouraged settlers to move upriver from the Gulf Coast settlements, and they established farms on the rich bottomland of Natchez territory.

Natchez leaders resented this appropriation of their land and in 1722 at-tempted to expel the French settlers. Troops suppressed the outbreak, and the Natchez remained quiet until 1729 when they struck back with great fury. Their warriors destroyed several military posts and settlements in their territory and massacred the garrisons, killing 250 Frenchmen and taking nearly 300 women and children hostage. Eventually a French and Choctaw army avenged the massacre several times over and recovered most of the hostages. French and Choctaw troops captured over 400 Natchez and sent them to the West Indies as slaves. Several Natchez survivors fled northeast and settled among the Chickasaws, Creeks, and Cherokees. By 1731 France had entirely erased the Natchez nation.[13]

The Invincible Chickasaws

The Chickasaws lived in northeastern Mississippi, remote from the Mississippi River. Thus they were ignored by the French in the early years of European expansion in the Gulf Coast region. Around 1700 British agents, following trader paths from Carolina, entered their villages. The First Chickasaw War, caused by the refusal of the Chickasaws to banish English traders from their towns, began in 1720. The French sent Choctaw troops to raid Chickasaw settlements, and the Chickasaws retaliated by attacking Choctaw towns and raiding French shipping on the Mississippi—the lifeline that connected the Gulf settlements and Louisiana with the Illinois Country and Canada. The Chickasaws succeeded in closing the river to French use for nearly four years. Colonial officials attempted to break the Chickasaw blockade by increasing the military pressure. French officers formed additional companies of Choctaw troops and led them against the Chickasaws. They paid a bounty of a gun, one pound of powder, and two pounds of bullets for each Chickasaw scalp. Nonetheless, by 1725 the Chickasaws remained unconquered, and commerce in Louisiana was at a standstill. French officials decided to call back their Choctaw raiders and make peace. A deceptive calm settled over the lower Mississippi Valley. Once again French boats navigated the Mississippi, and hunters and traders roamed the prairies and forests unmolested.

The Second Chickasaw War began in 1732 after the tribe refused to meet renewed French demands to expel the growing community of British traders from their territory and to turn over all Natchez survivors who had taken refuge there. Again French officials sent their Choctaw troops against the Chickasaws; this time they also imported Indian troops from the Illinois Country. The Chickasaws responded with a fury of retaliatory attacks against the Choctaws and the Illinois Country tribes, and they struck at French commerce on the Mississippi. By 1734 when they had virtually closed the river to French shipping, Governor Bienville of Louisiana wrote the French colonial office: "The entire destruction of this hostile nation...becomes every day more necessary to our interests, and I am going to exert all diligence to accomplish it."[14]

In 1736 Bienville planned a two-pronged attack on the Chickasaw settlements. One column of 400 French and Indian troops from the Illinois Country commanded by Major Pierre d'Artaguette, was to descend the Mississippi, land at Chickasaw Bluffs, and march east to the Chickasaw towns. A second column of 600 French regulars and nearly 1,000 Choctaws, commanded by Bienville himself, was to march north on the Tombigbee River Valley for an assault on the Chickasaw towns. Poor timing caused d'Artaguette to arrive first. The Chickasaws ambushed his column. Belatedly Bienville's regiment reached the Chickasaw towns where it suffered a smashing defeat.

Three years later Bienville made a third attempt to crush the Chickasaws. He mustered a regular army of 1,500 men from stations on the Gulf Coast and 1,500 regular and Indian troops from the north. Heavy rains held up the French advance at Chickasaw Bluffs, and Bienville finally had to abandon the campaign and withdraw. In 1752 the French made one final attempt to conquer the Chickasaw nation. A French army marched up the Tombigbee to the Chickasaws' fortified towns, was unable to dislodge the Indian defenders, and withdrew for the last time.

In 1763 French dominion over peoples and territory in North America passed to Great Britain and Spain. The French legacy among the Indian tribes included mixed Indian-French blood lines, a smattering of Roman Catholic religion in the French-Indian settlements in the Illinois Country and Louisiana, and widespread Indian fluency in the French language. The former French Indians soon found that, in the diplomatic disposition of their persons and territories the exploiters of one empire had simply been exchanged for another. And many Native Americans preferred the French over their new masters, revolted, and complicated the takeover process.

Other European nations competed with France, Spain, and Great Britain for dominion over Native Americans and their lands. For the first half of the seventeenth century Holland dominated the Mid-Atlantic seaboard and Hudson River Valley; the Dutch impact upon the Indian tribes of this region is the subject of Chapter Seven.

Notes

1. Kenneth D. McRae, "The French Empire in Canada: Image of the Old World," in *Three American Empires,* edited by John J. TePaske (New York, 1967), p. 61.
2. Sigmund Diamond, "An Experiment in 'Feudalism': French Canada in the Seventeenth Century," in *Ibid.,* p. 87.
3. Francis Parkman, "The French, the English, and the Indian," in *Ibid.,* p. 133.
4. *Ibid.*
5. "French Influence," in *Handbook of American Indians North of Mexico,* edited by Frederick W. Hodge (Washington, 1907), Vol. I, p. 475.
6. William C. MacLeod, *The American Indian Frontier* (New York, 1928), p. 301.
7. *Ibid.,* pp. 148–49.
8. George T. Hunt, *The Wars of the Iroquois: A Study in Intertribal Trade Relations* (Madison, Wisc., 1940), p. 65.
9. Arrell Morgan Gibson, *The West in the Life of the Nation* (Lexington, Mass., 1976), p. 245.
10. Quoted in Diamond, "An Experiment in 'Feudalism'," pp. 86–87.
11. Parkman, "The French," pp. 134–35.
12. "The Foxes," in *Handbook of American Indians North of Mexico,* edited by Frederick W. Hodge (Washington, 1907), Vol. I, p. 472.
13. P. F. X. de Charlevoix, *History and General Description of New France* (Chicago, 1962), Vol. I, pp. 97–102.
14. Arrell Morgan Gibson, *The Chickasaws* (Norman, Okla., 1971), p. 50.

Selected Sources

General works containing information on American Indians' role in the French empire in North America include Howard Peckham and Charles Gibson (eds.), *Attitudes of the Colonial Powers towards the American Indians* (Salt Lake City, Utah, 1966); Carl O. Sauer, *Sixteenth Century North America: The Land and the People as Seen by Europeans* (Berkeley, Calif., 1971); and Herbert E. Bolton and Thomas M. Marshall, *The Colonization of North America* (New York, 1935). The expanding dominion of New France over the Native Americans and their territories is detailed in H. A. Ennis, *The Fur Trade in Canada* (New Haven, Conn., 1930), Clarence Vandiveer, *The Fur Trade and Early Western Exploration* (Cleveland, Ohio, 1929), Paul C. Phillips and J. W. Smurr, *The Fur Trade* (Norman, Okla., 1961), 2 vols.; William T. Hagan, *The Sac and Fox Indians* (Norman, Okla., 1958), Francis Parkman, *Count Frontenac and New France Under Louis XIV* (Boston, 1902); John G. Shea, *History of the Catholic Missions Among the Indian Tribes of the United States, 1529–1854* (New York, 1881); Emma H. Blair, *The Indian Tribes of the Upper Mississippi Valley and Region of the Great Lakes* (Cleveland, Ohio, 1911), 2 vols.; Arrell Morgan Gibson, *The Chickasaws* (Norman, Okla., 1971); and *The Kickapoos: Lords of the Middle Border* (Norman, Okla., 1963); Norman W. Caldwell, *The French in the Mississippi Valley, 1740–1750* (Urbana, Ill., 1941); and P. F. X. de Charlevoix, *History and General Description of New France* (Chicago, 1962), 6 vols.

Studies of the fur trade and the expanding empire include Elizabeth A. H. John, *Storms Brewed in Other Men's Worlds: The Confrontation of Indians, Spanish, and French in the Southwest, 1540–1795* (College Station, Texas, 1975); George T. Hunt, *The Wars of the Iroquois: A Study in Intertribal Trade Relations* (Madison, Wisc., 1940); and Le Page Du Pratz, *The History of Louisiana* (London, 1763), 3 vols.

CHAPTER 7

HOLLAND AND THE
NATIVE AMERICANS

The great man wanted only a little, little land, on which to raise greens for his soup, just as much as a bullocks' hide would cover. Here we first might have observed their deceitful spirit.

Delaware tradition of their first contact with the Dutch on Manhattan Island, 1609

❥

Holland, like Spain and France, for a time held an empire in North America. Although Holland controlled only a small enclave of territory on the Atlantic seaboard and that for only a brief time—from 1609 to 1664—Dutch dominion was pervasive over New Netherland and the resident Native Americans.

During New Netherland's brief life, Indian tribes of the Hudson and Delaware River valleys were no less affected by the Dutch than were other tribes under Spain, France, and other powers. Through their Iroquois allies, Dutch goods and influence flowed to the Mississippi River and southward into the Ohio Valley. The Iroquois appetite for power, whetted by Dutch trade goods and backed with Dutch guns, loosed fierce Mohawks and Senecas across the western wilderness. From the Indians whose territory they crossed the Iroquois demanded tribute. They decimated the splendid Huron and Ottawa trading systems, uprooting the Peoria, Sac, Fox, and Potawatomi tribes and driving them to safer territory in the upper Mississippi Valley. For a time the Iroquois succeeded in disrupting the entire commercial order of New France.

THE DUTCH COLONIAL ESTABLISHMENT

By the late sixteenth century, Holland had become the most important mercantile nation of Western Europe, its huge maritime force scattered in trading ventures around the world. Dutch interest in North America began about 1598 when Hollanders, from trading ships anchored in the Hudson and Delaware rivers, began trading with the Mid-Atlantic coastal tribes for furs.

In 1609 a group of Amsterdam capitalists commissioned Henry Hudson, an English navigator, to explore the North Atlantic coast for a water passage through the continent. Hudson ascended several rivers flowing into the Atlantic, paying particular attention to a broad, south-flowing stream the

Chapter Opening Artifact: Red pipestone from Shiloh, Tennessee. (Courtesy National Park Service, Shiloh National Military Park)

Dutch named the Mauritius River and later renamed North River; it is now called the Hudson River. While Hudson failed, as had many before him, to find a water passage through the continent, his explorations in North America led the Dutch parliament, the States-General, to claim the territory from the St. Lawrence River to Virginia and to name it New Netherland.

The Land and Peoples of New Netherland

Holland's North American province was a rich land. From the tall trees in its dense forests shipbuilders could fashion masts, planking, and framing timbers for the Dutch fleet. New Netherland abounded in beaver, mink, and otter, which Dutch fur interests hoped could be exploited to challenge France's supremacy in prime pelt production. Offshore fisheries and seasonal whaling in Delaware Bay increased New Netherland's prospects for profits. Fertile valleys could provide grain and other foodstuffs for the projected colony of New Netherland as well as for the burgeoning population at home in Europe. Two great river systems—the Hudson (North River) and the Delaware (South River) and their tributaries—provided easy access into the northeastern quadrant of North America and comprised a communication resource of no small consequence.

A strategic resource in which New Netherland abounded, which the Dutch discovered shortly, was the local *sewan* or wampum manufactory. Indians near the Hudson and Delaware estuaries and on the adjacent islands gathered white periwinkles, small marine snails, and the tiny purple to black sections of inner clam shells and made beads by piercing and stringing them. Black beads were worth twice as much as the white. *Sewan* served as currency among the Indians, as well as jewelry; it could pay ransoms and tribute, seal contracts, atone for injuries. Made into a belt, it played a large role in Indian ceremonial diplomacy, and it recorded various public transactions. During pre-Contact times, Indians from Canada, the Mississippi Valley, and the area south of the Ohio River came to the Long Island area to trade for *sewan*. The Dutch soon commandeered its manufacture and used it to advantage in the fur trade.[1]

New Netherland's most striking resource, however, was an unusually large Indian population—perhaps 25,000—which if properly recruited, could perform essential labor for the colonial establishment, including gathering furs. Likewise, as consumers the Indians comprised a lucrative market for goods from Holland's factories.

The Indians of New Netherland were mostly Algonkian-speaking Lenape-Delaware tribesmen—Wappingers, Manhattans, Raritans, Tappans, Hackensacks, Pavonias, Esophus, Canarsees, Munsees—who lived around the shores and on the islands of the Hudson and Delaware estuaries. Along the upper Hudson dwelt the Mohicans, the most powerful tribe in New Netherland, and the most strategic for the early Dutch fur trade. Also important in the early Dutch fur trade were the Pequots who lived along the Connecticut River north of Long Island Sound. As the Dutch fur trade expanded inland, Hol-

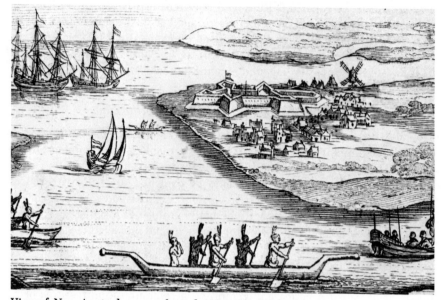

View of New Amsterdam west from the East River across the tip of Manhattan Island. (Courtesy of the New York Historical Society, New York City)

landers eventually came into contact with the Iroquoian-speaking Susquehannas of the upper Delaware Valley, and the Iroquois Confederacy tribes westward along the Mohawk Valley.

United New Netherland Company and the Indians

The center of early Dutch commercial activity was the Hudson and Delaware valleys. In 1614 the States-General chartered the United New Netherland Company and while making no provision for colonization, granted it trading privileges within New Netherland. In the year of its chartering, the United New Netherland Company sent out ships for North America carrying company agents, employees, and cargoes of trade goods.

With one exception, company traders worked from large ships, floating warehouses, riding at anchor in the Hudson and Delaware estuaries. They carried their trade goods, largely knives, hatchets, mirrors, vermilion, and textiles, in small boats and sloops up the Connecticut, Hudson, and Delaware rivers, trading with local tribes for their furs. Company employees remained in the field until they had made up a cargo of furs for their parent ship. The exception to this trade pattern developed on the upper Hudson River in the heart of Mohican territory. There United New Netherland Company agents founded Fort Nassau, complete with its own warehouses. The reserves of goods maintained in storage at Fort Nassau enabled traders to carry on a year-round commerce with local Indian hunters. In 1617, the year that the United New Netherland Company charter expired, a flood on the Hudson

142

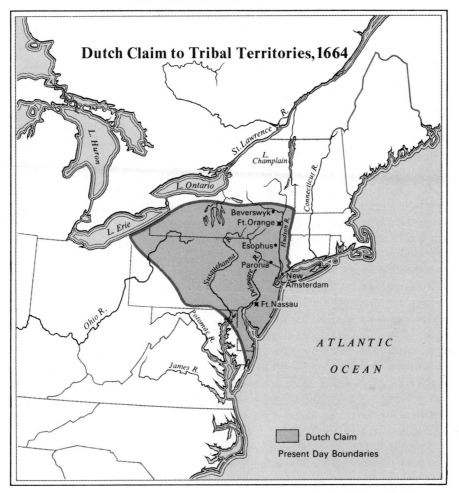

River swept Fort Nassau away. Thereafter trade with the Indian tribes of New Netherland continued, carried on until 1624 by independent traders.

The first Dutch venture as an imperial power in North America had considerable impact upon the Native Americans. Tribes in New Netherland were introduced to European textiles and metal goods, and they began overhunting wildlife in their territory to meet the Dutch traders' escalating demands for more pelts, a process which in less than a generation resulted in the extermination of most species of fur-bearing animals in the lower Hudson and Delaware valleys.

The Dutch West India Company and the Native Americans

In 1621 the States-General issued a charter to the Dutch West India Company. Its counterpart was the well-established and immensely successful Dutch East India Company which held a monopoly on trade with the Orient. The Dutch West India Company charter granted monopoly over trade with

West Africa (ivory, gold, and slaves), Brazil (sugar), and North America (furs). Government of the territory of New Netherland was also assigned to the Dutch West India Company. Thus the company was required to maintain political as well as enjoying commercial direction over Holland's territory in North America, its actions subject to review by the States-General.

Between 1621 and 1624 the Dutch West India Company directors formed a body of policy and rules to guide the economic and political management of New Netherland, much of it devoted to the maintenance of relations with the resident Indian tribes. The director-general, or governor, of New Netherland was responsible for maintaining relations with the native peoples; he was admonished to use great prudence and patience in this regard, to go to great lengths to preserve peaceful relations with the Indian tribes, and thus provide order and protect the fur trade. Company policy forbade Dutch citizens to participate in intertribal wars; they were to maintain neutrality so as not to prejudice the fur trade. The director-general was to use diplomacy whenever possible to settle differences and could resort to war against offending Indians only as a last resort. He was empowered to deal with the Indian tribes through treaties, negotiated "upon such conditions as shall be deemed most advantageous to the service of the company, without paying heed in such treaties to any one's private interests." Agents or employees of the company were required to abide by these agreements even if "by so doing they should be involved in war . . . and even be obliged to take the field." Dutch citizens were required to fulfill their promises faithfully to the Indians and not to offend them without cause "regarding their persons, wives, or property." And in all transactions, the natives were to be treated with "honesty, faithfulness, and sincerity, so that no cause for hostility might arise." Officials were to use presents to "draw the Indians into our service . . . to learn from them the secrets of that region and the condition of the interior. . . . In the absence of an adequate labor force, Indians were to be hired to work on the fortifications or other projects should they prove willing. Their wage, however, was set at half that paid to Dutchmen for the same work."[2]

Holland recognized Indian tribal sovereignty. Treaties were negotiated with Indian leaders, thus acknowledging the sovereign, independent status of the Indian tribes. Likewise Dutch administrators regarded Indians subject to the laws of their respective tribes; each tribe was expected to maintain a system of law and order sufficient to control its citizens. A corollary was application of the principle of extraterritoriality to the Indian nations of New Netherland, a practice widely used by the Dutch, British, and Portuguese in the Orient. The rule of extraterritoriality exempted Dutch citizens from jurisdiction of Indian law, but colonial regulations assured offended Indians speedy and effective justice to any Dutchperson who wronged an Indian. An extension of extraterritoriality was that "if in spite of all precautions an Indian wronged a Dutchman and his tribe failed to punish him, the Dutch officials were authorized to seek out the culprit and administer justice themselves."[3]

Holland also recognized Indian ownership of land in the European sense. Consequently legal necessity and expediency required that Dutch West India Company officials acquire formal title to lands from Indians by purchase.[4] Dutch colonial administrators also believed such action would counter the territorial claims of competing European powers. By the time Holland entered North America, several European nations had already established themselves there and were claiming vast portions of the continent. Dutch officials were concerned that Spain, France, and England would challenge their right to settle and trade in North America because

They had little chance of sustaining a claim themselves on the basis of right of discovery, which the English at first rested their case on; or donation from the Pope, upon which the Spanish claim rested. So they had to find something else. They decided to argue, against the claims of Spanish and English, that the Indian tribes or nations were owners of the land—as of course they were. Thus title could be obtained from the natives, they contended, only by conquest, or by gift or purchase.[5]

Rather than purchasing vast, amorphous territories, Dutch agents negotiated for only small parcels as required, including sites for trading posts and towns and later farming tracts for agricultural colonies. The Dutch West India Company charter conveyed no original land title. Ownership of the land in New Netherland remained with the resident Native Americans until extinguished by legal processes established under Dutch law. Land cessions by tribal leaders had to be "voluntary, not obtained by craft or fraud, lest we call down the wrath of God upon our unrighteous beginnings."[6]

THE INDIAN AND THE DUTCH

The Dutch West India Company began to fulfill the terms of its charter in 1623. Although the company was a commercial enterprise, it had been delegated political functions by the States-General which required the manager of the company in New Netherland, the director-general, and his council of advisors to provide government for the colony. The Dutch West India Company continued under its charter, with periodic revisions, until Holland was ousted from New Netherland by England in 1664.

The company's primary interest during the early years in New Netherland was the fur trade. However, within a decade the Dutch West India Company was ordered by the States-General to include expanded agriculture in its New World activity. Thus while the fur trade continued as a principal industry, farming gradually increased in importance in the lower Hudson Valley and on the estuary islands. Both the fur trade and agriculture brought momentous change to the Native Americans in New Netherland. Natives involved in collecting furs for Dutch traders piled up huge debts and became totally dependent upon European goods. Indians in the agricultural region were trapped by the expansion of Dutch farms onto their tribal estates.

The Fur Trade

Dutch West India Company ships carrying officials and traders began arriving in New Netherland in 1623. Among the passengers were thirty families of Walloons, French-speaking Calvinists from the southern Low Countries (now part of Belgium), who were expected to settle near the fur stations and raise food for the traders. Some of the colonists remained on Manhattan Island to form the town of New Amsterdam which became the principal port and fur entrepôt and the capital of New Netherland. Others settled on Long Island. Some Dutchmen continued north to the upper Hudson River where they established Fort Orange, a wilderness trading post, and the adjacent village of Beverwyck. A party of traders went to the Delaware River to establish the new Fort Nassau; another proceeded to the head of navigation on the Connecticut River and founded Fort Good Hope.

Traders found that the most popular items among Indian hunters were hatchets, hoes, knives, copper kettles, beads, mirrors, vermilion, rum and brandy, and duffels, a closely woven wool cloth from the looms of Duffel near Amsterdam. Dutch West India Company policy banned sale of guns and ammunition to Indians. Locally produced shell bead money, *sewan* or wampum, in popular demand even among remote tribes, also was a valued trade item.

Dutch traders, or Swannekens the Indians called them, spent most of their time at the posts negotiating with Indian hunters, called Wilden—wild people—by the Hollanders, for their pelts and maintaining a supply of trade goods. Many Swannekens married Wilden women and settled permanently in the villages near the trading posts. Beverwyck was a thriving Dutch trader settlement near Fort Orange. Early commercial contacts were widely dispersed although actual trade was concentrated among the Algonkian tribes of the lower Hudson, Delaware, and Connecticut estuaries, since until about 1630 furs were plentiful in these areas close to the posts and traders were not competing with farmers for land. Dutch traders themselves rarely trapped or hunted but maintained the trading stations and engaged Indians to harvest furs in the wilderness for them. Swannekens did explore new fur territories, contact tribes in remote areas, and urge them to come into Fort Orange, Nassau, Good Hope, and other posts to trade. Their explorations led them to the Kennebec River in Maine and along the Mohawk Valley to the settlements of the Senecas.

In 1623 tribesmen from remote regions responded to an invitation from Dutch West India Company agents to visit Fort Orange. Mohawks, Oneidas, Cayugas, and Senecas, with Ottawa delegates, convened and "made covenants of friendship...bringing presents of beaver and other peltry, and desired that they might come and have a constant free trade" with the Swannekens. For several years afterward the Indians "were all quiet as lambs, and came and traded with all the freedom imaginable."[7]

As the tribes of New Netherland increased their dependence upon European trade goods, they intensified their search for furs. Saturation hunting soon exterminated the fur-bearing wildlife on their home territories, and they intruded on the domains of neighboring tribes to hunt. As Delaware bands exhausted the pelt resources on the Hudson and Delaware estuaries, they trespassed on land in the upper Delaware Valley belonging to the Susquehannas and the inevitable bloodshed resulted. And Mohicans, favored by the Dutch in the early years of the fur trade in New Netherland, were contested by the Mohawks who, seeking a route to Fort Orange, caused additional bloodshed. As events developed, these contests for fur territory in New Netherland were minuscule compared to the large-scale and extended wars of conquest which the Iroquois Confederacy tribes soon would launch against the tribes west of the Great Lakes to serve the insatiable Dutch fur market.

Dutch traders observed the company rule of neutrality in Indian disputes and wars and avoided involvement in the Delaware-Susquehanna contest for the rich fur territory of the upper Delaware Valley. The one exception to this rule occurred in 1626. The Mohicans, supreme in their dominion over the Hudson Valley, were pitted in a bloody war against their ancient enemy the Mohawks and asked the Dutch, with firearms, to help them. Daniel Van Krieckenbeeck, in charge at Fort Orange, foolishly agreed and, with six men, accompanied a Mohican war party into Mohawk territory. At Beaver Falls the Mohawks ambushed the intruders, caused the Mohicans to flee in fright, and killed four Swannekens including Van Kriekenbeeck. Dutch officials in New Netherland saw the folly of this action and quickly restored peace with the Mohawks. The Mohican-Mohawk war continued until 1627 when the Mohawks triumphed, defeated the Mohicans, and drove them east of the Hudson River.

The lengths to which Hollanders would go to follow the rule of neutrality and maintain peace with the Indian tribes for the sake of the fur business is indicated by the Dutch response to the massacre at Swaanendael ("Valley of the Swans"), a Dutch West India Company settlement on the west shore of Delaware Bay. A dispute between local tribesmen and settlers in 1632 concluded in an Indian attack on the settlement which resulted in the death of thirty-two Europeans. Rather than mustering troops and marching against the offenders, officials of the Dutch West India Company called the Indians into a council where "a formal peace was ratified . . . by presents . . . and the astonished red men departed in great joy to hunt beavers for the Hollanders, who, instead of exacting a cruel retribution, had quietly let pass their inhuman offense."[8]

Increasingly the Dutch fur trade came to focus on Fort Orange. The Hudson River provided easy access into the portion of the continental interior which flanked French Canada on the St. Lawrence and drained on the French fur trade. The "Dutch soon learned that the Indians of the St. Lawrence Valley and the Great Lakes could travel down Lake Champlain to Fort Orange almost as easily as they could journey to Quebec, and that they particularly valued the seawant [wampum] manufactured by the Indians of Long Island," and the consistently high quality and reasonable prices of Dutch trade goods.[9]

During the 1630s substantive changes occurred in the Dutch fur trade and Indian policy. First, by that time the Hollanders and the Iroquois Confederation, largely through the Mohawks who were intermediaries for the Dutch with the other member tribes, had forged an alliance which endured for the remainder of Dutch hegemony in North America and subsequently was imparted to the English. In their dealings with the Indian tribes of New Netherland, the Dutch came to favor the Iroquois and to discriminate against the Algonkian tribes along the coast, to neglect, even scorn them. The fur trade, for which New Netherland had been established and which contributed most of the provincial revenue, was the basis for this differential treatment. The lower river tribes were of diminishing value to the Dutch because the fur supply in their territory had been exhausted. Their economic value as consumers of European trading goods thus failed to outweigh their destructive capacity, and they became expendable. The coastal tribes "bore the brunt of the European invasion" and received "only transitory benefits in return." From the Dutch viewpoint their only possession of value was their lands, where the Dutch were building towns and developing farms. But the Iroquois to the north and west were not in the path of Dutch settlement. There was no population pressure for land around Fort Orange, and thus land disputes there were rare. Indians and Dutch were dependent upon one another. The Iroquois remained powerful, and the Dutch worked assiduously to maintain their favor because the Iroquois had access to apparently unlimited fur resources.

To appease and strengthen the Iroquois the Dutch West India Company during the 1630s moderated its strict ban on sale of firearms and permitted its traders to supply firearms, judiciously, to Mohawk hunters. The Mohawks armed themselves and then distributed weapons to their fellow Iroquois, the Senecas, Onondagas, Oneidas, and Cayugas. Company rules forbade sale of firearms to Algonkian tribesmen near the Dutch settlements in the Hudson and Delaware estuaries.

Another change of considerable consequence in the Dutch imperial system during the 1630s was cancellation by the States-General of the Dutch West India Company fur-trade monopoly. Thereafter merchants, clerks, and farmers from New Amsterdam and other New Netherland settlements and adventurers from Europe entered the fur trade. By this time the fur supply of the lower country was largely exhausted, and the focus of the commerce was upon Fort Orange and the rich peltry supplied to that post by the Iroquois tribes, led by the Mohawks.

So many Swannekens entered the fur trade that competition for handling Iroquois furs became fierce. Independent traders, the *"bosch loopers"* (runners of the woods, not unlike the French *coureurs de bois*) often bested Dutch West India Company traders in the race for Iroquois-supplied pelts. They intercepted Indians in the forests on their way to Fort Orange and used brandy and other inducements to obtain their furs. Both tribal leaders and "honest traders" complained to Dutch West India Company officials because the renegade hunters were debauching Indian hunters with brandy and rum. The director-general and his council adopted an ordinance prohibiting *bosch looper* activity and ordered detachments of troops into the wilderness to enforce this rule.

Dutch commercial pressure upon the Iroquois for furs continued to be so great that by 1640 Confederation hunters had largely exhausted the beaver resources of their territory. They had to have furs one way or another; pelts were the currency which purchased at Fort Orange the guns, powder, shot, textiles, knives, hatchets, vermilion, and other European trade items which had become essentials in Iroquois households. The Iroquois had forever abandoned the old simple, self-sufficient, aboriginal life-style.[10]

To obtain the furs which they now required for their survival, the Iroquois turned to the fur-rich territory to the west. First they attempted to establish peaceful commerce with the tribes beyond the Great Lakes, offering Dutch goods from Fort Orange in competition with French goods from Canada. However, Iroquois traders found that the Hurons (Wyandots) in the St. Lawrence Valley were the supreme managers of the western fur trade. Their warriors carried French goods to the western tributary tribes to purchase their packs of beaver and otter skins. The Ottawas as their agents controlled the trade in the vast territory south of the Great Lakes and as far west as the Mississippi River.

Mohawk, Seneca, and other Iroquois emissaries attempted to negotiate trade agreements with the Hurons. But these proud people, whose great economic power and French arms had made insolent, refused. Thus the Iroquois, well armed by the Dutch, attacked Indian hunting camps in the western wilderness and robbed the lodges of furs, conquering several tribes and forcing them to pay annual tribute in furs. They preyed upon the trading fleets and plundered the magnificent Huron canoe brigades coming down the rivers laden with rich peltry from the north and west.

The Iroquois' restless, marauding quest for furs even threatened the French in Canada. During the 1650s, Mohawk and Seneca raiders occasionally attacked French settlements around Montreal, Three Rivers, and Quebec. Farming in New France suffered "as no Frenchman dared to dwell outside the fortified towns [and] most of the food for the colony had to be imported from France."[11]

Besides appropriating the furs of the vast Huron commercial network and decimating Wyandot communities near Quebec, Iroquois fur-trade legions continued their conquest of western territory. By 1654 they were in control of the north and south shores of Lake Erie. Some of their bloodiest campaigns took place there against cultural kinsmen, the Iroquoian-speaking Eries. Iroquois Confederation forces also drove south into the Susquehanna Valley, warring on the tribes of that region including the Munsees who had been supplied arms by Swedish traders on Delaware Bay.

By the close of the period of Dutch rule Mohawk, Seneca, Oneida, Onondaga, and Cayuga raiders ranged from the East Coast to the Mississippi Valley and from the St. Lawrence Valley south to the Ohio River and as far east as Maine, regularly raiding settlements on the Kennebec River, preying on the Abenaki tribe and scattered English settlements. Thus by arming the Iroquois Confederency tribes and providing a lucrative market for their furs, the Swannekens supplied these striving, ambitious Indians with the firepower and the motive "to subdue all their neighbors and achieve a pivotal position in intercolonial affairs."[12]

Missions

Holland's colonial establishment in the New World was a commercial venture, carried out by a group of capitalists organized as the Dutch West India Company. Thus it could hardly be expected to hold broader concerns of colonial development including winning Indians to the Christian faith. Nevertheless, the Dutch Reformed church, of which most of the Swannekens were members, did not lack a sense of missionary responsibility, and the Native Americans' spiritual state was not completely ignored, although the Dutch dethroned few tribal gods. But the "problem of saving Indian souls was never as pressing among the Dutch as it was in either New France or New England."[13]

Those persons coming to the New World as agents for the Dutch West India Company were admonished to "by their Christian life and conduct seek to draw the Indians and other blind people to the knowledge of God and his word." And officials and colonists were "encouraged to work for the Indians' conversion through education and provision of a good example in Christian conduct."[14]

Certain perceptive Hollanders found the tribesmen deeply religious and determined to retain their faith. One observed, "They are all free by nature and will not bear any domineering or lording over them," thus making them poor subjects for conversion to authoritarian Christianity.[15]

Domine Jonas Michaelius was the first minister to serve in New Netherland. He reached New Amsterdam in 1628 and was so preoccupied with Dutch communicants at Manhattan that "time did not permit him to conduct missions among the Indians." Besides, Michaelius found the Indians repugnant; he "was repelled by the ... first contact ... and dismayed at the prospect of making them Christians." He stated, "I find them utterly savage and wild, strangers to all decency, proficient in all wickedness and godlessness; devilish men, who serve nobody but the Devil." He concluded that the most productive approach "lay in abandoning the adults and getting control of their children, but the parents invariably opposed any such program." The Dutch Reformed divine promised to pray for their "eventual salvation, [to] keep a watchful eye over these people, [and] to learn what he could of their language, and to seek some means for their instruction." The Indians of New Netherland had little to fear from Michaelius who returned to Europe in a few years without converting a single one of them.[16]

Domine Johannes Megapolensis, a more compassionate and patient minister, arrived in New Netherland in 1642. He spent most of his ministry near Fort Orange on the upper Hudson River. While he did not neglect the members of the local Dutch Reformed congregation, he spent much time studying the Iroquois language and visiting with Mohawk and Seneca fur hunters who came to the post to trade. His patience was demonstrated in the case of a young Mohawk convert to the Dutch Reformed church. Megapolensis spent two years teaching him to read and write the Dutch language and instructing him in the Bible. About the time that the missionary regarded him ready to preach to his people, Megapolensis lamented that the youth "took to drinking brandy; he pawned the Bible, and turned into a regular beast, doing more harm than good among the Indians."[17]

Thereupon Megapolensis applied himself to learning the Mohawk language. In two years he was sufficiently fluent to preach to these people in their tongue. Indian hunters, in from the western wilderness, would stop to hear him preach. Megapolensis related:

When we have a sermon, sometimes ten or twelve of them, more or less, will attend, each having in his mouth a long tobacco-pipe made by himself, and will stand a while and look and afterward ask me what I am doing, and what I wanted that I stood there alone, and made so many words, and none of the rest might speak? I tell them that I admonished the Christians that they must not steal, nor drink nor commit lewdness and murder; and that they too ought not to do these things; and that I intend after awhile to come and preach to them, in their country . . . when I am acquainted with their language. They say, I do well in teaching the Christians; but immediately add, Why do so many Christians do these things?[18]

Swedish missionaries had been spreading Lutheranism among Indians on the Hudson and Delaware estuaries after the Swedes established themselves on Delaware Bay in 1638. Domine Megapolensis was contemptuous of the Lutheran effort and pointed to one of their missionaries in particular as an evil influence over the Indians of southern New Netherland: "The Lutheran preacher is a man of impious and scandalous habits; a wild, drunken, unmannerly clown; more inclined to look into the wine than into the Bible. He would prefer drinking brandy two hours to preaching one. What hope for the Indians?"[19]

Competitors for Empire

Among the North American neighbors of the Dutch were Frenchmen in Canada, Englishmen in Virginia and New England and, belatedly, Swedes on the Delaware River. Their presence and competitive commercial activity, which led to disruptive relations with the Indians of New Netherland, complicated matters for Dutch West India Company officials. The English claimed the Atlantic seaboard and regarded the Dutch as intruders, and traders from Virginia and New England regularly traded with the Hudson and Delaware estuary tribes. English settlements expanding from Massachusetts Bay Colony into Connecticut provoked the Pequots to resistance. English military recrimination led to the annihilation of this tribe in 1637 and destroyed the profitable Dutch trade in the Connecticut River Valley. Also many English settlers from Connecticut drifted onto Long Island, a portion of New Netherland; their expanding agricultural settlements contributed to the bloody Algonkian insurrections of the 1640s and 1650s. Dutch-allied Indians, particularly the Mohawks, raided deep into New England, forced the Abenakis and other tribes into rendering fur tribute, and carried off English captives. Officials at Boston regularly called upon the Dutch at Fort Orange to intercede with the Iroquois and restore the captives. Of course the most conspicuous example of Dutch relations with the English was the Anglo-Dutch war which led to the conquest of New Netherland by English forces in 1664 and the incorporation of this region into what became the British empire in North America.

The Dutch in New Netherland had only indirect relations with the French in Canada. Swanneken influence over the Iroquois Confederation tribes and the extension of their trade tentacles into the West through these middlemen created many problems for New France. Thus as Dutch surrogates the Iroquois maintained a steady military-commercial pressure on New France during the period 1640–1664. French officials in Canada periodically would lead a punitive expedition through the Seneca country. The Indians would sue for peace, sign a treaty of amity with the French to gain time to recover from the avenging thrust, then resume their plundering forays against the French and their Indian allies. The French attempted through Jesuit missions to tame the Iroquois, convert them, and to turn them to French purpose, but they rarely got anywhere. More often the Iroquois tortured and martyred the French Jesuits. The Dutch occasionally interceded by pressuring their Iroquois supporters to restore the captives brought south by the raiders or to free Jesuit fathers who were marked for the stake. These compassionate acts are explained by the fact that Protestant Dutchmen maintained their capacity for mercy for fellow Europeans, even though Roman Catholic.

Daring Swedish colonists, chartered for the Indian trade by their government as the New Sweden Company, defied Dutch claims to the territory of New Netherland and established a colony on Delaware Bay in 1638. The Scandinavians erected a post on the west shore of Delaware Bay, strategically situated to draw the fur commerce of a vast hinterland, and named it Fort Christina. Dutch West India Company officials at Fort Nassau, on the east shore of Delaware Bay, protested this intrusion and ordered the Swedes to leave. Fort Nassau was manned by only twenty men, and the Swedes ignored the order. They developed a lucrative trade with the tribes around Delaware Bay, underselling both Dutch and English traders. Finally in 1655 Dutch officials directed the construction of Fort Casimir on the West shore of Delaware Bay near Fort Christina and, with reenforcements, besieged the Swedes and forced them to evacuate. Dutch West India Company officials sold the recovered Delaware Bay territory to the city of Amsterdam which ruled the region for a few years as the colony of New Amstel with its principal settlement at the former Fort Christina.

Patroons and Native Americans

By 1630 officers of the Dutch West India Company were divided over the direction New Netherland should take. One faction was committed to continuing concentration on furs for short-term profits. The other, concerned over the rapid depletion of New Netherland's fur resources, promoted colonization as a long-term investment. Colonization advocates pointed to the very real threat of English expansion from Virginia and New England into New Netherland. They contended that populating the New Netherland wilderness with Dutchmen and diversifying its economy by adding commercial agriculture and other industries to the fur trade would discourage English encroachment.[20]

The colonization faction prevailed, and the Dutch West India Company devised the patroon system to populate New Netherland. A patroon, like a seignior in French Canada and a proprietor in the English colonies, received a grant of land from the Dutch West India Company in return for settling at least fifty Europeans above the age of fifteen in New Netherland. The patroon could select his tract any place in New Netherland except on Manhattan Island. After he had selected his estate, the patroon purchased that tract from the Indians claiming dominion over it. Thereupon the patroon with tribal leaders presented a document, describing the bounds of the grant and the price paid, to the director-general and his council. If they found that the transaction was executed according to company rules, they issued a deed of ownership to the patroon. Presumably the patroon would develop the grant from rent collected from his tenant colonists. Patroons established several settlements including Swaanendael on Delaware Bay, Pavonia on the north Jersey shore, and Rensselaerwyck on the upper Hudson River. Although patroons and their tenants were expected to concentrate on agriculture and stock raising, they were permitted to collect naval stores, manage fisheries and whaling enterprises, and participate in the fur trade.

The patroon system coupled with the termination of the Dutch West India Company monopoly of the fur trade had the desired effect. European population in New Netherland increased from less than 1,000 in 1630 to nearly four times that number in 1645. The effects of this change in the direction of the Dutch West India Company, the expansion of commercial agriculture, more intensive utilization of New Netherland's resources beyond the fur trade, and the taking of large tracts of land from the Indian tribes for agricultural purposes had a decisive impact upon the Native Americans.

ABORIGINAL INSURGENCY

Hudson and Delaware river Indians had consistently supported the Dutch by providing food and other essentials during the early days of colonizing New Netherland. Their cooperation had provided the foundation for the ultimate Dutch-Iroquois takeover of western wilderness commerce. However, the Dutch had increased in such numbers and their hunger for land had become so voracious that during the 1630s and 1640s, local tribesmen began to resent Europeans and tried to expel them. By this time Dutch power had increased, and the Indians had become so disorganized, reduced in numbers by disease and debauched by Swanneken brandy, that they were no match for the Dutch. Yet for twenty years they spiritedly sought to recover the territory and independence which their fathers had bargained away to Dutch colonists.

The Pavonia Massacre

Inevitably competition between Indian farmers and growing numbers of Dutch settlers for tribal lands created friction. To the Indians of New Netherland "land was like the air; it was everywhere and freely accessible to those who wanted to make use of it; like the ocean waters, it could not be disposed of by sale." During land negotiations, when Swannekens presented them cloth, hatchets, and other items of value, they believed that they were conveying to the Dutch only the right to use the land, that the Dutch were purchasing the right to share in its use with the Indian community. By these transactions the Indians did not intend to dispose of the land permanently or exclude themselves from its use. However, when they "purchased" land from Indians, the Dutch "expected to possess it exclusively as they did in Europe, and to deny the Indians further access if it so suited their purpose." Certainly exclusion from lands that the Indians regarded as the property of all was a major grievance of tribesmen against the Dutch.[21]

The lower river tribes also had other grievances. They were bitter at the favoritism the Dutch accorded the Iroquois Confederacy tribes in the fur trade, particularly their policy of providing the Mohawks, Senecas, and other Confederacy tribes with guns, while forbidding the sale of guns to them. They obtained weapons illegally, but because Dutch law forbade them to possess firearms, their weapons were always subject to confiscation by Dutch West India Company officials.

Officials declared that the lower river tribes did not need firearms because the Dutch would protect them. Yet Mohawk raiders, claiming prerogatives from their earlier conquest of the Mohicans, each year came south to collect their annual tribute from the river tribes, taking corn and their choice of women; the Dutch, anxious not to antagonize the Iroquois tribes, did nothing to protect the local Indians. The traditional Dutch policy of diplomacy and conciliation with the Indians was increasingly threatened as the Swanneken population in the Hudson and Delaware settlements increased. The lower river tribes became an ever greater obstacle to Dutch agricultural expansion. The Dutch did not consider Indian removal and concentration on reservations, separate from the expanding Swanneken settlements. Thus for these beleaguered Native Americans there was the grim choice of coexistence or extermination. The latter came to dominate Dutch policy.

In 1639 William Kieft became governor-general of New Netherland. His coming marked an end to the diplomacy-conciliation policy in Dutch-Indian relations. Kieft admittedly detested Indians, and he openly advocated extermination of the lower river tribes as the essential solution to the problem of keeping the path of Dutch expansion open. From the beginning of his administration Kieft set out deliberately to harass the Native Americans and provoke them to desperate acts.

Incidents mounted; interracial tensions escalated. Governor-General Kieft decided to impose an annual tax in corn on those Indians living near the downriver Dutch settlements, payable to the Dutch West India Company government at New Amsterdam. He claimed that the company faced heavy expenses for its fortifications and garrisons in New Netherland, and the Indians whom the Dutch had defended against their enemies should bear a portion of the expense. The Indians refused to pay the tax, but Kieft's threat to enforce it made them apprehensive.[22]

More settlers were taking more tribal land. Native Americans found themselves increasingly squeezed onto smaller tracts. Dutch livestock destroyed their corn fields; Indian farmers killed intruding cattle, horses, and hogs. A Dutchman shot an Indian for killing his livestock. The Indian's family retaliated by killing the Dutch farmer, claiming that Dutch West India Company officials had not brought the Swanneken to trial. Kieft then offered a bounty of ten fathoms of wampum, worth about four dollars, for the head of each of the Indians involved in this affair.

In 1642 Kieft raised an army and marched through the nearby Indian settlements to intimidate the tribesmen. Then during February 1643, a Mohawk party arrived to collect tribute from the surviving Mohicans, now living close to the lower-river Dutch settlements. The Algonkians rushed to safety in New Amsterdam and Pavonia ahead of the Iroquois host. However, the Iroquois, unrestrained by Dutch troops, sought out their prey, killed seventy, and took many women and children north as captives.

Kieft reminded the lower-river settlers of the Swaanendael massacre and declared that it was time for Dutch revenge. He dispatched eighty soldiers to Pavonia to complete the ghoulish work begun by the Iroquois. The "Slaughter of the Innocents" took place on the night of February 25. On Kieft's orders neither age nor sex was spared. An eye witness recounted:

Daybreak scarcely ended the furious slaughter. Infants were torn from their mothers' breasts and hacked to pieces in the presence of their parents and the pieces thrown into the fire and in the water, and other sucklings were bound to small boards and then cut, stuck, and pierced, and miserably massacred in the manner to move a heart of stone. Some were thrown into the river, and when the fathers and mothers endeavored to save them, the soldiers would not let them come on land but made both parents and children drown, children from five to six years of age, and also some decrepit persons.

The Dutch soldiers returned to New Amsterdam with thirty prisoners and eighty heads of massacred Indians. Governor-General Kieft thanked his men "by taking them by the hand and congratulating them." The prisoners were tortured in public and the eighty "gory heads with sightless eyes" were placed on display. "More vivid still perhaps, is the picture of the aged mother of Kieft's secretary, [Cornelius] Van Tienhoven.... When the many heads of the murdered ... Indians were laid on the street for public view, the old mother displayed her keen elation over the exploits of her murderously-inclined son by kicking the heads like footballs about the streets."[23]

The Pavonia massacre stirred widespread indignation and revolt among the downriver tribes. Small bands raided isolated Dutch settlements on Long Island and Delaware Bay; they also struck at English settlements in the nearby Connecticut River Valley. Swannekens rushed to the safety of New Amsterdam from the hinterland. Indian raiders maintained a light siege on Manhattan Island for over a year. While it was peace and business as usual with the Iroqouis on the upper Hudson at Fort Orange, economic life in the downriver part of New Netherland was at a standstill. No person dared to plow fields or tend livestock for fear of a swift, deadly strike by Indians.

Dutch and English troops led by Captain John Underhill, of Pequot War fame (see Chapter Nine), took the field and maintained pressure on the Indians during the warmer months, capturing ten Indians here, twenty there, placing them in chains, and sending them off to labor on plantations in the West Indies. During the winter of 1643–1644, the insurgent Indians collected in larger settlements. Underhill's tenacious campaigning devastated them. On Long Island his troops discovered two large encampments, surrounded each and, with surprise attacks by night, torched the lodges. As men, women, and children fled from the burning shelters, Underhill's marksmen shot them down. Indian refugees from New Netherland formed a third winter encampment in Connecticut near present-day Stamford. Underhill's men found their settlement and killed over five hundred men, women, and children there. The relentless pursuit maintained by the Dutch-English troops kept the Indians on the move. Troops destroyed their shelters and stored corn. Freezing and starving, the Indians urged their leaders to negotiate a peace.

Peace advocates in New Netherland pressured Dutch West India Company officials to end what they called "the vicious war," arguing that exterminating Indians was impracticable and unchristian. In the 1644 councils which produced a peace between the Europeans and Indians of the Hudson and Delaware estuaries, tribal leaders reproached the Dutch: "In the beginning of your voyages, you left your people here with their goods; we traded with them while your ships were away, and cherished them ... we gave them our daughters for companions, who have borne children and many Indians have sprung from the Swannekens; and now you villainously massacre your own blood."[24]

The Peach Wars

Although Algonkian tribal leaders and their Swanneken neighbors called a halt to hostilities in 1644, lasting peace did not come to New Netherland for the remainder of the period of Dutch rule in the New World. Remnants of tribes living near the downriver Dutch settlements carried deep resentments against their European conquerors, and they watched for opportunities for vengeance.

In 1647 Peter Stuyvesant became governor-general of the Dutch West India Company. While less committed to Indian extermination than Kieft, he was a stern defender of Dutch interests in New Netherland, had little sympathy for the Indian viewpoint, and retaliated with vigor at every sign of insurgency.

In 1655 a Dutch farmer killed an Indian woman for picking peaches from his orchard. The victim's family retaliated by killing the farmer; hostilities resumed and did not conclude until the final year of Dutch dominion in New Netherland. Dutch reaction to the peach-orchard incident was to prepare to arrest and punish the offending native family. Before they could do so, a large force of warriors mustered from the local tribes struck New Amsterdam and the surrounding settlements in a predawn attack. The raiders burned barns and houses, killed several Dutchmen, and captured 150 prisoners.

Peter Stuyvesant, last Governor-General of New Netherland. (Courtesy of the New York Historical Society, New York City)

Stuyvesant struck back with his militia, recovered many of the captives, destroyed several Indian settlements, and stationed companies of troops in the scattered Dutch farming communities.

After a deceptively quiet period, insurgency shifted to the territory of the Esophus Indians, a fertile agricultural region midway up the Hudson River, coveted by the Swannekens. Dutch pioneers had established farms and the town of Wiltwyck there. Resident Native Americans sought to drive out the Dutch settlers by burning their barns, killing their livestock, and terrorizing their households. Settlers appealed to Governor-General Stuyvesant who warned the Indians that unless they submitted to a peace council, he would annihilate them. A delegation of Esophus tribal leaders came to Wiltwyck to meet with Dutch officials. While the Indians slept, Stuyvesant's troops slaughtered them. Enraged Esophus Indians retaliated by capturing eight Dutch soldiers and burning them at the stake. They maintained a bloody, destructive siege on Wiltwyck for three years.

In 1660 Stuyvesant determined to end for all time the threat of Indian insurgency. He ordered each tribe living near the downriver settlements to leave a number of its children in Dutch custody at New Amsterdam as bond for the tribe's good behavior. Most Hudson and Delaware estuary tribes, by now battered and drastically reduced in numbers, submitted. However, the Esophus Indians refused. Stuyvesant gathered a large, well-armed expedition and captured several hundred Esophus men, women, and children whom he held at New Amsterdam as hostages until they agreed to comply with his demands. When Esophus leaders refused to negotiate, Stuyvesant sent the prisoners to the Caribbean to labor on plantations as slaves. Finally Dutch officials called in the Mohawks, and their awesome presence forced the Esophus Indians to conclude a peace treaty.

Indians on the middle Hudson continued to raid European settlements. Dutch recrimination and punishment were severe. Finally in 1664, Stuyvesant concluded a final treaty of peace with the Esophus. Its terms provided that the "Esophus country . . . now conquered by the sword" was ceded to the Dutch. By its terms no Indians were permitted "to approach the farms of the Christians." Stuyvesant exultantly marked the occasion by proclaiming "a day of general thanksgiving to the Almighty."[25]

In the year of the final Esophus peace treaty, English troops invaded New Amsterdam, forced Dutch West India Company officials to surrender, and integrated New Netherland into its chain of seaboard colonies. The English benefited greatly from the Dutch legacy. Swannekens had so reduced the Hudson and Delaware estuary tribes in numbers and in power that they could not resist the advance of English interests. And by inheriting the Dutch alliance with the Iroquois Confederation the English were able to continue the challenge to France for hegemony over the trans-Appalachian wilderness and, with indispensable Iroquois assistance, eventually drove the French from North America and captured their province of Canada and its western territory. However, before considering the English experience with seaboard tribes, it would be well to proceed to the north Pacific Basin where Russian fur traders were advancing across the Aleutian Islands into Alaska, claiming resident Aleuts, Eskimos, and Indians as Russian subjects.

Notes

1. John R. Brodhead, *History of the State of New York* (New York, 1853), Vol. I, p. 172.
2. Allen W. Trelease, *Indian Affairs in Colonial New York: The Seventeenth Century* (Port Washington, N.Y., 1971), p. 37.
3. *Ibid.*
4. Allen W. Trelease, "Indian-White Contacts in Eastern North America: The Dutch in New Netherland," *Ethnohistory* 9 (1962), p. 138.
5. William C. Macleod, *The American Indian Frontier* (New York, 1928), p. 195.
6. Trelease, *Indian Affairs*, p. 40.
7. Brodhead, *History of the State of New York*, p. 152.
8. *Ibid.*, pp. 220–21.
9. Trelease, *Indian Affairs*, p. ix.
10. George T. Hunt, *The Wars of the Iroquois: A Study in Intertribal Trade Relations* (Madison, Wisc., 1940), p. 35.
11. T. Wood Clarke, *The Bloody Mohawk* (New York, 1940), pp. 30–31.
12. Alice P. Kenney, *Stubborn for Liberty: The Dutch in New York* (Syracuse, N.Y., 1975), p. 27.
13. Trelease, *Indian Affairs*, p. 38.
14. C. A. Weslager, *Dutch Explorers, Traders and Settlers in the Delaware Valley, 1609–1664* (Philadelphia, 1961), pp. 107–108.
15. Ellis L. Raesly, *Portrait of New Netherland* (New York, 1945), p. 188.
16. Weslager, *Dutch Explorers*, p. 107, and Trelease, *Indian Affairs*, p. 39.
17. Weslager, *Dutch Explorers*, pp. 107–108.
18. Brodhead, *History of the State of New York*, pp. 375–76.
19. Macleod, *American Indian Frontier*, p. 345.
20. Kenney, *Stubborn for Liberty*, p. 23.
21. Weslager, *Dutch Explorers*, p. 69.
22. Brodhead, *History of the State of New York*, p. 293.
23. Macleod, *American Indian Frontier*, pp. 225–26.
24. *Ibid.*, p. 229.
25. Brodhead, *History of the State of New York*, p. 731.

Selected Sources

Holland's brief tenure in North America and the Dutch dominion over the Native Americans of New Netherland are chronicled in elaborate detail in John R. Brodhead, *History of the State of New York* (New York, 1853), Vol. I. Supporting studies of Dutch relations with the North American Indians include Allen W. Trelease, *Indian Affairs in Colonial New York: The Seventeenth Century* (Port Washington, N.Y., 1971); and two articles by the same author—"Indian-White Contacts in Eastern North America: The Dutch in New Netherland," *Ethnohistory* 9 (1962), pp. 137–46; and "The Iroquois and the Western Fur Trade: A Problem in Interpretation," *Mississippi Valley Historical Review* 49 (June 1962), pp. 32–51; T. Wood Clarke, *The Bloody Mohawk* (New York, 1940); Alice P. Kenney, *Stubborn for Liberty: The Dutch in New York* (Syracuse, N.Y., 1975); C. A. Weslager,

Dutch Explorers, Traders and Settlers in the Delaware Valley, 1609–1664 (Philadelphia, 1961); Ellis L. Raesly, *Portrait of New Netherland* (New York, 1945); J. Franklin Jameson (ed.), *Narratives of New Netherland, 1609–1664* (New York, 1909); and William C. Macleod, *The American Indian Frontier* (New York, 1928).

Dutch Indian policy and administration are the subjects of Henry H. Kessler and Eugene Rachlis, *Peter Stuyvesant and His New York* (New York, 1959); Edmund B. O'Callaghan, *History of New Netherland* (New York, 1855), 2 vols.; and Edward Manning Ruttenber, *History of the Indian Tribes of Hudson's River* (Albany, N.Y., 1872).

The Dutch and the Iroquois Confederation, particularly as related to the fur trade, are characterized in Cadwallader Colden, *The History of the Five Indian Nations of Canada* (New York, 1902), 2 vols.; and George T. Hunt, *The Wars of the Iroquois: A Study in Intertribal Trade Relations* (Madison, Wisc., 1940).

CHAPTER 8

RUSSIA AND THE
NATIVE AMERICANS

Woe to those who resisted him; he destroyed them without pity, deported them to desert islands, took away all their means of getting together, and mixed up their tribes, so they would be unable to plot any evil against the Russians. [The Indians] dreaded him; they looked upon him as a terror from heaven and, being unable to oppose him, were forced to become his slaves and forget their former freedom which they had but recently enjoyed without any restraint.

Alexander Baranov's treatment of Indians

Certainly no European empire could claim that it was truly humane in its treatment of American Indians; each debauched, exploited, and destroyed peoples and cultures. However, the Russians surpassed all others in barbarity, cruelty, and mindless destruction of Indian life. Russian rule in North America lasted from 1741 to 1867.

RUSSIAN NORTH AMERICA

Russian navigators sailing from bases on the eastern Siberian coast spent most of the first half of the eighteenth century exploring the Pacific Basin's northern waters. Reports of their maritime explorations led to an eventual extension of Russian dominion from Siberia into the Aleutian Islands, Alaska, and a portion of northern California. However, awesome navigational problems confronted Russian mariners. They claimed that "long stretches of rugged shoal-studded coast," constant storms, heavy fog, and damaging ice in winter made approaches to shore hazardous if not impossible over much of the region. Russian explorers reported that the islands, peninsulas, and mainland contained few harbors and even in the river mouths quiet anchorages were difficult because of the height and speed of the tides. Offshore waters were a maze of crosscurrents. Running at some distance from the coast in a steady drift eastward across the Pacific was the Japanese Current; closer to shore a countercurrent flowed westward. Added to the currents were raging tides,

Chapter Opening Artifact: Tlingit carved cedar pipe. (Courtesy Museum of the American Indian, Heye Foundation)

"almost unpredictable in the maze of islands and passages," which combined to "make up a labyrinth of eddies, cross currents and tide rips." An added menace for deep-hulled vessels was unseen pinnacles of rock thrusting hundreds of feet from the ocean floor to within a few feet of the surface. Winds, fogs, storms, contrary currents, and heavy tides confused navigators. Often ships were dashed to pieces on the rocks. Hulls, ripped open by hidden reefs, sank. It was many years before the Russians learned to navigate these waters with any degree of success, developed craft that were seaworthy in this region, accumulated accurate maps and charts, and trained pilots to navigate these treacherous waters. Thus, while the ultimate doom of local native peoples was sealed by the inevitable coming of the Russians, the difficulty of access to their territories provided the natives nearly half a century of respite.[1]

The Resources of Russian America

That portion of the Pacific Basin that became Russian North America, particularly the Alaskan mainland, was rich in timber and mineral resources. However, the Russians made only limited use of its natural riches. The Russian style of exploitation was an extension of the century-old quest for furs across Siberia. The *promyshlenniki*, fur hunters, had plundered the pelt-bearing creatures of Siberia, especially in search of the much-valued sable. By the 1730s the *promyshlenniki* had reached the shores of the sea of Okhotsk whose waters blended with the Pacific Ocean. The islands between Siberia and North America and the Alaskan mainland, abounding in fur resources, made the region extremely attractive to the *promyshlenniki*. In the offshore kelp beds lived sea otter in great numbers. Millions of fur seals collected each summer on the islands north of the Alaskan Peninsula. The Aleutian Islands and Alaskan Peninsula and mainland were populated with the blue fox, brown fox, the rare white or Arctic fox, beaver, bear, wolf, mink, and sable or marten. In the adjacent waters lived whales, sea lions, and many species of edible fish. Truly this portion of the Pacific Basin was a hunter's paradise. After the Russians arrived, the sea otter became the most sought-after pelt, surpassing even the sable. This "sea beaver" was a marine mammal that lived along the rocky and shallow coastal waters over a range from the North Pacific to Baja California.

The Native Peoples of Russian America

The Russians' penetration into North America and their almost complete reliance upon the fur trade brought them into contact with three different types of Native Americans—Aleuts, Eskimos, and Indians. The Aleuts, numbering perhaps 25,000 at the time of contact, occupied the chain of islands now named for them between Siberia and North America. There were also Aleut settlements on the north coast of the Alaskan Peninsula, on Kodiak Island, and on the tip of the Kenai Peninsula. Aleuts were sea-oriented. They

Etchings of an Aleut woman and man in the 1770s. (Harvard University Library)

hunted sea otters, sea lions, seals, small whales, and fish in swift-moving ma-neuverable, skin-covered craft called *bidarkas*. Each boat was fitted with two hatches or cockpits, one for the oarsman, the other for the harpooner. Aleuts were the greatest hunters of the Pacific Basin and also the most exploited and devastated of the native peoples under Russian rule.

Eskimos in Russian Alaska numbered perhaps 8,500 and lived in scattered settlements mostly on the Arctic Coast and on the shores of the Bering Sea, although there were also several Eskimo communities south of the Alaskan Peninsula on Kodiak and adjacent islands. Eskimos were also sea-oriented, hunting the seal, walrus, and whale from skin-covered craft called kayaks. In the warm season they collected and smoked fish, and in winter they used sleds pulled by dogs to hunt caribou on the tundra. The Russians' most direct contact with Eskimos was on Kodiak, the site of one of the largest Russian settlements in North America. Russian contact with other Eskimo settlements was largely through their trade goods carried by Aleut and Eskimo merchants to the more isolated regions. Most Eskimos were remote from the Russians and therefore escaped the devastation inflicted upon the Aleuts.

As the Russian traders moved eastward in search of new fur territories, they came into contact with the coastal-dwelling Indians, the Tlingits, Haidas, Kwakiutls, Tsimshians; interior-dwelling Athapascans; and Pomos of northern California. Russians had their most difficult relations with the Tlingits, whom they called Kolush.

The Tlingits were a maritime people, carrying on some hunting, but largely dependent upon the salmon as were their cultural kinsmen south along the coast at Vancouver and Puget Sound. The most expert boat builders in North America, the Tlingits constructed dugout-type canoes from huge cedar logs, each canoe up to seventy-feet long and capable of carrying forty to fifty persons. Fierce, independent people, they were never conquered by the Russians. Tlingits harassed the Russians until they disposed of their North American territory in 1867. The Russians also had limited contact with the Haidas and other coastal tribes south of the Tlingits.

As *promyshlenniki* obliterated the coastal and island fur resources, Russian trader parties entered Alaska's interior where they established small stations to trade with the Athapascans for beaver, mink, otter, and wolf pelts.

THE RUSSIAN IMPERIAL SYSTEM

By the 1730s *promyshlenniki* had crossed Siberia and were collecting furs around the shores of the Sea of Okhotsk and the Kamchatka Peninsula. At about the same time the Russian court at St. Petersburg was beginning to show interest in the regions east of Siberia and sponsored exploratory expeditions into the northern Pacific Basin. The czar sent the Danish navigator Vitus Bering on two voyages of exploration between 1720 and 1741. His discoveries and the subsequent occupation of the Aleutian Islands and portions of the Alaskan Peninsula and mainland by *promyshlenniki* provided the foundations for Russian claims to that portion of North America. Bering's crewmen returned to the Siberian coastal settlements from the 1741 expedition to North America with sea otter pelts which they had obtained from the natives in the lands they had just explored.

These fur trophies excited great interest among the *promyshlenniki* at Okhotsk, the principal Russian settlement in eastern Siberia. They constructed crude boats and attempted to reach the new bonanza fur country. Most of the boats and their crews were lost in the turbulent waters and on the shoals and rocks off the Aleutian Islands. In 1743 *promyshlenniki* finally made a successful expedition to the Aleutian Islands; six men returned with 1600 sea otter pelts, each worth about 300 rubles in the Russian fur market.

The Russian government at St. Petersburg claimed this north Pacific territory, recently explored by Bering and others, as national property. However, the court, preoccupied with internal concerns, left the development of Russian North America to private interests. The primary interest of the St. Petersburg government was that the *yasak*, the royal tribute of 10 percent of the value on all furs taken each year, be paid into the imperial treasury. Thus, the Russians' North American colonial policy lacked the interest, direction, and oversight of the national government at home. The result was chaos; the native peoples were left unprotected and at the mercy of the *promyshlenniki*.

Russian Exploitation Patterns

Muscovites occupied their newly discovered lands in the North Pacific in three stages. The first stage consisted of casual groups of individual hunters and traders in commercial expeditions to the eastern islands; by 1765 *ad hoc* companies formed by merchants at Okhotsk and Kamchatka, to stay for one season of trading ventures in Russian North America, replaced the individual enterprises; and after 1799 came the third stage, characterized by royal monopoly maintained by the Russian American Company.

Native Americans could expect the worst from their Muscovite masters who, for the most part, were acknowledged "riff-raff." Lack of law enforcement permitted *promyshlenniki* unfettered license. The national tradition for cruel treatment and gross exploitation of native peoples, which Muscovites had formed over the years in the conquest of the peoples of Siberia in their advance to the Pacific, was applied to Native Americans. A Russian tactic had been to use coercion to force subject peoples to do their will. In all three stages of Russian exploitation of the peoples and resources of North America, native peoples endured unspeakable impositions from the Russians, but the first stage was the most barbaric.

This first stage lasted for about twenty years after 1745. Russian fur traders moved from island to island doing some hunting themselves, but more and more impressing natives into their service. Aleuts were far superior to *promyshlenniki* in capturing fur-bearing creatures on the islands and in the sea. They also knew how to process the precious pelts to stand up under rough handling and the long passage across the Pacific from the islands to Okhotsk, thence across Siberia to the interior markets. After a few years of working the Aleutians, the *promyshlenniki* developed a common *modus operandi*: "On landing at a village hostages were exacted from the natives, generally wives and daughters of the principal men; the men were given fox traps . . . with which to go out for furs. Then the *promyshlenniki* lived the winter in the enjoyment of the primitive pleasures of a petty sultan of a barbarian harem. In the spring the furs were received from the trappers. If enough were not produced by the natives to satisfy the demand of the exacting masters, death was dealt out with as little compunction as it would be to any of the hunted animals. The traps were taken in, a few beads were given to the women; then sail was set for Kamchatka." Next year another ship came, and the process was repeated. At first Russian firearms terrified the natives and provided an initial advantage. When Aleuts in a particular village proved uncooperative, Russians killed the hostages or tortured recalcitrant males in the center of the village. During 1745 *promyshlenniki* executed fifteen natives on Attu as a public example.[2]

Through the years Russian fur men met increasing resistance from the natives, a growing mood in insurgency, and an escalating determination not to hunt for the Muscovite masters. By the early 1760s the annual pelt harvest from Russian North America had declined alarmingly. Russians themselves had to hunt: they scoured the more westerly Aleutians, finding fur-bearing animals increasingly scarce there. They became desperate in their demands upon the natives, but no amount of torture or mass execution seemed to produce the accustomed cooperation. New tortures and punishments had little effect. On Kanaga in 1757 the Russians punished two adult men for an incidence of resistance. When this did not produce the desired results, a *promyshlenniki* foreman led his men into the village where they "committed an awful butchery and then plundered and burned the village."[3]

By 1761 the *promyshlenniki* had reached the Fox Islands, the most easterly of the Aleutian group. There they established several more temporary trading stations before proceeding to Umnak, Unalaska, and Kodiak Island. Aleuts on these islands and Eskimos on Kodiak began to form a confederation to thwart the Russians.

A taste of resistance from long-suffering Aleuts, embittered by years of Russian excesses, was shown in 1761 on Umnak when *promyshlenniki* attempted to force native hunters to work for them and to impress young women into the Russian fur brigade as concubines. The Russians had to fight their way out of the village, and few survivors reached the ship anchored in the bay. Native leaders on Umnak, the Fox Islands, Unalaska, and Kodiak began to plot against the Russians. In 1762 five Russian trader ships sailed from Kamchatka for Russian North America. The Aleuts and southern Eskimos

North Pacific inlet—the habitat of the Aleuts. (Harvard University Library)

were ready for them. They skillfully lured the Russians inland to trade, ambushed parties in small boats from the parent ship coasting the bays and inlets searching for villages to trade for pelts, then boarded the anchored ships in the harbors and captured and burned them.

From 1762 to 1766 no Russian in North America was safe. Natives ambushed *promyshlenniki*, captured their trade goods, and burned their ships. However, even when the Aleuts seemed on the verge of triumph, the Russian reconquest was underway. Ivan Solovief, a leading trader from Okhotsk, was the self-appointed avenger whose mission was to punish the native peoples for revolting against Russian rule. He mustered several hundred well-armed *promyshlenniki* in a small armada, each vessel fitted with cannon, and began the systematic reduction of the more populous native settlements in the Aleutians, on Umnak and Unalaska. At one fortified village on Umnak his men destroyed the heavy palisade walls with gunpowder charges, then massacred all the men, women, and children. Island after island was combed for hiding Aleuts. The Russians selected certain young women as concubines and executed the remainder. Solovief completed his mission with relentless success, crushing for all time the Aleut will to resist.

Sir George Simpson, director of the Hudson's Bay Company, who frequently visited the nearby Russian American colonies, commented on the drastic decline in Aleut population following the revolt of the 1760s, speculating on why only about one tenth of these peoples survived into the nineteenth century. Granting some blame to the general trauma of the European Contact including the devastating effect of unfamiliar diseases, Simpson attributed the tragic depopulation of the Aleutians largely to the treatment by the Russians.

Added insight into this near annihilation of a people is provided by the Russian writer, S. S. Shashkov. He explained that the Russians were completely dependent upon the Aleuts for their skill in hunting the sea otter and preserving pelts. A large Aleut population was a threat to Muscovite dominion. Thus calculated reduction by extermination became conscious Russian policy, the ultimate aim to achieve an Aleut population level which the Russians could manage without threat of rebellion.

After the Aleut revolt, the Muscovite exploitation of Russian North America escalated. Businessmen at Okhotsk applied a more systematic management to the industry. Intensive hunting had virtually exterminated the fur-bearing creatures on the western islands. *Promyshlenniki* had to travel farther east in search of new hunting areas; greater distances from Okhotsk required improved ships and larger quantities of supplies, which in turn required greater capital. Okhotsk businessmen formed *ad hoc* trading companies which generated the required capital from the sale of shares in the venture. Soon after 1770 an average of 42 companies financed annual fur expeditions to Russian America. Nearly 1,000 *promyshlenniki*, operating from ships riding in protected anchorages, worked the bays and inlets of Russian America in small boats, searching for furs. At strategic locations they established small,

Aleut dwelling interior. (Harvard University Library)

temporary shore stations to store supplies; these they used only on a seasonal basis because as yet there were no permanent Russian settlements in North America.

Promyshlenniki did some trading for furs, but they found it difficult to provide goods which the natives desired. Trade goods most in demand were dentalium shell, small mirrors, and copper or brass wire which the native peoples formed into rings and coiled bracelets. Hatchets, knives, and guns were much sought by the natives, but the Russians had difficulty providing their own needs. Firearms and ammunition were particularly dear, so that using them as trade items was unthinkable. Russian goods were for the most part of low quality, and the great distances from sources of supply and the accompanying high transportation costs limited the variety and quantity of goods *promyshlenniki* could use in trading for furs. The natives also began to scorn the low-quality Russian goods; by the 1780s they were receiving high-quality, low-priced blankets, textiles, and metal goods including guns from American and British traders.

Thus the Russians were at a disadvantage in the fur trade. The *promyshlenniki* found that the most effective way to obtain furs was to hunt for pelts themselves, which they did occasionally, and to use Aleut hunters, now completely cowed and ready to do the Muscovite bidding, who provided most of the furs. Each spring Russian fur men collected them from their island villages and transported them, with their *bidarkas*, eastward to new fur territory on the Alaskan peninsula and mainland. Each *promyshlenniki* foreman would take a party of twenty to fifty Aleuts under his charge and work them for a season in Alaskan waters. In this way the Russians were able to collect enough furs to fill the holds of their ships and assure prosperity for the Okhotsk capitalists.

The Aleuts worked on the shares—one half of the furs taken each hunting season. However, *promyshlenniki* foremen recovered the Aleuts' share by assessing them high prices for their pitiably meager rations, a levy for protecting them from their enemies, and other unreasonable and outlandish charges. Thus in the new order the Aleuts were virtually enslaved.

Russian fur men with their Aleut hunters explored the bays and inlets of the Alaskan peninsula and mainland and sailed through the Bering Strait. In 1786 a Russian-Aleut hunting party discovered the Pribilof or Seal Islands, habitat for millions of fur seals, the greatest concentration of these creatures in the Pacific Basin. Thereafter, increasing numbers of seal furs joined sea otter pelts in the cargoes bound for Okhotsk. Aleuts also collected walrus teeth and sea mammal ivory which Okhotsk businessmen exported to Turkish and Persian markets.

British-American Traders and Russian-American Natives

For half a century, through their control of strategic territory and native peoples in the northern Pacific Basin, Muscovites were able to monopolize the sea otter and seal pelt industry. Then in 1778 Captain James Cook, the British navigator, explored the Pacific Basin. His crewmen brought to the attention of the world the fur riches of this region by displaying at Canton several sea otter pelts they had obtained from the natives on the North Pacific voyage. The enormous prices paid for these pelts at Canton stirred wide interest around the maritime world.

The first challengers in Russian North America were British traders. In 1785 a British brig from Macao traded in North Pacific waters for a valuable cargo of 500 sea-otter skins. Two years later three British commercial expeditions, one from Bengal, one from Bombay, and one from England, traded for furs off the Alaskan coast. And in 1788 American trading ships arrived.

British and American maritime traders lacked the Russian advantage of the services of Aleut hunters. Thus they had to obtain their pelts by trading with Indian hunters from shipboard, with obvious hazards. But they had the decided advantage of quality trade goods, particularly guns and ammunition, which every Indian hunter coveted.

By 1792 there were 21 non-Russian trading ships in the upper Pacific Basin, most of them from the United States. The maritime traders established the pattern of being out from home port for several seasons; it required two to three years of trading to fill their ships' holds with precious sea-otter pelts which they sold in the Chinese market at Canton. To escape the bitter cold, North Pacific storms, and grinding destructive ice, maritime traders wintered in the balmy Sandwich Islands (now Hawaii). Both American and British ship captains had their crews erect small shipyards on the beaches near Pacific

Northwest forests. There ships' carpenters constructed small shallow-hulled, swift-running sloops which could move in and out of the uncharted bays and inlets for the coastal trade, returning regularly to the parent ship to discharge pelt cargoes and take on trading stores.

The effects of the presence of American and British traders in Russian America were pervasive and sustained, particularly for the native peoples. Their activity forced the Russians to establish permanent settlements in their North American territory. Permanent occupation put more pressure on the native peoples than had the temporary, shifting seasonal trading stations which the natives were accustomed to. American and British traders supplied guns to the natives of the Alaskan coast and adjacent islands. Well-armed, they could prevent the Russians from advancing. American arms enabled Tlingits to maintain their independence. The entry of American and British maritime traders also had long-range diplomatic implications for the region and its native peoples, including the Russo-American and Russo-British treaties of 1824 and 1825. Also the Anglo-American maritime trader entry into Alaskan waters led to monopoly. For greater strength to thwart the intruders, the St. Petersburg court through a charter issued in 1799 formed the Russian-American Company, and granted to it monopoly management of Russia's North American territory and native peoples.

Shelikhov-Baranov and the Native Americans

During the late 1770s the entrepreneur Gregory Shelikhov came to dominate the fur trade scene in Russian America, and thus the lives of many thousands of native peoples. Under his leadership permanent Russian settlements were founded in North America. Shelikhov devised a system for the most intensive utilization possible of North American native peoples and fur resources. And he was responsible for the formation of a colony-wide monopoly through the Russian American Company.

In 1784 Shelikhov, in command of three ships and 200 men from Okhotsk, founded Three Saints on Kodiak Island, the first Russian settlement in North America. Kodiak soon became the focus of commercial activity in Russian North America. Through the years he brought several hundred additional Russian settlers to Kodiak and founded other settlements.

Beginning in 1790 Shelikhov set in motion three changes in his company's direction which had great impact on Russian North America and the Native Americans: amalgamation, leadership, and monopoly. Shelikhov was concerned about the inroads which American and British maritime traders were making in Russian fur commerce. The many competing fur companies complicated relations with the native hunters, reduced the effectiveness of the Russian efforts, and thus eased the way for foreign interlopers. To strengthen his fur enterprise in North America and to check the American and British traders, Shelikhov began to absorb competing fur companies in Russian North America. Thus where there had previously been over 40 companies, soon after 1790 there were only three, and shortly Shelikhov amalgamated these into the United American Company.

To direct his burgeoning fur empire, Shelikhov brought Alexander Baranov, a merchant-trader from Kargopol in North Russia, to Kodiak to manage his interests. Baranov became the moving force in Russian America, initially for Shelikhov enterprises, and later for the Russian American Company during its critical formative years. Baranov was ruthless and thoroughly dedicated to Russia's commercial success in North America.

Baranov reduced fur hunting to a science. He resettled entire villages of Aleuts on Kodiak and assigned all their inhabitants—men, women, and children—to company labor details. Most of the men were engaged in hunting and processing pelts; 1,500 Aleut hunters with 800 *bidarkas*, working under the direction of *promyshlenniki* foremen, were based on Kodiak. Food for the enlarged hunting crews and their families was a constant concern, and Baranov assigned some men to collecting fish and hunting sea lions. Women processed the flesh for food, the hides for boots, and the intestines they dried and stretched to be used as waterproof shirts for hunters working from *bidarkas*. The women and children cured and dried fish; dug, washed, and dried edible roots; and made garments for the hunters.

The Aleuts dreaded Baranov and did his bidding without hesitation. He led flotillas of Aleut hunters in *bidarkas* to the Bering Bay and Russian traders east to the islands off the Alaskan mainland. On Yakutat Bay he met Indians—the Tlingits—who, unlike the Aleuts, did not fear Baranov and were a constant source of problems for the Russians. Baranov found that he could not trade with them. They scorned his goods because they were able to obtain metal and textile items of superior quality more cheaply from American and English maritime traders. Thereupon Baranov brought a flotilla of Aleuts to hunt the rich sea otter grounds around the Alexander Archipelago. Tlingit leaders objected to this trespass and informed Baranov that the land and adjacent waters belonged to them and that the Russians were wrong to kill sea otters and take them away without offering compensation. After presentation of gifts the Tlingits permitted Baranov's hunters to proceed, but they kept a close watch on the Russians and their Aleut retainers.

On an expedition to Prince William Sound Baranov had another encounter with Tlingits. Well-armed warriors hit his camp on the beach in a night attack. The Indians wore armor of wooden rods bound together with leather thongs, large wooden hats, and masks representing heads of bears and other animals to protect their faces. The Russians' bullets did not penetrate the thick covering; the Tlingits killed two Russians and nine Aleuts and wounded fifteen.

While Baranov was shaping his North American enterprises, Shelikhov was at the imperial court in St. Petersburg seeking a royal charter granting him a monopoly of the fur business in Russian North America. He modeled his monopoly plan on the British East India Company. His appeal to the czar for the monopoly grant pointed to the threat to the Russian national interest posed by American and British traders poaching on Muscovite territory. And he deceitfully exploited Native American welfare. Reports had reached St.

North Pacific hunting craft—bidarka (top) and kayak (bottom). (Harvard University Library)

Petersburg of brutal treatment which Russian subjects had inflicted upon Native Americans. Shelikhov claimed that his proposed monopoly would assure better treatment. Much later the record was to reveal that in the early days of establishing himself on Kodiak, when natives resisted his efforts to impress them into hunting brigades, Shelikhov had ordered his *promyshlenniki* to gather people from several villages and select several men for punishment to serve as examples. However, to gain strategic support of certain court favorites, zealous members of the Russian Orthodox church, Shelikhov claimed that there was a critical need to establish missions in the colonies. He pledged that his proposed monopoly would have the commitment and the means to convert the natives. Thus with encouragement from the St. Petersburg court Shelikhov was to become the person most responsible for establishing missions in Russian Alaska.

Shelikhov died in 1795. His work for the cause of monopoly in Russian North America was carried forth at the imperial court by his widow. In 1799 the czar issued the long-sought charter, authorizing the Shelikhov interests to organize the Russian American Company to serve as the steward of the czar's lands and native subjects in the New World.

173

THE RUSSIAN AMERICAN COMPANY

The Russian American Company continued as the managerial agency for Russian North America until 1867. At first the company was headquartered at Irkutsk, but in 1801 the principal stockholders, including the czar himself, moved it to St. Petersburg. By the terms of its charter, the Russian American Company was required to treat the native peoples humanely, to protect them, and to support their conversion to Christianity. In return the natives were obligated to render the company tribute in service or furs. Many, particularly Aleuts, were to be conscripted for three-year terms of service to the company. All men over 18 and under 50 years of age were subject to call to serve in the hunting brigades. Those peoples not conscripted, including most of the natives on far-off islands and on the Alaskan Peninsula and the northern mainland around the Bering Sea and Arctic Ocean, were to render their annual tribute to the company in furs.

Baranov was named governor-general of the Russian American Company. He divided Russian America into hunting and trading districts or counters, centering on 16 settlements, the principal ones being Kodiak, Unalaska, Atka, Northern, and after 1811, Ross. Baranov distributed over 500 *promyshlenniki* and nearly 2,000 Aleut hunters and their families, and 26 sailors to man supply boats, in these settlements to collect furs by hunting, trading, and tribute collecting.

Under Baranov's driving leadership the Russian American Company challenged the British Hudson's Bay Company for first place in the world's fur business. During the life of the company (1799–1867), Russian, Aleut, and Indian hunters collected nearly 4,000,000 skins, of which more than 140,000 were sea otter and 2,500,000 seal, in addition to thousands of rare white or Arctic fox, blue and brown fox, otter, mink, marten, beaver, wolf, and bear skins. In 1803, Aleut hunters at Kodiak put together the largest shipment of furs on record—17,000 sea otter pelts valued at 1,200,000 rubles, consigned to Okhotsk.

Despite creditable commercial success, Russian American Company officials faced continuing and, as events proved, insurmountable problems which so weakened the company's effort that it felt compelled in 1867 to dispose of the North American territories and native peoples. The singular problem which stalked the Russian American Company throughout its life was the irrepressible Tlingits.

Tlingit Insurgency

The Indians the Russians called Kolush refused to comply with the Russian demand for tribute in furs. These fierce tribesmen were a source of continuing difficulty. They were dangerous not only because of their unconquerable spirit but also because of their access to firearms, even cannon, supplied by American and British traders, and they became skillful in the use of this weaponry.

The Tlingits controlled the strategic islands and strip of Alaskan mainland containing the prime sea-otter grounds in Russian North America. During the 1790s Baranov began to encroach upon their territory, first by hunting there and later by founding the settlement of New Archangel at Sitka. Russians antagonized the Tlingits by intruding upon their territory to hunt sea otters. Tlingits resented the superior hunting skill of the Aleuts, and they were concerned that the Russian-Aleut intruders would exterminate the furs which they required to trade with the Americans and British. Russians also appropriated their women. Baranov himself took an eighteen-year-old girl as his common-law wife; she bore him several children.

During 1802 Tlingit war parties ambushed Russian-Aleut hunting and trading parties throughout their territory. A large force swept into New Archangel and captured the town, burned all the buildings, stole 4,000 sea-otter pelts, and killed 20 Russians and 130 Aleuts. In 1804 Baranov returned with an armada, including Russian war ships with cannon batteries, 120 Russians, and nearly 1,000 Aleut militia. The batteries shelled the Tlingit positions at New Archangel and after much bloodshed Baranov's men were able to land, reestablish themselves on Sitka, and restore New Archangel.

Tlingits watched for another opportunity to torment the Russians. In 1805 warriors from this tribe raged through the Russian settlement at Yakutat, killing or capturing 22 Russians and many Aleuts. The following year Indians massed from several island and mainland coastal villages 2,000 men in 400 boats for another assault on Sitka. Baranov was away from New Archangel founding a new hunting station. Tlingit girls living at the fort warned Russian officials of the impending attack. Aware of the impossibility of success against the huge Native American force, the officers invited tribal leaders to a feast at the post. The lavish entertainment and gifts had the desired effect; the Indian plan to destroy New Archangel was deflected.

Nevertheless the Tlingits struck periodically. In 1808 Baranov moved the seat of company government from Kodiak to New Archangel. The inhabitants faced the threat of daily raids. Guerrilla attacks by Tlingit raiders made life uncertain on Sitka and the adjacent mainland. Russian and Aleut defenders had to ward off serious attacks in 1809 and 1813. Finally Baranov appealed to the Russian navy for protection, and in 1818 a warship patrolled the harbor at Sitka.

In councils Baranov urged Tlingit leaders to end their trade with the Americans and the British. The Tlingits refused, pointing out that Russian goods did not suit their taste. They expected guns, hatchets, knives, and quality blankets and textiles, including linen, which Muscovite traders could not supply. From their dealings with American and British sea merchants they had also come to expect special gifts and favors as bonuses for doing business.

In these councils Baranov also urged that as a means to better relations, the Tlingits place in his care hostages to be converted and educated in Russian ways. Tlingit leaders agreed to this only on the condition that the Russians also supply hostages. Thus Baranov presented two young mestizos in exchange for the nephew of a chief. This hostage exchange did quiet hostilities for awhile, and Tlingits actually traded with the Russians. When the Indians returned the Russian hostages, they demanded the chief's nephew in return, and the Russians complied.

The Tlingits also used nonmilitary tactics to confound and exploit the Russians. Nowhere were they more effective than through the much sought-after Tlingit women. "The Kolushan courtesan understands as thoroughly as the European dancer how to rob her admirer and one often sees a *promyshlen-niki* bankrupt himself to provide fine clothes for her, in spite of the efforts of the officers to try to prevent such mischief."[4]

But the military threat was the most devastating for the Russian American Company. As late as 1850 a Russian official complained that 500 well-armed Tlingits "live right by our settlement of New Archangel always ready to take advantage of our negligence. [At the] slightest provocation they would swarm out of their houses, their faces blackened with war paint, wearing hideous masks made in images of wild beasts, and shout defiance at their neighbors over the stockade." In 1863, only four years before the transfer of Russia's American holdings to the United States, Muscovite officials warned of the necessity to strengthen New Archangel "from the attacks of the Kolosh, this sword of Damocles eternally threatens Sitka."[5]

Russians and the California Indians

Besides the continuing Tlingit threat, Russians in North America faced the additional problem of a chronic shortage of food, caused in part by the forced diversion of native peoples from food gathering to fur hunting. In 1805 seventeen Russians and several hundred natives at New Archangel died of scurvy and starvation; similar conditions existed in the other settlements of Russian North America.

Shelikhov had anticipated food shortages, and he had attempted to establish agricultural production in the colonies adequate to support the fur industry. In 1794 he had imported 10 peasant families and cattle, poultry, seeds, and tools to Kodiak for the purpose of producing foodstuffs. When churchmen established missions in Russian North America, they conducted agricultural experiments, attempting to find food plants which would grow to maturity in the generally harsh environment, including the short growing season, of the northern Pacific Basin. They found that potatoes, turnips, and radishes did best. Wheat, oats, and rye generally failed; there were occasional crops of barley. Most of the potatoes were dried and ground into flour. Despite these efforts, farming did not prosper in Alaska. Stock raising failed, too.

Thus main reliance for food was upon nature—fish, sea-lion meat, and wild plants and roots collected by Aleut women and children at each settlement. When at peace with the Tlingits, the Russians purchased geese, ducks, and potatoes from them. Haida Indians from as far away as the Queen Charlotte Islands often visited Sitka, their boats laden with potatoes.

Baranov purchased large amounts of grain and other foodstuffs from American maritime traders who delivered cargoes of grain raised on farms in the United States. These sea merchants were finding it increasingly difficult to obtain sea-otter pelts in the Northwest Coast commerce. They were aware of the rich hunting grounds along the Pacific Coast from San Francisco Bay to Lower California. That this was Spanish territory, off limits to outsiders, was of small concern to the maritime traders. They negotiated with Baranov, delivering cargoes of foodstuffs to Russian North America in exchange for use of his Aleut hunters. In effect Baranov leased the natives to American ship captains for a season. The Aleuts hunted the bays and inlets each day and returned to the base ship at night. In 1803 one ship brought back to Sitka 2,200 sea otter skins, and between 1806 and 1812 ten ships with Aleut hunters took 25,000 sea-otter pelts in these southern waters. From this arrangement Baranov obtained much-needed grain and one half of the sea otter catch earned by his Aleut hunters.

Russian officials also tried to establish reliable sources of food in the Sandwich Islands but without success. Then in 1805 Count Rezanov, a Russian American Company stockholder, made an inspection of the "starving colonies." He ventured south to San Francisco where he obtained a supply of provisions from the Spaniards and shipped it to Sitka. Rezanov was impressed with the vast tracts of unoccupied land and mild climate north of San Francisco Bay, and he recommended that the company establish an agricultural colony there.

During 1812, 95 Russians and 80 Aleuts arrived at Bodega Bay; nearby they erected buildings which became Fort Ross, the beginning of Russian California. The Russians also occupied the Farallone Islands, a cluster of rocky atolls 30 miles offshore from Fort Ross. There Baranov stationed a group of Aleuts with a Russian foreman to hunt sea otters, seals, and sea lions, and to gather sea-bird eggs. Aleut hunting in the Farallones yielded 1,000 sea-otter pelts each year and 1,500 seal skins, plus large amounts of sea-lion meat and sea-bird eggs. At Fort Ross the Russians and Aleuts established vineyards, peach orchards, and grain fields.

Most of the agricultural work at Fort Ross was performed by local Indians, the Pomos. They were primarily migratory gatherers, subsisting in season on wild plants and roots of the interior; seeds and wild grains near the seashore; and shellfish. At first, perhaps out of curiosity, they met and cooperated with the Russians and voluntarily worked for them. As time went on, however, the Pomos fared no better than the Aleuts and other native peoples who had been absorbed into the Russian dominion. In July they were hired by the Russians, mainly for the harvest. But they were unskilled and unaccustomed to regular work; they quickly became bored and left. If the harvest failed, the Indian laborers were held responsible and forced to remain and redeem the lost crop with other work.[6]

The Pomos had escaped impressment by the Spanish padres into their mission system, but the Russians exceeded the Spaniards in disregard for common humanity. At first the Russians required them to furnish only 100 laborers each year. As the Europeans increased the amount of land in cultivation, they demanded more laborers until by 1835 the Pomos were required to supply 200 workers annually. The natives resisted Russian conscription in various ways. They burned grain fields and killed cattle. And they hid from Russian squads sent after them. When captured, "sometimes as many as 150 are driven together by force and are put to hard work in the fields. [They were fed] only flour for thin gruel. As a result of this scanty food and the hard labor . . . the Indians reach in the end a state of complete exhaustion."[7]

Fort Ross continued as the Russian American Company's southernmost outpost until 1841. Its bounty of grains and other foodstuffs was harvested at heavy cost to Pomo life and tribal vigor. Deaths from Russian-introduced diseases and the destructive labor conscript system reduced the Pomo population by one third between 1812 and 1841.

Missions in Russian North America

Shelikhov's efforts to obtain a monopoly of colonial economic development through the proposed Russian American Company, in which he stressed the hunger of the native peoples for the Christian message and salvation, stirred interest in imperial court and Russian Orthodox church circles. In 1793 Empress Catherine II issued a *ukase* directing that priests be sent to the Russian American colonies. The following year seven missionaries began to work among the natives in the Aleutian Islands and on Kodiak. During 1796 they established a church on Kodiak and began agricultural experiments in an attempt to relieve the threat of starvation there. In the same year the first Orthodox priest was martyred; Father Juvenali was killed by natives on Unalaska. Ships sent out from Okhotsk in 1799 to support the new missions sank with all missionary workers, supplies, and equipment lost. There followed a relaxation of the mission efforts, and by 1809 there was only one clergyman in the colonies.

The really intensive Russian Orthodox missionary effort in North America began in 1824 with the arrival of Ivan Veniaminoff in the Aleutian Islands. He was friendly and dedicated; he learned the native language, was much respected by the Aleuts and succeeded in converting nearly all of them. In 1834 Veniaminoff was transferred to Sitka to attempt to subdue the Tlingits by converting them to Christianity. His poorest results were among these fiercely independent people; most of them remained dedicated to their tribal religion. Their leaders explained that over the years they had observed the terrible things which Christian Russians had done to the Aleuts, and they were determined to reject Christianity. Veniaminoff persevered and finally converted 102 Tlingits, built a church for them at Sitka, and established schools for their youth.

Veniaminoff and other missionaries worked on native languages and were able to convert Aleut, Eskimo, and the Tlingit dialects to written form and and to publish books in these languages for use in the mission schools. Veniaminoff extended the missionary horizons of Russian America. Besides great success among the Aleuts and only modest success among the Tlingits, he also established missions among the Eskimos and Indian tribes of the interior. After the Russian fur hunters moved into the Bering Sea, Veniaminoff erected a northern headquarters at St. Michael, and from there missionaries penetrated the lower Yukon and Kuskokim basins. From the schools Veniaminoff established in the Aleutian Islands, on Kodiak, at Sitka, and at other locations in Russian America, native youth, most of them Creoles, went on to St. Petersburg to complete their education at the expense of the company.

Above all else, Veniaminoff was a constant critic of Russian treatment of Native Americans. His regular reports to the court at St. Petersburg related oppression in the colonies, and his complaints brought investigations by the czar's agents but, sadly for the native peoples, little improvement in treatment. Following the purchase of Russian Alaska in 1867 by the United States, Russian Orthodox missionaries continued their work in local churches, schools, and missions. As late as 1900 they were conducting six schools for native peoples in Alaska.

Last Days of the Russian American Company

Except for the humanity and intercessory influence of the missionaries, particularly Veniaminoff, and status of mestizos, it is difficult to find one redeeming quality in the Russian dominion over the north Pacific Basin native peoples. Granted Russians were not alone in oppressing these Native Americans. British and American maritime traders also corrupted them and debauched them with rum, brandy, and whiskey. And by 1835 American whalers entered the waters near Kodiak Island; ten years later they were in the Bering Sea. Crewmen from whaling ships disturbed sea-otter hunting, they raided native villages for supplies and women, and they burned the native peoples' precious supplies of driftwood to render oil from whale blubber. But these were intermittent torments, to be endured only occasionally. The dreaded Russian presence was constant.

Reports of abuses inflicted by Russian subjects upon native peoples reached the court in 1787, and a *ukase* issued which denounced the practices and warned traders to cease their oppressions. Court officials also sent out an expedition the following year, its members to observe firsthand the state of affairs in Russian America. The expedition's report stated that *promyshlenniki* "lord it over the inhabitants with more despotism than generally falls to the lot of princes, keeping the islanders in a state of abject slavery."[8]

The Russian American Company charter contained the wishes, and thus policy, of the imperial court as to treatment of aboriginal subjects in Russian North America. The company was required to protect the native peoples, watch over them as the agent of the czar, promote their welfare, and support their conversion to Christianity. The court permitted the company to conscript natives, but the charter made no provision for oversight or accountability. Thus there was little change in the treatment of natives except that Aleuts, who had become increasingly valuable to the company as hunters, received protective attention that was not accorded Tlingits, Eskimos, Pomos, and others within the Russian imperial orbit.

The status of mixed bloods or mestizos has varied among the several empires. Curiously, mestizos fared very well in the Russian system, perhaps better than mixed bloods in any other empire.

The Russian population in the colonies was never large; as late as 1860 they numbered only about 1,000. And very few Russian women migrated to North America, so the *promyshlenniki* took native wives. They were reported to have established homes in the settlements and "live comfortably, marrying ... native women, who are industrious and make good wives." Their offspring, mestizos, were identified as Creoles and received special recognition in the Russian American Company charter as Russian subjects, forming a "separate estate equal to the rank of commoner, that is, to a free station." Mestizos were exempt from tribute and labor conscripts and "had no obligation to the Russian American Company unless they had been educated at company expense in which case they had to serve for periods of ten to fifteen years." As educated members of colonial society in Russian North America, mestizos served as "ship masters, clerks and bookkeepers, and some rose to positions of eminence." One of them, Adolph Etolin, became governor-general of the Russian American Company. Thus they "escaped the fate of being caught between two cultures, the marginal status so common for persons of mixed blood in other European colonies."[9]

In 1867 the United States purchased the Russian territory in North America. "The ceremonial transfer of the fort of New Archangel to the American troops took place on October 18. The Indians followed the ceremony with great interest. Since they were not allowed in town, they embarked in their canoes and took positions in the harbor from which, in spite of the distance, they had a good view of the proceedings. They had only a vague idea of the implications and because of their acquaintance with American whalers, they were not inclined to regard it favorably. They watched the lowering and raising of the flags and listened to the thunder of the cannons and then quietly withdrew."[10]

Having examined the lot of native peoples under Russian dominion we now consider, in Chapter Nine, the fate of Native Americans under the dominion of Great Britain. British Indian policy is particularly important and instructive because it served as the model for the stance later developed by the United States.

Notes

1. Stuart R. Tompkins, *Alaska: Promyshlennik and Sourdough* (Norman, Okla., 1945), p. 5.
2. C. L. Andrews, *The Story of Alaska* (Caldwell, Idaho, 1938), p. 34.
3. Tompkins, *Alaska*, p. 51.
4. Aurel Krause, *The Tlingit Indians* (Seattle, Wash., 1956), p. 29.
5. Andrews, *Story of Alaska*, pp. 117, 119.
6. James R. Gibson, *Imperial Russia in Frontier America* (New York, 1976), p. 32.
7. S. B. Okun, *The Russian-American Company* (Cambridge, Mass., 1951), p. 143.
8. Andrews, *Story of Alaska*, p. 46.
9. Clarence C. Hulley, *Alaska, 1741–1953* (Portland, Ore., 1953), and B. D. Lain, "The Decline of Russian America's Colonial Society," *Western Historical Quarterly* 7 (April 1976), pp. 144–45.
10. Krause, *Tlingit Indians*, p. 46.

Selected Sources

The most detailed account of imperial Russia in North America, containing considerable detail on that nation's relations with native peoples is *History of Alaska, 1730–1885* by Hubert H. Bancroft (San Francisco, 1886). Other studies of Alaska and Native Americans during the period of Russian imperial dominion include Hector Chevigny, *The Great Alaskan Venture, 1741–1867* (New York, 1965); Clarence C. Hulley, *Alaska, 1741–1953* (Portland, Ore., 1953); C. L. Andrews, *The Story of Alaska* (Caldwell, Idaho, 1938); and Stuart R. Tompkins, *Alaska: Promyshlennik and Sourdough* (Norman, Okla., 1945).

Studies of Native Americans in the northern Pacific Basin and subject to Russian dominion include William H. Dall, *Tribes of the Extreme Northwest* (Washington, D.C., 1877); Sheldon Jackson, *Missionary Work Among the Indians of Alaska* (Washington, D.C., 1877); Aurel Krause, *The Tlingit Indians* (Seattle, Wash., 1956); Norman A. Chance, *The Eskimo of North Alaska* (New York, 1966); Nicholas J. Gubser, *The Nunamiut Eskimos: Hunters of Caribou* (New Haven, Conn., 1965); and B. D. Lain, "The Decline of Russian America's Colonial Society," *Western Historical Quarterly* 7 (April 1976), pp. 143–53, the last source particularly useful in explaining the role of mestizos in Russian colonial society.

The principal Russian exploitation apparatus was the Russian American Company. Its role in the process of managing Native Americans is discussed in Raymond H. Fisher, *The Russian Fur Trade, 1500–1700* (Berkeley, Calif., 1943); Hector Chevigny, *Lord of Alaska: Baranov and the Russian Adventure* (New York, 1942); James R. Gibson, *Imperial Russia in Frontier America* (New York, 1976); Henry M. Michael (ed.), *Lieutenant Zagoskin's Travels in Russian America, 1842–1844* (Toronto, 1967); S. B. Okun, *The Russian-American Company* (Cambridge, Mass., 1951); William R. Hunt, *Arctic Passage: The Turbulent History of the Land and People of the Bering Sea, 1697–1975* (New York, 1975); and Raisa V. Makarova, *Russians on the Pacific, 1743–1799* (Kingston, Ontario, 1975).

CHAPTER 9

BRITONS AND THE NATIVE AMERICANS

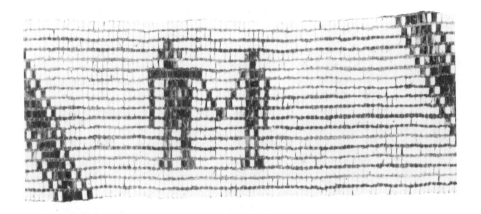

I have seen two generations of my people die.... I am now grown old, and must die soon.... Why will you take by force what you may have quietly by love? Why will you destroy us who supply you with food? What can you get by war? We can hide our provisions and run into the woods; then you will starve for wronging your friends. Why are you jealous of us? We are ... willing to give you what you ask, if you come in a friendly manner, and not with swords and guns, as if to make war upon an enemy. I am not so simple as not to know that it is much better to eat good meat, sleep comfortably, live quietly with my wives and children, laugh and be merry with the English ... than to run away from them and to lie cold in the woods, feed on acorns ... be so hunted that I can neither eat nor sleep.... Take away your guns and swords, the cause of all our jealousy, or you may all die in the same manner.

Powhatan's oration to English colonists at Jamestown, 1609

English dominion over territory and peoples in North America began in 1607 with a humble, struggling beachhead at Jamestown on the estuary of the James River in Virginia. Through the years English settlement spread north and south along the Atlantic seaboard to embrace the territory from Maine to Georgia. By 1763 Great Britain had vanquished other nations with colonies in the New World and thus controlled Florida, Canada, and the vast trans-Appalachian territory extending to the Mississippi River. Of the mercantilist nations lusting after overseas colonies, Spain, France, Holland, and Russia eventually retreated; only Great Britain survived in North America. Subsequently the thirteen seaboard colonies with the trans-Appalachian territory seceded from the British empire, but Great Britain maintained a degree of sovereignty over Canada into the twentieth century.

The longevity of the British empire has been due primarily to the pattern of occupation and development of its North American colonies. Britons, like the French and Dutch, came to the New World to trade with native peoples for furs and to exploit North America's readily extractable resources of minerals, lumber, and naval stores (pitch and turpentine), all enterprises in which tenure of the land was only temporary. However, Britons came primarily as families and as agriculturalists; they came to stay and their hold on the land,

Chapter Opening Artifact: Detail of the Delaware wampum belt presented to William Penn. (The Historical Society of Pennsylvania)

in a sense, was eternal. For this reason, more than any other, the British remained and the other imperial powers were forced out of North America. Other colonial powers concentrated on more transitory enterprises and did not establish this family-based pattern of settlement as the British did. Thus they failed to plant extended demographic roots. The British pattern of colonial settlement and development had an awesome impact upon Native Americans.

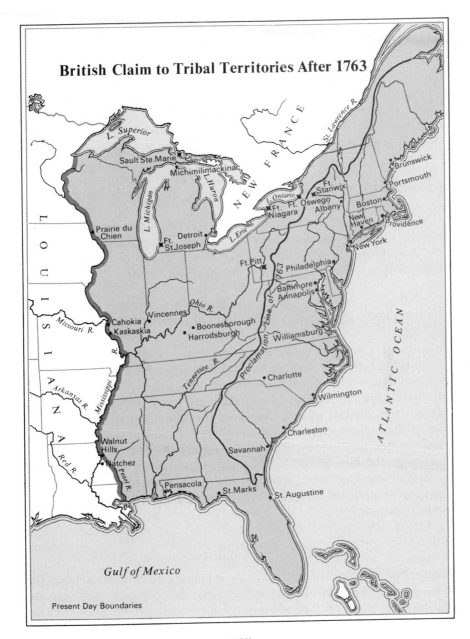

British Claim to Tribal Territories After 1763

Present Day Boundaries

Great Britain's long tenure in North America and its relations with the Indian tribes made British Indian policy the natural and lineal ancestor of the Anglo-American Indian relationship which began in 1776. British ethnic philosophy, Indian policy, and Indian relations were the foundation upon which the new American nation built its policy; phases of British Indian policy survive in the United States government's policies toward Native Americans into the 1970s.

The British occupation of the American mainland from Maine to Georgia and, after 1763, Florida, is a well-known part of Anglo-American history. This colonial zone was populated by many Indian tribes, their people crucial to British success as an imperial power. Ill-prepared colonists desperately needed Indians to guide and instruct them on survival in the American wilderness. The colonists turned to Indians to teach them planting techniques and culture of crops by which they could sustain themselves and eventually prosper, to hunt furs to enrich their trading establishment, to labor on their plantations, and to serve as colonial troops in the various wars Great Britain waged against European adversaries in North America. In view of their indispensability to European success in the New World it is surprising that Englishmen so ill-used Indians. The British Indian policy was exploitive and unnecessarily destructive and demeaning, and it was never executed in the best interests of Native Americans.

Until 1763 each of the thirteen British colonies pursued an independent course in handling Indians. However, regional patterns did exist, and one may characterize Indian policy in three useful, though perhaps overly simplified, divisions: New England, Mid-Atlantic, and Southern.

NEW ENGLAND COLONIAL INDIAN POLICY

From the St. Lawrence Valley south into Connecticut lived over a score of Indian tribes including Penobscots, Abenakis, Massachusetts, Narragansetts, Wampanoags, Confederated River Tribes, and Pequots. These tribes had a mixed economy of hunting, fishing, and agriculture and maintained trade relations with interior tribes by exchanging corn and dried fish for furs and copper. They also traded with the Long Island tribes for wampum. By 1620 when permanent English settlement in New England began, these tribes numbered only about 25,000. Tribal populations had been drastically reduced by scarlet fever and other epidemic diseases carried to New England by European traders and fishermen who preceded the Pilgrims and Puritans in Massachusetts.

Early Indian-English Relations

Three circumstances assured the English initial success in founding settlements in this portion of North America. First, the epidemics, occurring perhaps as late as 1610, had so reduced tribal populations near Cape Cod that the European settlers encountered only minimal competition for the land. Second, many Indians welcomed the English because they hoped to use them as allies to help defeat the powerful Pequots who lived in western Connecticut and who exacted tribute from most other New England tribes. And third, by 1620 the communication barrier between white and Indian had been broken by several Indians who spoke English. Squanto (Tisquantum) was one of a group of twenty Indians seized by an English trader in 1614 and taken to Malaga to be sold as slaves. Squanto escaped and returned to Cape Cod via Newfoundland. His ability to speak English substantially eased matters for the Pilgrims at Plymouth. He persuaded local tribes to help the suffering colonists during their first winter in New England. He also served as a strategic communication link between Pilgrims and Indians whereby the newcomers received land for settlement, trading privileges, seed, and instruction in planting.

Leaders of both Plymouth and Massachusetts Bay colonies hoped to coexist with the Indians, although on their terms. Their early intent was all peace and kindness; they did not consider Indians natural enemies but rather "unfortunate heathens." Officials of the Massachusetts Bay Company admonished their colonists, "Above all, we pray you to be careful that there be none in our precincts permitted to do any injury, in the least kind, to the heathen people; and if any offend in that way, let them receive due correction."[1]

Both the Pilgrims at Plymouth and the Puritans at Massachusetts Bay believed that Indians were capable of improvement and it was their sacred obligation to break the hold that Satan had upon them, to Christianize them through missions, conferring upon them the benefits of civilization so that they might live like Europeans. However, these English settlers did not believe that Indians would improve themselves voluntarily. Thus civilizing and Christianizing them would require jurisdiction over Native Americans, to displace their pagan law and make them subject to English colonial law which was the "law of God." This would regularize native life-styles, discipline the Indians, and make them receptive to Christian teachings. Clearly the early New Englanders had a pacifistic, if naive, attitude toward Native Americans.[2]

The Destruction of the Pequot Nation

West of the Massachusetts Bay and Plymouth settlements, escaping the devastating plague which had earlier stricken the coastal tribes, lived the Pequots, their tribal name an Algonkian word meaning "destroyer of men." Traders made contact with them soon after 1620. While bringing the weakened coastal tribes under English jurisdiction, law, and regulation appeared to be relatively easy, the Pequots proved to be another matter. And the Puritans were not about to allow any resistance to accepting what they believed was their divinely ordained theocracy.

Meanwhile, English traders from Virginia, working the Connecticut shore from an anchored ship, had frequently been attacked by Pequots. During

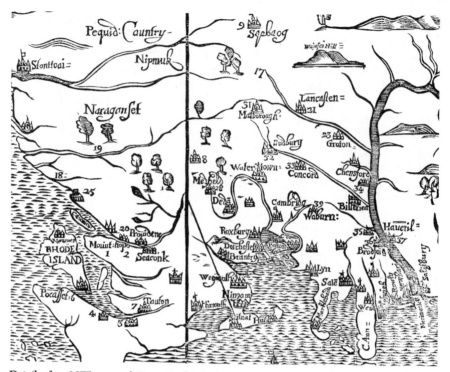

Detail of a 1677 map of New England showing the Pequot and other Indian nations. (Houghton Library, Harvard University)

a single raid the Indians killed nine traders and plundered their goods. In 1634 Massachusetts Bay officials claimed jurisdiction over the Pequots, attempting to force tribal leaders to sign a treaty acknowledging blame for the incident. By this pact the Pequots agreed to surrender the killers to the English for trial, to pay a fine of forty beaver pelts and thirty otter pelts, and to cede a large territory in Connecticut for English expansion.

For over two years Puritan officials waited for the Pequots to fulfill the terms of the 1634 treaty; tribal leaders had not surrendered the slayers of the Virginia traders, and they had paid only a portion of the fine. Incidents outside the Pequot nation led the English to press the Pequots to a settlement, which in turn precipitated the Pequot War.

In 1636 a small party of Indians raided another group of English traders in the Narragansett Bay area, killing one trader and capturing a store of goods. Massachusetts Bay authorities blamed the Narragansett Indians for the raid; the accused Indians fled to the Pequot country. Ninety Puritan militiamen marched into southwestern Connecticut, confronted Pequot leaders, and demanded the refugees. The Pequots refused and a battle ensued; several Pequots were killed and wounded, and two Englishmen were wounded. The whites seized a considerable amount of Indian property and returned to Boston. The enraged Pequots retaliated, ambushing traders, attacking isolated settlements, slaying thirty colonists, and carrying off many women and children as captives. In May 1637 the Massachusetts Bay General Court (legislature) declared war on the Pequots and officials mustered an army from the Massachusetts Bay, Plymouth, and Connecticut settlements, and the coastal tribes. Many Wampanoag and Narragansett warriors fought with the colonial militiamen against the Pequots to free themselves from the heavy tribute in furs and wampum which the Pequots collected from them each year.

Puritan-Indian columns campaigned over Pequot territory, burning villages and killing or capturing Indian residents. They laid siege to Mystic Fort, the principal settlement of the Pequots, and finally set fire to the dwellings, killing nearly 500 men, women, and children. They sold the captives for service as slaves in Boston households or for labor on southern colonial plantations.

Annihilation of the Pequots removed a threat to the security of New England colonists, and it opened new territory for their expansion. In a sense, a war to punish Pequots for resisting extension of English jurisdiction and law became a war of conquest, because it opened most of southern New England to settlement. Following the colonial victory, Puritan divine Increase Mather called upon his congregation to thank God that "we have sent six hundred heathen souls to hell."[3]

Puritan Guardians

In the early days of Puritan settlement, colonial officials seriously attempted to fulfill the Massachusetts Bay Company directive to provide prompt remedy for offense against the "heathen." The General Court of Massachusetts Bay adopted a code of rules to protect Indians against unfair trading and to prevent traders from supplying them with the principal sources of mischief—liquor and firearms. When Thomas Morton sold both to New England Indians, Puritan officials deported him to England, but Morton returned to New England and resumed trading contraband to the natives. This time authorities made a public display before hundreds of Indians in seizing his goods and burning his house.

Other portions of this Puritan code regulated relations of colonists with Indians. Authorities, concerned that Indian life-style might appeal to the less disciplined among them (as it had for the French *coureurs de bois*), adopted rules which forbade citizens of Massachusetts Bay to live on the frontier "without government." They were required to "move into town rather than to continue to live without community discipline among the Indian."[4]

From the beginning of European settlement to the present, the most vexing of all matters in relations between Indians and other settlers has been tenure and use of tribal land. Few Britons, and for that matter subjects of other European nations, understood the Native Americans' attitude toward land and landownership. The economy of most of the tribes of New England was a mixture of agriculture, hunting, gathering, and trading. Each maintained a common tribal estate which consisted of two parts. In one portion were the villages and cultivated fields; the other portion was the tribal hunting preserve, certainly less intensively used than the farmland but just as essential to tribal survival. This latter portion the English, with their agricultural orientation of intensive land use, regarded as "surplus," "unoccupied," "unused," and thus available for appropriation by landless Europeans.

The charter issued to the Massachusetts Bay Company, similar to grants made by the British crown to other companies founding colonies in the New World, ignored the presence of Native Americans. The king considered certain lands in North America, discovered by his subjects, as part of the royal estate, to be dispensed in a manner he determined. Thus it fell to the colonists settling on lands drawn from the royal estate in the New World to deal with the resident Native Americans.

Plymouth Company officers directed their settlers, should they require land claimed by Indians, "to purchase their title, that we may avail the least scruple of intrusion." The Puritans came to follow the Dutch precedent of purchasing land by token payment, although they rarely missed the opportunity to extinguish title to tribal lands by confiscation or conquest. Puritan rhetoric ordained that the Indians' resistance to their law, because it was "God's law," comprised blasphemy, the ultimate sin, and thus placed the offending Indians outside the pale of protection and their lands could be taken by force or conquest with impunity.[5]

Roger Williams, founder of colonies in Rhode Island, took the position that the monarch could not grant title to land which he did not own. "No king, not even Charles," he contended, "was invested with the right by virtue of their Christianitie to take and give away the Lands and Countries of other men." Williams required that for land transfers from Indians to colonists to be legal, they had to be supervised and approved by the constituted colonial authorities, and the Indian owners had to receive a fair price for the ceded territory.[6]

The General Court of Massachusetts Bay in 1643 adopted Williams' principle of supervised land transactions. Laws enacted by this body set rules for land sales, including the requirement for a "fair price," and stated that Indians could retain the right to hunt and fish on unused portions of ceded territory. Connecticut legislators adopted Indian land transfer regulations in 1640. Amendments to the basic law included provision for a fine of triple the value of land to be assessed against any person convicted of making unlawful purchases of Indian land. New Englanders righteously claimed that they "did not possess one foot of land . . . but what was fairly obtained by honest purchase of Indian proprietors," not counting, of course, the territory taken by military conquest.[7]

It is unlikely that Indians understood the transactions which conveyed their communally owned lands to private ownership. Many may have thought that they were merely selling the use of the land and not conveying exclusive and permanent possession. An important aspect of landholding in New England was the colonists' hope that by the example they set in private land-ownership they could convert Indians to abandon communal ownership and adopt the English system. This was regarded as an essential step in "civilizing the Indian in making him a property owner in the English sense," and it became a continuing, if vain, hope which survived into the twentieth century.[8]

Puritan Missions and Land Policy

From the beginning Puritans held mixed attitudes about whether or not Indians were capable of achieving salvation and thus being worthy of Christian attention. The dominating view was that Indians indeed could be saved. However, rank-and-file colonists maintained serious reservations which were to escalate into bias and genocide after the 1676 Indian revolt.

The prevailing view had been that the primary purpose for settling New England was to bring the Christian message to Native Americans there, to work for their conversion, and to defeat Satan. By Puritan canons, in order to be a church member and thus worthy of assimilation into English society, one had to submit to a complete conversion experience based upon a thorough knowledge of the Bible and the English style of living. Thus it was realized that the Indians' conversion would require a lengthy and "vigorous" effort. Eventually it was determined that to accomplish this, the Indians had to be isolated from their own life-style and placed on reservations where the de-tribalization process and conversion would take place.

The model for this type of segregated living was already developing. In 1638 colonial authorities founded a 1,200-acre reservation at New Haven as a protectorate to guard the surviving 47 members of the Quinnipiac tribe. Rules adopted by the English forbade the Quinnipiac Indians to leave their reservation or take any major step including sale of reservation land without government approval. The colonial wards could admit no "foreign Indians" to their reservations, and they were to report Indian plots. Reservation law prohibited sale of liquor, guns, shot, and powder to resident Indians. An English magistrate supervised the reservation.

Following the Pequot War, the victorious colonists forbade use of the tribal name, they erased Pequot place names, and they dispersed the few survivors who had not been sold into slavery to the other tribes. Eventually the Pequots sought to recover their tribal identity. In 1655 colonial authorities reunited the scattered elements and resettled them on reservations in southeastern Connecticut. Remnants of the other tribes were similarly consolidated. Colonial officials appointed Indian governors who, with English supervisors, managed the reservations. Indians on reservations paid annual tribute to the colonial governments.

The concentration of Indians on reservations provided colonists the means to reduce and eventually to appropriate tribal estates, all under the aegis of Puritan missions for the Indians' inherent benefit. Puritans called the reservations "plantations." Indians settled on these restricted tracts under the charge of missionaries were called "praying Indians." Missionary work was supported by the labor of Indians who lived on the reservations, colonial legislatures through supportive laws and funds raised locally, and by funds raised in England. In 1636 the Plymouth legislature adopted laws to support missions to the Indians; the legislative bodies for Massachusetts Bay and New Haven took similar action. The English government chartered two missionary societies—the New England Company (1649) and the Company for the Propagation of the Gospel in New England (1662)—"to move Indians from the power of darknesse and the kindom of Satan, to the knowledge of the true and only God." New England missions prospered for several years largely because these home-based organizations provided most of the fiscal support.

During the Golden Age of New England Indian evangelization (1640–1680) several outstanding men were attracted to Indian missions. By 1651 Thomas Mayhew, Jr., had begun mission conversion work among 3,000 Indians at Martha's Vineyard, an island off the coast of Massachusetts. When he died at sea, his father continued his mission work there. John Eliot, a Puritan clergyman, began during the 1640s to divide his time between his colonial congregation and Indians. Learning Algonkian from an Indian captive, he taught Indians in their own language. Eliot also published a grammar, a speller, a reader, a catechism, and his translation of the Bible in Algonkian.

Puritan missionary zeal extended to higher education. To fulfill the commitment in their charter to educate both English and Indian youths, Harvard trustees created an Indian college within the university. Several Indian students studied at Harvard, but most of them perished of various diseases. Only one Indian student graduated with a bachelor's degree during this early period. Puritan concern for missionizing Native Americans eventually faded, but interest in Indian education continued. The royal charter for Dartmouth College, issued in 1769, stated that the institution's purpose included "civilizing and christianizing the children of pagans."

Christian plantations for New England Indians began at Natick in 1651 when the Massachusetts General Court created an 8,000-acre reservation for the tiny Nonantum tribe. The following year, to confirm the hope that private ownership of land would abet the civilizing and christianizing processes, the General Court passed the first allotment act. Indian residents of this plantation, after demonstrating that they could live "civilly and orderly" received an individual allotment of land for farming and stock raising. The concept of "restricted allotment" or trust deed, in later times a widely applied restraint on sale of Indian land, was introduced in that the deed to each allotment was held in trust by the colonial government so that the Natick allottees could not sell their land. Natick Indians, with the help of colonial carpenters, constructed English-style residences on their allotments.

Between 1650 and 1670 the Massachusetts General Court, following the pattern of the Natick Christian Plantation, created several additional reservations. To manage this growing system of Indian reservations, the General Court in 1656 established the office of superintendent of Indian affairs for Massachusetts, who was to direct the civilization process for the Christian plantation residents. A model government unit was to be created, consisting of a reservation court similar to English county court on each plantation, staffed by Indian magistrates and the superintendent, with authority to handle cases growing out of major crimes committed on the reservation. Indians eventually were permitted to serve on juries and to have their testimony admitted in court. Daniel Gookin was the first superintendent of Indian affairs for Massachusetts.

By 1675 Puritan missions had converted over 2,100 Massachusetts Indians; nearly 3,000 Christian novitiates lived on Martha's Vineyard. In that year, Eliot, the elder Mayhew, Gookin, and other men devoted to the cause of Indian transformation saw most of their work annihilated by the Indian Revolt and its aftermath.

The Indian Revolt of 1675

By the 1670s Indians were becoming restless over English expansion. They saw the missions as a mockery. Puritans represented the reservation system as conceived and executed for Indian uplift and benefit, but Indians came to regard the system as a cruel way to take their land and destroy their culture. The restrictive reservation life was becoming increasingly objectionable to Indians, and their leaders resented the diminution of their influence and rights. Expanding English settlements meant extended English jurisdiction; Indians were becoming oppressed by the choking net of Puritan "blue laws" and the accompanying decline of their personal freedom. Word of the plight of coastal Indians spread to the frontier, and Puritan missionaries found western Indians reluctant to receive the Gospel and take up the new life on reservations.

Puritan leaders also detected a growing insurgency among Indians near their settlements. King Philip, head of the Wampanoag tribe, resented Puritan impositions and exactions, and because of his articulate denunciation of English exploitation of his people, he became the rallying point of escalating resistance. Philip made public protests to the expansion of Puritan jurisdiction. By 1670 perhaps 20 percent of the Indians of New England had been converted, but Christians and non-Christians alike were subject to English law. Attempts to force Indians to observe the Puritan sabbath and to abide by a legal code providing capital punishment for blasphemy were subjects of particular denunciation by Philip. He expressed resentment at the cultural change reservation life was producing in Indians, and he claimed that he could see virtually no benefit from this for the Indians. He charged that Native Americans faced ruin from the increasing English population in New

Caricature sketch of King Philip, patriot leader of the New England Indian war of independence against Massachusetts. (Engraving by Paul Revere, courtesy The American Antiquarian Society)

England and their growing demands for land.

In 1671 Puritan authorities arrested and fined Philip for his demonstrations of protest, and they disarmed his followers. Thereupon Philip increased his public protests, stressing how Puritans had destroyed Indian dignity and independence. He also began to conspire with Indians on reservations as well as with those on the frontier beyond the reach of Puritan law, urging them to join him in expelling their European oppressors and restoring Indian life-styles.

The insurrection, called King Philip's War, began in 1675 with well-armed

Indians raiding outlying English settlements. Colonists in Boston reacted toward the Indians in their midst in a manner similar to the response by Anglo-Americans to Japanese-Americans during the early 1940s. New Englanders demanded that colonial authorities concentrate all local Indians on military reservations. The Massachusetts General Court reduced the number of reservations from fourteen to five and directed the relocation of Christian Indians onto these smaller, closely guarded reservations. The Indian wards were forbidden to leave these compounds. Fifteen Christian Indians at Marlborough, suspected of plotting to join the Indian insurgents, were arrested and marched under heavy guard with ropes around their necks to Boston for trial. Evidence presented at their trial was unconvincing, and the magistrates ordered their release. The people of Boston were enraged. They formed a lynch mob, but the guards saved the prisoners and placed them on a military reservation.

Nipmucks and Narragansetts joined the Wampanoags in their war on the colonists. Philip's appeal reached far to the north; Abenaki warriors from Maine joined the Wampanoags in raids on the settlements. The insurgent warriors carried much pent-up rage into the war; many fought with great fury to the finish. Most of the Christian Indians remained neutral. Some offered to serve in the colonial army, and English commanders, after suffering repeated defeats in forest combat, finally engaged several Christian Indians as scouts. Their reconnaissance skill had a decisive effect on the colonial effort.

During 1676 resistance waned; Philip finally was defeated and slain. Colonial officials sold his wife and son, with hundreds of other surviving insurgents, into slavery. New Englanders preferred Indian slaves from the Carolinas and planned to ship their Indian captives there for an exchange or sale. They kept some Indian rebels in New England and sold them into servitude for periods ranging from ten years for adults to up to the age of twenty-five for children. The victorious colonists assumed title over much of western Massachusetts as war reparations.

Colonial attitudes toward Indians had been changing for some time, and the insurrection solidified negative views. Fewer Englishmen thought that Indians should or could be converted or civilized, and they renounced assimilation and intermarriage with the Indians. Increasingly Indians were regarded as members of an abandoned and threatening race. The recently concluded colonial war jelled the "bloodthirsty savage" image in the colonial mind. This attitude was nurtured by the railings of clergy against "the heathen" and published accounts of colonists allegedly held as Indian captives.

Cotton Mather horrified and inflamed his Puritan congregation with tales of "Indian bloodlust and cruelty," claiming that Indians had been "decoyed" here by Satan "in hopes that the gospel of the Lord Jesus Christ would never come here to destroy or disturb his absolute empire over them." Mather and other Puritan divines raged at Indian paganism, calling Indians "the accursed seed of Canaan" and charging that it was "the duty of Good Christians to

NARRATIVE

OF THE

MASSACRE, BY THE SAVAGES, OF THE WIFE & CHILDREN

OF

THOMAS BALDWIN,

Who, since the melancholy period of the destruction of his
unfortunate family, has dwelt entirely alone, in a
hut of his own construction, secluded from
human society, in the extreme western
part of the State of Kentucky.

"Great indeed, have been my afflictions; but, as it was the will of Heaven, I
ought not to murmur, but to say like him, whose afflictions were still greater, "the
Lord gave and has taken away, and blessed be his name."

Annexed are some well written Moral Instructions, of the venerable BALDWIN, to the bereaved and afflicted, how and where (from his own experience) they may find support and comfort amid the *severest trials* that may attend them in this "miserable world," and how to prepare themselves for endless enjoyments in that which is to come.

MARTIN & PERRY—PUBLISHERS—NEW-YORK.
1836.

Title page from a captivity narrative. (Houghton Library, Harvard University)

exterminate" them. Popular reading in the post-Indian-revolt period was Mary Rolandson's capitivity narrative which related her ordeal as an Indian prisoner, claiming that her treatment was barbarous and that her captors were cruel, wild, proud, and lustful savages.[9]

The Massachusetts General Court continued to adopt additional restrictions on Indians in New England. When an Indian and an Englishman met in the forest, the Indian was required immediately to place his weapons on the ground as a form of peaceful salute. Indians were stripped of additional lands and assigned to increasingly smaller reservations, more for security and punitive purposes and less for education and conversion. They could not leave the reservation without permission; a stiff prison term faced those who dared violate this rule. And Puritan authorities appointed English guardians to handle affairs for many Indians on reservations.

In addition, Puritan authorities continued to consolidate tribal remnants on new reservations in western Massachusetts to open more Indian land for settlers. Stockbridge was an example. Early in the eighteenth century the Housatonic Indians migrated to western Massachusetts and formed a settlement at Stockbridge. Colonial politicians supported a plan for a reservation at Stockbridge because it would provide frontier defense and Indians on this reservation would require less land than they would if they lived in the old style close to nature. The Great Awakening, a rekindling of colonial Protestant zeal, had produced momentary renewed interest in converting Indians. Missionaries hoped to transform Stockbridge into an old-style "Christian Plantation," convert the Housatonic Indians, and educate them to live within the engulfing English society. The Massachusetts General Court awarded the Housatonic a reservation embracing a township, six miles square, to be known as Stockbridge Reservation. The Housatonic came to call themselves Stockbridge Indians. In 1741 missionaries colonized a group of Mohawks at Stockbridge. By 1790 over 1,300 persons lived at Stockbridge, but few were Indians because frontier speculators had stripped the Stockbridge Indians of their reservation lands. The Stockbridge Indians drifted across the frontier, their descendants eventually settling in the northern half of territory which became the state of Kansas and in Wisconsin.

In the century after King Philip's War, other remnants of New England tribes coalesced for mutual protection. During the 1780s surviving Pequots, Mohicans, Narragansetts, Montauks, and Wampanoags confederated to form the Brotherton Indians, sold their lands, and moved beyond the western frontier of New England settlements.

By the eve of the American War of Independence, New England's reservation system had deteriorated to a pitiable state. When Massachusetts officials inspected Indian communities in that colony in 1746, they found the reservations in a deplorable condition. An act of the General Court in that year directed the appointment of three guardians for each of the colony's eight Indian reservation districts; these guardians were to lease Indian lands and disburse the proceeds for the support of impoverished Indians on the reservations.

The rate of Indian depopulation, constant throughout the colonial period, intensified in the eighteenth century. Colonial officials had recruited Indian soldiers for their armies to fight Great Britain's North American wars. Once away from the reservations, few Indians who survived combat ever returned to Massachusetts; most settled with other Indians on the frontier. Smallpox epidemics also took a heavy toll. And poverty and degradation, the result of loss of their tribal estates and their own life-styles, caused additional decline in Indian population. Colonial officials approved more and more purchases of allotted and reservation land by settlers. By 1781 only two "Christian plantations" survived.

MID-ATLANTIC COLONIAL INDIAN POLICY

The territory from Connecticut to Virginia, embracing the present states of New York, New Jersey, Pennsylvania, Delaware, and Maryland, was the home of Algonkian-speaking Indians. Holland and Sweden claimed this region; Dutch and later Swedish settlements were established in its northern and central portions. Virginians, working from trading ships anchored in the bays, traded each season with these tribes. Thus these Indians had been in contact with Europeans since early in the Colonial Era.

English settlement in the Mid-Atlantic region began in the 1630s when Charles I granted a vast tract on its southern margins to Lord Baltimore of the Calvert family. The Calverts founded the proprietary colony of Maryland. At the same time English settlers from New England began spreading southward across Long Island into Delaware Bay during Dutch and Swedish times.

In 1664 an English force occupied New Amsterdam and claimed New Netherland by right of conquest, the English crown designated the Duke of York primary proprietor, and the region was parceled into colonies. The northern portion became the colony of New York. John Berkeley and George Carteret were granted the territory that became the colony of New Jersey, and William Penn, a Quaker leader, later received territory west of Delaware Bay which became the colony of Pennsylvania. Subsequently Pennsylvania's three southern countries became the separate colony of Delaware.

Indians of the Mid-Atlantic Colonial Region

The several Indian communities in the coastal portions of this region were culturally similar segments of the Delaware tribe. Their band names included Raritan, Wappinger, Hackensack, Wicomoco, Minqua, and Nanticoke. Scattered along New York's Hudson River and on Long Island were remnants of formerly populous Algonkian bands, their numbers drastically reduced by wars with the Dutch and their Puritan allies from New England. Midway up the Hudson was a cluster of bands called the Esophus, battered by the

Dutch militia and much reduced in population and territory. And here and there along the Hudson were bands of surviving Mohicans. Many Indians from the Delaware Bay, the area of Dutch and Swedish settlements, had migrated westward into the Susquehanna Valley. Also on the western margins of the Mid-Atlantic region lived the Susquehanna and Shawnee Indians.

From the standpoint of military power, trade, and diplomacy, the most important Indians in the Mid-Atlantic region were those of the Iroquois Confederation, the five proud nations west of Albany along the Mohawk Valley. They had provided riches to the Dutch through the fur trade, and they had guarded the lower Hudson Valley settlements against French expansion from Canada. At the time of the English conquest of New Netherland, both the English and the French were avidly courting the Iroquois in the hope of winning their loyalty. In 1714 the Confederation absorbed an Iroquoian-speaking tribal remnant, the Tuscaroras, who were severely battered in their wars on the southern colonial frontier. Thereafter the Iroquois Confederation was known as the Six Nations.

Relations with the Mid-Atlantic Indians

An escalating population fed by steady migration from Europe and a high rate of natural increase following the English conquest of the Mid-Atlantic region placed great pressure on colonial governments to provide new lands for settlement. The crown regarded this region as a portion of the royal estate and granted full title to proprietors with no stipulation for recognizing tribal title or requiring that it be extinguished. Thus officials in each colony fashioned the policy for tribal land acquisition as well as the fur trade and general dealings with Native Americans.

Preliminary to the founding of Maryland was action by agents for the Calvert family in negotiating with the resident Wicomoco Indians, owners of the land on which Lord Baltimore selected to found his proprietary colony. Calvert family representatives presented to the Indians large quantities of cloth, axes, knives, hatchets, and other valued items in exchange for permitting them to form settlements in the territory granted to Lord Baltimore by King Charles I.

In Pennsylvania William Penn established the pattern of Quaker justice for dealing with Indians which became a tradition in that colony as long as the Society of Friends dominated its government. In 1682 Penn signed his first treaty with Delaware tribal leaders, beginning an extended period of good relations and scrupulously fair dealing in purchasing land for settlers. The 1682 pact acknowledged Indian ownership of land, denying the royal estate principle and providing the foundations for Quaker-Indian land negotiations. Eventually settlers found ways to evade Pennsylvania colony's laws regulating purchases from the Indians, including the negotiation of long-term leases with Indian landholders. The Pennsylvania colonial legislature banned this practice in 1729.

Painting depicting William Penn's negotiations with Delaware leaders in 1682. The negotiations acknowledged Indian ownership of the land and set a pattern for harmony between Indians and colonists in Pennsylvania. (Pennsylvania Academy of the Fine Arts, Joseph and Sarah Harrison Collection)

By 1700 in New York the English and Dutch population had increased to over 20,000; most of the colonists lived near New York City. Only a few pitiable Indians, survivors of a large Native American population of only a century before, squatted on lands at Manhattan, Long Island, and the edge of lower mainland settlements, the former vast tribal estates of their grandfathers and now the fee simple property of colonists. They subsisted by farming, hunting, fishing, and trading in the settlements. Colonial officials maintained no Indian reservations in this section of the colony.

The crown had directed New York governors to extinguish tribal title to as much land in that colony as possible to meet the growing demand for new settlement areas. They disposed of lands in the crown's name to those persons who would settle thereon and pay the patent fee and an annual quitrent. After colonial officials had extinguished aboriginal title to most of the arable land on the lower Hudson and in the immediate interior, including the rich Esophus lands, they began to negotiate for Iroquois territory along the Mohawk Valley. During the 1690s colonial officials purchased several huge tracts from the Mohawks; thereupon colonial settlement spread west from Albany.

Widespread corruption and fraud colored the dispensing of Indian lands obtained by these negotiations. One royal governor pocketed the patent fees paid by settlers. His only punishment when called to task was removal from office. The intense pressure for more Indian land, the variation in colonial land policy, and the resultant chaos and conflict persuasively demonstrated to the British government the critical need to replace permissive, individual colonial policies with a single Indian policy, particularly in the disposition of tribal lands and conduct of frontier trade.

Frontier Trade

Indian-colonial commerce in the Mid-Atlantic region varied with location. Indians who lived near the lower Hudson Valley and coastal settlements sold firewood, fish, shellfish, and venison at street markets. Many Indians, particularly those living on Chesapeake Bay, who hunted fur-bearing animals, moved inland to the valleys and western slopes of the Appalachians. There they mingled with Shawnees and other tribesmen who hunted over this vast wilderness.

Before 1700 colonial fur traders from Pennsylvania, New Jersey, and Maryland were following the coastal Indian hunters through the densely forested mountains into the country around the forks of the Ohio and proceeding cautiously into the French-dominated Ohio Country; by 1749 they had reached the Sandusky region in Ohio where they traded with the Shawnees. New York traders joined in exploring the western country; they urged the Shawnees and other local tribes to trade their pelts at Albany.

Iroquois hunters from the Mohawk Valley also explored the region in search of new fur territory. They roamed southward along the Pennsylvania and Virginia back-country to the Carolina border, raiding Indian settlements in their path. Delaware bands, who had moved across the mountains seeking refuge from the pressure of spreading English settlements, particularly suffered at the hands of these fierce raiders from the north. The Iroquois finally drove the Delawares into Ohio. A stream of Iroquois conquest also flowed westward around the southern shore of the Great Lakes. Senecas and other Iroquois resumed their wilderness wars on the Ottawas, Miamis, and other French-oriented Indians.

British traders, supported by Iroquois and coastal Indians, became the vanguard of British expansion into the trans-Appalachian West. They established trading stations near the forks of the Ohio (now the site of Pittsburgh) and began to attract Indians of the Old Northwest who customarily traded with the French. New York officials founded Fort Oswego on Lake Ontario at the mouth of the Oswego River. Shortly it became a popular trade center for tribes who in the past had carried their furs to French posts south of Montreal. British commercial expansion from their Mid-Atlantic colonies into the trans-Appalachian West threatened the French trading establishment in Canada.

The New World fur trade was important to both the French and the British. French colonists in Canada placed almost total reliance upon it for support. Agriculture was of primary importance to British colonists, but they depended upon the fur trade as their principal source of ready cash. While British traders rarely could match French style in maintaining relations with Indians, they enjoyed some advantages over their Gallic rivals. For the British, the fur trade was a free enterprise. All profits went to the traders. In French Canada, on the other hand, the fur trade was a government monopoly, requiring that a substantial portion of the proceeds be paid to the crown. English goods, including the prime items—firearms, cutlery, and textiles—were superior to French goods. Canadian traders faced the additional handicap of greater transport cost. Because of winter ice, seagoing ships delivering trade goods had access to Canadian ports via the St. Lawrence River only about half the year. The upper St. Lawrence and Ottawa rivers, the principal routes into the West, were punctuated by extensive rapids which required slow, expensive portage of cargoes. English goods moved by ship to colonial ports the entire year, and the Hudson River-to-Albany passage presented only occasional transport difficulties. Consequently, British traders could pay higher prices than French traders for furs, and their goods, besides being of higher quality, were on the average less expensive, costing the Indian hunter less than half what French goods cost. The difference in the price of furs and goods and the quality of goods lured Indian hunters from French traders and French trading stations. This threat to Canadian fur trade interests drove the French to wage four destructive wars on the British and their Indian allies in an attempt to drive them from the western wilderness and restore French supremacy.

Indian Missions

Indians in the Mid-Atlantic colonies escaped the intensive missionary efforts endured by the New England tribesmen. Generally the colonists in this portion of British North America lacked the evangelical fervor of their New England neighbors. Thus mission interest there was incidental, much as it had been under Dutch rule.

The so-called Duke's Laws, drafted on behalf of the primary proprietor for the governance of the land and people of the Mid-Atlantic colonies, made Indians subject to English jurisdiction and included the requirement that they observe the Christian sabbath. Indians were discouraged from practicing their own religion, not because they offended Christian sensibilities, but because colonists claimed that Indian worship disturbed the peace.

The Reverend Thomas James, minister at East Hampton, was one of the few colonial divines who seemed concerned for Indian spiritual welfare. For several years he attempted to convert tribes along the lower Hudson. In 1660 New England officials granted him funds to hire an interpreter to further his mission work. James's activities included composing an Indian catechism, but the enduring effect of his work was slight.

Dutch Reformed clergymen were the most active in Mid-Atlantic missions. In 1683 Domine Godfrey Dellius arrived in the colony of New York from Holland, and in a few years began mission work at his own expense west of Albany among the Mohawks. With the assistance of mixed-blood interpreters he studied the Iroquois language and translated portions of the Bible. Like Eliot, Dellius used the Roman alphabet to reduce spoken Iroquois to written form. Dellius became influential with the Indians of western New York, and in 1696 the governor appointed him commissioner of Indian Affairs for the colony.

Domine John Lydius continued Dellius' missionary work after 1700. He invited Mohawks to his home at Albany for prayer and singing. Domine Bernardus Freeman also devoted part of his time to missions. He settled in Schenectady for this purpose, became proficient in the Iroquois language, and translated the English *Book of Common Prayer* and portions of the Bible. Freeman attracted some Mohawk interest by his work.

Other missions among the tribes of the Mid-Atlantic region included those maintained by Anglicans and Moravians. In 1704 Anglicans completed a chapel in the Mohawk village nearest Schenectady and staffed it with an Anglican clergyman. Moravian missionaries began to minister to East coast Indians, particularly the Delawares during 1740. Their *modus operandi* was to collect Native Americans displaced by colonial expansion and resettle them in mission villages apart from the settlements. There the missionaries attempted to convert the Indians and instructed them in general education and vocational arts. The first mission settlements were in eastern Pennsylvania at Friedenshutten and Wyalusing. The pressure of white settlements forced them to relocate in western Pennsylvania where they established Friedenstadt. Thence they moved their Indian mission settlements to the Muskingum River in Ohio where they established three villages—Gnadenhutten, Salem, and Schoenbrunn.

New York colonial authorities became concerned over the persistent efforts of Jesuit missionaries from Canada among the Iroquois and appealed to clerical authorities in England and in New England for aid in expanding the work of the Dutch Reformed missionaries. They also urged clergy in New

York to establish missions on the frontier. They received no response to their appeals from any of these sources except the very limited aid from New England to assist James and the single Anglican mission.

The Jesuit mission stream into New York from Canada appeared to the British a dangerous, competitive force, strongly tinged with diplomatic and military considerations. Although the English arrived in Albany in 1664, the changeover from Dutch to English dominion enabled the French to make some inroad into the Iroquois communities through Jesuit missionaries. Some fur trade was also being diverted to Montreal.

The Iroquois, while not hostile to the English, were becoming more friendly with the French. Thus in each of the five nations of the Iroquois Confederation, particularly the Onondagas and Oneidas, there had evolved a pro-French faction. The Mohawks had remained the most friendly with the English, and when New York officials in 1676 urged the Iroquois to expel Jesuits from their settlements, their response was speedy, forcing the French clerics to abandon their missions and return to Canada. Through the years, as the British rather consistently faltered in their dealings of the Iroquois, the French party in each tribe grew in influence, and defections to the French cause increased.

In 1669 the Sulpicians founded a missionary settlement, St. Francis (Caughnawaga) for the Iroquois on the south bank of the St. Lawrence across from Montreal. Oneidas and Onondagas were the most numerous there, but the other Iroquois Confederation tribes were represented. By 1700 Caughnawaga had an Iroquois population of over 350 warriors and their families.

Indian Relations

The royal grants bestowed upon Mid-Atlantic proprietors the authority to rule the land as well as the peoples of their constituencies. Officials in the Mid-Atlantic area were not as intensively committed to make Indians subject to English law and courts as were those in New England.

In Pennsylvania the Quakers dealt with Indians kindly and fairly, their relations based upon Penn's treaty with the Delawares in 1682. Their laws protected Indians in their persons, property, and land from avaricious settlers. In 1726 the Society of Friends lost control of the Pennsylvania legislature, and the colony's era of unusual peace and goodwill with Native Americans, during which the Pennsylvania frontier had been largely free of major Indian raids except those carried out by the Iroquois on other Indians, came to an end. An indication of drastic change in treatment of Indians residing in Pennsylvania colony was adoption by the colonial government of a bounty law offering $130 for an adult male Indian scalp and $50 for an adult female scalp. Eight years later Pennsylvania colonial officials amended the scalp bounty law to apply to enemy Indians over 10 years of age.

In New York colony there were two different Indian groups: pitiable tribal remnants residing near the lower river settlements and on Long Island, and the proud and powerful Iroquois Confederation tribes on the western frontier. New York colonial officials fashioned policy for these two Indian communities. They governed lower river tribal remnants through a five-member Commission for Indian Affairs. The Duke's Laws forbade sale of guns, ammunition, and horses to these Indians, but in spite of this ban they had obtained firearms which they used for hunting. The colonial militia disarmed them during King Philip's War.

An entirely different policy was adopted toward the Iroquois Confederation tribes. In 1664 Iroquois leaders concluded a treaty with the English which continued the relationship which they had maintained with the Dutch, largely that of commercial benefactor. The British, however, claimed sovereignty over the territory and people of this portion of New York and presumed to bring the Iroquois under their jurisdiction. The Iroquois were generally contemptuous of this British assertion of sovereignty and refused to consider themselves Brtish subjects; rather they regarded themselves as citizens of an independent nation cooperating with the British. Occasionally British officials levied fines on Iroquois hunters for destroying property and livestock belonging to settlers. When the Iroquois submitted and paid the fines, they did so, they stated, because such action was compatible with tribal sense of justice and individual responsibilty and not because they had submitted to British law.

At Albany a second Commission for Indian Affairs supervised the colony's relations with the tribes there. The royal governor of New York delegated to these magistrates authority to regulate the western fur trade. They also supervised political and diplomatic relations with the western tribes. As conflict with the French intensified, political and diplomatic relations with the western Indians, centering on the Iroquois, became increasingly crucial to British tenure in this region. Thus the commissioners at Albany regularly sent envoys to the Oneida, Seneca, Onondaga, and Cayuga villages, and at Albany they held frequent grand councils with great ceremonial display and pageantry. Iroquois chiefs and head warriors resplendent in tribal attire and British colonials in dress uniform performed the respected protocol including exchange of gifts, an ancient custom among the Indians. Their gift to a single official might consist of packs of pelts worth in excess of 100 pounds, and the prudent recipient responded with lavish rejoinder.

French agents and missionaries from Montreal conspired with the displaced, scattered tribal remnants in New York and New England, casualties of settler expansion, inviting them to resettle on protected preserves in Canada. Around 1700 the New York colonial governor attempted to counter these appeals by setting aside several large tracts along the upper Hudson, withdrawing them from settlement, and urging these tribal remnants to settle there. Thus began the reservation system in the Mid-Atlantic region.

SOUTHERN COLONIAL INDIAN POLICY

British presence was established in the Southern colonies in 1607 with the founding of Jamestown in Virginia. Early settlers at Jamestown came to rely upon agriculture, largely the production and export of tobacco; only later did they place any appreciable reliance upon the fur trade. The expansion of agricultural settlement from the coast toward the interior applied constant pressure on the local Indian tribes, resulting in their displacement and, eventually, their virtual extermination. North Carolina and South Carolina were founded as proprietary colonies, less dependent upon agriculture and more upon frontier trade. Charleston became the great fur entrepôt for the South, its traders venturing over the vast interior to the Chickasaw towns near the Mississippi River. Thus, excluding Virginia, in the early South the trader more than the agrarian settler maintained contact with the Indian tribes, corrupted them and, in several instances, destroyed them. Georgia was founded in 1733 between South Carolina and Spanish Florida, where James Oglethorpe brought his colonists after negotiating with resident Creek Indians for the right to settle on a narrow strip of land around the mouth of the Savannah River. From this base trading and farming settlements expanded west across lands claimed by Creeks and Cherokees.

Indians of the Southern Colonial Region

An ethnic mix—Algonkians, Siouians, and Muskhogeans—occupied the lands eventually embraced by the Southern colonies. Coastal Virginia was the homeland of several Algonkian bands. At the time of English settlement the Pamunkey band, headed by Powhatan, was in the process of uniting some thirty other Algonkian bands into a confederacy. The English arrival had a propitious beginning. Few in number and completely unaccustomed to New-World living, the settlers were surprisingly well received by Powhatan who apparently planned to use them in his scheme to complete his confederacy. On Virginia's western margins roamed the Susquehannas, Shawnees, and Tuscaroras. Southward on the Carolina coast as far as Georgia were Catawbas, Yamasees, and Creeks. In the Carolina and Georgia backcountry were the populous and powerful Cherokees and additional Creek settlements. Eventually British trade tentacles and political power extended into the lower Mississippi Valley to embrace the Chickasaws and, to a limited degree, the Choctaws.

The Virginia Anomaly

The emphasis of most early Virginians on tobacco culture made that colony's Indian relationship different from that developing in the Carolinas and Georgia between traders and Indians. Virginia was a charter colony with a grant of land extending from the James River estuary inland, the charter amended to include a strip reaching to the "western sea," and a trans-Appalachian domain to the northwest along the Ohio River. Virginia Company officials admonished their colonists that, if they found it expedient to do

Early English sketch of Secoton, a Native American settlement on the Virginia coast near Roanoke Island. (The British Museum)

so, they were to recognize Indian title to the land and negotiate for the right to occupy new territory, and to do their utmost not to offend the Indians.

When Virginia Company settlers put ashore momentarily at Cape Henry, Indians of the Chesapeake tribe attacked them. It has been suggested that these Indians feared that the Europeans blamed them for the disappearance of the Raleigh colony, founded in 1585 on nearby Roanoke Island, and had come to punish them.

In contrast, at Jamestown Powhatan and his Pamunkey followers welcomed the colonists and punished the Chesapeake Indians for their unprovoked sally against the Englishmen. Powhatan's warm treatment of the

Matoaks als Rebecka daughter to the mighty Prince Powhatan Emperour of Attanoughkomouck als Virginia converted and baptized in the Chriftian faith, and Wife to the wor.ll M.r Tho: Rolff.

Pocahontas. (National Portrait Gallery, Smithsonian Institution, Washington, D.C.)

colonists lends credence to the view that he planned to use the Europeans and their awesome weapons in his drive to form the Algonkian confederacy.

During the first difficult year, Powhatan's Pamunkeys supplied food to the suffering colonists at Jamestown. Thereafter, however, the colonists attempted to make their Indian benefactors submit to Virginia Company rule and render an annual tribute. John Smith, a strong-willed colonial spokesman, was the principal advocate of this policy for which he nearly paid with his life. Smith enraged and insulted the Indians with his arrogant stance. Increasingly strained relations between the settlers and the Indians were eased in 1614 when Powhatan's favorite daughter Pocahontas married John Rolfe. Their union symbolized a bond between Indians and Englishmen, and it increased Powhatan's influence among the confederation tribes; this marriage indicated acceptance by Europeans of the chief's family as equals. Also it marked the beginning of an era of peace between colonists and Indians.

After Powhatan died in 1618, his brother Opechancanough became the confederation leader, and Indian-colonial relations deteriorated. English tobacco plantations increasingly encroached upon territory used by Indians for hunting and gathering. Recently arrived Anglican missionaries, who were attempting to convert and civilize the Indians, were particularly eager to enroll Indian children in their schools; Indian parents strongly objected.

In 1622 the confederation tribes lashed out against the settlers killing 350 Englishmen, about one third of the European population in the colony. The colonials fought back with a determined campaign which scattered the confederation tribes, destroyed granaries and settlements, and exterminated several of the smaller bands.

The colonists justified their retaliation by reiterating the natives' refusal to accept Christianity and European civilization. They conveniently concluded that their Indian neighbors were committed in their heathenism, were hopeless of redemption, and were thus an obstacle to the advance of superior European Christian civilization. The sooner they were destroyed the better, and harassment and extermination became a conscious policy of the colony. Virginia militia regularly marched through tribal settlements, killing Indians, seizing property, and destroying crops.

Colonial demands had become so oppressive by 1644 that the confederation Indians again made war on the Virginians. Opechancanough, now old and feeble, was carried on a litter to the scene of battle. A larger, better-armed English population made the Indians' chances for success remote and their conduct was marked by a grim fatalism and futility. However, the Indians preferred "a quick and honorable death to the indignities of living in subjection of the whites."[10]

The 1644 war was a bloody, destructive conflict for both settlers and Indians. Outraged Indians killed over 500 settlers while retaliatory militia compaigns killed at least twice that number of Indians. During 1646 colonial officials and Powhatan confederacy leaders negotiated a treaty which concluded hostilities. The treaty established a boundary separating tribal and colonial lands and pledged that Indians would be protected in the tenure of their lands. Thus began the reservation system in the South. The pact placed the surviving confederacy Indians under colonial law, their rights to be protected by Virginia courts. They were required to serve the colonial militia as scouts and auxilary troops. As a token of their submission to English rule, the vanquished Indians were to render an annual tribute of beaver skins to colonial officials.

The final Indian war in Virginia involving Powhatan confederacy tribes occurred in 1676. Pioneers from the Virginia and Maryland frontier waged a retaliatory war against the Susquehannas and then turned their wrath on other tribes closeby, including remnants of the Powhatan confederacy who, having fought with colonists against other Indians, now lived on the reservation assigned them by the treaty of 1646. Colonial successes in this frontier war opened the Virginia Piedmont to settlers.

Remnants of the Tidewater and Piedmont tribes roamed the Virginia frontier, beyond the settlement line, until 1715. In that year the colonial governor collected them, consolidated them into the so-called Monacan and Nottaway tribes, and settled them on a reservation at Fort Christina in southwestern Virginia near the Carolina border.

Indians and the Southern Seaboard Colonies

The Carolinas, founded in 1670, and Georgia, founded in 1733, were latter-day colonial establishments. Each colony saw some agricultural development, but the region's earliest economic emphasis was on trade in deer skins—leather—for which there was a sustained demand in British markets, and Indian slaves, most of them sold to Caribbean planters.

Charleston, founded in 1670 when 150 colonists from England and Barbados established a settlement at the mouth of the Ashley River, became the center for Southern colonial commerce. Traders furnished guns to coastal Indian hunters, most of them Yamasees, and sent them into the western wilderness to kill deer and to capture other Indians for sale in the Charleston slave market.

Bands of Yamasee hunters, led by Charleston traders, raided Tuscarora, Creek, and Cherokee settlements for slaves. After a few Cherokees had been captured and taken to Charleston, Cherokee leaders demanded that the captives be returned or they would obliterate the Carolina settlements. Thereupon Charleston traders enlisted Cherokees to strike the Euchees and other western tribes for slaves. Carolina traders and their aboriginal slave-hunting bands also preyed on Spanish mission settlements in Florida, capturing Timuca, Apalachee, and Guale Indians and carrying them off for sale in the Charleston slave market. The Florida Indians were defenseless because the Spanish refused to supply them with guns. One English-Yamasee raid in 1704 destroyed 13 missions, killed several hundred Spaniards and Indians, and netted 325 men, women, and children slaves. Traders even seized Indian wives and children to satisfy the debts of their husbands and fathers and sold them to slave dealers.

In 1712 a male Indian slave sold for about 20 pounds, a black slave brought twice that amount because it was claimed that he was more easily managed. And there was the ever present threat that the Indian slave would flee to the wilderness, an act which the African bondsman rarely committed. Not all Indian captives were sent off to Caribbean plantations. Some were kept on the mainland to labor for Carolinians. The colony of South Carolina in 1708 recorded 1,400 Indian slaves, about half the number of black slaves. A Carolinian justified the Indian slave trade on the grounds that "it both serves to lessen their number before the French can arm them and it is a more Effectuall way of Civilizing and Instructing."[11]

As the Carolinians extended their trade territory beyond the Appalachians, they concentrated more on the hide and pelt traffic and less on slaves. Leading columns of Indian bearers, each laden with a heavy pack of goods, the Southern colonial traders penetrated the interior via the Savannah River, thence over trader paths through the Creek nation. Eventually they reached the lower Mississippi Valley to trade with the Choctaws and Chickasaws. The Carolina trade connection with the Chickasaw nation brought strategic diplomatic and military advantages to the Britons in their struggle with the French for supremacy in North America.

Indian Insurgency

Frontier traders were scoundrels of the first order. However, colonial Carolinians seemed particularly depraved, surpassing all wilderness merchants except perhaps the Russian *promyshlenniki* for vicious exploitation, sharp practice, malicious cheating, and consistently callous treatment of Native Americans. Two tribes, the Tuscaroras and the Yamasees, in particular were treated so badly by Charleston-based traders that they rose in revolt and nearly annihilated the Carolina settlements.

In 1711 the Tuscaroras reacted with explosive fury against Carolinian traders for fraudulent trading practices and cruel slave raids on their towns and against settlers for peremptorily seizing their best tribal lands. For nearly two years colonists reeled from the forays. Finally, a colonial militia army, braced by a large force of Yamasee warriors, got the upper hand in 1713, devasted the Tuscarora country, killing many Indian insurgents and taking 400 prisoners. The survivors fled north to join their cultural kinsmen, the tribes of the Iroquois Confederation.

Two years later the Yamasees rose up against the Carolinians. The Yamasees lived closest to the English settlements, their warriors the most consistent supporters of the colonial interest, laboring for traders and providing fighting men to support English troops during the recently concluded Tuscarora War. Their support had been essential for the English victory. The Yamasees were resentful of their treatment by the British; the cumulative abuse, gross exploitation, and overall callous treatment inflicted upon them by colonial traders and settlers. English settlers took their best lands, and traders corrupted their honor, destroyed their physical vigor, made cripples of them while still young men, and violated their households.

Charleston traders engaged the Yamasee men as burden bearers, requiring them to carry seventy-pound packs for 300 to 500 miles, threading the highland paths into the western wilderness to trade with the Chickasaws and other lower Mississippi Valley tribes. For this wearing labor they were paid a mere pittance. And while the Yamasee men were absent on these commercial expeditions, traders bragged that they seduced their wives and daughters. Traders also addicted the Indians to rum and progressively debauched them, extending generous credit and permitting them to build up a debt which no burdener or hunter could ever hope to repay. Then the traders seized Indian wives and children and sold them in the Charleston slave market to settle these debts.

The insults, cheating, grossest of exploitation, debt, and seizure of wives and children fed a cumulative rage which erupted in 1715 in the Yamasee War. Catawbas and other neighboring tribes, similarly exploited and ill-used by the Carolina traders, joined the Yamasee revolt. The Yamasee War nearly destroyed the colony of South Carolina. Indian insurgents, to erase their debts in one bloody coup, attempted to assassinate the total trader community, and succeeded in slaying three fourths of them. They also fell upon the colonists in outlying settlements, killing 200 and driving hundreds of women and children into Charleston for safety.

Colonial officials charged that the Yamasees were in conspiracy with the Spaniards, and they put down the uprising with little quarter given, nearly exterminating these tribes and their allies. A census taken in 1761 revealed that only 20 Yamasees survived out of a population that in early colonial times numbered perhaps 5,000. The Catawbas, never numerous, were so battered that after the conflict they numbered less than 100 and were confined to a small reservation in the northern portion of South Carolina. The Tuscarora War and the Yamasee War cleared the Carolina frontier east of the Appalachians to white settlement.

Colonial Indian Policy

Carolinian Indian policy, permissive and opportunistic, dominated the territory south of Virginia. In Georgia a more humane Indian treatment system prevailed, but Georgia was founded so late in the colonial period that Charleston-based traders had already inflicted considerable damage upon resident native peoples, debauching them with rum and terrorizing them with slave-catching sorties. Carolinian policy was formulated by the proprietors. In 1670 they formed a managerial body of seven, including the governor, to adopt rules for the frontier trade and to deal with conflicts between colonists and Indians. Their rules included the requirement that each colonial trader obtain a permit or license to engage in the deer-skin trade and to catch and sell Indian slaves. The commissioners were to prevent Carolinians from enslaving and transporting certain friendly Indians. Carolina officials used treaties in dealing with the more powerful western tribes. Thus in 1693 they concluded a treaty of amity with the Cherokees. After 1680 the commission adopted rules that placed Indian nations under their direct protection and forbade the enslavement of any Indians living within 400 miles of Charleston. Also they banned use of rum in the Indian trade. Traders ignored or evaded both rules with impunity.

In the latter part of the seventeenth century, as their settlements approached the Piedmont, Virginians became interested in the trans-Appalachian frontier and wilderness commerce. Carolina traders demanded that their colonial government exclude Virginians from the western trade. In 1707 officials at Charleston adopted such a rule. Thereupon Carolinian military patrols intercepted Virginia traders, arrested them, and confiscated their goods. The Virginia colonial government protested these actions to the British government in London, and the privy council ruled that the Indian trade was "free and open" to all British subjects.

In 1707 the Carolinian Indian policy was extended and refined. It increased official surveillance over the licensed traders, again prohibited the sale of rum, and forbade traffic in free Indians, that is, those the Carolinians were obligated by treaty not to enslave. The rules provided for appointment of an agent who was to live in the Indian nations at least 10 months of each year. He was delegated broad powers to regulate trade and settle disputes between traders and Indians. As the Carolina settlements extended westward and the resident Indian tribes decreased in population from disease, debauchery, warfare, or migration, colonial officials resettled several surviving remnants on small reservations in the colony's backcountry.

Missions

Except for an initial burst of evangelical attention, there was little interest in converting southern Indians to Christianity. The charter for the Virginia Company stated that one of the objects of planting a colony in the New World was to bring civil order and the Christian religion to the heathen. James I, who issued the charter, pressed for an extension of Christianity among the Indians. And Virginia Company officials in London directed the colonial governor to take Indian children from their families, by force if necessary, and place them in a Christian setting. In 1619 fifty Anglican missionaries arrived in Virginia, and the council of Jamestown appropriated funds to educate Indian children in Christian living, mental improvement, and training for a vocation which became the triad goals of Indian education into the middle of the twentieth century. The superintendent for one of the Indian schools enthusiastically reported on the eve of the bloody war of 1622 that the "heathen children" were making "much progress in godliness." Several Indian youths were taken to England for further education.

However, Powhatan confederacy tribes did not convert easily. They were extremely reluctant subjects, demonstrating a strong devotion to their own religion. Indian parents were understandably opposed to missionaries taking their children and placing them in the homes of colonists to bask in Christian example and influence. Most Indians spurned Christian teachings; they tried the patience of missionaries.

The bloody war of 1622 was precipitated in part by missionaries antagonizing Indian parents over the transfer of their children to foster parents in colonial homes. For some time following the war Christian education was restricted to young Indian captives. As late as 1700 some Virginians were showing occasional interest in civilizing and converting Indians, particularly the youth. The College of William and Mary, founded in 1691, had a few Indian students.

During the pre-Anglo-American dominion period, the Moravians probably accomplished the most permanent results through their dedicated ministry to southern Indians. By the 1750s missionaries from this sect were active among Indians on the frontiers of North and South Carolina and Georgia. Also early in the eighteenth century, the Society for the Propagation of the Gospel in Foreign Parts did some work among the southern Indians, but lost interest in this field after 1754. The Society in Scotland for Propagating Christian Knowledge, largely Presbyterian, and the Company for the Propagation of the Gospel in New England and Parts Adjacent in America, headquartered in London and managed by Anglicans, in 1757 became interested in working among the Cherokees and their neighbors and agreed to support the work of two missionaries. The missionary branch in Virginia selected John Martin, a Presbyterian minister, as missionary to the Cherokees. He became the first British missionary to work among the Indians of the southern trans-Appalachian region. William Richards was appointed to assist Martin. In 1763 John D. Hammerer, a Lutheran missionary from Germany, arrived in North America and began work among the Creeks and Cherokees.

Beginning around 1500 the Indians progressively became subjects and their lands the colonial territories of Spain, France, Great Britain, Holland, and Russia. Each nation tried to transform Native Americans into submissive subjects by having them adopt European culture in place of their own. Tribes on North America's periphery, of course, felt these changes most strongly. But European influences, largely through trade, also filtered to the Indian tribes of the continental interior, but most of them escaped the drastic cultural alternatives inflicted upon the more exposed tribes. Thus it was left to a new nation, the United States, to absorb the continental interior, extend dominion over the resident tribes, and apply the transformation processes to them.

Notes

1. Harold E. Fey and D'Arcy Mc-Nickle, *Indians and Other Americans: Two Ways of Life Meet* (New York, 1970), p. 51.
2. Dwight W. Hoover, *The Red and the Black* (Chicago, 1976), p. 37; and Robert F. Spencer and Jesse D. Jennings, *The Native Americans* (New York, 1965), p. 496.
3. Alden T. Vaughan, "Pequots and Puritans: The Causes of the War of 1637," in *The American Indian: Past and Present,* edited by Roger L. Nichols and George R. Adams (Lexington, Mass., 1971), pp. 61–73.
4. Hoover, *Red and the Black*, p. 38.
5. Fey and McNickle, *Indians and Other Americans*, p. 51.

6. D'Arcy McNickle, *Native American Tribalism: Indian Survivals and Renewals* (New York, 1973), p. 32.
7. *Ibid.*
8. Hoover, *Red and the Black*, p. 21.
9. "English Influence," in *Handbook of American Indians North of Mexico,* edited by Frederick W. Hodge (Washington, D. C., 1907), Vol. I, p. 433.
10. Nancy O. Lurie, "Indian Cultural Adjustment to European Civilization," in *Seventeenth Century America,* edited by James M. Smith (Chapel Hill, N.C., 1959), pp. 53–54.
11. Charles Hudson, *The Southeastern Indians* (Knoxville, Tenn., 1976), p. 438.

Selected Sources

The chronicles depicting founding of the British colonial establishment in North America are substantially accounts of English relations with Native Americans. General studies of this ethnic interaction include A. L. Rowse, *The Elizabethans and America* (New York, 1959); Daniel J. Boorstein, *The Americans: The Colonial Experience* (New York, 1958); Charles M. Andrews, *The Colonial Period of American History* (New Haven, Conn., 1934–1937), 3 vols; and Wilbur R. Jacobs, "British-Colonial Attitudes and Policies Toward the Indian in the American Colonies," in *Attitudes of Colonial Powers Toward the American Indian*, edited by Howard Peckham and Charles Gibson (Salt Lake City, Utah, 1969).

Regional studies containing information on the impact of English colonial formation and expansion upon the Native Americans are abundant. Some of the more illuminating writings on Indian-English relations in New England include Alden T. Vaughan, *New England Frontier: Puritans and Indians, 1620–1675* (Boston, 1965); Douglas E. Leach, *Flintlock and Tomahawk: New England in King Philip's War* (New York, 1958); and by the same author, *The Northern Colonial Frontier, 1607–1763* (New York, 1966); Francis X. Maloney, *The Fur Trade in New England, 1620–1676* (Cambridge, Mass., 1931); Lloyd C. Hare, *Thomas Mayhew, Patriarch to the Indians* (New York, 1932); Charles M. Lincoln (ed.), *Narratives of the Indian Wars, 1675–1699* (New York, 1913); Howard Bradstreet, *The Story of the War with the Pequots, ReTold* (New Haven, Conn., 1933); Perry Miller, *Roger Williams: His Contributions to the American Tradition* (New York, 1962); and by the same author, *Errand into the Wilderness* (Cambridge, Mass., 1956).

Mid-Atlantic colonial-Indian relations are the subject of Allen W. Trelease, *Indian Affairs in Colonial New York: The Seventeenth Century* (Port Washington, N.Y., 1966); John R. Brodhead, *History of the State of New York* (New York, 1853), Volume I; George T. Hunt, *The Wars of the Iroquois: A Study in Intertribal Trade Relations* (Madison, Wisc., 1940); F. C. Wallace Anthony, *King of the Delawares: Teedyuscung, 1700–1763* (Philadelphia, 1949); T. Wood Clarke, *The Bloody Mohawk* (New York, 1940); Thomas J. Wertenbaker, *The Founding of American Civilization: The Middle Colonies* (New York, 1938); David M. Ellis, et al., *A Short History of New York State* (Ithaca, N.Y., 1957); Mathew P. Andrews, *The Founding of Maryland* (Baltimore, 1933); William Brewster, *The Pennsylvania and New York Frontier from 1720 to the Close of the Revolution* (Philadelphia, 1955); Edwin B. Bronner, *William Penn's 'Holy Experiment': The Founding of Pennsylvania, 1681–1701* (New York, 1962); and Wayland F. Dunway, *A History of Pennsylvania* (New York, 1948).

Southern colonial-Indian relations comprise interacting not only with the coastal tribes but, largely through South Carolina, involvement of the interior tribes (Cherokees, Creeks, Choctaws, and Chickasaws) as well. The basic study of Indian-settler relationships in early Virginia is Nancy O. Lurie, "Indian Cultural Adjustment to European Civilization," in *Seventeenth Century America*, edited by James M. Smith (Chapel Hill, N.C., 1959), pp. 33–60. General studies include Wesley F. Craven, *The Southern Colonies in the Seventeenth Century* (Baton Rouge, La., 1949); Lyman Carrier, *The Beginnings of American Agriculture* (New York, 1923); and Herbert L. Osgood, *The American Colonies in the Eighteenth Century* (New York, 1924–1925), 4 vols.

Studies of specific colonies in the Southern sector and their relations with Native Americans include Richard L. Morton, *Colonial Virginia* (Chapel Hill, N.C., 1960),

2 vols.; Archibald Henderson, *North Carolina* (Chicago, 1941); Robert L. Meriwether, *The Expansion of South Carolina, 1729–1765* (Kingsport, Tenn., 1941); and David D. Wallace, *The History of South Carolina* (New York, 1934), 2 vols.

The Southern Indians have received considerable literary attention; works which characterize their early relations with the British are David H. Corkran, *The Creek Frontier, 1540–1783* (Norman, Okla., 1967); by the same author, *The Cherokee Frontier: Conflict and Survival, 1740–62* (Norman, Okla., 1962); Verner W. Crane, *The Southern Frontier, 1670–1732* (Durham, N.C., 1928); Charles Hudson, *The Southeastern Indians* (Knoxville, Tenn., 1976); by the same author as editor, *Four Centuries of Southern Indians* (Athens, Ga., 1975); and John Phillip Reid, *A Better Kind of Hatchet: Law, Trade, and Diplomacy in the Cherokee Nation during the Early Years of European Contact* (University Park, Pa., 1976).

CHAPTER 10

INDIANS AND THE EUROPEAN IMPERIAL LEGACY

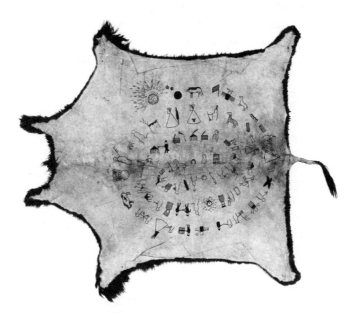

The white man . . . does not understand America. He is too far removed from its formative processes. The roots of the tree of his life have not yet grasped the rock and the soil. The white man is still troubled by primitive fears; he still has in his consciousness the perils of this frontier continent, some of its fastnesses not yet having yielded to his questing footsteps and inquiring eyes.

Luther Standing Bear's (Sioux) oration, 1896

In 1783 a new nation, the United States of America, emerged to claim dominion over great numbers of Native Americans and their vast territories and to become a serious competitor for hegemony in North America. The fact that a weak, struggling nation could survive, increase in power, and eventually displace other imperial powers is due in large measure to certain initial advantages which provided an ultimate crushing momentum. The new nation had inherited from several European proprietors a body of policies and methodology derived from two centuries of New World experience. Following three bloody, destructive wars, the recent and complete triumph of British arms over France had removed from the American scene the strongest and most menacing imperial competitor. These wars had progressively weakened France's ally, Spain, another formidable antagonist of the new American nation.

Perhaps most important of all, the Anglo-American nation survived because many powerful Indian tribes on its western frontier had been immensely weakened by two centuries of warfare with Europeans. It will be productive to take a look at the situation on the eve of American Independence and the cumulative effect of European influence on the tribes.

THE IMPERIAL WARS

Between 1689 and 1763 many Indian tribes were engaged by their European conquerors to fight four bloody wars (King William's War, 1689–1697; Queen Anne's War, 1702–1713; King George's War, 1739–1748; and the French and Indian or Seven Years' War, 1754–1763) as each of the imperial nations sought to expel its adversaries and to establish its colonial supremacy in

Chapter Opening Artifact: A Sioux painted buffalo robe showing the winter count or Calendar. (Courtesy Museum of the American Indian, Heye Foundation)

218

North America. In the first contest, Indians under Spanish dominion joined tribes allied with England to wage war on French Indian and colonial troops. In the three succeeding contests, British Indians, colonists, and some regular troops campaigned against French and Spanish Indian, colonial, and regular troops.

Indian Response to the Imperial Wars

Indian tribes were drawn into these four imperial wars because of self-interest, and they were also prodded to serve by officers who claimed that military duty was an obligation of subjects of the proprietary nation. Many Indians were lured into military service by bounties offered for enemy scalps or by the promise of regular pay, rations, blankets, and arms.

The first contest, King William's War, was fought largely in New England, northern New York, the St. Lawrence Valley, and lower Canada, and involved resident Indians and colonists. The war grew out of mounting French concern over increasing British trade advantages. The British were supplying better-quality goods than the French and were selling at lower prices. Indians who customarily supplied furs to French traders more and more were selling them to Iroquois traders from Albany. Likewise, there was a growing threat of Iroquois-British expansion into the trans-Appalachian country, territory claimed by France. Iroquois raiders and traders were the vanguard of this invasion. Thus it was clear to French colonial administrators that the Iroquois were absolutely essential to both English commercial and military success in the West. The Iroquois Confederation's strategic territory and military power protected English settlements in the lower Hudson Valley. Moreover, these tribes were the principal channel for the flow of furs from new areas in the West, so essential now that fur resources of northern New York and New England were largely exhausted.

France's strategy focused on eliminating this growing English threat to its western fur trade. The French plan was to concentrate on the Iroquois Confederation settlements, maintaining such a destructive military pressure that these tribes would shift their allegiance from the British to the French or, failing that, at least to force them to a pledge of neutrality.

French Indian and colonial troops raided some English settlements in New York and New England beginning in 1689, but they concentrated on Iroquois Confederation towns along the upper Mohawk Valley. Their strikes were answered by Indian and English armies from Albany or from New England posts marching against French installations in the St. Lawrence Valley. The severity and frequency of French attacks on the Iroquois Confederation settlements had a telling effect. One carried out in dead of winter of 1693 by French Indian and colonial troops on snowshoes caused widespread ruin and suffering. The invading host killed many persons, burned shelters, looted provision stores, and carried off many captives. A particularly destructive Indian-French raid in the Iroquois country during the summer of 1696 created great waste over the countryside with crops destroyed and many prisoners taken. Starving Indians dared not venture forth to tend crops or hunt for food, so complete was the Indian-French destruction of their territory. New York colonial officials rescued the Iroquois with supplies from Albany.

These tactics drove the Oneidas to seek peace with the French; the Onondagas, Senecas, and Cayugas wavered in their commitment to the English. And even the consistently dedicated Mohawks were broken and inclined toward peace with the French. Hostilities were concluded in 1697. French officials held several councils for the Iroquois in Montreal to which British colonial officials objected, charging that the Iroquois were their subjects and protocol required that the French apply through official English channels for permission to communicate with their Indian subjects. The Iroquois indignantly denied the British claim, pointing out that they were independent people, not subjects or children, but brothers, equal to Europeans and thus they would communicate and negotiate with whom they pleased. By 1700, following a series of councils with French officials at Montreal, the Iroquois leaders were swearing eternal friendship with the French, and they committed their nations to a stance of neutrality. French policy goals for the Iroquois had been achieved. Peace came to the Mohawk Valley.

The three succeeding imperial wars, concluded by the decisive British victory in the French and Indian War in 1763, spread across the British colonial area from Maine to Georgia and eventually into the Ohio and lower Mississippi valleys. Beginning in 1699 French colonial officials founded Biloxi and other settlements on the Gulf of Mexico. They hoped to link these vantage points with French Canada via the Great Lakes and the Ohio River Valley. With support from trans-Appalachian Indian tribes, pledged Iroquois neutrality, and assistance from Spaniards in Florida—a French ally after 1700— the French fashioned a menacing commercial-military pincers around the British seaboard beachhead.

King William's War involved French and British Indians and colonists in the New York, New England, and St. Lawrence Valley region of North America. The next conflict, Queen Anne's War (1702–1713), was waged on a broader geographical scale. It evolved from bitter French-British-Spanish rivalry in Europe, North America, and other regions of the world where these nations were striving for imperial supremacy. Local causes included French reaction to the threat of British commercial and territorial expansion in the trans-Appalachian West. In this contest Great Britain faced a most serious threat to colonial security, causing the British to marshal Indian-colonial military resources, both North and South, for defense against the French threat and for an attempt to break that nation's hold on the West.

In the North the Iroquois refused to take either side, maintaining a detached friendliness toward both France and Great Britain. Thus French Indians and colonists concentrated their raids on the region embraced by New Hampshire, Massachusetts, and Maine, inflicting on English settlements there an extended torment of desolated fields, stolen livestock, plundered and burned households, slain defenders, and women and children captives dragged off to Canada. No military action of consequence occurred in the Mohawk Valley. New York officials tried desperately to arouse the Iroquois to join British colonists in operations against Canada. As a final resort, Colonel Peter Schuyler, a prominent frontiersman respected by the Iroquois, took five Mohawk leaders to England. They were warmly received by Queen Anne. Court officials lavished praise and gifts upon the visitors, leading them to pledge to join in destroying the French in Canada. However, a subsequent invasion of the St. Lawrence Valley from New York miscarried, thus preserving the Iroquois pledge of neutrality.

In the South, French agents and traders from the Gulf Coast settlements sought to draw the Creeks, Cherokees, Choctaws, and Chickasaws into a military alliance against Great Britain. Cherokee leaders rejected the overtures, but Creek and Choctaw factions joined French colonists to ambush British traders moving over the paths between Charleston and the lower Mississippi Valley region. Great Britain's most important support in the Southern sector was the Chickasaw nation. From the beginning of French contact the Chickasaws had thwarted Gallic attempts to absorb them, like the Choctaws, into their colonial empire. British traders were welcomed in the Chickasaw nation and by 1700 were securely entrenched there. This provided Great Britain a strategic commercial-military enclave in the lower Mississippi Valley. Chickasaw fighting prowess, aided by arms from Charleston, erased the Choctaws and Creeks as threats to British security in the Southwest.

British and French representatives in Europe concluded Queen Anne's War in 1713. No antagonist had won a convincing victory over its adversary. Thus the peace was but a truce, a welcome respite from combat, enabling the principals to restore their spent vigor, refurbish their arsenals, and prepare for another round in the bloody struggle for dominion over North America.

King George's War (1739–1748) was another indecisive contest which produced no definitive result as to imperial supremacy in the New World but had dire effects upon those Native Americans drawn into its bloody vortex. In the war's prelude Iroquois leaders expressed uneasiness that even though they had maintained a neutral stance, more than likely French and Indian armies would eventually overrun their territory because it lay across the principal invasion routes to the British towns on the lower Hudson River. Therefore, they urged British colonial officials to build defensive posts in their country. The British responded in 1728 by constructing several fortifications including a stone-walled post at Oswego on the eastern shore of Lake Ontario. French colonial officials protested military construction charging that several of the new posts were on French territory. And they countered the British action by extending their military frontier south of Montreal in 1731, erecting Fort St. Frederick at Crown Point on the west side of Lake Champlain.

As Anglo-French relations deteriorated and resumption of hostilities loomed, British colonial officials repeatedly attempted to engage the Iroquois actively to defend the northern frontier of their North American empire, but these tribesmen were determined to maintain their neutrality. At the urging of the British Board of Trade, Colonial leaders in 1744 convened at Lancaster, Pennsylvania, in council with Iroquois leaders in a final effort to draw them from their neutral position. The Lancaster council produced little benefit for the cause of colonial defense because the Iroquois could not be dissuaded. Tribal spokesmen pointed to the folly of allying with the individualistic British colonies which were so completely committed to following an independent, disunited, destructive course against a foe which was unified in purpose. They observed that for nearly a century their warriors had defended New York from invasion; their British alliance had produced little but bitter suffering and progressive decimation of their fighting men and of the Confederation's military power.

When King George's War began, French Indian and colonial troops from the vantage of Fort St. Frederick maintained relentless pressure upon British interior settlements. During a three-month period in 1745 settlers on the Massachusetts-northern New York frontier endured 27 invasions. In one giant offensive the invaders captured, burned, and looted Saratoga, and carried off over 100 women and children captives to Canada.

Eventually a few Mohawks joined the British in military operations against the French, largely through the influence of William Johnson, an Irish trader and land speculator at Albany who, through his marriage to a Mohawk, could expect enduring support from his wife's family. Johnson mustered a force of Mohawks and colonial troops for a strike at Crown Point. The offensive faltered because of lack of coordination with other colonial columns and a political quarrel between the New York governor and legislature over frontier defense appropriations resulting in failure of the colonial legislature to appropriate funds for Johnson's campaign. Thereupon Johnson financed small, nuisance-type raids against French supply lines on the northern frontier from personal resources.

In the South during King George's War, Cherokees remained steadfast in their British alliance and warred on the French Choctaw and Creek factions. Westward in the lower Mississippi Valley the Chickasaws preyed on French river traffic, closing the Mississippi to French shipping and cutting communications between the French provinces of Canada and Louisiana for the duration of the war.

Hostilities abated in 1748, neither side gaining an impressive advantage, the peace again a respite to regroup for the final contest, the French and Indian War (1754–1763), which would determine imperial supremacy in North America. During the interlude both French and British interests rushed to establish positions of strength in the trans-Appalachian West.

The French were unified, single-mindedly committed to protecting their claim to the western territory for the fur trade. The British, as usual, were divided, not only in colonial goals and management, each of the thirteen colonies pursuing an independent and generally divisive course, but also in that they sought to serve incompatible interests—the fur trade community and the agricultural settler community, each demanding that its needs receive primary attention. In the great military contest that evolved between these titan powers, Indians from the seaboard settlements as well as those in the immediate interior and in the trans-Appalachian West became involved and suffered immensely in serving these competing powers.

During the 1740s British traders began to establish themselves in strength near the forks of the Ohio. George Croghan, a Pennsylvania trader, in 1741 took a pack train of goods from Harrisburg over the mountains and founded several Western trading stations, the principal one, which came to be called Logstown, 18 miles below the forks of the Ohio. Croghan's engagés, most of them Delaware and Shawnee Indians, ranged west to the Wabash River and northwest to Lake Erie's south shore. The quality of Croghan's goods, at prices lower than those charged by French traders, made him a favorite with Indian hunters and a serious threat to French traders. In 1748 Croghan negotiated with the Shawnees, Delawares, and Wyandots the Treaty of Logstown in which they pledged their allegiance to the British.

Speculators were close on Croghan's heels. Agricultural settlers had made a break into western Indian lands during the 1730s when British colonial officials began constructing fortifications in the Iroquois country, at the Iroquois' request, following Queen Anne's War. Soon the Iroquois Confederation tribes rued the day they had made the request because garrisoned posts in their country encouraged settlers from the lower Hudson River settlements and New England to take up land around the forts. The Indians got a foretaste of what to expect from British settlers, most of whom, after 1776, would become citizens of the new American nation. Already they were manifesting an expansionism and a voracious appetite for land, qualities which became the essence of the new American republic's national ethos and which would win for the country the nickname "Great Land Animal."

Prospering frontier settlements led British speculators to attempt to establish a forward colony on the Ohio River. The Iroquois had claimed this territory by right of conquest. By the Treaty of Lancaster (1744) they transferred their claim to the Ohio River Valley to Great Britain, and by the Treaty of Logstown (1748) the Shawnees, who held occupancy rights to the region, authorized the British to establish settlements there. British and colonial officials also justified their westward expansion by authority of land grants made by the crown to Virginia and other seaboard colonies which extended their territories beyond the Appalachian Mountains. During 1749 the British crown granted to the Ohio Company of Virginia, a group of British and colonial businessmen, a 200,000-acre tract in the Ohio River Valley. The company was required to fortify the tract and settle at least 200 families thereon within seven years.

French response to the British fur trader and settler expansion into the trans-Appalachian country was prompt and devastating. Colonial officials from Canada first reaffirmed alliances with the western Indian tribes, stressing the seriousness of the British threat to Indian interests. Their timing was opportune because the western tribes were already feeling the pressure of British settlement in some parts of their territories. The French had the advantage because they placed only subtle stress upon the tribes of this region and made few demands for land. Their colonial population numbered only about 80,000 persons, most of them thinly distributed over southern Canada, the Old Northwest, and the Mississippi Valley. On the other hand the British population was more than ten times that, and it was increasing dramatically, numbering well over 1 million in the first third of the eighteenth century, and exceeding 2 million by American Independence in 1776.

British speculation in frontier lands had become a public mania. Thus Indians justifiably were concerned over settler expansion on their lands, and their mounting apprehension caused many to shun the advantages of high-quality goods at lower prices provided by British traders in favor of the French who promised to protect their land tenure. Many tribal remnants in the path of British expansion in the trans-Appalachian West had only recently been forced beyond the mountains by the expansive seaboard settlements. The so-called Western Delawares were an example. They readily cast off the British trader benefits and became the strongest defenders of French interests around the forks of the Ohio.

Besides arousing the western tribes against the British, Frenchmen raided their scattered western trading stations. French frontier patrols of colonial rangers and parties of Ottawas and Delawares attacked and looted the stations, seized the furs, burned the stockades, executed the Indian engagés, and sent the divested traders into the forest without firearms or knives.

Another French mode of response to British intrusion was to reassert France's claim to the region. French officials traveled along the length of the Ohio River, stopping at the mouth of each tributary to bury lead plates containing declarations of Gallic ownership of all territory drained by these streams. The French also fortified the northern portions of the trans-Appalachian region. Canadian and Indian workmen built a line of posts from Lake Erie to the forks of the Ohio, including Fort Venango on the Allegheny River. In the spring of 1754 Virginia officials sent a work crew to the forks of the Ohio to construct a fort to guard the settlers expected momentarily. A French force arrived, drove off the workmen, destroyed their breastworks, and erected a more substantial post which they named Fort Duquesne.

The French and Indian War was triggered on July 3, 1754, when a militia force from Virginia approached the forks of the Ohio with orders to recover the strategic site. A large French colonial and Indian column intercepted the Virginians on the approaches of Fort Duquesne at Great Meadows, forcing them to capitulate and withdraw.

British colonial officials expected regular troops from England momentarily, but for the time being they planned military actions around colonial and Indian troops. They tried to engage the Iroquois Confederation tribes as well as remnants of Indian tribes from New England and from the lower Hudson River Valley in New York, Delaware bands still living close to the Pennsylvania settlements, and Cherokees and Chickasaws in the South to apply military pressure on French positions from Canada to the Gulf of Mexico. British strategy called for early strikes at three points: through the lower Mississippi Valley where, from their powerful position in the Chickasaw nation, warriors from that Indian community would close the Mississippi and cut off Louisiana and the Gulf of Mexico from the French Northwest and Canada; through the tongue of trade territory opened by Croghan in the upper Ohio River Valley; and via the St. Lawrence River Valley into New France's heart at Quebec and Montreal.

British colonial officials regarded the Iroquois as essential to the success of their operations in the North, but Confederation leaders announced their intention to stay aloof from the imperial conflict. The British government, eager to win the active support of these outstanding Indian warriors, prodded colonial officials to meet in council with Iroquois leaders to press them for a commitment for military support. In 1754 delegates from governments of seven colonies met with Iroquois Confederation leaders at Albany. The Albany Congress proceedings produced little benefit for British military goals. The Indian delegates, unmoved by British appeals, pointed to continuing colonial disunity and the likelihood that the British could hardly properly defend themselves, let alone their Indian allies. Iroquois leaders were also antagonized by speculators at the Albany Congress who kept pressing them to cede certain tribal lands while the very survival of the British empire in North America was in peril. Despite Iroquois disinterest William Johnson continued to urge them to support the British cause, and before the year was out Confederation leaders hesitantly agreed.

French colonial officials had the advantage of greater Indian military resources in the North and the promise of Creek and Choctaw and some Cherokee support in the South. Their northern Indian allies included the Chippewas, Ottawas, Miamis, Abenakis, Caughnawagas (Mission Iroquois), Wyandots, Shawnees, and Western Delawares.

Major campaigns by both British and French forces began in 1755. The Chickasaws successfully drove a wedge between Louisiana and Canada by gaining control of both banks of the Mississippi River at Chickasaw Bluffs (now Memphis). This victory severed the French western lifeline. Also they put heavy military pressure upon the French-allied Choctaws and Creeks.

On all other fronts, British fortunes went into a decline. Their attempt to conquer the country around the forks of the Ohio failed miserably. General Edward Braddock, British commander in North America, mustered a 2,000-man army of regulars and Virginia militia and marched up the Potomac River Valley to Fort Cumberland, thence down the Monongahela Valley toward Fort Duquesne. Woodsmen slashed a road through the dense forest to permit passage of Braddock's supply wagons and artillery. On July 9, 1755, French and Indian troops engaged Braddock's column ten miles from Fort Duquesne. The ensuing battle ended in heavy British casualties and a stunning defeat. General Braddock was among those slain, and only about 500 regular troops survived to beat the hasty retreat up the Monongahela to Fort Cumberland.

French and Indian troops maintained pressure on British positions from

Lake Champlain to western Lake Ontario. During the summer of 1756 the Marquis de Montcalm, commander of French forces in North America, took Fort Oswego with an Indian-colonial army. The fall of this strong point in the West had dire consequences for the British. Iroquois Confederation leaders, hestitant and uncomfortable in their renewed commitment to the British, rushed to Montreal to negotiate a peace pact with French officials. They excused their withdrawal from the British commitment by pointing to ineptness of British leadership and disunity among the colonies. Only the Mohawks remained firm in their commitment to the British. The Iroquois' return to neutrality opened much of the territory north and west of Albany to French Indian and colonial troops, whose brutal, devastating raids along the Mohawk Valley forced settlers to flee to Albany.

In the South, too, except for control of the lower Mississippi River by the Chickasaws and their sorties against pro-French Choctaws and Creeks, the British faced a grim future. The war effort in the South was weakened by independent military actions of Virginia and South Carolina and by the escalating colonial Indian trade rivalry. Charleston mercantile interests were alarmed that traders from Virginia, North Carolina, and Georgia threatened their monopoly of trade with the western tribes.

In many respects the conflict between Virginia and South Carolina over the trade with the western Indian tribes was as bitter as the broader contest with the French. The tribes were restive and divided because of the influence of the traders. Charleston traders and Cherokee hunters were locked in a heated dispute over the pricing of goods and deer skins. Cherokees were dependent upon traders for guns, powder, shot, textiles, and other essentials. To bring the Native Americans to terms the South Carolinians installed a trade embargo. The Cherokees responded by inviting Virginia and Georgia traders, even French traders, to their nation so that they might become independent of the Charleston traders. It also led the Cherokees, who had been steadfast in their loyalty to the British, to form a small but active French faction which regularly visited French officials at New Orleans.

The divided, uncoordinated purposes of the colonies led to additional confusion among the southern tribes. Each colonial government negotiated treaties with the Cherokees and other southern tribes, and confused and divided the Indians in their loyalties, less to Great Britain and more to this colony or that. Thus, while the governor of Virginia was meeting with certain Cherokee leaders seeking to persuade them to furnish fighting men to support British western operations, the governor of South Carolina was entertaining other Cherokee leaders to discuss the strengthening of South Carolina's defenses. A force of 600 Cherokee warriors did serve in the British army, defending the Virginia frontier and campaigning in the Ohio River Valley against the Shawnees and other French-allied tribes.

Out of the general chaos in the southern colonies during the French and Indian War the British cause enjoyed, besides the Chickasaw successes and Cherokee military assistance, singular support from the colony of Georgia.

This support was largely the result of the judicious leadership of Governor Henry Ellis in dealing with the western tribes. He used diplomacy and trade to draw many Creeks from their French alliance and from their attachment to Spaniards in neighboring Florida. Ellis vigilantly regulated trade to reduce abuses by traders and disputes with Indian hunters, and he provided prompt redress of injustices committed by British traders. Through his skillful and conciliatory administration of frontier affairs, he strengthened the British cause immensely in the Southwest, and Augusta, Georgia, became a thriving center for the Indian trade.

In the North French colonists and their Indian legions seemed invincible, able to sweep all before them in New England to the coast and in New York along the Hudson Valley, threatening Manhattan Island. The northern seaboard colonies were truly menaced. Then fortunes of war began to turn for the British during 1758. The most decisive British action was maintaining a tight blockade of French ports in North America, choking off the flow of vital guns, ammunition, and other military essentials for Indian troops and preventing landing of regular troop reenforcements from Europe. Gradually French Indian allies, with no means to continue the conflict, faded into the forests. General John B. Forbes led an army from the Pennsylvania settlements over a freshly cut road to Fort Duquesne. French colonial forces, greatly reduced by loss of essential Indian troops, evacuated the post ahead of the British advance. Forbes renamed the post Fort Pitt. Also in 1758 the British government sent Baron Jeffrey Amherst and General James Wolfe to North America to direct the growing Indian-colonial-regular army. The revitalized forces captured several French posts including Fort Frontenac, successes which caused many wavering Indian troops to return to the British ranks. Hostilities concluded in 1759–1760 with the British attack and capture of Quebec and Montreal.

By the terms of the Treaty of Paris, signed February 10, 1763, France ceded Canada, plus all territory, except New Orleans, in the trans-Appalachian region west to the Mississippi River, to Great Britain. Spain, which had belatedly entered the war as an ally of France, ceded Florida to the victorious Britons. Thereby Great Britain emerged the supreme imperial power in North America. The enlarged territory with increased numbers of Indians and harsh lessons of painful experience of 150 years of laissez-faire and disunited administration of Native Americans caused officials in the British government to move in the direction of centralized Indian policy. However, before Great Britain could formulate and apply this integrating policy, it had to cope with two costly Indian uprisings.

The Wars for Indian Independence

No sooner had Great Britain's colonial-Indian-regular armies triumphed over France and Spain and their Indian allies than the British were confronted with aboriginal insurgency in the Northwest and in the South. Fifteen years before the American War of Independence the Native American combatants were seeking independence. The Indian outbreak in the Old Northwest was the action of confederated tribes centering on the Ottawas. The Cherokees were the Southern insurgents.

Cherokee leaders had agreed to provide troops for service in the French and Indian War if the British would build and garrison posts in their country to protect their families from French and Creek raids while the warriors were absent. British engineers erected Fort Prince George (present mid-South Carolina) and Fort Loudoun (present eastern Tennessee) on Cherokee territory. Thereupon the Cherokee council mustered 600 warriors who marched north for service near the forks of the Ohio.

As in the case of fortifications in the Iroquois country, the Cherokees soon realized that they had erred. British administration of their internal affairs, hardly discernible before, noticeably tightened after the military stations were completed and garrisoned and this interference became a source of anxiety for Cherokee leaders. Trader abuses of Cherokee hunters continued to provoke strong resentment. And the expansion of settlement on the eastern margins of the Cherokee territory added to tribal grievances against the British.

A precipitating cause of the Cherokee war of independence was a massacre that occurred during 1760 in the mountains of western Virginia. A party of Cherokees who had completed their term of service in the British army were returning home. Virginia militiamen, hunting Indians to collect the bounty their colonial government paid for enemy scalps, ambushed the Cherokee party, killing forty warriors. Outraged Cherokees bloodied the western borders of Virginia and the Carolinas and forced evacuation of the frontier region. Tribal leaders stated that the purpose of their war on the British was to throw off imperial rule and recover their independence.

Baron Amherst, supreme commander of British forces in North America, sent Colonel Archibald Montgomery and 1,500 highlanders, who had just completed campaigns in western Pennsylvania, New York, and Canada, against the Cherokees. The Scots took a heavy toll among the Cherokees, but the Indians valiantly resisted the invasion of their country. Oconostota, a great Cherokee warrior, devised a retalitory strategy by Indian defenders which so battered Montgomery's column that the British were forced to evacuate.

Following the expulsion of Montgomery's army, the Cherokees applied a long and determined siege on Fort Loudoun. When the garrison faced death by starvation, the officers capitulated to Oconostota. Following the surrender, some soldiers were executed, but Oconostota protected most of the captives, intending to use them to remove the cannon from Fort Loudoun's battlements and drag the heavy guns over the mountains for use in the siege he intended to lay at Fort Prince George.

Meanwhile Cherokees as well as Virginians and Carolinians had wearied of war, and late in 1760 the principals struck a truce. Then during 1761 an army of 3,000—British light infantry, Royal Scots, Carolina rangers, and

Indian troops—returned to Cherokee territory to punish the insurgents. The invading host burned towns, destroyed corn fields, and forced the Cherokees into the highland forests. Their guerrilla strikes at the army's flanks and supply train punished the intruders, too. However, the Cherokees lacked adequate weaponry to continue an extended resistance struggle, and finally late in 1761 Cherokee leaders and British officials concluded a peace pact. By it the Cherokees pledged to submit to British dominion and to permit British troops to reoccupy the existing forts and to build new ones in the nation as required. Questions of justice were to be resolved by military officials at the posts and not by colonial politicians in Virginia, North Carolina, or South Carolina. And as reparations of war, the British took from the Indians a huge tract of their eastern territory for use by settlers.

Indian striving for freedom from British rule was equally intense among the tribes in the region west of Albany. Wars between the various empires had drastically reduced tribal populations; combat and war-induced conditions of tribal dislocation and suffering from hardship, starvation, and disease produced a one-fourth to one-half decline in the populations of the Wyandots, Ottawas, Miamis, and Shawnees.

Western Indians were apprehensive as tidings of the French capitulation reached them. Many were stunned and felt abandoned. Without the French they had no ally to help them resist the expanding British settlements. Some of the tribes had been French partisans for a century or more; they could not believe that their patron at Montreal had been conquered. French traders lurked about their villages fanning hopes that France would return and deliver Indians from their new British master and spreading rumors that the British planned to exterminate the Native Americans and take their lands for settlers moving westward from the seaboard.

Several tribal remnants including the Delawares had only recently migrated from the coast to escape the threat of total destruction. They were apprehensive that under British rule they faced a repetition of abuse from traders, the trespassing of white settlers on their lands, and appropriation of their recently established tribal territories.

Rumors of plans to exterminate Indians and appropriate their lands were based on disturbing events on the frontier. Surveyors appeared in the region. Settlers in their wake opened wilderness farmsteads. Extermination as British policy was confirmed in the orders of the supreme commander of British forces in North America, Baron Amherst. In his view the western tribes by their French alliance during the recent war had "misbehaved," and his duty was to punish them. Amherst directed staff officers to use large dogs and a primitive form of germ warfare on Indians. Officers at Fort Pitt took blankets from soldiers who had smallpox in the post hospital and distributed them among the Delawares. Soon a smallpox epidemic raged among frontier Indians.

The tribal leaders were enraged. Likewise they were embittered by intense prejudice that whites, particularly settlers, held toward Indians. The Paxton

Boys, vigilante renegades on the Pennsylvania frontier near present-day Harrisburg, were an especially violent example. A small group of surviving Susquehannas and other Indians had settled in a village in Lancaster County where the Paxton Boys found them and executed most of them, killing the rest, who had taken refuge in the Lancaster jail, shortly after. Benjamin Franklin called these miscreants "Christian white savages." The Paxton Boys also denounced Moravian missionaries who provided shelter and care for Indian refugees in Philadelphia. Paxton spokesmen delivered an angry "remonstrance" to Pennsylvania colonial officials denouncing the practice of protecting and "maintaining . . . at public expense his majesty's perfidious enemies."[1]

Discontent among Indians in the Old Northwest increased when they found that they could not obtain supplies, particularly powder and shot required for subsistence, on credit from the British posts as had been their practice during the French regime. Baron Amherst, as another means of punishing the western Indians for recently making war on the British, had directed that they be denied credit.

A message of hope for Indian regeneration came from a Delaware mystic who claimed that he had received a mandate from the Great Holy Force Above which directed him to reveal to all Indians the way to freedom from their torment. The primary requirement was that Native Americans shed European ways and things and recover the old way of life valued by their ancestors. Their reward for this restoration would be the miraculous disappearance of their British oppressors.

Pontiac, an Ottawa Indian who refused to abandon the hope that the French would return and assist in driving out the British, became leader of the discontented Indians. He appropriated the nativistic teachings of the Delaware prophet and fashioned a pan-Indian association committed to rebelling against British rule. Besides Ottawas, Pontiac's principal military support was drawn from the Potawatomis, Senecas, Wyandots, Delawares, Shawnees, Miamis, and Kickapoos.

In May 1763 Pontiac's warriors began their war for independence by attacking British positions from Fort Pitt and Detroit west to St. Joseph and Michilimackinac. He laid large-scale sieges to the British strong points at Detroit and Fort Pitt. The insurgents captured post after post in the West, destroying British garrisons at Sandusky, Presque Island, and Michilimackinac. At the Battle of Bloody Run on July 31, 1763, Pontiac's warriors defeated and inflicted heavy losses upon a large British force. Settlers on the frontiers of New York, Pennsylvania, Maryland, and Virginia fled to the safety of seaboard settlements. Over 2,000 troops and settlers were slain in this Indian war for independence.

The British reconquest, centering on two armies led by Colonel Henry Bouquet and Colonel John Bradstreet, began during the spring of 1764. Two years later Pontiac met with Sir William Johnson and negotiated a treaty providing for termination of resistance. Thereupon the British government pardoned Pontiac for leading the revolt. With peace in the transmontane territory British officials began the formulation of a policy for Native Americans and their lands which would serve the broader interests of the empire.

NATIONALIZED INDIAN POLICY

The chaotic state of British-Indian relations in the prelude to the French and Indian War and the near disaster this posed for the British establishment in North America led the home government in the 1760s to nationalize its Indian policy. The new practices would replace the particularistic, divisive, and destructive methods used by the colonies in dealing with the Indian tribes. Not only was this a drastic departure from the 150-year-old laissez-faire practice of permitting each colony to maintain its own Indian policy, but it also provided the foundation for policy adopted after 1776 by the new American nation. And the responses of British subjects in the North American colonies to these substantive Indian policy changes give a hint of what the attitudes of citizens of the new American union would be after 1776.

Origins of Integrated British Policy

Well before the British government enunciated its centralized Indian policy in 1763, several of the colonies had voluntarily associated to formulate a more effective way of dealing with the Indians. The Confederation of New England, founded in 1643, managed Indian affairs in the northern colonies for over forty years. During the 1680s the escalating French-Indian threat and the need for coordinated colonial diplomacy with the powerful Iroquois Confederation led the northern colonial officials, including those from New York, to replace the Confederation of New England with the Dominion of New England.

On several occasions before 1760 the British government demonstrated concern over intercolonial divisiveness in Indian relations, particularly relating to trade and tribal land acquisition, and the enervating effect this had upon the British effort to confront the threat of French and Spanish empires in North America. A royal commission in 1664 studied colonial-Indian relations and rendered a report highly critical of the colonies for harsh treatment of Native Americans. The Board of Trade, the British government agency responsible for colonial affairs, in 1721 recommended that a governor-general for the colonies with supreme authority in Indian and military affairs be appointed in order to achieve coordination of the colonial effort. While this plan was passed over, the crown did accomplish some coordination through royal governors who, as direct agents of the king, were expected to protect the empire's interest over local colonial interest. Increasingly the British government also took over the role of principal supplier of annual gifts to Native Americans. Colonial governors were responsible for distributing these royal gratuities to the annual councils with tribal leaders. Sadly there occurred widespread malfeasance by colonial officials in the discharge of this function, a sordid theme which runs through the chronicle of the American Indian into the twentieth century—those serving as trustees for Indian property consistently converting it to their own use.

Other examples of attempts by the British government to integrate Indian affairs included royal decrees issued regularly after 1720 to various colonial governors directing them to cooperate in regulating the Indian trade. Officials for the colonies of Virginia, North Carolina, New York, and Pennsylvania met at various times to discuss trade, frontier defense, and maintaining the Iroquois alliance. The Council of Lancaster (1744) and the Albany Congress (1754) were instances of British officials attempting to force colonial politicians to formulate a unified Indian policy in order to improve North American defenses against France and Spain and their Indian allies.

There were limited instances of voluntary cooperation by the colonies with the crown in the conduct of Indian affairs. Joint British-colonial efforts extended the military frontier into tribal domains, constructing and garrisoning forts, and administering the tribes from these posts. There was also occasional British-colonial cooperation in settling jurisdictional questions through treaties with the western tribes whereby Indian leaders were required to turn over Indians accused of killing British subjects. However, as a substitute for ultimate punishment for the crime, or as resolution of the offense, the Indian defendant could in most cases absolve his guilt by delivering a Frenchman or his scalp to British officials. In several instances British and colonial officials joined to designate a single ruler or head of state for the scattered towns of an Indian nation. Thus English puppet government in the Cherokee nation began in 1730 with the appointment of Motoy, of Great Tellico, as emperor of the Cherokees. This practice was important for administrative convenience and for symbolism in that it signified Cherokee subservience to the British crown. Colonial governors appointed local tribal leaders to the ranks of captain and ensign for service to the king. Each of these practices not only increased British efficiency in administration of Indian affairs, but also represented a progressive diminution of tribal self-determination and sovereignty.

British Indian Policy

The most comprehensive change in British policy toward the Indians began in 1755 with publication of the Atkin Report and Plan. Edmond Atkin, a businessman and member of the South Carolina colonial governor's council, prepared a design for improving Indian administration. He wrote,

The importance of Indians is now generally known and understood. A doubt remains, not, that the prosperity of our Colonies on the Continent, will stand or fall without interest and favor among them. While they are our friends they are the cheapest and strongest barrier for the Protection of our Settlements; when Enemies they are capable by ravaging in their method of war, in spite of all we can do, render these Possessions almost useless.

Cherokee visitors to London, 1762. The torsos of these Indians were copied from engravings of Mohawks who visited England in 1710, although the heads were probably Cherokee portraits. The Europeans tended to stereotype the American Indian in this way. (Smithsonian Institution, National Anthropological Archives)

Atkin pointed to France's growing power among the tribes and explained that French officials

had centralized control over trade and related activities, used men of training and experience at points of contact with the Indian people, and had singleness of purpose, which was to promote French interests. . . . The French have accordingly taught the Indians to consider our Colonies as so many separate communities, having no concern with each other. Whence it hath arisen that the Indians in Peace and Amity towards one of the colonies have at the same time behaved as enemies towards the people of another. Some of the Colonies have made no regulations at all in Indian affairs. . . . Seldom if at all have they sent proper persons to look into them. But the management of them hath often been left to Traders, who have no skill in Public Affairs, are directed only by their own Interests, and being generally the loosest kind of People are despised and held in great Contempt by the Indians as liars and persons regarding nothing but their own Gain.[2]

Atkin's recommendations for nationalizing Indian policy and placing it under the direction of the crown was followed to a degree. In 1755 the British government established the Indian superintendency system. Sir William Johnson was appointed superintendent for Indian affairs in the Northern Department which included the territory west of the Appalachians and north of the Ohio River. Atkin was appointed superintendent for the Southern Department, the territory west of the Appalachians and south of the Ohio River. In 1762 John Stuart replaced Atkin as southern superintendent. There was also an agent, called a commissary, who lived with a tribe. He represented the crown in that tribe and reported to the superintendent.

In 1763 the British government assumed exclusive jurisdiction over the tribes. Each tribe was considered an independent nation, its citizens subject to tribal law and exempt from British law. Thus assimilation was rejected. Official relationships between each tribe and the crown were defined by treaties, negotiated exclusively by royal representatives and tribal leaders. Power to regulate trade, settle tribal land questions, and other matters pertaining to Indians was stripped from the individual colonies, and the British government formulated a single royal Indian policy, enforced by crown-appointed agents and superintendents. The new policy included the reservation system in that it established a vast Indian Country between the Appalachian Mountains and the Mississippi River for the exclusive use of Indians. Resident Indian tribes were acknowledged owners of this land. A royal proclamation, issued in 1763, confirmed the grant and forbade settlement west of a line formed by the drainage divide of the Appalachians; all persons who had encroached beyond that boundary were to leave. Any future cession of Indian land had to be negotiated by representatives of the crown with tribal leaders. The Indian trade was to be regulated by a single code of rules enunciated by the crown. Only traders licensed by the commissary or superintendent and royal troops and officials were permitted to enter the Indian Country.

Before the British government could fulfill its policy for guarding Indians and their lands from its subjects, the thirteen American colonies revolted, seceded from the British empire, and established an independent nation, the United States. One cause of this American War for Independence was the attempt by the British government to take management of Indian affairs from the colonies and to check the assumed right of colonists to expand, unimpeded, into the Indian Country. Interestingly, the government formed by the seceding colonies soon adopted a nationalized Indian policy virtually identical to that which the British government belatedly had attempted to establish.

THE LEGACY OF THE EMPIRES

There were many similarities in treatment of Indians by Spain, France, Holland, Russia, and Great Britain, the differences being in degree of exploitation. The Indians' experience under these different nations had included depopulation, detribalization, and destruction of traditional cultures. In addition, shifting ruler nations produced differing policies and resulting confusion, uncertainty, and altered status. Such was the case in the Mid-Atlantic region when in 1664 England conquered New Netherland, as well as after 1763 for Indians under Spanish rule in Florida and under French rule in the trans-

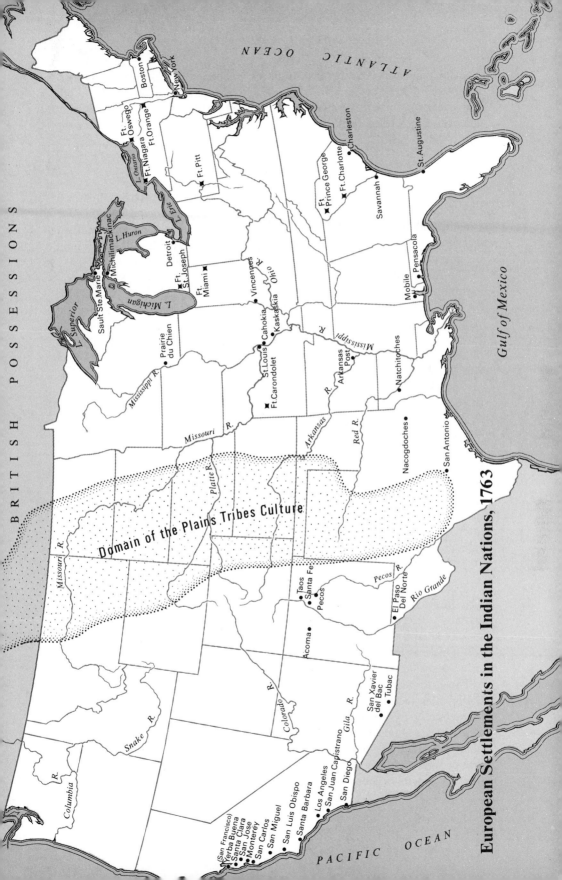

European Settlements in the Indian Nations, 1763

ATLANTIC OCEAN

Gulf of Mexico

PACIFIC OCEAN

BRITISH POSSESSIONS

Boston
New York
Oswego
Ft. Niagara
Ft. Orange
L. Ontario
Ft. Pitt
L. Erie
Prince George
Ft. Charlotte
Charleston
Savannah
St. Augustine
Pensacola
Mobile

L. Huron
L. Michigan
L. Superior
Sault Ste. Marie
Michilimackinac
Detroit
Ft. St. Joseph
Ft. Miami
Vincennes
Ohio R.
Kaskaskia
Cahokia
St. Louis
Prairie du Chien
Mississippi R.
Ft. Carondelet
Missouri R.
Arkansas Post
Mississippi R.
Natchitoches
Arkansas R.
Red R.
Nacogdoches
San Antonio

Domain of the Plains Tribes Culture

Missouri R.
Platte R.
Arkansas R.
Pecos R.
Taos
Santa Fe
Pecos
El Paso Del Norte
Rio Grande
Acoma
Colorado R.
Gila R.
San Xavier del Bac
Tubac
Snake R.
Columbia R.

San Luis Obispo
Santa Barbara
Los Angeles
San Juan Capistrano
San Diego
(San Francisco)
Yerba Buena
Santa Clara
San Jose
Monterey
San Carlos
San Miguel

Appalachian West. And the new American nation, in its swift territorial thrust westward to the Pacific, would soon absorb all British Indians in the West, and eventually native peoples ruled by Spain, Mexico, and Russia, further complicating life for resident Indians as they were forced to cope with the new order.

Indian Demography

Life as a subject of France, Spain, Holland, Russia, or Great Britain was a luxury Native Americans could ill afford. It brought them no recognizable benefit, and the cost in human life was excessively high. Because of their isolated existence in the Western Hemisphere, Native Americans had not built up any natural resistance to alien infections or epidemic diseases.

The Indian, despite a capability for near superhuman feats of strength and endurance, was extremely susceptible to many alien infections introduced by Europeans. True, service as combat soldiers in the armies of the ruling powers reduced Indian numbers. But military action probably accounted for no more than a 10 percent decline on average in Indian populations. Wars of conquest against certain tribes because they refused to submit to European rule led to the virtual elimination of certain groups including the Pequots at the hands of God-fearing Puritans in New England, and the Natchez at the hands of vengeance-driven French settlers in the lower Mississippi Valley.

However, diseases were the principal destroyers of aboriginal populations. Virtually every tribe which came into direct contact with Europeans suffered at least a one-fourth decline in population, several one-half or more. Smallpox, measles, scarlet fever, venereal infections, and, after 1840, cholera periodically raged in epidemic proportions. Alcohol (rum, brandy, and raw frontier whiskey), a prime trade item, was a destroyer of vitality and life of the first magnitude. And loss of traditional native life-styles and tribal estates, with attendant dislocation, poverty, and degradation increased aboriginal death-rates and further reduced tribal populations.

Native American Image and Status

The image a European power held of Native Americans determined the Indians' sociopolitical status under the various nations claiming dominion over them and their territory. The Indians' curiosity, hospitality, sharing, and willingness to assist the colonists soon changed to disillusionment and resentment, occasionally rising to intense hate and desire to destroy the intruders.

The European attitude toward Indians varied by nation and time. Under the Spanish most Indians were subjects of the crown and, although exploited unmercifully by Spanish colonists, from their status as subjects had limited rights and a legal, recognizable place in society. Under Russian administration, Native Americans occupied a position in the imperial caste system below that of serfs and, except for mestizos, were treated with great inhumanity by their Muscovite masters. Dutch law provided some protection for the Indians of New Netherland. Their status, from the Dutch viewpoint, was primarily that of colonial laborers serving the Dutch West India Company. Indian status under French colonial law was that of subjects and, except in the lower Mississippi Valley where agriculture was pursued and Indians suffered accordingly, Native Americans generally received better treatment than under any other colonial system. The fur trade was the foundation of France's prosperity in the New World, and Indian men as hunters and Indian women as processors of pelts, making them marketable, were for the most part valued and protected. Under British rule, the Indian image and hence status varied in place and time. And the British image was most important because, after 1776, for nearly 3 million subjects, it became the Anglo-American image.

Increasingly, Indians and colonists became alienated from each other. Rather than coexist with the Indians and assimilate them through civilization, Christianization, and intermarriage, a dual pattern of existence developed. Increasingly British Indian policy maintained two separate societies. This separation was dramatically confirmed in 1763 by the royal proclamation which established the vast western Indian reservation and segregated Indians from Englishmen, the Indians subject to tribal law, and Indian-British relations defined by treaties. All this was an acknowledgement of the failure of coexistence and assimilation.

Interracial Coupling and the Mestizo

The imperial legacy spawned no greater social problem than that of the mestizo, the offspring of the inevitable mingling of Native Americans and Europeans. The mestizo tragedy, a social stigma conjured by British colonial society, was carried across the continent by the succeeding Anglo-American nation. The mestizo's pejorative identity of "breed" or "halfbreed" was perhaps a covert manifestation of the social scorn directed at the interracial relationship which conceived him, but in any case "half-breed" was generally an incorrect reference because many so-called half-breeds were in fact more or less than half Indian. Thus "mixed blood" is a more precise and certainly less invidious usage.

In Spanish and French territories Indians and mestizos or mixed bloods were accepted and had a place in colonial society. The French practice of assigning identity, status, and social place to Indians and mixed bloods is explained, perhaps by oversimplification, in the easygoing Gallic nature which maintained no crippling inhibitions toward peoples of differing color and culture. Spaniards came to the New World after several centuries of contact and experience with peoples of differing color and culture—Moors and Jews— in their midst. Iberians, largely from the provinces of Castile and Aragon, led in conquering and assimilating large numbers of both ethnic groups. They continued this multiethnic approach in the New World conquest, mating with Indian women. Thus much of the population in Mexico and the southwestern United States, identified as Mexican or Spanish-American, is mestizo, a blend of Indian and Spaniard. By Spanish and later Mexican practice, Indians and mestizos had a place in society, which was denied them in the British and American legal and social contexts. Even the Russians, despite the *promyshlenniki's* harsh treatment of Native Americans, accorded mestizos a place in their colonial society and treated them well.

The Indian's and mestizo's status in British colonial society varied with time, place, and the group, especially since the British community embraced English, Irish, and Scots, and the social tastes of Irish and Scots might well, and probably did, differ in several regards from that of the English. However, the English view toward Indians, and mestizos in particular, hardened into bias which became the official position of the British government as manifested in the exclusionist Indian policy of the 1760s. And this official British position became the dominating prejudice of the new Anglo-American nation, coloring the attitudes of its citizens and guiding the direction of its Indian policy.

In the early colonial period, Native Americans and English settlers mingled freely, and it was expected that eventually Native Americans, culturally and biologically, would be assimilated into the English social stream. Some intermarriage took place, particularly in the South, the most celebrated nuptials occuring in 1614 when Pocahontas, daughter of Powhatan, head of the Indian state in whose territory Jamestown was founded, and John Rolfe were wed. At the time there was no conspicuous prejudice or scorn toward interracial marriage. Actually colonial officials in Virginia and the Carolinas publicly urged intermarriage of English persons and Indians, expecting the blending of the races to breed the "Indian problem" out of existence. However, no widespread intermarriage took place, not because of social or legal interdict, but probably because of the colonials' agricultural economy. Indian women were valuable companions in the forest as mates of hunters and traders, skilled in wilderness living and economically essential as processors of furs. However, colonial farmers judged women's marital qualifications less on their ability to live successfully in the forest and more on their competency for assisting with hard farm work. Thus a principal deterrent to interracial marriage was economic, not the social stigma of Indianness. Furthermore, many English settlers migrated to the New World as families.

The English came to hold ambivalent views toward Native Americans, particularly Indian women. In Europe they persevered in the romantic noble-savage image. They cherished the legend of Pocahontas, the Indian princess, and urged uniting of the races through marriage. The legend started with Captain John Smith's *General Historie* in which he reported that he was once surrounded by thirty naked young girls, whose bodies were painted different colors and decorated with a few feathers. They tormented him by performing a sensuous dance around the fire.

The myth of love in the woods . . . persisted, and the Indian princess became the European symbol for America. As portrayed in pictures, she was handsome, vigorous, naked to the waist, and armed with a bow and arrow. She was believed to be a descendant of the Indian Queen, who was the symbol for the Western hemisphere and who was depicted as an Amazon carrying a club with an arrow-pierced head of a man lying near her feet. The legends of the Indian Queen and Pocahontas demonstrate the fascination of the European with the physically attractive but savage women who could bridge the gap between red and white.[3]

Colonists in day-to-day relations with Native Americans progressively became less romantic in their attitude toward Indians. Escalating Indian insurgency and devastating colonial recrimination fed the image of bloodthirsty savages, intensified alienation of the races, and attached a social stigma to Indianness. Encouragement for interracial marriage and assimilation changed to demands for segregation and even extermination. And increasingly strict Protestant moral codes and an expanding sense of superiority of Englishmen toward Indians discouraged creation of a legitimate mestizo class in British colonial society. To the pejorative references "breed" or "halfbreed" was added "squaw," a derogatory allusion to the Indian woman. Colonists in their ignorance of Indian social ways or disregard of the privileged position occupied by women in most tribes put her down as an unattractive drudge, a marital slave. Many Englishmen secretly savored the Indian woman's mystique; publicly scorning her, they privately regarded her as an exotic creature, forbidden fruit; and surreptitiously they lay with her.

A phase of interracial relationships hardly touched upon at all except in terms of rape, torture, and general ill-treatment was that between Indian men and Englishwomen. The colonial era's sexist writings are nearly silent on the subject of colonial women being interested in or attracted to Indian men. Scattered legal references, discreetly composed and succinctly stated, can be found of New England women being arrested and punished for seducing Indian men serving as slaves in their households. William T. Hagan presents one of the rare literary allusions to this phenomenon in discussing Baron Amherst's condition of surrender for the insurgent Northwest tribes. Indian leaders were required to return all captives, a condition

striking at family ties. The tribesmen were most unwilling to surrender their captives. Many of them had been held for several years and had become adopted members of Indian families; a number of the women now had Indian children and were as reluctant to leave them as their husbands and adopted relatives were to see them go.[4]

The Scottish, Scotch-Irish, and Irish segments of the British population in the New World had fewer inhibitions, were more like Frenchmen and Spaniards in ethnic sensibilities, and mingled more freely with Native Americans. Sir William Johnson, an Irishman, married two Indian women, one of them Molly Brant, sister of Joseph Brant, the Mohawk patriot. In the Southwest, large numbers of Scottish traders lived among the Cherokees, Creeks, Choctaws, and Chickasaws. They took Indian wives, and in each tribe there grew a large community of mestizos with familiar family names like Rogers, Vann, Ross, Colbert, McGillivray, Grayson, Chisholm, Adair, McIntosh, and McCurtain. Denied a place in the expanding Anglo-American society because of the stigma of their Indianness, these mestizos turned their restless energies to becoming leaders of their host Indian nations in the troubled removal era.

State of Indian Life-style

The pervasive dissemination of European technology must rank with insensitive government policy and alien disease as prime destroyers of Indians and their cultures, their weakened state making Anglo-American expansion easier. Indians understandably were quickly drawn to trader goods. They had always relied on stone, wood, animal skin and hide, and bone for making shelter, clothing, tools, weapons, and other essentials. The only metal used by Native Americans in prehistory was sheet copper, and it was of limited consequence. European goods of metal, glass, and cloth were truly revolutionary innovations to Indians. They saw the technological advantage of European goods and quickly came to value and demand metal axes and hatchets to fell trees to construct shelters, boats, and other wooden items; steel knives as substitutes for flint chips and flakes to skin animals and do a host of other jobs; metal hoes to prepare gardens for sowing and to cultivate food crops; iron cooking pots to replace pottery vessels; fishhooks; firearms, in many cases superior to their own bows and arrows, lances, and darts, for hunting and warfare; and textiles, more adaptable for blankets and garments than animal skins and hides. Another commodity for which Indians quickly built up a taste, a compulsive craving in fact, was alcohol—rum, brandy, whiskey— which traders provided in prodigious quantities and which set in motion a chain of debauchery, degradation, and destruction.

Most of the trader-supplied goods quickly became essentials. Moreover, ownership was a status symbol within the tribe. As Indians became inextricably dependent upon traders for these items and would go to any length to accumulate trader goods, they began to neglect basic family, clan, and tribal duties. Each Indian man became a commercial hunter spending most of his time in the forest seeking fur-bearing animals. In a sense he became a competitor with fellow tribesmen. The old cooperativeness and open sharing, particularly with the aged, passed. He shunned ancient duties of instructing the young and transmitting tribal tradition. Increasingly he became detached from the old ways and responsibilities, less group-oriented and more individualistic. His wife (or wives) became a part of this new way of life, shifting from household, family, and garden responsibilities to the time-consuming processing of furs to trade for the sought-after merchandise. These pervasive, basic changes in culture eventually produced individual and group confusion, disorientation, and anxiety.

Increasingly detached from the old, Native Americans found themselves unable to cope with the new, in part because the ruling Europeans provided no real preparation for the Indians' transition from one life-style to another. Indian religion was strongly slanted toward regular individual observance of fasting, propitiation, and meditation. In the rush for furs Indians increasingly neglected these rites, adding to personal disorganization and increasing cynicism.

The furious quest for the means to obtain trader goods also disturbed the cohesiveness of family, clan, and tribe. In some cases these essential group units were destroyed by dislocations perpetrated by the trader. He customarily extended generous credit to a group of families. They became deeply in his debt, utterly dependent upon him. His power over them was his ever ready threat to withhold goods, including rum, if they failed to do his bidding. As saturation hunting destroyed fur-bearing resources of the tribe's traditional territory, the trader moved his debtor-wards to new hunting areas, separating them from clan and tribal life and from the essential individual and group renewal rituals.

Other bulwarks of Indian life-style, tribal sovereignty and self-government, were also casualties of European conquest and were part of the cumulative process of cultural decline. Policies of the European nations claiming dominion over New World peoples reduced tribal self-determination and power and in some cases eliminated them altogether. The pattern began with colonists extending benevolent protection to the tribe, declaring tribal members to be vassals or subjects of their sovereign. And under the claim of protecting the tribe, the colonial government progressively reduced the tribes' governmental functions and extended jurisdiction over tribal citizens and their territory. Finally colonial officials became directly involved in tribal governance, assuming functions and prerogatives of established tribal leaders, interfering with orderly functioning of the tribal government, consolidating ancient tribal divisions, replacing decentralized, particularistic town government patterns with integrated tribal units headed by a single ruler, called emperor or king, appointed by the colonial authorities.

Thus, European control erased Indian self-determination, and Indian dependence upon traders disturbed and at times destroyed their ancient self-sufficiency. In reverberating rings these changes corrupted the native life-style, led to neglect of essential family, clan, and tribal duties and observances, and caused pervasive personal and public disorientation and decay. If the Indian resisted the trader, saturation hunting over his range by other Indians and traders soon destroyed the wild creatures that had provided him food, shelter, and clothing. He and his tribe were reduced to a state of poverty not of his making.

The continuum of tribal tradition and pride, transmitted through a chain of many generations, had sustained Indianness. The sudden decline of many tribes, some in less than a century, can be accounted for in part by the fact that the adult generation, which should have been propagating and preserving age-old tribal values, became enraptured by European ways and things. They thus broke the chain, the continuum of ethnic tradition, and set in motion a progressive deterioration which made Native Americans easier marks for mounting imposition and exploitation which would be their lot under the rule of their next ruler, the United States.

Anomaly of the Plains Tribes

A striking exception to the general cultural decline among Indians following European contact was the response of the various groups who belatedly settled the Great Plains. This region's interior location, its awesome isolation,

A Plains tribe camp scene with a dog travois used to transport household goods in the foreground. (Smithsonian Institution, National Anthropological Archives)

and its lack of trees, made it less attractive for European exploitation than North America's more accessible regions. Thus European explorers, traders, and missionaries had only slight knowledge of the Great Plains, a vast grassland which overlay the continental heartland from Canada to the Rio Grande. It was the principal habitat for the bison or buffalo, huge hairy beasts, which ranged in vast herds on a seasonal north-south migration. Around 1700 over 30 different Indian tribes entered the Plains and forged a hybrid culture which increased their power, extended their ethnic longevity, and enabled them to become the most resistive of any Indian communities to Anglo-American conquest.

In pre-Contact times few Indian tribes lived on the Great Plains. Bands of Apache hunters roamed its southern margins, and there were scattered agricultural settlements in the Plains' fertile river valleys—of Mandans in the Missouri River Valley, Pawnees in the Platte River Valley, and Wichitas and Caddoes in the Canadian and Red River valleys. Hunters from communities on the Great Plains' margins occasionally came into the grasslands to hunt buffalo. They stalked their quarry on foot, using decoys and traps as well as the surround, and occasionally they stampeded bison over cliffs.

The horse was the grand catalyst which revolutionized the life-styles of the thirty-odd tribes which migrated to the Great Plains around 1700; with the bison it comprised the economic foundation for Plains Indian culture. Europeans reintroduced the horse into the New World beginning around 1500. Within two centuries these animals were gravitating onto the Great Plains from all directions, some as carriers of European traders and goods. But the prime source of horses for tribes settling the Great Plains was the Spanish empire in North America, especially the settlements along the Rio Grande. In spite of efforts by Spanish officials to ban traffic in firearms and horses, in various ways the Indians obtained both. Native Americans learned to breed, train, and use horses; mounted and mobile, they could traverse in a day on horseback many times the distance that had been possible on foot. By 1700 those tribes that already lived on the Plains, the Plains Apaches, Wichitas, Caddoes, and Pawnees, had adopted the horse. Wichitas and Caddoes continued in agriculture, but Pawnees for the most part gave up farming to become skilled buffalo hunters and horse thieves. Several tribes from other regions also adopted the horse and moved to the Plains. Sioux and Cheyenne farmers from the upper Mississippi Valley, Blackfeet agrarians from north of the Yellowstone, and Comanche and Kiowa hunters-gatherers from the Rocky Mountains and, from the East, woodland-dwelling Osages, Poncas, Otoes, Missouris, and other Siouian-speaking tribes took up permanent residence on the grasslands and contributed to the formation of the hybrid Plains culture.

Their social, political, economic, and religious synthesis was keyed to the Great Plains milieu, to the horse and the buffalo. Virtually all the tribes adopted the evolving common practices which became the trademarks of Plains culture. Language, however, was an exception, as each tribe retained its orignal spoken language. Hence, in order to communicate with each other, the Plains people developed a common manual sign language. Also, reflecting local military supremacy, the strongest tribe's language came to dominate its particular region, becoming a sort of *lingua franca*. On the northern Plains this language was the Plains Dakota Siouian dialect, while the Comanche tongue dominated the Southern Plains.

Except for the grass lodges of the Wichitas and the earth lodges of the Pawnees and Mandans, the adaptable and mobile buffalo-hide tipi became the shelter for the Plains tribes. Each buffalo-hunting Indian family transported its tipi covers, lodge poles, household impedimenta, and personal property on the travois, a platform lashed to two long poles secured to the sides of a horse.

The social organization formed by the blending of these diverse peoples on the Plains is called the Composite Tribe, defined as a "breakdown in culture with a subsequent readaptation." Their social organization was a response to their migratory economy and life-style. Thus most tribes came to practice a mixed descent reckoning, some from the father's line, others from the mother's. Marriage rules were necessarily flexible, there was no matrilocal or patrilocal mandate as found in many tribes; a young couple could live with either side of the family. Polygyny became common, because women became increasingly essential for processing buffalo robes, hides, and meat, and ranked with horses as the chief sources of wealth. On horseback the hunter could kill in a day many more bison than had been possible in prehorse times; thus he required additional household help to process the daily kill. Captives performed some of this work, but most of it was done by the hunter's several wives and children.[5]

Each tribe was a group of bands, a practical association for hunting and subsisting according to the pattern of bison migrations. Most of the year these animals grazed over the Plains in small groups but during the late summer rutting (mating) season "they came together in huge herds that blackened the Plains." The Indians responded with a parallel social cycle, uniting for the summer encampment and for the conduct of tribal business and ceremony.[6]

Although the tribal members were scattered in small hunting bands most of the year, they maintained tribal identity by use of a common language and through nonkinship sodalities or societies, a substitute for kinship clans. There were groupings for both men and women, identified by functions—some societies specialized in the dance, some in crafts, others in the martial arts. The military sodality was the elite association of the tribe; each warrior society governed itself with an elaborate set of rules and practiced complicated rites. Members of the warrior societies served as tribal police and enforced the rules adopted by the older men in council pertaining to matters of public interest, including moving the village, setting the departure date for the hunt, and the conduct of councils with representatives of other tribes. Most violators of the consensus regulations were punished by public scorn, but in serious breaches the warrior society members fined the accused by seizing property and administering public whippings.

In the warrior society, "warfare became as ritualized as medieval knighthood." The ritual and pageantry of Plains warriorhood included a hierarchy of honors centering on the coup, or strike. The coup count, the record of the warrior's feats of daring, skill, and bravery, was most important in gaining public esteem. Each warrior member of the sodality sought to exceed all others in daring, reckless exposure to the greatest hazard, and thus gain the greatest public recognition. There was special merit for coup count when the enemy was not slain but only touched by the daring warrior with special wand or baton called the coup stick. Accumulated brave deeds or coups yielded political power and was the avenue to band and tribal leadership.[7]

Plains Indian religion placed great stress on individual and group metaphysical experience. Individual observance of religious canons included faith in the power of visions for gaining individual guidance so that each individual continually sought visions. The search for visions often included isolation and self-torture. By punishing the flesh, members believed, one edified the spirit, thus sharpening it, making it more receptive to the vision which would provide guidance for future actions. Focus of warrior power was the sacred medicine bundle containing strengthening fetishes, feathers, and other items

A Great Plains travois, the principal mode of transportation used by tribesmen of the Plains culture for moving family shelter and household and personal effects. (International Museum of Photography, George Eastman House)

with supernatural character, all enclosed in a cured otter skin. Group religious observance included several tribal and pan-Indian rites, chief of which was the Sun Dance, an annual group renewal festival. Their worship focused upon the bison; the pageants, dances, and propitiatory witnesses were offered to placate the great bison force and assure its annual replenishment on the Plains.[8]

The Plains tribes rarely had direct contact with European or Anglo-American traders until after 1800, largely because they were so isolated and because it was unsafe for non-Indians to venture onto the Plains. Thus these tribes escaped the influences which peoples in other parts of America had faced. Nonetheless, besides the horse, they were readily receptive to certain European and Anglo-American items. Occasionally *comancheros*, Iberian traders from the Rio Grande settlements, ventured eastward onto the Plains to trade with the tribes there. And French and later British and Anglo-American traders had some limited contact with Plains Indians. But it was largely through the Wichitas and other Indian middlemen that guns, knives, hatchets, kettles, cloth, vermilion, beads, and other goods flowed to the Plains

A Comanche warrior. (Smithsonian Institution, National Anthropological Archives)

where resident Native Americans paid for them with buffalo robes and hides, and plunder, captives, horses, and mules swept up in raids on Spanish settlements in northern Mexico. Another source of goods for the Plains tribes was the annual Taos, New Mexico, fair.

This striking exception of the Plains tribes to the general trend of tribal degradation, depopulation, and cultural deprivation following European Contact is a matter of considerable moment in Indian history. The Plains tribes, largely free of imperial domination, adapted certain European items to their peculiar needs, notably the horse, and they flourished, became prosperous and powerful, and thus were able to offer the most effective resistance to being conquered by the upcoming Anglo-American westward advance.

Fate of British Indian Policy

While Plains Indian culture was evolving in the North American heartland, the eastern tribes continued to feel colonial expansion, even after the British government had established a protective policy during the 1760s. Before the new Indian policy had a fair trial, it suffered several mortal blows. One was retraction of the policy on Indian trade. Powerful trader groups pressured colonial governors and legislators who in turn pressed the crown to rescind the rule which had nationalized the Indian trade, and in 1767 control of trade was returned to the colonies. Another mortal blow was colonial attitude and noncompliance. The Proclamation of 1763 caused great concern among colonial speculators and settlers. No less a figure than George Washington, a speculator in western lands, assured the troubled colonists that the proclamation was only a passing expedient "to quiet the minds of the Indians." Settlers ignored the dividing line and poured into the transmontane Indian Country. British officials responsible for enforcing the rule against settler intrusion declared that the task was impossible.[9]

A preview of land appropriation by military conquest, soon to become a mainstay of United States Indian policy, was played out during 1774 in Lord Dunmore's War. The Iroquois Confederation tribes claimed by right of conquest the land around the forks of the Ohio River. By the Treaty of Lancaster (1744) and the Treaty of Fort Stanwix (1768) leaders of the Six Nations ceded this area to the British crown. Shawnees were the principal Indian occupants at the time. Settlers subsequently poured into the territory south of the Ohio River (which became Kentucky), then a western county of the colony of Virginia. Settler-Indian relations deteriorated. Mutual depredations included the killing by Kentucky pioneers of the family of Logan, a Cayuga leader married to a Shawnee woman. The frontier contest which followed is called Lord Dunmore's War. Shawnee warriors led by Cornstalk attempted to drive the intruding colonists east of the mountains. Lord Dunmore, royal governor of Virginia, ordered an army into the troubled territory. At Point Pleasant, near the mouth of the Kanawha River, one of Dunmore's columns met and defeated the Shawnees. As spoils of victory the Virginians forced the Shawnees to permit peaceful settlement of Kentucky.

The third mortal blow to fulfillment of British Indian policy goals was the American War of Independence, precipitated in part by the threat of British attempts to commandeer dealing with the Indians, their lands, and trade, to protect them from entrenched colonial interests. The rise of the Anglo-American nation as ruling power over Native Americans is the subject of Chapter Eleven.

Notes

1. Wilbur R. Jacobs, "British Colonial Attitudes and Policies Toward the Indian in the American Colonies," in *Attitudes of Colonial Powers Toward the American Indian*, edited by Howard Peckham and Charles Gibson (Salt Lake City, Utah, 1969), p. 85.
2. See Wilbur R. Jacobs (ed.), *Indians of the Southern Colonial Frontier: The Edmond Atkin Report and Plan of 1755* (Columbia, S.C., 1954).
3. Dwight W. Hoover, *The Red and the Black* (Chicago, 1976), pp. 36–40.
4. William T. Hagan, *American Indians* (Chicago, 1961), p. 24.
5. Peter Farb, *Man's Rise to Civilization* (New York, 1968), p. 152.
6. *Ibid.*, p. 153.
7. *Ibid.*, p. 156.
8. *Ibid.*, pp. 163–66.
9. Jacobs, "British-Colonial Attitudes," p. 96.

Selected Sources

Accounts of the wars for imperial supremacy in North America include Howard H. Peckham, *The Colonial Wars, 1689–1762* (Chicago, 1964); Norman W. Caldwell, *The French in the Mississippi Valley, 1740–1750* (Urbana, Ill., 1941); Verner W. Crane, *The Southern Frontier, 1670–1732* (Philadelphia, 1929); Theodore C. Pease (ed.), *Illinois on the Eve of the Seven Years' War, 1747–1755* (Springfield, Ill., 1940); Jack M. Sosin, *Whitehall and the Wilderness: The Middle West in British Colonial Policy, 1760–1775* (Lincoln, Neb., 1961); Francis S. Philbrick, *The Rise of the West, 1754–1830* (New York, 1965); and Clarence W. Alvord, *The Mississippi Valley in British Politics* (Cleveland, Ohio, 1916), 2 vols.

Indian viewpoint on the colonial era, including perspectives on Native American insurgency, is found in Howard H. Peckham, *Pontiac and the Indian Uprising* (Princeton, N.J., 1947); David H. Corkran, *The Cherokee Frontier: Conflict and Survival, 1740–62* (Norman, Okla., 1962); and by the same author, *The Creek Frontier, 1540–1783* (Norman, Okla., 1967); John Phillip Reid, *A Better Kind of Hatchet: Law, Trade and Diplomacy in the Cherokee Nation During the Early Years of European Contact* (University Park, Penna., 1976); Arrell Morgan Gibson, *The Kickapoos: Lords of the Middle Border* (Norman, Okla., 1963); and by the same author, *The Chickasaws* (Norman, Okla., 1971).

The genesis of British Indian policy is traced in George L. Beer, *British Colonial Policy: 1754–1765* (New York, 1907). The experiences of colonial officials assigned the mission of applying the new policy to aboriginal America are detailed in a group of biographies of the principals: John R. Alden, *John Stuart and the Southern Colonial Frontier* (Ann Arbor, Mich., 1944); James T. Flexner, *Mohawk Baronet: Sir William Johnson of New York* (New York, 1959); Milton W. Hamilton, *Sir William Johnson: Colonial American, 1715–1763* (Port Washington, N.Y., 1976); and Arthur Pound, *Johnson of the Mohawks* (New York, 1930). Wilbur R. Jacobs, *Indians of the Southern Colonial Frontier: The Edmond Atkin Report and Plan of 1755* (Columbia, S.C., 1954), details the problem of Native Americans from the colonial American viewpoint.

Studies on the impact of British administration upon the Indian tribes include Clarence W. Alvord, *The Illinois Country, 1673–1818* (Springfield, Ill., 1920); Georgiana C. Nammack, *Fraud, Politics, and the Dispossession of the Indians* (Norman, Okla., 1969); and two works by Wilbur R. Jacobs—*Dispossessing the American Indian: Indians and Whites on the Colonial Frontier* (New York, 1972); and *Diplomacy and Indian Gifts: Anglo-French Rivalry along the Ohio and Northwest Frontier, 1748–1763* (Stanford, Calif., 1950).

The Plains tribes anomaly is depicted in Peter Farb, *Man's Rise to Civilization* (New York, 1968); Ernest Wallace and E. Adamson Hoebel, *The Comanches: Lords of the South Plains* (Norman, Okla., 1952); Mildred Mayhall, *The Kiowas* (Norman, Okla., 1962); Donald J. Berthrong, *The Southern Cheyennes* (Norman, Okla., 1963); and R. B. Hassrick, *The Sioux* (Norman, Okla., 1964).

CHAPTER 11

INDIANS UNDER
ANGLO-AMERICAN
DOMINION
1776–1800

I admit that there are good white men, but they bear no proportion to the bad; the bad must be the strongest, for they rule. They do what they please. They enslave those who are not of their color, although created by the same Great Spirit who created us. They would make slaves of us if they could, but as they cannot do it, they kill us! There is no faith to be placed in their words. They are not like the Indians who are only enemies while at war and are friends in peace. They will say to an Indian, "My friend! my brother!" They will take him by the hand, and at the same moment destroy him. . . . Remember! that this day I have warned you to beware of such friends as these. I know the long knives; they are not to be trusted.

Pachgants' oration (Delaware), 1788

▼

Toward the close of the eighteenth century a new nation displaced Great Britain as ruler of large numbers of peoples and their vast territories in North America. Leaders of those Indian tribes who lived astride the expansion path of the infant United States quickly learned that the new nation's leaders showed little originality in their approach to dealing with them, their lands, and other resources. Rather they copied techniques used by European nations, particularly those developed by Great Britain during the 1760s. It soon became apparent that in its relationships with Indians the United States was no less imperial than Spain, France, Russia, or Great Britain. The ideals of human rights for all people, expressed in the Declaration of Independence, the Preamble to the Constitution and the Bill of Rights, had yet to be extended to Indians. This chapter traces the foundations of the new nation's Indian policy.

INDIANS AND THE AMERICAN REVOLUTION

The United States, born of secession from the British empire by the thirteen colonies, had engaged in a bloody war against Great Britain to achieve national independence. Many Indian leaders perceived grim irony if the Anglo-American independence effort succeeded, because it threatened tribal independence—Indians on the frontier had already seen the restless expan-

---

Chapter Opening Artifact: Wooden Cherokee Booger mask. (Courtesy Museum of the American Indian, Heye Foundation)

sionism of British colonials most of whom, after 1775, became citizens of the new American republic. Aware that their tribal interests would be endangered should the insurgent colonies triumph, most Indians who lived on the colonial borders joined the British in their attempt to crush the revolt. The British failure had awesome consequences for Native Americans.

Indian Soldiers in the American Revolution

British officials in North America at first underestimated the determination and capability of American rebels to conduct military operations of any magnitude against crown forces. They regarded British regulars and Loyalist or Tory troops as adequate to crush the insurgent colonials. Thus it appeared that for the first time in over a century Indians would not be mustered as soldiers to protect European imperial interests.

American leaders, convened in the Continental Congress, acknowledged the importance to the war of Indian nations on their borders, but followed the British stance of neutrality or noninvolvement of Native Americans in the struggle. They did, however, express their concern on how to gain and preserve the goodwill of neighboring tribes. On July 12, 1775, a five-man committee including Phillip Schuyler of New York and Patrick Henry of Virginia presented a resolution, adopted by the Continental Congress, which stated that "securing and preserving the friendship of Indian nations, appears to be a subject of the utmost moment to these colonies." The insurgent leaders at that time were most concerned over the stance of the Six Nations, the Iroquois Confederation. In their communications with these tribes Colonial leaders stressed that the conflict was a "family quarrel" which the Indians should shun.[1]

During 1776, General Thomas Gage, commander of British forces in North America, began to feel rebel military pressure on his defensive positions in New England, and he changed British policy regarding use of Indian troops against the insurgent Americans. He ordered British officials in Canada to raise an Indian army and send it against the New England frontier settlements to divert rebel military attention. He also directed British agents in Florida to muster the southern Indians. John Johnson, Sir William Johnson's successor, began recruitment of an Indian army in the North while John Stuart marshaled the Cherokees, Creeks, Choctaws, and Chickasaws, supplying them from the British arsenal at Pensacola, for strikes against the southern colonial settlements. In urging the northern and southern tribes to render military assistance, British agents pointed to the steady flow of American pioneers along the Mohawk Valley and southward across the mountains into the Watauga and Holston settlements of eastern Tennessee and onto Indian lands, their numbers increasing each month, particularly in those frontier districts soon to be known as Tennessee and Kentucky. After Mohawk and Shawnee leaders had committed their tribes to aid the British, they sent Indian emissaries south to assist British agents in winning military support from the southern tribes.

Learning of Gage's orders and the mounting tribal shift from neutrality to preparation for war against the colonies, Colonial leaders also turned to Native Americans for support. Officials in the insurgent government charged that British agents were inciting Indians against them, and they published reports that crown officials had urged Mohawks to "feast on a Bostonian and drink his blood." During May 1776 Congress changed its policy and sought military alliances with the frontier tribes.[2]

Formation of a standing committee on Indian affairs in the Continental Congress marked the beginning of the national bureaucracy for Indian affairs. On the recommendation of this committee the Continental Congress created three departments to conduct its relations with the Indian nations—one department was assigned jurisdiction over the Northwest tribes, a second department was to direct relations with the Southwest tribes, and the third department was responsible for looking after the tribes in the Fort Pitt area (at the forks of the Ohio, now Pittsburgh). Initially each department was headed by a committee of commissioners charged with maintaining regular contact with the western tribes and countering British influence among them—Northwest Department, three commissioners; Southwest Department, five commissioners; and Central Department, three commissioners. Later Congress changed this structure to follow the old British pattern of two commissioners, one in charge of the tribes north of the Ohio River, the other in charge of those south of it. The Continental Congress also voted modest sums to purchase gifts for distribution at councils to be held with tribal leaders and funds to support Indian students at Dartmouth and Princeton colleges. The new state governments duplicated much of the work of the Continental Congress in Indian affairs, most of them maintaining state Indian agents among the tribes and performing those functions in Indian trade and lands which had been their prerogatives during colonial times.

British agents easily bested their American rivals in winning Indian allies. American agents were handicapped in relations with the frontier tribes by the poverty of their new nation. They lacked the resources in gifts and other considerations that Indian leaders and their warriors had come to expect as a part of maintaining a cooperative relationship. The Americans rarely could provide the weapons and ammunition needed by the Indian troops. British agents, on the other hand, were able to supply gifts, arms, and other expected considerations in abundance. And their repeated warnings of American expansion onto Indian hunting grounds were confirmed by the extension of American settlements in the trans-Appalachian region while the war was still in progress.

Almost all tribes that engaged in the American War of Independence fought for Great Britain. Only the Oneidas, Tuscaroras, and a few Mohawks provided limited military support for the Americans. At one time it appeared that the Colonial cause might win the Delawares. American commissioners made a treaty with the leaders of this tribe at Fort Pitt on September 17, 1778. The Delawares agreed to permit American armies to pass through their country to attack British posts on the Great Lakes; the tribe contracted to sell American forces corn and horses; and warriors were permitted to enlist in the American army. This pact was short-lived because soon the Delawares became antagonized and shifted to the British side.

British commanders concentrated their use of Indian troops in the West, while regulars and German mercenaries campaigned on the seaboard. From 1776 to 1783 the frontier was bloodied time and again by sweeping strikes carried out by Indian soldiers led by British and Tory officers. Counterslashes against Indian and British settlements in the Northwest were carried out by vengeance-seeking frontier militia.

The Cherokees were among the first Indian troops to do the British bidding. Warrior bands from this populous Indian nation struck hard at the Watauga settlements in July 1776. James Robertson and John Sevier rallied the harried settlers, collecting them at Sycamore Shoals on the Watauga and at Eaton's Station on Long Island in the Holston River, and constructing a strong log fort at each location. The Cherokee raiders, led by the highly respected warrior chieftain Dragging Canoe, maintained a tight siege on the Watauga forts for nearly three weeks. Finally Robertson and Sevier led the cooped-up settler militia in a counterattack that broke the siege and forced the Cherokees to withdraw.

Cherokee raids on the American settlements extended from the Watauga-Holston frontier in the trans-Appalachian region eastward into Virginia, North Carolina, South Carolina, and Georgia. During the late summer of 1776 militia columns from each of these new American states joined with a western army mustered from the Watauga and Nolichucky settlements in Tennessee to carry out a retaliatory campaign against the Cherokees. The American armies desolated the Cherokee country in western North and South Carolina and eastern Tennessee, burning villages and destroying crops. These operations crushed Cherokee military power; thereafter only on isolated occasions were raiders from this tribe able to strike at the American settlements.

During 1777 the victorious Americans extracted from reluctant Cherokee leaders two agreements—the Treaty of DeWitt's Corner and the Treaty of Long Island—obligating the Cherokees to cede all tribal territory in western South Carolina and that portion of their range east of the Blue Ridge Mountain divide in North Carolina, and reiterating their cession of the Watauga and Nolichucky settlement districts in eastern Tennessee.

Along the Mohawk Valley and Lake Champlain district, avenues for American armies invading Canada or for British-Indian armies entering the United States, was another military sector engaging a large number of Indian troops. Sustained campaigning there desolated the Iroquois country and drastically reduced tribal populations. During 1777, American forces supported by Oneida and Tuscarora troops attempted to drive a British-Indian army from the approaches to Fort Stanwix but were defeated at the Battle of Oriskany. That same year American troops, again with Oneida and Tuscarora support, defeated General John Burgoyne's large Indian-British invading force. In 1778 an Indian army, largely Senecas and Cayugas led by British officers, invaded the Wyoming Valley of Pennsylvania and the Cherry Valley of New York, massacred settlers and burned their towns and farms. Enraged survivors appealed to General George Washington, commanding the Continental Army, for succor. He responded by ordering General John Sullivan to lead a large force of regulars to punish the Iroquois Confederation tribes. Sullivan's troops went to their task of desolating the Six Nations' settlements, killing men, women, and children, burning villages, destroying fields of corn and other foodstuffs, and cutting down orchards. His officers' toast for the campaign was "Civilization or death to all American savages." The Iroquois survivors fled to Canada.[3]

Most of the British Indian troops were assigned to the Ohio Valley–Kentucky sector. There the most notorious and successful agent for furthering the British cause through the use of Indian troops was Henry Hamilton, Lieutenant-Governor of Canada. From his Detroit headquarters, Hamilton supplied Indian armies with guns, ammunition, knives, hatchets, blankets, and provisions; he fired them to fury pitch with warnings of the Indians' grim future if the land-greedy rebels won the war, and launched them on devastating campaigns against settlements on the Allegheny and Monongahela rivers and across the Ohio River into Kentucky. Settlers called Hamilton the "Hair Buyer" because he was reputed to pay his Indian followers a bounty for each rebel scalp—man, woman, child—that they delivered to Detroit.

British Indians kept Kentucky, a western county of Virginia and an area of continuing expansion of settlements, in a stage of siege from 1776 to 1782. Virginia officials sent troops at times to help pioneers in their defense. The raids during 1776 were probing actions, but in 1777 they became sustained, destructive, extended campaigns of terror and death for Kentuckians.

American commanders regularly tried to drive through the Northwest Indian defenses to take Detroit, the source of terror for the Anglo-American frontier. During 1778 General Edward Hand led an army from Fort Pitt, campaigning as far north as the Shawnee and Delaware settlements at Sandusky and destroying villages and corn fields. The Indians faded ahead of his advance, and at no time was he able to force them to battle. Major George Rogers Clark led a small army of Virginians and Kentuckians down the Ohio to Kaskaskia, then moved obliquely toward Detroit, capturing Vincennes, but his required supplies and reinforcements failed to arrive and he was forced to abandon his campaign. In his conquest of Vincennes he captured Hamilton who had ventured from Detroit to command the defense of this Wabash settlement. Clark sent Hamilton to Virginia in irons. However, the lieutenant-governor was replaced by officers just as committed as the "Hair Buyer" to using Indian troops to destroy frontier Americans.

American commanders at Fort Pitt attempted again to penetrate the Indian country at the southern approaches to Detroit. During October 1778, Commandant Lachlan McIntosh marched nearly 1,000 troops from Fort Pitt on a campaign intended to terminate in the conquest of Detroit. His column halted on Big Beaver Creek, only fifty miles northeast of Pittsburgh to erect Fort McIntosh as a forward base. North of this post the Americans located and destroyed several Indian villages, but at no time were they able to make contact with the enemy—Indian or British. The cold of winter forced McIntosh to call in his troops and return to Fort Pitt.

Detroit continued to be the base for British-Indian frontier operations. Colonel Alexander McKee, a particular favorite with the Northwest tribes, succeeded Hamilton as commander of Indian troops. His aides included Simon Girty, leader of the western Tories. Several times between 1780 and 1782 McKee led Indian armies out of Detroit into Kentucky. The enemy columns slipped past the thin Ohio River defenses to burn, plunder, and desolate the new settlements. Their bloodiest coup occurred during June 1780 when a 1,000-man army of Indian troops swarmed into the Kentucky settlement of Rundle's Station, burned the fort and killed 200 men, women, and children. Clark hurried from his Kaskaskia headquarters to Kentucky, mustered an army, and marched north of the Ohio River. There the Americans cut a swath of death and destruction among the Shawnee and Delaware Indian settlements at Chillicothe and Piqua. An Indian army led by Simon Girty moved up to intercept the Kentuckians at Piqua and was annihilated. The Americans attempted to collect from the corpses scalps equal in number to those taken at the Rundle Station massacre.

During 1780 Clark's men constructed a post below the mouth of the Ohio River inside Chickasaw territory. Named Fort Jefferson, the new station was garrisoned by 100 troops. Settlers collected around the fort and started farms. Chickasaw scouts discovered the American outpost and reported it to British officials. Before the close of 1780 a Chickasaw-Tory army swept into the settlement, drove the settlers inside the post, burned their cabins, and laid siege. The Chickasaws sealed the routes supplying Fort Jefferson, killed or captured stragglers from the garrison, and at one time subjected the post to such a close and protracted surveillance that only the timely arrival of reinforcements saved it from destruction. In desperation Clark's besieged detachment and the settlers fought their way out of Fort Jefferson in June 1781, abandoning it to the Chickasaws.

After their defeat in 1777, the Cherokees remained at peace with the Americans except for the dissident Chickamaugas—headed by Dragging Canoe and Bloody Fellow—who longed for vengeance on the Colonial pioneers. During 1778 British agents delivered guns, powder, and shot from the Pensacola arsenal to the Chickamauga towns. Thereupon Dragging Canoe and his followers moved against the American settlements, closing the Wilderness Road—the principal link between Virginia and Kentucky—and driving the Watauga and Holston river settlers into forts. Colonel Evan Shelby collected a frontier army of 600, invaded Chickamauga territory in the Tennessee River valley and wreaked such a destructive fury on their settlements that the Cherokees sued for peace. Occasionally thereafter warriors from certain sections of the Cherokee nation, feeling the pressure of Anglo-American expansion, attempted to expel the settlers. However, they resorted to military action only on their own behalf and not as British allies. Nevertheless, late in 1780, Watauga militiamen desolated Cherokee towns on the upper French Broad River on the pretext of avenging Cherokee raids on their settlements. The Americans forced the vanquished Cherokees to cede additional territory for settler expansion.

Lord Cornwallis, supreme British commander in North America, surrendered to General George Washington on October 18, 1781, at Yorktown, and for all intents and purposes hostilities between Great Britain and the United States were over. However, the war continued in the transmontane region with unabated fury long after Cornwallis' capitulation. British raids and retaliatory American strikes made a wasteland of the Ohio River Valley, the Indian tribes suffering heavy population losses much like the Iroquois Confederation tribes in the Mohawk River Valley. And during 1782 while negotiations between American and European representatives at Paris were progressing toward a diplomatic conclusion of the American Revolution, guerrilla warfare continued in the trans-Appalachian region. In 1781 Seneca war parties from the North and Delaware-Shawnee raiders from the West preyed on the settlements of western Pennsylvania. Early in the spring of the following year a 300-man militia collected from the survivors, driven by desire for vengeance, campaigned west of the Allegheny River into the Ohio Country. Their line of march took them to Gnadenhutten, a Moravian missionary outpost among the Delawares in central Ohio. Ninety peaceful Indian converts were at this station. The Pennsylvania militiamen executed most of them—men, women, and children. The few survivors fled to Canada, settling along the Thames River in southern Ontario where their descendants live today.

Later in the same year, Colonel William Crawford led an army from Fort Pitt into the Ohio Country to search out and destroy Indian settlements suspected of providing manpower for heavy raiding in the settlements around Fort Pitt and in eastern Kentucky. An Indian army trapped Crawford's column, scattered it, and captured several Americans including the commander. Crawford and the other captives were turned over to the Delawares who tortured and mutilated the Americans, then burned them at the stake.

The Indian effort on behalf of the British attempt to crush the American independence movement was more than nuisance-type raiding; Indian power mustered by British officers decidedly hampered the American cause. Their destructive strikes against American settlements from Canada to Florida made it nearly impossible for American agents to recruit fighting men from the frontier regions for service in the Continental Army; thus Indian power reduced troop strength for military service against British armies on the seaboard. Furthermore, General Washington was compelled to detach regiments from his pitifully small Continental Army to reinforce Fort Pitt. And he found it necessary to postpone major operations against British forces in the East during 1779 in order for a detachment from his Continental Army led by General Sullivan to carry out his expedition against the Six nations.

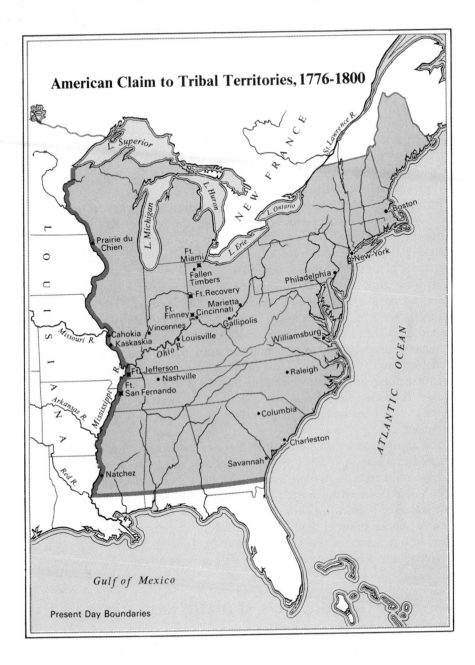

American Claim to Tribal Territories, 1776-1800

Present Day Boundaries

Legacy of the American Revolution for the Indian Tribes

The diplomatic settlement that ended the American Revolution, which was concluded on September 3, 1783, at Paris, made no mention of Indian tribes, either as British allies or as proprietors of the territory British diplomats ceded to the new American nation. The new country covered all territory between the Atlantic Ocean and Mississippi River, and from the Great Lakes to the Florida border. A treaty proviso that Tories receive restitution or proper compensation for their property confiscated by American authorities inadvertently had tremendous implications for Native Americans because crown officials anticipated that Americans would be reluctant to fulfill this clause. The British therefore retained control of Detroit and other posts situated in the American Northwest Territory as a sort of surety bond. Its presence in the Northwest provided Britain with a continuing influence over the resident Indian tribes and worked to thwart the advance of American settlers into that part of the new nation's territory.

British use of Indian armies in campaigns against the American settlements had led to counterstrikes which depopulated the once great and powerful tribes on the colonial borders. The Iroquois Confederation was reduced to shambles by American armies never again to muster its awesome power. Remnants of this once grand community settled on reservations in Canada or in New York or drifted into the Ohio River valley to escape their new American masters. Other tribes, including the Cherokees, had attacked American settlements as British allies. They now lived on territory claimed by the United States. In the eyes of the victors their actions smacked of treason; retaliatory campaigns against them by western militia had consistently ended in defeat for the Indians. These campaigns were generally concluded by treaties calling for cessions of tribal land to the Americans, ostensibly extracted from the Cherokees as reparations for making war on their new masters. This became a common method for opening new western lands to settlement.

The campaigns against American frontier settlements by British Indian armies had a lasting effect. Frontier militia matched its enemy in destruction and general barbarity in their retaliatory strikes. At the close of hostilities the British and Tories withdrew to Canada, but the Indians remained in territory that was now within the national domain of the United States. The image, born in colonial times of the Indian as a deadly, skulking, bloodthirsty savage, came to full flower in the American War for Independence in the West. It survived for at least a century in the minds of most Americans.

NATIVE AMERICANS AND THE NEW MASTER

The American government, acknowledged by the Treaty of Paris as successor to Great Britain as sovereign of the territory of the thirteen former colonies and western territory to the Mississippi River, sought to apply its dominion over the resident Native Americans. Two of the most pressing matters facing the new government were to gain from the Indian tribes an acknowledgment of submission to the United States and to establish a single, coordinated national Indian policy. The latter was complicated by several states continuing to exercise prerogative in Indian affairs including negotiating for tribal lands, regulating trade, and performing other acts which the national government regarded as exclusively its province.

Origins of the Indian Affairs Bureaucracy

As indicated, the Continental Congress in its role as the central governing body for the insurgent colonies, had conducted relations with the Indian nations through a committee on Indian affairs. Its Board of War received reports from Continental Army officers in contact with the tribes on the frontier; these reports in turn were submitted to the Continental Congress committee. Initially Congress had divided the frontier into three districts, each under a committee of commissioners. However, volume of Indian relations was slight because most of the tribes had little peaceful contact with the Anglo-Americans.

During the war a committee in the Continental Congress had drafted the Articles of Confederation to guide the new government. The section pertaining to Indian affairs represented a compromise among the member states—determined to retain traditional prerogatives in regulation of trade, tribal land acquisition, and other matters pertaining to Indians—and Continental Congress leaders who desired to establish a single, national policy for dealing with the Indian tribes. Thus in the nation's beginning many Indian tribes were subject to two Indian policies because the states shared this responsibility with the national government. The Articles of Confederation section pertaining to Indian affairs stated that Congress had "the sole and exclusive right and power of . . . regulating trade and managing all affairs with Indians, not members of any of the states, provided that the legislative right of any state within its own limits be not infringed or violated."

Under authority of this section of the Articles of Confederation, Congress in 1786 adopted an ordinance which assigned the management of Indian affairs to the secretary of war. The ordinance created two departments, one with jurisdiction over the tribes west of the Hudson River, the other with jurisdiction over those south of the Ohio River. Each department was headed by a superintendent. Two deputies assisted each superintendent by maintaining regular contact with the tribes in the wilderness and regulating trade through the licensing system.

With this limited administrative machinery Congress attempted to assert itself with those Indian nations within its national territory. The new government's principal concern was tribal territory, the prize most sought by settlers and state governments. In 1779 the Continental Congress had adopted a resolution which declared that no Indian land could be transferred except by consent of Congress. Because this resolution conflicted with local prerogative, state governments and the extra-legal governments forming in the western territory ignored it, and their militias continued to seize vast tracts from the Cherokees and other tribes under the pretext of exacting reparations of war.

In 1783 Congress, still under the Articles of Confederation, issued a proclamation which forbade settlement of lands or purchase of lands outside state jurisdiction and inhabited by Indians. Subsequently to placate the mounting rage of the tribes north of the Ohio River over widespread expansion of settlements, Congress included in the Northwest Ordinance of 1787 this high-sounding but ineffective clause:

The utmost good faith shall always be observed towards the Indians; their land and property shall never be taken from them without their consent; and in their property, rights and liberty, they shall never be invaded or disturbed, unless in just and lawful wars authorized by Congress; but laws founded on justice and humanity shall from time to time be made, for preventing wrongs done to them, and for preserving peace and Friendship with them.

The Tribal Land Dilemma

The situation of tribal land with respect to state and territorial boundaries varied; some of it, like the Iroquois territories in western New York, was within the established bounds of states. However, by this time most tribal land was west of the Appalachians. Even there the claimed title of certain states intruded and complicated matters for the Indian nations as well as the national government. The central government, which was the sovereign of the national territory, as acknowledged by the Treaty of Paris in 1783, actually owned or held title to only a portion of that national territory. Both state and national governments acknowledged that Indian tribes had some rights, perhaps those of transitory tenants, to the land. But those rights could be extinguished by due process, generally token payment. The great and continuing obstacle to the national government's acquiring title to the land in the territory west of the Appalachians was the determination of several state governments to pursue claims to western lands founded upon colonial charters and crown grants. Finally in 1781 these states agreed to cede their claims to western lands to the national government. However, Congress soon found these cessions hedged with reservations and conditions. Several states, including Virginia, with claims to lands north of the Ohio River based on colonial charters, reserved huge tracts of western land to compensate troops for military service and to pay state war debts, substantially reducing the amount of land available to the central government. North Carolina and Georgia first agreed to cede their western lands to the central government then reneged, thus extending state bounds and state control over these frontier districts as guaranteed to them under the Articles of Confederation. Thereupon officials in these states disposed of the western lands to settlers and speculation companies with the result that there was little land left south of the Ohio River for the national domain. Virginia, North Carolina, South Carolina, and Georgia had seized Cherokee and Creek land during the war as reparations and punishment for supporting the British. After the war North Carolina and Georgia continued to nibble at the surviving Indian lands, appropriating vast tracts and assigning them to land speculation companies for distribution to settlers.

The poverty-stricken national government had designs on these western lands. Confederation leaders expected to sell tracts from the national estate to land companies and settlers and use the proceeds to pay off the national war debt and provide much-needed revenue for operating the new government. Because virtually all the transmontane lands which the states had promised to cede to the national government were occupied by Indians, their title had to be quieted. And after North Carolina and Georgia reneged on their cession of western lands and proceeded to dispose of them under state powers, most of the land available for national use was north of the Ohio River. It was there in negotiations with resident tribes that the national government attempted to resolve the land dilemma.

The Organic Treaties

Soon after conclusion of the Treaty of Paris, officials in the American government appointed commissioners to conduct councils with the Indian tribes on the frontier. The purpose of these negotiations was twofold: the tribes to abrogate their loyalty to Great Britain and establish an official relationship with the United States; and, for several tribes, to cede portions of their tribal territories to the United States.

Leaders of the Northwestern tribes were the first to meet with American commissioners. They expected that the boundary set by the Fort Stanwix Treaty in 1768 would continue to be the line separating Indians and Anglo-Americans. Spokesmen for the Six Nations and other tribes protested that settlers were already streaming across this boundary and that surveyors were plotting tracts for speculators. And they declared their reluctance to discuss a diplomatic settlement with the United States until the contested area was cleared of intruders.

The American viewpoint on the direction negotiations should take in the Confederation Congress crystallized. Most national leaders agreed that these Indians, by their alliance with the American enemy (Great Britain), had violated their pledges of neutrality to the United States, had waged "unprovoked war" upon the new nation, and thereby had annulled the 1768 Fort Stanwix Treaty and had forfeited their title to territories in the Northwest. As a consequence the United States by "right of conquest" had absolute title, free of tribal "residual interest," to a 30 million-acre tract extending from the Ohio River north to Lake Erie and including all of Ohio except the northwestern corner.

The new nation lacked funds to extinguish Indian title to land by money and goods payment as had been the custom from early colonial days. Thus, American officials, pressed by their citizens for more land, had to stress their right to take the land by conquest. Philip Schuyler, a general and national leader, was concerned, not about the new government taking Indian land but about the extent of land to be taken. He feared that taking too much land at that time would incite the Indians to resume their war on the United States, a contest which the young, struggling nation could ill afford. Rather than intemperate appropriation at that time Schuyler urged peaceful negotiation and drawing a new boundary between Indian and American territory which would satisfy settlers' immediate land needs; then, with patience, he believed the Indians would eventually voluntarily move on west as game became depleted, and their abandoned lands could be obtained in less expensive ways than war.

George Washington's view was similar to Schuyler's "gradualism" policy. He recommended that the tribes be informed that the territory they occupied now belonged to the United States, and that "exact justice" would permit the Americans to expel them from these lands because they had made war on the United States. However, the new nation desired to be "merciful" and would, therefore, draw a "reasonable" boundary between Indian and settler territory, permitting the Native Americans to retain "some of their lands for themselves." Like Schuyler, he opposed driving them from the country, as proposed by officials from New York and certain other states, because doing so would mean a bloody, expensive war. He recommended "an orderly expansion which would compel the Indians to retire"; then the United States could obtain their lands without resort to military action.[4]

In 1784 Congress appointed commissioners to negotiate with the northern tribes. Since these tribes were expected to cede lands to the national government to permit settlement to proceed westward and because the national government's financial resources were so limited that it had no means to pay for the desired territory, the commissioners were to proceed with the "conquered territory" strategy; the United States as victor could set boundaries as it chose.

The commissioners negotiated four treaties with the northern tribes. The first, the Treaty of Fort Stanwix with the Six Nations on October 22, 1784, provided for peace with the United States and acceptance of American dominion, cession of tribal lands in western New York and Pennsylvania, and abandonment of claims to territories west of Fort Pitt. The Treaty of Fort Stanwix confirmed the loyal Oneidas and Tuscaroras in their New York lands although state officials shortly pressured them to surrender their treaty-protected lands in exchange for smaller reservations. On January 21, 1785, Wyandot, Delaware, Chippewa, and Ottawa leaders signed the Fort McIntosh Treaty which provided for peace between the United States and these tribes and brought them under American dominion; the signatory tribes ceded their lands to the United States and a reservation for each was created in the Northwest Territory. In a council held at the mouth of the Great Miami early in 1786 Shawnee chiefs concluded the Fort Finney Treaty with American commissioners, by which these Indians submitted to American suzerainty, agreed to peace, ceded certain territory in the Northwest to the new nation, and accepted a fixed reservation. In each of these three pacts, the American government pledged to keep settlers off Indian lands, and the Muskingum

Red-Jacket: Seneca war chief, orator, and statesman. (Smithsonian Institution, National Anthropological Archives)

River was set as the boundary for settlement. To thwart American trespass west of the river, General Joseph Harmar constructed Fort Harmar at the mouth of the Muskingum.

Soon leaders of the Northern tribes, particularly Six Nations spokesmen, renounced these treaties, began to confer with British agents at Detroit, and threatened to attack settlers in the ceded territory. American officials became alarmed. Secretary of War Henry Knox was concerned that the United States, by persisting in taking land by its claimed right of conquest, had agitated the northwestern Indians. To placate them he recommended that officials extinguish tribal claims to the western territory described in the recent treaties by payment in goods. Congress appropriated funds to purchase goods to distribute to the northwestern tribes and in 1789 commissioners held a council at Fort Harmar. By the Fort Harmar Treaties, concluded on January 8, 1789, with the Six Nations and the northwestern tribes, the United States abandoned the right-of-conquest principle and paid for the lands ceded by the recent treaties. The Fort Harmar Treaties confirmed the earlier disputed treaties and renewed the land cessions.

While one group of commissioners was concluding peace settlements with the northwestern tribes, another was attempting to conclude similar treaties with the southern tribes. In late 1785 and early 1786 American officials met with leaders of the Cherokee, Choctaw, and Chickasaw nations at Hopewell along the Keowee River on the South Carolina frontier. Creek leaders, bitter at Georgia for extravagant land exactions and resentful at national officials for failing to protect them against state trespass, refused to participate in the proceedings. By the Treaties of Hopewell with the Cherokee, Choctaw, and Chickasaw nations, tribal leaders agreed to peace with the United States, acceptance of American dominion, and permission for the United States to manage tribal affairs in such manner as it might "think proper." The treaties defined tribal boundaries and permitted cession to the United States of small tracts as sites for military and trading posts. Thus the Chickasaws ceded to the United States a five-mile tract at the lower Muscle Shoals on the Tennessee River. During 1790 Creek leaders traveled to New York City (then the national capital) and concluded a basic treaty of peace with American officials. Thereby most of the tribes near the American settlements acknowledged United States suzerainty and began official relationships with their new rulers.

The vexing difficulties national commissioners met in dealing with the northern tribes were exceeded by the complications arising from negotiations with the southern tribes, largely because of aggressive state action in Indian affairs. Already Virginia commissioners had negotiated with the Chickasaws and other tribes for tracts on the Tennessee River, and agents from North Carolina, South Carolina, and Georgia roamed the wilderness dickering with tribal leaders for lands. North Carolina and Georgia officials were particularly troublesome. They claimed that the Hopewell Treaties complicated their negotiations with tribal leaders and spoiled their plans to accommodate the land needs of their citizens. Georgia officials bitterly resented national agents dealing with Cherokees and Creeks in that state; they alluded disparagingly to the "pretended treaty" of Hopewell and accused national commissioners of violating "the sovereignty and legislative rights" of Georgia as guaranteed by the Articles of Confederation. The Georgia legislature, in a preview of its strong anti-Indian, antifederal stance of the 1820s and 1830s, adopted a resolution stating "that all and every act and thing done or intended to be done within the limits and jurisdiction of this state by said commissioners . . . shall be and same are hereby declared null and void."[5]

Cabals and Conflicts

These organic treaties with Indian nations who lived in territory claimed by the United States permitted the signatory tribes a precious truce to rest from the turmoil of war, repent their submission to the new American nation, and contemplate their future. International neighbors of the United States—Great

Britain in Canada and Spain in Florida—offered the conquered Indian nations sympathy, shared concern for the surging, swarming tide of Anglo-American settlers flowing into the West, and alluring if deadly alternatives.

British agents and troops from adjacent Canada at Detroit and other posts they still occupied in the American Northwest, kept alive the hope of an early American collapse, largely through fiscal insolvency, and with Indian help, British recovery of the lost colonies and western territory. They continued to distribute to Indians from the United States guns, ammunition, blankets, and other supplies.

British officials in councils with leaders of the Northwest tribes scorned the American doctrine of right of conquest for taking Indian land and encouraged Native Americans in the view that, by the terms of the Treaty of Fort Stanwix (1768), they were the sole proprietors of the land in the West and that only by purchase could tribal title to this land be extinguished. Governor General of Canada Lord Dorchester personally assisted the tribes. He provided reservation homes for scattered bands of Iroquois Confederation tribes and Delawares, casualties of the American War for Independence. He ordered troops from Detroit to construct Fort Miami in the Ohio Country in order to have a supply post closer to the Northwest tribes, and he announced a plan to form a huge Indian reservation in the territory between the Great Lakes and the Ohio River.

During the 1780s several Indian patroit leaders like Joseph Brant (a Mohawk), Little Turtle (a Miami), and Blue Jacket (a Shawnee), stirred nationalism among the Northwest tribes. They worked to form an Indian confederation to strengthen the tribes in their resolve not to negotiate with land-hungry Americans. Brant went to England seeking military assistance for this confederation.

Leaders of the confederated tribes decided that treaties with the United States were null if signed by a single tribe; a land cession treaty had to reflect confederacy consensus. Tecumseh later applied this idea to the formation of his confederacy. By 1786 confederation leaders forbade chiefs of any member tribe to cede land unilaterally to the Americans, and they required American agents to consult with confederacy spokesmen and not with leaders of the individual tribes. The Northwest Confederacy rejected the American government's right-of-conquest doctrine and repudiated all treaties—the 1784, 1785, and 1786 pacts—based upon that premise. Confederation leaders declared the Ohio River to be the boundary between the United States and Indian territories.

American plans had proceeded for settling and developing the territory west of Pittsburgh and north of the Ohio River, now known as the Northwest Territory. Congress had passed a series of laws culminating in the Northwest Ordinance of 1787 to provide for the orderly survey, sale, settlement, and governance of this region. National officials had sold huge tracts of the Northwest Territory to land companies; their agents were selling farmsteads to prospective pioneers in the eastern United States and in Europe; surveyors

Joseph Brant, Mohawk leader of intertribal resistance to early American expansion in the Old Northwest. (Harvard College Library)

were plotting the lands in accordance with national law; and settlers were occupying the disputed territory.

British-armed Indians from the Northwest Confederation tribes—Wyandot, Delaware, Shawnee, Miami, Ottawa, Chippewa, Potawatomi, Kickapoo, and Six Nations remnants—ravaged the intruding settlements, cutting a bloody swath from Chillicothe to the gates of Fort Harmar. One estimate claims that between 1783 and 1790 over 1,500 Ohio Country settlers perished in the renewed frontier war.

In 1790 President Washington called on Kentucky, Virginia, and Pennsylvania to send militia forces to the Northwest to pacify the frontier. During that summer General Josiah Harmar mustered nearly 1,500 troops, motley and undisciplined, and marched them toward the Maumee River. Enroute his army destroyed several Indian villages; Miami, Shawnee, and Kickapoo snipers nagged at Harmar's flanks in the dark forests below the Maumee. On September 19, a large Indian force struck from ambush, killing nearly 200 militiamen and sending the survivors in dreadful rout southward toward the Ohio River settlements.

The next year President Washington directed Governor Arthur St. Clair to lead an army against the confederated Northwest Indians. St. Clair's army of 3,000 six-month enlistees, most of them from eastern cities, marched into the wilderness during the autumn of 1791 and constructed a line of support bases. On November 3 near the Maumee River massed Indian defenders struck St. Clair's army in a surprise attack, precipitating a confused, bloody retreat even worse than the previous year's disaster. Over 630 Americans died in battle, and nearly 300 were wounded. The survivors fled to Fort Jefferson, one of the support bases, while the Indians followed up their smashing triumph over the American army with furious attacks on white settlements, forcing the pioneers to evacuate to the Ohio River towns.

Once again President Washington determined to destroy the Indians who were fighting the advance of American settlement in the Northwest. He assigned General Anthony Wayne to command the new army of conquest. Wayne subjected his men to intensive training and stern discipline; then during the autumn of 1793 he marched them into the Northwest. The American army occupied the territory above Fort Jefferson, constructed Fort Greenville, and wintered there, continuing their combat drill.

Nearby on the Maumee River the British had erected Fort Miami to guard the approaches to Detroit. Over 2,000 Indian soldiers from the Northwest tribes collected at this post to meet the expected American spring offensive. During the spring and summer of 1794 Wayne's men edged north, occupying more territory, turning back fierce Indian assaults on their lines, but not panicking and rushing to retreat as had the previous armies. In August 1794 at Fallen Timbers Indian troops from the confederated tribes and Wayne's men were locked in decisive combat. The Indian defenders suffered a disastrous defeat. To their surprise and chagrin the British troops at nearby Fort Miami offered no direct support; while the fighting was going on in the North American wilderness, American and British officials in London were concluding a pact, the Jay Treaty, which provided for British evacuation of Detroit and the other posts on American soil no later than June 1, 1796.

American power in the Northwest was established once and for all when Wayne's men constructed Fort Wayne at the head of the Maumee following their victory. During 1795 Wayne's officers collected tribal leaders at Greenville. There they signed the Treaty of Greenville by which on behalf of their tribes the leaders ceded most of Ohio to the United States. In return the United States distributed $20,000 worth of goods to the signatory tribes and pledged an annuity of $10,000 to be shared by the subdued tribes, including the Delawares, Potawatomis, Wyandots, Shawnees, Miamis, Chippewas, Ottawas, and Kickapoos.

The Southern tribes—Cherokees, Creeks, Choctaws, and Chickasaws—felt similar pressure from the spread of Anglo-American settlements. Their leaders filed protests with national government officials demanding the protection promised them by the Hopewell Treaties, and on occasion they took matters into their own hands and attacked pioneer outposts. And like the Northern tribes these Indian communities coalesced into a mutual-protection confederation, committed to guard their territories from appropriation by the new Anglo-American nation. Leader of the Southern Indian Confederation was Alexander McGillivray, a Creek mixed-blood chief who was deeply attached to the land of his forebears.

Spanish officials in neighboring Florida and Louisiana, worried that American expansion in the Southwest might eventually engulf their provinces, attempted to control the Southern Indian Confederation and turn it to serve their purpose, the Indian nations to form a vast defensive cordon insulating Spanish territory from American invasion. Spanish agents won McGillivray and leaders of several other Indian tribes who regularly met in councils with officials at Mobile, Pensacola, and New Orleans for direction. Spain like Great Britain enhanced its power in the Southwest by building military posts on American soil close to the Indian allies to supply them with arms and ammunition and to incite them to attack American settlements. The principal Spanish post on American soil was Fort San Fernando on the Mississippi River at Chickasaw Bluffs, now the site of Memphis.

The Southern Indian Confederation and Spanish anti-American strategy collapsed during the 1790s and, to the southwestern Indian's distinct disadvantage, led to uncontested United States supremacy there. This reverse for the southwestern Indians was brought about by successful American counterdiplomacy which won the loyalty of McGillivray, leader of the confederation. In 1790 he visted the nation's capital at New York City by invitation of President Washington. Federal officials feted him and awarded him the rank of brigadier-general, United States army, with an annual salary of $1,200. McGillivray continued as Spanish agent and patriot leader of the Southern Indian Confederation, but with considerably less vigor. His death in 1793 broke the most important link Spaniards had with southern Indians.

Another cause of the collapse of the Indian confederation was the success of Americans in pacifying the Cherokee nation. A growing segment of that populous tribe had come to accept peace and American presence in their territory. The die-hard group, the Chickamaugas, perhaps seeing the inevitability of the American advance, began during the 1790s to drift west of the Missisippi River into Spanish territory and to settle permanently along the Arkansas and St. Francis rivers.

An additional cause of the decline of the Southern Indian Confederation and the downfall of Spanish influence in the Southwest was the pro-American stand of the Chickasaw nation. Long attached to the British in colonial times, the Chickasaws accepted the Americans after the Treaty of Hopewell and, except for a small pro-Spanish faction, they consistently refused to join McGillivray's Indian confederation. Creek war parties regularly invaded the Chickasaw domain in attempts to intimidate the Chickasaws into joining the Spanish-Indian alliance against the Americans. When soon after 1790 Piomingo, the Mountain Leader, appealed to frontier politicians in the Tennessee settlements for aid, they generously supplied powder and shot. Piomingo held firm. His American-armed warriors defeated the Creek invaders and destroyed all hope of forcing them into the alliance. Their towns also served as strategic centers for American agents in the Southwest.

The southwestern Indians lost their Spanish support in 1795 when officials from that nation concluded with American commissioners the Treaty of San Lorenzo. Just as the Jay Treaty required British forces to withdraw from American posts in the Northwest, strategically close to the insurgent northern tribes, so by the terms of this pact Spain agreed to withdraw from American territory on the east bank of the Mississippi River north of thirty-one degrees latitude.

EVOLVING INDIAN POLICY

The recent military battering suffered by Indian nations in the trans-Appalachian West and their forced witness to the rush of settlers onto their ceded territories was only a revealing foretaste of more devastating losses to come. By 1812 they would be involved in another bloody, destructive war with the United States, more decisive than the conflict just ended. In the interim the government for the new American nation was altered in form; it acquired the power to make it more effective and efficient in management of Indian affairs. Between 1789 and 1812 it formulated a body of policy which endured into the twentieth century.

Constitutional and Ideological Foundations

From experience in Indian affairs officials in the national government quickly learned the folly of sharing responsibility for Indian affairs with the states. The new constitution, which went into effect in 1789, attempted to remedy the weaknesses of the old Articles of Confederation in sharing sovereignty with the states in Indian affairs.

The new basic law delegated to Congress exclusive power in Indian affairs. In its early exercises of this power Congress reiterated the 1787 Northwest Ordinance which committed the national government to treat the Indian nations within its territory with the "utmost good faith" and to formulate "laws founded in justice and humanity . . . for preventing wrongs being done" to the Indians and "for preserving peace and friendship with them." In 1789 Congress established the Department of War. The statute made the cabinet secretary in charge of that agency responsible for matters pertaining to Indians as "entrusted to him by the President."

The United States government came to recognize each Indian tribe as a sovereign entity and to deal with it separately. As an autonomous community, each Indian nation governed its tribal citizens and conducted internal affairs by traditional methods. Anytime a change in relations between the tribe and the United States was required—such as making peace, altering trading privileges, or more importantly, ceding tribal lands—a treaty was negotiated by the President through his agents and ratified by the Senate, much like pacts with foreign nations. This practice in effect committed the United States to separation of the races as a part of its Indian policy. There were national leaders, notably Thomas Jefferson, who regarded racial separation a temporary phase; through the process of gradualism Indians eventually would become "Americanized," acculturated, and thus assimilated into the white Anglo-American nation.

George Washington, Henry Knox, and Thomas Jefferson provided leadership in Indian policy formulation—Indian rights, status, education, and land use—and their viewpoint provided the ideological bases for national Indian relations. Of these three, Secretary of War Knox was the most profound and, from the Indian viewpoint, protective. Knox stated on several occasions, "The Indians being the prior occupants, possess the right of the soil. It cannot be taken from them unless by their free consent, or by the right of conquest in case of a just war." Several government officials recommended that the Indian tribes resisting expansion of American settlements be annihilated by federal armies. Knox denied that the United States had "a clear right consistent with the principles of justice and the laws of nature, to proceed to

Henry Knox, early advocate of allotment in severalty. (Harvard College Library)

destruction or expulsion" of Indians. "It is presumable that a nation solicitous of establishing its character on the broad basis of justice would not only hesitate at, but reject every proposition to benefit itself, by the injury of any neighboring community, however contemptible it might be."[6]

In spite of the grandiose statement of the 1787 Ordinance regarding Indian rights and sanctity of tribal land titles, utopian hopes for ultimate absorption of Indians into Anglo-American society and supporting comments by national leaders, most of the government's Indian policy from 1789 to the middle of the twentieth century was directed to contriving legal means for obtaining tribal land. Above all else Indian tribes were landowners, proprietors of vast tracts which they held in common. The "Great Land Animal," as John Randolph later called the Anglo-American settler, wanted that land. Numbers of settlers increased phenomenally during the post-revolutionary period; their land needs escalated geometrically. Most Americans were farmers. Technological advances and expanding grain and fiber markets led American farmers to shift from subsistence agriculture, which required only a patch in a wilderness clearing, to commercial agriculture, which required several hundred acres for each rural family.

Little regard for "utmost good faith" permeated the frontier districts where Native Americans and pioneers were locked in a savage but unequal contest. Each Anglo-American settler was a sovereign: he was endowed with the franchise. As a voter he chose territorial delegates, congressmen, and senators. In the nation's capital they formulated laws and policy which served his needs. Native Americans lacked this strategic power. They were forced to rely upon the goodwill, fairness, and sense of justice of public officials. And of course to retain their offices, these public officials had to conform to the wishes of their voting constituencies which, more often than not, ran counter to tribal interests. Thus American Indian policy became marked by violations of "utmost good faith" which muddied the national honor. Even the "civilization" and "assimilation" phases of Indian policy, by changing the Indian lifestyle and thus reducing their need for land, became nonviolent, legal means for acquiring additional frontier tracts for settler-voters.

Anglo-American land greed became a national madness. Officials followed a schizo-like stance. On the one hand they righteously expostulated the duty of this Christian nation to protect the Indians' interests. At the same time federal agents on the frontier were directed "to permit no opportunity to pass" to extinguish Indian rights to all the land westward to the Mississippi River. Indian land could be purchased, or it could be taken by force of arms; the 1787 Ordinance stated that the national government could appropriate tribal territory by "just and lawful wars authorized by Congress."

However, it was assumed that "just and lawful wars" would be rare occurrences. Therefore, other means were contrived, including reducing the tribal estates through "civilization." President Jefferson in 1803 stated,

I consider the business of hunting has already become insufficient to furnishing clothing and subsistence to the Indians. The promotion of agriculture, therefore, and household manufacture, are essential to their preservation, and I am disposed

271

to aid and encourage it. This will enable them to live on much smaller portions of land. . . . While they are learning to do better on less land, our increasing numbers will be calling for more land, and thus a coincidence of interests.[7]

The "civilization" process was expected to transform Indians into yeoman farmers. A fundamental value of this hard-working agrarian class was private, individual ownership of land. Colonial leaders in New England had experimented with private ownership of land by Indians as a civilizing influence. Secretary of War Knox recommended adoption of this revolutionary practice for Native Americans in the national period. Aside from drastically reducing the Indian estate, thereby making available, without resorting to arms, immense tracts for Anglo-American settlers, allotment in severalty, as the process of assigning Indians individually owned farmsteads was called, would be an instructive instrument of "civilization" and hasten the Indians' transformation from children of the forest to steady yeoman farmers, ready to be integrated into mainstream Anglo-American society.

The Bureau of Indian Affairs

Just as Indian policy formulated by federal officials during the 1790s extended into the twentieth century, so did the government agency created to carry out this policy. As indicated, in 1789 Congress created the Department of War and assigned primary responsibility for Indian affairs to the secretary of war. The reasoning was that the Indian nations cumulatively possessed great military power, their leaders were regularly in touch with foreign agents, and collectively they comprised a serious military threat to the United States.

Several officials assisted the secretary of war in dealing with the Indian tribes including (after 1806) the superintendent of Indian trade, who directed the Federal Factory System, and the territorial governors, appointed by the President, each of whom served as superintendent for Indian affairs in his territory. In 1824 Secretary of War John C. Calhoun created by executive order the Bureau of Indian Affairs, headed by the commissioner of Indian affairs. An act of 1832 provided statutory authority for this office, the commissioner of Indian affairs to be appointed by the President and to have "direction and management of all Indian affairs, and of all matters arising out of Indian relations." When in 1849 Congress created the Department of the Interior, the statute transferred the Bureau of Indian Affairs to that department where it has remained ever since.

In its early years the national government maintained contact with Indian nations through army officers stationed at remote frontier posts. They frequently served as federal commissioners, presiding at councils with tribal leaders and negotiating treaties with these tribes on behalf of the United States. Secretary of War Knox believed that the interests of the nation would be better served by federal Indian agents living among the tribes. He established the Indian agent system in 1796 when upon his recommendation the President appointed Benjamin Hawkins as Creek agent and superintendent of southern Indians.

Beginning with this appointment in 1796, the agent roster increased to twelve in 1812; by 1832 it contained three territorial governors acting as superintendents of Indian affairs, and about 100 agents, subagents, interpreters, and blacksmiths. Hawkins, the first agent, has had no peer in the Indian service. He spent twenty years with the Creeks, protected them from trespass by expanding Georgians, and succeeded in keeping peace between them and the United States despite the complications of that Indian nation's proximity to the troubled Spanish Florida border.

During the years of maximum Indian power (1789 to 1815) the agent's primary function was to maintain the Indian nation's friendship, distribute gifts and annuities, and watch for British and other foreign intrigue. He was required to live with the tribe to which he was assigned. From their side the Indian nations maintained relations with the United States through delegations of tribal leaders who regularly visited Washington to call on the President. In the days when Indian power comprised collectively a serious military threat to the security of the young United States, these visits were in nature diplomatic delegations.

Congress passed several laws to guide the emerging bureaucracy in staffing the wilderness mission and handling Indian relations for the nation. Laws adopted in 1790, 1793, and 1796 were basic—each was "to regulate trade and intercourse with the Indian tribes, and to preserve peace on the frontier" by providing for licensing traders, protecting Indians from white trespass, controlling the liquor traffic, and defining the Indian country. Each Congress adopted legislation regulating Indian-Anglo-American relations until 1834 when Congress consolidated these rules in the Indian Intercourse Act. Interestingly, the 1799 statute directed the secretary of war to make certain that Anglo-American intruders and squatters on Indian lands, who were also voters, were removed "with all the humanity which the circumstances will possibly permit."

A persistent concern of early Congresses was trade. As early as 1775 the Continental Congress had conceived a plan for public trading houses and in 1776 purchased goods for use in a national frontier trade system. All unlicensed traders were banned from trafficking with the tribes. The 1786 ordinance had divided the trans-Appalachian region into two divisions, each headed by a superintendent, assisted by deputies who enforced the trade regulations and licensed traders. The 1790 law retained the licensing system. Then in 1796 Congress created the Federal Factory System by adopting legislation directing construction of trading posts ("factories" in the language of the day) in the wilderness at public expense, situated convenient to the Indian tribes and manned by federal employees. At the peak of operation there were 28 such posts on the frontiers.

The national government established the Federal Factory System because its agents were failing in their attempts to win the favor of Indian nations through diplomacy. Hopefully trade would accomplish the goal to achieve their commitment to the United States. Officials found it almost impossible to control the actions of the independent traders in the wilderness. The potential collective military power of the Indian tribes was awesome; the threat to harmonious relations with the United States posed by the wilderness trader with his penchant for provoking the tribes by sharp trading practices was very real. The United States profited from previous experiences of several imperial nations which guided creation of the government-financed and managed Indian trade system. France had maintained a successful and profitable government monopoly of the fur trade in North America for a century and a half. And Great Britain and Spain subsidized trading posts on the American borders, using commerce to turn Indians against expansive Anglo-Americans.

Congress provided original capital of $150,000 to fund the Federal Factory System and by 1800 posts at Coleraine on the Georgia frontier and Tellico on the border between Tennessee and the Cherokee nation were completed, manned by federal workers, and doing business with frontier Indians. Between 1802 and 1804 four additional "factories," including one at Detroit and another at Chickasaw Bluffs were started; shortly a post at Chicago was functioning, and by the close of 1809 there were posts in the trans-Mississippi West at Arkansas Post, Belle Fontaine, Natchitoches, and Fort Osage.

Government traders paid Indian hunters full market value for their furs and sold them high-grade metal, textile, and glass goods at cost. Sale of liquor to Native Americans was forbidden. Federal Factory System rules concerning credit varied. It was found that generous credit extended to Indians at the frontier posts could be used to obtain title to tribal land for settlers, and national leaders quite openly used the system for this purpose. President Jefferson regularly admonished federal employees at the government houses to extend more and more credit to the Indians so that they would more readily cede their lands to the United States to pay their mounting debts.

Later Federal Factory System employees were directed to permit only cash transactions. Most Indians required credit, and the rule change led many of them to turn to private traders who functioned largely on a credit system. Also, in spite of rules to the contrary, Indians could obtain alcohol from most private traders. Volume of business began to decline at the government trading posts after 1812. As American fur men moved into the trans-Mississippi West, they formed companies with considerable political power. In 1822 Congress abolished the Federal Factory System.

Americanization and the Indian

Besides trying to win the Indians' loyalty through subsidized trade, federal policy goals included transforming them into civilized mortals cast in the mold of the Anglo-American yeoman farmer. In spite of the "bloodthirsty savage" image held by most Americans, there were national leaders who persistently believed that the most desirous way of solving the new nation's "Indian problem" was to assimilate them. To be worthy of social and biological membership in mainstream society, the Native American had to become civilized through education. This early national concern for Indian education became embedded in federal Indian policy; although reasons for its support varied over time, education continues to the present as the great and ultimate hope for the Indian.

The principal protagonists of Indian education were certain federal officials and spokesmen for missionary societies supported by various American religious bodies. At first these two groups of Indian education advocates went their separate ways in providing civilization opportunities for the Indian nations. Federal support for Indian education began in 1793 when Congress responded to President Washington's recommendation and appropriated $20,000 to be used to purchase domestic animals and farming implements for issue to Indians and for vocational instruction. However, misapplication of these funds intended to benefit Indians—an increasingly common practice among federal officials serving as trustees of Indian resources—was charged when agents allegedly used this money to buy gifts and to entertain tribal leaders for purposes of influencing them to favor land cessions.

Provision for educating tribal youths became a common clause in treaties between the United States and the Indian nations; a 1794 pact with the Oneidas and Tuscaroras committed the federal government to provide funds for educating the youth of those tribes. Beginning in 1802 Congress occasionally appropriated funds, varying from $10,000 to $15,000 per annum, to promote "civilization" among the Indian nations.

In the immediate postrevolutionary period the new nation's religious bodies showed a strong missionary interest in the Indians of the trans-Appalachian region. Moravian, Quaker (Society of Friends), Baptist, Episcopal, Methodist, Congregational (formerly Puritan), Presbyterian, and Dutch Reformed churches launched missionary programs to convert Indians. Most active and successful in the early years were the Moravians, who had also been so active in colonial times. Several religious bodies formed special missionary societies, including the Society for Propagating the Gospel among Indians (1787), Society of the United Brethren for Propagating the Gospel among the Heathen (1787), the Northern Missionary Society (1797), the Connecticut Missionary Society (1798), the Massachusetts Missionary Society (1799), the Western Missionary Society (1802), the United Foreign Missionary Society (1817), and the Missionary and Bible Society of the Methodist Episcopal Church in America (1820). The ecclesiastical organization serving longest and most effectively among Native Americans was the American Board of Commissioners for Foreign Missions, known as the ABCFM or American Board, founded in 1810 and representing the ecumenical effort of Congregationalist, Presbyterian, and Dutch Reformed churches.

Clergy from the missionary societies established themselves among the Indian nations, preached, and attempted to win converts among the adults. Many missionaries attempted to protect Indian rights by complaining to a generally unresponsive public. They also maintained schools for Native American youth; literacy was important for reading Scriptures. Educated Indians became tribal leaders, better able to deal with the expanding Americans.

But missionaries were also a divisive influence in the Indian nations. Their influence was felt in tribal affairs and government. In some cases to hasten the conversion and transformation of life-style, missionaries established separate colonies of Indian converts. Other missionaries simply moved into the tribal territory, erected schools and churches, and attempted to function in the midst of daily tribal life. Missionaries inevitably weakened the tribes by creating schisms, causing Indian nations to fragment into the Christian party and the Pagan party (those committed to retaining old customs). These factions often studiously avoided each other, even living apart. Also the sectarianism of competing missionaries in a single nation further confused and divided the Indians. Thus the presence and teachings of Christian missionaries in an Indian nation often served the purpose of Anglo-American expansion by dividing and thus weakening the tribe, confusing the members and making them easier marks for federal agents seeking their lands.

The separate directions followed by the federal government and the missionary societies in spreading Christian Anglo-American civilization among the Indian nations began to abate in 1819 when Congress adopted a statute creating an Indian civilization program. This measure called for an annual appropriation of about $10,000 for the support of Indian education. The funds were divided among those missionary societies maintaining schools in the Indian nations. To be accredited, missionary schools were required to offer agriculture, reading, writing, and arithmetic to Indian students. Federal officials regarded conversion an essential part of the civilization process. Therefore missionaries were also permitted to preach Christian doctrine to Indians.

Ironically, by the time that the federal and private educational missions coalesced to transform Indians through Anglo-American Christian civilization and thus make them worthy of assimilation into the national society, federal policy changed to a stance of separation of the races. The national government decided to remove those Indian nations which lay in the path of spreading settlement to the remote western wilderness. The saga of Indian removal, the genuine American Tragedy, is the subject of Chapter Twelve.

Notes

1. Harold E. Fey and D'Arcy McNickle, *Indians and Other Americans: Two Ways of Life Meet* (New York, 1970), p. 55.
2. Jack M. Sosin, "The Use of Indians in the War of the American Revolution: A Re-Assessment of Responsibility," in *The American Indian: Past and Present*, edited by Roger L. Nichols and George R. Adams (Waltham, Mass., 1971), p. 107.
3. William T. Hagan, *American Indians* (Chicago, 1961), p. 38.
4. Walter H. Mohr, *Federal Indian Relations, 1774–1788* (Philadelphia, 1933), pp. 100–101.
5. *Ibid.*, p. 148.
6. Fey and McNickle, *Indians and Other Americans*, p. 57.
7. P. L. Ford (ed.), *The Writings of Thomas Jefferson* (New York, 1892), Vol. 3, p. 214.

Selected Sources

The Indian role in the American War for Independence is traced in Jack M. Sosin, *The Revolutionary Frontier, 1763–1783* (New York, 1967), and "The Use of Indians in the War of the American Revolution: A Re-Assessment of Responsibility," in *The American Indian: Past and Present*, edited by Roger L. Nichols and George R. Adams (Waltham, Mass., 1971); Marshall Smelser, *The Winning of Independence* (Chicago, 1972); Donald Higginbotham, *The War of American Independence: Military Attitudes, Policies, and Practice, 1763–1789* (New York, 1971); John R. Alden, *The American Revolution, 1775–1783* (New York, 1954); and *The South in the Revolution* (Baton Rouge, La., 1957). Thomas P. Abernethy, *Western Lands and the American Revolution* (New York, 1937); and Paul C. Phillips, *The West in the Diplomacy of the Revolution* (Urbana, Ill., 1913).

Surveys of Native American history which discuss the origins of American Indian policy include Wilcomb Washburn, *The Indian in America* (New York, 1975); Harold E. Fey and D'Arcy McNickle, *Indians and Other Americans: Two Ways of Life Meet* (New York, 1970); and William T. Hagan, *American Indians* (Chicago, 1961). The most useful study of federal Indian policy evolution is Francis Paul Prucha's *American Indian Policy in the Formative Years: The Indian Trade and Intercourse Acts, 1790–1834* (Cambridge, Mass., 1962). Supportive works on this subject are Walter H. Mohr, *Federal Indian Relations, 1774–1778* (Philadelphia, 1933); George D. Harmon, *Sixty Years of Indian Affairs: Political, Economic, and Diplomatic, 1789–1850* (Chapel Hill, N.C., 1941); and S. Lyman Tyler, *A History of Indian Policy* (Washington, D.C., 1973).

Trade, tribal land, and Indian education are discussed in Ora B. Peake, *A History of the United States Indian Factory System* (Denver, 1954); Walter H. Blumenthol, *American Indians Dispossessed* (Philadelphia, 1955); Reginald Horsman, *Expansion and Indian Policy* (Ann Arbor, Mich., 1967); Wilcomb Washburn, *Red Man's Land, White Man's Law* (New York, 1971); Katherine C. Turner, *Red Men Calling on the Great White Father* (Norman, Okla., 1951); Robert F. Berkhofer, Jr., "Protestants, Pagans, and Sequences Among the North American Indians, 1760–1860," in *The American Indian: Past and Present*, edited by Roger L. Nichols and George R. Adams (Waltham, Mass., 1971), and *Salvation and the Savage: An Analysis of Protestant Missions and American Indian Response, 1787–1862* (New York, 1972).

CHAPTER 12

INDIANS UNDER
ANGLO-AMERICAN
DOMINION
1800–1828

Accursed be the race that has seized on our country and made women of our warriors. Our fathers from their tombs reproach us as slaves and cowards. I hear them now in the wailing winds . . . the spirits of the mighty dead complain. Their tears drop from the wailing skies. Let the white race perish. They seize your land, they corrupt your women, they trample on the ashes of your dead! Back whence they came, upon a trail of blood, they must be driven.

Tecumseh's Appeal to the Southern tribes,
Grand Council, Tukabatchi Town in Alabama,
October 1811

As we have seen, the American Indian was a tragic casualty of imperial expansion, first by the European nations and, after 1776, increasingly by the United States. The rise of the American nation on the Atlantic seaboard and its rapid expansion into the trans-Appalachian interior produced drastic change in attitude toward the Indian. American pioneers entered the wilderness as families. Their society was agrarian-based; the father, mother, and many children of each family provided the labor required to open a frontier farm. Thus, American pioneers did not need the Indians. However, because of their rapidly expanding population and changes in agricultural technology and markets, they needed the Indians' land.

These aggressive, expansive pioneers desired to settle the vast trans-Appalachian territory belonging to powerful Indian nations whose tenure in this land had been guaranteed by treaties with the United States government. As the western settler population increased, resident Indian tribes found themselves engaged in a bitter, sustained contest for control of this land. Settlers regarded Indians as hazardous barriers to fulfillment of their land needs. A mounting concern of national leaders was formulation of a frontier policy which would satisfy the increasing land needs of pioneer citizens and, at the same time, protect the Indian nations from annihilation.

Chapter Opening Artifact: Pueblo brown-ware jar. (Courtesy Museum of the American Indian, Heye Foundation)

JEFFERSONIAN INDIAN POLICY

In the evolution of public processes and techniques, or policy, for Native Americans two men exercised the greatest influence: Thomas Jefferson and Andrew Jackson. Their dominating wills, their values and political philosophies, and their political goals strongly colored the nation's Indian policy. Jeffersonian influences were strongest in the period 1800–1828.

The Jeffersonian Philosophy

President Jefferson did not subscribe to the popular view that Indians were inferior; he believed that "in body and mind" they were "equal" to whites. The essence of Jeffersonian Indian policy was coexistence and gradualism, that is, the steady if slow accommodation of Indians to Anglo-American lifestyle through the transforming process of civilization, culminating in their actually intermarrying into the dominant Anglo-American society.

Jefferson's stress on civilization for Indians became almost an obsession; he believed that for the future of the race it was absolutely essential that they give up hunting, which required vast territory, and adopt the yeoman-farmer style of Anglo-American life, which required only a fraction of the amount of land that a hunting economy needed. Only by this land-use change

Etching from the Patrick Gass journal depicting early federal contact with trans-Missouri tribesmen by representatives of the Lewis and Clark expedition, 1804–1806. (Houghton Library, Harvard University)

and by the acceptance of civilization could "they be absorbed to their infinite advantage, within the American population." Jefferson believed that "civilization would bring peace" between Indians and settlers. Thus under his leadership the national government placed its "greatest hope in its policy of bringing civilization to the Indians." Jefferson constantly urged tribal leaders to change their life-style in order to require less land for their people. He directed governors of the Northwest Territory, Michigan Territory, and Indiana Territory to "promote energetically" the national government's plan for civilizing Indians, and he authorized the assignment of blacksmiths and other artisans to cooperative Indian tribes to maintain plows and other implements for Indian apprentices. He encouraged missionaries to take part in the Indian civilization process. In 1803 he directed the Cherokee agent to erect a schoolhouse for Gideon Blackburn, a Presbyterian missionary, to enable him to instruct Cherokee children. The number of tribal schools increased until in 1824, twenty-one with nearly 1,000 Indian sudents, were functioning.[1]

Jeffersonian Indian policy fitted well with the growing land needs of Anglo-American pioneers. It accepted the inevitability of their advance across the frontier with the national government maintaining firm though regularly changing boundaries through an orderly, managed progression of settlements, made possible by periodic land openings. New settlement zones would be created from new cessions by Native American proprietors.

Jeffersonian Indian policy, while answering the voracious land needs of frontier settlers did attempt to reconcile Anglo-American expansion into the western wilderness with the interests of the Indians. It was naive but well intentioned. Only when pressed did he falter in his protectiveness toward the Indian tribes, as in cases when he attempted to obtain tracts desired by settler-voters and tribal leaders refused to comply. Then he directed managers of federal fur trade factories to advance generous credit to native hunters of that tribe, permitting them to build up debts that only cessions of land by the tribal government could liquidate.

Despite Jefferson's strong commitment to Indian civilization, the program was never successful. At no time was it ever sufficiently supported, fiscally or politically, by Congress and officials in the government. Cynical politicians regarded the nation's "Indian problem" as soluable through the steady advance of hardy American pioneers; in due time extermination rather than assimilation would rid the nation of this vexing complication to its expansion, growth, and development.

Jeffersonian Policy and Removal

The lack of evidence of noticeable progress in Indian civilization during his tenure as the nation's chief executive led Jefferson to consider alternatives for protecting Indian interests and making tribal land available for settlement by Anglo-American pioneers. Jefferson preferred that the eastern Indians remain on their progressively diminished tribal territories and support themselves by agriculture. However, after the United States acquired the vast trans-Mississippi province of Louisiana, he considered colonizing certain eastern Indians there. In each Indian nation Jefferson found that there were spirited factions who seemingly could not cope with the settler tide relentlessly advancing across established boundaries onto tribal territories which the national government had pledged to protect from trespass. Jefferson urged these recalcitrants to consider exchanging eastern lands for wilderness tracts west of the Mississippi River. Thus for eastern Indians removal appeared as an alternative to life on a compressed tribal estate, attempting to coexist with Anglo-American neighbors.

Portions of Jefferson's Indian policy persisted after he left the presidency. The policy of his immediate successors—James Madison, James Monroe, and John Quincy Adams—continued in varying degrees the Jeffersonian style and mode for managing the Indian tribes. Gradually, however, removal and segregation by exile into the trans-Mississippi wilderness eclipsed coexistence and assimilation as cornerstones of federal management of the eastern tribes. The War of 1812 was a major precipitant of the public demand that the Native Americans in the trans-Appalachian region be exiled to the western wilderness.

NATIVE AMERICANS AND THE WAR OF 1812

The War of 1812, involving fighting men from several Indian tribes as well as British and American armies, in many respects was a resumption of the war which began in 1776. Much of the national fury which precipitated the American declaration of war was stirred by the awesome and threatening British-supported Indian league formed among the tribes of the trans-Appalachian West.

Origins of the Conflict

In both the Old Northwest and the Old Southwest federal commissioners had achieved spectacular successes in reducing the domains of certain tribes to meet the escalating demands of an ever-growing pioneer population for more land on which to establish settlements and open farms. In the Old Southwest federal treaties with the Cherokees, Creeks, Choctaws, and Chickasaws had yielded cessions for roads, several of them strips of land five miles wide for rights-of-way across Indian nations as well as sites for military and trading posts, transportation rights on navigable rivers in the Indian nations, and territorial cessions for accommodating expanding settlements. By the Treaty of Holston in 1791 Cherokee leaders ceded land on the Tennessee-North Carolina border, right-of-way for a road to the Cumberland settlements, and navigation rights on the Tennessee River. Then during 1798 by the Treaty of Tellico, concluded at Tellico Blockhouse in eastern Tennessee, the Cherokees ceded three tracts, one in the Cumberland Mountains and two south of the

Holston River. By the Tellico pact the United States pledged on its "sacred national honor" to guarantee and protect the remainder of the Cherokee country "forever." The Creeks, too, felt continuing pressure for additional land cessions from both the national government and the state of Georgia. Boundaries for their nation had been set by the Treaty of New York in 1790. Four years later Georgia officials seized huge blocks of Creek territory as compensation for state troops on active duty guarding the frontier to prevent Creek retaliation against Georgians squatting on tribal lands. Creek leaders protested to national officials, and in 1796 they concluded with federal commissioners the Treaty of Colerain which confirmed the boundaries set by the Treaty of New York. This in effect restored the lands seized by Georgia officials, and it represented one of the very few occasions on which federal officials interceded on behalf of Indians, forcing a state to rescind action taken against tribes. The more westerly situated Choctaw and Chickasaw nations also suffered some territorial compression during this prelude to the War of 1812.

However, at this time, most of the pressure on the tribes for land cessions occurred in the territory north of the Ohio River. There William Henry Harrison, governor of Indiana Territory, continued to press the tribes to cede more and more land to accommodate the onrushing tide of settlers. A shrewd negotiator, by 1809 he had completed fifteen treaties calling for substantial cessions of territory by the Piankeshaws, Weas, Delawares, Potawatomis, Miamis, Kickapoos, Ottawas, and other tribes. Following each cession, the signatory tribes simply retreated to diminished tribal territories until by 1809 they had virtually no land remaining and some tribes, following surrender of the last fragment of their homeland, were required to move onto the surviving domains of neighboring tribes. At Fort Wayne in 1809 Harrison concluded a treaty with Delaware and Potawatomi leaders which ceded 3 million acres of tribal land in Indiana to the United States in exchange for $7,000 and an annuity of $1,750. The Fort Wayne Treaty marked the high point of Harrison's treaty-making success and became the principal cause of bloody prelude to the War of 1812 on the trans-Appalachian frontier.

Tecumseh and the Prophet

Harrison's treaties and the advancing tide of settlers had scattered, confused, and intimidated the Indians of the Northwest tribes. However, their deliverance seemed imminent when two Indian nationalists—Tecumseh and Elskwatawa the Prophet—appeared. These brothers, of mixed Shawnee-Creek parentage, provided the leadership which transformed destitute, rum-soaked, desolated Indians into proud, hardy warriors, committed to destroy the Anglo-American intruders.

Tecumseh and the Prophet lived in a small Shawnee settlement near Greenville, Ohio. In 1805 they began to preach their ideas of Indian renaissance through nativism, restoration, and pan-Indianism (an antecedent of Red

Tecumseh—Shawnee chieftain, nonpareil orator and statesman, leader of the Pan-Indian movement, 1800–1812. (Field Museum of Natural History, Chicago)

Power), which committed their followers to expulsion of Anglo-Americans from tribal territories. Tecumseh and the Prophet focused upon Indian renewal and territorial recovery and their doctrine that no individual or tribe could alienate title to land held in common by all Indians of a region. Their Indian restoration teachings rejected Jeffersonian civilization and assimilation; their pan-Indianism became a program of confrontation with the expanding Anglo-Americans.

In 1808 Tecumseh and the Prophet moved to the ruins of Kithtippecanoe, an old Indian town on Tippecanoe Creek in Indiana Territory. The settlement came to be called Prophetstown and was a center for the various tribes of the Northwest Territory. Beginning with 140 followers, the Prophet and Tecumseh began an evangelistic crusade that inspired the periodic migration of thousands of Indian families to the council grounds on the edge of Prophetstown. There the listeners were entranced with the oratorical brilliance of Tecumseh and the mysticism of the Prophet, each focusing his special talents on the theme of Indian nationalism. They described and interpreted the woes of the Indian; both pointed to rampant internal divisions and the abandonment of certain old customs that had been sources of Indian strength. The debauchery and poverty of the tribes, in fact every torment of the moment, were attributed to the American advance in the Northwest.

The Prophet was more zealous than Tecumseh, sometimes using mystical seizures to render messages from the Great Holy Force Above. Through him the Great Holy Force Above promised that soon Indians would have the means to destroy every American. The Prophet assured his attentive audiences that he had been endowed with the power to cure diseases, confound enemies, and stay the arm of death in sickness or on the battlefield. The Great Holy Force Above, he claimed, had ordained a new way of life for Indians, and all must purify themselves and adopt it. No follower was to have any dealings with the Americans. The British were to be considered the friends of Indians, the Americans their enemies.

Tecumseh's stability complemented his brother's volatility. Avoiding the emotional, dramatic technique of the Prophet, Tecumseh maintained a rational approach to the Indians' problems. His legalism was persuasive. He claimed no special access to the Great Holy Force Above, but taught with directness; drunkenness and vice were condemned, the white customs were to be shunned, and each warrior must return to certain old customs. As a symbol of rejection of white culture, Native Americans should cast off textile clothing and wear skins as of old. Each warrior was to reform his personal conduct in order to recover his physical, moral, and spiritual strength.

Since most of the Indian-American friction grew out of the issue of land tenure, Tecumseh directed his attention first to retaining what was left of Indian lands, and second to recovering lands in American possession. The basis for Tecumseh's argument was that in the beginning the Great Holy Force Above had provided the land for the use of all Native Americans. No single tribe was intended to be the sole proprietor of a given area; all land was ordained to be held in common. Therefore, no tribe or fraction of a tribe could presume to transfer title of land to the United States without the common consent of all Indians.

Most of the Indian attenders returned to their home villages to ponder the teachings of Tecumseh and the Prophet and to relate them to their fellow Indians. They returned from time to time to receive an interpretation of the most recent revelation by the mystical Elskwatawa or an exposition from the eloquent Tecumseh. Many, however, accepted Indian nationalism so completely that they separated from their tribes, built lodges for their families at Prophetstown, and settled there permanently. By 1811 nearly 1,000 warriors from the Northwest tribes lived at Prophetstown.

After the Fort Wayne Treaty negotiations Tecumseh personally confronted Governor Harrison and repudiated the treaty "on the ground that all the land belonged to all the Indians, and that not even the whole membership of a single tribe could alienate the property of the race." He warned Harrison to keep surveyors and settlers out of the tract ceded by the Treaty of Fort Wayne. There ensued a two-year impasse. Harrison realized that if Tecumseh's will prevailed, Indians in northwestern Indiana would permanently "exclude the United States from further expansion."[2]

In 1811, Tecumseh, accompanied by a Kickapoo escort, visited the Indian tribes south of the Ohio River and urged them to join him in his cause to check the American expansion. At councils with the Choctaws, Chickasaws, Creeks, and Cherokees he pointed to the menace of the onrushing white horde. His orations usually included this bitter denunciation:

The white race is a wicked race. Since the days when the white race first came in contact with the red men, there has been a continual series of aggressions. The hunting grounds are fast disappearing, and they are driving the red man farther and farther to the west. Such has been the fate of the Shawnees, and surely will be the fate of all tribes if the power of the whites is not forever crushed. The mere presence of the white man is a source of evil to the red men. His whiskey destroys the bravery of our warriors, and his lust corrupts the virtue of our women. The only hope for the red man is a war of extermination against the paleface. Will not the warriors of the southern tribes unite with the warriors of the Lakes?

Of all the Southern tribes, Tecumseh's message appealed only to one faction in the Creek nation, the Red Sticks.[3]

While Tecumseh was in the South, Governor Harrison determined to break the impasse and march on the pan-Indian settlement of Prophetstown. Mustering an army of 1,000 he moved on the intertribal town on Tippecanoe Creek, arriving on November 6, 1811. At dawn next day 400 warriors began a series of suicidal assaults on Harrison's lines. The Americans fell back, finally rallied, and turned the charges, causing the attackers to retreat. The Prophet's medicine had failed them; they did not have the power to turn back the enemy's bullets or stay the arm of death, and 38 of their fellow warriors lay dead on the battlefield. Their retreat was complete; they even abandoned the village. Harrison's army collected nearly 150 dead and countless wounded, burned Prophetstown, and returned to Vincennes, claiming victory.

After Harrison's army dispersed the confederated Indian community at Prophetstown, the aroused Indians fell upon the American settlements in the Northwest with great fury, forcing the pioneers to flee to the safety of Vincennes and other fortified towns. American officials, including Governor Harrison, charged that the Indians were supplied with arms, blankets, and provisions and incited to wage war on the American settlements by British agents at Fort Malden—a post on the Canadian side of the Detroit River built after the British evacuation of Detroit.

The Northwest Tribes in the War of 1812

Americans in the Northwest reacted to the devastating Indian raids by pleas to the national government for relief and protection. Various groups in the East and South with grievances against Great Britain in other matters joined the settlers in their demand for national retaliation. Thus on June 18, 1812, Congress voted to declare war on Great Britain.

The secretary of war directed General William Hull, commander of the

Scene from the War of 1812 showing Indians involved in combat. (Anne S. K. Brown Military Collection, Brown University Library)

western army, to capture Fort Malden and bring the adjacent portion of Canada under American control. Hull with his 2,000-man army made a slow, hesitant thrust toward the objective. General Isaac Brock, British commander in this Canadian sector with a combined Northwest Indian and British North American regular army cut Hull's supply line, causing the timid American to fall back toward Detroit. On August 16, Brock marched into Detroit with his army and Hull capitulated. The fall of Detroit, coupled with the Indian-British conquest of Fort Dearborn at the southern tip of Lake Michigan appeared to spell doom for the American cause in the Northwest.

Combined Indian-British armies began to probe south to the approaches of Fort Wayne and Fort Harrison in Indiana. The national government, in hopes of mitigating the effects of Hull's demoralizing surrender, assigned Governor Harrison the task of blunting the invasion and driving the enemy back into Canada. For the remainder of 1812, Harrison directed his attention to strengthening the interior line of Northwest defenses. The next step in the American reconquest was to gain control of Lake Erie which bristled with British guns mounted on the lake flotilla. On September 10, 1813, in a bloody three-hour battle, U.S. Naval Lieutenant Oliver H. Perry's gunners swept the British from Lake Erie. The naval threat removed, Perry transported Harrison's army of 5,000 men to the Canadian shore. The American invaders met the Indian-British army on the Thames River on October 5, 1813, and inflicted a smashing defeat; among those slain was Tecumseh. The Battle of the Thames was decisive for Native Americans. Besides losing their greatest leader, the contest marked the end, for all time, of Indian-British power in the Old Northwest. For the remainder of the war, fighting men from the Northwest tribes, shorn of any substantive British support, continued their resistance struggle against the Anglo-Americans through guerrilla-type strikes against outlying settlements north of the Ohio River.

The Southwest Tribes in the War of 1812

As indicated, the only Indians south of the Ohio River who seriously considered the anti-American teachings of Tecumseh were members of the Red Stick faction of the Creek nation. Led by William Weatherford, a worthy successor of the earlier Creek leader Alexander McGillivray, the Red Sticks ravaged the frontier settlements of western Georgia and Alabama during 1813–1814. Red Stick power reached its climax with the conquest of Fort Mims, a post on the lower Alabama River. Over 500 persons died in the attack. General Andrew Jackson, commander of military forces south of the Ohio River, mustered an army of 5,000 militia from Tennessee and Kentucky—augmented with regiments of loyal Creeks, Cherokees, Choctaws, and Chickasaws—and campaigned through the Creek country to avenge the Fort Mims massacre. The Red Stick Creeks concentrated at Tohopeka, a fortified town on the Horseshoe Bend of Tallapoosa River in central Alabama. On March 27, 1814, Jackson's army surrounded the town. While cannon fire swept the battlements, loyal Creek, Choctaw, Cherokee, and Chickasaw fighters flanked the defenders downriver. The offensive vice tightened; over 800 Creeks were slain at the Battle of Horseshoe Bend.

General Jackson convened the leaders of the Creek nation at Fort Jackson on August 9, 1814. He made clear that he held the entire Creek nation responsible for the Red Stick insurgency and took from the Creeks by the Treaty of Fort Jackson—as a sort of reparations of war—22 million acres of land in southern Georgia and central Alabama.

Cherokee, Choctaw, loyal Creek, and Chickasaw companies served with General Jackson's army in the defense of New Orleans which concluded hostilities for the War of 1812 south of the Ohio River. To their dismay, the leaders of these tribes soon learned that their reward for loyal service to the United States was a growing expectation that they surrender their lands and exile themselves into the trans-Mississippi wilderness. The War of 1812, concluded by the Treaty of Ghent on December 24, 1814, in a real sense ended, from a military standpoint, the Indian problem in the eastern United States.

BEGINNINGS OF TRIBAL EXILE

Following the War of 1812 there occurred a phenomenal burst of Anglo-American settlement and development in the Old Northwest, Old Southwest, and Mississippi Valley. The region's ultimate destiny, however, according to local politicians was retarded by the continuing presence of Indian nations who occupied choice lands. Moreover, with admission of more and more states to the Union, the power of the West in national political affairs was growing. The region's ever-larger delegation of congressmen and senators was unanimously committed to exiling resident tribes into the trans-Mississippi wilderness. They were supported by citizen delegations from the frontier communities who regularly visited Washington to present petitions and memorials to this effect to the President and other officials. They stressed that a proper punishment for the treasonable conduct of the tribes for supporting Great Britain in the recent war would be total surrender of their lands as reparations, and emigration.

The Ideology of Dispossession

Thus national leaders increasingly were pressured to compromise the Jeffersonian policy of coexistence, civilization, and assimilation with escalating demands for expropriation and removal. Various solutions to this vexing dilemma were offered. One was to continue the policy of coexistence and ad hoc compression of tribal estates through cessions to satisfy settler demand, the tribesmen retreating to ever-reduced territories. State governments, and territorial governments aching to become states, objected, claiming that this arrangement permitted the unconstitutional practice of states existing within states.

Another suggested solution was allotment in severalty, dividing communally owned tribal lands into 80- to 160-acre homesteads and placing each Indian family on an allotment; the national government would then absorb the surplus lands into the public domain for settlement by its citizens. And assimilation advocates believed that adoption of this plan by Native Americans would be a major step along the road to civilization. Puritans in New England had used allotment in their attempts to convert Native Americans from common (tribal) to private individual ownership of property. Former Secretary of War Henry Knox had urged its application as a civilizing device. Secretary of War William H. Crawford continued this advocacy. In 1816, when removal increasingly was considered as the most desirable solution to the Indian problem, he proposed that allotment in severalty be offered to Indians as an alternative to removal. This he believed would overcome objections of those who had expressed a determination not to emigrate. By treaties concluded with the Cherokees in 1817 and 1819 and with the Choctaws in 1820, provision was made for voluntary allotment in severalty to heads of Indian families; 311 Cherokees and 8 Choctaws applied for allotments under these provisions.

Allotment was rejected by settlers and their spokesmen in Congress; nothing short of removal would satisfy them. Several well-intentioned public officials including Thomas McKenney, head of the Bureau of Indian Affairs, and William Clark, superintendent of Indian affairs at St. Louis, came to regard removal as a necessary and humane step to preserve Native Americans from extermination and the only way that the civilization process could continue: "Only if the Indians were removed beyond contact with whites could the slow process of education, civilization, and Christianization take place."[4]

Clark cogently observed,

The relative condition of the United States on the one side, and the Indian tribes on the other [had drastically changed. Before the War of 1812] the tribes nearest our settlements were a formidable and terrible enemy; since then, their power has been broken, their warlike spirit subdued, and themselves sunk into objects of pity and commiseration. While strong and hostile, it has been our obvious policy to weaken them; now that they are weak and harmless, and most of their lands fallen into our hands, justice and humanity require us to cherish and befriend them. [The eastern tribes should be taught by government agents to] live in houses, to raise grain and stock, to plant orchards . . . to establish laws for their government, to get the rudiments of common learning, such as reading, writing, and ciphering . . . the first steps toward improving their condition. [To accomplish this] the tribes now within the limits of the States and Territories should be removed to a country beyond [the Mississippi River] where they could rest in peace.[5]

President James Monroe agreed with Clark. He concluded that "To civilize them was essential to their survival"; however, this was a "slow process and could not be attained in the territory where the Indians then resided." Unlike certain of his successors, Monroe did not advocate forceful expulsions, because that would be "revolting to humanity, and utterly unjustifiable." His logical solution to the moral dilemma of Indian emigration was:

The hunter or savage state requires a greater extent of territory to sustain it, than is compatible with the progress and just claims of civilized life, and must yield to it. [Therefore,] it was right that the hunter should yield to the farmer, for the earth was given to mankind to support the greatest number of which it is capable, and no tribe or people have a right to withhold from the wants of others more than is necessary for their own support and comfort.[6]

The nation's judiciary also played a role in defending appropriation of the Indian estate. Jurists as well as officials in the executive and legislative branches of the national government had respected the position on Indian land tenure stated by former Secretary of War Knox:

The Indians, being the prior occupants, possess the right of the soil. It cannot be taken from them unless by their consent, or by the right of conquest in case of a just war. To dispossess them on any other principle would be a great violation of the fundamental laws of nature.[7]

As was to happen from time to time in later years when the President and Congress failed to protect tribal interests as required by treaty stipulation, Native American leaders appealed to the federal courts for remedy. Their test case of the Knox principle, *Johnson's and Graham's Lessee* v. *McIntosh*, reached the United States Supreme Court in 1823. The decision added to the growing defense for dispossessing the eastern tribes by enhancing the federal government's position in the management of tribal lands. Chief Justice John Marshall wrote the opinion which defined the nature of Indian land title. The court concluded that the national interest in all the land within the United States came from the right of discovery which it had inherited from Great Britain, France, and other European sovereigns who had at one time held land which the United States had acquired. Thus the ultimate legal title to this territory was vested in the United States. By this decision the resident Indian nations held the right of occupancy to certain territories which, by court definition, was subordinate or inferior to the right of discovery. Title through right of discovery did not extinguish the rights of the native inhabitants; they had a "legal as well as a just claim to retain possession of the soil and to use it according to their own discretion" until the sovereign, the United States government, properly extinguished their title. In other words, the Indian nations held a sort of overlay of title to the land which had to be erased before the land could be placed in the public domain and opened to settlers.

Some politicians justified seizure of tribal estates on grounds that the national government had an absolute title to all land embraced by the United States. Eventually this view triumphed.[8]

These ideological convolutions were necessary for Jeffersonians in their strained efforts to resolve their haunting indecision over Indian status. Were Indians persons in a constitutional sense, and thereby the beneficiary of constitutional protection in their rights as were other persons within the American community? Likewise Jeffersonians were uneasy over the basic inconsistency on the one hand of Anglo-American tradition of sacredness of property rights and what had become the callous expropriation of Indian estates.

There was a growing ideological gap between Jeffersonians who dominated the leadership of the national government and Anglo-American pioneers exposed to day-to-day hazards of wilderness living. Increasingly the viewpoint of the latter group on Indians and other matters of public concern was being felt in national affairs. A lusty, growing minority by the early 1820s, they would finally triumph in 1828, mustering sufficient electoral power to put Andrew Jackson into the White House. However, for the time being frontier settlers ignored constitutional and moral questions as they related to Native Americans. They expected and demanded that their government punish the Indian nations for their treasonable association with Great Britain during the War of 1812 and that this punishment consist of appropriating tribal lands and exiling all Indians to the trans-Mississippi wilderness.

To Indians of the trans-Appalachian West, prospects for any sort of satisfying existence there in the postwar period were grim indeed. Their collective military power had been destroyed. This alone, as Clark admitted, kept the United States in a position of reluctant deference toward the Indian nations. Now that their favored status was lost, they could expect the worst from the victorious United States. For all appearances Great Britain was finally prepared to accept the United States as a peer nation rather than an insurgent colonial child expected eventually to return, voluntarily or otherwise, to the imperial home. Thus the Indian tribes no longer held the balance of power between the United States and Great Britain. The disastrous defeat of the French by Great Britain in the 1760s had cost the Indian nations what at the time appeared to be an indispensable ally against British expansion. However, during and after the American War for Independence Great Britain became the ally of the trans-Appalachian Indians against the expanding Anglo-Americans. But it became clear after 1815 that this relationship had ended. No longer was there a European nation to be an ally against the United States. Indian power declined proportionately. Parenthetically, insurgent factions among the southern tribes lost a source of support, although admittedly weak and uncertain, from Spanish officials in Florida. Anglo-American invasions of Florida began during the War of 1812 and continued until 1819 when the United States absorbed Florida.

BEGINNINGS OF REMOVAL

Finally national leaders reached the decision to remove the eastern tribes to the trans-Mississippi West. Under present conditions fulfillment of the three-part Jeffersonian policy of coexistence, civilization, and assimilation was impossible. Rapid extension of Anglo-American settlement across the frontier had created disorders and distractions and posed such a serious threat to Native Americans, even to that of extermination, that idealistic Jeffersonian coexistence was absolutely impossible; civilization and assimilation were thus foolish dreams. The Jeffersonians concluded that it would be best for Native Americans to cede their eastern territories (which would quiet the noisy demands of settlers) to the United States and relocate in the western wilderness. And with a fresh start, isolated from the destructive influences of pioneers, they could resume the federally sponsored civilization program.

Therefore, removal, tribal exile, and aboriginal segregation became the focus of national Indian policy. Jefferson had been the first chief executive to advocate removal to certain factions of the eastern tribes, and between 1804 and 1825, limited relocations of several tribes under federal auspices had been carried out. However, President James Monroe was the first to propose to move all eastern Indians west of the Mississippi River. He presented his Indian colonization plan to Congress in January 1825. It included tribal relocation at government expense and assignment to the emigrating Indians of western territory at least equal in extent and quality to the lands they were vacating in the East. Above all else Monroe insisted that the tribes had to consent "voluntarily" to cede their eastern lands and emigrate.

The Voluntary Exiles

Long before the eastern Indian nations were relocated under federal government removal programs, Native Americans from both north and south of the Ohio River were moving into the trans-Mississippi territory. During colonial

American Claim to Tribal Territories, 1800-1828

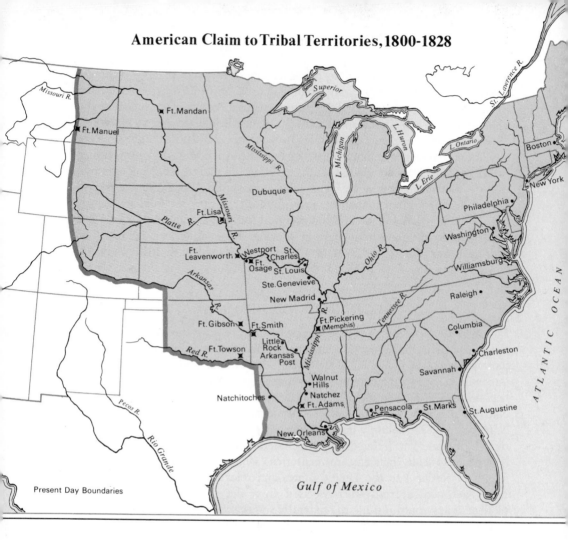

times bands of Kickapoos, Shawnees, Delawares, Sac and Fox, Miamis, and Ottawas had migrated from the Great Lakes region across the Mississippi River in the company of French and British traders. Then, soon after Spain received Louisiana from France in 1762, Spanish officials at St. Louis, the administrative center for upper Louisiana, found that Osage power threatened their hold on this region. They established an alliance with Kickapoos who were drifting across the Mississippi in increasing numbers. The émigrés protected the Spanish settlements in Missouri until after 1800. Following American independence bands of Kickapoos and other Northwest tribes, scorning what they considered contamination by "Long Knives" (American frontier settlers) joined their kin in the trans-Mississippi territory.

In 1794 The Bowl, a Cherokee, led an ambush of Anglo-American settlers on the Tennessee River. For this so-called Massacre of Muscle Shoals, The Bowl and his followers were ostracized by the Cherokee council. To escape retribution by frontier militia as well as their people, The Bowl and his warriors, with their families, crossed the Mississippi into Spanish territory and settled on the St. Francis River in what became Arkansas Territory. This group became the nucleus for additional Cherokee settlement in the West.

Soon after the United States acquired the province of Louisiana, Spanish officials on the northern frontier of Mexico formed a defense system in Texas which included settling emigrant tribes from the United States along rivers at strategic points to front the expanding Americans and to protect the Texas settlements from destructive Comanche raids. Colonel Antonio Cordero received several bands of Cherokees, Shawnees, Kickapoos, and Delawares and resettled them on land granted to the émigrés by the Spanish king. Most of their settlements were on the Sabine and Angelina rivers in east Texas. Chief Bowles and his Cherokee followers from Arkansas dominated this confederated Indian community.

Removal of the Northwest Tribes

The relocation of Indian communities from the Northwest Territories did not occur in a single year. As late as the 1840s tribal remnants from this region were still being relocated to the trans-Mississippi West. Moreover, some Northwest Indian tribes withdrew to lands so unattractive to settlers that they completely escaped removal to the West; late in the twentieth century residual communities of Potawatomis, Menominees, and certain other tribes still remain in isolated portions of the Old Northwest.

The first step in the process of liquidating tribal estates in this region and removing resident tribes to the trans-Mississippi territory occurred during 1815. This was, in a sense, a resumption of the work of former Governor Harrison of the Indiana Territory, whose progress in erasing title to tribal lands had been arrested by Tecumseh's powerful protest of the Treaty of Fort Wayne in 1809. American victories in the Northwest during the War of 1812 had settled the issues raised by Tecumseh's confrontation with Governor Harrison.

During the summer of 1815, leaders of the Northwest tribes met with federal commissioners at Portage des Sioux in Illinois Territory. The treaties that resulted from this council provided officially for resumption of American dominion over the tribes. All parties agreed that every injury or act of hostility by either party towards the other was "forgiven and forgotten," and each party pledged "perpetual peace and friendship." The next step was for American commissioners to negotiate cession treaties. Federal officials were particularly anxious to secure a strategic tract of over 2 million acres between the Illinois and Mississippi rivers. During the War of 1812 Congress had reserved this land for military bounties, and holders of land warrants were demanding an opportunity for redemption. Between 1816 and 1818, government commissioners obtained cessions to portions of this tract from the Peorias, Kaskaskias, and several smaller tribes.

A considerable portion of the bounty lands, however, was held by the Kickapoos. This powerful pro-British tribe also controlled enclaves of territory on the Wabash River in the Indiana Territory and the rich Illinois and

Sangamon river country in north central Illinois. After much delay by tribal leaders and a good deal of pressure by the commissioners, in 1819 the Kickapoos finally agreed to exchange their Illinois and Wabash lands for a domain in the trans-Mississippi territory. Nearly 2,000 Kickapoos moved west of the Mississippi River during 1819; but two renegade bands repudiated the cession treaties, refused to consider removal, and remained in Illinois.

One band, numbering 250 and led by Mecina, was particularly incensed by the Treaty of Edwardsville. Mecina adamantly refused to acknowledge that the Kickapoo homeland had been surrendered to the United States. With the vigor of a fanatic, he regularly recited to Superintendent Clark the doctrine of Tecumseh, denying that his tribe or any other could unilaterally sign away tribal lands and "the resting places of the bones of their ancestors." Mecina's Kickapoo band preyed on the edge of the advancing line of American settlement in Illinois, looting isolated farmhouses, stealing horses, and shooting cattle and hogs. In 1824, a settlers' association in Fulton County, Illinois, complained in a petition to Congress that the continuing Kickapoo presence was a serious threat to life and property. Federal troops and Illinois militia units responded to the settler appeals, and close and constant military surveillance caused Mecina to lead his Kickapoo followers reluctantly across the Mississippi.

Another recalcitrant Kickapoo band of about 250 members lived along the Vermilion River. Their leader was Kennekuk, a self-styled prophet. He taught his followers to lead a simple, peaceful life of meditation and to disregard the swirling pressure of the American settlements. Each of Kennekuk's disciples was required to undertake a strict regimen of fasting and general rejection of materialism and to return to the ancient life-style in which the individual lived close to nature. Kennekuk promised his followers that by seeking "simple virtue" each would have as his reward eternal life in a holy place free of torment and American settlers. By means of passive resistance, Kennekuk defied the removal requirements of the 1819 treaties. His quiet determination and captivating oratory caused Clark and other officials charged with the duty of clearing Indians from the Northwest to indulge the Kickapoo prophet and his people. Endowed with abundant native ability, Kennekuk was exceedingly skilled in the art of delay; each time Clark pressed him to take his followers west of the Mississippi, Kennekuk assured Clark that it was his wish to comply with the demands but because the corn "was yet in the milk" or because of illness in his band, or more often than not, because the Great Holy Force Above had advised that this was not the time to move, the prophet remained in Illinois. Not until the spring of 1834 did Kennekuk lead his Kickapoo band from their Vermilion River homeland toward the West.

The Kickapoo cessions, accomplished by the treaties of 1819, cleared the lands most directly in the path of expanding American settlements. The next tribes to feel the pressure for surrender of Northwest lands were the Sac and Fox, who occupied western Illinois and Wisconsin, the Chippewas, who held the territory along the south shore of Lake Superior, certain Sioux communities west of the Great Lakes, Potawatomi bands in the area south of Lake Michigan, and Winnebagos on the Wisconsin River. Superintendent Clark and Lewis Cass, governor of Michigan Territory, met in council with leaders of these tribes at Prairie du Chien, Wisconsin, in 1825. The resulting treaties provided for continuing peace between the tribes and the United States, a confirmation of tribal territories in the Northwest, and a commitment to future reduction of these territories.

The Prairie du Chien treaties were timely from the viewpoint of American expansion. The completion of the Erie Canal and the extension of mining and agricultural settlements in western Illinois and Wisconsin in 1825 accelerated the Americanization of the vast tracts in the Old Northwest. Within ten years after the signing of the Prairie du Chien treaties virtually all Indians had been cleared from this portion of the Northwest. The Sac and Fox, Winnebago, Sioux, and most Potawatomi bands had been colonized west of the Mississippi River. The Chippewas had retreated far into northern Wisconsin and the Menominees had been pushed beyond the Green Bay area.

Two incidents marred the evacuation of Indian tribes from the Northwest. Discovery of rich lead deposits on the western border of Illinois and Wisconsin during the 1820s caused a rush of miners and farmers into the territory of the new bonanza. Before long mining camps and farms were appearing on lands claimed by the Winnebago and Sac and Fox Indians. Red Bird, a patriot leader of the Winnebagos, prepared his people to resist this miner-settler intrusion. During 1827 he led several raids on the mining settlements, but was thwarted on each occasion by spirited local defense. Regular army units joined militia forces to destroy this threat to the Illinois-Wisconsin mining settlements. Red Bird and Winnebago warriors fell back into the interior and finally were trapped between two American columns on the upper Wisconsin River. Red Bird's capitulation ended the Winnebago threat for all time.

The second incident centered on a massacre of Sac and Fox Indians known as the Black Hawk War. Under pressure from miners and farmers a band of Sac and Fox Indians led by Black Hawk ranged the country between the Illinois and Wisconsin rivers. During the summer of 1831 the line of American settlements extended into their territory, and Black Hawk collected his people, numbering about 1,000 men, women, and children, and settled them near the old tribal grounds at Rock Island. Federal officials urged Black Hawk to move across the Mississippi River into Iowa; and when the Sac and Fox leader refused, troops marched into the village and forced the Indians to cross the river. But during the spring of 1832, Black Hawk and his band returned to their land in Illinois, bringing not only warriors but women and children as well. Settlers regarded the move as an invasion and in great panic demanded that state and federal officials protect them. Illinois militia units marched against Black Hawk's band and engaged the Indians in several minor battles but were unable to turn them back. Finally, federal troops from the Illinois posts and Jefferson Barracks in Missouri moved in. Black Hawk led his people north into the wilds of Wisconsin, hotly pursued by regular

Black Hawk, Sac and Fox chieftain, resisted removal of his people to the trans-Mississippi West. (The Warner Collection of Gulf States Paper Corporation)

army units and militia. Cornered on the Bad Axe River and exhausted and hungry from their long march, the Indians made a last stand. The carnage that followed, precipitated largely by the militia components of the converging host, left over 300 Indians dead. Black Hawk was taken prisoner of war.

On August 7, 1832, General Winfield Scott met with Sac and Fox leaders at Fort Crawford. Their deliberations produced a treaty providing for the cession by the Sac and Fox of a strip of territory fifty miles wide on the west bank of the Mississippi River along the future eastern border of Iowa; this strip, the Black Hawk purchase, was to serve as a buffer to restrain the Sac and Fox from returning to Illinois.

Federal officials continued to collect scattered bands of Old Northwest tribes and relocate them beyond the Mississippi River until mid-century. However, most of the Indian survivors of the War of 1812 had been exiled to the western wilderness by 1830.

Scene from the Black Hawk War. The Sauk are shown being fired on as they attempt to return to their homes. (The New York Public Library)

Removal of the Southwest Tribes

Citizens in the Old Southwest demanded no less strongly than those in the Old Northwest that the national government remove the Indian tribes from their regions. By 1821 the Cherokee nation numbered somewhat over 20,000, the Choctaw nation about 22,000, the Seminole nation 4,000, the Creek nation over 22,000, and the Chickasaw nation approximately 5,000. These Native Americans occupied valuable lands and, according to business and political leaders, held up settlement and development in the states where they lived. Each of the Indian nations also maintained a tribal government that had jurisdiction over members and, by treaty with the United States, the tribal citizens and tribal governments were exempt from state laws. To state leaders these tribal governments challenged state sovereignty and comprised, in a sense, states within a state; in some cases there was more than one nation within the borders of a single state, and each one exercised complete sovereignty within its own area.

By the 1820s successive land cessions negotiated by federal commissioners and tribal leaders had substantially reduced the tribal domains in the Old Southwest, with the result that the Cherokees were concentrated in eastern Tennessee, northwestern Georgia, and eastern Alabama; the Creeks in western Georgia and Alabama; the Choctaws in southern Mississippi and southwestern Alabama; the Chickasaws in northern Mississippi and northwestern Alabama; and after 1819, the Seminoles in Florida.

The Cherokees were the first of the southern tribes to succumb to pressure from national officials and accept a western domain. Georgia officials had consistently urged federal officials to fulfill that portion of the Georgia Compact, concluded in 1802, whereby in return for ceding its western lands to the United States, the federal government was to extinguish tribal title to Indian lands in the state. In 1817 at the Cherokee Agency in Tennessee, Cherokee leaders George Lowry, Charles Hicks, and Going Snake met with federal commissioners Andrew Jackson, Joseph McMinn, and David Meriwether; they negotiated a treaty providing for cession of one third of the remaining eastern lands of the Cherokee nation in exchange for a tract of equal size in northwestern Arkansas between the White and Arkansas rivers. Emigration was voluntary; by 1835 about 6,000 Cherokees had moved west.

The Choctaws were the next to commit themselves to vacating their eastern lands and migrating to the West. Chief Pushmataha and other Choctaw leaders met with an American commission headed by General Jackson at Doak's Stand on the Natchez Trace, a national road running diagonally across Chickasaw and Choctaw lands, connecting Nashville with settlements near the mouth of the Mississippi River. The agreement issuing from the council provided that, in return for surrendering to the United States about a third of their eastern domain, the Choctaws were to receive a vast tract of territory west of the Mississippi. The treaty pledged the United States government to supply to each emigrating Choctaw warrior a rifle, bullet mold, camp kettle, blanket, ammunition sufficient for hunting and defense for one year, and payment for any improvements he left in his ancestral home. Pushmataha insisted on the inclusion of a clause providing for 54 sections of Choctaw land to be surveyed and sold at auction, the proceeds to go into a special fund to support schools for Choctaw youth in the new country. Their western home extended from southwestern Arkansas to the western border of the United States, at that time the one hundredth meridian, and was bounded on the north by the Canadian and Arkansas rivers and on the south by the Red River.

While federal officials were hopeful that the Choctaws would remove at once and tribal leaders knew full well that total removal was inevitable, the treaty had made removal voluntary. Therefore, less than one fourth of the tribe moved west under its terms. Most members remained in Mississippi since the Choctaws had surrendered only about a third of their eastern lands and still possessed a sizable domain in Mississippi.

By 1828 Indian colonization had stalled. Most of the tribes of the Old Northwest had been relocated west of the Mississippi, and those factions of the populous Southern tribes willing to emigrate had done so. However, large numbers of Native Americans in Georgia, Alabama, and Mississippi refused to join the exodus; they were determined to remain on their compressed eastern domains. Their lives were profoundly influenced by the election of 1828 which brought Andrew Jackson to the presidency.

Notes

1. Reginald Horsman, *Expansion and American Indian Policy, 1783–1812* (East Lansing, Mich., 1967), p. 106.
2. See Arrell M. Gibson, *The Kickapoos: Lords of the Middle Border* (Norman, Okla., 1963), pp. 52–63.
3. Arrell M. Gibson, *The Chickasaws* (Norman, Okla., 1971), p. 96.
4. Francis Paul Prucha, *American Indian Policy in the Formative Years: The Indian Trade and Intercourse Acts, 1790–1834* (Cambridge, Mass., 1962) p. 225.
5. Gibson, *The Chickasaws*, pp. 160–61.
6. Prucha, *American Indian Policy*, p. 227.
7. D'Arcy McNickle, *Native American Tribalism: Indian Survivals and Renewals* (New York, 1973), p. 52.
8. Jerry Muskrat, "The Constitution and the American Indian: Past and Prologue," *Hastings Constitutional Law Quarterly*, 3 (Summer 1976), pp. 664–65.

Selected Sources

Insights into Jeffersonian Indian policy are provided by Reginald Horsman, *Expansion and American Indian Policy, 1783–1812* (East Lansing, Mich., 1967); Francis Paul Prucha, *American Indian Policy in the Formative Years: The Indian Trade and Intercourse Acts, 1790–1834* (Cambridge, Mass., 1962), and "The Image of the Indian in Pre–Civil War America," *Indiana Historical Society Lectures, 1970–1971* (Indianapolis, 1971); Bernard W. Sheehan, *Seeds of Extinction: Jeffersonian Philanthropy and the American Indian* (New York, 1973); George D. Harmon, *Sixty Years of Indian Affairs: Political, Economic, and Diplomatic, 1789–1850* (Chapel Hill, N.C., 1941); S. Lyman Tyler, *A History of Indian Policy* (Washington, D.C. 1973); and Wilcomb Washburn, *Red Man's Land, White Man's Law* (New York, 1971).

The Native American role in the War of 1812 is detailed in Glenn Tucker, *Tecumseh, Vision of Glory* (Indianapolis, 1936); Freeman Cleaves, *Old Tippecanoe: William Henry Harrison and His Times* (New York, 1939); Francis F. Bierne, *The War of 1812* (New York, 1949); William T. Hagan, *The Sac and Fox Indians* (Norman, Okla., 1958); and Arrell M. Gibson, *The Kickapoos: Lords of the Middle Border* (Norman, Okla., 1963).

Accounts of early Indian removals are Grant Foreman, *Last Trek of the Indians* (Chicago, 1946), *Indian Removal* (Norman, Okla., 1942); *Indians and Pioneers* (New Haven, Conn., 1930), and *The Five Civilized Tribes* (Norman, Okla., 1934); Gloria Jahoda, *The Trail of Tears* (New York, 1975); and Annie H. Abel, *Indian Consolidation West of the Mississippi, Report of the American Historical Association for 1906.*

CHAPTER 13

INDIANS UNDER
ANGLO-AMERICAN
DOMINION
1828–1840

You have taken me prisoner. . . . I am much grieved, for I expected, if I did not defeat you, to hold out much longer, and give you more trouble before I surrendered. . . . I fought hard. But your guns were well aimed. . . . My warriors fell around me. . . . I saw my evil day at hand. The sun rose dim on us in the morning, and at night it sunk in a dark cloud, and looked like a ball of fire. That was the last sun that shone on Black Hawk. His heart . . . no longer beats quick in his bosom. He is now a prisoner to the white men; they will do with him as they wish. But he can stand torture, and is not afraid of death. . . . He has done nothing for which an Indian ought to be ashamed. He has fought for his countrymen . . . against white men, who came year after year, to cheat them and take away their lands. You know the cause of our making war.

Black Hawk's (Sac and Fox) capitulation
at Prairie du Chien, Wisconsin, August 27, 1832

The lusty, growing pioneer constituency, which during the latter portion of the Jeffersonian era had increasingly injected its viewpoint on Indian policy and other matters of public concern, finally triumphed in 1828, garnering sufficient electoral power to launch folk hero Andrew Jackson into the presidency. Jackson was a faithful mirror of their values, attitudes, and goals. The overpowering issue among pioneers in the Old Southwest, the region south of the Ohio River, was completion of Indian removal. Satisfaction of their immense land needs was thwarted by populous Indian nations which occupied choice agricultural territories. They looked to the day when the Old Southwest would be cleared of Indian tribes and the lands opened to settlement as had occurred in the Old Northwest. Now that their champion Andrew Jackson was the nation's highest official, they expected action.

Frontier settlers no longer had to contend with Jeffersonians and their caution and patience in handling Indian matters and their genuine concern for Indian rights, which had slowed the ejection process. Pioneers, scornful of the finer constitutional and moral points of Indian policy, rejoiced. Now that Jackson was the nation's chief executive, their hearts' desire would be met; his ascendancy assured a direct and complete solution to what frontier editors

Chapter Opening Artifact: Navajo woven blanket. (Courtesy Museum of the American Indian, Heye Foundation)

euphemistically called the "Indian problem." Their consuming, overpowering concern throughout Jackson's tenure as President was completion of Indian removal; all other matters, national and international, were of lesser import.

JACKSONIAN INDIAN POLICY

Thomas Jefferson and Andrew Jackson have exercised the major influence on American Indian policy; their legacy has lasted into the twentieth century. Permissive Jeffersonian Indian policy directed tribal relations in the period 1800 to 1829 when Jackson took office. Jacksonian philosophy and values, particularly their suppressive, segregationist aspects, have remained strong in the federal government's policies toward Indian tribes ever since, but Jeffersonian principles of coexistence, civilization, and assimilation, have periodically reappeared to a greater or lesser degree.

The Jacksonian Philosophy

Whereas Jeffersonians formulated a pluralistic frontier policy which sought to satisfy the escalating land desire of pioneers and at the same time protect the Indian nations from annihilation, Jacksonians were monistic and exclusionist. Jackson was obsessed with satisfying his frontier partisans, meeting their demands for vacating Indian lands and moving resident Native Americans into the trans-Mississippi wilderness.

For many years before he became President, Jackson was active in southwestern frontier affairs, including service to the national government as a commissioner in negotiations for compression of tribal lands with leaders of the southern Indian nations. He became a spokesman for American frontier settlers with their hatred of Indians and desire for Indian-owned land. Jackson and his partisans committed themselves to work for the day when Indians would disappear. They denounced Indians as "wretched savages," and "unworthy stewards," their lands were portions of the earth "destined by the Creator" for the creative use of vigorous Anglo-American farmers. They saw Indians as "a degraded brutal race of savages, whom it was the will of God should perish at the approach of civilization." The Manifest Destiny of the young country to expand to the Pacific would include driving the Indians from the earth.[1]

Jackson scorned use of treaties in dealing with the Indian nations. He regarded Native Americans as "subjects of the United States with no sovereignty of their own." To Jackson, Indians had no right to the soil or domain "except the mere possessory right that had been granted to them by the liberality and humanity of the United States." He repeatedly stressed that Indians should be completely subject to the laws of Congress. However, he overlooked the fact that the segregation of Indians that he also advocated required duality, the maintenance of two societies through the treaty process.[2]

Proud and heady from wide acclaim on the frontier as a military hero, Jackson began to express his anti-Indian views freely. "The opinion that Indians were entitled to occupy the land until their right was purchased from them in lawful negotiations was not practical," he believed, "because too many Indians were refusing to negotiate." He commented to President James Monroe in 1817,

I have long viewed treaties with the Indians an absurdity not to be reconciled to the principles of our government. The Indians are subjects of the United States, inhabiting its territory and acknowledging its sovereignty, then is it not absurd for the sovereign to negotiate by treaty with the subject? I have always thought, that congress had as much right to regulate by acts of legislation all Indian concerns, as they had of territories; there is only this difference, that the inhabitants of territories, are citizens of the United States and entitled to all the rights thereof; the Indians are subjects and entitled to their protection and fostering care, the proper guardian of this protection and fostering care is the legislature of the Union.[3]

Monroe replied,

The view which you have taken . . . [to remove the southern Indians forcibly] is new but very deserving of attention. . . . A compulsory process seems to be necessary, to break their habits, and civilize them, and there is much cause to believe that it must be resorted to, to preserve them.[4]

Jacksonian Indian policy, derived from the President's experiences with the Indian nations of the southwestern frontier, was coercive, exploitive, and cheapening. Even as President he regularly traveled to the Southwest to attend councils where federal commissioners were attempting to negotiate removal treaties; his purpose was to apply personal pressure on reluctant tribal leaders to capitulate to government demands. Jackson had studied the southern tribes' leadership, assumed that he had discovered their weaknesses, and coached commissioners in their dealings with the tribes, including use of bribes to quench "cupidity" of certain chiefs. He regularly ordered agents to withhold annuities from Indians. The annuity was the annual cash payment the United States was to pay tribal members or leaders. The money was rightfully due by treaty obligation, and the Indians used it to purchase livestock, tools and implements, and personal needs, and to pay debts to traders. Jackson instructed agents to inform expectant Indians that the annuity would not be paid until their nation had done his bidding which was to remove promptly to the Indian Territory. Their annuity cash would be paid to them at Fort Gibson or Fort Towson in the western wilderness. When the situation required, Jackson directed commissioners to use federal troops to exclude antiremoval chiefs and factions from council grounds when treaty negotiations were underway; missionaries were also banned because they were suspected of urging tribal leaders not to sign away their lands and move to the Indian Territory. He also authorized his commissioners to use public funds to purchase beeves and barrels of whiskey for entertaining the Indians during the council proceedings.

Jacksonian policy included selective enforcement of the law. Decisions of the United States Supreme Court rank with the Constitution as the supreme law of the land. Jackson defied this principle and ignored a landmark ruling in 1832 (*Worcester* v. *Georgia*) which if enforced would have restored constitutional law and fairness to federal treatment of the Indian nations. Until that time the United States had recognized that the cause of the Indian against the pioneer was just. Jackson's action told frontier settlers all over the West that they could proceed with presidentially sanctioned impunity against the property, person, and land of Indians. Following the decision Jackson "warned the Southern tribes that they would find no solace if they remained on their old land and continued on their pretensions of sovereignty. . . . the arms of this country can never be employed to stay any state of this Union, from the exercise of those legitimate powers which attach, and belong to their sovereign character."[5]

Jacksonian Indian policy was also patronizing and paternalistic. Some observers have claimed that an enduring effect of Jackson's policies toward Native Americans has been to create a dependence among the Indians which has been termed infantilism. Aggression, exploitation, and verbalization built infantilism as he "promised to rescue his 'red children' from the advancing tide of white settlement in the east, protect them in the west." Jacksonian Indian policy "extended the paternalism which had structured Indian policy for his predecessors. . . . His paternal language was largely free of the exterminatory rhetoric which had marked his earlier career. It more closely resembled the rhetoric used in the Washington, Jefferson, and Monroe administrations." The difference was in intensity of application. His predecessors had used paternal language more as innocent metaphor. With Jackson this language was a genuine expression of his estimate and image of Native Americans. His policy forced Indians to adopt a new definition of their identity.

It defined them as children, which in fact they were not. It forced the tribes into childish dependence upon a white father. This was particularly devastating in a liberal culture which had eliminated legitimate hierarchal authority and believed that "manly independence" offered the only proper basis for relations among men. When such a society imported the father into politics, it was likely to impose an insecure and overbearing paternal domination. To insist that Indians be shown "their real state of dependence" upon government was . . . to infantilize them. Infantilization provides the major significance of the call for paternal authority.[6]

The Indian Removal Act

President Jackson gave his personal attention to driving the Indians to the far frontiers of the country. Besides visiting councils in the Old Southwest where tribal leaders were considering removal treaties, Jackson also pressed Congress to adopt legislation which would legitimize the exile and federal appropriation of the remaining tribal territories for conversion to public domain lands for settlers. Consideration of his removal plan by the Congress

transformed that body into a national forum where supporters of the Jeffersonian protectionist viewpoint raged at Jacksonian partisans who fostered
coercion as the ultimate resort in negotiations with the recalcitrant southern
tribes. One of the Native Americans' most ardent defenders was Congressman
Henry R. Storrs of New York. He exposed the Jacksonian "fallacy of pretending to remove the Indians for their own good from a community where
they had pleasant homes, churches, and schools to a wilderness where hostile
tribes would be their only neighbors."[7]

Secretary of War Lewis Cass expressed the belief in aboriginal denigration
which Jackson partisans in the Congress took up. He scorned the Jeffersonians'
protectionist view, claiming that they were creating a "romantic" illusion,
drawing their "balderdash" from the writings of Jean Jacques Rousseau and
James Fenimore Cooper, "lunatic dreamers" who depicted Native Americans
as "noble savages." Cass argued, "It is difficult to conceive that any branch of
the human family can be less provident in arrangement, less frugal in enjoyment, less industrious in acquiring, more implacable in their resentments,
more ungovernable in their passions, with fewer principles to guide them,
with few obligations to restrain them, and with less knowledge to improve
and instruct them."[8]

Voices in the Congress challenged the Jacksonians' demeaning of Native
American capabilities. Theodore Frelinghuysen of New Jersey rejoined, "It
is not now seriously denied that the Indians are men, endowed with kindred
faculties and powers with ourselves; that they have place in human sympathy,
and are justly entitled to a share in the common bounties of a benignant Provi-
dence. And, with this conceded, I ask in what code of the law of nations, or
by what process of abstract deductions, their rights have been extinguished?"
And Edward Everett of Massachusetts thundered,

Whoever read of such a project? Ten or fifteen thousand families, to be rooted up,
and carried a hundred, aye, a thousand miles into the wilderness! There is not such
a thing in the annals of mankind. . . . To remove them against their will, by
thousands, to a distant and different country, where they must lead a new life, and
form other habits, and encounter the perils and hardships of a wilderness. . . .
They are planters and farmers, they are tradespeople and mechanics, they have
cornfields and orchards, looms and workshops, schools and churches, and orderly
institutions.[9]

Jacksonians insisted that the removal plan they supported was really philanthropy in disguise. Since clergy were much respected, highly regarded,
and attentively listened to by nineteenth-century Anglo-Americans, Jacksonian
strategists mustered supporting testimony for total removal from several eminent divines including the Reverend Jedidiah Morse, who had first advocated
aboriginal colonization as a Christian action in 1822, and the zealot the Reverend Isaac McCoy, utopian designer of the New Canaan for Native Americans in the western wilderness. Thomas L. McKenney, head of the Office
of Indian Affairs, organized several prominent New York clergymen into the
Board for Emigration, Preservation, and Improvement of the Aborigines to

support Jackson's removal plan. McKinney and the Board for Emigration publicly insisted that their concern was "only to preserve the Indians from complete degradation and enable them to improve and civilize themselves outside of contact with the whites.[10]

Several nationally organized religious bodies denounced the proposed action and submitted petitions and memorials to the Congress and officials in the government urging regard for Indians' rights and enforcement of current treaties protecting those rights. One of the most powerful and influential ecumenical associations in the nation was the American Board of Commissioners for Foreign Missions. Its secretary, Jeremiah Evarts, composed and published essays under the name "William Penn" opposing the Jacksonian approach to Indian affairs. These counterefforts were to no avail. Jackson's influence prevailed, and the Indian Removal Act became law during 1830.

The Indian Removal Act was more an articulation of national intent than a detailed guide for aboriginal colonization in the trans-Mississippi West. It contained congressional sanction of blanket removal of Native American communities in the eastern United States. The chief executive was to decide whether removal would be voluntary or required. Since Jackson's views on this matter were well known, it was accepted that coercion would be applied where required.

The Indian Removal Act marked the beginning of a growing regimentation of Indians by the national government. Already Congress had adopted a number of laws relating to Indians, but they were largely limited to fulfillment of treaties, a duty assigned Congress by the Constitution. Congress had also adopted laws creating the federal bureaucracy for handling Indian affairs, as well as Indian intercourse acts for regulating trade and the activities of non-Indians in the Indian country. Jackson's Removal Act was, as will shortly be apparent, of a very different nature.

INDIAN COLONIZATION AND THE WESTWARD MOVEMENT

Considerable migration had occurred among Indians before passage of the Indian Removal Act. Following the War of 1812 federal agents prepared to establish reservations for the émigrés over a wide territory on the western margins of what soon would become Arkansas, Missouri, and Iowa. On the maps of the day this region was designated vaguely as the "Indian Country." This land belonged to the Osage, Quapaw, Oto, Missouri, Kansa, and other resident tribes. Between 1803 and 1825 federal officials, particularly William Clark, the superintendent of Indian affairs at St. Louis, concluded treaties with these tribes providing for drastic diminution of their domains to make room for the emigrating Indians. The resident tribes retreated to reduced domains on the western margins of this vaguely defined Indian Country. As indicated in Chapter Twelve, a series of treaties concluded between 1815 and 1820 with tribes from the Old Northwest and the Old Southwest assigned vast tracts of the Indian Country to emigrating eastern Indians as their homes "forever." Kickapoos, Delawares, and other Northwest tribes were assigned new homes in what became Missouri; that portion of the Cherokee nation willing to emigrate, under their 1817 treaty, was assigned to northwestern Arkansas; and those Choctaws willing to emigrate under their 1820 treaty were assigned a domain extending from southwestern Arkansas to the one hundredth meridian. The eastern tribes established settlements in the Indian Country and began a new life of farming, stock raising, hunting, and trading.

Native American–Settler Contest for the Indian Country

Even before federal commissioners had concluded these early removal treaties, Anglo-American settlers had established themselves in the trans-Mississippi territory and begun competing with the immigrant Indians for the land. Clearly, in the period immediately following the War of 1812, the intent of certain federal officials was to use a goodly portion of the Mississippi Valley as an Indian colonization zone for relocated eastern tribes. The bitter Native American–settler contest for the Indian Country showed a lag in communication and a lack of coordination among government leaders, because at the very time that officials in the War Department were negotiating treaties of removal with certain eastern tribes and relocating them on permanent reservations in the Indian Country, the processes of American frontier expansion were at work in the same region.

Moreover, the expansion of the settler frontier was actively aided by leaders in the Congress. The treaties negotiated with the Kickapoos and other tribes of the Old Northwest are good examples of this conflict in national purpose, policy, and action. In 1819, when the leaders of the Indian communities surrendered their lands in the Old Northwest and accepted permanent reservations in Missouri Territory, that territory was already passing through the familiar American frontier metamorphosis and was only two years from statehood. Other cases illustrating this dichotomy in national purpose include the Cherokee and Choctaw treaties, which assigned them vast tracts south of Missouri Territory in a region which was being organized by the Congress as Arkansas Territory, legally open for Anglo-American settlement.

Thus, two opposing streams of development were occurring in this region at the same time, and the national government was a party to both. New territories were being created to accommodate pioneer-settler demands, and these new political entities were being prepared for admission to the Union. And western Missouri and Arkansas were becoming a checkerboard of reservations settled by tribes from the Old Northwest and the Old Southwest. The immigrant Indians comprised a barrier to the American settlers, and in a very real sense they arrested the seemingly irrevocable developmental pattern common to Western America. The self-governing Indian communities were states within emerging states. Inevitably, the Anglo-American settlers coveted the

Chippewa pictograph. The animals in this picture symbolize the clan totems in agreement on the issue of demand for restoration of lands taken by the national government. The lines from the eyes of the bird to the eyes of the creatures behind it, and from its heart to theirs, signify the unity of views on the accord. (New York Public Library)

fertile lands of the reservations. The settlers and the Indians were soon locked in a bitter contest for the reservation lands.

It was, as always, an unequal contest; when Indian-white interests were in conflict, the settlers always triumphed. Whatever their apologists might have said, more than anything else, the settlers' victories were due to the fact that they were voters while the Indians were not. By his ballot exercise, the settler could choose the territorial delegate to Congress, through whom he had a voice in the formulation of the law and policy to serve his personal and local interests. Missouri and Arkansas congressional delegates continued to press their constituents' cause: clearing their territories of the Indian communities. Once the Indians were gone, they could achieve the ultimate for their territories—statehood in the American Union.

While their spokesmen in Washington were doing their bidding by making legal the appropriation of Indian land they so ardently coveted and arranging to relocate the resident tribes farther west in the wilderness, bands of raiding settlers regularly terrorized the Indian communities of western Missouri and Arkansas, hoping to make life so miserable for the Indians that they would surrender their reservations and move west. Settlers burned Indian towns, violated Indian households, and ran off tribal livestock.

Local courts and friendly juries protected settler rights in any contest over livestock and other property seized in these raids. And, if the Indians resisted and drove off the intruders, an "Indian war" justified calling federal troops from Fort Smith and other frontier posts into the reservation to quell the "uprising." On the Arkansas frontier, local citizens poached game on Cherokee lands. They slaughtered buffalo solely for tallow and bears for oil, and stench from the rotting carcasses carried into the Cherokee towns.

Formation of Indian Territory

In 1825 Secretary of War John C. Calhoun determined to end the recurring tribal relocations. He described to President Monroe the tragedy of periodic uprooting of the tribes to serve the American settlers' lust for land. "One of the greatest evils to which they are subject is that incessant pressure of our population, which forces them from seat to seat. To guard against this evil ... there ought to be the strongest and most solemn assurance that the country given them should be theirs, as a permanent home for themselves and their posterity." Jefferson and other national leaders had been accustomed to regard the land between the Atlantic Ocean and the Mississippi River as more than adequate for the settlement needs of the American people. Therefore, they and many others were surprised that American expansion had crossed the Mississippi River into a new region. Even so, the vast empty portions of the Mississippi Valley, for the most part north of Missouri, contained such an attractive land reserve that it was inconceivable to most government leaders that the land needs of the American people would ever extend beyond the Mississippi Valley. There was also in the minds of the nation's leaders a growing sense of "national completeness," that the Mississippi Valley would mark the absolute western limit of Anglo-American settlements. Moreover, the widely read accounts of federally sponsored expeditions beyond the Mississippi Valley characterized much of the West as the Great American Desert. The region became fixed in the public mind as a vast, inhospitable waste, unfit for Anglo-American pursuits and, therefore, a suitable homeland for displaced Indians.[11]

Calhoun recommended that President Monroe set aside the region west of Missouri and Arkansas as a permanent reserve; there the federal government could colonize the tribes remaining in the eastern United States as well as those presently living in Arkansas and Missouri. Monroe and his successors followed Calhoun's recommendation. With the support of Congress, an extensive Indian colonization zone was withdrawn from settlement. Located west of Missouri and Arkansas, it was bounded on the north by the Platte River, on the south by the Red River, and extended to the western boundary of the United States, at that time the one hundreth meridian to the Arkansas river, and along that stream to the Rocky Mountains. It was restricted to use by the Indian nations and was named variously the Indian Country and, by 1830, the Indian Territory. In 1825 the Choctaws ceded their lands in southwestern Arkansas Territory; and three years later the Cherokees ceded their lands in northwestern Arkansas Territory and made their final move to the Indian Territory. The Missouri tribes, including the Kickapoos and Delawares, relocated in the northern portion of the Indian Territory which in 1854 became Kansas Territory.

Indian Territory Before 1854

ROCKY MTS

UNORGANIZED TERR.

IOWA

MISSOURI

ARKANSAS

TEXAS

LOUISIANA

Missouri R.

Big Sioux R.

Laramie R.

Platte of Nebraska R.

South Fork

Solomon Fork

Grand Saline Fork

Kansas R.

Arkansas R.

Neosho R.

Cimarron

North Fork

Canadian R.

Washita R.

North Fork Red R.

Red R.

Verdigris R.

Grand R.

Western Boundary of the United States

Omaha

Pawnee

Otoes

Otoe and Missouri

Iowa

Sauk and Fox
of Minnesota

Kickapoo

• Kickapoo Agency

• Ft. Leavenworth

Delaware Outlet

Delaware Agency

Delaware and
Wyandot Reserve

Kansas

Potawatomi
Agency

Ottawa

Peoria and Kaskaskia

Shawnee

Wea and
Piankasha

Sauk Fox
Agency

Miami

Kansas Agency •

Sauk and Fox of Mississippi

Potawatomi

New York Indians

• Ft. Atkinson

O s a g e

Drum Creek
Agency

Cherokee
Neutral Lands

Medicine Lodge •

Quapaw

Seneca

Cherokee Outlet

Cherokee
Nation

Tahlequah

• Park
Hill

Tullahassee Mission

• Ft.
Gibson

Seminole Nation

Creek
Nation

Creek Agency

Arkansas R.

Wichita Agency
• Ft. Cobb

Seminole
Agency

Edward's
Post

Camp
Holme

• Skullyville

Canadian R.

Greer
County

Leased
District

Chickasaw
Nation

• Perryville

Choctaw Nation

• Ft. Arbuckle

Boggy
Depo •

Doaksville

Eagle-
town

Tishomingo •

Armstrong
• Academy

• Ft. Towson

• Ft. Washita

Red R.

100°

100°

0 25 50   100   150   200

Scale of Miles

PACIFICATION OF THE INDIAN TERRITORY

Creation of the Indian Territory and passage of the Indian Removal Act demonstrated the determination of national leaders to complete removal of the southern Indian nations. Chiefs of the Five Civilized Tribes faced great pressure from government commissioners. They parried this pressure by refusing to consider removal until the new tribal domains in the Indian Territory were made safe for settlement. They pointed to the presence of fierce bands of Kiowas and Comanches on the Indian Territory's western margins. These Plains Indians resented the prospect of emigrant Indians settling close to their hunting grounds, and they had sent to the eastern settlements dark threats of extermination of intruders. Leaders of the southern tribes also objected to the boundaries within the new Indian Territory which, they charged, were ambiguous and overlapping.

An added threat to peace and safety for Indian immigrants was the large community of Osages still living along the Verdigris and Grand rivers in territory assigned to the southern Indians. The Osages had only partially relocated, and several of their towns remained on Cherokee land. These served as bases for raids on Cherokee and Choctaw settlements in western Arkansas and eastern Indian Territory. Thus, before the national government could effectuate removal of the southern Indians, its officials had first to remove the objections and quiet the concerns of the leaders of these tribes.

The Stokes Commission

To accomplish this purpose, Congress passed an act in 1832 authorizing the President to appoint a three-member commission to expedite removal of the southern Indians. Jackson selected Montfort Stokes of North Carolina as chairman, Henry R. Ellsworth of Connecticut, and John F. Schermerhorn of New York as members. The group became known as the Stokes Commission, after the chairman. Fort Gibson at the mouth of Grand River was to be the commission's headquarters. The War Department provided the commission with a military arm because its work would be accomplished by use of force if peaceful means failed. Military action was thought likely, especially in dealing with the Osages, Kiowas, and Comanches.

Major Henry Dodge had been ordered to recruit a battalion of heavily armed cavalry, called the Mounted Rangers, for service in the Illinois-Wisconsin Black Hawk War of 1832. By the time this special force had been raised and trained, its services were no longer required east of the Mississippi River, so the secretary of war ordered three companies of Mounted Rangers to Fort Gibson to assist the Stokes Commission in establishing peace on the Indian Territory frontier and settling the immigrant tribes.

By early 1833 the three members of the commission were at Fort Gibson, ready to carry out their duties, the first of which were fairly simple. A band of Seneca Indians needed a reservation home. This once-powerful tribe from

New York, like so many others, had been desolated by Anglo-American expansion. Remnants of the Seneca nation lived in the rough, mountainous portions of western New York and Pennsylvania. Others had drifted into Ohio, near Sandusky. In 1831 they ceded their Ohio lands to the United States, and in 1833 the Stokes Commission had to find a reservation home in the Indian Territory for them and for a band of Shawnees, reduced in power like the Senecas, and recently affiliated with this tribe. The commissioners assigned the Senecas and Shawnees a 127,000-acre reservation north of the Cherokee nation between the Missouri border and Grand River.

The commission had also been instructed to look into reports that the Quapaws were destitute and needed help. In 1818 this tribe had ceded to the United States all claim to land south of the Arkansas River and east of the Kiamichi River. The commissioners found that about 200 impoverished Quapaws were living among the Caddoes on the Red River. They negotiated a treaty with the Quapaw chiefs, in which they agreed to locate on a 96,000-acre reserve north of the Senecas between the western boundary of Missouri and the Grand River.

The Stokes Commission next settled the Cherokee-Creek boundary controversy. Cherokee and Creek leaders met with the commissioners at Fort Gibson and produced an amicable solution. In 1826 a faction of the Creek nation in Alabama had signed a removal treaty and settled on a domain in eastern Indian Territory near Fort Gibson. Two years later the Western Cherokees exchanged their lands in northwestern Arkansas for a domain in Indian Territory adjacent to the Creek lands. The boundary separating Creek and Cherokee territories was poorly defined. A new boundary was drawn between the two nations which gave the Creeks some of the land between the Verdigris and Arkansas rivers that had been claimed by the Cherokees.

Such small problems were relatively easily solved. Dealing with the Osages, however, was a very different matter. Whereas the Stokes Commission had found harmony and conciliatory attitudes in their negotiations with the Cherokees, Creeks, Senecas, Shawnees, and Quapaws, they met only hostility and obstruction from the Osages. In February 1833 the commission held its first council with the Osage tribal leaders at Chouteau's Post on the Grand River near Salina. The proceedings recessed briefly and resumed at Fort Gibson in March. For three weeks the Osage chiefs bitterly denied Cherokee and Creek charges that they had burned cabins and stolen the horses and other property of immigrant Indians. Repeatedly the commissioners attempted to persuade Osage leaders to set a time when they would move their villages from the Cherokee nation to the northern domain assigned them by the treaty of 1825. Growing federal military power at Fort Gibson and continuing surveillance of their villages by Dragoon patrols caused Osage leaders to resettle their people during 1836 on treaty-assigned lands just north of 37 degrees in the northern half of the Indian Territory.

The Stokes Commission made two efforts before 1834 to contact the Plains tribes. Columns of Mounted Rangers had been sent to the Wichita Mountains in the southwestern portion of the Indian Territory to deliver invitations to the Kiowas, Comanches, Wichitas, and Caddoes to meet at Fort Gibson with federal officials. Both missions had failed. However, prospects brightened early in 1834 when officers at Fort Gibson ransomed a young Kiowa girl captive, Gunpandama, from the Osages through a frontier trader named Hugh Love for $200. The Stokes Commission members hoped to use Gunpandama as the means of gaining access to the unapproachable Kiowas and Comanches.

The Dragoon Expedition

The federal military force in the Indian Territory was strengthened by the arrival of a new type of unit called Dragoons. The First Dragoon Regiment was organized late in 1833 and was commanded by Colonel Henry Dodge. A core of experienced men for the unit came from the disbanded Mounted Rangers. Most of the recruits were from Boston, New York, Philadelphia, Baltimore, and St. Louis.

After a brief training period, the Dragoon Regiment prepared for an expedition to the buffalo country. To date, it was the most colorful and awesome military force mustered on the western frontier. The splendid Dragoon trappings and accoutrements were calculated to make a lasting impression on the Kiowas and Comanches and to intimidate them into making a treaty of peace and amity with the United States. Colonel Dodge's magnificent column, with guidons flying, rode out of Fort Gibson on the morning of June 15, 1834. A wagon train contained commissary supplies, ammunition, gifts for the Indians, the Kiowa captive Gunpandama, and George Catlin, the Philadelphia artist. Disaster stalked the Dragoon expedition from its first day. Summer heat came early to the Southwest in 1834, and the Dragoons suffered in their heavy uniforms. By the time the regiment arrived at Camp Washita, midway between Fort Gibson and Wichita Mountains, nearly half the men were ailing—some from heat stroke and exhaustion, others from a gastrointestinal malady. At Camp Washita Dodge selected 250 effective men and proceeded to the Wichita Mountains.

There he succeeded in drawing the Kiowas, Comanches, Wichitas, and Caddoes into council. His return of Gunpandama established good relations; the gifts he distributed helped, too, and by patient negotiation he extracted from the leaders of these tribes a promise to remain peaceful and to meet soon with American officials in a treaty council. Catlin, although ailing, rode west with Dodge; he visited the Indian villages while Dodge's councils were in progress, sketched the people and camp scenes, and kept a daily journal. He later published both the journal and sketches in a two-volume work titled *Letters and Notes on the Manners, Customs, and Condition of the North American Indians*, an important pioneer work on the native peoples of the trans-Missouri region.

Between 1835 and 1837 leaders of the Kiowas, Comanches, Wichitas, and Caddoes met with federal agents and negotiated their first treaties with the

United States. They accepted the Anglo-American nation as their sovereign and protector and pledged to live at peace with their new neighbors, the emigrating southern Indian nations. Because traffic between the American frontier settlements and the Rio Grande towns was increasing, the commissioners also exacted an assurance of unmolested passage for traders and their caravans through the buffalo range.

Having pacified the Indian Territory, settled boundary disputes in the new land, and met other objections to removal, federal agents increased pressure on leaders of the southern tribes to cede their eastern lands and emigrate. While eventually the national will triumphed, for the time these intimidative actions by public officials only provoked Indian patriots in each of the Five Civilized Tribes to unremitting determination not to comply. Political considerations forced the national administration to desperate steps to break this impasse including deceitful diplomacy and bloody military recrimination which did not conclude until 1842.

RESUMPTION OF INDIAN COLONIZATION

Leaders of the southern tribes had reluctantly ceded to the United States by successive treaties large tracts of land to accommodate settler demands, retaining in each case a cherished homeland core of territory. By 1820 the Cherokees had surrendered most of their lands in western North Carolina, South Carolina, and Tennessee and retained a domain in northwestern Georgia centering on their tribal capital at New Echota. The Creeks had surrendered their lands in southern Georgia and retained a homeland core in Alabama. The Seminoles, only recently under United States jurisdiction, were in the process of accepting reduced territory in Florida. The Choctaws had ceded much of their territory in southern and central Mississippi and were on the verge of agreeing to another large cession. And the Chickasaws, once lords over much of Tennessee, Kentucky, northern Alabama and northern Mississippi, had retreated through successive land cession treaties to a small domain in northern Mississippi and northwestern Alabama. On these reduced domains these Five Civilized Tribes, as they are known, made their last stand to preserve the land of their ancestors from the settler onslaught.

Tribal Strategies

Leaders of the southern tribes developed various strategies to protect their lands and the right to remain in the East. One tactic was cooperation with federal officials and support of the national interest. They studiously supported the United States in its international goals. During the War of 1812 these tribes remained loyal to the United States, politely rejecting Tecumseh's plea for Indian brotherhood and war on the Americans. And the Cherokee, Choctaw, Creek, and Chickasaw nations each formed a regiment which joined

Major General Andrew Jackson's army to guard the southwestern frontier against British invasion. One Creek faction, the Red Sticks, accepted Tecumseh's gospel and made war on the American settlements in the Southwest; however, loyal Creek, Cherokee, Chickasaw, and Choctaw regiments in Jackson's army smashed the Red Sticks at the Battle of Horseshoe Bend.

Another tribal strategy was coexistence—the hope held by leaders of the southern tribes that they could so order their lives that Anglo-Americans would be willing to accept them as worthy neighbors. Thus Cherokee, Creek, Choctaw, and Chickasaw leaders urged great changes among their people. Adopting white customs in dress and industry, the Indians established successful farms, plantations, and businesses in their nations; many became prosperous slave owners. In addition, they changed their political systems from traditional tribal governments to governments based upon written constitutions with elected officials, courts, and other elements of enlightened polity.

Tribal leaders welcomed missionaries to their nations, not necessarily because they found their tribal deities inadequate, but rather because missionaries, besides being ministers of the gospel, were also teachers. Missionaries established schools, which allowed many Indian youths to complete basic studies locally and then continue their education in colleges in the Northeast. Soon in each Indian nation there developed a corps of elitist leaders, most of whom were better educated than whites in the neighboring settlements and able to work with white counterparts in the professions, industry, business, and politics.

The Cherokee advance illustrates the substantive changes among the southern tribes generally. By 1830 their nation was divided into two sections—the Eastern Cherokees in northwestern Georgia and committed to remain there; and the Western Cherokees, formerly living in northwestern Arkansas, and after 1828 in the northeastern section of the Indian Territory. The drastic cultural change discussed here applies largely to the Eastern Cherokees.

The Eastern Cherokees emulated their white neighbors, and a great number were prominent and wealthy as slave owners and operators of grain and lumber mills, plantations, stock farms, and other businesses within the Cherokee nation. A northern visitor during the 1820s observed that many Cherokees lived

in comfort and abundance, in good houses of brick, stone, and wood. We saw several houses built of hewn stone, superior to any we had ever seen before. The people seemed to have more money than the whites in our own settlements; they were better clothed. The women were weaving, the men cultivating corn, and raising beef and pork in abundance; butter and milk everywhere. We were at an election for delegates among the Cherokees to form a constitution. They were orderly, and well behaved.[12]

Schools, most of them operated by Congregationalist, Presbyterian (American Board), and Moravian missionaries, instructed Cherokee children in the rudiments of learning. Sequoyah, the Cherokee genius, had invented his syllabary, an 86-symbol alphabet that reduced the Cherokee language to written form. A tribal newspaper, the *Cherokee Phoenix*, edited by Elias Boudinot, a mixed-blood Cherokee, appeared for the first time in 1828; its columns were printed both in Sequoyah's syllabary and in English. Sequoyah's syllabary was so well received and it stirred such intense pride among Cherokees that it is said that their nation achieved near total literacy in less than 5 years. The Cherokee nation abolished its tribal government in 1827 and formed a constitutional republic. Pathkiller, the last of the full-blood Cherokee hereditary tribal chiefs, was replaced by Charles Hicks, a brilliant mixed blood who was the chief author of the constitution.

Leaders of the Cherokees and other southern tribes could not comprehend, in their hope to coexist and adapt to the rapid changes swirling about their nations, that their success in altering tribal ways and their progress in education, business, and polity only aroused envy and antagonism among their Anglo-American neighbors. Indian progress was regarded as a threat. What leaders of the southern tribes did not understand was that nineteenth-century Anglo-Americans feared, scorned, and rejected any peoples unlike themselves in culture and physical characteristics.

Anglo-American Counterstrategies

Citizens in Georgia, Alabama, and Mississippi regarded resident Indians as barriers to furthering their material goals. Indians occupied rich agricultural lands which they wanted, especially in an era of rapid expansion of cotton growing. Thus Georgians, Alabamans, and Mississippians developed counterstrategies to force the Indians into exile, and they used state and federal apparatus to accomplish their goal. Whites were voters in state and federal elections while Indians were not. At the state level, citizen will was reflected in legislatures which adopted laws to abolish tribal governments functioning in each state. Between 1828 and 1830 the legislatures of Georgia, Alabama, and Mississippi enacted laws calling for arrest and imprisonment of tribal leaders if they attempted to exercise the duties of their offices. The only purpose for which tribal councils could meet under these repressive state laws was to discuss surrender of tribal lands and removal to the West. Indian testimony was not admissable in state courts. Thus, settlers could depredate with impunity on Indians, their households, and property, and Indians had no remedy in state courts. The clear intent of these laws was to make life so miserable for the Indians that in self-defense they would move to the West.

The national government was bound by treaties with these tribes by solemn constitutional pledge to protect the Indians in their person, property, and land from trespass by its citizens or the states. Indian leaders, well aware of the treaty protection the federal government had pledged to them, pleaded with national leaders to fulfill the treaties and protect them from state and citizen tyranny. The failure of federal officials to respond to Native American entreaties for protection was another manifestation of Anglo-American citizens' advantage over the Indians as voters in the federal system. They elected representatives and senators to the United States Congress committed to fulfilling their goal of removing all sign of Indians from their states. Their representatives and senators pushed for adoption of laws which would legalize the appropriation of tribal lands and removal of Indians, the classic example being, of course, the Indian Removal Act. Southerners also favored presidential candidates who were committed to support this aim. Their strategies triumphed over those of the southern Indian nations.

The Cherokee Removal

The Cherokee Treaty of 1817 was the first agreement with a southern Indian nation to contain a provision for migration to the West. Although many treaties had been negotiated with the Cherokees, Creeks, Choctaws, and Chickasaws before 1817, each of them providing for cession of territory to the United States, until then the cessions had amounted to a diminution of the tribal estates; the Indians continued to live on their reduced domains. And since only a portion of the Cherokee nation migrated under the terms of the 1817 treaty, additional negotiations were required to clear all the Cherokees from the eastern United States. But government-sponsored tribal migration did begin with the 1817 treaty, and it was to serve as a model for negotiations with the other southern tribes.

Difficulties for Cherokees mounted. During 1829 gold was discovered in the mountains of northern Georgia within the Cherokee nation. The state legislature passed a law forbidding Cherokees to prospect or mine gold on their own lands. The gold discovery set off a mad stampede; over 3,000 whites stormed across the Cherokee domain, wrecking fences, violating households, and creating general chaos. When Indians brought charges against the intruders for trespass, stock theft, or violation of person, the Georgia courts refused to acknowledge their petitions on the grounds that their testimony was incompetent and inadmissible.

Eleven missionary teachers were arrested for failure to obtain state permits to teach in the Cherokee nation. Georgia courts gave the accused the choice of following the requirements of the law or going to prison for four years. Nine missionaries bowed to the state requirement; only Samuel A. Worcester and Elizar Butler refused. Cherokee leaders and Worcester and Butler appealed to the federal judiciary for relief. The year before, the Cherokees had urged the United States Supreme Court to rule on the constitutionality of the application of Georgia state laws to them. They had based their case on the claim of immunity from state law on the proposition that the Cherokee nation was a foreign state; therefore the United States Supreme Court would have original jurisdiction in the action. Chief Justice John Marshall prepared the court's decision in *Cherokee Nation v. Georgia* (1831); the court lacked original jurisdiction, he said, because the Cherokee nation rather than being a foreign state was a "domestic dependent nation." In 1832 the Cherokees and Worcester and Butler appeared before the court for a resumption of consideration of the question of Indian status within state jurisdiction. Marshall also prepared this decision (*Worcester* v. *Georgia*) which declared the state laws under which the two missionaries were imprisoned as well as the other tribal regulatory statutes null and void and ordered the prisoners released.

The Cherokees and other southern tribes were elated. At last, they believed, they would receive the justice they merited and the protection against oppressive state action guaranteed them by treaties with the United States. However, their hopes were dashed when President Jackson refused to enforce the court's decision. Tribal leaders reminded Jackson of his constitutional responsibility. Thereupon he answered, incorrectly, that he was powerless in the matter and that the only hope for the Indians was to accept their fate and move to the West. The President's failure to fulfill his constitutional duty destroyed the will of many Indians to attempt to adapt to the surging settlement about them; they eventually capitulated and prepared to move to the Indian Territory.

During 1834 the Georgia legislature authorized the survey of Cherokee lands and the disposal of most of the choice parcels in the nation by a state lottery. The estates of leading Cherokees including Principal Chief John Ross were confiscated and taken over by white planters. Spring Place Mission, long a center of learning and culture in Cherokee tribal life, was included in the lottery. The Georgian who drew this property converted the mission into a frontier tavern! In the year of the land lottery, the Georgia militia marched to the Cherokee capital at New Echota, seized the printing press and type of the *Cherokee Phoenix*, and smashed the equipment. Suppression of the *Phoenix* was excused on the grounds that it had advocated resistance to removal.

This harassment added to growing Cherokee indignation, and there developed in the nation a group who saw removal to the West as the lesser of two evils. The leader of this faction was Major Ridge, one of the wealthiest Cherokees and speaker of the Cherokee National Council. His followers included his son John Ridge as well as Elias Boudinot and his brother Stand Watie. Ridge's group came to be called the Treaty Party and consisted mostly of mixed bloods. The group opposing removal, the more numerous, were full bloods; they took the name Ross Party from their leader, Principal Chief John Ross.

Federal commissioners continued to offer the Cherokees various and ever more favorable removal treaty terms. During 1835, when Chief Ross refused the national government's offer, American agents headed by John Schermerhorn turned to leaders of the Treaty Party; at New Echota on December 29 he negotiated a treaty of removal. The Ross Party members warned the Treaty Party followers that if they affixed their names to the Treaty of New Echota, they would in effect sign their death warrants. The removal partisans signed nonetheless, and the United States Senate ratified this pact despite the public knowledge that it represented only a minority of the Cherokee nation's will.

By the terms of the Treaty of New Echota, the Cherokees sold their eastern domain, consisting of over 8 million acres, for $5 million. They were confirmed

Painting of the Cherokees' Trail of Tears. (Woolaroc Museum)

in joint ownership with the Western Cherokees of their lands in the Indian Territory and were obligated to move within two years after ratification. The federal government was to pay the cost of removal and promised to support the immigrants for one year after their arrival in the West. The Ross Party refused to accept the treaty and declared that its members were not bound by it because it had been negotiated by a minority of the nation. Only about 2,000 Cherokees, most of them members of the Treaty Party, migrated peacefully under the terms of the Treaty of New Echota. When 1838 arrived and it was clear that the Ross Party Cherokees were determined not to migrate, United States troops were ordered to the Cherokee nation to collect the Indians and forcibly relocate them in the Indian Territory. The Georgia militia assisted the federal troops in this massive Indian roundup.

The story of the Cherokee Trail of Tears is an epic of misery and death. An eye witness recalled

The troops were disposed at various points throughout the Cherokee country, where stockade forts were erected for gathering in and holding the Indians preparatory to removal. From these, squads of troops were sent to search out with rifle and bayonet every small cabin hidden away in the coves or by the sides of mountain streams, to seize and bring in as prisoners all the occupants. . . . Families at dinner were startled by the sudden gleam of bayonets in the doorway and rose to be driven with blows and oaths along the weary miles of trail that led to the stockade. Men were seized in their fields, or going along the road, women were taken from their [spinning] wheels and children from their play. In many cases, on turning for one last look as they crossed the ridge they saw their homes in flames, fired by the lawless rabble that followed on the heels of the soldiers to loot and pillage.[13]

About 5,000 Cherokees had been ruthlessly uprooted and marched to the Indian Territory when Chief Ross appealed to American officials to permit him and other Cherokee leaders to supervise the removal. They formed the exiles into travel parties of 1,000 persons each, and the removal proceeded in a more orderly and humane fashion. Even so, their march to the West was marked by the gravestones of the perishing; the tribal population was reduced by at least 25 percent by the ordeal. Several hundred Cherokees escaped the army's dragnet; they hid out in the dense upland forests near their old homeland, and in modern times their descendants are known as the Eastern Cherokees of North Carolina.

The Choctaw Removal

The Choctaws in Mississippi suffered the same fate at the hands of state government as the Cherokees in Georgia. During the 1820s the state of Mississippi followed the same pattern as Georgia of applying negative persuasion in its attempt to force the Choctaws to vacate their lands and migrate. The Mississippi legislature adopted laws abolishing tribal governments; chiefs who exercised their tribal duties faced prison terms. Indians were made subject to state law. When tribal leaders appealed to federal officials for protection from state action as guaranteed by treaties with the United States, they were told that the national government was powerless to protect them. White settlers did their bit to make life miserable for the Choctaws. They squatted on tribal lands, daring the Indians to evict them; they stole and killed Indian livestock and carried away other property with impunity. Law-enforcement officers and the courts intervened only when white predators had to be protected from Indian wrath.

Reluctant as they were to leave the lands of their ancestors, Choctaw leaders saw the futility of attempting to thwart such a powerful combination of private citizens and state officials. High federal officials, including the President, had made it clear that the Indians could expect no protection from the national government. Therefore, in 1830 Choctaw leaders met with federal commissioners at the Dancing Rabbit Creek council ground and signed a definitive removal treaty. By the terms of this pact the Choctaw nation ceded to the United States all tribal lands in Mississippi. In return the government bound itself to pay the cost of the Choctaw relocation, provide a payment to the tribe of $20,000 annually for a period of twenty years, finance the education of forty Choctaw youths each year, and pay to the Choctaw nation the sum of $50,000 to establish new schools in the Indian Territory. The Treaty of Dancing Rabbit Creek contained an allotment clause to placate those Indians who refused to consider removal—some full bloods because their land was a bounty from the Great Holy Force Above and to dispose of it would violate a sacred ordinance; some mixed bloods because of economic interests they had established in productive plantations. Allottees received land assignments or allotments determined by size of family and other considerations, each somewhat over 640 acres in size. Allottees were required to separate from the Choctaw nation and agree to submit to state law. About one fourth of the Choctaw nation population requested allotments. Federal agents in collusion with state land speculators failed to register the Indian allotment selections and shortly the allottees were landless and in poverty; most of them proceeded to the Indian Territory to rejoin their kin. Those remaining in the East in the twentieth century are known as the Mississippi Choctaws.

The Choctaw removal was less traumatic than the Cherokee removal, but intense suffering seemed the common lot of all emigrating parties, mostly because of poor planning by supervisory government agents. Most of the emigrants were on the trail in the middle of a harsh winter; temperatures regularly fell to zero, and several parties of Choctaws had to march through six inches of snow. Cholera, smallpox, malnutrition, and other maladies devastated the columns on their westward march. One witness to the Choctaw exodus recalled a column of emigrating Indians passing his farm. The Choctaw party had to cross two deep rivers near the farm, both nearly impassable in any case.

This they had to perform or perish, there being no provision made for them on the way. This, too, was to be done in the worst time of weather I have ever seen . . . a heavy sleet having broken and bowed down all the small and much of the large timber. And this was to be performed under the pressure of hunger, by old women and young children, without any covering for their feet, legs, or body except a cotton underdress. . . . In passing, before they reached the place of getting rations here, I gave a party leave to enter a small field in which pumpkins were. They would not enter without leave, though starving. These they ate raw with the greatest avidity.[14]

While suffering Choctaws were struggling west over their Trail of Tears to the Indian Territory enduring freezing temperatures, ice, snow, sleet, mud, scarce rations, and cholera, Elbert Herring, head of the Bureau of Indian Affairs in the War Department commented, "The humane policy, exemplified in the system adopted by the government with respect to the Indian tribes residing within the limits of the United States, which is now in operation, is progressively developing its good effects; and, it is confidently trusted, will at no distant day, be crowned with complete success."[15]

The Creek Removal

The Creek nation had a similar removal ordeal. This tribe had two great divisions: the Lower Creeks, mixed bloods who were led by the McIntosh family; and the Upper Creeks, who were full bloods led by Opothleyaholo. Because their domain had been reduced by regular cessions of tribal land in 1814, 1818, and 1821, the Creek Council in 1823 adopted a law prescribing the death penalty for any of its citizens who signed away Creek lands without approval of the Council.

Nonetheless, increasing settler depredations and incessant pressure from federal officials caused Chief William McIntosh to meet with an American commission at the Indian Springs, Georgia, council grounds in 1825. There he signed the Treaty of Indian Springs, providing for additional cessions of tribal territory in exchange for a new Creek domain west of the Mississippi. McIntosh's justification was that the Creek nation had to migrate and soon. At present the government was willing to pay for the Creeks' eastern lands, but, he warned, before long the Americans would

take them and the little band of our people, poor and despised, will be left to wander without homes and be beaten like dogs. We will go to a new home ... till the earth, grow cattle and depend on these for food and life ... and we shall grow and again become a great nation.[16]

Upper Creek chiefs led by Opothleyaholo refused to approve the Treaty of Indian Springs. The Creek council ordered McIntosh's execution, and the order was carried out in summary fashion. A hundred Creek warriors surrounded McIntosh's home, set fire to the dwelling, and, when heat and flames flushed McIntosh into the dooryard, they shot him to death.

The Senate ratified the Treaty of Indian Springs, but before President John Quincy Adams could put the agreement into effect, he learned of the circumstances surrounding the negotiations. At his invitation a Creek delegation headed by Opothleyaholo journeyed to Washington. This delegation was authorized by the Creek council to negotiate with the President the question of ceding tribal lands; its members were therefore exempt from the treatment McIntosh had received. The willingness of the Creek government to proceed with an action that had been unacceptable only a few months before was undoubtedly the result of the threat of civil war within the Creek nation. The Lower Creeks were aching to avenge McIntosh's death, and Opothleyaholo believed it prudent to allow the dissidents to migrate. He therefore negotiated the Treaty of Washington in 1826 whereby the Creeks exchanged a portion of their remaining eastern lands for a domain in the Indian Territory near Fort Gibson. Most of the Lower Creeks migrated under the terms of this treaty.

Federal commissioners persisted in pressuring the Creeks to agree to a definitive treaty of land cession and removal, and land-hungry settlers assisted them by carrying on a merciless campaign of harassment. Squatting on Creek lands, stealing Indian livestock, and tormenting the Creeks until they fought back, they created incidents that were characterized as savage Indian reprisals. Like Georgia and Mississippi, the Alabama legislature abolished the Creek tribal government and made all Indians subject to state law which did not protect Indians from white aggression but did protect whites from Indian retaliation.

By 1832 the Creek chiefs were finally persuaded of the futility of attempting to live in the land of their ancestors, and Opothleyaholo headed a tribal delegation to Washington to negotiate a final removal agreement. By the second Treaty of Washington, the Creek nation in Alabama was dissolved. Tribal members had the option of joining their kin in the West at once—in which case the government would pay the removal expense—or remaining in Alabama and receiving allotments, which varied in size from 320 to 640 acres. The United States government pledged to expel white intruders and insure that the Indian allottees could reside on and use their lands. In exchange for title to its tribal estate in the East, the Creek nation was to receive an annuity of $12,000 for five years and $10,000 for the next fifteen years.

The Creeks accepting allotments were granted a five-year period in which to try living under Alabama law. Only 630 Creeks prepared to emigrate to the Indian Territory; most of the Creeks elected to try this new way of living. And it was new to them, for like other tribes, the Creeks had always held their lands in common. Few of the Creeks understood the intricacies of private land-ownership, and the whites exploited their ignorance. There were widespread land frauds and attachments for false debt; dispossession was frequently ordered by courts friendly to white land seekers. And the federal government utterly failed to insure the Creek allottees the peaceful use of their lands. Settlers continued to harass the Indians; and when individual Creeks attempted to defend their homes and drive off their oppressors, they were arrested by state officers for assault and disorderly conduct. Finally, in 1836, a unified resistance developed around a Creek chief named Eneah Emothla. The encroaching settlers became alarmed, appealed for protection, and United States troops came to Alabama to put down the so-called Creek Rebellion.

The Creek Rebellion was used as a justification for the wholesale removal of the nation from Alabama. Squads of soldiers swarmed over the countryside rounding up Indians and collecting them in heavily guarded concentration camps until a party of 1,000 or so had accumulated. Then they were marched overland under military guard to the Indian Territory. Torn from their homes, forced to abandon improvements and most of their personal belongings, the Creek immigrants suffered more than any other tribe on their Trail of Tears. The army captured nearly 2,500 chiefs and warriors who were classed as hostile and were therefore considered dangerous. During the bitterly cold winter of 1836–1837 many in this group were bound in shackles and driven on foot to Fort Gibson. One party of 300 Creeks was taken down the Alabama River to the Gulf of Mexico, transported to the Mississippi, and placed on a river boat that had been condemned as unsafe. Upriver the rotting craft sank, and all passengers were lost. By the spring of 1837, 15,000 Creeks had reached the West. Over 3,500 had died in the winter cold on the way west. The severe weather, lack of food, and general suffering killed virtually all infants as well as many small children and old people.

The Chickasaw Removal

Like the other Southern Indian nations, the Chickasaws were surrounded by Anglo-American settlements, and government officials sought to persuade tribal leaders to sign a removal treaty. Successive cession agreements with the United States had already drastically reduced Chickasaw territory when an 1818 treaty cut off their range in western Kentucky and Tennessee and restricted them to northern Mississippi and northwestern Alabama. Through the years government commissioners encouraged the chiefs to cede this last vestige of their once vast domain. Like the other tribes, the Chickasaws suffered harassment, and, in the usual pattern, the Mississippi legislature dissolved their tribal government and made all Chickasaws subject to state law. The chiefs were aware that removal was inevitable, but they shrewdly held out just long enough to wring from the government by far the best removal treaty negotiated with any southern Indian nation.

During October 1832 at the Chickasaw council house on Pontotoc Creek in northern Mississippi, tribal leaders signed a treaty with President Jackson's representatives providing for the cession of all Chickasaw lands east of the Mississippi River as soon as a suitable home in the West could be found. By the terms of the Treaty of Pontotoc, the federal government was to survey the Chickasaw nation; then each Indian family was to be assigned a homestead as a temporary residence until the western home was found. The remainder of the land was to be sold at public auction, the proceeds to go to the Chickasaws.

Chickasaw delegations visited the trans-Mississippi territory from time to time searching for a tribal home. The Choctaws encouraged them to settle in their domain west of Arkansas. Officials in the federal and state governments urged the Chickasaws to make a decision, but the chiefs were not to be hurried. Finally, in January 1837 Chickasaw and Choctaw leaders signed the agreement known as the Treaty of Doaksville; the Chickasaws agreed to settle among the Choctaws.

Prodded by government officials, the Chickasaws began migrating in the spring of 1837, and by 1840 most of them had arrived in the Indian Territory. With a shorter distance to travel and the wise management of their removal by tribal leaders, the Chickasaw relocation was the most peaceful and orderly experienced by any of the Southern tribes. Indian families were able to collect most of their personal property, slaves, and livestock for transfer to the West. One report told of 7,000 Chickasaw horses gathered at Memphis waiting for transportation to the west bank of the Mississippi. But even with their well-organized removal, they did not escape suffering and disease. Cholera struck some of their emigrant camps, and many suffered from spoiled meat and grain rations issued them by unscrupulous government contractors.

The Seminole Removal

The last of the Southern tribes to be colonized in the West were the Seminoles of Florida, southern Georgia, and Alabama. They were sedentary town dwellers, their government consisting of a head chief and a council with moderate power. The nation was divided into bands, each named for the captain of the band. Some of the leading band chiefs, who at the time of removal defended the right of the Seminoles to remain on the land of their ancestors, were Osceola, Alligator, Jumper, Coacoochee (Wildcat), and Micanopy.

The Seminoles first came under American jurisdiction in 1819, when Spain ceded Florida to the United States. Immediately thereafter Americans moved into Florida Territory and began demanding that the government remove the Seminoles and open their rich coastal lands to settlement. In 1823 the Seminoles signed their first treaty with the United States. By the Treaty of Tampa they agreed to move onto the swampy interior east of Tampa Bay. This satisfied the whites only briefly, and in no time at all they were demanding that the federal government remove the Seminoles altogether, claiming that the Indians stole their slaves and livestock and were a menace to the settlements.

In 1832 United States Commissioner James Gadsden met with the Seminole chiefs and negotiated the Treaty of Payne's Landing, by which the tribe was obligated to evacuate Florida when their leaders found a suitable home in the western country. The Indians had three years in which to make the move, and the United States government agreed to pay the cost of removal and subsistence for one year after arrival in the West, and to pay the nation $15,400 for the land surrendered in Florida, plus $3,000 a year for fifteen years.

A delegation of seven Seminole chiefs traveled to the West in search of a new home. Creek leaders invited them to settle on their lands west of Fort Gibson. After some hesitation the Seminole delegates signed the Treaty of Fort Gibson in 1833, accepting the Creek offer. By the terms of the Treaty of Payne's Landing, the Seminole grace period ended in 1835. Osceola headed a faction that refused to be bound by the removal treaties, but a portion of the nation agreed to move, and federal officials made preparations accordingly. Osceola and other patriot leaders were angered by the removal activities, and they killed one of the signers of the Treaty of Fort Gibson. Agent Wiley Thompson had Osceola arrested and placed in irons. After a brief confinement, Osceola was released, and shortly afterward he and a band of followers shot Thompson, an army officer, and several civilians near Fort King, and ambushed a column of 110 soldiers on the road near the post. Only three men escaped the Seminole trap. The Fort King massacre set off the Seminole

War which lasted until 1842. No settlement was safe, and soldiers who went after the fierce Seminoles did so at great peril. Osceola promised that his warriors would fight "till the last drop of Seminole blood had moisted the dust" of their homeland.

In the meantime, peaceful Seminoles appeared every month or so to be outfitted for emigration. Four hundred people departed from Tampa in April 1836. Under Osceola, the resistance faction carried on a fierce, unremitting war against the United States army and the Florida settlements. In 1836 General Thomas Jesup was placed in command of troops for what the government hoped would be the final campaign against the Seminoles. Unable to bring the elusive warriors to bay, he called a peace council, and the chiefs came in under a flag of truce. In violation of the truce agreement Osceola was seized by troops guarding the camp and sent to Fort Moultrie at Charleston, South Carolina. The unconquerable war chief died there in a dark prison cell in January 1839, but his followers continued the war under Wildcat and Bowlegs. This protracted struggle was one of the costliest wars the young American nation had yet seen. Finally in 1842 the hazards of flushing Seminoles from their swamp hideouts caused the federal government to call off the contest. A community of Seminoles was allowed to remain permanently in Florida.

A census of the Seminole camps near Fort Gibson in 1842 showed that in ten years the federal government had managed to remove 3,000 Seminoles from the Old Southwest. Some came peacefully, most by coercion. The cost was high: $20 million was spent in keeping an army in the field from 1835 to 1842; 1,500 soldiers were killed; and countless others were maimed for life. Each Seminole removed to Indian Territory (man, woman, child), cost the government $6,500, a private fortune in 1842. Looking at these statistics another way, for every two Seminoles removed to the West, the army paid with the life of one soldier. No one knows the exact cost in terms of Seminole lives, but the Seminole removal brought to a close one of the blackest periods in American history. The Trail of Tears of the Southern tribes and the other Eastern Indian communities who were ruthlessly uprooted to make way for the "Great Land Animal" ranks among the tragedies of the ages.

The chief executive who presided over the most sordid phase of this exile stated in his Farewell Address to a grateful nation on March 4, 1837:

The States which had so long been retarded in their improvement by the Indian tribes residing in the midst of them are at length relieved from the evil . . . and this unhappy race—the original dwellers in our land—are now placed in a situation where we may well hope that they will share in the blessings of civilization and be saved from degradation and destruction.[17]

Notes

1. Francis Paul Prucha, *American Indian Policy in the Formative Years: The Indian Trade and Intercourse Acts, 1790–1834* (Cambridge, Mass., 1962), p. 225; Helen Hunt Jackson, *A Century of Dishonor* (New York, 1881), new edition (Williamstown, Mass., 1973), p. vi.
2. Prucha, *American Indian Policy*, p. 234.
3. Harold E. Fey and D'Arcy McNickle, *Indians and Other Americans: Two Ways of Life Meet* (New York, 1970), pp. 62–63.
4. *Ibid.*
5. Ronald N. Satz, *American Indian Policy in the Jacksonian Era* (Lincoln, Neb., 1975), p. 13.
6. Michael Paul Rogin, *Fathers and Children: Andrew Jackson and the Subjugation of the American Indian* (New York, 1975), pp. 207–209.
7. D'Arcy McNickle, *Native American Tribalism: Indian Survivals and Renewals* (New York, 1973), p. 73.
8. Gloria Jahoda, *The Trail of Tears* (New York, 1975), p. 42.
9. *Ibid.* pp. 44–45.
10. Prucha, *American Indian Policy*, p. 237.
11. *American State Papers: Indian Affairs*, vol. 2, p. 544.
12. Arrell M. Gibson, *Oklahoma: A History of Five Centuries* (Norman, Okla., 1965), p. 111.
13. *Ibid.*, p. 117.
14. Jahoda, *Trail of Tears*, p. 86.
15. *Report of the Commissioner of Indian Affairs for 1831*, p. 172.
16. Gibson, *Oklahoma*, p. 88.
17. James D. Richardson (ed.), *Messages and Papers of the Presidents* (Washington, D.C., 1896–1899), Vol. 2, p. 541.

Selected Sources

The origins and application of Jacksonian Indian policy are presented in Ronald N. Satz, *American Indian Policy in the Jacksonian Era* (Lincoln, Neb., 1975); Wilcomb Washburn, *Red Man's Land, White Man's Law* (New York, 1972); Francis Paul Prucha, *American Indian Policy in the Formative Years: The Indian Trade and Intercourse Acts, 1790–1834* (Cambridge, Mass., 1962), and "Andrew Jackson's Indian Policy: A Reassessment," *Journal of American History*, 56 (December 1969), pp. 527–39. The concept of Jacksonian-induced infantilism is provocatively treated by Michael Paul Rogin, *Fathers and Children: Andrew Jackson and the Subjugation of the American Indian* (New York, 1975). Also see Herman J. Viola, *Thomas L. McKenney, Architect of America's Early Indian Policy: 1816–1830* (Chicago, 1974). Of the vast literature devoted to Indian removal, the following selections provide both scope and substance: Gloria Jahoda, *The Trail of Tears* (New York, 1975); Arrell M. Gibson, *America's Exiles* (Norman, Okla., 1976), and *The Chickasaws* (Norman, Okla., 1971); Mary Elizabeth Young, *Redskins, Ruffleshirts and Rednecks: Indian Allotments in Alabama and Mississippi, 1830–1860* (Norman, Okla., 1961), and "Indian Removal and Land Allotment: The Civilized Tribes and Jacksonian Justice," *American Historical Review* 64 (October 1958), pp. 31–45; George D. Harmon, *Sixty Years of Indian Affairs: Political, Economic, and Diplomatic, 1789–1850* (Chapel Hill, N.C., 1941); Wilson Lumpkin, *Removal of the Cherokee Indians from Georgia*, 2 vols. (New York, 1907); Angie Debo, *Rise and Fall of the Choctaw Republic* (Norman, Okla.,

1934), and *The Road to Disappearance* (Norman, Okla., 1941); Arthur H. De-Rosier, *The Removal of the Choctaw Indians* (Knoxville, Tenn., 1970); Grace S. Woodward, *The Cherokees* (Norman, Okla., 1963); Edwin C. McReynolds, *The Seminoles* (Norman, Okla., 1957); Grant Foreman, *The Five Civilized Tribes* (Norman, Okla., 1934), and *Indian Removal* (Norman, Okla., 1932); and Althea Bass, *Cherokee Messenger* (Norman, Okla., 1936).

The constitutional status of Native Americans in the removal crisis is analyzed by Jerry Muskrat in "The Constitution and the American Indian: Past and Prologue," *Hastings Constitutional Law Quarterly* 3(Summer 1976), pp. 657–77. See Wilcomb Washburn (ed.), *The American Indian and the United States: A Documentary History*, 4 vols. (New York, 1977) for primary materials on this era. Also see R. David Edmunds, *The Potawatomis: Keepers of the Fire* (Norman, 1978); and Patricia K. Ourada, *The Menominee Indians: A History* (Norman, 1979).

CHAPTER 14

INDIANS UNDER ANGLO-AMERICAN DOMINION 1840–1861

There was a time when our people covered the whole land as the waves of a wind-ruffled sea cover its shell-paved floor. But that time has long since passed away with the greatness of tribes now almost forgotten. I will not mourn over our untimely decay, nor reproach my paleface brothers with hastening it. . . . Every part of this country is sacred to my people. Every hillside, every valley, every plain and grove has been hallowed by some fond memory or some sad experience of my tribe. Even the rocks which seem to lie dumb as they swelter in the sun . . . thrill with memories of past events connected with the fate of my people. The braves, fond mothers, glad-hearted maidens, and even little children, who lived here . . . still love these solitudes. Their deep fastnesses at eventide grow shadowy with the presence of dusty spirits. When the last red man shall have perished from the earth and his memory among the white men shall have become a myth, these shores shall swarm with the invisible dead of my tribe. . . . At night when the streets of your cities and villages shall be silent, and you think them deserted, they will throng with the returning hosts that once filled and still love this beautiful land.

Prophesy by Seattle (Dwamish-Salish) at the Port Elliot Council, 1855

♥

The Anglo-American nation, by the time it was seventy years old in 1846, had swept from the Atlantic seaboard to the Pacific shore. Its citizens took great pride in their prodigal achievements. Besides conquering this vast geographic area and adapting to its differing environments, they had removed the humans who stood in the way of their private and public goals. By the 1830s the national government, responding to popular demand, had erased Indians from virtually all the territory between the Atlantic Ocean and the western border of Missouri. This erasure—by war and disease and exile—had been singularly thorough; only a few tiny Indian communities survived in remote sections of the eastern United States that held little appeal for white settlers.

National leaders believed that with the creation of the Indian Territory and its settlement by the eastern tribes they finally had found the solution to the Indian problem. But events very soon proved that the Indian Territory was a major miscalculation. Federal agents were concerned that several tribes had

Chapter Opening Artifact: Paiute basket with rounded shoulder, black decoration. (Courtesy Museum of the American Indian, Heye Foundation)

been required to move twice, some three times, in order to accommodate the land demands of encroaching Anglo-American settlements. Therefore they urged the President and Congress that once settled in the Indian Territory, Indians should never again be required to move. Thus by presidential order the Indian Territory was withdrawn from settlement and placed off limits to Anglo-American pioneers.

In the past such an order had been no deterrent to white settlement, but now there was good reason for federal officials to feel secure in tribal tenure of the Indian Territory. First there was wide public acceptance of the idea of "National Completeness," a belief that with the Atlantic seaboard, Old Northwest, Old Southwest, and Mississippi Valley populated, organized, and integrated into the national life, the United States had reached the westernmost limits of land required by its citizens for agricultural pursuits. The organized national territory was regarded as adequate for the foreseeable land needs of the nation; the American people would not require any land west of Missouri. Moreover, published accounts of federally sponsored explorations by military and scientific specialists describing the country west of Missouri stressed its inhospitable environment, its trackless wastes, towering mountains, and severe climate; they fixed firmly in the American mind the concept of the Great American Desert. Thus it was widely acknowledged that the limits of effective American occupation—"National Completeness"—had been achieved. The public image that a vast wasteland existed west of Missouri helps to explain the generosity of national leaders in setting aside a substantial portion as a resettlement zone for the eastern tribes. They clearly believed that low value of the region in the public's mind would forever protect the uprooted Indians from competition with Anglo-American settlers for land. Shortly afterward, unforeseen events began to occur west of the Indian Territory, shattering the illusion of "National Completeness." Anglo-American territorial expansion resumed; it brought western Indian communities under United States dominion, and they came to suffer similar torments and impositions endured by the eastern tribes only recently exiled to the Indian Territory.

THE INDIAN TERRITORY

The nation's Indian colonization zone extended from Missouri's western border to the limits of the United States which, during the 1830s, was the one hundredth meridian; the Platte River marked its northern boundary; the Red River the southern boundary. Tribal land assignments by federal agents had divided the Indian Territory on the thirty-seventh parallel, the present boundary between Kansas and Oklahoma.

Indian Territory was a misnomer. At no time in its existence as a geographic-political entity in the Anglo-American community did it have a territorial form of government. In 1834 and on several other occasions proposals were submitted to Congress for the political organization of the Indian Territory along the lines of an integrated territorial government as a prelude for the formation of an Indian state. The idea for such a territory had first appeared in the writings of the Reverend Jedidiah Morse, a pioneer advocate of an Indian state, and the Reverend Isaac McCoy, who proposed a utopian Indian community called New Canaan. The Indian Territory throughout its existence remained a fragmented maze of self-governing Indian communities, the political systems varying from the ancient tribal forms of the Shawnees to the constitution of the Cherokees.

Colonizing Northern Indian Territory

In the northern portion federal agents had resettled many local tribes, including the Osage and Kansa, onto smaller domains to make room for the emigrating eastern Indians. Native Americans from the Old Northwest were concentrated in this portion of the Indian Territory and included Potawatomis, Peorias, Wyandots, and Kaskaskias. Many relocated tribes came directly from the Old Northwest. Many Old Northwest tribes, including Kickapoos, Delawares, Shawnees, and Sac and Fox, which had first been settled in what became Missouri and Iowa, subsequently were forced by settler pressure and government negotiation to remove a second time onto new domains in this segment of the Indian Territory.

North of the immigrant tribes in the Missouri and Platte river valleys were the so-called Border Indians—Iowas, Otos, Missouris, Omahas, and Pawnees —agriculturalists who for centuries had lived on the eastern margins of the Great Plains, became skilled horsemen and, in season, hunted buffalo. The Pawnees particularly were acknowledged excellent judges of quality horses and became notorious along the western border as inveterate stock thieves.

The northern portion of the Indian Territory was much more of a cultural collage than the southern portion, and because of this ethnic mix, federal agents found it more difficult to administer. Their task was complicated by its proximity to the hunting range of the fierce Sioux, Cheyennes, and Arapahoes. Swift-riding warriors from these tribes regularly preyed on the Border Indians and the more westerly immigrant Indians for livestock, women, and weapons. The constant threat of these forays discouraged the émigrés beginning life anew in the western wilderness.

Another complication for the tribes of the northern half of the Indian Territory was the location of their lands astride what became the two most heavily traveled routes in the West. A trader's road, the Santa Fe Trail, linked the western Missouri border towns of Westport and Independence and the Rio Grande settlements, crossing the northern Indian Territory to Bent's Fort in southeastern Colorado. The principal immigrant roads to the Mormon communities in the Great Basin, to the Oregon Country, and to California crossed the northern half of the Indian Territory. Inevitably this ever increasing human stream across Indian lands interrupted the adjustment attempts of immigrant tribes and was distracting and destructive to peace and order;

travelers stripped the Indians of livestock and other property with impunity and diminished their wood and grass resources.

Fort Leavenworth, established in 1827, was garrisoned with Dragoons after formation of these mounted trooper units in 1834. They assisted in the removal of several tribes to the northern half of the Indian Territory and provided some protection to the immigrant Indians, although the troops were too few in number and their task too great to provide complete protection from Sioux-Cheyenne-Arapaho raids and damage by travelers from the wagon trains crossing their lands to the West. As shall be discussed further subsequently, the northern half of the Indian Territory had a brief life, existing as an Indian haven only until 1854.

The Hitchcock Mission

The cruelty that the southern tribes suffered on their Trail of Tears resurfaced in the shockingly revealing but futile Hitchcock mission. By the removal treaties with the eastern tribes the government had promised to pay the cost of relocating each of the tribes, including food and provisions for the Indians during the emigration and for one year after arrival in the West. But the federal government was not giving a gift to the Indians by these promises: Treasury Department clerks had calculated the estimated expense of each relocation, and federal commissioners then deducted this estimate from the offers they made for tribal lands.

Government officials had delegated most of the job of feeding and transporting the Indians to private contractors, and those Indians who survived the Trail of Tears claimed that much of their suffering and high death rate in transit were due to corrupt contractors who enriched themselves at the Indians' expense. Critics claimed that "at so much per head it was entirely a business proposition with the contractors . . . the removal of the Indians was not a great philanthropy, but was carried out with the same business considerations that would characterize the transportation of commodities of commerce from one point to another."[1]

Vast sums of public money were paid to contracting firms, newly formed to render this service to the government; it was later revealed that most of the contractors were friends and relatives of officials high in the government. The contracts customarily called for the following: "the ration of bread shall be one pound of wheat flour, Indian meal, or hard bread, or three quarters of a quart of corn; the meat ration shall be one pound of fresh meat, two quarts of salt to every hundred rations. The transportation shall be one six-horse wagon and 1500 pounds of baggage to from 50 to 80 persons. The provisions and transportation shall be of the best of their kind. The average daily travel shall not exceed twelve miles."[2]

Angry protests by tribal leaders and charges of profiteering and fraud published in eastern newspapers embarrassed the federal government and forced it to investigate the charges. The secretary of war ordered Major Ethan Allen

Hitchcock to look into the complaints. Concerning his appointment, the eminent anthropologist John R. Swanton has said: "Since ... the national administration was willing to look the other way while this criminal operation [the removal] was in progress, it made a curious blunder in permitting the injection into such a situation of an investigator as little disposed to white-wash iniquity as was Ethan Allen Hitchcock."[3]

Major Hitchcock began his investigation of removal abuses during November 1841. A highly perceptive investigator, he confided to his journal that news of his mission had preceded him, and there was much curiosity about his business in the Indian Territory. He added that one of the contractors who had settled on the border "came here so poor that a man with a $400 claim against him was glad to settle for $100. Now he owns a considerable number of Negroes and has offered $17,500 for a plantation." Hitchcock's exhaustive investigation yielded evidence of "bribery, perjury and forgery, short weights, issues of spoiled meat and grain, and every conceivable subterfuge was employed by designing white men."[4]

Hitchcock took his findings to Washington; there he prepared a report with 100 exhibits and filed the hefty document with the secretary of war. "Committees of Congress tried vainly to have it submitted to them so that appropriate action could be taken; but it was stated that too many friends of the administration were involved to permit the report to become public. It disappeared from the files and no trace of it is to be found." Swanton's comment on the fate of the Hitchcock report was, "The fact that it did not allow the report to be made public and its mysterious disappearance from all official files proves at one and the same time the honesty of the report and the dishonesty of the national administration of the period."[5]

The fate of transplanted eastern tribes was soon shared by those west of the Indian Territory. During the 1830s the comforting calm of "National Completeness" began to wane, and the expansive Anglo-American nation resumed its march toward the Pacific, bringing the western Indian nations under United States dominion.

Colonizing Southern Indian Territory

As the southern Indians—Cherokees, Choctaws, Seminoles, Creeks, and Chickasaws—recovered from the trauma of removal and adjusted to the southern Indian Territory wilderness, they turned to establishing the essentials of orderly existence, including government and economy. For some time they had lived near European and Anglo-American settlements with which they had cultural and economic interaction, even intermarriage. By the time of removal each Indian nation had a large community of mixed bloods who tended to be the principal proponents of change. On the eve of their removal the Southern Indian nations had established organized governments with functioning executive, legislative, and judicial branches. They maintained schools, in some cases with strong missionary support. Increasingly, they sustained themselves by stock raising, agriculture, and trading, relying less upon the primitive arts of hunting, fishing, and gathering. Most Southern Indians had adopted so-called citizen dress—the costume of neighboring Anglo-American settlers. Many of the prosperous mixed bloods were slave owners. In many ways the political, economic, and social patterns of Southern Indian society on the eve of removal were similar to those of their settler-neighbors.

The Cherokees, Choctaws, Chickasaws, Creeks, and most of the Seminoles energetically transformed the southern portion of the Indian Territory wilderness and planted there constitutional government, formal education, economy, slaveholding, and certain other familiar Anglo-American institutions. The Southern Indians therefore may be regarded as carriers of Anglo-American culture into the West like frontier settlers in the adjacent border settlements of Missouri, Arkansas, and Texas.

Like other Western pioneers, the Southern Indians, many with slave labor, established farms, ranches, and plantations in the virgin valleys, uplands, and prairies of the Indian Territory. They founded towns, businesses, and newspapers, and began river steamer, stage, and freight transport systems.

At first the southern Indian Territory was divided into three parts—the Cherokee nation in the north, the Creek nation in the center, and the Choctaw nation in the south. These boundaries changed during the late 1830s as the Seminoles and Chickasaws relocated in the West. For a time the central portion was designated as the Creek-Seminole nation, and the region south of the Canadian and Arkansas rivers as the Choctaw-Chickasaw nation. After years of strong urging by Chickasaw leaders, that nation in 1855 was permitted to withdraw from the Choctaws and form a separate, independent Chickasaw nation in the central third of the old Choctaw nation, the latter retaining the eastern third as a homeland territory. The Seminoles also became disenchanted with their status as a minority group in the more populous Creek nation and urged separation. The resistance leader Wildcat was particularly irreconcilable and, as a protest against what he regarded as the inferior status of his people in the Creek nation, he led a group of Seminoles and their slaves to northern Mexico. At the invitation of the Mexican government Wildcat's band settled in Coahuila. In a few years the chief and many of his followers returned to the Indian Territory, but several remained in Mexico and their descendants, locally called Muskogees, live there to this day. Finally the Creeks relented and permitted the Seminoles to withdraw onto territory of their own and to form their independent government. The treaty authorizing this change was concluded in 1856; it defined the Seminole territory as a tract between the North Canadian and Canadian rivers and extending from the ninety-seventh to the one hundredth meridian.

Tribal leaders formed governments for their nations. Activities of the tribal governments were concentrated in their national capitals—Tahlequah for the Cherokees, Doaksville for the Choctaws, Tishomingo for the Chickasaws, North Fork Town for the Creeks, and Seminole Agency for the Seminoles.

The governmental system created by the Cherokees was similar to that used by the other tribes. The Cherokee nation was governed by a constitution which divided the government into three coordinate sections: an elected principal chief, an elected bicameral legislative branch called the National Council, and an appointed judiciary of a supreme court and lesser courts. The nation was divided into local government units called districts, similar to counties; each was administered by elected officials, including commissioners and a sheriff.

The Cherokees maintained a public school system for the nation's youth. It offered elementary and grammar (secondary) school work and was directed by a national superintendent of public instruction. Books and other learning materials were published both in English and Cherokee—in the Cherokee syllabary invented by Sequoyah during the 1820s. The *Cherokee Advocate*, a weekly newspaper printed in both English and Cherokee, was published at Tahlequah beginning in 1844.

Samuel A. Worcester, a missionary-teacher supported by the American Board of Commissioners for Foreign Missions who had been jailed in Georgia for teaching in Cherokee schools without a state license, established Park Hill, a missionary settlement near Tahlequah. The compound included a school, church, and the Park Hill Press, a publishing house established by Worcester with printing equipment he had brought to the Indian Territory from the East. Park Hill Press did a thriving business publishing books, pamphlets, the *Cherokee Almanac*, and other items.

Similar governmental and educational institutions arose among the other nations in the Indian Territory. The southern Indians were the first pioneers, even preceding the Texans, to establish the familiar agricultural frontier in the West. Cotton produced on Indian Territory plantations was shipped from landings on the Arkansas and Red rivers aboard steamers to ports on the Gulf; grain and livestock from Indian Territory farms and ranches made their way to markets on the southwestern border in Missouri, Arkansas, and Louisiana.

As in the case of the tribes settled in the northern Indian Territory, those to the south faced a growing tide of traffic across their lands, produced by the resumed territorial expansion of the Anglo-American nation. Four heavily traveled highways into the West crossed the southern Indian Territory. The oldest was the southerly Santa Fe Trail from Fort Smith along the Arkansas and Canadian valleys into New Mexico, terminating at the Rio Grande settlements. This was primarily a traders' highway. The Texas Road carried the greatest volume of traffic. Laterals of this popular travel artery extended from the headwaters of Grand River into Missouri, then southwest across the Cherokee, Choctaw, and Chickasaw nations, crossing Red River at the mouth of the Washita. It was the principal north-south route for settlers bound for Texas. The trans-continental Butterfield Overland Mail Company crossed a portion of Indian Territory on its route from St. Louis and Memphis to San Francisco via El Paso; twelve stage stations were situated between Fort Smith on the northern edge of the Choctaw nation and Colbert's Ferry on the Red River in the Chickasaw nation. The California Road was the fourth highway to the West crossing the southern Indian Territory; troops from Fort Smith and Fort Gibson surveyed this passage for use by gold seekers rushing to California beginning in 1849. Originating at Fort Smith it followed the Arkansas and Canadian valleys, one branch running due west to Santa Fe, the other bending southwest to Doña Ana on the Rio Grande for connections with the Gila River route to California. Before the gold fever ebbed, perhaps 5,000 persons followed the California Road across the Indian Territory on their way to camps on the Sacramento.

While the increased traffic across their domains had an unsettling, distracting effect upon the southern tribes, much as it did the tribes in the northern Indian Territory, they were better able to cope with the hordes of travelers. Being more business-oriented, Cherokees, Choctaws, Creeks, Seminoles, and Chickasaws profited from outfitting emigrant trains with wagons, mules, horses and oxen, camp equipment, and provisions for the journey. The gold fever hit the Five Civilized Tribes, too, especially the Cherokees, and several hundred Indians made the trip to the West Coast gold fields.

ANGLO-AMERICAN EXPANSION AND NATIVE AMERICANS

The region west of the Indian Territory was the home of many Indian groups with widely varying life-styles. Bordering the Indian Territory was the range of the Plains tribes. Having universally adopted the horse, Plains Indians were mobile and dangerous, a formidable barrier to outsiders who ventured

"The Piegan." (Peabody Museum, Harvard University/Photograph by Edward Curtis, 1910)

into their domains. The Plains tribes lived largely by hunting buffalo, raiding, and by trading in the frontier settlements of Texas, New Mexico, the Indian Territory, and in the British trading communities of the far north. The Sioux nation occupied a region extending across western Minnesota into the Dakotas. For years they controlled passage up the Missouri River to the Rocky Mountains. The Cheyennes and Arapahoes dominated the territory between the Platte and Arkansas rivers, and south of the Arkansas roamed the Comanches and Kiowas. The core of their settlement was in the Wichita Mountains of southwestern Oklahoma, but they roamed across most of the Southwest. Comanche-Kiowa raider bands struck at settlements from the Indian Territory to the Spanish towns on the Rio Grande and south across Texas into northern Mexico.

Scattered throughout the Plains were settlements of tribes with a mixed

Paiute woman weaver seated outside a brush shelter. (Smithsonian Institution, National Anthropological Archives)

economy of hunting and agriculture. These included the Mandans near the great bend of the Missouri River and the Wichitas and Caddoes in the Red River valley. Texas supported a large and varied aboriginal population. In the east along the headwaters of the Angelina and Sabine rivers were the Hasinai, a confederacy of fifteen to twenty tribes; around the Gulf Coast were several Native American communities including the Karankawas and Tonkawas; the Caddodacho Confederacy of about twenty tribes occupied central Texas; Jumanos lived in the Rio Grande Valley; and Lipan Apaches roamed across northwest Texas. Far to the north, Blackfeet, Crows (or Absarokas), Utes, Arikaras, and Shoshonis lived in the Rocky Mountains but moved seasonally onto the Plains to hunt buffalo. Sacajawea, the gifted young woman who served as interpreter-guide to the Lewis and Clark expedition, was of the northern Shoshoni tribe.

The plateau and desert country between the Rocky Mountains and the Sierra Nevadas had but a sparse Indian population, and each tribe developed an economic system and life-style compatible with the generally harsh, inhospitable environment of this portion of western America. In the north, on the Columbia Plateau, lived the Nez Percés and Salish (or Flatheads). After European contact, the Nez Percés became excellent stock raisers and produced a new American breed of horse—the Appaloosa. During the nineteenth century, the Nez Percés were the most illustrious Indian patriots of the West. Their attempts to stem the tide of American expansion onto Indian lands were epitomized by their great leader Chief Joseph.

In the Great Basin of Utah and Nevada lived the Gosuite, Paiute, Yuman, and Mohave tribes, and bands of Shoshonis and Utes. The paucity of game in this region forced many of these tribes to eat insects, snakes, and lizards, and to burrow for nourishing roots; hence the rather derogatory nickname "Digger Indians."

Between the Pecos River and the Colorado River there were several populous and powerful tribes. Some were sedentary, others migratory. The eastern sedentary tribes of the Southwest were called Pueblos (Spanish for "towns") after their residences—large multifamily dwellings constructed of adobe brick or stone with fortifications to fend off attacks by Utes and other marauding tribes. They practiced intensive agriculture, irrigating their crops with water drawn from the rivers near their villages. The Pueblo community consisted of Keresan and Tanoan settlements on the upper Pecos and Rio Grande rivers of New Mexico, and Hopi, Acoma, and Zuñi settlements in western New Mexico and eastern Arizona. The principal sedentary tribes to the west of the Pueblos were the Pimas and Papagos on the Salt, Gila, and lower Colorado rivers. Unlike the Pueblos, the Pimas and Papagos dwelt in sizable villages of thatch houses. They, too, practiced intensive irrigated agriculture.

The most recent arrivals in the Southwest were the Apaches and Navajos—both of Athapascan stock—who ranged over western New Mexico and Arizona. The Apaches were especially wide-ranging wanderers. Fierce in battle and virtually unconquerable, they were the scourge of the Spanish-Mexican

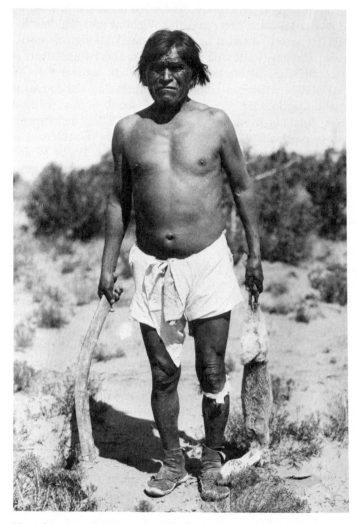

Hopi hunter. (Smithsonian Institution, National Anthropological Archives)

frontier and helped discourage American expansion into the Southwest until the last quarter of the nineteenth century. The Apache nation was divided into several bands including the Chiricahuas, Mimbreños, Jicarillos, San Carlos, Coyoteros, and Mescaleros. The Navajos, who were somewhat less migratory than the Apaches, practiced some agriculture and were receptive to stock raising. Soon after the Spanish arrival Navajo families developed sizable herds of horses and flocks of sheep.

Perhaps the most populous and diverse aboriginal community in the West was in California. Its population at the time of European contact is estimated to have been 150,000. The many small tribes comprising this ethnographic complex included the Modocs, Karoks, Yuroks, Shastas, Hupas, Pomos, Miwoks, and Chuwash. They subsisted on acorns, fish, roots, and small game, and their principal craft was making baskets from native sedges. The Spanish found most of these tribes docile and readily integrated them into ecclesiastical communities so that many came to be called Mission Indians.

The Pacific Northwest tribes were also numerous and varied in culture. Their economic life centered on fishing, usually for the ubiquitous salmon. The tribes of this region—which included the Klamaths, Walla Wallas, Chinooks, Salish, Umpquas, Spokans, and Yakimas—were renowned for their skill in basket and mat weaving, woodworking technology, and the potlatch ceremony—a prodigious, competitive giving of gifts.

The first of the western tribes to come under American rule were those in Texas and then the Oregon Country.

Conquest of the Texas Indians

In 1819 while Texas was still a Spanish border province, officials in New Spain (Mexico) opened the territory north of the Rio Grande to settlement by aliens. The Mexican nation, following independence in the revolution of 1821, continued this practice. Most immigrants to Texas came from the United States, primarily from Missouri, Kentucky, Tennessee, Louisiana, Mississippi, and Alabama; they carried with them their anti-Indian bias. Following a successful revolt in 1836, Anglo-American settlers established the Texas Republic.

Officials of the Texas Republic had three Indian communities to deal with: the indigenous tribes of the Hasinai and Caddodacho confederacies; the immigrant tribes consisting largely of Cherokees, led by The Bowl but also including bands of Kickapoos, Shawnees, and Delawares from the Old Northwest, living on lands granted to them by the Spanish in eastern Texas along the Sabine River; and bands of Comanches and Kiowas from haunts in the Wichita Mountains of the southwestern portion of the Indian Territory, each season ranging across central Texas southward into the Mexican state of Coahuila to raid settlements for captives and livestock. As Texas pioneers increasingly took up land in the range of their raids, these fierce predators turned their fury on Texan farms, ranches, and towns.

The Indian policy of the Texas Republic copied the United States policy except that Texan officials refused to recognize Indian title to land, claiming that the Republic of Texas held absolute title to all land within its jurisdiction. Indian policy of the Texas Republic permitted Native Americans the grim choice of emigration, expulsion, or extermination.

With no public restraint, Texas settlers carried out a merciless campaign of harassment and intimidation toward their Indian neighbors, driving them from south-central Texas into the northwestern wilderness. By the time of the annexation of Texas to the United States in 1845 the Texas tribes had been reduced to fragments of once populous Indian nations. And as shall be indi-

345

cated subsequently, their ordeal at the hands of the expansive Texans did not end with annexation of Texas by the United States.

The second aboriginal community in Texas was the composite emigrant group residing in eastern Texas, consisting of Cherokees, Kickapoos, Shawnees, and Delawares, who occupied rich farming lands coveted by Texans. Republic officials accused the Indians of conspiring with Mexican agents who were seeking the reconquest of Texas, and in 1839 used this justification for a bloody campaign mounted by the army of the Texas Republic to drive these Native Americans from Texas. After a spirited defense, Cherokee, Kickapoo, Shawnee, and Delaware émigrés abandoned their thriving East Texas settlements and fled south into Mexico and north to the Indian Territory.

The third community of Indians Texans had to cope with—Comanches and Kiowas—became such a menace to expanding settlements that during most of the Republic period much of the public income of the Texan nation was spent maintaining a frontier army, the Texas Rangers, in a futile attempt to check devastating raids by the marauders from north of Red River. Comanches and Texans engaged in a long and bloody contest for central Texas that was not definitely decided until 1874. On several occasions Comanche military power threatened San Antonio and other large Texas settlements as a part of their extended war.

The United States annexed Texas in 1845. Thereupon the United States as sovereign could have been expected to take over management of the Texas tribes. However, there were several complications. First, a stipulation in the annexation compact permitted Texas to retain its public lands, thwarting the United States in attempts to fulfill its role as primary and exclusive director of Indian relations. Also, following annexation the Texas legislature enunciated the state's position on Indian affairs: it recognized no tribal title to land in the state, and it denied the right of the federal government to negotiate any treaty with an Indian nation without the consent of the state. Curiously the federal government acceded to these conditions in that it proceeded most cautiously in attempting to assert its dominion over the surviving Texas Indian tribes. During 1846 Texas congressional representatives objected to a treaty concluded between federal commissioners and leaders of the Texas tribes providing for reception of these Indian communities under United States protection and administration, and for regulating trade and relations generally by the federal government. The ratification vote failed.

As the Indian-settlers contest for land intensified, Texas state officials in 1848 finally established a temporary boundary separating Anglo-American and Indian settlements; each group was directed to respect the boundary line guarded by companies of Texas Rangers. Both Texans and Indians violated the boundary. Settlers raided Indian communities and ran off tribal livestock. Indians ambushed surveyors and wagon trains on lands they claimed. The frontier of north-central Texas became so bloodied that state officials appealed to the United States army for assistance in maintaining peace.

Texan leaders had adamantly refused to concede Indian title to land in the state until 1854 when the legislature finally acknowledged United States direction over resident tribes and ceded land on the Brazos River in far northwestern Texas for two small reservations to enable federal agents to concentrate remnants of the Texas tribes. State leaders also demanded that federal officials remove the Comanche-Kiowa threat to the westward-moving line of settlement in central Texas. Federal military officials directed construction of a group of forts athwart the Comanche-Kiowa trails in north-central Texas and at strategic points along mail, stage, and freight routes between San Antonio and Preston and El Paso. Among these posts were Fort Belknap, Fort Chadbourne, Fort Davis, Fort Phantom Hill, Fort Quitman, Fort Stockton, Fort Bliss, and Fort Worth.

Federal agents also used diplomacy in their attempts to pacify the Comanches and Kiowas. In 1853 they met with several leaders of these tribes at Fort Atkinson (near present Dodge City, Kansas) and renewed the 1835 pact of peace and pledge not to molest overland traffic. Any treaty with these tribes would be difficult to enforce largely because of their system of government; for example, the Comanches were divided into twelve autonomous bands, and rarely were all bands represented in negotiations with federal agents. In addition, federal officials attempted to persuade the Comanches and Kiowas to settle upon reservations, abandon their migratory buffalo-hunting, raiding existence and adopt agriculture and stock raising. For this purpose agents leased from the Choctaws and Chickasaws the western third of their domain between the ninety-eighth and one hundredth meridians and designated it the Leased District, a reservation home for the Comanches and Kiowas.

Resourceful Comanches and Kiowas simply used the Leased District as a sanctuary for supporting their continuing depredations into Texas and northern Mexico. Their sweeping raids on ranches, farms, and towns to the south netted horses, mules, and women and children captives. The raiders brought the plunder to their villages in the Leased District. At least two retaliatory campaigns were carried out against these raider bands before the Civil War. One strike was made by a Texas Ranger force under Captain John S. Ford; the other by a United States army cavalry column under Major Earl Van Dorn. In the late spring of 1858 Ford's men crossed Red River into the Leased District and attacked a Comanche village near the Wichita Mountains and killed 76 Indians. Then during September 1858 Van Dorn's cavalry scoured the Leased District for Native Americans. His Tonkawa scouts found a Comanche camp near Rush Springs, a watering point in the southeastern corner of the Leased District. Van Dorn's cavalry struck during the night while the Comanches were asleep; the surprise attack killed 60 Indians.

For the time being the Leased District tribes were quiet. The year after the military strikes against the Comanches and Kiowas, federal agents faced a crisis of another sort among the Indians. The surviving remnants of the confederated Texas tribes (including Wacos, Tonkawas, Anadarkos, Tawakonis, Ionis, Keechis, and Caddoes), recently concentrated onto the two Brazos reservations, were under siege—the line of pioneer settlement had reached the edge of their reservation, and Texans were demanding that the Indians be removed or face extermination. Hurriedly, federal agent Robert S. Neighbors collected nearly 2,000 Brazos Reservation Indians, and escorted by a United States army force, he conducted them to a new home in the Leased District. Federal officials constructed Fort Cobb to protect the immigrant Indians and Wichita Agency to administer their affairs. Thus by 1859 Texas was virtually cleared of Native Americans; only tiny pockets of isolated Indian settlements remained. However, until 1874 fierce tribesmen from the north continued to torment the westward-extending Texan settlements with swift, terrorizing raids.

Conquest of the Oregon Country Indians

Native Americans in the Pacific Northwest were also engulfed by white settlers. For some time they had maintained a seasonal contact with British traders from Canadian posts and from Fort Vancouver on the lower Columbia River. In 1811 American traders attempted to siphon off some of this rich interior fur trade by establishing Astoria at the mouth of the Columbia River. However, British economic and military power forced them to evacuate, and British domination of the Oregon Country continued. Then during the mid-1830s American missionaries began to penetrate the Oregon Country, and because British agents regarded their ministration to the Indian tribes as no economic threat, they permitted them to remain. However, as matters worked out they were but the vanguard of an invasion by Anglo-American settlers. Methodist missionaries led by Jason Lee settled at French Prairie and concentrated on Native Americans in the Willamette and lower Columbia river valleys. American Board missionaries, led by Marcus and Narcissa Whitman, settled inland near the junction of the Snake and Columbia rivers. Waiilatpu became their headquarters station.

Roman Catholic missionaries also entered the Oregon Country to minister to the resident tribes. The first were from Canada. Arriving in 1838, they founded missions at Cowlitz on Puget Sound and at Misqually midway between the sound and the Columbia River. Shortly they were joined by Roman Catholics from Missouri; the most famous was Father Pierre Jean De Smet who, by 1842, had established the most successful Christian missions in the Pacific Northwest. De Smet worked principally among the Flatheads and Pend Oreilles in the Coeur d'Alene and Bitterroot mission districts. Catholic missions in the Oregon Country during this period far exceeded Protestant missions in lasting commitment, service, and results. The most important reason for the Catholics' success was their single-mindedness of purpose—solely to serve the Indian tribes. The Protestants were torn by mixed interests—serving the Indian tribes and sharing the promise of the Oregon Country with fellow Christians in the states.

Protestant missionaries in the Oregon Country became precursors of American expansion and settlement. For their vocational training programs for Indian youth, missionaries imported cattle, horses, and mules from California. They established flourishing orchards and broad fields of grain. These training farms, undertaken to instruct Indian students in farming and stock-raising techniques, demonstrated the fertility of the soil and generally favorable conditions for successful agriculture in the Oregon Country. The expanding mission staffs increasingly spent their time developing farms and livestock herds for their personal benefit to the detriment of their ministry to the Indians. Missionary workers corresponded with families and sponsoring church congregations in the East. Their letters, full of descriptions of the superlative bounty of the Oregon Country, were often shared with newspaper and magazine editors who published them for a wider constituency. Missionaries also regularly returned to the states to raise money to support their work in Oregon and to recruit additional workers for the missions; these became promotional junkets for Oregon. In 1838, four years after the founding of the mission at French Prairie, Jason Lee journeyed to the East on a fund-raising venture. He returned to Oregon with fifty men, women, and children, certainly more persons than were needed for the Methodist mission staff in the new country.

Each year white migration to the Oregon Country increased; in 1843 over 3,000 pioneers trekked to Oregon. They established farms, towns, and local and eventually territorial government. Resident Indians were steadily swept aside into more remote territories. Then an incident at Waiilatpu Mission on November 29, 1847, marked the beginning of a long, bloody war which reached the familiar conclusion of defeated tribes: drastically reduced Native American population and reduction in tribal lands. Accumulated grievances of the upper Columbia River tribes against expansive Anglo-Americans focused momentarily upon Waiilatpu Mission. A raging measles epidemic had swept through the Cayuse tribe. Several Cayuse children, carriers of the disease, were students at the Waiilatpu Mission school. Grieving Cayuse warriors fell upon the mission and killed Whitman, his wife Narcissa, and twelve mission workers. To the Oregon Country settlers the Whitmans became martyrs. Messengers from the Oregon settlements rushed to the eastern United States to appeal for relief and protection. Public expressions of sympathy for the Whitmans and indignation over the massacre led Congress to create a territorial government for Oregon militia and federal troops to seek vengeance against the Indians. This incident was exploited for years as justification for reducing Oregon tribal estates and concentrating Native Americans there on reservations.

As a part of the conquest and compression process, during the 1850s the War Department directed construction of a cluster of military posts in Oregon and Washington. The principal posts in Oregon were Fort Dalles, Fort Stevens, Fort Umpqua, and Fort Lane; in Washington Fort Steilacoom, Fort Taylor, Fort Walla Walla, Fort Bellingham, Fort Cascades, Fort Chekalis, and Fort Colville. These military bases supported regular and militia forces in their campaigns against insurgent Indians who mounted an ever stiffening resistance to expanding Anglo-American settlements.

The Indian-settler contest in the Oregon Country, precipitated by the Whitman massacre, lasted until nearly 1860. Following the Waiilatpu Mission attack, 500 volunteers marched through the Cayuse country, pressuring tribal leaders to surrender the warriors involved in the massacre. A military commission tried 5 men and found them guilty, and on June 3, 1850, troops executed them by hanging. However, Native American resentment smoldered, and incidents continued to mount in the familiar Indian-settler contest for the land. Inevitable tribal defeat led to cession treaties which compressed tribal farming, hunting, and fishing territories. Renewed Indian raids on Anglo-American settlements throughout Washington and Oregon led to joint retaliatory campaigns by regular and militia troops, defeat of the aboriginal insurgents, and further reductions in tribal living space as punishment for making war on the Americans.

Between 1850 and 1855, a series of actions against the Shastas and other tribes near the Rogue River drastically reduced the Indian population in eastern Oregon, opened new lands to settlement, and cleared the overland passage to California. Regular and militia forces battered the tribes in the Puget Sound area and ended Indian resistance to settlement expansion.

The surge of the mining frontier to the east, to be discussed subsequently as it pertained to Indian conquest and compression, caused the Snakes, Palouses, Coeur d'Alenes, Spokans, and Yakimas to take to the warpath. In 1858 Colonel E. J. Steptoe and 150 militia campaigning in the Palouse country were attacked and nearly annihilated at Pine Creek by a large force of Spokans. Later that year Colonel George Wright and 600 regulars marched through the country to crush rising Indian resistance. On September 5 on the Spokan Plains his troops defeated a force of warriors from several tribes and captured and slaughtered 800 horses. A month later at the Walla Walla Council, Wright met with the leaders of the Snake, Coeur d'Alene, Spokan, Yakima, and Palouse tribes. He demanded from the tribes and received 4 insurgent leaders. The humiliating defeat and execution of their principal leaders pacified these tribes. Compression of their lands and resettlement on reduced territories under rather regular military surveillance led to peace east of the Cascades.

Conquest of the Southwestern Indians

Anglo-American occupation of the Great Basin and Southwest placed upon the resident tribes a destructive pressure similar to that suffered by Oregon Country Indians. By treaty with Great Britain in 1846, the Mexican War, which ended in 1848, and the small Gadsden Purchase of 1853, the United States completed its continental spread to the Pacific shore. These territorial additions brought many new Indian nations under its direction. However, most of the region with its Great American Desert image was viewed as worthless by Anglo-American farmers. Thus Native Americans in the vast continental reaches west of the Indian Territory, excluding Texas, Oregon, and the Great Basin (to the surprise of all, flourishing under Mormon occupation) could have escaped any appreciable Anglo-American influence or reduction in tribal lands for perhaps a century. But in January 1848 a completely unexpected discovery of gold on the American River in northern California had immediate and enduring effects upon the western tribes. News of the discovery set off a stampede of fortune-seeking immigrants, first from the coastal settlements and soon from the eastern United States and throughout the world. By the end of 1849 over 100,000 persons had arrived on the West Coast; in 1852 California's population exceeded 250,000. In the miners' surging, reckless quest for the precious metal, both the fragile Sierra environment and the native inhabitants were casualties.

Much of the mining activity occurred north of San Francisco in territory largely undisturbed by Spaniards or later by Mexicans. The sudden appearance of hordes of single-minded, gold-smitten miners was traumatic for resident Indians. Most of the emigrant miners were Anglo-Americans and, as in Texas and Oregon, most had little sympathy for Indians. But the rate of destruction of California Indians exceeded that in Texas and Oregon; in fact, it was more precipitous than anywhere else in North America at any time.

The rate of conquest and the scope of appropriation of tribal lands in California was shocking; the Indian population there declined from an estimated 150,000 in 1848 to about 30,000 in 1861. The conquest of the Modocs is but one example. The Modocs occupied the Tule Lake region on the California-Oregon border where they were caught in a squeeze between the southward expanding Oregon settlements and the northward march of the mining frontier in California. Heavy traffic between the Oregon towns and the California mining settlements flowed through Modoc territory. During the 1850s attacks by warriors from this tribe on immigrant and supply trains yielded considerable plunder and claimed an estimated 100 American lives. California and Oregon militia supported by regular troops were determined to remove this hazard to easy passage between the two settlement areas. Their furious retaliatory campaigns in the Tule Lake area reduced the Modoc population by at least half and made the tribe an easy mark for dispersal and, eventually, removal to the far-off Indian Territory in the post–Civil War period.

Those Native Americans who escaped the militia campaigns of the miners faced a fate that would have made death in the warfare merciful. The first session of the California legislature, in 1850, enacted a statute titled "Act for the Government and Protection of Indians." It provided that Indians could be impressed into legal indenture for forced service and labor; this practice was particularly applied to children and young women, the latter primarily as concubines. And outright sale of Native American captives was common in California from 1850 until 1863 when the act was repealed to conform with the national emancipation proclamation. It is estimated that 10,000 Indians were indentured or sold for forced labor before repeal of this bondage statute.

From 1851 to 1852, federal agents concluded eighteen treaties with California Indian leaders providing for reducing tribal estates and relocating several thousand Indians out of the path of mining expansion. However, the Senate refused to ratify the treaties claiming that because the United States had "purchased" California from Mexico, the resident Indian tribes had no "usufructuary" rights (that is, rights of use) to the land they occupied as tribal territory. Finally in a desperate move to prevent complete annihilation of the Indians, federal agents in 1853 set aside a limited number of reservations, but these were also largely failures because the national government did not provide the protection required to restrain the rapacious miners. The secretary of war stationed regular troops on several reservations but "the conflict between state and federal laws hampered the actions of the soldiers, and the corruption and venality of Indian agents in charge of reservations was so great that the money appropriated by Congress to operate the reservations was rarely spent for the Indians' welfare."[6]

The lure of mining riches which had brought this plague to the California Indians soon involved other western tribes. Thousands of miners failed to find their Eldorado in the lodes of the Sacramento, but still obsessed with the gold bug, they crossed the Sierras into Nevada, found the Comstock bonanza, and then scattered over the West from Arizona and New Mexico northward. They roamed through the Great Basin and Rocky Mountains into the Columbia and Snake river country, a restless pack of prospectors each driven by the eternal hope and conviction that at the turn of a canyon in some remote western wilderness he would find the mother lode. And many wandering miners did find rich gold and silver fields throughout the West. Their discoveries caused thousands of new fortune seekers to rush to mining camps in Colorado, New Mexico, Arizona, and Utah, and from eastern Oregon and Washington into Idaho and Montana.

Mining towns led to founding of the supporting industries of farming, ranching, lumbering, and transportation of equipment and other needs of miners. Clusters of population in the mining camps eventually coalesced into political groups demanding recognition by Congress, which led to formation of territorial governments and eventually admission to the Union as states. The consequences for the Indian tribes were direct and disastrous. Citizens of the new western territories and states came to have the same expectations as citizens in the eastern states—that their national government erase Indian title to local lands and concentrate the resident Indian tribes onto smaller domains, even removing them to another part of the country.

To protect its citizens and to maintain peace on the trans-Missouri frontier, the national government tightened its control over the tribes. Congress expanded the bureaucracy for Indian affairs by creating several agencies for the West: the Upper Platte Agency for the tribes of the Arkansas and Platte river valleys, the Brazos Agency and its successor the Wichita Agency for the displaced Texas tribes in the Leased District, and agencies for the Great Basin tribes at Salt Lake City and for the New Mexico tribes at Sante Fe.

Federal presence in the region west of the Indian Territory was considerably strengthened to back up the Indian agents. The secretary of war directed construction of military posts to guard the new settlements and trails connecting them with the East. Besides the military posts in Texas and on the Pacific Coast, army engineers erected Fort Washita and Fort Arbuckle in

Rose Emerson, a young Yuma mother, and child. (Courtesy the American Museum of Natural History)

the Indian Territory as intermediate posts to protect the California Road and the Doña Ana Road. Fort Stanton, between the Pecos and the Rio Grande, Fort Bliss, and Fort Fillmore, succeeded by Fort Yuma on the Colorado River completed the southern trail defenses against Comanche and Apache attack. Several protected lines of travel also radiated from Fort Leavenworth on the western border of Missouri in the northern section of the Indian Territory. Fort Riley and Fort Mann in Kansas and Fort Union and Cantonment Burgwin in New Mexico protected the Santa Fe Trail to the Rio Grande. Fort Kearny and Fort Grattan in Nebraska, Fort Bridger and Fort Laramie in Wyoming, and Fort Hall in Idaho protected traffic along the great immigrant highway. Posts off the trails protecting interior settlements in New Mexico and Arizona were Fort Craig, Fort McLane, Fort Thorn, Fort Breckenridge, Fort Buchanan, Fort Defiance, and Fort Mohave. These stations placed federal military power near the Utes, Apaches, and Navajos. Discovery of gold in the southern Rocky Mountains led to the establishment of Fort Garland on the Colorado-New Mexico border near La Veta Pass and Fort Wise near Bent's Fort on the Arkansas River. Fort Wise provided the army a strategic post near the Cheyenne and Arapaho tribes who were being pressured by an influx of miners attracted by the Pike's Peak gold rush.

This growing military presence failed to intimidate many of the Western tribes. Expanding settlements in their territories and increasing traffic across their hunting ranges led these beleaguered Indians to react with retaliatory strikes and threats of all-out war against the intruders. To reduce the prospects for this eventuality, Commissioner of Indian Affairs Luke Lea in 1850 recommended compression of tribal territories by assigning the western tribes to reservations away from settlements and immigrant highways. He stipulated that each reservation should have precise boundaries and that all resident tribes be required to remain thereon, under threat of prompt military action against those who disobeyed. Lea justified the appropriation of tribal lands by the position that only by forcing the Indians to "cease their wandering ways" and settling them on reservations where closer bureaucratic oversight was possible "could the great work of regenerating the Indian race be accomplished." According to Lea's plan tribes would be required to remain on these reservations until their "good conduct may supercede the necessity of such restrictions." Federal agents assigned to duty on these reservations were expected to transform the peripatetic buffalo hunters into sedentary farmers and stock raisers through vocational education.[7]

Lea's reservation plan marked a departure from the established federal policy for eastern Indians of "removal" from territories and states occupied by Anglo-Americans and their concentration in an "Indian Country." Removal for a time at least gave way to resettlement on reservations, "islands of land usually within the larger area they once possessed."[8]

Thus the Native American conquest, compression of tribal estates, and relocation of survivors onto drastically reduced reservations, applied by federal officials to the Indians of Texas, Oregon, and California, became the pattern applied to all Western tribes caught in the rapid Anglo-American sweep to the Pacific Shore. While fulfillment of Commissioner Lea's plan for assigning all Western tribes to restricted military reservations was not achieved until after the Civil War, important beginnings in the conquest of the tribes and compression of their lands began during the 1850s. By 1856 federal agents had concluded 52 treaties with western Indian leaders; each provided for a compression of Native American territories and assignment of tribes to reservations. Two of these negotiations illustrate the beginnings of this reservation assignment policy.

In 1851 when leaders of those tribes tributary to the Upper Platte Agency gathered at Fort Laramie, Agent Thomas Fitzpatrick extracted from them a series of treaties which began the reduction of tribal lands in the central and northern Great Plains and along the eastern slope of the Rocky Mountains. The signatory tribes pledged that their warriors would not attack the

Fort Laramie, site of the Northern Plains Indian Councils. (University of Wyoming Library, Laramie, Wyoming)

immigrant trains, freight caravans, and mail stages crossing their domains, and they agreed to permit construction of military posts at designated locations therein. The Mandans and Gros Ventres accepted reservations east of the Yellowstone, the Crows west of the Powder River, the Blackfeet in northwestern Montana, and the associated Cheyennes and Arapahoes between the North Platte and Arkansas rivers along the eastern slope of the Rocky Mountains. In return for these concessions, the signatory tribes were to receive a combined annuity of $50,000 for fifty years, subsequently reduced to fifteen years by the United States Senate.

The second major pact illustrating Lea's reservation system was concluded during 1855 by Isaac Stevens, governor of Washington Territory and ex-officio superintendent of Indian affairs, with the Blackfeet nation, a group of four tribes with a strong military tradition and intense, unremitting hostility to Anglo-Americans since their brush with members of the Lewis and Clark expedition in 1806. Their pact with the United States provided that in return for accepting a reduced range and agreeing to remain thereon, the United States pledged to pay the Blackfeet nation an annuity of $20,000 for ten years and $15,000 each year for educating tribal youth. Blackfeet leaders agreed to permit the United States government to establish schools and military posts in their territory and assured safe passage of immigrants through their lands.

These treaties which forced the western tribes into reduced territories and permitted the beginnings of bureaucratic control and increased military surveillance had the effect of diminishing Native American freedom of action and limiting tribal sovereignty. Apprehensive tribesmen repented their pacts with the United States and struck back; the decade of the 1850s became one of the bloodiest in the history of the American frontier. Military campaigns against Native Americans in Texas, Oregon, and California have already been discussed. As Anglo-Americans settled other portions of the trans-Missouri region, largely drawn by the rapid spread of the mining frontier, Indian patriots valiantly defended their homelands, but their courage was for naught; there followed the inevitable retaliatory military action, tribal defeat, and further reduction of tribal lands as punishment for making war on the United States.

Soon after the conquest of New Mexico, the Anglo-American army was faced with an Indian revolt. On January 19, 1847, Pueblo Indians and Spanish-Americans in the settlements between Santa Fe and Taos rebelled against United States rule. The natives were embittered by cruel treatment inflicted upon them by the army of occupation, mostly Missouri militiamen, who insolently appropriated beef, grain, and women. In swift strikes the Indian-Mexican rebels assassinated Governor Charles Bent and twenty other Americans at Taos. Colonel Sterling Price collected an army of 500 from the occupation troops at Santa Fe, marched on the rebel strongholds at La Cañada and Taos and, following heavy fighting, snuffed the revolt. His men executed fifteen Indian insurgent leaders.

The Anglo-American conquerors of the Southwest also had trouble with other Indians in New Mexico and Arizona. Soon after the conquest, American military officials met with Navajo, Pueblo, Ute, and Apache leaders who acknowledged United States suzerainty and committed their peoples to peace. However, increased mining activity and mounting immigrant traffic across the Southwest antagonized the tribes. Soon their reprisals against immigrant trains, mail stages, and freight caravans crossing their territories and raids on the intruding settlements kept federal troops in the field most of the time. In 1854 Jicarilla and Ute parties threatened Taos. Troops from Fort Union in northern New Mexico pursued the raiders into their mountain haunts, located their villages, and destroyed great quantities of provisions, blankets, and equipment, captured a large herd of horses, and dispersed the Indians. Thereafter until the Civil War northern New Mexico remained relatively quiet.

During the 1850s, Mescalero Apaches were a continuing threat to the settlements in eastern New Mexico. And Comanches, deflected from their traditional raiding territory in Texas and northern Mexico by new, stiffer military frontier defenses, added to the turmoil of the territory east of the Rio Grande. These fierce raiders from the southwestern part of the Indian Territory ranged into the Pecos Valley, at times threatening settlements near the Rio Grande. United States troops campaigned across southeastern New Mexico during 1855 and pacified the Mescalero Apaches, but the Comanches were able to defeat or elude the forces sent against them.

Western Apache and Navajo marauders also preyed upon the new mining camps of New Mexico and Arizona, sometimes extending their forays east to the Rio Grande, forcing abandonment of several towns. On one occasion Navajos attacked Fort Defiance and held it under an extended siege. Warriors from several Navajo bands tormented intruding miners and preyed on Spanish-American *placitas* west of the Rio Grande with relative impunity until the Civil War. The militarization of New Mexico during that struggle sealed the doom of the Navajo nation as a military power.

The two most deadly Apache groups were the Mimbreños led by Mangas Coloradas, and the Chiricahuas, led by Cochise. They ranged across southern New Mexico and Arizona southward into the Sierra Madres of northern Mexico, for centuries raiding north Mexican settlements and ranches. Mexican officials offered cash bounties for Apache scalps; captive Apaches were sold to perform slave labor in Mexican mines. Several Anglo-Americans joined Mexicans in the Apache scalp and slave traffic. This, added to growing immigrant traffic across their territories, intruding mining settlements, and the treatment accorded Mangas Coloradas and Cochise by federal military officers, miners, and territorial officials enraged the Apaches and drove them to loose their militant fury upon Anglo-Americans. They were not finally subdued until Geronimo's capitulation in 1886.

The sedentary Pimas and Papagos along the Gila and Salt rivers of southern Arizona, because Anglo-Americans had no desire for their desert land, were largely left alone for the time being. Their principal threat during the 1850s came from mining settlements along the Santa Cruz River, and immigrant travel across their lands on the Gila route to the Pacific Coast was an intermittent nuisance.

In the Great Basin, Ute, Shoshoni, and Paiute tribesmen occasionally raided Mormon settlements in Utah, miner communities in Nevada, and the growing overland traffic. Mormon and miner militia, supported by a growing federal military force, regularly campaigned against Indian marauders. In 1860, Shoshoni and Paiute war parties nearly succeeded in closing all trails in the Great Basin region; they were to be dealt with decisively during the Civil War.

During the decade of the 1850s several Native American and federal military confrontations took place in the northern Great Plains, most of them brought on by Sioux raids on overland traffic and settlements on the eastern edge of the Dakotas. In late 1854 a Brule Sioux party was attacked by a small United States force under Lieutenant John Grattan as punishment for allegedly attacking an immigrant train. The Sioux reacted by killing every man in Grattan's column. In August 1855 General William S. Harney led a force of 1,200 troops against the Brule Sioux, engaged them at Ash Hollow on the North Platte, and defeated them. The bitter contest between the Sioux and settlers for control of the land west of Minnesota and Iowa also required action by United States troops. A temporary peace was achieved in 1859 when federal commissioners concluded a treaty with the Yankton Sioux; by its terms the tribe ceded to the United States a large tract in southeastern Dakota Territory.

In the reduction of the western tribes during the bloody decade of the 1850s, military action was the principal destroyer of Native American life, but the army had a ghoulish ally in epidemic diseases which drastically reduced tribal populations and thus Indian resistance. Measles, smallpox, and Asiatic cholera were introduced among the western Indians by westward-moving Anglo-Americans. The former had no appreciable resistance to these diseases; each cut a terrible swath in most tribal populations. Four different smallpox epidemics raged among the trans-Missouri tribes between 1835 and 1860; the Mandans were reduced from an estimated 1,600 to 100, and the Blackfeet nation, originally numbering about 4,800 suffered a 50 percent decline. Asiatic cholera was a dreaded destroyer among the tribes of the southern Great Plains; the Comanche and Kiowa tribes with a combined population of about 5,000 suffered a similar decline from this malady.

While much Anglo-American effort during the decade of the 1850s was directed at taking far western tribal lands, the Indian Territory, did not escape notice. The railroad builders were approaching the Mississippi Valley and soon would require land for construction right-of-way west of Missouri. The most attractive transcontinental routes crossed Indian Territory. Thus even the "perpetually reserved" Indian Territory became a casualty of American expansion.

REDUCTION OF THE INDIAN TERRITORY

During the early 1850s transportation interests exerted great pressure upon national politicians to open the Indian Territory for railroad construction. The expansionists triumphed. The Kansas-Nebraska Act of 1854 directed that the Indian Territory be partitioned, and the northern half was organized into Kansas and Nebraska territories.

Fate of the Northern Indian Territory

In 1853 the President directed Commissioner of Indian Affairs George W. Manypenny to negotiate cession treaties with the tribes in that portion of the Indian Territory north of thirty-seven degrees, the Potawatomis, Wyandots, Kickapoos (Kennekuk's passive followers, to distinguish them from their fierce kin who ranged over the western part of the Indian Territory, Texas, and northern Mexico), and others, remnants of once great and powerful tribes from the Old Northwest but by this time weak, disorganized, and poorly led. Consequently, they were easy marks for federal agents urging them to sign treaties surrendering their communally owned reservations and accepting individual allotments. By their signatures tribal rights and title were abrogated, and vast tracts were opened to railroad development and settlement.

Manypenny traveled to the Indian Territory and held councils with the leaders of the tribes whose lands were in the line of the railroad's advance. He urged tribal leaders to repeal treaties containing solemn pledges that "forbade the creation of any organized territory" within the lands granted them by their removal treaties. He found that there were few squatters in this part of the Indian Territory which led him to observe that in no way was the region under "pressure of population which had in the past given a justification to many of the removals. . . . It was a political demand that he was serving, to remove the obstacle to railroad building." The commissioner reported that "without enthusiasm" leaders of the Sac and Fox, Kickapoos, Delawares, Shawnees, Kaskaskias, Peorias, Piankeshaws, Weas, and Miamis, and the Omahas, Otos, and Missouris signed the 1853 treaties ceding northern Indian Territory lands and accepting reduced territories or allotments. About half the tribes refused to cede all their lands; in compromise they accepted reduced reservations within the limits of their old domains. In July 1853 the General Land Office opened a branch in Kansas Territory for the sale of the Indian lands opened by the Manypenny treaties. Feeling regret and some shame for his success in dealing with the northern Indian Territory Native Americans, Manypenny wrote, "By alternate persuasion and force some of these tribes have been removed, step by step, from mountain to valley, and from river to plain, until they have been pushed halfway across the continent. They can go no further; on the ground they now occupy the crisis must be met, and their future determined." This was not the final relocation for these harried folk; at the close of the Civil War they would be required to remove again.[9]

359

Fate of the Southern Half of the Indian Territory

The portion of the Indian Territory between thirty-seven degrees latitude and the Red River, and from Fort Smith west to the one hundredth meridian, was the domain of the southern tribes. It, too, was coveted by railroad developers. At the same time that the Kansas-Nebraska Bill, which partitioned Indian Territory and opened the northern half to settlement, was under consideration by Congress, that body also was considering a bill to organize the southern half of the Indian Territory. The proposal provided for a survey of the domains of the Cherokees, Choctaws, Creeks, Seminoles, and Chickasaws, the assignment of an allotment to each tribal citizen, and the sale of surplus land to settlers. The bill required the creation of three territories—Cherokee, with its capital at Tahlequah, Muskogee with the capital at Creek Agency, and Chatah, with the capital at Doaksville. As soon as the mixed Indian-settler population of the three territories had made satisfactory progress in self-government, the three territories were to be fused into the state of Neosho. The bill was defeated, and the southern half of the Indian Territory was spared, at least temporarily. The proposal failed primarily because of the intense opposition of articulate southern Indian leaders who had spent much time in Washington lobbying against its adoption.

Unfortunately, the subsequent error of these same Indian leaders in signing alliances with the Confederate States of America provided the federal government leverage in 1866 to begin the process of diminishing the much-coveted Indian Territory lands of the southern tribes. While the Civil War in the West devasted the southern tribes, it had dreadful consequences for most other Native Americans, too. Their vicissitudes in this great struggle are the subject of Chapter Fifteen.

Notes

1. Arrell Morgan Gibson, *Oklahoma: A History of Five Centuries* (Norman, Okla., 1965), p. 188.
2. *Ibid.*
3. Grant Foreman (ed.), *A Traveller in Indian Territory: The Journal of Ethan Allen Hitchcock* (Cedar Rapids, Iowa, 1930). p. 7.
4. *Ibid.*
5. *Ibid.*, p. 12.
6. Robert F. Heizer (ed.), *The Destruction of California Indians* (Santa Barbara, Calif., 1974), pp. vi–vii.
7. Robert A. Trennert, Jr., *Alternative to Extinction: Federal Indian Policy and the Beginnings of the Reservation System, 1846–51* (Philadelphia, 1975), p. 56.
8. S. Lyman Tyler, *A History of Indian Policy* (Washington, D.C., 1973), p. 73.
9. Frederic L. Paxson, *History of the American Frontier, 1763–1893* (New York, 1924), pp. 431–32.

Selected Sources

Changing federal Indian policy in the age of expansion is traced in Robert A. Trennert, Jr. *Alternative to Extinction: Federal Indian Policy and the Beginnings of the Reservation System, 1846–51* (Philadelphia, 1975); George Dewey Harmon, *Sixty Years of Indian Affairs: Political, Economic, and Diplomatic, 1789–1850* (Chapel Hill, N.C., 1941); and S. Lyman Tyler, *A History of Indian Policy* (Washington, D.C., 1973). The concept of "National Completeness" as it related to Indian policy is introduced in Frederic L. Paxson, *History of the American Frontier* (New York, 1924).

Grant Foreman's writings, particularly *Advancing the Frontier, 1830–1860* (Norman, Okla., 1930), *The Five Civilized Tribes* (Norman, Okla., 1934), *Indian Removal: The Emigration of the Five Civilized Tribes of Indians* (Norman, Okla., 1932), *Indians and Pioneers* (1936), and *Sequoyah* (1938) depict the evolution of the Indian Territory and the colonization of the southern tribes in the southern half of this resettlement zone. Tribal histories describing specific removals include Angie Debo, *The Rise and Fall of the Choctaw Republic* (Norman, Okla., 1934), and on the Creek nation, *The Road to Disappearance* (Norman, Okla., 1941); Grace S. Woodward, *The Cherokees* (Norman, Okla., 1963); Edwin C. McReynolds, *The Seminoles* (Norman, Okla., 1957); and Arrell Morgan Gibson, *The Chickasaws* (Norman, Okla., 1971).

Colonizing the northern half of the Indian Territory is discussed in William E. Unrau, *The Kansas Indians* (Norman, Okla., 1971); Bert Anson, *The Miami Indians* (Norman, Okla., 1970); William T. Hagan, *The Sac and Fox Indians* (1958); Arrell Morgan Gibson, *The Kickapoos: Lords of the Middle Border* (Norman, Okla., 1963); and John Joseph Mathews, *The Osages: Children of the Middle Waters* (Norman, Okla., 1961).

Federal military conquest of the western tribes before 1861 is the subject of Robert M. Utley, *Frontiersmen in Blue: the United States Army and the Indian, 1848–1865* (New York, 1967); Percival G. Lowe, *Five Years a Dragoon ('49 to '54) and other Adventures on the Great Plains* (Norman, Okla., 1965); Dorman H. Winfrey (ed.), *Texas Indian Papers, 1846–1859* (Austin, Texas, 1960); George A. McCall, *New Mexico in 1850: A Military View* (Norman, Okla., 1968); Robert F. Heizer (ed.), *The Destruction of California Indians* (Santa Barbara, Calif., 1974); Edward E. Dale, *The Indians of the Southwest* (Norman, Okla., 1949); John W. Caughey, *History of the Pacific Coast* (Lancaster, Pa., 1933); and George W. Fuller, *A History of the Pacific Northwest* (New York, 1921).

Federal action in partitioning Indian Territory and opening its northern half to settlement is discussed in Roy Gittinger, "The Separation of Kansas and Nebraska from the Indian Territory," *Mississippi Valley Historical Review* 3 (March 1917), pp. 442–61; James C. Olson, *History of Nebraska* (Lincoln, Neb., 1955); and William F. Zornow, *Kansas: A History of the Jayhawk State* (Norman, Okla., 1957).

CHAPTER 15

NATIVE AMERICANS
AND THE CIVIL WAR

Whereas the Government of the United States has been broken up by the secession of a large number of States composing the Federal Union ... and Whereas the Lincoln Government, pretending to represent said Union, has shown by its course toward us, in withdrawing from our country the protection of the Federal troops, and ... a total disregard of treaty obligations toward us. ... Therefore, Be it resolved by the Chickasaw Legislature assembled ... *That the dissolution of the Federal Union ... has absolved the Chickasaws from allegiance to any foreign government whatever; that the current of the events of the last few months has left the Chickasaw Nation* independent, *the people thereof free to form such alliances, and take such steps to secure their own safety, happiness, and future welfare as may to them seem best. ... Resolved, that the Governor of the Chickasaw Nation be, and he is hereby instructed to issue his proclamation to the Chickasaw Nation, declaring their* independence.

Chickasaw Declaration of Independence, May 25, 1861

During the fifteen years preceding 1860, a period of the rapid settlement of the trans-Missouri West, the federal government had increasingly resorted to military action to implement its Indian policy. Federal and militia troops had always been an ultimate weapon for achieving national purpose, but in the past, public officials for the most part had first applied nonmilitary pressure upon tribal leaders. Negotiations in wilderness councils and occasionally in Washington where discussions might even include the President and other high government officials were time-consuming, patience-wracking protocol, more often than not ending in treaties granting Anglo-American demands.

The sweep of the mining frontier across the West had been startlingly rapid; the frenzied rush of fortune-seeking Anglo-Americans had greatly disturbed Indian patterns; mining settlements in tribal territories threatened the very lives of resident Indians. Confrontations occurred and in virtually every case ended in military action. Geographic isolation also was a factor in this sudden increase in resort to military action to accomplish national objectives.

Chapter Opening Artifact: Haida cloth blanket trimmed with red cloth, decorated with buttons and dentalium shells representing a bear. (Courtesy Museum of the American Indian, Heye Foundation)

In the Old Northwest and Old Southwest, even in the more remote Mississippi Valley, the Indian-settler contest for land had been tempered by a continuum of Jeffersonian benevolent protectiveness, which at times even softened the harsh Jacksonian Indian policy. But the western mining, farming, and ranching regions were even more remote from the seat of national government, and miners were desperate men, recklessly seeking personal fortunes. In their rush to riches they plundered and destroyed—forests with axes and careless fires, mountainsides with their erosive hydraulic pressure, and Native Americans with firearms, whiskey, and disease. In California Indians faced the added torment, sanctioned by state law, of impressment as slave workers and assignment to Anglo-Americans to labor in mines and on farms and ranches. Westerners wanted direct, immediate action in solving problems. They had little patience with Indian leaders who were reluctant to cede home territories for the expanding mine, farm, and ranching settlements, and to relocate their people on drastically diminished reserves. They had no respect for Indians who were determined to perish if necessary to defend their homelands. They held Indians in glowering contempt and denounced them as heathen savages, due no more consideration than cornered beasts. To Anglo-Americans Indians were obstacles to be removed as quickly as possible in order that the business of western development could proceed.

This escalation in military action against Native Americans by the United States government lasted from 1845 to 1886 and may be divided into three periods. The first, 1845–1861, and discussed in Chapter Fourteen was by far the most important in terms of accomplishment of objectives, especially in the rate of tribal conquest and reduction of Indian lands. The second, 1861–1865, and the subject of this chapter, was a time when curiously, Union troops raised in the western states and territories to fight Confederates and Confederate troops raised in the western states and territories to fight Union troops were used to continue the conquest of the western tribes. And the third period, 1866–1886, concluded by the capitulation of the indomitable Apache leader Geronimo and popularly regarded as the most important period in the conquest process, was in fact a dramatic epilogue to a long and bloody chronicle, a time for federal consolidation with the United States army following up the military advantages it had gained over the western tribes during the more productive first and second periods.

This chapter details the second period, from 1861 to 1865, and attempts to explain the anomaly of Indian involvement in the Civil War. This strange chronicle begins with Confederate military objectives. Southern leaders were keenly interested in the trans-Missouri region, where by 1861 most Indians were concentrated. Thus Confederate attempts to fulfill the goals of their new nation in the West would directly and indirectly affect the resident Indians.

Southern leaders had two broad goals: (1) to separate from the United States in order to pursue an independent national life, free of pressures and threats of the abolitionist crusade and the laws of Congress, and (2) to absorb that part of the West recently denied it as an area for expanding its institutions, particularly slavery. Confederate planners developed a bold and broad design for the West. Its primary purpose was to provide a continuous land corridor across Texas, the Indian Territory, New Mexico, and California to the Pacific shore. The gold and silver mines of Colorado and Nevada and the transportation and communication routes crossing Utah to California also made these intermediate territories attractive to Southerners. The attempt of the Confederate States of America to fulfill its goal of independent existence was challenged militarily by the federal government, leading to the Civil War. And the attempt of the Confederacy to fulfill its western objectives drew most of the West and many of the Indian tribes into the maelstrom of this epochal conflict.

THE INDIAN AS A DIRECT PARTICIPANT IN THE CIVIL WAR

The Indian Territory was a surprisingly promising region for essential supplies for the Confederacy. A Confederate supply officers' survey of Indian Territory resources reported that its farms, plantations, and ranches could provide beef, hides, horses, and grain, as well as salt and lead—items particularly important for the new nation. The report claimed that the rich mines of the Indian Territory's northeastern border yielded sufficient lead to supply the total small arms needs for all the Confederate armies in the field. The combined population of the five Indian commonwealths—the Cherokee, Seminole, Creek, Choctaw, and Chickasaw nations—was nearly 100,000. The South saw the nations as a source of troops to guard its western border.

The Confederate Treaties

Paradoxically, leaders of the southern Indian nations signed treaties of alliance with the Confederate States of America, even though the leading secessionist states—Georgia, Alabama, and Mississippi—had heaped insult, harassment, and untold suffering on these same tribes during the removal era. Possibly time had healed old wounds and dimmed painful memories. Also, the United States government, and President Andrew Jackson, had formally shared the blame for the agony of their Trail of Tears. Through the years Cherokees, Creeks, Choctaws, Seminoles, and Chickasaws had developed an animosity toward the federal government especially for its slowness in making annuity settlements and its general neglect of treaty obligations. During the spring of 1861, the secretary of war had ordered all posts in the Indian Territory abandoned, an action which greatly disturbed tribal leaders. Not only did it violate treaty pledges, but it left the region exposed to possible invasion from Confederate Texas or Arkansas.

Likewise, tribal leaders were disturbed by the election in 1860 of Abraham

Lincoln as President. His campaign workers, notably William H. Seward, in order to appeal to Free Soil voters, had recommended appropriating the land of the Five Civilized Tribes and opening it to white settlers. Furthermore, Lincoln's government was committed to abolishing slavery; hence, many tribal leaders, like other slaveowners, faced substantial loss of investment.

Southern influence was strong in the Indian Territory. Many mixed bloods had emulated Southern culture, establishing a replica of antebellum elegance based on slave labor. Because of the flow of navigable rivers, the economic orientation of Indian planters was to markets in the South. Most tribal annuity funds, income of proceeds from sale of eastern tribal lands held in trust by the federal government, were invested in enterprises in Southern states. Indian agents assigned to the Five Civilized Tribes all were southerners, many prominent Indian families had blood ties with southerners, and just as the Union was abandoning the Indian Territory, the Confederacy was showing strong interest in it as a source of supply for critical items and manpower for Southern armies.

The Confederate government commissioned Albert Pike, prominent Arkansas editor and attorney, to negotiate treaties of alliance with the Indian nations. He visited the tribal capitals, held councils with the leaders of the Five Civilized Tribes, and successfully concluded treaties with the Choctaw, Chickasaw, Creek, Seminole, and Cherokee governments. By these pacts each Indian nation terminated its relationship with the United States, thereby in a sense seceding from the American community, and was accepted into the Confederate States of America. The Confederacy pledged to protect the tribes in the tenure of their lands, to assist in the defense of the Indian Territory, and to accept annuity obligations and other pledges made to them by treaties with the United States government. Leaders of the Five Civilized Tribes agreed to support the Confederate cause and to raise armies for border defense. The Choctaws and Chickasaws were to raise a regiment, the Creeks and Seminoles a regiment, and Cherokees two regiments. The Confederate secretary of war placed Albert Pike and Douglas Cooper, the Choctaw-Chickasaw agent, in command of the Indian regiments.

From these councils Pike traveled to the western end of the Indian Territory and met with the Caddoes and other tribes attached to the Wichita Agency, and with several Comanche bands. The Pike treaties with these western tribes brought them, too, under Confederate dominion. He distributed gifts to the assembled tribes and pledged arms and supplies throughout the war. The signatory chiefs promised to stay out of Texas and instead to raid Union settlements in Kansas.

The Neutral Indians

Choctaws and Chickasaws were united in supporting the Confederacy, but Creeks, Seminoles, and Cherokees were divided. Their differences were similar, a split primarily between mixed bloods and full bloods, and derived from long-standing bitterness over the issues of removal and cession of eastern lands. Leader of the defecting tribes was the Creek chief Opothleyaholo. He refused to meet with Pike and showed his disdain for the Confederate cause by calling a general council of Indian Territory tribes. At the gathering Opothleyaholo strongly recommended that Indians follow a course of neutrality and shun "this white man's war."[1]

Civil War hostilities broke out in the eastern United States in April 1861, and the first blood shed in Indian Territory came during November from an attempt by Confederate Indian troops to force Opothleyaholo's followers to join the Confederate cause. Opothleyaholo had established a settlement for his neutral partisans—about 8,000 men, women, and children—on the Deep Fork River in the Creek nation. Confederate leaders, equating neutrality with sympathy if not active support for the Union cause, regarded Opothleyaholo's settlement on the Deep Fork as a menace to the security of the Indian Territory. On two different occasions, Colonel Cooper's Confederate Indian cavalry attempted to drive the neutral tribes from Indian Territory. Each time, Opothleyaholo's fighters defeated the Confederate attackers, first at the Battle of Round Mountain on November 19 and again at Chusto Talasah on December 9.

Cooper appealed for reinforcements and received 1,600 fresh cavalry from Fort Gibson and Fort Smith. On December 26, 1861, the strengthened Confederate force reached Opothleyaholo's camp at Chustenalah in the upper part of the Creek nation. They ringed the neutral Indian encampment and, at the signal, swept like a tide over the battlements. Brave fighting was no replacement for supplies and ammunition, depleted by the two previous battles, and the defenders were unable to hold their positions. Confederate troops stormed through the camp, captured most of the wagons, equipment, and livestock, and scattered Opothleyaholo's people over the heavily timbered hills of the northern part of the Indian Territory. A fierce snowstorm during the night after the battle caused great suffering among the survivors. Eventually they reached Union Kansas, and soon thereafter warriors from Opothleyaholo's refugee column, dressed in federal uniform as troops in the First and Second Union Indian Brigades, returned to Indian Territory determined to wreak vengeance on their Confederate tormenters.

Confederate Indian Disasters

In early March 1862 the Union army in Missouri and Kansas began a drive against Confederate border defenses, causing Confederate commanders in the trans-Mississippi department to rush men, artillery, and supplies to check the advance. On March 6 Union and Confederate armies collided at Elkhorn Tavern near the Indian Territory-Arkansas boundary. The Union army triumphed in the Battle of Pea Ridge in a bloody two-day engagement inflicting massive casualties upon the Confederates. Colonel Stand Watie, with his regiment of Cherokee Mounted Rifles, won one of the few victories attrib-

Stand Watie, Cherokee Confederate General. (Courtesy the Oklahoma Historical Society)

uted to the Confederates; Cherokee troops captured the strategically positioned Union artillery batteries that had rained destruction and death upon the Southern ranks. Watie's men also held their position on the broad Confederate line and helped cover the general withdrawal.

The Union victory at Pea Ridge sealed the doom of the Confederate cause in the West and cut mightily into its human and material resources. In their retreat, Confederate troops had abandoned heavy guns, tents, and other essentials. Survivors falling back to Fort Smith and Fort Gibson deserted in large numbers, and many joined the Union army. Gloom permeated the border. Never again would Confederate recruiters meet with much success there. Stand Watie and other Confederate commanders from bases in the Indian Territory continued to carry out strikes along the Missouri-Kansas border. Some produced fleeting successes, but never permanent results. Federal commanders took advantage of Confederate weaknesses in the West to complete the conquest of that region; the campaigns that led to their victories reduced the Indian Territory to a wasteland and caused additional suffering for its residents.

The Indian Expedition

During the spring of 1862, Union forces in Kansas were bolstered by Wisconsin and Ohio volunteer cavalry and infantry regiments and an artillery battery from Indiana. These troops and two Kansas brigades, plus two Indian regiments recruited from Opothleyaholo's followers, were formed into the Indian Expedition. In the course of a thrust in 1862 into the Cherokee nation, the Indian Expedition invested Tahlequah, capital of the Cherokee nation, captured Principal Chief John Ross, and returned to Kansas. The Indian Expedition in 1863, commanded by General James Blunt, resumed its conquest, driving down Grand River valley to Fort Gibson, capturing that post and converting it into a base to support additional operations against Confederate Indians.

During the summer of 1863, a large Confederate force from nearby Fort Smith led by Colonel Cooper moved on Fort Gibson. Blunt marched his troops out to meet the Southern army. At the Battle of Honey Springs, fought on July 17, Blunt's superiority in artillery forced Cooper's Confederate Indian army to withdraw. Thereupon Blunt took the offensive, crossing the Arkansas River into the Choctaw nation, capturing and burning the Confederate depot at Perryville, and thereby opening the road to Fort Smith. Blunt's Indian Expedition troops then marched east, easily taking Fort Smith on September 1. The fall of Fort Smith to Union forces ended major engagements in the Indian Territory. Thereafter, Union and Confederate commanders reassigned most of the men from the border to the armies of General Ulysses S. Grant and General Robert E. Lee, respectively, east of the Mississippi. Both Union and Confederate officials maintained just enough troops on the western border to protect their established positions in a holding action.

Guerrilla Warfare in the Indian Territory

The joint reduction in military strength in the Indian Territory created a stalemate there for the remainder of the war, but action continued in bloody, internecine strife and guerrilla warfare. The Arkansas-Canadian river line became the boundary separating Union and Confederate Indian forces.

Three types of guerrilla bands stalked the border in the period between 1863 and 1865: the free companies, the Quantrill band, and Stand Watie's raiders. The free companies were groups of local renegades, outcasts from the Indian nations. These brigands flourished in the general anarchy of the border, stealing cattle and horses and plundering and burning both Union and Confederate communities. Free-company depredations added to the disorders plaguing this border region during the last two years of the war.

Colonel Charles C. Quantrill had been commissioned by the Confederate government to raise a private army to harass Union border settlements in Kansas and Missouri and to counter the Jayhawkers, private raider bands from Kansas. Quantrill acquired a dreadful reputation on the Indian Territory border. His most notorious coup was the sacking of Lawrence, Kansas, on August 21, 1863. But Quantrill and his bushwackers raided indiscriminately, attacking Union and Confederate settlements with equal fury. From time to time the Quantrill band roamed over Indian Territory and northern Texas spreading destruction and slaughter wherever they rode.

Cherokee Colonel Stand Watie's activities were distinguished from those of the Quantrill band and the free companies by their concentration on military objectives. His men destroyed dwellings and barns only when they were used by the enemy for headquarters, billeting troops, or storing supplies. His favorite targets were the mule-drawn Union supply trains running between Fort Scott in Kansas and Fort Gibson. He preyed on this lifeline not only because of its military aspects, but also because the plunder he swept up could be distributed among Confederate Cherokee, Creek, and Seminole refugees scattered in camps along Red River in the Choctaw nation and in northern Texas. Watie's raids made feeding the garrison at Fort Gibson, plus the 16,000 Union Cherokees, Creeks, and Seminoles who had collected there, a serious problem for federal officials. Watie tormented the garrison and refugees with the prospect of mass starvation by controlling the military road that connected Fort Gibson and Fort Scott.

During the spring of 1864, the Confederate War Department reorganized its Western armies, creating the Indian Cavalry Brigade, consisting of the First and Second Cherokee Regiments, the Creek Squadron, the Osage Battalion, and the Seminole Battalion. Watie was placed in command and appointed brigadier general, the only Indian to achieve this rank in either Union or Confederate armies. Watie's Confederate Indian troops were active until the end of the war. From his bases south of the Canadian River he sent squads of mounted raiders into Union territory. Federal details sent out to cut hay for the thousands of cavalry mounts at Fort Gibson were always in peril. Finally, to feed the starving horses and mules, Union officers sent great herds of them under heavy guard to graze on the prairie flats near the post. Watie's raiders regularly swooped down to drive the animals across the river, with the result that cavalrymen at Fort Gibson became foot soldiers.

After the conquest of Arkansas and Fort Smith, Union officers attempted to provision the troops and refugees at Fort Gibson by sending supply steamers up the Arkansas River. In June 1864 Watie's scouts discovered the slow-moving *J. R. Williams* toiling upstream toward the Fort Gibson landing on Grand River. At Pleasant Bluff in shallow water, just below the mouth of the Canadian, Watie's troopers swept from ambush and captured the vessel with a cavalry charge. Great quantities of provisions, uniforms, and medical supplies fell to the Confederates by this feat.

Watie's greatest stroke of the war occurred during September 1864 at the Cabin Creek crossing on the Fort Scott-Fort Gibson military road in the Cherokee nation. The Cherokee general carefully positioned his men on the approaches to the ford and surprised and defeated a large Union army. His victory included capture of a huge supply train of 300 wagons laden with essential supplies and provisions for the beleaguered garrison and the Union refugees at Fort Gibson. By a skillful decoy Watie's men eluded a Union relief column from Fort Gibson and drove the prize into Confederate territory where the stores of food, medical supplies, clothing, and blankets were distributed among Confederate Indians in the refugee camps.

Watie became cynical toward the Confederacy for what he regarded as its neglect of Native American interests, but this in no way affected the vigor of his defense of the Confederate cause in Indian Territory. The Cherokee general charged that while "the Indian troops ... had been true to the South from the very first," Confederate officials at Richmond had acted as though it were "immaterial" whether Indian troops were adequately equipped and provisioned. He claimed that "no vigorous effort had been made" by the Confederacy to assist his army in driving "the enemy from Indian Territory." General Watie charged that Union troops in the Cherokee nation had

desolated the land and robbed the people, until scarcely a southern family is left east and north of the Arkansas River. . . . The promised protection of the Confederate government, owing, I am compelled to say, to the glaring inefficiency of its surbordinate agents, has accomplished nothing; it has been a useless and expensive pageant; an object for the success of our enemies and the shame of our friends. I fear that we can reasonably look for no change for the better, but that the Indians will have at last to rely upon themselves alone in the defense of their country. I believe it is in the power of the Indians unassisted, but united and determined, to hold their country. We cannot expect to do this without serious losses and many trials and privations; but if we possess the spirit of our fathers, and are resolved never to be enslaved by an inferior race, and trodden under the feet of an ignorant and insolent foe, we, the Creeks, Choctaws, Chickasaws, Seminoles, and Cherokees, never can be conquered.[2]

Despite these efforts to keep Confederate hopes alive, Union arms triumphed. General Robert E. Lee surrendered to General Ulysses S. Grant at Appomattox Court House, Virginia, on April 9, 1865. General E. Kirby Smith, commander of Confederate troops west of the Mississippi, capitulated on May 20. Preparations for surrendering Confederate Indian forces began on May 15, 1865, when Israel G. Vore, Confederate Indian agent for the Creeks, invited Native American leaders to meet at Council Grove on the North Canadian River. When Union forces threatened to disperse this meeting, delegates from the Five Civilized Tribes and Great Plains tribes met at Camp Napoleon near present Verden on the Washita River. Representatives at the Camp Napoleon Council adopted a compact of peace among all the tribes and in effect prepared themselves to present a united front against the United States in the forthcoming postwar settlement.

The Camp Napoleon Council paved the way for additional surrenders. On June 19, the Choctaw leaders surrendered at Doaksville. Stand Watie signed a capitulation agreement for Confederate Cherokees at Doaksville on June 23 and was the last Confederate general to surrender. Governor Winchester Colbert surrendered Confederate Chickasaw and Caddo troops on July 14. The Confederate Indians, defeated and reduced to abject poverty by the war, with each of their nations a wasteland, awaited the terms of the victor. These would first be announced at the Fort Smith Council in September 1865.

THE INDIAN AS AN INDIRECT PARTICIPANT IN THE CIVIL WAR

The border tribes varied in the degree of their involvement in the Civil War. The Cherokee, Creek, Seminole, Choctaw, and Chickasaw nations were actively and openly engaged in the conflict, their fighting men armed and organized in military regimen, in Confederate or Union uniform, campaigning under the Confederate or Union banner. Wichita, Caddo, Osage, Shawnee, Delaware, Seneca, and Quapaw tribesmen served with Watie and other Southern Indian commanders, but their role was somewhat more marginal, functioning largely as scouts and spies for the Indian regiments. Westerly neighbors of the Five Civilized Tribes, the Comanches and Kiowas, also served the Confederate cause, but only occasionally or indirectly. Several Comanche bands were committed to the Confederate cause by treaties negotiated by Albert Pike. Confederate officials at Wichita Agency also supplied Comanches and Kiowas ammunition, arms, and blankets and encouraged them to strike at settlements in Union Kansas and to prey on communication lines crossing the central Great Plains. Thus in occasionally doing the bidding of these agents, Comanches and Kiowas, while not in uniform and not bound by military regimen, did serve the Confederate cause.

Comanche and Kiowa Confederate Support

Comanches and Kiowas were buffalo hunters and raiders. Their hunting and raiding range on the Great Plains extended southward from the Arkansas River Valley across Texas into northern Mexico. Their annual forays against the Texan towns and settlements in the Mexican state of Coahuila netted plunder and horses, and women and children captives. These tribesmen also desolated Spanish-American settlements between the Pecos and the Rio Grande in New Mexico, and they occasionally tormented the tempting settlements of the Five Civilized Tribes.

Comanche treaties with the Confederacy committed them to stay out of Confederate Texas and to turn their predatory fury upon Union Kansas. Although some Comanche and Kiowa bands persisted in raiding north Texas settlements, for the most part during the period 1861–1865 they ranged west and north of their Wichita Mountain sanctuary. Supported by Confederate arms and ammunition, most Comanche and Kiowa bands hunted over the Texas Panhandle, at that time an unsettled buffalo range, north into the Arkansas River valley, and they raided Union settlements and communication lines in Kansas and New Mexico.

Battle of Adobe Walls

In the early stages of the Civil War, New Mexico and Arizona were conquered by armies from Texas and became Confederate territories. Subsequently, Union armies from Colorado and California expelled the Confederates and restored these territories to the Union. Thereafter federal officials maintained the region as the Military Department of New Mexico, its function to thwart any renewed Confederate drive across the Southwest to the Pacific shore. Thus for the war's duration New Mexico and Arizona remained in a state of military occupation. Companies of California and New Mexico volunteer regiments garrisoned posts and camps from the Pecos River to the Colorado River.

The major problem facing Union commanders in New Mexico was supply. At that time the region was sparsely populated; its limited agricultural production was inadequate to support the large Union military establishment stationed within its borders. Thus the troops were completely dependent upon outside sources; isolation complicated the supply problem. The department's principal material source was Fort Leavenworth in northeastern Kansas; its lifeline a traders' trail that led southwest from the border settlements to the Rio Grande. Nearly every month caravans of mule-drawn freight wagons laden with provisions, ammunition, and other essentials for Union troops stationed in the Southwest, under heavy cavalry guard, moved over this road to New Mexico.

Comanche and Kiowa raiders regularly attacked the caravans. Their swift strikes stampeded mule teams which stranded or wrecked wagons and slowed the progress of the convoys, forced delays, and created serious shortages of food and munitions in New Mexico. The predators occasionally captured wagons and plundered and burned them. Their raids on this Union supply line created grave concern in New Mexico; Union commanders were faced with the real prospect of having to abandon the region. General James H. Carleton, Union commander of the Department of New Mexico, steadily increased the cavalry guard for the supply trains. His troops established Fort Bascom on the Canadian River in eastern New Mexico as a cavalry support station for troops guarding the road. During 1864 Comanche and Kiowa raids on the Santa Fe road became so threatening that Carleton directed Colonel Kit Carson to march a force of 350 New Mexico and California troops with two howitzers onto the Great Plains and seek out and destoy the raiders.

After several indeterminate brushes between swift-riding Comanche and Kiowa raiders and Carson's men, Ute and Jicarilla Apache scouts in late autumn 1864 located a large Comanche-Kiowa encampment on the Canadian River in the Texas Panhandle near the ruins of an old trading post called Adobe Walls. On November 25 Carson's men struck the village in a surprise attack. Fierce counteraction by Native American defenders nearly overwhelmed Carson's ranks and forced his men to retreat. He later admitted that the column was saved from annihilation only by the timely use of the two howitzers. Carson's gunners charged the small cannon with grapeshot and fired them at point-blank range, turning the Indians and covering Carson's withdrawal.

For the duration of the war Comanche and Kiowa raiders harassed Union supply and communication lines crossing their hunting domain, but sufficient amounts of military goods reached the beleaguered Union garrisons in the Southwest to enable the troops to maintain their positions. And a time of reckoning was nearing for the Comanches and Kiowas. At the Little Arkansas Council held late in 1865 in south-central Kansas, they were called to task for their role in the Civil War as Confederate allies. However, in the postwar settlement, Comanches and Kiowas fared much better than most of the tribes west of them who also had been caught up in the Civil War.

THE INNOCENT CASUALTY OF THE
CIVIL WAR

The Civil War produced a thorough militarization of the West which had dreadful effect upon the Indian nations. In 1861 President Abraham Lincoln called on the western states and territories to raise volunteer infantry and cavalry regiments. Every state and territory north and west of Texas and the Indian Territory mustered troops for Union service. Kansas volunteer regiments participated widely in Civil War operations, particularly in the Indian Territory sector. California regiments were scattered over the West. Union military units also were formed in Washington, Oregon, Colorado, Nebraska, Utah, and Nevada. These units were to be kept on active duty in constant readiness for assignment in the East. But because they were not yet needed for eastern combat and because after 1862 the Confederate threat in the West had been crushed, the volunteer troops were used against Indians. Infantry and cavalry regiments throughout the West continued the process of conquest and reduction of tribal territory that the regular army had begun in the period from 1848 to 1861. Moreover, settlement and development continued in the West while bloody combat enveloped the eastern United States. Mining frontier expansion was primarily responsible for keeping this development process alive; discoveries of rich mineral deposits in Idaho and Montana during 1862 and 1863 precipitated a new gold rush. The movement of great numbers of people and ever-increasing quantities of machinery and general freight across Indian land precipitated incidents. Mining exploration and development also continued in Colorado, New Mexico, and Arizona and provoked the Indian tribes of those territories.

In addition, the general business of the war—the flow of guns, ammunition, uniforms, and other essentials for equipping and maintaining the western volunteer military establishment—added to the traffic from the Mississippi Valley to Colorado, the Great Basin, the Northwest, the Southwest, and the Pacific Coast. The Confederate attempt to push through to the Pacific had closed mail, immigrant, and freight routes in the Southwest, diverting the transcontinental traffic to the northern routes and adding to the volume of activity there. These factors, as well as the occupation of additional tribal lands by the new mining settlements, placed tremendous pressures on the western Indian communities. They resisted, and the period between 1861 and 1865 was a bloody time of continuing conquest, pacification, and compression of tribal lands, a process made more direct and effectively certain by the militarization of the West as an outgrowth of the Civil War. Union volunteer regiments raised in the western states and territories to fight Confederates, as they waited for the call to duty in the East, sharpened their combat skills by fighting Indians. In this way many additional Native Americans were caught up in the Civil War.

Campaigns in the Pacific Northwest

The processes of conquest, pacification, and reduction of tribal territories had largely been completed for the tribes in California, Oregon, and Washington in the earlier period (1846–1860). Therefore, volunteer troops from California were assigned duty in Utah to guard the overland routes and communications and for combat in the Department of New Mexico. In both regions California troops were rather constantly engaged in compaigns against Indians. Volunteer infantry and cavalry companies recruited in Oregon and Washington watched the border tribes, primarily the Modocs, and they continued to maintain pressure upon the Spokans, Snakes, Cayuses, and other tribes east of the Cascades. Following the discovery of gold and silver in Idaho and Montana in 1862 and 1863, they guarded the roads connecting coastal towns with mining camps in the districts of the new bonanzas.

Campaigns in the Great Basin

In Utah and Nevada the Shoshonis, Bannocks, and Utes, like other western tribes, were pressured and provoked by the increased traffic across their lands and the extension of the mining frontier during the war. Raider bands from these tribes preyed on the stages and freight caravans operating between the Platte River and Fort Bridger. They also attacked mining camps and Mormon agricultural settlements. Their strikes threatened isolated ranches and mining camps; Union officials feared that these Indians would destroy sections of the transcontinental telegraph line.

Mormon troops guarded the telegraph line, escorted mail stages and freight caravans through the troubled zone, and campaigned against these Indians until relieved by California volunteer troops. During October 1862 General P. E. Connor and the Second California Volunteer Regiment entered Utah and established Fort Douglas near Salt Lake City. Detachments of California troopers launched campaigns against the Shoshonis and Bannocks. In the Bear River campaign of January 1863 Union troops killed 368 Indians and took 160 women and children captives. This action destroyed Indian power in northern Utah and southern Idaho and removed a threat to transcontinental roads and communications. California and Nevada troops garrisoned Fort Bridger and other posts along the immigrant routes, guarded the telegraph line and convoyed mail stages and freight caravans.

During the same period in western Utah and Nevada, Pahvants, Utes, and Goshutes attacked mail coaches and freight caravans and cut down isolated prospecting parties. An intensive campaign during 1863 by California and Nevada troops also conquered these tribes. Thereupon federal officials negotiated treaties with them and other Great Basin Indian communities providing for peace with the United States and pledges to permit safe passage for mail stages, freight caravans, and immigrant trains through their territories.

The conquest treaties also contained clauses permitting construction of a transcontinental railroad across tribal lands and reducing some tribal territories to permit the establishment of new mining and agricultural settlements. In return for these considerations, the government pledged to protect the signatory tribes and to issue at once to all tribal members gifts of clothing, provisions, and other goods, and to pay each tribe for twenty years an annuity in goods ranging in value from $1,000 to $5,000. In this way was the Great Basin pacified.

Campaigns in the Southwest

The most extensive operations against western tribes in this period were carried out in the Department of New Mexico. The First California Regiment, the famous California Column, commanded by General James H. Carleton and supported by New Mexico volunteer companies commanded by Colonel Kit Carson, comprised the attack group in this region. As indicated, Colorado and California troops had expelled Texas Confederate forces from the territory between the Pecos and the Colorado rivers during 1862. Confederate troops had antagonized many Navajo and Apache bands during their brief occupation of New Mexico and Arizona, and these tribesmen were venting their wrath in raids upon Spanish-American settlements across the region.

Along the valley of the Rio Grande and eastward into the Guadalupe Mountains of western Texas ranged the Mescalero Apaches. Before the Civil War, United States army forces from Fort Bliss and Fort Stanton and Indian agents from Santa Fe had established relations with these tribes. In 1861 the Confederates entered the country and provoked the Indians to all-out war. The Texans showed poorly in their campaigns against the Apaches. The Indians cut off and destroyed entire companies and captured substantial stores of provisions and weapons. Well-armed and more deadly than ever, the Mescalero Apaches were at the peak of their military power when the California Column reached New Mexico in 1862. In a single month, August 1862, Mescalero parties killed 46 settlers, carried scores of children into captivity, and ran off herds of cattle, horses, mules, and sheep. These sweeping raids caused Spanish-Americans to abandon their *placitas* and to flee to the garrisoned towns for protection.

On October 11, 1862, Carleton ordered several company commanders to mount a campaign against the Mescaleros. "There will be no council held with the Indians," he told his troops. "The men are to be slain whenever and wherever they can be found. Their women and children may be taken prisoner. . . . I trust that these demonstrations will give these Indians a wholesome lesson."[3]

Relentless pressure by California and New Mexico troops during the winter of 1862–1863 forced the Mescalero Apaches to abandon their country. Many fled to Mexico. Over 400 members of this tribe surrendered to Carleton's forces. General Carleton directed that a forty-square-mile area at Bosque Redondo on the lower Pecos River in eastern New Mexico be set aside as a military reservation and internment zone for the Indian prisoners and ordered construction of a post, Fort Sumner, on the grounds. The garrison, two companies of cavalry and one company of infantry, was to mount a constant guard and enforce residence at Bosque Redondo once the Indian prisoners were brought in. Carleton was optimistic about the future of the Bosque Redondo military reservation as an Indian concentration center not only because of its isolation from the settlements but because of the open plains

Navajo prisoners of war at Fort Sumner, New Mexico, are helping construct an adobe building, under military guard. This photo is from the period 1865–1868. (Museum of New Mexico, Santa Fe, New Mexico)

country for miles in every direction which made surveillance over the Indian captives easier for the troops.

The successful relocation of the Mescalero Apache captives on the Pecos led Carleton to decide to concentrate other tribes in his jurisdiction which he regarded a menace to peace and order, especially the Navajos, at Bosque Redondo. The Navajos occupied a large territory in western New Mexico and eastern Arizona. Prospectors were making gold and silver strikes with increasing regularity across the Southwest. News of the mineral discoveries attracted miners who established settlements near the new mines. Navajos and other tribes were rising against this trespass in their territory, and Carleton regarded forced evacuation of the new mining districts to be the only means of maintaining peace and order. Navajo retaliation for miner trespass extended to raiding settlements near the Rio Grande and preying on overland traffic.

On Carleton's orders the Navajo campaigns began in the spring of 1863. Colonel Carson and New Mexico volunteers carried out most of the conquest work; as Mexican scouts discovered Navajo settlements the troops marched in, drove off the defenders and captured stored grain, burned crops, destroyed orchards, and scattered flocks of sheep, cattle, and horses. Fierce resistance of the Navajo bands gradually faded under the punishing military pressure. They reluctantly capitulated, and Carson's men escorted them to Bosque Redondo.

The Navajo removal to Bosque Redondo was completed during 1864. By that time there were just under 10,000 Indians at this internment center. The Indian prisoners were expected to raise their food from garden plots and fields opened on the reservation, but the hot sun and drought conditions withered most of the corn and other food crops. The internees suffered untold misery from heat, malnutrition, and disease. They were on the verge of starvation most of the time, saved by occasional issues of government rations of low-grade flour, corn, salt pork, and beef. Stagnant, brackish water standing in the river channel bred mosquitoes, and most of the internees were stricken with malaria and dysentery. Troops at Fort Sumner infected many of the Indian women with syphilis and gonorrhea which in turn spread widely among the other interned Indians. An estimated one fourth of the Indian residents at Bosque Redondo perished before they were finally released in 1868 and permitted to return to their homeland west of the Rio Grande.

Attempting to cope with and control the western Apaches was another matter. During the 1850s, these tribes, mostly Chiricahuas and Mimbreños, had been pressed by the extension of the mining frontier into western New Mexico and southern Arizona and by the increase in California-bound traffic through their lands. Their retaliatory raids had threatened to prevent expansion of the mining frontier in their territory and to close the overland passage to California. These proud and fierce people were unremittingly committed to thwart the American attempts to cross and to occupy their territory. They were the most difficult of all the Indians of the Department of New Mexico to

Navajos on the "Long March" to Bosque Redondo, by Edward Curtis. (Library of Congress)

deal with, and at no time did Carleton's program of conquest and containment at Bosque Redondo succeed with them.

The California Column saw its first combat with the western Apaches in 1862. Chiricahua and Mimbreño warriors preyed on the column in its advance to the Rio Grande, killing scouts and messengers caught away from the main column. At Apache Pass an advance force of 125 men was confronted by about 300 Indians. The California troops were pinned down and were saved from annihilation only by the column gunners who lobbed cannister shot into the highland battlements occupied by the Indians and forced them to withdraw.

Between 1862 and 1865 Union troops and western Apache warriors fought many battles. Countless Indians were slain, in the process taking their toll of troops and settlers. But for Carleton's men it was like fighting phantoms; the swift-moving Apaches struck here, there, and were eternally a threat, unconquerable. Although they campaigned constantly against them, the California and New Mexico troops were unable to establish military dominance over the western Apaches. Their conquest was not completed until 1886.

Campaigns in the Rocky Mountains

The Indian tribes of Colorado Territory also suffered conquest and reduction of their lands during the Civil War. The Utes occupied the attractive San Luis Valley in southern Colorado. They attempted to defend their lands against mining, agricultural, and ranching settlements but were defeated by Colorado volunteer troops. Finally Ute leaders met with federal officials in October 1863 and exchanged their San Luis Valley lands for a new domain west of the Continental Divide and remote from the settlements.

One of the most tragic results of the militarization of the West during the Civil War occurred in eastern Colorado on Sand Creek. The expanding mining frontier in Colorado Territory, proliferation of ranches along the Platte River, and the general increase of traffic crossing the Great Plains into the mining settlements on the eastern slope of the Rocky Mountains led to demands that the Cheyenne-Arapaho range, assigned by the Treaty of Fort Laramie in 1851 and extending from the Platte to the Arkansas, be reduced. In 1861, leaders of these tribes signed the Treaty of Fort Wise in which they accepted a much-reduced reservation in southeastern Colorado. The new Cheyenne-Arapaho domain, called the Sand Creek Reserve, was bounded by Big Sandy Creek and the Arkansas River and was about ninety miles wide. It was described as the "most dry and desolate region" in the territory and, from the settler viewpoint, it was ideal because it was isolated from the principal east-west roads into Colorado. The War Department directed the construction of Fort Lyon on the reserve to serve as the center for managing the Indians. The Cheyennes and Arapahoes retained the right to hunt on unoccupied portions of the ceded territory.

The Indians, who depended upon the buffalo for subsistence, found the Sand Creek Reservation intolerable. The increasing traffic across the buffalo range to the Colorado settlements diverted the bison herds, and the animals became increasingly difficult to find. Several tribesmen turned to raiding ranches along the Platte and stage and freight traffic between Fort Kearny and Denver.

Early in 1864 Colorado Governor John Evans sent word to the Cheyennes and Arapahoes to return to their reservation or "suffer the consequences." That autumn, 500 Cheyennes, led by Black Kettle, returned to the Sand Creek Reservation. On November 29, Colonel John M. Chivington marched 900 men of the First Colorado Volunteer Regiment to the reservation and carried out a swift surprise attack on Black Kettle's village. Two hundred Cheyenne men, women, and children died in the carnage. The commissioner of Indian affairs denounced Chivington's action as a massacre in which Indians were "butchered in cold blood by troops in the service of the United States."[4]

The militarization of Colorado produced by the Civil War temporarily pacified the territory, substantially reduced the Indian barrier to settlement and development, and drastically compressed tribal lands there.

Civil War Legacy of Retaliation

Two additional incidents, widely separated geographically but a part of the second stage of conquest, should be considered. Not only do these incidents conclude this segment of the bloody, sordid chronicle of Indian suppression and compression, but also each provides useful perspective on the third period of Native American conquest.

The first incident occurred on the Minnesota frontier where settlers had occupied territory guaranteed by federal treaty to the Santee Sioux. Tribal disillusionment with the United States government for its failure to fulfill treaty pledges to protect their tenure in these lands and flagrant disregard by federal officials of other treaty obligations led to a destructive war. Little Crow was the principal leader of the Santee Sioux uprising in which it is estimated that Indian insurgents killed 700 settlers. The number of Indian casualties is unknown but far exceeded those of the settlers. Regular and militia troops finally defeated the Sioux, arrested their leaders and, on December 26, 1862, executed 38 of them by hanging. Military officials scattered the remaining Sioux prisoners. Those regarded as most dangerous were held in military prison. Some of the more peaceful ones were sent to small reservations in Iowa, Nebraska, and Dakota Territory. During the uprising several hundred Sioux also fled to Canada and to Dakota Territory where they joined Sioux kin to become a source of concern to the United States army during the next decade.

The other incident occurred in western Texas at the Battle of the Concho. The southern Kickapoos, numbering about 600 and distinguished from the peaceful followers of Prophet Kennekuk in northern Kansas, roamed the western margins of the Indian Territory hunting buffalo and trading with the Plains tribes. Both Union and Confederate agents had attempted to muster southern Kickapoo warriors into their frontier armies, but these tribesmen nourished a bitter hatred for the United States and its citizens. Wishing to be free from the solicitations of both Union and Confederate agents, they decided to join a band of their tribe living in the north Mexican state of Coahuila. These émigrés had lived in Mexico since 1839 when the Texan army drove them from their Sabine River homeland.

During the summer of 1862 the southern Kickapoos proceeded west and then turned south just beyond the one hundredth meridian, taking every precaution to escape detection by Texan Confederate patrols. They traveled without incident until, late in December 1862, they arrived on the Little Concho River in southwestern Texas. There they paused to rest and to restore their horses. A mounted Confederate battalion assigned to frontier defense sighted their trail sign, moved upon the unsuspecting encampment, noted the

Indians' large herd of horses and struck at it. Warned of the danger, the warriors rallied quickly, recovered the horse herd, then drove back repeated cavalry charges. After 16 Texans had been shot from their saddles, the battalion retreated. The Kickapoos gathered their camp gear and hastened on to Mexico.

The Mexican government made a grant of land to the Kickapoos in the state of Coahuila on the Remolino River, in return for which the Kickapoos agreed to defend the northern frontiers of Mexico against Comanche and Apache raiders. This group of émigrés—known subsequently as the Mexican Kickapoos—in retaliation for the unprovoked attack on the Concho, carried on a ruthless war against Texas from their settlements in Mexico. They were quieted only after Colonel Ranald Mackenzie and the Fourth Cavalry made their famous raid into Mexico in 1873.

Although the Santee Sioux and Kickapoo experiences, like many other Indian involvements, were peripheral to the Civil War, they illustrate its widely dispersed character; these incidents involved Union and Confederate military units, and are a part of the military record of that conflict. Few Native Americans escaped its impact or the postwar settlement which is called Reconstruction.

INDIANS AND RECONSTRUCTION

Reconstruction is the process developed by the victorious national government to deal with its vanquished enemies. While it applied more specifically to the eleven states of the Confederacy, to a degree it also applied to many Indian tribes who likewise were regarded as enemies of the United States. As indicated, several Indian nations had made war on the United States directly, as in the case of the Five Civilized Tribes, or indirectly as in the case of the Plains tribes. Thus the same punitive attitude against the eleven states of the Confederacy was applied to several Native American communities, the degree of punishment depending upon the vigor and constancy of their support of the Confederacy. Therefore, in the postwar settlement the Five Civilized Tribes suffered more severe penalty than the Comanches and Kiowas.

Postwar Settlement for the Five Civilized Tribes

Since 1862, officials in the Union government, anticipating eventual victory, had been working out a system known in history as Reconstruction for dealing with the Confederate States of America. Inasmuch as the Confederacy and its satellite, the Indian Territory, had seceded from the American Union, government leaders regarded this separation as treason, and their Reconstruction program had many punitive elements. Broadly, the system devised by Congress to enable the Confederate components to resume their place in the

Union was based on the theory that the Confederacy was a conquered province and that its people must submit to the terms set by the conqueror.

The Reconstruction plan devised for Indian Territory was not exactly the same as that for the states of the Confederacy, but it was similar. The Indian Territory's Reconstruction plan was conceived by two senators from the state of Kansas—James Lane and Samuel Pomeroy. Their scheme for reconstructing Indian Territory reflected the bitterness and vindictiveness Kansans generally held toward the Five Civilized Tribes for joining the Confederacy. At the same time this action by the Five Civilized Tribes gave Kansans an excuse to carry out a long hoped-for objective. Some of the best land in Kansas was held by Indian tribes; Kansas until 1854 had been the northern half of the Indian Territory, and a score of tribes from east of the Mississippi had been colonized there. Kansas settlers coveted these Indian lands and demanded the removal of the tribes to what was left of the Indian Territory so that the Kansas reservations could be opened to settlement. Thus, the association of the Five Civilized Tribes with the Confederacy provided a convenient excuse for taking land from the Indians as a penalty for secession and relocating the Kansas tribes thereon.

Beginning in 1862, Senators Lane and Pomeroy began introducing bills in the Congress to achieve this purpose, and in February 1863 they achieved passage of the legislation which came to be the Reconstruction program for Indian Territory. Basically the Lane-Pomeroy plan authorized the President to suspend treaties with the Five Civilized Tribes, to appropriate certain portions of their domains, and to direct the removal of the tribes from Kansas to the Indian Territory.

During the summer of 1865, summons went out to the leaders of the Confederate tribes to meet with United States commissioners at Fort Smith in early September. The United States delegation to the Fort Smith Council included Dennis N. Cooley, Commissioner of Indian Affairs. Although the council was primarily concerned with contriving a postwar settlement for the Five Civilized Tribes, representatives from other tribes attended. Therefore, besides tribal delegations from the Creek, Choctaw, Chickasaw, Cherokee, and Seminole nations, there were spokesmen from the Osage, Wichita, Caddo, Seneca, Shawnee, Quapaw, and Wyandot tribes.

The Fort Smith Council convened on September 8 and lasted thirteen days. The United States commissioners opened the council with the statement that the Five Civilized Tribes had violated their treaties with the United States, had thereby forfeited all rights under these treaties, and that each tribe must consider itself at the mercy of the United States. Commissioner Cooley stated the conditions for resuming relations with the United States: (1) each tribe must enter into a treaty for permanent peace and amity among themselves and with the United States; (2) slavery must be abolished and steps taken to incorporate the freedmen into the tribes as citizens with rights guaranteed; (3) each tribe must agree to surrender a portion of its lands to the United States for colonizing tribes from Kansas and elsewhere; and (4) tribal leaders must agree to the policy of uniting all tribes of the Indian Territory into a single, consolidated government.

As expected, the leaders of the Five Civilized Tribes dominated the council proceedings. The Cherokees, Creeks, and Seminoles were represented by northern and southern delegations. The most energetic delegations spoke for the Cherokees. Principal Chief John Ross, who had recently arrived from Philadelphia where he had remained in protective custody of federal officials following his capture at Tahlequah in 1862, spoke for the Union viewpoint. The Confederate viewpoint was expressed by Stand Watie and Elias C. Boudinot.

Watie objected to the Union Cherokee law that confiscated all Confederate Cherokee property. As a solution to apparent irreconcilable difference and bitterness between the two factions, Watie proposed that the United States government divide the Cherokee nation into two separate jurisdictions, one for Union Cherokees, the other for Confederate Cherokees. Ross and the Union faction objected to this proposal, and finally the Confederate Cherokees were placated by the promise by federal commissioners that the final Reconstruction treaty would include a provision annulling the confiscation law.

The tribal delegations were shocked at what they regarded as extreme federal demands and deliberately delayed the proceedings. Each delegation claimed that it lacked authority from its government to negotiate a final settlement. When it became apparent that he would be unable to conclude Reconstruction treaties at Fort Smith, Cooley recessed the council, calling for a resumption of negotiation at Washington the following year. His reasoning was that the tribal delegations could be more easily managed far from the influences and pressures of their fellow tribesmen. Before the Fort Smith Council closed, however, the commissioners did negotiate a simple treaty of peace with the tribes through which the Confederate treaties were repudiated and allegiance to the United States was restored.

During 1866, the Five Civilized Tribes through their delegations reluctantly submitted to the Reconstruction treaties in Washington. Since the Choctaws and Chickasaws signed a joint treaty, only four agreements were negotiated. In most respects the treaties were similar. A common provision established peace with the United States and other tribes. Each treaty contained a clause abolishing slavery and granting tribal citizenship to blacks with all the rights of Indians, making provision for them in land and other benefits. Each tribe agreed to grant railroad rights-of-way to enable chartered companies to construct north-south and east-west lines across Indian Territory. Each tribe subscribed in principle to the development of a unified government for Indian Territory and pledged to initiate this movement by participating in an annual intertribal council. By the Reconstruction treaties the United States could establish courts in the Indian Territory with jurisdiction in cases involving non-Indians, and provision was made to compensate Union Indians for property losses due to war.

In keeping with the Lane-Pomeroy Reconstruction plan, each of the four treaties also contained clauses providing for the cession of tribal lands. The Seminoles surrendered their entire domain of 2,170,000 acres to the United States for fifteen cents an acre. They purchased a new nation of 200,000 acres on the western border of the reduced Creek nation for fifty cents an acre. The federal government took the western half of the Creek nation, paying the tribe thirty cents an acre for the 3,250,000 acres appropriated. The Choctaw-Chickasaw treaty provided for the cession of the Leased District for $300,000. The Cherokees ceded the Neutral Lands in southeastern Kansas, which they had purchased from the United States by the New Echota Treaty in 1835, and the Cherokee Strip. This ribbon of territory in southern Kansas, two and one-half miles wide, extending west from the Cherokee Neutral Lands to the one hundredth meridian, was the result of an error in an early boundary survey. The federal government was to auction these lands and turn the proceeds over to the Cherokees. The federal government also in effect took an option on the Cherokee Outlet, a six-million acre reserve tract adjacent to the Cherokee nation proper, by asserting a right to settle tribes from other parts of the United States there. Until final decision, however, title to the Outlet remained with the Cherokees. In addition, the Cherokees agreed to permit the federal government to colonize certain tribes on land east of ninety-six degrees longitude in the Cherokee nation proper.

The seeds of destruction for the Five Civilized Tribes were sown by the Reconstruction treaties. The agony of war was augmented by the ordeal of Reconstruction and by necessary adjustment to new ways of life brought to Indian Territory by the railroads and the increasing stream of settlers. In fewer than twenty-five years a network of railroad lines covered the Indian nations. Cattlemen, boomers, then homesteaders followed; and in 1907, the process of tribal dissolution begun in the 1830s was consummated when the last surviving remnant of Indian Territory was fused with Oklahoma Territory to form the new state of Oklahoma.

Postwar Settlement for the Plains Tribes

During 1865 several federal commissions traveled to the West to study conditions among the Indian nations and to conclude settlements with tribal leaders. The groups included, besides the commission to the Five Civilized Tribes, a joint congressional committee and a commission to the Plains tribes.

The recent militarization of the West and dreadful mauling volunteer troops had inflicted upon several of the Indian tribes, using them as surrogate Confederates, were conspicuous manifestations of the Civil War legacy in the trans-Missouri region. Reports of reckless and unnecessary destruction of Native American life and seizure of Indian lands by these predacious frontier armies filtered to the eastern United States. The near annihilation of Black Kettle's southern Cheyenne band at the Sand Creek Massacre by Colorado volunteer troops under Colonel Chivington particularly had provoked a public outcry in the East. In 1865 congressional leaders appointed a joint committee to investigate conditions among the Indians and to recommend a definitive policy for final settlement of what national leaders still called the "Indian problem." Senator James R. Doolittle of Wisconsin was named chairman of the seven-man investigatory body. The members traveled through the West interviewing Indians, pioneers, and military officers, and observing conditions of the tribes firsthand. The Doolittle Committee's report was not published until 1867; thus its impact applies to the third and final period of tribal conquest and compression. However, the members' arrival on the frontier in 1865 was timely because they were able to observe the destructive effects of Civil War mobilization and militarization upon the Indian tribes.

One of the federal commissions appointed in 1865 to conclude postwar settlements with the western tribes was assigned to the central and southern Great Plains region for negotiations with the Comanches, Kiowas, Cheyennes, Arapahoes, and Kiowa-Apaches. This peace commission, which included Thomas Murphy, head of the Central Indian Superintendency, and General William S. Harney, engaged Jesse Chisholm, a Cherokee mixed blood, and Black Beaver, a Delaware, both frontier traders and frequently employed as guides and scouts by federal military, cartographic, and scientific expeditions. They were to seek out the chiefs of the Comanches, Kiowas, Cheyennes, Arapahoes, and Kiowa-Apaches and summon them to a council to be held at the mouth of the Little Arkansas River near present site of Wichita, Kansas. The Little Arkansas Council began on October 10, 1865. Tribal delegations included Black Kettle, Little Raven, Seven Bulls, and Little Robe for the Cheyennes and Arapahoes; Rising Sun, Buffalo Hump, and Ten Bears for the Comanches; Lone Wolf, Black Eagle, and Stinking Saddle Blanket for the Kiowas; and Poor Bear, Iron Shirt, and Wolf Sleeve for the Kiowa-Apaches. By the Little Arkansas Treaties these tribes ceded to the United States their claims to territory north of the Arkansas River. The Cheyennes and Arapahoes were assigned a reservation between the Arkansas and the Cimarron rivers in southwestern Kansas and the northwestern corner of the Indian Territory. The Comanches and Kiowas were assigned to a reservation which extended across the western end of the Indian Territory from the ninety-eighth meridian across the Texas Panhandle to the meridian of 103 degrees west, flanked by the Cimarron and Red rivers. By the Little Arkansas Treaties the Kiowa-Apaches were confederated with the Cheyennes and Arapahoes.

As matters worked out, these treaties were only truces, brief interludes in an unfolding saga of defeat, desolation, and destruction for the Plains tribes. Anglo-American trespass on their treaty-assigned lands, their attempts to expel the intruders, and settler appeals for protection brought these tribes into a bloody and final contest with the United States army, within a decade ending in their collective defeat and confinement upon much smaller military reservations, and subjected to a process of Americanization by force. The denouement of Indian military power is the subject of Chapter Sixteen.

Notes

1. Arrell Morgan Gibson, *Oklahoma: A History of Five Centuries* (Norman, Okla., 1965), p. 198.
2. *Ibid.*, p. 208.
3. Carleton to West, October 11, 1862. *War of Rebellion Records*, Series One, Vol. 15, p. 580.
4. See Stan Hoig, *The Sand Creek Massacre* (Norman, Okla., 1961), for an account of Chivington's action and its aftermath.

Selected Sources

The anomaly of American Indian involvement in the Civil War is a neglected subject but sufficient readings can be derived from scattered sources to provide some perspective on and understanding of this curious circumstance. The primary source on Native Americans' role in the Civil War is *United States Official Records, War of Rebellion*. Documents relating to Union and Confederate Indian relations are found throughout this collection; Series One, Volume 3, is devoted to the Civil War in Indian Territory. The pioneer studies are Annie H. Abel, *The American Indian as a Slaveholder and Secessionist* (Cleveland, 1915), *The American Indian as a Participant in the Civil War* (Cleveland, 1919), and *The American Indian Under Reconstruction* (Cleveland, 1925).

Native American involvement in the Indian Territory sector of Civil War operations is detailed in Wiley Britton, *The Civil War on the Border* (New York, 1899); see also his *The Union Brigade in the Civil War* (Kansas City, Mo., 1922), and *The Aftermath of the Civil War* (Kansas City, Mo., 1924); Arrell Morgan Gibson, *Oklahoma: A History of Five Centuries* (Norman, Okla., 1965); Edwin Bearss and Arrell Morgan Gibson, *Fort Smith: Little Gibraltar on the Arkansas* (Norman, Okla., 1969); Rachel C. Eaton, *John Ross and the Cherokee Indians* (Menasha, Wisc., 1914); Frank Cunningham, *General Stand Watie's Confederate Indians* (San Antonio, Texas, 1959); Mabel Washbourne Anderson, *Life of General Stand Watie* (Pryor, Okla., 1915); and Edward E. Dale and Gaston Litton (eds.), *Cherokee Cavaliers* (Norman, Okla., 1939).

Information on guerrilla warfare in Indian Territory during the Civil War is provided by Jay Monaghan, *Civil War on the Western Border* (Boston, 1955); and William E. Connelley, *Quantrill and the Border Wars* (Cedar Rapids, Iowa, 1910).

Impact of the Civil War upon the Five Civilized Tribes is found in Grace S. Woodward, *The Cherokees* (Norman, Okla., 1963); Edwin C. McReynolds, *The Seminoles* (Norman, Okla., 1957); Angie Debo, *Rise and Fall of the Choctaw Republic* (Norman, Okla., 1934), and for the Creeks, *The Road to Disappearance* (Norman, Okla., 1941); and Arrell Morgan Gibson, *The Chickasaws* (Norman, Okla., 1971).

Basic work on the Civil War in the trans-Missouri West and its effect on the Indian tribes is Ray C. Colton, *The Civil War in the Western Territories* (Norman, Okla., 1959). See also William A. Keleher, *Turmoil in New Mexico, 1846–1868* (Santa Fe, N.M., 1952); Martin H. Hall, *Sibley's New Mexico Campaign* (Austin, Tex., 1960); Aurora Hunt, *Major General James Henry Carleton* (Glendale, Calif., 1958); Arrell Morgan Gibson, *The Life and Death of Colonel Albert Jennings Fountain* (Norman, Okla., 1965); Robert M. Utley, *Frontiersmen in Blue: The*

United States Army and the Indian, 1848–1865 (New York, 1967); Fred B. Rogers, *Soldiers of the Overland ... General Connor and His Volunters in the Old West* (San Francisco, 1938); Mildred Mayhall, *The Kiowas* (Norman, Okla., 1962); Ernest Wallace and E. Adamson Hoebel, *The Comanches: Lords of the South Plains* (Norman, Okla., 1952); Donald J. Berthrong, *The Southern Cheyennes* (Norman, Okla., 1963); Stan Hoig, *The Sand Creek Massacre* (Norman, Okla., 1961); Robert H. Jones, *The Civil War in the Northwest: Nebraska, Wisconsin, Iowa, Minnesota and the Dakotas* (Norman, Okla., 1960); Arrell Morgan Gibson, *The Kickapoos: Lords of the Middle Border* (Norman, Okla., 1963); Roy W. Meyer, "The Canadian Sioux: Refugees from Minnesota," *Minnesota History* 41 (Spring 1968), pp. 13–28; and Donald Chaput, "Generals, Indian Agents, Politicians: The Doolittle Survey of 1865," *Western Historical Quarterly* 3 (July 1972), pp. 269–82.

A Civil War episode exceeding Sand Creek in needless waste of Native American life was Bosque Redondo. Two works which illuminate this sordid experiment by Union commanders are Lynn R. Bailey, *Bosque Redondo, An American Concentration Camp* (Pasadena, Calif., 1970); and Gerald Thompson, *The Army and the Navajo: The Bosque Redondo Reservation Experiment, 1863–1868* (Tucson, Ariz., 1976). Edmund J. Danziger, Jr., *Indians and Bureaucrats: Administering the Reservation Policy during the Civil War* (Urbana, Ill., 1974) examines the problems of Native American management during the period 1861–65.

CHAPTER 16

END OF INDIAN
MILITARY POWER

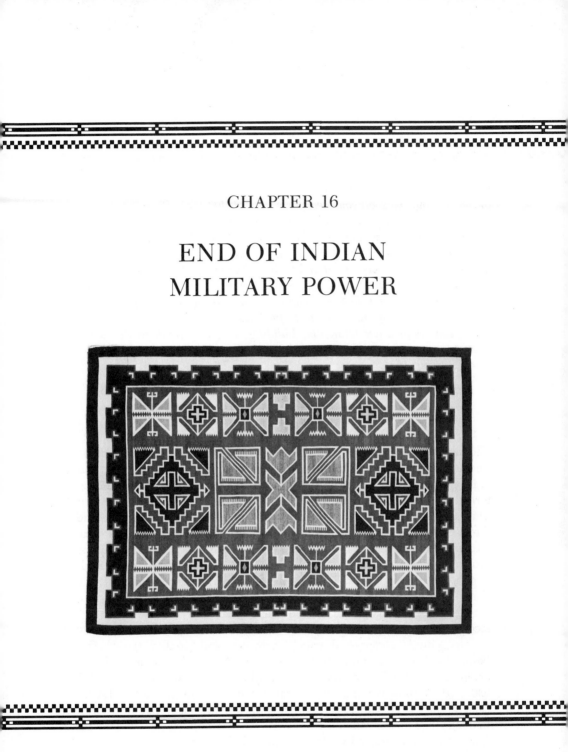

Behold, my Brothers, the spring has come; the earth has received the embraces of the sun and we shall soon see the results of that love! Every seed is awakened. . . . It is through this mysterious power that we too have our being and we therefore yield to our neighbors, even our animal neighbors, the same right as ourselves, to inhabit this land. Yet, hear me, people, we have now to deal with another race—small and feeble when our fathers first met them but now great and overbearing. . . . Possession is a disease with them. These people have made many rules that the rich may break but the poor may not. . . . They claim this mother of ours, the earth, for their own and fence their neighbors away; they deface her with their buildings. . . . That nation is like a spring freshet that overruns its banks and destroys all who are in its path. We cannot dwell side by side.

Statement by Sitting Bull (Sioux) at the Powder River Council, 1877

The third and final period of tribal conquest came during the years 1866–1886. The national government, having preserved the Union in 1865 by final triumph of its armies over the forces of the secessionist Confederate States of America, turned its attention to completing the military conquest of the western tribes. This process, begun in 1846, had already substantially reduced the Indian threat to American expansion in the West and had opened vast new areas to settlement and development. The first phase in this conquest and compression process took place, we have seen, between 1846 and 1860 and was carried out largely by regular troops. Their efforts were particularly successful in California, Oregon, and Washington where, except for scattered pockets of resistance, Indian military power was no longer a factor to be reckoned with. The second phase of the conquest, from 1861 to 1865, further reduced Indian military power, compressed tribal territories, and pacified the Shoshonis, Bannocks, Utes, and other tribes near the Oregon-California roads. Campaigns against the Cheyennes and other tribes of Colorado, Nevada, and Utah scattered the Indians and reduced their domains. In New Mexico and Arizona, General James H. Carleton's conquest and containment policy at Bosque Redondo had destroyed the Mescalero Apache and Navajo will to resist. The western Apaches had yet to be dealt with decisively.

Chapter Opening Artifact: Two Grey Hills rug, by Daisy Touglechee, 1948, Navajo. (Courtesy the Denver Art Museum, Denver, Colorado)

As the national government prepared to undertake the third phase of western conquest and compression, which lasted from 1866 to 1886, federal officials could, for the first time since American independence, conclude with some certainty that the time was near when the Indian would no longer be a military threat to the consummation of American purposes.

CHANGING FEDERAL INDIAN POLICY

The third and final period of conquest was a time of rapid change in federal policy with a number of new methods conceived and applied, each aimed at bringing the "Indian problem" under federal control, reducing the Indians' landed estate for the benefit of Anglo-American settlers, and concentrating Indians on reservations so that Americanization processes could proceed. The practice of colonizing Native Americans in the reduced Indian Territory was resumed, and Indian military power was destroyed by defeating the last tribal resistance, reducing their lands, and confining their leaders in federal prison.

Federal Commissions and the Indian

During the final period of tribal conquest several federal tribunals were commissioned to investigate conditions among the tribes and to find administrative solutions for the "Indian problem." The first of these groups to contact the western tribes was a joint select congressional committee, the Doolittle Committee, its activities described in Chapter Fifteen. The Doolittle Committee's findings, published in 1867 as the *Report on the Condition of the Indian Tribes,* concluded that the continuing Indian resistance in most cases was due to unlawful settler intrusion and hunter trespass on tribal territories and precipitate actions by overzealous military officers. The committee further stated that in its judgment it was no longer feasible to allow the western tribes a free, roving existence. To prevent Indian wars and to establish peace in the West, the Indians would have to give up the nomadic life, accept limited reservations, and "walk the white man's road." The Doolittle report became the guide for leaders in both the legislative and executive branches of the national government for developing the final answer to the "Indian problem," its recommendations serving as the basis for federal reservation assignments and additional reductions in tribal territories.

In June 1867 Congress authorized formation of the Peace Commission, its assignment to travel to the West and continue the study of problems in Indian relations revealed by the Doolittle Committee report and to seek solutions to these problems. Above all else the function of the Peace Commission was to end Native American resistance to the Anglo-American advance. Peace Commission members, who included Commissioner of Indian Affairs

393

Nathaniel G. Taylor and Senator John B. Henderson of Missouri, inspected the work of the federal agents and interviewed tribal leaders. They negotiated several treaties which committed the signatory tribes to cede their lands and accept limited reservations. One class of these cession treaties applied to tribes in Kansas and Nebraska who subsequently moved to reservations in the Indian Territory so that settlers could homestead on their vacated lands. Another class of cession treaties substantially reduced lands of the tribes of the northern, central, and southern Great Plains which opened a corridor for railroad construction through the heart of the continent. Each treaty included a commitment by the federal government to assist the tribes to become self-sustaining through agriculture and stock raising. Agents were to issue tools, implements, seed, and livestock to the reservation dwellers and to teach them to become agrarians. The reservations assigned by the Peace Commission to the western tribes survived until application of the General Allotment Act of 1887.

Peace Policy versus Force Policy

The Doolittle report's castigation of federal officials for unnecessary use of military force to implement Indian policy led to a brief experiment with the "Peace Policy" as a substitute for the War Department's "Force Policy." Shortly after his inauguration President Ulysses S. Grant met with a delegation of nationally prominent churchmen, most of whom were Quakers (members of the Society of Friends). These spiritual leaders pointed out that a century of force had failed to solve the Indian problem, and they urged resort to more peaceful alternatives. Grant was impressed by their argument, and he invited leading religious denominations to recommend clergy and prominent laymen to serve as officials in the Bureau of Indian Affairs and as agents on the reservations.

Use of churchmen as government agents was compatible with the federal government's Americanization (acculturation) program fashioned to change Native Americans from the "primal" state to "civilization." National leaders believed that an essential step in this process was conversion to the Christian faith; daily exposure of reservation Indians to Christian agents setting upright examples would aid this process. They regarded the upgrading of Indian agents to be essential. The federal bureaucracy responsible for Indian tribes, the Bureau of Indian Affairs in the Department of the Interior, was embarrassed by a sordid history of corruption, particularly at the agent level where considerable sums of money and large quantities of valuable goods for annuity payments, beef contracts, and other valuable considerations were handled each year and adequate oversight was difficult if not impossible. It was believed that agents from religious bodies would be less susceptible than civilian agents to malfeasance. This was a major reason for Grant's support of the "Peace Policy" which would permit churchmen to become agents.

Methodists and representatives of other religious bodies supplied "Peace Policy" agents, but because most of them came from the Society of Friends, they were commonly called "Quaker Agents." Quakers assigned to duty in Indian Territory included Enoch Hoag, head of the Central Superintendency; Brinton Darlington served as agent for the southern Cheyennes and Arapahoes until succeeded by another Quaker, John D. Miles; Laurie Tatum worked among the Comanches and Kiowas; Jonathan Richards served at Wichita Agency; Hiram W. Jones administered the Quapaw Agency; and Isaac T. Gibson worked with the Osages. Tatum related his experiences as Comanche-Kiowa agent in a book titled *Our Red Brothers,* published in 1899. Quakers also served as teachers at government schools on the new reservations. Thomas C. Battey, who taught at the Comanche-Kiowa school, described his experience in a book titled *A Quaker Among the Indians,* published in 1875.

However, not enough qualified churchmen responded. Though religious leaders committed their churches to supply the agents, they found it difficult to recruit laymen and clergy who would go to the West and live and work among the Indian tribes. It was charged that "Protestants had never enjoyed much success in their missionary work among the tribesmen"; they "found harvesting souls in Africa and the Orient more rewarding." The "Peace Policy" discriminated against Catholics in that they were allocated only a small number of the agent positions even though they provided considerably more funds for Indian work than any other religious body. This discrimination against Roman Catholics caused divisions in the "Peace Policy" movement and contributed to its early demise.[1]

Grant, searching for another source of Indian agents above the common politician class, appointed army officers to several of the agent positions. This threatened the partisan patronage prerogative, and Congress in 1870 passed a law forbidding appointment of military officers to these positions.

"Peace Policy" advocates in the federal government faced continuing conflict with the "Force Policy" clique headed by General of the Army William Tecumseh Sherman, whose maxim was "Americanization at the point of a bayonet." This group was cynical of "Peace Policy" resort to patience and humanity in dealing with Indians. "Force Policy" advocates claimed that Indians responded only to force or the threat of force. Thus the western tribes "should be managed by those best qualified to use force." Finally, responsibility for aboriginal management was divided. "Peace Policy" agents were to be supreme on the reservations; the army was delegated discretionary power over Indians caught off the reservations. Understandably this duality in federal Indian policy created confusion for Indians and dilemmas for officials.[2]

Board of Indian Commissioners

Another experiment in Indian policy administration was formation of the Board of Indian Commissioners by Congress in 1869. The board, to consist of 10 prominent citizens appointed by the President, was to be nonpartisan. Its function was to remove politics and corruption from the Indian bureaucracy and improve Indian administration. As an advisory agency to the secretary of the interior and the commissioner of Indian affairs, the board was to investigate conditions among the tribes and recommend reforms to appropriate federal agencies. Board members or their hired investigators spent considerable time in the West inspecting the reservations and watching for agent malfeasance. For years this was the only protective voice the Indians had in a generally unresponsive government. However, the Board of Indian Commissioners' inspectors were too few, their time too limited, and the task too great to produce pervasive benefit for Native Americans.

End of the Treaty Process

After its tour in the West the Peace Commission had recommended that the use of treaties in carrying on relations with the Indian tribes be ended. Furthermore, the United States House of Representatives, required to appropriate funds provided for in treaties concluded by federal agents with tribal leaders and ratified by the Senate, declared its determination to have "equal voice" in Indian matters and thus contributed to the demise of the treaty process for Indian tribes. However, the immediate cause was a United States Supreme Court decision popularly known as the Cherokee Tobacco Case. The Cherokee Reconstruction Treaty of 1866 included a clause which permitted tribal citizens to produce, manufacture, ship, and market any product throughout the United States without restraint, exempt from any federal tax. In 1868, Elias C. Boudinot and Stand Watie purchased a tobacco factory at Hannibal, Missouri, and moved it to Boudiville, near the Arkansas line in the Cherokee nation. Boudinot and Watie produced chewing tobacco, snuff, treated leaf, and pipe tobacco. Although they sold their products all over the United States, their principal market was in the nearby southwestern states.

Tobacco dealers in Missouri, Arkansas, and Texas complained that the untaxed and thus cheaper Cherokee tobacco threatened their businesses. Congress responded by passing revenue laws annulling the Cherokee tax exemption. A posse of federal deputy marshals, responding to a complaint from the commissioner of internal revenue in Washington, seized the Boudinot-Watie tobacco works and arrested the Cherokee owners. The Indian defendants were convicted in federal district court but gained a hearing in the United States Supreme Court on a writ of error. Attorneys for the Cherokees claimed an invasion of rights under the historic principle that the United States Constitution and treaties comprised the supreme law of the land, superior to laws of Congress. The high court handed down its famous Cherokee Tobacco Case decision in 1870. The justices in effect drew a distinction between treaties made with foreign nations and Indian tribes, declaring that the 1868 revenue laws did supersede the Cherokee treaty of 1866, thus upholding the lower court's ruling. Soon after the Cherokee Tobacco Case decision, Congress passed an act which provided that no future treaties would be negotiated with the Indian tribes. Thereafter, all Indians were subject to the laws of Congress and the administrative rulings of the President.

This alteration in Indian policy was indeed revolutionary. From earliest colonial times, the tribes had carried on relations with the European nations through treaties; after American independence, the United States continued this practice. The very act of negotiating diplomatic agreements with the Indian nations ascribed to them a sovereign status. In early United States history the tribes were numerous and powerful, the nation was relatively weak, and it was feasible for the federal government to recognize the sovereign status of Indian communities through treaties. By 1870, however, Indian power had suffered a progressive erosion while there had been a concomitant increase in Anglo-American power. The massive military power buildup by the Union during the Civil War and the national military potential after demobilization, plus improvement in military weapons and tactics, made it unnecessary to continue this practice which national leaders had come to regard as cumbersome and inconvenient. Thus in March 1871 Congress passed legislation providing that "No Indian nation or tribe within the territory of the United States shall be acknowledged or recognized as an independent nation, tribe, or power with whom the United States may contract by treaty; but no obligation of any treaty made is hereby invalidated or impaired." Thereafter any change in relations with any Indian tribe was carried out by executive order or act of Congress. Needless to say, this change was a staggering blow to the prestige and pride of the Indian nations.

Indian communities responded in various ways to these new federal policies. Some, including the Five Civilized Tribes, reluctantly accepted the new order and attempted to recover from the ruin of war and the pain of Reconstruction to fashion a new life. Remnants of once great Indian nations like the Osages and Kansas accepted life anew and permitted federal officials to colonize them on reservations in the Indian Territory. They settled there peacefully and created no particular difficulty for federal agents except that they studiously avoided being Americanized. However, many tribes had to be decisively defeated by United States troops and their leaders sent off to military prison before they submitted to the new order on restricted military reservations.

THE PEACEFUL INDIANS

The Five Civilized Tribes of Indian Territory, having moved a considerable distance along the "white man's road," faced in the postwar era the same problems as the rest of the former Confederacy—providing for former slaves, now freedmen, resolving internal disorders and lawlessness, reorganizing tribal governments along the lines set by the victorious Union government, and coping with rapid economic development, focusing upon railroad building. Their life-style contrasted dramatically with those of many western tribes being colonized by federal agents upon reservations near their settlements on lands taken from them by the Reconstruction Treaties.

The Five Civilized Tribes Under Reconstruction

The Five Civilized Tribes spent the quarter century after 1865 in attempted rehabilitation. Leaders of these Indian republics labored to retrieve from the ruin of war the internal strength, order, and progress their nations had enjoyed before 1861.

When hostilities ceased in Indian Territory during the early summer of 1865, the people of the Five Civilized Tribes were scattered. Most of the men of military age were serving in Union or Confederate regiments. The war had scattered the civilian population. Union refugees, most of them Creeks, Seminoles, and Cherokees, were in camps in Kansas or near Fort Gibson. Confederate refugees were dispersed along Red River in the Choctaw and Chickasaw nations and in northern Texas. Disease, particularly cholera, struck both Union and Confederate refugee camps. This dreaded malady also swept through several Union Seminole and Cherokee communities. Malnutrition was widespread, and hundreds of Indians perished of starvation during the winter of 1865–1866. This, added to the thousands who died of wounds and disease on the battlefield, in camp and on the trail, plus the high death rate in the refugee camps, reduced the population of the Five Civilized Tribes by 25 percent or more.

The Choctaws and Chickasaws fared best because only the northern perimeters of their nations suffered Union desolation. But their resources had been severely taxed as they attempted to relieve the hunger and suffering of the Confederate Cherokee, Creek, and Seminole refugees.

The three Indian nations north of the Canadian River were a melancholy wasteland. Throughout the war foraging armies had ranged over the Cherokee, Creek, and Seminole nations. Poor quartermaster systems in both Union and Confederate armies were the combatants' excuse for living off the land and the people. Looting by free companies and guerrilla bands brought additional destruction and appropriation of property. The misery of the Five Civilized Tribes continued after the Confederate capitulation. Though the country north of the Canadian River was under Union occupation, over 300,000 head of cattle worth nearly $5 million were gathered up by well-organized stock theft rings and driven to Kansas. Subsequently, many of these animals were slaughtered and sold to government contractors at Fort Gibson for feeding Union refugees.

Confederate refugees were hesitant to return to their homes north of the Canadian and the Arkansas rivers because they feared reprisals from Union tribesmen. When they finally returned, they found their farms, plantations, towns, schools, and churches in ruins. Houses and barns were charred piles of rubble, stone chimneys marked homesites like stark sentinels, fields were taken by weeds and scrub growth, fences were destroyed, and movable property including plows and tools were gone. Indian Territory was a scene of desolation, a wasteland.

The principal postbellum problem facing the Five Civilized tribes, aside from grinding poverty and pervasive ruin due to war, was rampant lawlessness. Before 1861 these five Indian republics had maintained well-organized governments which supplied exemplary law and order and led visitors to comment that life and property were safer in Indian Territory than on the streets of Philadelphia or St. Louis. After the war the tribes lacked the financial means to carry on effective government. The chief source of support for the tribal governments had been the annuity payment—the annual income from the invested proceeds of eastern land sales paid by the United States government. Treaties with the Confederacy had cut off this flow of money. The treaties of 1866 provided for resumption of annuity payment, but as usual federal officials were slow in paying.

The Cherokee, Creek, and Seminole governments faced the added problem of factionalism. Organized Confederate and Union partisans were struggling to gain control of the government in each of these nations. This divisiveness decreased tribal strength almost to the point of anarchy, with the result that disorders and lawlessness flourished. It was a trying period for those attempting to recover from the ravages of war.

The five Indian republics were under military occupation like the rest of the former Confederacy, but troops in the Indian Territory were spread thinly over the region. Most United States forces were concentrated on the western border to pacify the Plains tribes and were thus of little help in maintaining order in the five nations. As a part of the Reconstruction program's military control, officers from the regular army administered the Cherokees, Choctaws, Creeks, Seminoles, and Chickasaws as tribal agents, and they remained in charge until 1870 when the federal government adjudged these tribes reconstructed and assigned civilian agents to Indian Territory. The Indian agents were under the direct supervision of the head of the Southern Superintendency with headquarters at Fort Smith. In 1869, the Southern Superintendency was abolished. Thereafter, tribal agents reported directly to the commissioner of Indian affairs. The four agencies of the Five Civilized Tribes (Cherokee, Creek, Seminole, and Choctaw-Chickasaw) were consolidated in 1874 into the Union Agency under a single federal official, the superintendent of the Five Civilized Tribes, with headquarters at Muskogee in the Creek nation.

In the absence of restraint, every type of desperate character and renegade flourished in the Indian Territory. A principal source of disorder immediately following the war was the freedman. The Radical Republicans in control of the national government sought to gain for the former slaves of Indian Territory all the political rights enjoyed by Indians, plus an equal share in tribal annuities, lands, and other benefits. This policy was included in the Reconstruction Treaties of 1866. In addition, congressional leaders seriously considered colonizing former slaves from the Confederacy on lands taken from the Five Civilized Tribes. While it never did so, the "forty acres and a mule" idea was spread abroad and had the effect of encouraging black immigration from Texas, Louisiana, Arkansas, and Missouri to Indian Territory. These vagabonds formed colonies of their own by squatting on Cherokee and Choctaw lands or gathering in the settlements of the ex-slaves of the Five Civilized Tribes.

Indian Territory was poverty-stricken, and there was no means of providing the residents of these black communities with gainful employment. To survive, many of the former slaves raided corn cribs and smokehouses of Indian householders and stole chickens, cattle, hogs, and horses. The Choctaws and Chickasaws formed vigilante committees to stop this thievery.

The lack of law and order in Indian Territory after 1865 also attracted white renegades. The western border during the Civil War had produced a bumper crop of wild, lawless men and women. While the war was in progress, they found a shadowy excuse to rob, burn, rape, and plunder as members of the Quantrill gang and other semiofficial guerrilla bands. The close of hostilities ended this license, but these miscreants, unable or unwilling to take up a law-abiding way of life, continued their lawless activities. Many used the Indian Territory as a sanctuary from which to raid banks, stagecoaches, trains, and businesses in adjacent states. Herds of cattle and horses gathered from Texas ranches were driven into the Indian Territory for resale to dealers with no compunctions about brand registrations and bills of sale. These desperadoes likewise killed and robbed Indian Territory citizens. Choctaw-Chickasaw vigilantes did succeed in capturing and executing a group of Texas horse thieves, but crime was too widespread and the gangs too powerful and well organized to be contained by the limited resources of the Indian nations.

Railroad construction across the Indian Territory after 1870 brought additional disorder. Each of the railheads and construction camps became a Satan's paradise. These migrant communities contained, in addition to the rough-and-ready, brawling construction crews, a regular assortment of tinhorn gamblers, thieves, prostitutes, whiskey sellers, and assorted hoodlums. Gibson Station, a typical rail camp, was reputed to have at least one killing each night. At Caddo, a rail town on the Missouri-Kansas-Texas in the southern Choctaw nation, fifteen killings were committed with impunity in less than a year.

The reputation of Indian Territory as "The Robbers' Roost," "The Land of the Six-gun" spread far and wide, and its condition was neatly summarized in the widely broadcast slogan: "There is no Sunday west of St. Louis—no God west of Fort Smith." Tribal leaders, finally convinced of their inability to cope with this crisis in crime, appealed to federal officials for help in ridding their nations of this torment. In their entreaties they pointed out that no traveler was safe, and citizens faced daily peril.[3]

Federal officials responded to these pleas in 1871 by moving the Western Arkansas Federal District Court from Van Buren to Fort Smith and appointing Isaac Parker presiding judge. In a very short time Parker was known around the world as "the hanging judge of Fort Smith." He appointed 200 United States deputy marshals who traveled all over the Indian nations singly and in squads in a massive outlaw roundup.

The federal court at Fort Smith and the deputy marshals eventually purged the Indian Territory of crime, but Indian citizens came to fear and hate this law-enforcement agency. Many tribal leaders charged that the court and the deputy marshals, once vital for the well-being of Indian Territory, gradually had become an instrument of tyranny. Most of the conflict grew out of questions of jurisdiction. The federal district court at Fort Smith held jurisdiction in all criminal matters where one or both parties were non-Indian, and all cases where federal laws allegedly had been violated. As the Indian nations recovered from the ruin of war and Reconstruction, each reorganized its government and appointed Indian officials to enforce tribal laws. Indian offenders were then tried in tribal courts.

The most famous incident of conflict between federal and Indian courts was the Going Snake Courthouse affair. On April 15, 1872, the Cherokee nation court at Going Snake Courthouse was in session to try a tribal citizen, Ezekial Proctor, for the murder of a fellow Cherokee. During the trial, a posse of deputy marshals from Fort Smith arrived. The federal officers entered the log courthouse and attempted to take Proctor with them to Fort Smith for trial on another charge. Cherokee officials resisted, there followed a lively gun battle, and eleven men were slain—seven marshals and four Cherokees. The exchange wounded the judge, a juror, and several spectators.

In declaring their resentment of the Fort Smith court and its army of deputy marshals, Indian leaders charged that tribal rights were ignored, and that federal officials manufactured charges in order to drag innocent Indians to Fort Smith to enable marshals to collect their mileage and per diem fees. To alleviate the problem of distance, federal officials in 1889 placed the western Choctaw nation and the Chickasaw nation under the jurisdiction of the federal district court at Paris, Texas.

Matching law-and-order problems as obstacles to restoring tribal governments were internal divisions. The Choctaw and Chickasaw nations had been virtually unanimous in their commitment to the Confederacy and stood united in the postwar era. By contrast the Cherokee, Seminole, and Creek nations were seriously divided. Union and Confederate factions were so embittered and alienated that they established separate settlements. However, temperate Indians moved into leadership positions in the Cherokee and Seminole nations, the hatreds of war passed, and reconciliation became possible. As pressure from home seekers and federal officials to open tribal lands to settlement increased, the factions closed ranks to strengthen their nations against this threat. Wartime animosities seemed less important.

The Creek nation, on the other hand, was torn by insurgency until the demise of the Five Civilized Tribes as political entities in 1906. The tradition for restoration of old customs—nativism—established by the late Opothleyaholo, and irreconcilable resistance to the rapid postwar change occurring in all the Indian nations, were continued by a succession of full-blood Creek leaders who were unremittingly committed to resist even to the death the mixed bloods and their attempts to institute change in the Creek nation. Among the first postwar leaders was Oktarsars Harjo Sands who voiced tribal resentment and discontent with the Creek Reconstruction Treaty by which the federal government took half of the nation's territory. He also attacked constitutional changes which Sands said did away with cherished tribal ways which he was committed to preserve. Sands led a number of armed revolts in the Creek nation, on one occasion capturing the nation's capital at Okmulgee. In 1872 Sands died, but his work for nativism was continued by Isparhechar who also led several bloody uprisings. As late as 1890 regular cavalry were garrisoned at Fort Gibson, combat-ready to quell outbreaks among the Creeks. Isparhechar was succeeded by Chitto Harjo who continued resistance to change and worked for restoration of old ways. Harjo's insurgency focused on the revolutionary allotment in severalty which destroyed the ancient common ownership of tribal land.

Despite these internal divisions and continuing outbreaks, the five nations eventually recovered from the ruin of war. Educational leaders restored tribal school systems. Old businesses were resumed; new ones were established. The rich resources of the Indian Territory—timber, coal, lead, zinc, and by the turn of the century, petroleum—attracted national attention and investment. The great energizer for the Indian Territory's economic advance was railroad construction. By the close of the century, the Indian nations were laced by a transportation grid which brought rapid change to the sole surviving portion of the nation's Indian colonization zone.

The five nations were obligated by their Reconstruction treaties to work for an eventual united territory, complete with a single territorial government. Federal officials urged leaders in this direction, but local interests, fearing sacrifice of tribal sovereignty and privilege, prevented the development of enthusiastic support for this treaty obligation. As federal pressure for its fulfillment increased, tribal leaders finally began holding intertribal councils to consider the issue. A strong practical reason why the tribes did not move rapidly toward development of an inclusive territorial government was that this step would require that railroads that were being built through the Indian Territory be granted substantial right-of-way land grants from the various tribal domains. It was common knowledge among all tribal leaders that railway companies strongly supported the organization of a territorial government for the Indian Territory.

Tribal recalcitrance caused Congress to act. Senator Benjamin F. Rice of Arkansas introduced a bill providing for organizing "the Territory of Oklahoma." This bill alarmed Indian leaders. They forwarded strong resolutions against the Rice bill to Congress, but it became abundantly clear that either the Indians would act or the action would be taken for them, perhaps on terms not to their liking. As a result, the Intertribal Council was summoned to meet at Okmulgee in emergency session on September 27, 1870. Forty delegates attended. A committee headed by Cherokee William P. Ross, Princeton graduate and gifted writer, editor of the *Cherokee Advocate* and former principal chief, was assigned the task of drafting a constitution for the proposed unified Indian Territory and future Indian state. Ross's committee composed the Okmulgee Constitution, a well-drafted document which included a bill of rights. The delegates adopted the constitution and it was submitted to Congress; that body refused to approve it on the grounds that the Five Civilized Tribes were unduly insisting that the United States honor treaty rights, and as one observer put it, "Congress was unwilling to concede the measure of independence for Indians set in the terms" of the Okmulgee Constitution.[4]

Yet another problem faced by the Five Civilized Tribes in the postwar era was that of adjusting to the drastic reduction of their domains, required by the Reconstruction treaties. Added to the trauma of territorial loss was the problem of adjusting to new tribal neighbors, colonized on these appropriated lands from other sections of the United States.

The Second Trail of Tears

One of the Civil War settlement goals of Kansas leaders had been to punish the Five Civilized Tribes for their Confederate alliance by taking their lands and settling thereon those tribal remnants still living in Kansas and Nebraska which, until 1854, comprised the northern half of Indian Territory. Federal officials broadened the resettlement plan to include Native Americans from throughout the West so that by 1880 67 different tribes occupied the Indian Territory. For many tribes this forced move to the Indian Territory represented their fourth relocation in 50 years. It was an uprooting which produced considerable suffering and hardship, reminiscent of the melancholy "Trail of Tears" of the 1830s.

Published demands by frontier editors that the federal government remove resident tribes to Indian Territory, epitomized in a Topeka, Kansas, newspaper during 1867, echoed editorials of Georgia, Alabama, and Mississippi two generations before. One anti-Indian column denounced Kansas tribesmen as "a set of miserable, dirty, lousy, blanketed, thieving, lying, sneaking, murdering, graceless, faithless, gut-eating skunks . . . whose immediate and final extermination all men except Indian agents and traders, should pray for."[5]

One of the larger communities assigned to Indian Territory was the Osage nation. In earlier times the Osages lived in the northeastern portion of the Indian Territory, but they had been relocated into what later became southern Kansas in order to make room for the emigrating Cherokees. Osage chiefs signed a treaty with federal agents in 1865 which made preliminary arrangements for removal to the Indian Territory, and in July 1870, the United States Congress passed a law providing for an Osage reservation in the Cherokee Outlet. A definite assignment consisting of 1,700,000 acres between the ninety-sixth meridian, the western boundary of the Cherokee Nation proper, and the Arkansas River in the Cherokee Outlet, was made the following year.

The removal agreement included a provision that those Osage mixed bloods who had advanced along the "white man's road" could receive allotments on the Osage reservation in Kansas and remain, thereby becoming landowners and citizens of the United States. Their treatment at the hands of land-hungry Kansans following assignment of allotments was much like the harassment which Georgians inflicted upon Cherokees 35 years earlier. The commissioner of Indian affairs reported that very shortly the mixed-blood allotments were overrun by settlers.

Outrages and persecutions perpetrated upon them . . . shames humanity. All except eight have abandoned their homes, or taken what they could get for them. Some of their homes were burnt by mobs of white men; one half-breed died from injury received. . . . The murderers were arrested, went through the forms of a trial, and were discharged. The eight still remaining will probably lose their land, as they have not the means to engage in a long contest at law.[6]

Between 1871 and 1872, 1,500 Osages returned to the Indian Territory. Their domain, although extensive, was rough upland meadow and hill country, most of it apparently fit only for grazing. Ironically, the Osage reservation, considered one of the poorer and less desirable tribal assignments, became one of the richest tracts in the world. In later years, vast oil deposits were found beneath this rough, hilly, grass-covered domain, and the Osages for a time were the wealthiest community in the United States. For years every man, woman, and child on the tribal roll received over $10,000 annually from oil royalties.

The Kansas (Kaws), related to the Osages by language and culture, disposed of their reservation in Kansas by successive treaties, and during 1872 agreed to relocate in the Indian Territory. A 100,000-acre tract in the northwest corner of the Osage reservation was assigned to them, and during 1873 the 500 members of this tribe settled on their Indian Territory home. The commissioner of Indian affairs placed the Osage and Kansas tribes under the supervision of the Osage Agency at Pawhuska.

Another postwar agency developed from the assignment of the Sac and Fox tribes to the Indian Territory. Formerly two separate tribes living in the Old Northwest, these people numbered about 6,500 in 1825, but ravaged by frontier wars and disease, they had been reduced to fewer than 1,000 in 1865. In February 1867 about 500 members of these tribes assented to a treaty through which they exchanged their lands in Kansas for a 480,000-acre tract in the Indian Territory, west of the Creek nation between the Cimarron and the North Canadian rivers. By 1869 these Algonkian-speaking tribes were settled on their new lands, opening farms and adjusting to life in the Indian Territory.

The Sac and Fox Agency, established to administer the affairs of this affiliated tribe, soon had attached to it 4 additional tribes who were settled near the Sac and Fox—the Potawatomis, Absentee Shawnees, Iowas, and Mexican Kickapoos. Certain segments of the Potawatomi tribe in Kansas signed a treaty with the United States in 1867, agreeing to relocate on a reservation in the Indian Territory, and a tract of 575,000 acres just west of the Seminole nation was assigned to them. When these Native Americans, numbering about 450, reached their new home, they found that a band of Shawnees, known as the Absentee Shawnees, already occupied the northern portion of their domain. An arrangement was worked out providing for joint occupation, with the Kansas immigrants settling in the central and southern portions of the reservation.

The Iowas from the Kansas-Nebraska border began drifting into the Indian Territory during 1876, protesting federal government pressure that they agree to liquidate their northern reservation by allotment. The Iowas collected in a community in the Sac and Fox country, their status uncertain. Finally in 1883 by presidential executive order a 225,000-acre reservation between the Cimarron and Deep Fork rivers was established for the 185 members of this tribe.

The Ponca Agency supervised several tribes collected on land west of the Osages and Kansas including Poncas, Pawnees, Otos, and Missouris, for a time the Nez Percés, and the Tonkawas. The Poncas, Siouian-speaking people from Dakota Territory, lived briefly in Nebraska. In 1876 Congress passed an act that provided for the relocation of the 680 members of this tribe on a reservation in the Indian Territory. The Ponca migration began during 1877. Chief Standing Bear led his people first to the Quapaw reservation in the northeastern part of the Indian Territory where they remained while tribal leaders looked over the Cherokee Outlet for a permanent home. They finally decided upon a 100,000-acre tract between the Chikaskia and Arkansas rivers.

Hardship and suffering marked every tribal relocation, but none surpassed the Ponca removal for sublime pathos. Soon after the Poncas arrived in Indian Territory, Standing Bear's little son died. The grieving Ponca leader felt compelled to inter his child in the land of his ancestors. A mounted escort of 30 mourning Ponca warriors accompanied the wagon bearing the chief and the shrouded remains of his son. This slow-moving column alarmed settlers on the frontier; they feared an Indian outbreak and appealed to the military for protection. General George Crook and a cavalry force went after the Poncas, arrested the party and lodged the Indians in the Omaha jail to await return to Indian Territory.

For once, however, some people on the frontier took the side of the Indian. When it became known why the Poncas were off their reservation, the people of Omaha provided legal counsel for the Indians. Their attorneys sought a writ of habeas corpus in United States district court. Local papers stirred public interest to such levels that the courtroom was filled with spectators. Government attorneys asked that the petition for the writ be denied on the grounds that an Indian was not a person within the meaning of the Constitution and therefore could not invoke the right of habeas corpus. Nevertheless, the judge ruled that the Indian was a person and thus entitled to the same protection as a non-Indian. Standing Bear's party was released and permitted to proceed to the Ponca burial ground.

The Otos and Missouris, Siouian-speaking people closely related to the Iowas, had fused into one tribe by 1854 when they received a reservation on the Nebraska-Kansas border. This northern domain was taken from them by congressional action in 1880 and tribal leaders were forced to find a new location. The Oto-Missouri removal to Indian Territory, involving about 400 members of that tribe, occurred between 1880 and 1883. At first they squatted on lands in the Sac and Fox country, but in 1882 tribal leaders purchased a 130,000-acre tract in the Cherokee Outlet south of the Poncas.

The largest Indian community which federal agents settled in the Ponca Agency jurisdiction were the Pawnees, who mustered a population of more than 2,000 at the beginning of their removal in 1873. The year before, the Pawnee reservation in Nebraska was appropriated by the United States, and bands from this tribe began drifting into Indian Territory searching for a home. About 300 Pawnees settled temporarily near the Wichita Agency on the Washita River. In 1874, Pawnee chiefs selected a 283,000-acre reservation between the Arkansas and Cimarron rivers. Most of their land was in the Cherokee Outlet, although the southern portion extended into the area ceded by the Creeks in 1866.

The Tonkawas, a Texas tribe, had been moved from south of the Red River to the Leased District during the general relocation of Texas tribes in 1859. The tribe numbered about 350 at the time. The Tonkawas were harassed by the Kiowas, Comanches, Kickapoos, and other powerful southern Plains tribes who claimed that they were cannibals. The truth of the matter was that Tonkawas were excellent scouts and trailers, widely used by frontier military units in searching out the villages of resisting tribes. Consequently the Kiowas, Comanches, and Kickapoos scorned the Tonkawas and used the charge of cannibalism as an excuse to harass them. In 1862 during a raid on the Wichita Agency the Tonkawas were nearly exterminated. The survivors, numbering about 100, fled to Fort Griffin in Texas and remained there until 1884 when Indian Bureau officials arranged for their relocation in the Indian Territory. The Tonkawas settled temporarily in the Sac and Fox country. The following year they were located permanently on a 91,000-acre reservation in the Cherokee Outlet near the Chikaskia River.

By its Reconstruction Treaty with the Cherokees, the federal government gained the right to settle certain tribes east of the ninety-sixth meridian in the Cherokee nation. A community of Delawares, numbering about 1,000, had been assigned a reservation in northern Kansas while that area was a part of the Indian Territory. An agreement negotiated in 1867 permitted the Delawares to settle among the Cherokees in return for payment of $280,000 to the Cherokees. While a 158,000-acre tract was set aside for the Delawares in the northern Verdigris River valley, it was not in the nature of a separate reservation, since the Delawares were adopted by the Cherokees and soon became full citizens of that nation. Also in 1867 a band of Shawnees, numbering 722, ceded their lands in Kansas and worked out an agreement with the Cherokees similar to that negotiated with the Delawares. This Shawnee community settled in the upper Cherokee nation near Grand River.

The Quapaw Agency had a number of tribes under its jurisdiction. The reservation area, situated in the far northeastern corner between the Neosho and Grand rivers and the Missouri border, was carved out during 1832 and 1833 by treaties with the Quapaws, Senecas, and a small band of Shawnees. Following the Civil War, surplus Quapaw, Seneca, and Shawnee land was taken by the federal government to establish reservation homes for small tribes being relocated from Kansas reservations. These tribes included the Wyandots, Peorias, Miamis, and Ottawas. Most of these relocations occurred by treaties negotiated in 1867.

By 1890 the Indian Territory contained 21 separate reservations administered by 8 agencies: the Kiowa-Comanche Agency at Fort Sill, the Wichita-Caddo Agency near Anadarko, the Cheyenne-Arapaho or Darlington Agency near Fort Reno, the Ponca Agency near Ponca City, the Osage Agency at Pawhuska, the Sac and Fox Agency near Stroud, the Quapaw Agency, also known as the Neosho Agency, at Wyandotte and later at Miami, and the Union Agency for the Five Civilized Tribes at Muskogee. Each agency had at least 2 tribes under its jurisdiction, and several agencies had 5 more.

Most of the tribes settled peacefully on their assigned reservations and gave the agents no particular trouble, except for their determined efforts to continue intertribal visits, horse racing, gambling, feasts, religious observances, and dances, and their calculated attempts to avoid farming and other detribalization programs. The buffalo-hunting Plains tribes and certain other western groups, however, followed a course of active resistance; they refused to submit to restricted reservation life, and thus were periodically targets for the fury of the United States army's "Force Policy."

THE RESISTIVE INDIANS

An immediate postwar concern of the federal government was pacifying the vast territory of North America's heartland—the Great Plains, which extended from Canada to the Rio Grande. This country was the buffalo range and the home of America's most powerful surviving tribes. Fierce northern Cheyennes and Sioux dominated the northern Plains; southern Cheyennes and Arapahoes ruled the central Plains; and Kiowas and Comanches roamed over the southern Plains. These tribes had felt the lash of American military might during the Civil War period of tribal conquest and compression, but in 1866 they still controlled vast domains. Each tribe possessed superb fighting power and a strong will to resist American occupation. Federal officials on their side felt compelled to clear the Plains hunting range in order to open a wedge for the advancing transcontinental railroad, which would soon link the Mississippi Valley with the Pacific shore.

Conquest of the Southern Plains Tribes

In spite of the Little Arkansas Treaties, which contained pledges of mutual peace and protection, the soil of the new Kiowa, Comanche, Cheyenne, and Arapaho domains was bloodied by contests between Indian defenders and settlers. The reduced hunting ranges assigned the tribes by the Little Arkansas Treaties were endangered by the failure of the Senate to ratify these pacts. Moreover, the refusal of federal officials on the western border to protect tribal territorial rights guaranteed by these pending treaties put the Indians under heavy pressure from land-hungry settlers pressing into the eastern margins of the assigned domains. The flow of traffic along old trails across these tribal ranges increased; American hunters slaughtered the buffalo, so essential to the survival of these tribes, for hides.

Within two years, federal officials could see that the tribal domains assigned by the Little Arkansas Treaties would have to be reduced to satisfy the expanding land desires of settlers and railroad builders. Widespread trespass and intrusion on treaty-assigned ranges were clear violations, which irritated the Indians, and when federal troops failed to protect their rights, the tribes assumed this function themselves.

Retaliatory strikes by Indians against intruders caused federal commanders to campaign against the tribes. In April 1867 General Winfield Scott Hancock led a large cavalry and infantry force across western Kansas. On the Pawnee Fork, his troops captured and burned a Cheyenne village of 250 lodges. The infuriated Indians, in retaliation, stopped almost all travel across western Kansas; survey parties for the Kansas Pacific Railroad were held up for a month. Constant and intense campaigns against the Kiowas, Comanches, Cheyennes, and Arapahoes throughout the summer of 1867 made the Indians ready for a truce which came in October 1867 at a grand council on Medicine Lodge Creek, 70 miles south of Fort Larned in southwestern Kansas, just north of the Indian Territory border.

Principal Indian spokesmen at the Medicine Lodge Council included Stumbling Bear, Satank, and Satanta for the Kiowas; Ten Bears and Little Horn for the Comanches; Wolf's Sleeve and Brave Man for the Plains Apaches; and, for the Cheyennes and Arapahoes, Black Kettle, Whirlwind, and Tall Bear. This was the most colorful assemblage ever gathered on the southern Plains. Buffalo-hide tipis were scattered along the stream banks for miles. Over 7,000 Indians gathered to watch their chiefs match wits with the federal commissioners and to receive gifts of cloth, paint, and beads sent to them, according to the issue sergeant, by their Great White Father in Washington. Members of the federal Peace Commission included Commissioner of Indian Affairs Nathaniel G. Taylor, Senator John B. Henderson of Missouri (chairman of the Senate committee on Indian affairs), Samuel F. Tappan, John B. Sanborn, General Alfred Terry, General William S. Harney, and Colonel Christopher C. Augur. The importance of the Medicine Lodge Council was indicated by the presence of several newspaper correspondents who covered the proceedings.

The treaties negotiated during the Medicine Lodge Council are very important historically, but the Indian oratory, reflecting the pathos of harassed people, also provided a rare insight into the character of these raiders of the Plains. The American commissioners warned that the buffalo would soon disappear and that, for their own good, the chiefs must lead their peoples to settled lives on reservations in the Indian Territory and set examples by taking up farming and peaceful living. Ten Bears and Satanta gave the most forceful responses.

The first to speak was Satanta, the Kiowa chief who was acknowledged as "the orator of the plains. . . . He was a tall man and good-looking, with plenty of long shiny black hair, dark piercing eyes, a consuming vanity, and a quick temper. His presence was commanding and he was able to sway the councils of his people. He was respected, too, as a warrior." He faced the commissioners and declared:

All the land south of the Arkansas belongs to the Kiowas and Comanches, and I don't want to give away any of it. I love the land and the buffalo and I will not part with any. . . . I have heard you intend to settle us on a reservation near the [Wichita] mountains. I don't want to settle there. I love to roam over the wide prairie, and when I do, I feel free and happy, but when we settle down we grow pale and die. . . . I don't like that, and when I see it, my heart feels like bursting with sorrow. I have spoken.

Ten Bears spoke next.

The Comanches are not weak and blind, like the pups of a dog when seven sleeps old. They are strong and far-sighted, like grown horses. . . . There are things which you have said to me which I did not like. They were not sweet like sugar, but bitter like gourds. You said that you wanted to put us upon a reservation, to build us houses and make us medicine lodges. I do not want them. I was born upon the prairies, where the wind blew free, and there was nothing to break the light of the sun. I was born where there were no enclosures and where everything drew a free breath. I want to die there, and not within walls. I know every stream and every wood between the Rio Grande and the Arkansas. I have hunted and lived over that country. I lived like my fathers before me, and like them, I lived happily.[7]

These rhapsodic speeches had little effect upon the commissioners; before the council closed the chiefs had reluctantly assented to drastically reduced territories. By the terms of the Medicine Lodge Treaties, the Kiowas and Comanches were assigned a reservation in the Leased District on lands taken from the Choctaws and Chickasaws by the Reconstruction Treaties of 1866. The 1,200 Kiowas and 1,700 Comanches received a 3 million-acre domain. In addition, 300 Kiowa-Apaches confederated with the Kiowas and Comanches and agreed to settle on their reservation. The Cheyennes and Arapahoes were assigned a reservation in the Cherokee Outlet, bounded by the Cimarron and Arkansas rivers. Those Indians, numbering about 2,000 Cheyennes and 1,200 Arapahoes, actually settled south of the designated reservation on the North Canadian River. An executive order in 1869 established a new Cheyenne-

Arapaho reservation, containing nearly 5 million acres; south of the Outlet line and between the ninety-eighth and one hundredth meridians, it extended to the Kiowa-Comanche line on the Washita.

In 1872 the Cheyenne-Arapaho domain was reduced by about 600,000 acres when federal officials established a reservation on the Washita River for about 1,100 Wichitas, Caddoes, absentee Delawares, and remnants of the Texas tribes—Keechies, Anadarkoes, Ionies, and Wacoes. These Indian settlers had been colonized in the Leased District before the Civil War.

War Department officials and General of the Army William T. Sherman and field commanders Philip Sheridan and Ranald Mackenzie were convinced that these and many other Western tribes were still untamed and that they would remain on reservations only after their war-making potential had been completely destroyed. Therefore, while "Peace Policy" agents worked on the reservations attempting to lead their charges along the "white man's road," the military developed a standby "Force Policy." New military posts were constructed at strategic points over the Great Plains, in the Rocky Mountains, and in the Southwest as support bases for regular cavalry and infantry units, which were held in readiness to strike at errant tribes.

Federal officials failed to deliver the rations and other considerations promised by the commissioners at Medicine Lodge Council. Kiowa, Comanche, Cheyenne, and Arapaho warriors claimed that the failure of the United States to keep its pledge excused the tribes from observing the treaties, and during 1868 small bands, well-mounted and heavily armed, left the reservations to roam over the Plains hunting buffalo and occasionally raiding settlements in western Kansas, Nebraska, and Texas. Troops found it almost impossible to confront the scattered, fast-moving parties. In the late summer of 1868 General Alfred Sully's column finally located a village of Kiowas and Comanches in the North Canadian Valley but the strength of the encampment caused him to beat a hasty retreat to Fort Dodge.

Federal commanders on the western frontier determined on a winter campaign, a stroke they expected to be effective for several reasons. First, the Indians would be concentrated in large villages for winter quarters. Second, they would not be expecting trouble, because federal troops usually left them alone during the colder months, mostly because the Indians were quiet then. And third, the Indians would be unable to defend themselves as effectively as during the spring and summer because their horses would be weakened by sparse winter forage.

The winter campaign was planned to begin at Fort Supply, one of the new Indian control posts in the Cherokee Outlet at the junction of Beaver River and Wolf Creek. Federal troops from Fort Lyon, Colorado, Fort Bascom, New Mexico, and the Nineteenth Kansas Cavalry were to join the Seventh Cavalry at Fort Supply. However, in late November 1868, a heavy snowstorm swept into the southern Plains and delayed the troops converging from Colorado, New Mexico, and Kansas. Colonel George Armstrong Custer, commander of the Seventh Cavalry, was anxious to move on the Indians' winter encampments, located nearly 100 miles due south of Fort Supply, before they learned of the winter campaign. Therefore, he proceeded south with his troopers, a military band, and three scouts—California Joe and two Osage trackers—over the cold, snow-covered Plains of the western Indian Territory.

On the morning of November 27, 1868, Custer's scouts located a large Indian village on the upper Washita. The Seventh Cavalry surrounded the settlement, smashed it with a roaring dawn attack, and caught the sleeping Indians by such complete surprise that only the slightest resistance was possible. The massacre that followed was identified in the official reports as the Battle of the Washita. Cheyenne Chief Black Kettle, who had miraculously escaped death at the Sand Creek Massacre in eastern Colorado in 1864, was among the 102 Cheyenne warriors, and many women and children, slain in the Washita Massacre. Custer's troopers slaughtered the village herd of 800 Indian ponies, burned every lodge in the encampment, and gathered up over 50 women and children as prisoners.

General Sheridan followed up the Washita campaign with a thrust south into the Leased District. From their base at old Fort Cobb, 1,500 troops rounded up scattered bands of Kiowas and Comanches, forcing the Indians to establish their camps near Fort Cobb, where the soldiers could watch them. While in the area Sheridan selected the site for a new post on the edge of the Wichita Mountains; he named it Fort Sill. Sheridan's devastating winter campaign and the relentless watch his troopers maintained over the tribes appeared to pacify the warriors. But an undercurrent of discontent was evident by 1870 and threatened to flower into a full-scale uprising. Congress had reduced appropriations for purchasing rations for the reservation tribes, and the agents had to permit small bands of Indians to go to the Plains to hunt buffalo. The warriors were sickened and angered at what they saw. A great demand for buffalo hides and robes in eastern markets had attracted white hunters, who roamed up and down the Plains slaughtering thousands of bison each day, taking only the hides and leaving the carcasses to rot.

Another disturbing influence that produced great unrest among the tribes was the fact that several bands had not yet come to the reservation to surrender to the military. The deadliest group still free was the hostile Quahada Comanche band led by the famous Quanah Parker, son of a Comanche chief and a white captive from Texas. Warriors from the Quahada band frequently slipped into the Kiowa-Comanche reservation and taunted the peaceful Indians, calling them cowards and "squaws," the height of Indian derision, and urging them to join Quanah in his resistance to white domination. Beginning in 1870, small parties began slipping away from the reservation to attack the settlements. Usually the warriors made their way on foot to make detection more difficult. Once across the Red River, they prowled about the ranches and stole horses and weapons. Then, armed and mounted, they began their work of death and destruction. One of the more famous raids was carried out in 1871 by a party of Kiowas led by Satanta, Satank, and Big Tree. Near Jacksboro, Texas, they plundered and destroyed a wagon train, killing the teamster crew.

There were raids more destructive than the Jacksboro incident, but its aftermath was of fundamental significance for the future of the Plains tribes. The three leaders, Satanta, Satank, and Big Tree, were arrested soon after their return to the reservation and held for trial in Texas. This marked a drastic departure from the established practice and became a precedent; thereafter leaders were held personally responsible for actions of their followers. Satanta, Satank, and Big Tree were shackled and hauled by wagon across the Red River. Satank slipped his bonds and attempted to kill one of his guards, but was shot by the cavalry escort. Satanta and Big Tree were tried and sentenced to death as punishment for the killings at Jacksboro, but the Texas governor commuted the sentences to life imprisonment. The Kiowas petitioned state and federal officials to parole their chiefs. Finally, federal officials agreed to use their influence to gain freedom for Satanta and Big Tree, in exchange for which the Kiowas and Comanches were to remain on their reservation and keep the peace. The agreement set the release date for late in 1873. The tribes scrupulously observed the terms, and Satanta and Big Tree were paroled as promised.

The return of the famous raider chiefs to the Kiowa-Comanche reservation seemed to be a signal for renewed depredations. The year 1874 was a bloody one on the southwestern frontier; the many engagements between bands of mounted Indians and wide-ranging cavalry units became known in military history as the Red River Wars. Federal commanders launched a major offensive during 1874 to end once and for all the military strength of the southern Plains tribes. General Nelson A. Miles was placed in command of a force that contained eight troops of cavalry—including Colonel Mackenzie's famed Fourth Cavalry—four companies of infantry, a battery of artillery, and a company of guides and scouts, principally Delawares. His orders were to comb the region between the Cimarron and Red rivers for Indians off the reservations. Between August and December 1874 Miles's army maintained a relentless pressure upon the Indians; one by one the resisting bands came into Fort Sill or Fort Reno to surrender. The last to capitulate were the Quahada Comanches, led by Quanah Parker.

Three things happened to each band: the troops at Fort Sill and Fort Reno appropriated the Indians' horses, disarmed the warriors, and arrested the chiefs. Satanta, having broken parole, was returned to prison in Texas. Seventy-two raider chiefs were placed in irons and hauled under heavy guard to military prison at Fort Marion in St. Augustine, Florida. Finally, the warriors of the fierce southern Plains tribes, leaderless, disarmed, and stripped of their horses, were thoroughly pacified. They settled down to the dull routines of reservation life, demoralized by the drastic change in life-style confronting them but studiously thwarting the attempt of the agents to lead them along the "white man's road."

Conquest of the Northern Plains Tribes

The United States army also applied its "Force Policy" to Native Americans living on the Northern Great Plains. During 1865 federal commissioners had attempted to negotiate with the Sioux and northern Cheyennes in order to complete the railroad construction corridor through the central Great Plains. General Grenville Dodge managed to meet with some Sioux bands and drew from them a pledge of peace, but he was unable to contact a sufficient number of band leaders to negotiate a definitive treaty. Finally, in June 1866 a delegation of Brule and Oglala Sioux headed by Red Cloud met with American officials at Fort Laramie. Federal demands upon the northern Plains tribes included assent to improvement and fortification of a traders' trail known as the Bozeman Road, which ran from Fort Laramie to the newly discovered Virginia City, Montana, mines. The Bozeman Road led northwest along the Powder River on the east side of the Big Horn Mountains, then across the headwaters of the Yellowstone and over Bozeman Pass into the mining country. Because it traversed the prime buffalo hunting range of the Sioux, Red Cloud refused to hold discussions with United States officials on any subject until federal officials abandoned their plan to improve and fortify the Bozeman Road. On this note, the Fort Laramie council of 1866 ended.

In 1866 Colonel Henry B. Carrington led a force of regular cavalry and infantry into the Powder River country to guard the Bozeman Road. His troops erected three posts along the road—Fort Reno, Fort Phil Kearny, and Fort C. F. Smith. Red Cloud's warriors made travel on the Bozeman Road risky; freighters and miners used it at great peril. So intense was the Sioux pressure on this artery that, on several occasions between 1866 and 1868, they choked off all travel. Sioux parties also closely watched the military posts on the Bozeman Road and made it difficult for troops to escort caravans over the road and guard the posts at the same time. Fort Kearny, particularly, was in a stage of siege most of the time.

Two incidents from a long list of engagements along the Powder River road illustrate the determination of the Sioux to exclude Americans from their hunting grounds. Sioux raiders regularly attacked details sent out from the post to cut wood. On December 21, 1866, they attacked a wood detail near Fort Kearny. When Captain William J. Fetterman led a cavalry force of 80 men to rescue the woodcutters, Sioux raiders decoyed the riders into a trap and killed every man in the column. Soldiers on the Bozeman Road regarded the Fetterman Massacre a senseless waste of lives. Captain Fetterman, when ordered to rescue the woodcutters, had proudly declared that with 80 men he could ride through the entire Sioux nation.

Some months later, on August 2, 1867, at the Wagon Box Fight, the attitude was different. Thirty troopers commanded by Captain J. N. Powell were guarding a crew of woodcutters working near Fort Kearny when the inevitable Sioux attack came. Captain Powell's response to the raid indicated the new respect the troops had for Sioux warriors and the caution they now employed in combat. Rather than answer the Indians' challenge to pursue them on horseback, Powell directed his men to circle the wood wagons, which were turned on their sides and used as impromptu fortresses to protect the riflemen while they rebuffed the fierce Sioux charges. Powell's men held off the Sioux until relief arrived from Fort Kearny.

Finally during April 1868 Sioux and northern Cheyenne leaders met with the federal Peace Commission at Fort Laramie. The treaties negotiated at the council provided that the federal government would abandon the Bozeman Road and other travel routes and military posts in the Sioux hunting range. In return, the Sioux and northern Cheyennes accepted fixed reservations in the Dakota, Montana, and Wyoming territories, with a hunting annex in the Big Horn-Powder River region. The northern Plains tribes pledged peace with the United States and unimpeded passage for construction of railroads.

The Fort Laramie Treaty of 1868 was followed by a general increase in activity north of the Platte River, associated with the survey and construction parties of the railroads. Inevitably, incidents occurred between Indians and workmen, immigrants, and soldiers; according to the Sioux the trouble was due to trespass and general disregard for the Indian rights guaranteed by the

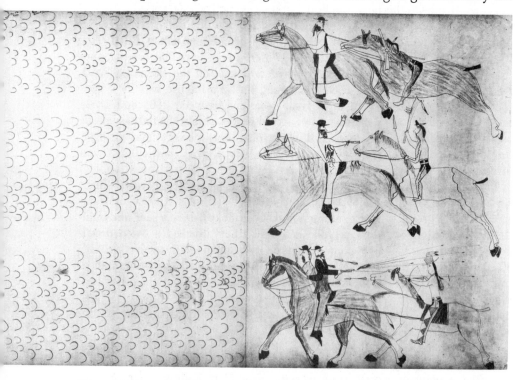

Pictograph drawn by Red Horse at the Cheyenne River Agency in South Dakota, 1881. He shows the Indians charging the white soldiers in Major Reno's column in the Battle of Little Bighorn. (Smithsonian Institution, National Anthropological Archives)

Fort Laramie Treaty. The increased activity on the northern Plains disturbed the buffalo and made hunting more difficult; the Indians had to range over wider areas to find the buffalo. Hunters in the employ of railroad companies also killed buffalo to feed the rail construction crews, and hide hunters slaughtered the huge, hairy beasts for the skins, leaving the carcasses to rot. The tribes who were dependent upon the bison for food, shelter, and clothing were incensed. Federal officials on the Plains actually encouraged extermination of the buffalo—the "Indians' commissary." The reasoning was that as long as there were buffalo to hunt, the Indians would have an excuse to leave the reservations. Once the animals were eradicated, Native Americans would become dependent upon government rations and farming for subsistence. Military commanders claimed that all too often the Indians mixed the buffalo hunt with raids on immigrant trains and rail construction crews.

Thus in the final stage of conquest federal officials encouraged deliberate extermination of the buffalo. This practice figured prominently in the ultimate defeat of the Indians because it destroyed their economic foundation for survival and action, including military resistance. Another factor which contributed to the ultimate conquest of resisting Indians was application of new technology to Indian campaigns. Firearms manufacturers had developed rapid-fire weapons, both sidearms and rifles, which the War Department finally adopted as standard equipment for the Indian-fighting army. Now the troopers had a singular combat advantage over their less well-armed foes. Railroad extension was also a factor in the final conquest. The first transcontinental line, the Union Pacific and Central Pacific, was completed in 1869; shortly, several others paralleled it on the north and the south. These main lines and connecting spurs made it possible to move troops quickly from one point to another in a matter of hours which, in prerailroad times, may have required days or weeks. The conquest noose tightened about the few surviving free tribes.

Throughout the period between 1868 and 1876, Sioux and northern Cheyenne warriors brushed with the military. One of the most dramatic contests was the Battle of Beecher's Island. In September 1868 Colonel George A. Forsyth rode out from Fort Wallace in western Kansas into eastern Colorado with 50 men to scout for Indians. While camped on the Arikaree River, they were surrounded by a large Sioux and Cheyenne party. Forsyth's men set up a sand-pit breastworks on an island in the river and fought an eight-day battle; they were nearly wiped out before the Indians withdrew. The defenders were able to turn back charge after charge only because of their superior firepower provided by new repeating rifles and a large supply of ammunition.

The time of reckoning and defeat approached for the northern Plains peoples just as it had for the southern Plains tribes. Incidents leading up to the climax began in 1874. The first was precipitated when prospectors from the mining towns in Montana and Idaho claimed that they had found rich gold deposits in the Black Hills, in the heart of the Sioux reservation in Dakota

Territory. In 1874, Colonel Custer led the Seventh Cavalry through the Black Hills, ostensibly to answer Sioux complaints and expel intruders, but really to escort a geological reconnaissance to confirm the gold find. The Sioux were also pressed from the north by the construction of the Northern Pacific Railway which, by 1872, had reached the Missouri River at the Mandan villages. Increasing numbers of miners entered the Black Hills during 1875. The Sioux threatened retaliation against the intruders, and federal officials attempted unsuccessfully to purchase the Black Hills from the Indians.

Sioux bands left their reservations in protest and reportedly were preparing to sweep through the country and destroy the prospectors. Federal agents sent messages to the Indians ordering them to return to their reservations by February 1, 1876, or face military action. The bands who received the message ignored it. The principal leaders in the Sioux nation at this time were Crazy Horse—Red Cloud's successor to Oglala military leadership after the latter determined on a course of peace following the Fort Laramie Council—and Sitting Bull, leader of the Hunkpapa group of Teton Sioux.

During the winter of 1875–1876, federal commanders on the northern Plains planned a punitive expedition into the Sioux country. Three columns were to converge on the principal Sioux concentration, believed to be on the Big Horn River and its tributaries. One column under General George Crook was to move north out of Fort Fetterman, Wyoming, into Montana. A second column under Colonel John Gibbon was to march east from Fort Ellis, Montana. The third column, commanded by General Alfred Terry, and including the Seventh Cavalry led by Colonel Custer, was to move from Fort Abraham Lincoln in Dakota Territory west to the Big Horn. Crook marched his column out of Fort Fetterman along the old Bozeman Road in March of 1876. On two occasions his men came upon scattered Sioux villages; they destroyed over 100 lodges, but fierce Indian counterattacks slowed his advance toward the rendezvous on the Yellowstone. After the first encounter, in March, Crook returned his men to Fort Fetterman to recuperate. His contacts with the Sioux were inconclusive, but they held him up, destroyed the element of surprise, and made impossible the coordination required for the success of the overall campaign. Nonetheless, the other two columns met on the Yellowstone at the mouth of the Powder River, and scouting reports confirmed a large encampment of Sioux in the valley of the Little Big Horn.

Terry sent Custer and 12 troops of the Seventh Cavalry to close retreat at the south end of the valley. On June 25, he came upon the Indian settlement. Dividing his column into 4 sections and placing 3 in position to check flight from the village, he led the fourth section—consisting of 225 men—along the Little Big Horn River toward the village. En route, Sioux and northern Cheyenne defenders intercepted the attack force. Custer and every trooper in this section were slain. The dispersed sections of the Seventh Cavalry were pinned down and saved from extinction only by the timely arrival of elements from the main force.

Sioux exultation at the victory over the Seventh Cavalry was brief. Massed federal troops forced the Sioux and northern Cheyennes to abandon their encampment on the Little Big Horn and relentlessly pursued the retreating Indians. Band leaders surrendered and led their followers back to the reservations. Crazy Horse was shot down during 1877 in what was reported to be an escape attempt. Sitting Bull and a group of followers fled to Canada; they returned to the Sioux reservation in Dakota Territory in 1881. By the end of 1876 the northern Plains, like the southern Plains, were quiet and peaceful. The tribes had been subdued, the barrier to settlement and development had been removed. The military conquest of the western tribes was nearly completed. Peripheral resistance to Anglo-American dominion posed by the Modocs, Mexican Kickapoos, Nez Percés, Utes, and western Apaches, was dealt with in a summary fashion by the federal military establishment.

The Conquest of the Modocs

The surviving members of the Modoc tribe lived on the Klamath Reservation on the California-Oregon border. In 1869 President Grant appointed Methodist Albert B. Meacham as "Peace Policy" agent for the Oregon tribes. Meacham's strong commitment to lead the Klamath Reservation Indians along the "white man's road" and his intensive suppression of tribal customs an-

Apache mercenary serving with the U.S. Army during the Modoc conquest in 1872. (U.S. Signal Corps, National Archives)

417

tagonized the Modocs. Kenitpoos, better known as Captain Jack, led a group of protesting Modocs off the reservation in 1870. When local citizens became alarmed and appealed for protection, troops were rushed to the troubled zone. The Modocs took refuge in the Lava Beds near Tule Lake and successfully defended themselves.

In April 1873 Modoc leaders met in council with a peace commission which included General Edward R. S. Canby and Meacham. During the proceedings, the Indians killed Canby and wounded Meacham. Thereupon, a force of 1,500 troops moved in for the kill, and Captain Jack surrendered on June 1, 1874. An army court martial tried and convicted him and 3 other Modoc leaders, and they were executed by hanging. The resisting Modocs were shipped off to the Indian Territory as prisoners of war and were settled on Quapaw Agency lands. In 1909, the Modocs were permitted to return to the Klamath Reservation, although about 50 chose to remain in Oklahoma, the former Indian Territory.

The Conquest of the Mexican Kickapoos

Beginning in the spring of 1865, the Mexican Kickapoos, claiming that Texas had declared war on the tribe by the attack at Concho River, launched a ten-year offensive against Texas. The campaign was unmatched for calculated vindictiveness and destruction of life and property. Before Kickapoo vengeance was finally satisfied, marauding bands from the Coahuila sanctuary across the international boundary had destroyed millions of dollars' worth of property, killed hundreds of Texas citizens, carried countless children into captivity, and completely desolated entire counties on the Texas side of the Rio Grande. The war also embroiled the United States in a dispute with Mexico when federal troops trespassed on Mexican soil to raid the Kickapoo settlement; the incident provoked a diplomatic tiff that involved an embarrassed Congress, the secretary of state, and the President.

In response to petitions, letters, and memorials from distressed and suffering Texans along the Rio Grande, the national government in 1873 paid serious attention to the Mexican Kickapoos. Colonel Ranald Mackenzie, fresh from victories over the Comanches in the North, arrived on the Rio Grande in the spring of 1873 with his famous Fourth Cavalry and orders to smash the Kickapoos. On May 17, the cavalry moved out of Fort Duncan and crossed the river into Mexico to make a surprise attack on the Kickapoo settlement near Nacimiento on the Remolino River. Scouts had reported that most of the warriors were away hunting and raiding. The next day, the troopers reached the Remolino and struck the villages in a lightning-swift attack. In a matter of minutes the settlement was a shambles. The troopers burned the dwellings, "ruin and desolation now marked the spot—a cyclone could not have made more havoc or a cleaner sweep" where scarcely an hour before had stood the prosperous villages of the Mexican Kickapoos.[8]

Mackenzie's mission had been accomplished. The soldiers gathered fifty women and children captives and beat a hasty return to the Rio Grande. The captives were held at Fort Gibson to lure the warriors to Indian Territory. Shortly thereafter, 317 Kickapoo husbands, parents, and relatives of the prisoners moved from Coahuila to the Indian Territory. Agents settled them on lands on the Sac and Fox reservation. Nearly 400 Kickapoos remained in Mexico, but they had been generally pacified by the Mackenzie raid.

The Conquest of the Nez Percés

Extension of the mining frontier into Idaho and Montana during the 1860s displaced many tribes occupying the territory between the Rocky Mountains and the Cascades; it also produced the inevitable reduction of Indian lands. One tribe, the Nez Percés, who had an unbroken record of peace with the United States, was particularly exploited during this period. A treaty with the United States, negotiated in 1855, had guaranteed perpetual tenure of their territory on the tributaries of the Snake River. But soon the press of settlement led to demands for Nez Percés' land, and in 1863 federal commissioners negotiated a treaty with selected tribal leaders providing for the cession of the Wallowaw country, valued by the Nez Percés for its salmon-filled streams and the rich pastures on which they grazed their herds of cattle and horses. This treaty assigned the tribe a small reservation at Lapwai near Lewiston.

The Nez Percés living in the Wallowaw country refused to move. In 1877 settlers trespassed on Nez Percés territory; the Indians killed 13 intruders, and federal troops came to drive the Indians to Lapwai. Chief Joseph collected his Nez Percés band of 200 warriors, with their women and children, and fled to evade the military dragnet. They roamed over Idaho, Wyoming, and Montana on a 1,300 mile sweep, pausing occasionally to inflict embarrassing defeats on the pursuing army. At the Battle of Big Hole, Nez Percés warriors defeated Gibbons' troops. Tenacious columns led by Crook, Gibbons, and General O. O. Howard continued the pursuit and finally forced the Nez Percés to a stand in the Bear Paw Mountains of north-central Montana. On October 4, 1877, after a five-day battle, to save the women and children from freezing, Chief Joseph surrendered. Federal authorities sent the Nez Percés to the Indian Territory as prisoners of war and settled them in the Cherokee Outlet on the Salt Fork River. In 1885 they were permitted to return to the Northwest to the Colville Reservation in Washington.

The Conquest of the Utes

Repression of tribal customs by government agents produced a revolt on the Ute reservation in western Colorado. The victims of earlier conquest and relocation, the Utes, who numbered about 3,600, occupied a tract on the White River west of the Continental Divide. Portions of the reservation contained timber, some minerals, and scattered agricultural lands. Colorado statehood in 1876 fired in the citizens a strong desire for the lands included within the reservation. Politicians campaigned on the slogan "The Utes Must Go!" Ouray, the principal tribal leader, urged the Utes to bend a bit and to rely more on farming in order to protect their claim to the White River Reservation.

In 1879, Agent Nathan Meeker established a program of comprehensive detribalization for the Utes. Douglas, an old warrior chief, led a revolt that resulted in the killing of Meeker and 11 other whites. Ute warriors later defeated an invading military force of nearly 200 men, killing 14 soldiers. Thereupon, a large federal and state militia force marched through the Ute country and mercilessly drove the Indians to a new reservation in Utah Territory at Uintah and Ouray. Only a small group of Utes was permitted to remain in southwestern Colorado.

The Conquest of the Apaches

The western Apaches were the last Native Americans to capitulate. By 1871, the federal government was ready to deal decisively with these peoples. Vincent Colyer, representing the Bureau of Indian Affairs and the Board of Indian Commissioners, traveled to the Southwest and laid out 4 reservations— one in New Mexico Territory and 3 in Arizona Territory—for concentrating the Apaches. He assigned the fierce Chiricahuas and Mimbreños to the San Carlos Reservation on the Gila River. Next, federal officials attempted to send word to the scattered Apache bands directing them to locate promptly on the reservations.

General Crook with a large force of cavalry and infantry ranged across New Mexico Territory and Arizona Territory, pressing the scattered bands to comply. Most Apaches submitted to reservation life, but a few restless holdouts watched for the opportunity to escape its confines. Beginning in 1874, Victorio, a Mimbreño Apache who had served with Mangas Coloradas, led the bolder spirits, rarely numbering over 50, on destructive raids against the scattered settlements and ranches of the Southwest. Over 2,000 troops were in the field most of the time between 1874 and 1880 pursuing this wily Apache guerrilla. In 1880 he was slain in northern Mexico by Mexican frontier troops.

The elderly Nana succeeded Victorio and led the raiders briefly until Geronimo emerged as the leader. Geronimo's depredations in the Southwest led to massed operations against him in 1883; he was forced to surrender and return to the reservation. In 1885, he again left the reservation at the head of a band of fewer than 50 men and about 100 women and children. Over 4,000 troops, operating in small parties, searched for this Apache band. Finally, in 1886, Geronimo surrendered. Following his capitulation federal officials sent him and nearly 500 other Apaches to military prison at Fort Pickens in Pensacola, Florida. In 1887, the Apaches were removed to Mount Vernon Barracks, Alabama, where one fourth of them died of tuberculosis and other diseases.

Apache prisoners-of-war in ankle shackles, after 1880. (Smithsonian Institution, National Anthropological Archives)

Finally, federal officials moved the Apaches to the Kiowa-Comanche Reservation in the Indian Territory and placed them under the guns of Fort Sill. Their status as prisoners of war continued until 1913.

The conquest of the Indians had begun in 1500 as Spain, France, Holland,

Geronimo's Apache band on the way to military prison in Florida in 1886. (U.S. Signal Corps, National Archives)

Russia, Great Britain, and the United States successively attempted to integrate Native Americans and tribal territories into their imperial systems. Anglo-American victories over the western Apaches in 1886 destroyed the last vestige of Indian military power. In defeat's aftermath federal officials forcibly assigned the vanquished tribes to reservations, a melancholy fate which made death at the hands of the conqueror seem merciful. The ordeal of reservation life is the subject of Chapter Seventeen.

Notes

1. William T. Hagan, *American Indians* (Chicago, 1961), p. 111.
2. Henry E. Fritz, *The Movement for Indian Assimilation, 1860–1890* (Philadelphia, 1963), p. 71.
3. Arrell Morgan Gibson, *Oklahoma: A History of Five Centuries* (Norman, Okla., 1965), p. 221.
4. *Ibid.*, p. 234.
5. Hagan, *American Indians*, p. 104.
6. Gibson, *Oklahoma*, p. 241.
7. *Ibid.*, pp. 238–39.
8. Arrell Morgan Gibson, *The Kickapoos: Lords of the Middle Border* (Norman, Okla., 1963), p. 243.

Selected Sources

The final conquest of aboriginal America includes Native American travail under Reconstruction, the second Trail of Tears or renewed tribal colonization in the Indian Territory, new federal policy for managing the subdued tribes, and the last military campaigns by federal troops against resisting Indians. The victorious Union government applied Reconstruction to the Five Civilized Tribes as a punishment for supporting the Confederacy during the Civil War. Principal work on this subject is Annie H. Abel, *The American Indian under Reconstruction* (Cleveland, 1925). Reconstruction is also discussed in *The Rise and Fall of the Choctaw Republic* (Norman, Okla., 1934), *And Still the Waters Run* (Princeton, N.J., 1940), and *The Road to Disappearance* (Norman, Okla., 1941), all by Angie Debo; Grace S. Woodward, *The Cherokees* (Norman, Okla., 1963); Morris L. Wardell, *A Political History of the Cherokee Nation* (Norman, Okla., 1938); Edwin C. McReynolds, *The Seminoles* (Norman, Okla., 1957); Arrell Morgan Gibson, *The Chickasaws* (Norman, Okla., 1971); Edwin C. Bearss and Arrell Morgan Gibson, *Fort Smith: Little Gibraltar on the Arkansas* (Norman, Okla., 1969); and W. David Baird, *Peter Pitchlynn: Chief of the Choctaws* (Norman, Okla., 1972).

Postbellum colonization in the Indian Territory is a major subject in Frederick W. Hodge (ed.), *Handbook of American Indians North of Mexico* 2 vols. (1907; reprint ed. New York, 1959); William E. Unrau, *The Kansas Indians* (Norman, Okla., 1971); Arrell Morgan Gibson, *The Kickapoos: Lords of the Middle Border* (Norman, Okla., 1963); John J. Mathews, *The Osage: Children of the Middle Waters* (Norman, Okla., 1961); William T. Hagan, *The Sac and Fox Indians* (Norman, Okla., 1958); Douglas C. Jones, *The Treaty of Medicine Lodge* (Norman, Okla., 1966); and Muriel H. Wright, *Guide to the Indian Tribes of Oklahoma* (Norman, Okla., 1951).

Postwar federal Indian policy changes are traced in Henry E. Fritz, *The Movement for Indian Assimilation, 1860–1890* (Philadelphia, 1965); Francis P. Prucha, *American Indian Policy in Crisis: Christian Reformers and the Indian, 1865–1900* (Norman, Okla., 1976); Robert M. Utley, "The Celebrated Peace Policy of General Grant," *North Dakota History* 20 (July 1953), pp. 121–42; Roy W. Meyer, *History of the Santee Sioux: United States Indian Policy on Trial* (Lincoln, Neb., 1967); Peter J. Rahill, *The Catholic Indian Missions and Grant's Peace Policy, 1870–1884* (Washington, D.C., 1953); Elsie M. Rushmore, *The Indian Policy During Grant's Administration* (Jamaica, N.Y., 1914); Edward E. Dale, *The Indians of the Southwest: A Century of Development Under the United States* (Norman, Okla., 1949);

and Richard N. Ellis, *General Pope and U.S. Indian Policy* (Albuquerque, N.M., 1970).

The final Native American conquests are described in William H. Leckie, *The Military Conquest of the Southern Plains* (Norman, Okla., 1963); Donald J. Berthong, *The Southern Cheyennes* (Norman, Okla., 1963); Mildred Mayhall, *The Kiowas* (Norman, Okla., 1962); Ernest Wallace and E. Adamson Hoebel, *The Comanches: Lords of the South Plains* (Norman, Okla., 1952); Wilbur S. Nye, *Carbine and Lance: The Story of Old Fort Sill* (Norman, Okla., 1937); Robert C. Carriker, *Fort Supply, Indian Territory: Frontier Outpost on the Plains* (Norman, Okla., 1970); Dorothy M. Johnson, *The Bloody Bozeman: The Perilous Trail to Montana's Gold* (New York, 1971); Robert M. Utley, *Frontier Regulars: The United States Army and the Indian, 1866–1891* (New York, 1973); and *The Last Days of the Sioux Nation* (New Haven, Conn., 1963); James C. Olson, *Red Cloud and the Sioux Problem* (Lincoln, Neb., 1965); C. M. Oehler, *The Great Sioux Uprising* (New York, 1959); Robert A. Murray, *Military Posts in the Powder River Country of Wyoming, 1865–1894* (Lincoln, Neb., 1968); George E. Hyde, *Red Cloud's Folk: A History of the Oglala Sioux Indians* (Norman, Okla., 1937); Stanley Vestal, *Sitting Bull: Champion of the Sioux* (Norman, Okla., 1957); Robert Emmitt, *The Last War Trail: The Utes and the Settlement of Colorado* (Norman, Okla., 1954); Francis Haines, *The Nez Perces, Tribesmen of the Columbian Plateau* (Norman, Okla., 1955); Merrill D. Beal, *"I Will Fight No More Forever":* *Chief Joseph and the Nez Perces War* (Seattle, Wash., 1963); Alvin M. Josephy, *The Nez Perces Indians and the Opening of the Northwest* (New Haven, Conn., 1965); Keith A. Murray, *The Modocs and Their War* (Norman, Okla., 1968); Ralph H. Ogle, *Federal Control of the Western Apaches, 1848–1886* (Albuquerque, N.M., 1940); Arrell Morgan Gibson, *The Life and Death of Colonel Albert Jennings Fountain* (Norman, Okla., 1965); and Angie Debo, *Geronimo: The Man, His Time, His Place* (Norman, Okla., 1976).

CHAPTER 17

NATIVE AMERICAN NADIR: THE RESERVATION ERA

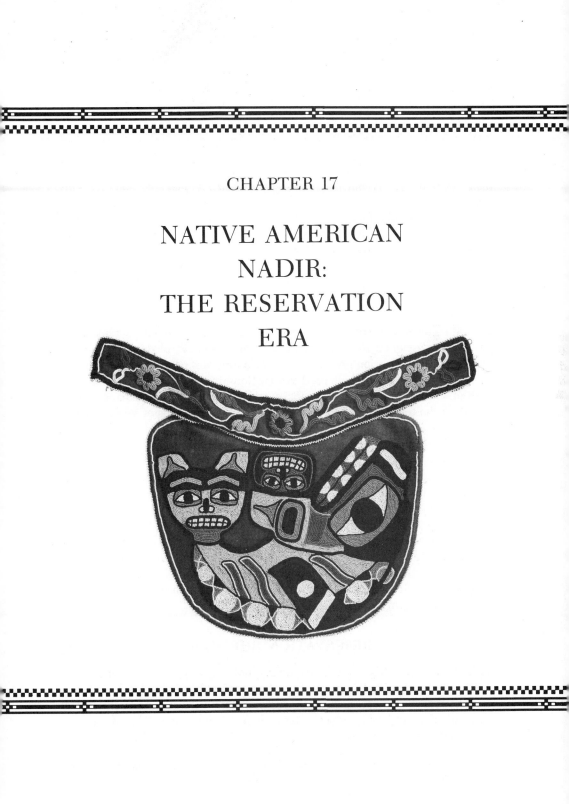

Once we were happy in our own country and we were seldom hungry, for then the two-leggeds and the four-leggeds lived together like relatives, and there was plenty for them and for us. But the Wasichus [white men] came, and they have made little islands for us and other little islands for the four-leggeds, and always these islands are becoming smaller, for around them surges the gnawing flood of the Wasichu.

Black Elk (Sioux) on reservation life, 1890

Once the rebellious tribes had been conquered and forced to remain on government-assigned reservations, federal agents could begin in earnest to apply the detribalization processes. The technique was not new. From colonial times Anglo-Americans had used reservations to remove Indians from the path of settler expansion. In the 1850s, swift transcontinental expansion had absorbed the territories of the western tribes. The demands of white citizens that Native Americans be removed from lands they desired led federal officials to begin the reduction of tribal territories and to assign the Indians to reservations, principally in California, the Pacific Northwest, and in the Rocky Mountains. Federal officials continued the policy of making reservation assignments during the Civil War; witness the Bosque Redondo ordeal of the Navajos and Mescaleros Apaches.

For many tribes the reservation era covered the period 1867 to 1887. It was an ordeal to be endured. In these twenty years, the federal government expected magically to transform the tribes from free, roving hunters and raiders to settled, peaceful, law-abiding wards made self-sufficient by the adoption of agriculture and stock raising. The reservation was to be the focus for tribal management and reformation.

RESERVATION RHETORIC

In its stance on public matters, including Indian policy, the national government reflected public opinion. And the American public in the late nineteenth century was almost unanimous in its view that Indian nations should be stripped of their lands and colonized on restricted reservations where detribalization could proceed.

Chapter Opening Artifact: Man's beaded bib or chest ornament—Tlingit. (Courtesy Museum of the American Indian, Heye Foundation)

Reservation Rationale

At least four viewpoints can be discerned in the public rationale for assigning Native Americans to reservations. First, the general public had more than a passing interest in the process of concentration and transformation of Indians. Nineteenth-century Anglo-American society maintained a public defensiveness toward ways that differed from established cultural values and practices. Thus tribal life-styles were regarded as threatening unchristian primitivism, and the national government was expected to expurgate them. Concentrating Indians on restricted reservations would permit their forced Americanization to proceed in an efficient manner. Native American transformation was essential because, in the public view, Indianness was an evil and comprised a threat to cherished national values. This was a survival of the Puritan view that Indians were a temporal manifestation of Satan, their nature-steeped customs a fatal diversion seeking to seduce Christian citizens. Assimilation, the biological absorption of Native Americans into the Anglo-American community, was an empty phrase as it had been from earliest colonial times. The general public was unyielding; theirs was a closed society, and they scorned the thought of absorbing Indians.

Thus Americanization, the detribalization and cultural transformation of Indians, was in reality not intended to make Indians worthy of intermarriage by Anglo-Americans, but rather for the vague purpose of "their own good." Anglo-Americans held the same expectation of blacks in Africa and natives of other parts of the world outside the pale of Christendom.

A second viewpoint, held by the growing numbers of westerners who lived next to the Indian nations, expected the federal government to concentrate tribes on reservations outside their state or territorial limits in the Indian Territory. Confined on reservations there and guarded by federal troops, Indians would no longer be a threat to regional peace and orderly development; their evacuated territories thereby would be opened to exploitation by stock growers, farmers, lumbermen, miners, railroad builders, town developers, and land speculators.

A third viewpoint, held by a small group of humanitarians, supported assigning the Indian tribes to reservations in order that Native Americans might be transformed by the civilization process, which to them meant "total integration in the dominant society." They were committed to complete assimilation of Indians into the Anglo-American mainstream. These humanitarians "sought to remold the Indian's conception of life . . . his system of values. If this could be changed, assimilationists reasoned, the Indian would then become like the white man." The humanitarians were largely ignored in the early reservation period, but their numbers and their influence over Indian policy gradually increased, and before the close of the nineteenth century they were able to produce substantive changes in Indian policy. They were in part responsible for the policy adopted after 1887 of liquidating many reservations, a step they regarded as being in the Native Americans' best interests.[1]

427

The fourth viewpoint, expressed by the managers of the reservation system—bureaucrats assigned the duty of containing Indians on reservations and transforming them through programs of Americanization—simply perceived reservation-confined Native Americans as a part of the continuing "Indian problem." Reservations were the proper punishment for those who had resisted Anglo-American expansion. For the most part Bureau of Indian Affairs officials were cynical toward the Indians' prospects, impersonal in dealing with them; many were corrupt as trustees in handling Indian property and funds, and all of them were impatient to conclude the task of transformation. Commissioner of Indian Affairs John Q. Smith in 1876 reflected this bureaucratic impatience:

The civilization or the utter destruction of the Indians is inevitable. The next twenty-five years are to determine the fate of a race. If they cannot be taught, and taught very soon, to accept the necessities of their situation and begin in earnest to provide for their own wants by labor in civilized pursuits, they are destined to speedy extinction.[2]

Reservation Goals

The interplay of these viewpoints yielded a set of policy goals for federal officials assigned to manage the reservations and their tribes. In many respects it was a replay of Jeffersonian doctrine that Indians were capable of civilization and ultimate assimilation. And, as in the early days of national development, in spite of talk that reduction of tribal territory was for the benefit of Indians, in fact as in earlier times, it really served to benefit Anglo-American settlers.

Thus the late nineteenth-century reservation system was to Americanize Indians according to a formula, requiring at least 25 to 30 years to complete. This formula consisted of 5 steps.

First: Self-sufficiency, and to achieve it the Indian was to be converted from hunting . . . to farming. [Stock raising was added later as an alternative.] His acquisitiveness was to be stimulated in a last stage by the introduction of private property. Second: Isolation [i.e. separation of the Indian from] the vicious, unscrupulous whites, who not only teach him their base ways, but defraud and rob him, and, often without cause, with as little compunction as they would in killing a dog, take his life. Third: Education, particularly of the manual labor variety. Fourth: Christianity, without which, that generation of Americans considered true civilization impossible. . . . Fifth. A system of law, to protect the individual property rights of the Indian as he evolved from communal ownership.[3]

THE AGENCY OF AMERICANIZATION

To fulfill these goals, the federal government maintained a bureaucracy with administrative authority flowing from the Department of the Interior through its Bureau of Indian Affairs to regional superintendencies, thence to agents on the reservations. Indian agents on the reservations enforced a growing body of law derived from administrative rulings of the secretary of the interior and the commissioner of Indian affairs, the laws of Congress, and federal court decisions. A citizen body, the Board of Indian Commissioners, watched over the management of reservations from their offices in the East and occasionally conducted field inspection of reservations, either in person or through hired investigators.

Reservations

These tribal territories, regarded as temporary residences while the Indians underwent their civilization training, had been assigned to the tribes by federal agents under authority of treaties and administrative rulings. Generally each reservation served as the home of a single tribe although in several cases more than one tribe occupied a common tract. Also, several reservations were often administered by a single agency. Reservations varied in size from tiny rancherías of less than 100 acres in California to the giant 14 million-acre Navajo reservation sprawling over portions of Arizona, New Mexico, and Utah. Federal officials had concentrated the greatest number of tribes—67—in the Indian Territory. There were also reservations in Minnesota, Iowa, Kansas, Nebraska, North and South Dakota, Colorado, Wyoming, Montana, Idaho, Nevada, Oregon, and Washington.

The Personnel

The Indian agent was the principal administrative official on the reservation. His duties included managing tribal property and funds, distributing annuities and rations, and supervising the Americanization process by eradicating tribal ways of life—polygamy, native religion, dances, rituals, and rites. He was expected to require his charges to abandon Indian garb and to accept "citizen dress." As a part of the detribalization process he was expected to suppress use of native language. Indians who persisted in the old native customs were to be punished by having their rations withheld. Children in government schools who faltered and used their tribal language were punished. In recent times Comanches have complained bitterly that when they were children their teachers literally "whipped the Comanche out of us."

To assist the Indian agent in leading Native Americans across the cultural threshold to the enriching bounty of Anglo-American civilization was the agency staff consisting of a clerk, physician, reservation farmer (vocational agriculture instructor), and a teacher. The Indian men were taught farming and animal husbandry, the women various household crafts; the native couples were to fuse into rural families recast in the Anglo-American prototype. On several reservations, the secretary of war directed the construction of military posts garrisoned with infantry and cavalry companies battle-ready to carry out the government's will against recalcitrant Indians. Later the agents were supported by squads of Indian police recruited from the young men of the tribes.

Where several tribes were attached to a major agency, as the Sac and Fox Agency or Ponca Agency, the Bureau of Indian Affairs established a sub-agency headed by a deputy or subagent for each of the assigned tribes. The agency compound on each reservation was centrally located to enable the staff to maintain optimum oversight of the Indians. Its components included agency grounds, agent's office building, storage sheds for rations and tools, a stable and dispensary, a school building, demonstration farm, church, and staff dwellings.

The Indian agent was the strategic official in the transformation process. Through the years this position had undergone a drastic change in function and authority. In the early life of the United States when collective Indian power was awesome, the Indian agent was more like a diplomatic official representing the United States to a particular Indian nation, living at the center of tribal government at the pleasure of the host tribe. However, Indian power had progressively diminished and Anglo-American power had concomitantly escalated to the point where, by 1875, the Indian agent, reflecting the drastically increased power of his government, had become to many Indian nations "the central authority figure in place of the Indian chief formerly looked to by the tribe for leadership."[4]

However, the agent's position among the Indians to whom he was assigned was diminished by the almost universal propensity of holders of this position for corruption. Each year the agent as tribal trustee handled considerable sums of Indian money, controlled issuance of contracts for agency improvements, livestock, farming equipment, rations, and seeds, and the leasing of tribal land. For most appointees to this position, the temptation was just too great. Indians were daily witnesses to this malfeasance and abuse of public trust, and they came to scorn and denounce those officials who were expected to set the example for them. Of course, not every agent was corrupt; there were a few honest, dedicated men in the Indian service. V. T. McGillicuddy, Oglala Sioux agent from 1879 to 1886, a man of great ability and unremitting integrity, won the respect of Indians on this potentially difficult and dangerous reservation. However, most Indian agents were susceptible to the temptations for the enhancement of their personal fortunes and this weakened the Americanization program on the reservations because Indians could not be expected to follow the directions of those whom they held in grand contempt.

Concerned citizens and serious-minded public officials attempted to overcome the image of incompetent and corrupt Indian agents. Henry B. Whipple, Episcopal bishop of Minnesota, a constant critic of Native American management, pointed out that "political patronage had a corrupting influence on Indian administration," which particularly centered on the agent, the federal official in day-to-day contact with the Indians. Thus the example he set was most crucial. Whipple explained that as western congressmen used their influence over federal patronage to reward supporting local politicians, one of the most sought-after positions was Indian agent because of the "tradition on the border that an Indian agent with fifteen hundred dollars a year can retire upon an ample fortune in four years. Indian funds were squandered by fraudulent contracts and ... schools were a sham. He urged "an end to the system of political appointments" stressing the importance of selecting as agency employees only persons of "purity, temperance, industry, and unquestioned integrity."[5]

President Grant had attempted to offset the image of corruption in the Indian service by using churchmen as "Peace Policy" agents, and the quality of reservation officials consequently improved. The spoils system was restored to the Indian service after 1877. Thereupon agents and reservation vocational and educational staffs, assigned the task of leading Indians along the "white man's road," were partisan appointees, and the quality of performance deteriorated accordingly. One writer has charged that after 1877 most agents were corrupt and that their staffs consisted of "instructors in agriculture who had never farmed, clerks who couldn't write, and teachers too dissolute or incompetent to hold positions in other schools."[6]

Periodic attempts were made by reform-minded department heads to purge corruption from the Indian service, but the spoils system, acknowledged as the prime cause of the problem, persisted. Finally in 1891 an executive order placed Indian school personnel, including superintendents, and agency physicians under the classified civil service. Five years later other reservation employees were removed from the spoils system. Then an act in 1893 permitted the commissioner of Indian affairs to eliminate the position of Indian agent by placing school superintendents in charge of agencies. However, this reform was not implemented for fifteen years.

Education

From colonial times an occasional concern of the emerging Anglo-American nation had been the education, civilization, and ultimate absorption of those Native Americans caught in the destructive avalanche of settler expansion. During Jefferson's presidency the government held education as the foremost means for preparing Indians for assimilation. Through the years Congress had appropriated token funds to provide minimal education for a limited number of young Indians. However, during the period before the Civil War, church-sponsored missionary groups, particularly the American Board of Commissioners for Foreign Missions, supported in part by these public funds, maintained the schools for Native Americans.

Those federal officials in charge of Americanizing Indians designed the postwar reservation education program to instruct both adults (in farming, animal husbandry, and homemaking in the Anglo-American mode) and children (intensive instruction based on a comprehensive basic education and vocational curriculum). Very soon federal administrators regarded Indian adults as hopeless protégés, and increasingly they placed emphasis upon educating Indian youth, regarded as more malleable than their parents.

Through the years Congress increased funds for Indian education from

$140,000 in 1870 to nearly $2 million in 1900. By the close of the nineteenth century, over 20,000 Indian students were enrolled in 148 boarding schools and 225 day schools. These institutions were maintained by federal funds, tribal funds, and missionary funds. Mission schools functioned under contract with the Bureau of Indian Affairs, which provided an annual subsidy until the 1890s when federal support was withdrawn. Thereafter sectarian schools for Native Americans were supported by mission and tribal funds.

Indian children attended boarding schools and day schools. Government agents and reformers preferred the off-reservation boarding school because it removed the Indian child for long periods from the influence of the aboriginal home environment. Army Captain Richard H. Pratt founded Carlisle Indian School at Carlisle Barracks, Pennsylvania, in 1879 to demonstrate to the public that Indians were educable. Carlisle became the model for off-reservation boarding schools established in the Indian Territory, Nebraska, Oregon, New Mexico, Arizona, and other western states and territories with large Indian populations.

Indian schools were of the vocational-manual labor type. The curriculum included instruction in reading, writing, arithmetic, spelling, and other basic education subjects. One half of each day was spent in vocational-manual labor duty in the shops and fields of the school. Each school was expected to be self-sufficient, the students to raise its food, dairy, and poultry products. Girls worked in the kitchen to learn homemaking. The school regime was steeped in military discipline. Students dressed in cadet uniforms, they drilled in military formation each day, and they marched to class, to the mess hall, and to labor in the fields. Instructors applied harsh discipline in the dormitory, the classroom, and on the school grounds. They punished errant Indian children for speaking in their tribal language and for slips in rules with whippings and denial of food.

Captain Pratt dominated the reservation education process for nearly 2 decades. As an extension of the acculturation goals he developed the Outing System. When students at Carlisle and other off-reservation boarding schools completed their training, school officials placed them with white rural families near the schools for a three-year period. The federal government paid the host family $50 a year for each student's medical care and clothing. The student's labor at farm work and household chores was regarded sufficient compensation for the home benefits he received from the Outing System.

Indian parents were terrorized by the threat of their children being snatched from them and sequestered in some remote boarding school. In typical bureaucratic fashion, to protect the annual congressional appropriation for each school, agents and agency police, even United States cavalry, every autumn seized children and hauled them off to school, over their parents' protests, thereby filling the quotas at each institution. Agents punished uncooperative parents by placing them in the reservation jail, or withholding their rations and annuities. Indian children were held at the boarding schools for periods of from 4 to 8 years, often in a state of semiconfinement, isolating them from

An 1880s Indian student from the Carlisle School—before matriculation and after. (Smithsonian Institution, National Anthropological Archives)

Indian parents and tribal environment, even denying them visits to home and parents during designated vacation periods.

Soon after 1900 the Bureau of Indian Affairs relaxed its policy of extended separation of Indian children from families in remote, off-reservation boarding schools by increasing the number of boarding schools and day schools on the reservations, closer to the Indian students' homes. Also during the 1890s, federal officials placed an increasing number of Indian children in public schools near the reservations, reimbursing school districts for the education costs.

In his autobiography Talayesva, a Hopi Indian and periodically a student in reservation schools, recalls his experiences with and feelings about the federal government's Americanization program. The Hopis were divided into "Hostiles" and "Friendlies" depending on their submitting to Americanization and permitting their children to attend the day school at New Oraibi and the boarding school at Keams Canyon Agency. His sister was the first in the family to attend school. After enrollment, the teacher cut her hair, burned her clothes, and gave her a new outfit and a name, Nellie. She detested school and escaped to her family, hiding out from agency police for about a year. Officials finally discovered her and forced her to return to school. The teachers had forgotten her old name, and called her Gladys. Talayesva's brother was able to avoid school for several years. Eventually tribal police captured him and placed him in the New Oraibi school. The teachers cut his hair, burned his clothes, and named him Ira.

Eventually federal agents discovered Talayesva and he, too, was forced to attend school. His family's willingness to permit his enrollment at the distant Keams Canyon boarding school suggests that confinement to reservation had so compressed the Native Americans' land base that, once prosperous and self-sufficient, they had become pauperized; many families were so poverty-stricken that they could not provide adequate food and clothing for their children. The Indian Service schools provided both. Talayesva's father admonished him, "Son, don't try to run away from here. You are not a good runner, and you might get lost and starve to death. We would not know where to find you, and the coyotes would eat you." Teachers cut his hair, burned his clothes, gave him Anglo clothing, and named him Max. Talayesva detested his new name and the following year when the teacher asked his name and he was silent, the instructor said, "Well, your name shall be Don."

Talayesva described the annual student roundup. Agency police rode into Oraibi and

surrounded the village, with the intention of capturing the children of the hostile families and taking them to school by force. They herded us all together at the east edge of the mesa. Although I had planned to go later, they put me with the others. The people were excited, the children and the mothers were crying and the men wanted to fight.

Talayesva recalled that happiest times were going home.

It was a joy to get home again, to see all my folks, and tell about my experiences at school. I had learned many English words and could recite part of the Ten Commandments. I knew how to sleep on a bed, pray to Jesus, comb my hair, eat with a knife and fork, and use a toilet. I had learned that the world is round instead of flat, and it is indecent to go naked in the presence of girls, and to eat the testes of sheep or goats. I had also learned that a person thinks with his head instead of his heart.[7]

A continuing criticism of schools was that the graduates became objects of ridicule among their people and "returned to the blanket." They found that much of what they had been taught—vocational skills of printing, baking, tailoring, leather work, masonry, and drafting—had little application to reservation life. In retrospect, critics claimed that the education phase of the federal government's Americanization program for Indians failed. It suffered from irregular attendance, high dropout rate, lack of motivation, and general defeatism on the part of Indian students.

Religious Transformation

Federal managers of the Americanization process regarded conversion of Native Americans to the Christian religion as vital for their passage along the "white man's road." Indian religion was a pervasive force in their life. Reformers believed that it was absolutely essential to eradicate Indian religion, not only because it was pagan, but also because it clearly was a protective bastion of tribalism to which Indians increasingly turned for respite from the trauma of reservation life.

Missionaries had worked among Native Americans for centuries, although the British and Anglo-Americans were much less successful than the Spanish, French, and Russians. In spite of a record of very limited success among the Indian tribes, the religious bodies after 1866 were permitted to work on the reservation in two capacities: first, to serve as Indian agents during the "Peace Policy" period; and, second, to continue attempts to convert the reservation tribes.

"Peace Policy" agents were expected to replace the longstanding image of corruption in the Indian service with honest administration, and they were permitted to encourage Christian missions on the reservations. Many religious bodies including Friends (Quakers), Methodists, Baptists, Presbyterians, and Episcopalians provided churchmen for service on the western reservations as "Peace Policy" agents and teachers. Some of the early "Peace Policy" agents were outstanding, notably Quaker Laurie Tatum, who worked with the fierce Comanches and Kiowas. However, critics charged that for most "Peace Policy" agents conversion was more important than civilization and they were "more interested in 'Sunday religion' than the kind which lasts seven days a week."[8]

Very soon federal officials became aware that sectarian bickering was spoiling the system, and many were shocked at the intense competition among religious bodies for public recognition, their lack of Christian charity, and their pettiness. One critic of the "Peace Policy" has charged that because of sectarian preoccupation this experiment "failed to produce any discernible improvement and reform" for Indian welfare.[9]

To be included in agency assignments became a status symbol among American religious bodies. Churches competed for particular appointments. Divines grumbled and complained over their assignments. Church leaders became embittered when their denominations were passed over in the appointments. Protestant religious bodies dominated the appointments to the exclusion of Roman Catholics in spite of the fact that the latter contributed well over one half of the funds for missions on Indian reservations. Catholics received only 7 of the 94 initial agency appointments.

Federal officials shed the troublesome ecclesiastical connection in 1876 and the following year returned to the venerable spoils system to select Indian agents and other staff for the Americanization programs on the western reservations. However, missionaries—including Congregationalists, Methodists, Presbyterians, Friends (Quakers), Episcopalians, Baptists, Unitarians, and Roman Catholics—continued to work among the tribes after 1877, although with considerably less vigor.

American religious bodies thereafter found the "Chinaman on the banks of the Yangtze...a more romantic and challenging figure" for missionary effort than the pitiful Indian of the West. One federal official berated the nation's churches for their feeble interest in reservation Indians, claiming that the churches and missionary societies of America spent millions on foreign missions annually and less than $10,000 on American Indians. The few churches that responded to the reservation opportunity often confused the Indians by their sectarian divisiveness. Chief Joseph would not permit missionaries among his people, declaring, "They will teach us to quarrel about God as the Catholics and Protestants do. . . . We may quarrel with men . . . but we never quarrel about God. We do not want to learn that."[10]

Moreover, many Indian leaders were quick to detect the contradictions and duplicity of American society, which provoked their scorn toward missionary efforts. A Sioux leader, when asked to permit missionaries to work among his people, answered, "It is your people, who you say have the Great Spirit's book, who bring us the fire-water. It is your white men who corrupt our daughters. Go teach them to do right, and then come to us and I will believe you."[11]

Missionaries, like teachers, with fanatical vigor went about the task of attempting to eradicate heathenish tribalism. They denounced Indian dress, long hair, dances, festivals, native rites, and plural marriage, all of which the divines regarded as manifestations of the devil, the sooner stamped out the better for Christian security. Missionaries could not understand that Indians were deeply religious, but on their own terms and in their own style; that most Native Americans found their ancient tribal religion adequate. Only it could provide them inner strength to cope with the surging, changing world about them. Most Indians could distinguish between the missionaries' preaching, which they scorned, and the teachings of Christ which they respected and integrated into their emerging religious synthesis. Like most reservation educators, most missionaries failed to uplift and improve the Indian tribes.

Tightening the Administrative Noose

Because tribal governments, which continued to function on the reservations, comprised a bastion of nativism and a prime source of opposition to the federal Americanization program, agents spared no effort to suppress and destroy them. They deposed tribal leaders, in some cases going so far as to separate chiefs from their people by placing them in remote military prisons, forbade tribal councils to meet, proscribed application of tribal common law and social controls, and replaced aboriginal tribunals with federally mandated courts.

In the early days of the American nation, when Indian power was awesome and the United States recognized Indian tribes as self-governing, sovereign entities, most federal laws pertaining to Indian tribes were passed to fulfill treaty obligations. However, through the years, by conquest and diplomacy, the United States reduced Indian power, and increasingly the Indian tribes became subject to the broad will and certainly the protection of the United States. The United States Supreme Court ruled in *Cherokee Nation* v. *Georgia* (1831) that the aboriginal communities were domestic dependent nations, bearing to the United States a relationship like wards to a protective guardian, and in *Worcester* v. *Georgia* (1832) that the Indian nations were self-governing principalities immune from state jurisdiction. Before 1840, laws pertaining to Indian tribes were of a broad policy nature, as illustrated by the statute creating the Federal Factory System, the series of intercourse acts regulating relations between Indians and non-Indians, and the Indian Removal Act.

As Indian power declined after 1846 under the pressure of Anglo-American territorial conquest and expansion, the volume of laws pertaining to Indians and progressively eroding tribal sovereignty and prerogative, increased. Federal regimentation of the Indian nations escalated perceptively after 1860 as federal officials applied a growing body of laws and administrative decrees to the Indian tribes. An act of 1862 permitted the commissioner of Indian affairs to remove uncooperative tribal leaders and to appoint those willing to do the bidding of federal officials. The law which destroyed tribal sovereignty and the foundations for the functioning of Indian tribal governments was the 1871 statute terminating the treaty process and making Native Americans completely subject to federal laws and administrative rulings. Thereafter the volume of controlling legislation increased, more and more aimed at destroying tribal governments, displacing tribal common law with federal law, and transferring Indians from tribal jurisdiction to Anglo-American jurisdiction.

After 1876 the administrative noose on Indian institutions tightened rapidly both internally (within the reservation) and externally (off the reservation). Internally the pressure came from an intensive and pervasive Americanization program. The tribes, desolated after their defeats by Anglo-American arms, stripped of their homelands, and forcibly assigned to drastically reduced territories called reservations, daily witnessed the great power of federal agents. And they were shamed by certain of their people collaborating in the Americanization process as members of the reservation police force and as judges on the reservation Courts of Indian Offenses.

Origins of the Indian reservation constabulary force go back to the 1860s when agents on the western reservations began using squads of uniformed Native Americans to maintain order in their jurisdictions. By the 1870s Indian police, recruited from the warrior community of each tribe, were on active duty on the western Apache, Navajo, Sioux, and Blackfeet reservations. In 1878 Congress established a system of native police throughout the Indian service, and by 1890 squads of Indian law-enforcement officers, in military uniform and on federal salary, were on duty at 59 agencies. Indian police were expected to set an example for fellow Indians by cutting their hair, wearing neat military uniforms on duty and civilian dress off duty, eschewing native religion and rites, and having only one wife. Their duties included maintaining order on the reservations, expelling intruders, and suppressing the whiskey traffic. In addition, the Indian police were to assist the agent, teachers, and missionaries in applying the Americanization program by vigilance for any sign of tribalism, helping to destroy the power and influence of the chiefs, and suppressing tribal religion, dances, and festivals.

Ration day at Pine Ridge Reservation in South Dakota. (The Denver Public Library, Western History Department)

To assist agents and Indian police in eradicating nativism on the reservations, Secretary of the Interior Henry M. Teller in 1883 created a system of Courts of Indian Offenses. Teller was upset that polygamy persisted among the reservation tribes in spite of strenuous public efforts to root it out. Likewise, he was distressed at the "continuance of the old heathenish dances, such as the sun-dance" which he claimed "led to a war spirit and demoralized the young," and the enduring influence of aboriginal priests—medicine men as the Anglos called them—whom he blamed for fostering nativism, for keeping Indian children from attending school, and for promoting "heathenish customs." He expected the Courts of Indian Offenses, working with the Indian police on the reservations, to suppress tribal practices "repugnant to common decency and morality," and to "put a stop to the demoralizing influence of heathenish rites." Each Court of Indian Offenses consisted of three judges appointed from the ranking officers of the local reservation police force or three other Indians the agent selected. The tribunal could impose fines and jail sentences on those Indians who persisted in the old customs of dancing, observing tribal religions, and practicing polygamy, or for gambling and drunkenness. Teller instructed the Native American jurists to adjudge any Indian who refused "to adopt the habits of industry, or to engage in civilized pursuits or employments, but habitually spends his time in idleness and loafing . . . a vagrant and guilty of a misdemeanor." Sentences were subject to review by the agent and the commissioner of Indian affairs. The Five Civilized Tribes, New York Indians, Osages, Pueblo Indians, and Eastern Cherokees were not required to adopt Teller's Indian court system.[12]

On a number of occasions Indians were subjected to martial law. During the 1862 Santee Sioux uprising in Minnesota, military commissions had tried Indian insurgents and ordered their execution. And in 1874 a military commission had tried and convicted Modoc leaders and ordered their execution. In the course of the conquest of the southern Plains, Satanta, Satank, and Big Tree were arrested by army authorities and consigned to Texas civilian authorities for trial on charges of violating state homicide laws. Military commissions at Fort Sill and Fort Reno in the Indian Territory had attempted to try 72 raider chiefs after their capture during 1874–1875, but the United States attorney general ruled that a state of war could not exist between a nation and its wards and that a military commission could be resorted to only during a state of war. Thus war department officials ordered the 72 Native American leaders committed to military prison without trial.

Tribal tribunals which, by custom and treaty guarantees, had handled offenders of Indian common law, were in the process of being destroyed. Courts of Indian Offenses handled only minor, petty offenses, but jurisdiction for major crimes committed by Indians on reservations was in limbo. As indicated, some Indians charged with major crimes had been turned over to state authorities for trial and punishment, and military commissions had tried, convicted, and executed Native Americans. The federal court at Fort Smith, Arkansas, exercised expanding jurisdiction over the Five Civilized Tribes and others of the Indian Territory. Later, federal jurisdiction over the Indian Territory was expanded to include federal courts at Paris, Texas, and Wichita and Topeka, Kansas. Subsequently, federal courts were established at Muskogee, McAlester, and Ardmore in the Indian Territory, further enlarging federal jurisdiction over the resident tribes.

Congress took its most comprehensive step in expanding federal jurisdiction over Indians in 1885 with the passage of the Major Crimes Act to remedy a defect exposed in the Americanization program in 1883 in the Supreme Court case of *Ex Parte Crow Dog*. By this ruling, Crow Dog, a Brule Sioux, was freed on a charge of killing Spotted Tail. The court ruled that federal jurisdiction did not apply to this case because the alleged offense was committed on a reservation, and the court presumed that the defendant had been punished by the local law of the tribe. This inadvertent reassertion of Brule Sioux sovereignty ran counter to the federal government's Americanization program and, from the viewpoint of Indian service officials, was a major setback to detribalization. Congress supportively remedied this in 1885 by adopting the Major Crimes Act. It provided that an Indian committing crimes against person or property of another Indian—murder, manslaughter, rape, assault with intent to kill, arson, burglary, or larceny—was subject to the laws of the territory or state where the crime was committed, the Native American defendant to suffer the penalty imposed on a non-Indian. The Major Crimes Act was challenged and on appeal to the United States Supreme Court in 1886 in *United States* v. *Kagama;* the nation's highest tribunal rendered in favor of detribalization by sustaining the statute.

Concentration

Supported by laws and court decisions, federal officials responsible for transforming Native Americans searched for additional ways to accelerate detribalization. One that was widely used during the decade 1875–1885 was concentration. Concentration was applied to several tribes on western reservations and it took two forms. One consisted of consolidating tribes from several reservations onto a common, reduced reservation administered by a single agency. Western congressmen, like Georgia, Alabama, and Mississippi congressmen in another political age, attempted to purge their states and territories of Indians. Justification for this form of concentration included claims from settlers living near the reservations that Indians there were continuing threats to peace. Concentrating Native Americans onto smaller reservations would enable federal officials to maintain closer surveillance over them. Furthermore, consolidating agencies would result in economy of administration which appealed to many congressmen. Not mentioned was the obvious benefit to settlers in opening vacated reservation lands.

During the 1880s Congress appropriated funds to finance the removal and consolidation of the western tribes and agencies onto 5 reservations. Federal agents prepared to colonize the Sioux, western Apaches, Nez Percés, Poncas, Pawnees, and several other tribes on reservations in the Indian Territory. Poncas, Nez Percés, and Pawnees were relocated there, and their vacated lands in Nebraska, Dakota Territory, and the Northwest opened to settlement.

This form of concentration, however, was halted before all the tribes designated for relocation were moved. A rising reform movement in the eastern United States joined with congressional delegations from Missouri, Arkansas, Texas, and Kansas to oppose further consolidation of western reservations and colonization of the displaced tribes in the Indian Territory. The former was motivated by humanitarian considerations, the latter by security and business imperatives. Political and civic leaders in the states bordering the Indian Territory objected to further consolidation because they claimed that additional colonization of western tribes in the Indian Territory would crowd the Indian nations there and create unrest and insurgency. They also looked to the early opening of the Indian Territory to Anglo-American settlement which they believed would improve regional business conditions. Concentrating additional Native Americans from western reservations into Indian Territory would complicate and delay this advent.

The other form of concentration, reducing the assigned reservation area and concentrating the Indians thereon, was carried out with greater success. Federal officials accomplished this under the guise that concentration provided improved administration. Thus the federal government was able to open immense tracts of surplus land to Anglo-American settlers. Tribal casualties of this form of concentration, of territorial compression, included the Crows whose Montana reservation was reduced by 4 million acres, and the Utes who lost nearly 5 million acres in southwestern Colorado. By this time there was no frontier or unoccupied wilderness to which Indians could be exiled as had been the case earlier. Thus they were finally settled on compressed reservations in the general area of their traditional homelands; then these were progressively reduced through the process of concentration, each reduction another step in the old and familiar process of Anglo-American appropriation of Native American lands. The ultimate form of concentration and compression of the tribal estate was allotment in severalty; beginning in 1887 federal officials partitioned the remaining reservation lands into 160-acre homesteads for Indians, taking surplus lands for settlers.

The Alaskan Indians

The Native American community under Anglo-American dominion was enlarged in 1867 when the United States purchased Alaska from imperial Russia. At the time, Alaskan natives numbered about 30,000 and included coastal-dwelling Tlingits and interior-dwelling Athapascans. Federal officials assumed that their policy for Indians in the contiguous United States extended to Alaska. However, their remote location enabled those in Alaska to escape the intensive Americanization program forced on their counterparts in the contiguous United States. In 1923 a federal report on Alaskan Native Americans admitted that "for a long time after the cession of the territory, Congress took no particular notice of the natives." Nonetheless, Presbyterian, Russian Orthodox, Episcopal, Roman Catholic, Methodist, Moravian, Baptist, Quaker, and Lutheran missionaries worked among Native Alaskans maintaining 82 missions and 24 schools for them. Russian Orthodox and Presbyterian missionaries provided the most facilities, each group supporting 16 missions and schools.[13]

Transfer of Indian Administration

After the United States army had completed its final tribal conquest, army officers contemplated the vanquished Native Americans with nostalgia and with an inexplicable protectiveness. They rated mounted Indians the best light cavalry in the world, adding "there is no frontier these days ... all our Indian wars are ... over. Those beautiful beasts ... will die out and nobody will ever know what splendid cavalry they could make." Following tribal conquest and concentration on reservations, army protectiveness was manifested in military officers' persistent attempt to obtain control of the administration of Indian policy and direction of the aboriginal transformation process. They recalled that until 1849 Indian affairs had been under War

Department management. Their troops having just crushed the Indians, they regarded Americanization on reservations as an extension of the military function.[14]

Military men were habitually contemptuous in their attitude toward civilian administrators. They saw nothing but inefficiency in the conduct of Indian affairs by the Interior Department. As late as 1891 the military claim was that the soldier on the frontier was "almost the only class of federal officials . . . free of the taint of political corruption," while the civilian official was "the incarnation of everything . . . scandalous in administration." General of the Army William Tecumseh Sherman believed that "'three generals could settle the current Indian difficulties in an hour," and both officers and enlisted men believed that "Indians would profit from army control."[15]

Interior Department officials countered with reforming strategies to retain the functions of the Bureau of Indian Affairs. President Grant supported both civilian and military positions. His "Peace Policy," the use of churchmen as Indian service officials and agents, was meant to offset the low public image of civilian Indian agents and to remove corruption of the spoils system from administration of Indian affairs. He supplemented civilian "Peace Policy" assignments by appointing several army officers as Indian agents. Neither practice survived the 1870s. Liberal Republican Carl Schurz, Secretary of the Interior for the period 1877–1881, conscientiously attempted to reform the Indian service and upgrade the quality of agents, but to no avail.

Congress, too, was caught up in the contest for control of the Americanization process. After 1870 for nearly two decades, the House of Representatives regularly passed legislation providing for transfer of Indian affairs from the Interior Department to the War Department, and the Senate just as regularly defeated the proposal.

Public opinion increasingly was becoming a factor in the formulation of public policy, and officials from both the Interior Department and the War Department sought wide citizen support for their respective positions. In 1881, a national essay contest on the question of the Indian and the Army was won by Captain Edward Butler with a paper which was published in national periodicals "defending United States-Indian relations from the founding of the Government and urging institution of a system of forceful education by the army which would reluctantly accept the duty of improving upon the weak civilian administration." Several civilian officials, active and retired, countered the army's campaign to regain control of Indian administration. George Manypenny, former Commissioner of Indian Affairs, wrote *Our Indian Wards,* an exposé of army relations with Indians. In answer to the question of army fitness to manage the Americanization process, Manypenny pointed out that in 1887, when the army numbered 25,000 men, nearly 12,000 soldiers were convicted of gambling.[16]

Reformers outside the government were divided on the issue of transfer. One group, completely disillusioned at the prospects of cleansing corruption from the Bureau of Indian Affairs, favored transfer to the War Department.

This faction included William Welsh, the Philadelphia philanthropist and acknowledged "leading champion of the Indians," Edward Everett Hale, and Herbert Welsh, secretary of the Indian Rights Association. On the other hand Alfred B. Meacham and Thomas A. Bland, editors of *Council Fire Magazine,* which stressed Indian self-determination, strongly opposed transfer of Indian affairs to the War Department.

Civilian federal officials continued to seek ways to defeat transfer. One alternative, seriously considered during the 1880s, was to refurbish the image of civilian management of Native Americans by changing jurisdiction through formation of a new agency separate from both Interior Department and War Department. However, administrative timidity and power of vested interests consistently forced those with the power to improve Indian management to return to the position of attempting to reform the existing bureaucracy. Yet, military influence persisted in the Americanization process. The practice of appointing former military officers as Indian agents was resumed and military drill, uniform, decorum, and martial regulations became an intrinsic part of Indian school operation.

This bitter intragovernmental contest for control of Native American alteration was costly for the advocates of Indian transformation. It confused Native Americans, further destroyed their morale, and assured ultimate failure of Americanization goals during the reservation era. And in a twisted way it helped those Indians who persisted in their determination to retain their Indianness because the transfer contest made total application of the Americanization program impossible as federal officials spent considerable valuable time defending their actions against public attacks by the military. Pressure on the tribes decreased.

THE RESERVATION ORDEAL

As indicated, for many tribes the reservation era covered the period 1867 to 1887. In these twenty years the federal government expected to accomplish the magical transformation of Indians from free, roving hunters and raiders into settled, peaceful, law-abiding wards, made self-sufficient by the adoption of agriculture and stock raising. The reservation was to be the center for tribal management and reformation. However, from the Indian viewpoint, the reservation experience matched, and in some cases exceeded, the somber "Trail of Tears" for needless, agonizing want, unthinkable suffering, and personal and group decline to the brink of destruction. Demographers, sociologists, and anthropologists have claimed that the Anglo-American nation exceeded all others in causing native population decline. By 1890 the Indian population of the United States had been reduced from an estimated original 1,500,000 to less than 250,000. Their numbers declined drastically during the reservation era due largely to the unhealthy conditions.

The shock of defeat in battle and loss of territory, of being forcibly required

Tribal poverty and the reservation ordeal. (The Huffman Pictures, Miles City, Montana)

to submit to daily surveillance, and enduring overt and covert pressure to abandon Indianness and become hybrid Americans, devastated Native American will. Sudden destitution was traumatic, too, as the tribes went from prosperity to poverty when federal agents concentrated them on reservations. Tribes were deprived of the land base which had provided their economic, political, and military power and strength. To Native Americans the reservation was a prison, a reform institution; the penitentiary aspect of reservations varied from large compounds where only moderate coercion and repression were applied to isolated military prisons with cellblocks.

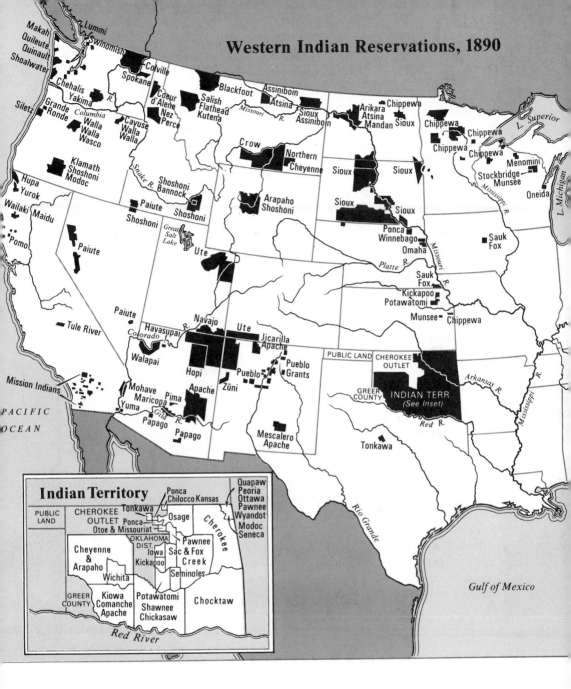

Western Indian Reservations, 1890

Makah
Quileute
Quinault
Shoalwater
Lummi
Swinomish
Chehalis
Yakima
Colville
Spokane
Coeur d'Alene
Blackfoot
Assiniboin
Atsina
Salish
Flathead
Kutena
Arikara
Atsina
Mandan
Chippewa
Sioux
Assiniboin
Chippewa
Chippewa
Chippewa
Chippewa
Chippewa
Menomini
Stockbridge
Munsee
Oneida
L. Superior
L. Michigan
Siletz
Grande
Ronde
Columbia
Walla
Walla
Wasco
Cayuse
Walla
Walla
Nez
Perce
Missouri R.
Crow
Northern
Cheyenne
Sioux
Sioux
Mississippi R.
Klamath
Shoshoni
Modoc
Hupa
Yurok
Wailaki
Maidu
Pomo
Snake R.
Shoshoni
Bannock
Paiute
Shoshoni
Shoshoni
Great
Salt
Lake
Ute
Arapaho
Shoshoni
Sioux
Sioux
Ponca
Winnebago
Omaha
Sauk
Fox
Platte R.
Missouri R.
Paiute
Paiute
Sauk
Fox
Kickapoo
Potawatomi
Munsee
Chippewa
Tule River
Havasupai
Navajo
Colorado R.
Ute
Jicarilla
Apache
PUBLIC LAND
CHEROKEE
OUTLET
Arkansas R.
Mississippi R.
Walapai
Hopi
Pueblo
Pueblo
Grants
Zuñi
GREER
COUNTY
INDIAN TERR.
(See Inset)
Mission Indians
Mohave
Maricopa
Yuma
Pima
Apache
Papago
Gila R.
Papago
Mescalero
Apache
Tonkawa
Red R.
PACIFIC
OCEAN

Indian Territory

PUBLIC
LAND
CHEROKEE
OUTLET
Ponca
Otoe & Missouriat
Tonkawa
Ponca
Chilocco
Osage
Kansas
Cherokee
Quapaw
Peoria
Ottawa
Pawnee
Wyandot
Modoc
Seneca
Cheyenne
&
Arapaho
OKLAHOMA
DIST.
Iowa
Kickapoo
Sac & Fox
Pawnee
Creek
Seminoles
Wichita
GREER
COUNTY
Kiowa
Comanche
Apache
Potawatomi
Shawnee
Chickasaw
Chocktaw
Red River
Gulf of Mexico

Rio Grande

Indian Prisoners of War

In the federal government's attempts to reform Indian character and eradicate
Indian culture, many Native Americans were deemed dangerous, were classed
as prisoners of war, and were held on military reservations, guarded by heavily
armed federal troops. Several leaders were regarded as being so threatening
to peace and order on the reservations that they were committed to eastern

military prisons, among them 72 band leaders of the Comanche, Kiowa, Cheyenne, and Arapaho tribes following their capitulation to federal commanders in the Indian Territory in 1875. This practice of isolating and separating leaders from their people aided the federal policy of destroying tribal government by breaking the hold of chiefs on the bands comprising each tribe. In the case of Geronimo's band of western Apaches, nearly 500 men, women, and children and their leader were regarded as such a threat to the peace and order of Arizona and New Mexico that they were removed first to Florida military prisons and then to Vernon Barracks in Alabama. Finally these Apache exiles were placed under the guns of Fort Sill on the Kiowa-Comanche Reservation in southwestern Indian Territory, their status as prisoners of war continuing until 1913.

However, the example of the 72 chiefs stripped from their Kiowa, Comanche, Cheyenne, and Arapaho followers and sent off to military prison in 1876 best illustrates the determination of federal managers of the tribal transformation process to end for all time the influence and power of Indian leaders over their people. During the final conquest of the southern Plains tribes (1874–1875), General Sherman had recommended that leaders of the resisting bands be separated from their people, tried by a military commission, and placed in military prison as punishment for making war on the United States.

Captain Richard H. Pratt, Tenth Cavalry, was placed in charge of the Indian prisoner program. Pratt used Indians, government scouts, certain army officers, and enlisted men at Fort Sill and Fort Reno, and Mexican and Anglo-American captives liberated by the conquest, as informants for selecting those to be punished. Pratt was required to honor those pledges of immunity from punishment made during the conquest by officers to band leaders who surrendered voluntarily, who cooperated with officials in urging surrender of certain recalcitrant band chiefs, or who provided incriminating information to Pratt.

President Grant favored trial of the accused Indians by a military commission. However, the attorney general ruled that a military commission could be used only in a state of war, and a state of war could not exist between a nation and its wards. Frontier wrath against Indians was so intense that Pratt believed it impossible to obtain an impartial trial before a jury in the civilian courts of Texas and Kansas. It was therefore concluded best to punish those leaders Pratt rated the most notorious by "arbitrarily sending all of them to some remote fort to be held indefinitely as prisoners of war."[17]

A de facto military commission headed by Pratt screened several hundred Comanches, Kiowas, Cheyennes, and Arapahoes and others on the two reservations. The commission directed that 72 Indians (33 Cheyennes, including one woman, 2 Arapahoes, 27 Kiowas, 9 Comanches, and a Caddo) as "ring leaders in marauding" be committed to Fort Marion Military Prison in St. Augustine, Florida. Each of the 72 prisoners was fitted with chain shackles at the post blacksmith shop and transported by military wagon and railroad to St. Augustine. Two died in escape attempts en route. Pratt and George Fox, a government interpreter from Fort Sill, remained with the prisoners throughout their stay in Florida. The Indian prisoners, shackles in place, were lodged in cells, euphemistically called casemates, their cell block guarded by an army detail. Each day the guards marched the prisoners from their cells for an exercise session in the high-walled courtyard next to the casemates. Soon after their arrival, the writer Sidney Lanier visited Fort Marion and observed the prisoners. He commented, "Each had his ankles chained together, but managed to walk like a man, withal. They are confined—by some ass who is in authority—in the lovely old Fort, as unfit for them as they for it. It is in my heart to hope sincerely that they may all get out."[18]

If the prisoners maintained surface poise, they suffered physical ailments and anxieties and resentments which they screened from the viewing public. The Florida environment, so unlike that to which they were accustomed, severely reduced their vitality and affected their health. The prisoners were lonely for wives, children, relatives, and friends. And they felt intense bitterness at being imprisoned while, as they repeatedly charged to Pratt, much worse offenders lived the free life in the Indian Territory.

Prisoners' rage at being punished while Indians they claimed were more guilty than they had received preferential treatment by the military during the prisoner selection and were permitted to remain free, slowed their adjustment to life at Fort Marion. Wives and relatives of the St. Augustine prisoners protested to agents and other officials, and there was finally an investigation of the prioner-selection process. Pratt admitted that the charges were well grounded, but he pointed to the promises of immunity to certain acknowledged raiders made by his superiors. The army defended the prisoner-selection process and responded to the complaints with "The delicate duties devolving upon" the officers at Fort Sill and Fort Reno "incident to this transfer of the hostile Indians to the care of the troops, and in the discriminating between those who were deservedly to be regarded as friendly and those not entitled to consideration . . . seem to have been discharged . . . with discretion and good judgment." The St. Augustine prisoners nursed resentment toward those who escaped punishment and the prisoner-selection process created intratribal rifts and divisiveness which remained long after their release and return to the reservations.[19]

Pratt worked to improve the lot of the prisoners and established a school within the cell block. Local matrons instructed the Native Americans in reading and other fundamentals. The students developed some interest and competency in the emerging Indian art. They were also instructed in the vocational crafts of carpentry, baking, masonry, and tailoring. After three years in prison, Pratt transferred 17 Indians to Hampton Institute in Virginia, and 5 young men he placed in private homes, 4 of them at Park Hill near Utica, New York, under the care of the Episcopal church.

The prisoners had been committed for indeterminate sentences, and regularly Pratt urged officials in the War and Interior departments to set the time for releasing them. He pointed out that enforced separation from family and

447

people was oppressive for the Indians, he praised their progress, and he urged clemency. Finally in 1878 federal officials decided that the prisoners had been punished sufficiently and ordered their release from St. Augustine Prison and return to the Indian Territory. The joy of the exiles in being restored to their people was noticed by one of the Indian agents who exulted, "There has been a very great change in these people, not only in their appearance but a complete and thorough reformation in every particular. Their profession of a thorough reformation I believe to be sincere, and I have the highest hopes of their further good conduct, and of good results to follow their example and teaching." Pratt was not so optimistic. He complained that his high hopes were dashed when they were returned to their agents, "to again become a very part of the reservation herds with their people, under the scant and lax methods of progress the Indian system provides."[20]

Detribalization

Reformers and bureaucrats who fashioned the aboriginal Americanization program ignored Indian diversity—the fact that on the new reservations were scores of tribal communities with vastly differing life-styles and languages—and applied a monolithic formula, a single transformation model, to all Native Americans. Federal planners observed the so-called melting pot which had transformed millions of European immigrants into American citizens and assumed that it had erased their ethnic quality and differences and that it would work for Indians.

During the last quarter of the nineteenth century, there arose a number of religious and social reform groups committed to Native American betterment, broadly called "Friends of the Indian." All except one followed the same monistic approach and supported federal officials in their Americanization program to erase all sign of Indianness. Only the National Indian Defense Association, headed by Thomas A. Bland, editor of *Council Fire Magazine*, thought to ask the Indians what their preferences might be in the transformation process. The National Indian Defense Association "opposed rather than encouraged governmental action on the theory that Indians should be left alone." Above all else this group stressed self-determination. Other than it, Native Americans had no public defender; they were captives of the system, of drastic cultural change unilaterally conceived and applied.[21]

As indicated, agents, teachers, and missionaries in applying the detribalization process worked to eradicate Indian religion and life-style, to transform the economy of each Indian family, and to destroy tribal institutions, particularly government. In addition, workers in the Americanization program placed great emphasis upon eliminating external signs of Indianness, including names and personal appearance.

Missionaries had attempted to rename Native Americans since colonial times. Furthermore, mixing of races over the years had produced a large community of mixed bloods with Anglo-American, French, and Spanish surnames in several tribes, especially the Five Civilized Tribes where over one half of the members had Anglo-American family names. However, most Indians placed on reservations during the postwar era had only their aboriginal names. Teachers, missionaries, and agents believed that an essential step in civilization was to eradicate Indian identity. Names of the reservation Indians were derived from nature and descriptive, and some of them were difficult for English-speaking people to pronounce. Most Native Americans on reservations also lacked surnames which made it difficult to organize them in the Americanization program which stressed family surname as basic identity. Teachers and missionaries continued to rename children in their schools, but they stressed first names—Morning Star to Mildred or Stands-in-the-Timber to Stanley. Then during the reservation era and the succeeding allotment-in-severalty era officials made a comprehensive attempt to rename Indians and provide each a surname. Examples of the surnames invented include American Horse to Horse, Spotted Horse to Spotted, All Runner to Runner, Black Wolf to Blackwulf or Blackwell, Brave Bear to Braveber, Big Nose to Bignus, and Black Owl to Blackall.[22]

Another external symbol of Indianness that attracted considerable attention from officers was dress and hair style. Reservation Indians were pressured to abandon tribal attire and take on what agents called "citizen dress." Hair was a vexing problem. Most Indian men wore their hair long for cosmetic effect; it provided a source of the male ego, and some ascribed supernatural significance to long hair. But to agents, long hair was a symbol "of resistance to the civilization process." The Mescalero Apaches were among the last of the reservation tribesmen to submit to the haircut. Their agent first directed members of the reservation Indian police force to cut their hair or face discharge. Slowly, reluctantly, they conformed. The rest of the warriors of the tribe, "gorgeous in paint, feathers, long hair, breechclouts and blankets," ignored the agent's demands until he threatened them with "confinement at hard labor." After six weeks he could report that "every male Indian had been changed into the semblance of a decent man."[23]

Thus, Native Americans, stripped of ethnic pride, humiliated by picayune impositions, and shorn of tribal moorings, eventually complied with repressive reservation routines. For most of them it was surface compliance with a detestable system while they covertly, inventively contrived strategies of evasion, the subject of Chapter Eighteen. However, some Indians seem to have accepted their fate and seriously attempted to relate to the new order by collaborating with federal agents, serving as reservation police and judges to suppress aboriginal life-style, supporting missionaries and joining reservation churches, and voluntarily enrolling their children in government schools.

Tribal fragmentation produced factions, identified on some reservations as "Conformists" and "non-Conformists," on others as "Progressives" and "non-Progressives," or "Pagans" and "Christians." This growing dichotomy abetted a federal policy goal of individualizing the Indians, alienating them from their heritage, and isolating them from the tightly knit, comforting, supportive

Sioux village on the Dakota Territory Reservation, 1891. (Library of Congress)

extended family, clan, band, and tribal identity and association, eventually
destroying tribal government so that the Indians would have no alternative
but to join the societal mainstream.

Erosion of tribal force had been in process for some time. Termination of
the treaty process, military conquest, assignment to reservations, and loss
of territory all contributed to individual and group disorientation and malaise.
The ancient consensus, the tribal cement, was shattered by the intrusion of
so many new, complex issues into the simple aboriginal political apparatus.
Observers of the process of aboriginal decline on reservations suggest that
Native Americans in the new order "lacked the opportunity to put space
between them and the alien culture or to destroy its representatives among
them without destructive reprisal." The traumatic impact of loss of tribal territory including the unpleasant realization that "the physical limits of their
world constricted, and with the shrinking of their world there was a cor-
responding loss of social momentum. Societies which had been highly ver-

satile in their adaptation to place and circumstance [in the prereservation era were] suddenly immobilized. The people, as tribes and bands, moved into an era where their voices were rarely heard and their power for decision was largely destroyed."[24]

Great Expectations

The reservation system forcibly compressed Native Americans on reservations and subjected them to an intensive Americanization program in an attempt to transform them into dutiful Anglo-American apprentices, poised on the threshold of the dominant society. Its mission was largely a failure due less to Indian cussedness or negativism and more to the strength, resiliency, and attractiveness of Indian culture, its mystical essence which would not expire in spite of intensive, sustained assaults upon it. Another factor, rarely considered, was that Indians possessed natural intelligence, some richly so, which enabled them to observe and to judge the relative merits of the Anglo-American culture which they were expected, even required, to accept. Most adult Indians found it pietistic, legalistic, obsessively materialistic, and downright unattractive. It promised Native Americans a bland, repressed, puritanical life-style. And many of its advocates were so patently corrupt that most Native Americans scorned this cultural alternative.

But there were other reasons why Indians failed to shape up, to conform to the reservation-derived model. They lacked faith in the system. A chain of duplicity, deceit, exploitation, and opportunism over the centuries had forged a tradition among Indians of distrust of Anglo-American overtures. Talayesva, the Hopi, recalled that he

grew up believing that whites are wicked, deceitful people. It seemed that most of them were soldiers, government agents, or missionaries, and that quite a few were Two-Hearts. The old people said that the Whites were tough, possessed dangerous weapons, and were better protected than we were from evil spirits. . . . They were known to be big liars too. They . . . tricked our war chiefs to surrender without fighting, and then broke their promises. . . . [The Hopis believed that whites] needed to be reminded daily to tell the truth. I was taught to mistrust them and to give warning whenever I saw one coming.[25]

Federal policy reflecting what the American people expected of Native Americans had frequently changed to the detriment of Indian peoples. Many Indians also refused to subscribe to the Americanization program because they were insulted by the contemptuous, ethnocentric attitudes of federal officials. Intelligent Indians were enraged at congressmen arrogantly demanding that reservation dwellers conform and become self-supporting, and soon, because that body was weary of having "for years footed the bills that maintained them in idleness, filth, immorality, and barbarism," when in fact the United States government presumptively served as trustee for Indian property including proceeds from land cessions. Thus in most cases when

451

congressmen allocated funds to Indians for rations, clothing, education, livestock, and tools, they were simply determining unilaterally what expenditures should be permitted from Indian trust funds.[26]

Congressmen and officials in the Bureau of Indian Affairs were unyielding in their determination to force Indians on reservations to become self-supporting through agriculture. Lack of progress in this regard was a regular cause for denunciation and threats of public abandonment. What federal officials did not understand was that Indians were reluctant to make extensive agricultural improvements on reservation lands for several reasons. A principal deterrent to conscientious application was cultural; it was sociologically unsound to expect rapid transformation of reservation people from hunting to agriculture. Such drastic change in aboriginal life-style required time, patience, and substantive family role change because in many Indian communities farming was regarded as "women's work." Also, in a very short period many of the tribes had been moved from one reservation to another, and talk of further concentration continued.

Rulings by federal officials on the question of tribal title to reservation lands also destroyed incentive among Indians to clear and open fields and perform other laborious tasks required to establish farms on virgin land. These administrative decrees defined Indians on reservations as tenants, having only limited rights to use the land and resources of the area assigned, which compromised absolute title in the tribe. An attorney general's opinion in 1819 held that Indians could not even "alienate the natural productions of the soil, the timber growing on it . . . the use of Lands permitted to the Indians is . . . intended for their subsistence and looking to their personal occupation of it, although they have the right to cultivate and sell the crops which are the production of their own labours, they have no more right to sell the standing timber . . . than they have to sell the soil itself." And during 1885 a ruling by the secretary of the interior held that "the right of the Indians to the reservations ordinarily occupied by them is that of occupancy alone." They were permitted to clear the land for farming and cut wood for fuel but were forbidden to "cut growing timber, open mines, quarry stone, etc. to obtain lumber, coal, building material, etc. solely for the purpose of sale. . . . In short, what a tenant for life may do, upon lands . . . Indians may do on their reservations."[27]

Another deterrent to Indians shaping up and becoming self-supporting yeoman farmers in the pioneer Anglo-American tradition was environmental limitation. Most reservations were located in arid regions of marginal agricultural potential, generally not highly valued by Anglo-American settlers. The unreasonable, unyielding expectation of Congress and the Bureau of Indian Affairs was that they become farmers in spite of all manner of acknowledged natural limitations upon agrarian success. Most of the northern reservations were in a climatic zone of short growing season with perennial threat of crop-killing early frosts and freezes. Many southern reservations were in an arid region where blistering summer droughts were a common occurrence. If this were not enough, there was the deterrent of pervasive poverty. As indicated, most Native Americans, only recently affluent and independent with vast tribal territories, many horses and buffalo robes, and prodigious dried meat stores, were quickly reduced to destitution and dependence by the reservation ordeal. They lacked capital to purchase seed, draft animals, plows, and other farming essentials. Congressional appropriations from tribal funds to purchase some of these needs were siphoned off by agent and contractor graft and only a token distribution was possible. Eventually federal agents relented their agricultural preoccupation by permitting reservation Indians to take up stock raising, for which much of the region containing the reservations was suitable. However, the success of this venture was limited by the perennial shortage of food on reservations. More often than not immediate need for subsistence to survive forced aboriginal stockmen to slaughter their small breeding herds to feed starving Indians.

Indians discerned and were angered by the double standard applied to them. For example, during a severe drought on the Northern Plains, Anglo-American homesteaders near the Pine Ridge Reservation evacuated their claims and "were glad to get back to some of the more prosperous parts of the country . . . and the country was absolutely abandoned" by settlers. However, federal officials "expected of an Indian that he shall make a living and thrive under the same conditions and upon the same kind of land that the educated and prepared white man failed."[28]

Native Americans on reservations also faced periodic distractions from non-Indian intruders—traders, squaw men (non-Indian husbands of Indian women), stock growers, permit holders, and home seekers—which further deterred their measuring up to federal policy expectations. Traders had been with the Indian tribes since early colonial times. As wilderness merchants they provided essentials and nonessentials to Indians, and they were often sources of controversy. From earliest days of the republic federal law had attempted to regulate their relations with Native Americans. The image of Indian traders was similar to that of the Indian agent—corrupt, venal, bent on cheating Indians by overcharging and maintaining "crooked" debt records. Their gravest transgression was providing liquor to Indians. Reformers regarded the trader "a relic of barbarism and an obstruction to the progress of Indian civilization." For the Americanization program to succeed they expected reservation agents to watch closely traders and protect Indians from exploitation by fixing fair prices on goods and suppressing traffic in liquor, arms, and ammunition. Agents and Indian police were expected to require traders to close business on Sundays and at all times "ban gambling, demoralizing dances [and] other practices or amusements hurtful to the Indian" on the premises and to assure that it was not a "resort of loafers." New Indian service rules required that traders be "sober, respectable people, whose conduct and example . . . will tend to elevate the Indians morally and socially." While a few traders abided by the rules, most persisted in sharp dealing. They debauched reservation Indians and were for the most part a cause of aboriginal decline.[29]

The squaw man gained the privileges and benefits of tribal citizenship including free use of tribal land and exemption from taxes. By 1877 it was reported that 700 white men had married Cherokee women, 60 had taken Creek wives, and 1,500 were married to Choctaw and Chickasaw women. One intermarried Chickasaw imported 100 white families as tenants on his vast Washita Valley farm. In 1886 a string of squaw man-managed farms, worked by white and black tenants, extended 50 miles along the Washita Valley. Many squaw men dabbled in tribal politics to maintain the status quo and thus protect their personal advantage.

The booming range cattle industry of the postwar era placed great pressure upon western grasslands. Indian lands often were attractive for expansion; by 1885 many of the reservation ranges were under lease to Anglo-American ranchers. A portion of every reservation in the Indian Territory west of the lands of the Five Civilized Tribes had been leased by Texas cattle raisers; virtually every acre of grass on the Kiowa-Comanche and Cheyenne-Arapaho reservations was leased to stockmen. For a time the most extensive ranching enterprise in the West was in the Cherokee Outlet. While the federal government had taken the eastern third of the Outlet from the Cherokees for the purpose of relocating tribes, about 6,500,000 acres of choice grassland remained unassigned. In 1883 Cherokee officials and officers of the Cherokee Strip Live Stock Association, a combine of ranchers representing over 100 individuals and corporations owning more than half a million cattle, concluded an agreement providing for the lease of the Cherokee Outlet for an annual payment of $100,000; in 1888 this was increased to $200,000. Stockraiser intruders were distracting to certain tribes in their progress along the "white man's road," but the money ranchers paid to Indians as rental for grazing land was vital for Native American welfare. Revenues of the Cherokee Strip Live Stock Association supported Cherokee nation schools and other tribal functions. And lease money paid by Texas cattlemen to the tribes of the western Indian Territory provided funds to feed and clothe destitute Indians.

The permit holder was found in the land of the Five Civilized Tribes. Federal law forbade entry into any Indian nation or reservation without proper authority. To meet the requirements of the law, or to evade it, governments of the Five Civilized Tribes worked out an arrangement known as the permit system which licensed outsiders and legalized their presence in the Cherokee, Creek, Seminole, Choctaw, and Chickasaw nations. Tribal leaders justified this as necessary to replace slaves who had been liberated by the Civil War. Indian Territory enterprises required labor, and the permit holders were expected to provide it. The permit laws allowed non-Indian mechanics and laborers and their families to settle and work in a particular nation upon purchase of an annual license costing $2.50 for laborers and $5.00 for mechanics and farmers. Sale of permits became an important source of revenue for the tribal governments. The cumulative effect of the so-called silent migration of permit holders on the Indian nations became clear in 1907 when the Indian Territory was joined with Oklahoma Territory to form the state of Oklahoma. The Choctaw nation alone had a reported population of 200,000; Indians numbered only about 30,000. At statehood Oklahoma had a population of about 1,500,000; the domain of the Five Civilized Tribes, comprising at statehood the eastern half of Oklahoma, had a population of about 750,000, with the ratio of non-Indians to Indians at least seven to one.

The most pernicious intruder on the Indian reservations was the home seeker who, during the 1880s, joined railway companies, banking houses, and western business enterprises to press the national government to open certain reservations. The Indian Territory, by this time a crazy quilt of nations and reservations, was the most sought-after settlement area. Because railroads, banks, and large business combinations were generally unpopular with the public, a direct campaign by these interests to open Indian reservations to settlement would probably have aroused suspicion. The home seeker, more closely connected with the image of American democracy, therefore became the stalking horse for the commercial interests on the premise that once the reservations were opened, all, including the home seeker, would benefit. Because authority for removing legal barriers to settlement of Indian lands had to come from Congress, railroad companies and other interested parties diligently pressed the national legislature to act on their behalf. In the West their agents formed home-seeker colonies, supported covertly by railroad and general business interests, on the Kansas and Texas borders of the Indian Territory. Led by Captain David L. Payne, "Prince of the Boomers," bands of home seekers periodically invaded Indian Territory on Boomer raids. Newspaper correspondents accompanied them. Federal troops ejected all the gangs of intruders, but their demonstrations against barriers to settlement in the Indian Territory were widely publicized. Promoters flooded the East with Boomer literature which proclaimed the promise of prosperity and success for home seekers once the Indian reservations were opened to settlement. The campaign to open the Indian Territory, launched in 1879, went on for ten years. The Boomer raids and general disorders of home-seeker activity distracted tribes and caused them to defer improving their reservation lands. After 10 years of intensive activity the Boomers triumphed. Congress passed the Dawes Allotment Act in 1887 providing for partitioning Indian lands; 2 years later the first of the Indian Territory tracts was opened to homesteaders.

An Indian View of Reservation Life

Most Indians silently endured the reservation experience, their muted thoughts on this ordeal communicated through their haggard faces, their defeated spirits. A few spoke out, and their statements have been translated and preserved. One of the most eloquent was an oration by the Shoshoni head man Washakie, delivered in 1878 to Governor John W. Hoyt of Wyoming Territory.

I cannot hope to express to you the half that is in our hearts. They are too full for words. Disappointment; then a deep sadness; then a grief inexpressible; then, at times, a bitterness that makes us think of the rifle, the knife and the tomahawk, and kindles in our hearts the fires of desperation—that sir, is the story of our experience, of our wretched lives. The white man, who possesses this whole vast country from sea to sea, who roams over it at pleasure, and lives where he likes, cannot know the cramp we feel in this little spot, with the undying remembrance of the fact, which you know as well as we, that every foot of what you proudly call America, not very long ago belonged to the redman. The Great Spirit gave it to us. There was room enough for all his many tribes, and all were happy in their freedom. But the white man had, in many ways we know not of, learned some things we had not learned; among them, how to make superior tools and terrible weapons, better for war than bows and arrows; and there seemed no end to the hordes of men that followed them from other lands beyond the sea. And so, at last, our fathers were steadily driven out, or killed, and we, their sons, but sorry remnants of tribes once mighty, are cornered in little spots of the earth all ours of right— cornered like guilty prisoners, and watched by men with guns, who are more than anxious to kill us off. Nor is that all. The white man's government promised that if we, the Shoshones, would be content with the little patch allowed us, would keep us well supplied with everything necessary to comfortable living, and would see that no white man should cross our borders for our game, or for anything that is ours. But it has not kept its word! The white man kills our game, captures our furs, and sometimes feeds his herds upon our meadows. And your great and mighty government . . . does not protect us in our rights. It leaves us without the promised seed, without tools for cultivating the land, without implements for harvesting our crops, without breeding animals better than ours, without the food we still lack. . . . I say again, the government does not keep its word! And so after all we can get by cultivating the land, and by hunting and fishing, we are sometimes nearly starved, and go half naked, as you see us! Knowing all this, do you wonder, sir, that we have fits of desperation and think to be avenged?[30]

A Non-Indian View of Reservation Life

Late in the nineteenth century the author Hamlin Garland spent several years visiting western reservations. His observations of the lot of confined Indians confirm Washakie's despair. Garland characterizes reservations as "corrals" or "open air prisons" where the

original owners of the continent have been impounded by the white race. Most of the reservations are in the arid parts of the Great Rocky Mountain Plateau; a few are in timbered regions of the older states like Wisconsin and Minnesota. Speaking generally, we may say these lands are relatively the most worthless to be found in the State or Territory whose boundaries enclose the red man's home, and were set aside for his use because he would cumber the earth less there than else- where. [However,] scarcely a single one of these minute spots is safe to the red people. Every acre of land is being scrutinized, and plans for securing even these miserable plots are being matured.... The Sioux, the Blackfeet, and the Northern Cheyennes live practically the same life. They have small, badly-ventilated log or frame hovels of one or two rooms, into which they closely crowd during cold weather. In summer, they supplement these mierable shacks by canvas tepees and lodges, under which they do their cooking, and in which they sleep. Their home life has lost all its old-time picturesqueness, without acquiring even the comfort of the settler in a dug-out. Consumption is very common among them because of their unsanitary housing during cold weather. They dress in a sad mixture of good old buckskin garments and shoddy clothing, sold by the traders or issued by the government. They are, of course, miserably poor, with very little to do but sit and smoke and wait for ration day. To till the ground is practically useless, and their herds are too small to furnish them support. They are not allowed to leave the reservation to hunt or to seek work, and so they live like reconcentrados. Their ration, which the government by an easy shift now calls a charity, feeds them for a week or ten days and they go hungry till the next ration day comes round. From three to seven days are taken up with going after rations. These words also apply to the Jicarilla Apaches, and to a part of the Southern Utes. Each tribe, whether Sioux, or Navajo, or Hopi, will be found to be divided, like a white village, into two parties, the radicals and the conservatives—those who are willing to change, to walk the white man's way; and those who are deeply, sullenly skeptical of all civilizing measures, are often the strongest and bravest of their tribes, the most dignified and the most intellectual. They represent the spirit that will break but will not bow. And, broadly speaking, they are in the majority. Though in rags, their spirits are unbroken; from the point of view of their sympathizers, they are patriots.[31]

Friends of the Indian

Anglo-American society, saturated with the Protestant ethic of performance and Darwinian natural selection, was largely desensitized to the Native American's pitiful state on western reservations, although occasionally a critic emerged to challenge the nation's repressive Indian policy. One pioneer voice for better conditions for Indians was John Beeson, an English immigrant who settled in Oregon. He was shocked at Anglo-American settlers and local newspapers which said that Indians "had nothing in common with humanity but the form," and he publicly challenged political candidates who urged "extermination" of the Oregon Indians. In 1855 during the Rogue River Wars Beeson regarded the settlers "aggressors" and took the Indian side in public debates. For this he was bitterly denounced, his life was threatened, and he moved to the eastern United States where, in 1858, he published *A Plea for the Indians*. Beeson continued to urge Indian reform into the 1870s.[32]

Another pioneer critic of Native American management was Henry B. Whipple, Episcopal bishop of Minnesota. Whipple was the strongest and most persistent voice for Indian reform before the Civil War. In the postwar era, many persons previously active in bettering life for blacks and in the abolitionist movement began to voice concern for Native Americans. During the late 1860s Lydia Maria Child wrote several pamphlets urging humane

Helen Hunt Jackson, author and reformer whose *Century of Dishonor* (1881) stirred reform of federal Indian policy. (The Huntington Library, San Marino, California)

treatment of Indians. Harriet Beecher Stowe helped found the Connecticut Indian Association, and Wendell Phillips actively supported Indian reform until his death in 1884. Samuel F. Tappan, a Boston abolitionist, moved to Colorado Territory in 1860 and developed a strong interest in Indian policy reform.

However, the person who touched the public heart strings and launched a national "Friends of the Indian" movement was Helen Hunt Jackson. She may be regarded as a pioneer muckraker because, like the author-critics of the early 1900s, she used her literary talent to expose a public evil and to urge corrective action. In 1881 she published *A Century of Dishonor*, an emotional treatise which exposed and denounced federal Indian policy and which served the cause of Native American reform in much the same way that *Uncle Tom's Cabin* served the antebellum crusade for blacks. Mrs. Jackson wrote in *A Century of Dishonor* that the purpose of her book was to "show our cause for national shame in the matter of our treatment of the Indians." In 1884 she published *Ramona*, a work of fiction depicting the plight of California Indians, which also had a wide and extended public appeal.[33]

But for exceptions to be noted, the critics who stirred reformers to mount the "Friends of the Indian" movement wholeheartedly supported the federal government's Americanization program. To them Indianness was a base, primitive survival which had to be eradicated before the Native American could be transformed and assimilated. The thrust of their reforms then was that reservations, rather than being a focal point for the transformation process, were really a public disgrace which had to be abolished with alternatives found for transforming the Indians.

Rare were those persons who saw redeeming qualities in aboriginal lifestyle and defended the Indians' right to retain it. Thomas A. Bland and Alfred B. Meacham, lecturers and editors, were champions of self-determination for the Indians and urged that they be consulted in the matter of Americanization. Hamlin Garland was a constant Indian advocate who resented the federal government applying "measures of Saxon virtue" to Native Americans. He respected Indian life-style, urged that it and native crafts be preserved, and he stated that his writing, fiction and nonfiction, was dedicated to "one underlying motive . . . to show the Indian as a human being, a neighbor."[34]

Before the reservation system had survived that 25-year period which federal officials regarded as the time required to detribalize and transform Indians into wholesome apprentices for Anglo-American society, it was exposed and denounced as an immense public failure. The alternative method to produce transformation, regarded as foolproof by "Friends of the Indian," was applied to those who survived the reservation ordeal, beginning in 1887. However, before considering allotment in severalty, which was equally devastating for most Indians, those strategies of evasion which many Native Americans contrived to mitigate reservation ennui and malaise will be examined.

Notes

1. William T. Hagan, "Indian Policy after the Civil War: The Reservation Experience," *Indiana Historical Society Lectures, 1970–1971* (Indianapolis, 1971), p. 36; and Margaret Szasz, *Education and the American Indian: The Road to Self-Determination, 1928–1973* (Albuquerque, N.M., 1974), p. 8.

2. *Report of the Commissioner of Indian Affairs for 1876*, pp. 15–20.

3. Hagan, "Indian Policy," p. 23.

4. Wilcomb E. Washburn, *The Indian in America* (New York, 1975), p. 209.

5. Henry E. Fritz, *The Movement for Indian Assimilation, 1860–1890* (Philadelphia, 1963), p. 39.

6. William T. Hagan, *American Indians* (Chicago, 1961), pp. 125–29.

7. Wayne Moquin and Charles Van Doren (eds.), *Great Documents in American Indian History* (New York, 1973), pp. 278–85.

8. Loring B. Priest, *Uncle Sam's Stepchildren: The Reformation of United States Indian Policy, 1865–1887* (New York, 1969), p. 39.

9. *Ibid.*, p. 38.

10. Hagan, *American Indians*, pp. 127–29.

11. *Ibid.*

12. *Report of the Commissioner of Indian Affairs for 1880*, pp. 11–30.

13. D'Arcy McNickle, *Native American Tribalism: Indian Survivals and Renewals* (New York, 1973), p. 61.

14. Kenneth Kay, "Gunga Din, Danny Deever, and the U.S. Cavalry," *Army* 27 (April 1977), pp. 48–49.

15. Priest, *Uncle Sam's Stepchildren*, p. 16.

16. *Ibid.*, pp. 24–25.

17. Richard H. Pratt, *Battlefield and Classroom: Four Decades with the American Indian, 1867–1904*, edited with an Introduction by Robert M. Utley (New Haven, Conn., 1964), pp. 104–105.

18. Charles R. Anderson and A. Starks (eds.), *Sidney Lanier Letters* (Baltimore, 1945), vol. 4, p. 198.

19. *Report of the Secretary of War for 1874*, p. 42.

20. *Report of the Commissioner of Indian Affairs for 1878*, p. 59; Also see Pratt, *Battlefield and Classroom*, p. 179.

21. Priest, *Uncle Sam's Stepchildren*, p. 86.

22. See Lonnie E. Underhill and Daniel F. Littlefield, Jr. (eds.), *Hamlin Garland's Observations on the American Indian* (Tucson, Ariz., 1976) for an account of the Indian renaming effort.

23. Jack D. Forbes (ed.), *The Indian in America's Past* (Englewood Cliffs, N.J., 1964), p. 114.

24. Robert F. Berkhofer, Jr., "Protestants, Pagans, and Sequences Among the North American Indians, 1760–1860," *Ethnohistory* 10 (Summer 1963), pp. 201–16; and McNickle, *Native American Tribalism*, p. 62.

25. Moquin and Van Doren, *Great Documents*, p. 278.

26. Forbes, *The Indian in America's Past*, p. 114.

27. Wilcomb E. Washburn, *Red Man's Land, White Man's Law* (New York, 1971), p. 62.

28. Moquin and Van Doren, *Great Documents*, p. 295.

29. *Report of the Commissioner of Indian Affairs for 1889*, p. 30; and Francis Paul Prucha, *American Indian Policy in Crisis: Christian Reformers and the Indian, 1865–1900* (Norman, Okla., 1976), pp. 197–202.

30. Moquin and Van Doren, *Great Documents*, pp. 235–36.

31. Underhill and Littlefield, *Hamlin Garland's Observations*, pp. 167–69.

32. See Fritz, *Movement for Indian Assimilation*, for sketches of the pioneer reformers, including Beeson.

33. Helen Hunt Jackson, *A Century of Dishonor* (New York, 1881); reprinted (Williamstown, Mass., 1973), p. 7.

34. Underhill and Littlefield, *Hamlin Garland's Observations*, p. 50.

Selected Sources

General studies which contain information on the reservation era are Angie Debo, *A History of the Indians of the United States* (Norman, Okla., 1970); D'Arcy McNickle, *Native American Tribalism: Indian Survivals and Renewals* (New York, 1973); Harold E. Fey and D'Arcy McNickle, *Indians and Other Americans: Two*

Ways of Life Meet (New York, 1959); Alvin Josephy, *The Indian Heritage of America* (New York, 1968); William T. Hagan, *American Indians* (Chicago, 1960); and selected articles in Frederick W. Hodge (ed.), *Handbook of American Indians North of Mexico*, 2 vols. (Washington, 1907–1910); reprinted (New York, 1959).

Federal policy which supplied the foundations for establishing reservations and their administration are the subject of Robert W. Mardock, *The Reformers and the Indian* (Columbia, Mo., 1971); Henry E. Fritz, *The Movement for Indian Assimilation, 1860–1890* (Philadelphia, 1963); S. Lyman Tyler, *A History of Indian Policy* (Washington, D.C., 1973); Francis Paul Prucha (ed.), *Americanizing the American Indians: Writings by the "Friends of the Indian," 1880–1900* (Cambridge, Mass., 1973), and *American Indian Policy in Crisis: Christian Reformers and the Indian, 1865–1900* (Norman, Okla., 1976); Loring B. Priest, *Uncle Sam's Stepchildren: The Reformation of United States Indian Policy 1865–1887* (New York, 1969); and Jennings C. Wise, *The Red Man in the New World Drama: A Politico-Legal Study with a Pageantry of American Indian History*. Edited with an Introduction by Vine Deloria, Jr. (New York, 1971).

The Indian reservation ordeal is described in William T. Hagan, *United States-Comanche Relations: The Reservation Years* (New Haven, Conn., 1976); Donald J. Berthrong, *The Cheyenne and Arapaho Ordeal: Reservation and Agency Life in the Indian Territory, 1875–1907* (Norman, Okla., 1976); Edward Everett Dale, *The Indians of the Southwest: A Century of Development Under the United States* (Norman, Okla., 1949); Angie Debo, *Geronimo: The Man, His Time, His Place* (Norman, Okla., 1976); William E. Unrau, *The Kansa Indians: A History of the Wind People* (Norman, Okla., 1971); Arrell Morgan Gibson, *The Kickapoos: Lords of the Middle Border* (Norman, Okla., 1963); Mildred P. Mayhall, *The Kiowas* (Norman, Okla., 1971); John J. Mathews, *The Osages, Children of the Middle Waters* (Norman, Okla., 1961); Francis Haines, *The Nez Perces: Tribesmen of the Columbia Plateau* (Norman, Okla., 1955); and Muriel H. Wright, *A Guide to the Indian Tribes of Oklahoma* (Norman, Okla., 1951).

The classic attack on the reservation policy, which precipitated wide public interest and sustained support for Indian reform, was Helen Hunt Jackson, *A Century of Dishonor: A Sketch of the United States Government's Dealings with Some of the Indian Tribes* (New York, 1881); reprinted (Williamstown, Mass., 1973). Three works which trace the extension of federal law and judiciary to Native Americans are William T. Hagan, *Indian Police and Judges: Experiments in Acculturation and Control* (New Haven, Conn., 1966); Monroe E. Price, *Law and the American Indian* (Indianapolis, 1973); and Felix S. Cohen, *Handbook of Federal Indian Law* (Washington, 1942); reprinted (Albuquerque, N.M., n.d.). Also see Marvin E. Kroeker, *Great Plains Command: William B. Hazen in the Frontier West* (Norman, Okla., 1976).

Postbellum use of Indian lands by outsiders is the subject of William W. Savage, Jr., *The Cherokee Strip Live Stock Association: Federal Regulation and the Cattleman's Last Frontier* (Columbia, Mo., 1973); and H. Craig Miner, *The Corporation and the Indian: Tribal Sovereignty and Industrial Civilization in Indian Territory, 1865–1907* (Columbia, Mo., 1976). Also see William W. Savage, Jr. (ed.), *Indian Life: Transforming an American Myth* (Norman, Okla., 1977).

CHAPTER 18

STRATEGIES OF EVASION

Our religion seems foolish to you, but so does yours to me. The Baptists and Methodists and Presbyterians and the Catholics all have a different God. Why cannot we have one of our own? Why does the agent seek to take away our religion? My race is dying. Our God will soon die with us. If this new religion [the Ghost Dance] is not true then what matters?

Sitting Bull (Sioux) on Indian religion, 1889

Indian policy, in the European and Anglo-American mind, became a set of processes for directing, controlling, and transforming Native Americans, and for appropriating their territory. Indian policy has another side, however. Native Americans formulated policy and strategy to guide their relations with both the European nations and the United States. In colonial times the policy of Indian nations centered on diplomacy, confederation, and military action to confront the intruding European nations and to protect their territory and interests, to guard tribal security.

After 1776 the United States became the principal adversary for Indian nations on the North American continent. Tribal leaders continued their well-established policy of confederation, diplomacy, and military action to thwart Anglo-American territorial designs. Later several Indian nations, particularly the southern tribes, expanded their policy to include coexistence in an effort to cope with the expansive United States.

However, as we have seen, with the ultimate triumph of Anglo-American arms and appropriation of tribal territories, the Indian nations were forced to settle on reservations. There they were required to submit to a transformation process called "Americanization" which included the destruction of their tribal governments and the erasure of Indianness. Native Americans were desolated by reservation life, but many refused to submit to the new order passively. They contrived imaginative strategies to relieve the boredom of reservation life and to evade the Americanization process. As tribal governments were suppressed under the new order, planning was left to individual Indians either as leaders of resistive groups, or as solitary rebels. However,

Chapter Opening Artifact: Cherokee woven river-cane basket. (Courtesy Museum of the American Indian, Heye Foundation)

reservation rules were strict and most of their acts of evasion remained secret.

One of the most serious obstacles to Indian recovery from defeat and the desolating effect of reservation life was the question of status. Native Americans had been transformed from free individuals with virtually complete self-determination to repressed subjects in a monolithic bureaucratic mold. Their old rights were abolished and new rights, promised under the Anglo-American regime, were held in abeyance until, in the judgment of federal officials, the Indians had been detribalized. Bishop Whipple, one of the few advocates of Native American rights in this period, charged that through the years, "Pledges solemnly made . . . have been shamelessly violated," so that Native Americans "had no redress but war," and now that they were conquered and concentrated on reservations as virtual prisoners of the American government, they had no rights before the law. "The Indian is the only human being within our territory who has no individual right in the soil. He is not . . . protected by the law. [He] has no standing before the law. A Chinese or a Hotentot would have, but the Native American is left pitiably helpless."[1]

The basic question of whether the federal government had the right to hold Indians forcibly on reservations was settled in the Standing Bear decision of 1879. In this case the federal judiciary acknowledged the right of a "peaceful Indian to come and go as he wishes with the same freedom accorded to a white man." However, this rule was largely ignored by federal officials managing the reservations. Agents demanded that Indians remain on the reservations, and they punished those who left without permission. A few Indians, however, were permitted to leave the reservations to work and to go to school. Although many charged that the federal government had no "statutory authority for confining Indians on reservations administrators simply used 'wardship' to justify the practice." In 1890 the confinement of Indians to the reservations was given official sanction in a decree issued by the commissioner of Indian affairs: "The Indian not being considered a citizen of the United States, but a ward of the nation, he can not even leave the reservation without permission."[2]

Hamlin Garland, another Native American advocate, claimed that the status of the Indian was

anomalous [because] he is neither man, brute, nor neighbor. He is told by the Commissioner that he is free to do as other men; but when he seeks to leave the reservation he is ordered back by the agent. He is forbidden to visit in numbers exceeding five or ten; he is ordered not to dance, and admonished to wear his hair short. He is told that he must not use paint on his face, and a hundred other useless indignities and restrictions are put upon him.[3]

Thus most Indians were cooped up on reservations, forcibly restrained, their activities severely restricted. They responded to this drastic change in various ways, some in personally demeaning, destructive ways, others in frivolous time-consuming pursuits, but a good many in creative, restorative ways.

RETROSPECTIVE RESPONSES

Many Indians reacted to the unpleasantness of reservation life with a near-zealous commitment to old customs. Because the old practices were banned by federal administrative rules and laws of Congress and because they were watched by reservation police and faced arrest and jail terms for practicing old customs, Indians performed them secretly. Some of the retrospective responses to reservation life were by groups, others by individuals; some were for harmless entertainment—visiting, horse racing, gambling; others were destructive—addiction to alcohol in an attempt to escape sordid reality of reservation life; some were uplifting—the observance of cherished religious rites; others were exciting—performing frontier tableaus for itinerant Wild West exhibitions and medicine shows in the eastern United States and in Europe.

Group Response

Reverence for old ways and a calculated determination to preserve them in spite of the sanctions and punishment, was a widely used resort among the reservation tribes. Indian practices of courtship, marriage, including polygyny, clan and band rules regulating property ownership and inheritance, and observance of sacred rites, rituals, and festivals of native religion were continued. Many of the tribes of the Indian Territory defied federal agents and observed the Busk, the green corn festival, and other tribal and personal renewal rites.

The Plains tribes concentrated on reservations in the nation's heartland from the Canadian border to Red River practiced individual rites of the search for visions and group rites of the Sun Dance. At the annual Sun Dance, holy men presided over the rites; regularly they gestured to the sky urging intercession by the "Great Mystery," and they directed the warrior participants in their physical sacrifices and prayers rendered through dancing and chanting. Warriors made vows to the Spirit of the Sun. They were bound by actions and pledges made publicly at the ceremony to fulfill their oaths. It was a social time for the gathering of the tribe or tribes, for presentation of infants at "first rites," a time for individual and group renewal. The Sun Dance had originally been a source of supplication for success on the hunt and in combat, but during the reservation period it became only a pageant. However, it remained significant for Native Americans as they sought through the Sun Dance to find the means to cope with the new order through ritual.

Sun Dance paraphernalia included the sacred pole or altar, the figure of a buffalo bull cut from rawhide, the figure of a man to represent the enemy, certain fetishes, and consecrated tobacco, pipes, vermilion, and sweet grass for incense. Tribes attempting to observe the Sun Dance during the reservation era found it difficult to obtain the prescribed buffalo head and hide. The once-vast bison herds had been exterminated by commercial hunters, and only

Sioux sun dancer. (Smithsonian Institution, National Anthropological Archives)

a few buffalo survived on Great Plains ranches. For their Sun Dance in 1887 the Kiowas had to purchase a buffalo bull head and hide from Charles Goodnight, a Texas Panhandle rancher, for the sum of fifty dollars. The other difficulty was obtaining permission to hold the Sun Dance. Bureau of Indian Affairs officials had banned the Sun Dance and authorized agents to call on military commanders at local posts for troops to suppress any attempt to hold the ritual. Any Indian observing the Sun Dance or any other ritual or feast was guilty of violating federal rules and was to be punished by the agent by withholding rations for ten days. Subsequent offenses were punishable by withholding rations for up to thirty days and a jail term of up to thirty days. Sun Dancers continued to hold their sacred rites, but in secret places on the reservation.

Popular social pastimes for reservation Indians included, after a few of their horses were restored to them, racing and games of chance. Many Native Americans were avid gamblers, wagering on horses and cards. They quickly learned the various games of chance with playing cards. Traditional games of chance, with peach and plum pits and shells shaken in a flat bowl or basket, were also widely played. Indian gamblers wagered everything of value; many, when stripped of worldly possessions, tried to recoup by wagering on their honor as bond.

Visiting was another favorite way to while away the time. Families spent days or weeks traveling about the reservation sharing gossip and humble rations with friends and relatives. Also, when permitted, Indian families visited tribes on nearby reservations. Bureau of Indian Affairs rules, issued in 1892, banned visiting because it was thought to produce idleness, loafing, and needless talk. Indians found visiting were to be classed as vagrants, guilty of a misdemeanor, and punished by a jail term.

Indian resourcefulness in deriving some pleasure from the new order included transforming the periodic beef ration issue into a simulated buffalo hunt. These occasions became gala affairs for the late buffalo hunters, a vicarious delight, as "The cattle were driven out of the corrals, pursued over the prairies, and killed in flight by excited warriors on horseback." An Indian Rights Association official witnessed a beef issue in 1886 and "was appalled by what he saw." This spectacle was so cherished by Indians that a principal of a government school rewarded his Indian students for good conduct by dismissing classes for the next beef issue. Federal officials in charge of the Americanization program regarded this a "brutalizing spectacle." In their view "beef-killing day on an Indian reservation is a spectacle which is a disgrace to our civilization. . . . It can not but serve to perpetuate in a savage breast all the cruel and wicked propensities of his nature. It is attended with scenes enacted in the presence of the old and the young, men, women, and little children, which are too disgusting for recital." To end this "savage sport" the commissioner of Indian affairs in 1890 ordered agents to maintain slaughterhouses convenient to the reservations for processing ration beef, from which women and children were excluded.[4]

Many reservation Indians simply decided to escape the reservation ordeal either by returning to the tribal homeland or by exile to another country. The Nez Percés illustrate the use of passive pressure on the federal government. Following Chief Joseph's capitulation to United States army officers in 1879 he and his followers were taken as prisoners of war to the Indian Territory and placed on a reservation on the Salt Fork River in the Cherokee Outlet. Chief Joseph claimed that the capitulation agreement pledged that upon surrender the Nez Percés would be permitted to return to their homeland in the Pacific Northwest. The Nez Percés maintained a steady pressure on federal officials to honor the pledge and finally in 1885, after years of passive resistance to reservation routines, the Nez Percés were permitted to return home.

The Poncas illustrate the peaceful flight form of reservation escape. During 1879 Standing Bear led a party of Poncas from their Indian Territory reservation to the old Ponca homeland on the Northern Plains. They were arrested and their plight received public notice when a federal court in Omaha, in the course of a habeas corpus proceeding on their behalf, rendered the famous Standing Bear decision which defined the Indian's status. The Standing Bear decision and the Ponca plight became a national *cause célèbre* which galvanized reform groups in the East and fused them into the Friends of the Indian movement, to be discussed in Chapter Nineteen.

Another example of escape, this one an armed outbreak, was exodus of the northern Cheyennes from the reservation in the Indian Territory which they shared with the southern Cheyennes. In 1878, to escape dreadful conditions on the reservation, a band of northern Cheyennes led by Dull Knife made a desperate attempt to return to their northern homeland. Dull Knife informed officers at Fort Reno that his people intended to return to their old territory and that they hoped to avoid trouble along the way, but they were armed and would resist to the death any attempt to force them to return to the Indian Territory pesthole. Their passage across Kansas and Nebraska alarmed frontier communities and federal and state military units combed the Plains for the fugitives. However, Dull Knife cleverly eluded the troops and the northern Cheyennes finally reached their old homeland. The fate of Dull Knife's band was in limbo for some time; federal officials finally permitted them to remain and assigned them a new reservation on the Tongue River in Montana.

Another form of reservation escape was exile to another country. Today remnants of many Indian tribes from the United States live in Canada and Mexico, enduring protests to their treatment by the Anglo-American nation. One of the largest groups that sought a haven in Canada during the reservation era were the Sioux and northern Cheyenne followers of Sitting Bull following their victory over the Seventh Cavalry at the Battle of the Little Big Horn in 1876. Indian tribes from the United States also took refuge in Mexico, including a large contingent of Kickapoos, originally from the Great Lakes region, and Seminoles from Florida and the Indian Territory. During the reservation period Kickapoos were forcibly returned to the United States following the Fourth Cavalry raid, led by Colonel Ranald Mackenzie, on their settlements in Coahuila, Mexico, in 1873. However, many Kickapoos subsequently returned to Mexico where they live today.

Individual Response

Many Indians seeking to escape traumatic reservation routines found comfort and solace in individual activity. Some took refuge in the past. Many clung to the empty hope "that the past shall come back again—the illimitable prairie, with vast herds of the vanished buffalo, the deer, the antelope, all the excitement of the chase, and the still fiercer thrill of bloody struggles with rival savage men." This dream was abetted by "oft-repeated recitals from the older men of their own deeds of valor and the achievements of their ancestors."[5]

Some Indians escaped the ennui of reservation life through alcohol. Traders, in blatant defiance of federal law and sometimes in collusion with agents, maintained an ever-ready supply of whiskey for sale or exchange to Indians. The personal degradation and destitution that often resulted fed the Anglo-American's stereotype of the Native American as the "drunken Indian," a derelict committed to a course of self-destruction. After the Indian made such a shameful spectacle of himself, the whites concluded that it was better to hide him on a reservation rather than bring him into the mainstream.

Some Indians, however, sought gainful employment and by hard labor escaped the debilitating reservation boredom. They hauled freight for the agencies and worked for ranchers as herdsmen. Military officers valued Indian riders as the "best light cavalry in the world" and hired them to serve as scouts for infantry and cavalry regiments. Delaware, Osage, Pawnee, and Apache warriors were particularly sought for this type of work.[6]

Indians also performed for Wild West exhibitions and medicine shows which toured the nation and Europe during the late nineteenth and early twentieth centuries. Several western figures including William F. Cody (Buffalo Bill) and Gordon Lillie (Pawnee Bill) became impresarios who put together extremely successful frontier extravaganzas. Indians attired in colorful warrior bonnets, buckskin leggings, and face paint, mounted on swift ponies with flashing lances reenacted western epics under the big tent. Buffalo Bill Cody became the unexcelled showman, the most successful exploiter of Indians and frontier themes for public entertainment.

Each year during the 1880s, Cody employed from 75 to 100 Indians, mostly Sioux, for his itinerant Wild West exhibition. In 1885, he signed Sitting Bull, home from Canadian exile, and the leader of the Indian victory over the Seventh Cavalry at the Battle of the Little Big Horn became a grand attraction for eastern audiences.

Native Americans also were employed as entertainers for itinerant medicine shows, their purpose to attract crowds to the "good doctor's" sales pitch for Indian Sagwa, a panacea. For many years medicine show themes based on the Indian lore were popular in the East and drew huge crowds. Dr. N. T. Oliver, known professionally as Nevada Ned, a Kickapoo medicine show pitchman, explained that the Indian was usually romantic in ratio to the distance separating him from the frontier; whereas the Indian was loathed in the West, the East saw in him the noble savage. Indians performing dances and displaying arts and crafts drew the crowds to the medicine show tent where the pitchman, a buckskin-clad frontiersman billed as "world-famous Indian fighter, scout, and medicine man," made his pitch to the crowd, proclaiming that his bottled panacea was based on secret Indian formulas.

King of the road on the medicine show circuit was the Kickapoo Medicine Company, a partnership organized in 1881 by Texas Charlie Bigelow, peerless promoter from the Lone Star State, and Colonel John Healy, whose favorite maxim was "What fools these mortals be." Exploiting eastern audience fascination with western lore, Healy and Bigelow organized 30 intinerant troupes, each consisting of from 10 to 30 Indians (men, women, and children) in the charge of a frontier scout and "good doctor" named Kit Carson, Nevada Ned, or Yellowstone Joe from the Golden West, resplendent in buckskins, flowing hair, and a booming, persuasive voice. The "scout" served as interpreter, guide, and manager for the troupe and doubled as the medicine man for the Kickapoo Sagwa pitch. The Kickapoo Medicine Company bottled its cures in New Haven, Connecticut. Company officials contracted with federal agents for Indian performers, pledged protection, good care, and 30 dollars a month and keep for each Indian. Most of the Kickapoo Medicine Company Indians were from isolated bands of New York Iroquois and Canadian Indians; a few, notably Pawnees, were actually from the Indian Territory. But at no time did a genuine Kickapoo ever grace a Healy-Bigelow troupe. Kickapoos were fierce, arrogant, Anglo-hating tribesmen fresh from the Mackenzie raid in northern Mexico, and at the time brooded as prisoners of war on their tiny Deep Fork Reservation in the Indian Territory. When asked why this particular tribal name had been selected, Nevada Ned explained, "The word 'Kickapoo' tickled Healy's ear."[7]

The opportunity to travel with a Wild West exhibition or a medicine show troupe gave Indians a welcome change from the tedium of reservation life. Seeing new places, the excitement of performing before crowds, and receiving recognition, applause, public approbation for their feats of daring on horseback and marksmanship skills, and a monthly income understandably were preferable to reservation life.

Federal officials soon came to denounce the use of Indians as public performers. Agents claimed that Sitting Bull and other Indians were virtually incorrigible after performing on Wild West exhibition tours. Reformers protested that the "image presented of the Indians was the wrong one. The glorification of the savage past was hardly a way to lead the Indians down the paths of decorous white civilization." Commissioner of Indian Affairs Thomas J. Morgan denounced Indian participation in public exhibitions.

[While government schools] elevate, the shows degrade. The schools teach industry and thrift, the shows encourage idleness and waste. The schools inculcate morality, the shows lead almost inevitably to vice. The schools encourage the Indians to abandon their paint, blankets, feathers, and savage customs, while the retention and exhibition of these is the chief attraction of the shows.

Morgan ignored the freedom of movement for Indians guaranteed by the Standing Bear decision and directed agents to "discourage in the strongest terms" Indians joining Wild West and medicine show troupes. This directive virtually banned Indian participation, but it had little effect. One way or another impresarios continued to use large numbers of Indians for their exhibitions until well past 1900.[8]

In their continuing attempts to cope with the new order, to develop some meaning for life, and to break reservation monotony, Indians resorted to several, perhaps all, of these group and individual responses. However, the most productive results for reconstruction and rehabilitation came from the regenerative responses which also attracted many reservation-bound Native Americans.

REGENERATIVE RESPONSES

Most Indians were deeply spiritual; religion dominated their lives; and they continued to resort to the metaphysical in their attempts to recover from reservation-induced personal and group desolation, disintegration, and ruin. Nativism, the restoration of uncorrupted Indian life-style, was the dominant theme in Native American reconstruction. Even in early colonial times Indian messiahs appeared with divinely inspired guidance for coping with the new order. Their messages of hope generally included the promise of divine intervention and restoration of the old order when Indians were free of imperial domination. Certainly the expansive, shattering dominion of the new Anglo-American nation increased Indian resort to supernatural intervention through tribal prophets.

Establishing the Messianic Tradition

As had subjugated nations in other ages and places, Indian tribes under European and Anglo-American dominion produced leaders who claimed supernatural powers which provided them the gift of prophesy and the mission of restoration. Some Native American prophets claimed that the Great Holy Force Above had directed them to preach overt defiance. Some called upon Indians to rise up and destroy their oppressors as the first step in achieving the Indian millenium; others advocated passive resistance, even peace, toward their masters, promising supernatural intervention through cataclysmic action to destroy the ruling enemy. Each prophet provided a system of worship to reinforce his teachings, based on traditional religion but frequently including some Christian elements and symbols. All the revelations required individual purification, including rejection of corrupting new customs and things, particularly abstention from use of alcohol, leading a life of self-denial to restore ancient physical and spiritual purity, vigor, and harmony. Thereby Indians would become worthy of salvation which would include divine intervention to destroy the intruders and to restore the lost Indian way of life.

Popé, the seventeenth-century Pueblo Indian patriot, was one of the first Native American messiahs. He claimed to have experienced a heavenly visitation which provided him a god-ordained mission. His prophesy was that,

472

the Indian millenium being near, it was the sacred duty of Indians to fulfill the prophesy by uniting, rising up, and destroying their Spanish oppressors. In 1680 Popé led the Pueblo tribes in a war of independence from Spanish rule. The insurgents triumphed, expelled the Iberian colonists, and for a time restored Indian supremacy along the Rio Grande; subsequently, they were savagely reconquered.

During the mid-eighteenth century a mystic called the Delaware Prophet sought to assuage and restore the scattered, defeated remnants of the Delaware Confederacy, casualties of British colonial expansion on the Atlantic seaboard and thereafter fugitives in the trans-Appalachian wilderness. He pointed to corruption and shameful decline in the once great and powerful Delaware nation. He admonished Native Americans to reject Europeans, their customs and things, and return to the aboriginal life centering on native religion. The Delaware Prophet claimed that he regularly received visions from the Great Spirit who spoke his divine will through him. To win the Great Spirit's blessing of deliverance from their imperial masters, they must obey his instructions revealed through the Delaware Prophet. The form of worship ordained by the Delaware Prophet included the requirement that each follower use a prayer stick engraved with hieroglyphic symbols. Following his teachings would restore aboriginal strength, and eventually Native Americans would achieve the power to expel the Europeans.

It is believed that Pontiac, the rebel who led the tribes of the Old Northwest against the British at the close of the French and Indian War, drew on the widespread influence of the Delaware Prophet, deriving considerable military strength from his spiritual unification of the Old Northwest tribes. However, Pontiac altered the Delaware Prophet's anti-Europeanism, portraying Great Britain as the enemy of Native Americans and France as the Indians' "brother."

All across the continent during the last quarter of the eighteenth century Indians increasingly resorted to messianic revelations to gain deliverance from the imperial nations. In southern California, Chumash Indians formed a restoration movement which spread to neighboring tribes north toward the Cascades and east into the Sierras, threatening Spanish dominion in the Far West. The American War of Independence had a devastating effect upon the Indian tribes in the trans-Appalachian territory. Their numbers drastically reduced, stripped of home territories, and scattered by the victorious Anglo-American nation, these refugees were highly susceptible to Indian messiahs. Moreover, during the war the massacre of Christian Indians, most of them Delawares, at Gnadenhutten by American troops discredited the work of Christian missionaries among the trans-Appalachian tribes and provided native prophets special advantages in winning converts.

One of the most popular Native American messiahs in this troubled age was Handsome Lake, a Seneca prophet, who during the 1790s began to preach the "Great Message" to the battered survivors of the Iroquois Confederation. His teachings consisted of rejection of Anglo-American customs and things, self-purification, a sacrificial, abstemious life, and return to native deities. Reward for compliance would be restoration of cherished old ways.

A second Delaware Prophet appeared to continue the ministry of hope and restoration for this scattered Indian nation and for other rootless Native Americans in the troubled Old Northwest. He stressed simplicity, abstinence, rejection of European and Anglo-American culture, and ceremonial purification as the means to recover ancient vigor, honor, and power. Thus they would be worthy of the Great Spirit's promise to assist them in destroying their oppressors and restoring an uncorrupted aboriginal life-style.

The second Delaware Prophet was a messianic bridge connecting the early aboriginal prophetic tradition with Elskwatawa, the Shawnee Prophet and brother of the incomparable Tecumseh, who forged the nineteenth century's most powerful pan-Indian association. The Shawnees, like the Delawares and scores of other tribes, their eastern lands taken by the expansive Anglo-American nation, were exiles in the trans-Appalachian wilderness.

About 1795 Elskwatawa began to have visions which included visitations with the Great Holy Force Above. He received the command to serve as interpreter and transmitter of these teachings for Indian salvation. After ten years of determined effort he finally attracted an appreciable number of disciples. Eventually Elskwatawa claimed to be the reincarnation of one of the principal deities in the Algonkian pantheon. He preached the necessity for Indian purity by rejecting Anglo-American culture and by abstinence from alcohol and other corruptions introduced to Indians by the "Long Knives," their American enemy.

Elskwatawa denounced any mingling with whites. His teachings banned intermarriage because he believed that white blood was evil; it corrupted Indian nature. He claimed that for those he had sanctified, he had the power to cure illness and turn the enemy's bullets in battle. He preached pan-Indian living and what he called "The Way." His ritual included secret rites of the "living fire," sacred icons, and mystic beads. The Shawnee Prophet explained that Indian problems were the result of their abandonment of tribal deities and old cherished customs and their corruption by adopting European and Anglo-American culture. The way to recover primitive virtue and thus be worthy of the Great Spirit's promise of Indian restoration was to follow the Prophet's teachings and achieve purification. Then they would be worthy of the Great Spirit's promise to assist them in destroying their white enemies. Elskwatawa taught that those who failed to accept and comply with his teachings also would be destroyed in the judgment. The restored Indians would live in an aboriginal utopia.

The Prophet's influence peaked around 1810 with the formation of the pan-Indian settlement at Kithtippecanoe near the Wabash River in Indiana Territory. At times over 8,000 Indians gathered there to hear the Prophet's most recent revelation. The involvement of Elskwatawa's pan-Indian community in armed conflict with the United States, beginning in 1811 at the Battle of Tippecanoe and continuing in the War of 1812, brought defeat to the Indians, death to Tecumseh, and disillusionment to Elskwatawa's disciples.

Several Indian prophets and messiahs appeared during the war's dreadful postlude as the victorious United States exiled the defeated eastern tribes into the trans-Mississippi wilderness, adding to their gloom and defeatism. Kennekuk, the Kickapoo Prophet, was the most successful spiritual leader during this melancholy era. His doctrine of nonviolence and passive resistance to the expansive United States was in marked contrast to the traditional Kickapoo stance of intense bitterness, ferocity in combat, and unremitting resistance to the Anglo-American advance. Kennekuk and his disciples ignored official demands that they vacate their eastern lands and migrate to the trans-Mississippi West. He claimed regular communication with the Great Holy Force Above who revealed divine will for Kennekuk and his followers. They were required to return to the ancient Kickapoo culture, to live abstemiously, and to worship in long meditations with the aid of prayer sticks. Kennekuk taught his followers not to cede their eastern territory and move west as ordered by the federal government but to remain on the land of their ancestors because compliance would offend the Great Spirit.

Reservation-Era Prophets

The tradition for Indian messiahs to appear in times of ethnic distress and offer a message of hope, a way to recovery, and preparation for restoration was well established when the federal government began its policy in the post–Civil War period of concentrating the Indian tribes on reservations. Their deplorable plight predictably produced several messiahs who attempted to mitigate their brothers' suffering and to provide them solace and hope. The principal prophets were Smohalla, Squsachtun, Tavibo, and Wovoka.

Smohalla, a Shahaptian Indian from the Columbia River region, began his messianic career in 1850 when he received metaphysical visitations directing him to protect Native Americans from Anglo-American settlers who were swarming over the Oregon Country. Eventually Smohalla evolved a set of beliefs centering on what is called the Dreamer Religion, from its followers' practice of spending long periods in meditation. Smohalla's teachings included prophesying the millenium with the resurrection of Indians, living and dead, into a mighty force which would destroy their white oppressors, followed by a restoration of the Indian world. He emphasized the need for periodic purification from Anglo-American corruption, personal cleanliness, abstention from alcohol, recovery of old customs, and respect for nature and Indian deities. Smohalla was adamantly opposed to the yeoman-farmer agricultural model set by Anglo-American settlers and urged on Indians by Christian missionaries. His anti-American sentiment was intensified after the Pacific Northwest tribes were crushed by federal and settler militia armies in the wars of 1855–1856, but he was not taken too seriously by Indians or whites until the federal government began to apply its program of territorial compression and reservation assignment to the Pacific Northwest tribes after the Civil War. His influence then increased markedly. Smohalla added a militant note to his teachings, urging overt resistance to reservation life and the federal government's Americanization program. Smohalla scorned the type of hybrid person the federal government was seeking to derive from the reservation-bound Indians; his apostles emphasized, "Their model of a man is an Indian. They aspire to nothing else." Smohalla and his disciples went from reservation to reservation preaching resistance as a manifestation of devotion to the revealed teachings of the Great Holy Force Above. He assured the pitiful reservation wards that the Great Spirit was coming to rescue them from their torment by destroying the white oppressors. He was regularly jailed, but federal harassment only intensified his determination to spread the message of resistance and hope for Indians. When admonished and threatened with prison for encouraging reservation Indians not to work in the fields like their Anglo-American neighbors, Smohalla answered, "My young men shall never work. Men who work can not dream, and wisdom comes to us in dreams . . . you ask me to plow the ground. Shall I take a knife and tear my mother's bosom?" Smohalla's Dreamer Religion is one of several Indian sects formed in the reservation era which survive today.[9]

Squsachtun, called John Slocum by white neighbors, was a Native American prophet in the Puget Sound area who founded the Indian Shaker religion in 1881. Squsachtun's gift of prophesy came from experiencing a long trance during which he was miraculously transported to heaven where he received the divine commission to return to earth and instruct Indians on how to escape destructive reservation life, overcome the trauma of losing aboriginal ways, and achieve salvation. Infusing his doctrine with Christian elements he had learned from missionaries, Squsachtun taught his followers to believe in God and Christ and a heaven and a hell, but for sacred teachings they were to depend upon his prophesy. His Shaker Indian faith was exclusive; it was for Indians only. Followers were called Shakers because in the course of meditative worship their bodies shook or moved in "nervous twitchings" which was a symbolic brushing-off of their sins. Many times federal agents arrested and imprisoned Squsachtun and his disciples for thwarting the Americanization program among Northwest Indians, but the Shaker Indian sect flourished and survives today.

The restoration cult which provided Native Americans the most attractive metaphysical means to escape the ugly reality of reservation life was the Ghost Dance religion. It originated with the messianic teachings of Tavibo, a Paiute Indian in Nevada. In 1870 during a mountain-top mediation vigil near his village Tavibo received a vision from the Great Holy Force Above which designated him earthly agent to carry forth the tidings to Indians that deliverance was imminent. White tormentors of the Indian—teachers, missionaries, government agents, traders, ranchers, and farmers—would be destroyed in one grand cataclysmic earthquake. Only Indians would be spared. Restoration of the old order in nature and tribal life would follow. Tavibo shared this promise of deliverance and restoration with his people, but as they

476

doubted his experience and ridiculed him, he gained only a few converts. Soon he returned to the mountain where he received a second revelation which was much like the first in promise of deliverance and restoration, but it contained more detail. Tavibo related that the cataclysm would swallow up both whites and Indians, but on the third day Indians would be resurrected. Thereafter, they would live forever in a restored aboriginal world. Still Tavibo did not gain the following he expected, so to the mountain he ventured again and received a third revelation. He related to his people that the Great Holy Force Above was so incensed at the lack of faith by Native Americans that by the third dispensation only those Indians who believed would be resurrected. The doubters, with whites, were consigned to eternal punishment. Bannocks, Utes, Shoshonis, and some Paiutes now began to take notice of Tavibo's prophesies, but before his following reached an appreciable size, he died.

Tavibo's son, Wovoka (Jack Wilson), continued his father's work and prophesy. He refined Tavibo's doctrine, added his own, and established a full-blown religious system that came to be called the Ghost Dance religion. Wovoka's addition to Tavibo's revelations included the claim of his death and ascension to heaven where he was designated the messenger for the new messianic cult. Thus Wovoka revealed that because Christ had come to white men but they had killed him, the Great Holy Force Above, God, returned Christ to the earth, this time to the Indians in the person of Wovoka; thus he was the Native American messiah. His ritual included frequent bathing as ceremonial cleansing, living abstemiously, and rejecting alcohol and other destroyers. Wovoka's teachings forbade war or violence in any form. Indians were to live in eternal peace, practicing brotherly love to all other Indians. He also forbade mourning because, he revealed, the dead would soon return; thus mourning was a waste of time. Wovoka repeated Tavibo's promise that white men would disappear, and "the living and dead Indians would be reunited in a restored world where all would live in happiness, free from misery, death, and disease." The restoration promise included reconstruction of the natural world Indians cherished. Grass would again grow on the prairies, lately scarred and torn with the white man's plow; buffalo and other game would flourish, and the free, happy life of old would return. Ghost Dance followers worshiped through meditation, prayer, chanting, and dances to be performed at intervals of five consecutive days, scheduled by Indian holy men, the dance above all other expressions to demonstrate worthiness for the restoration. Because the group ritual transfixed participants and produced a mild, mass hypnosis, the ritual was called the Ghost Dance.[10]

The Ghost Dance Religion

Word of Wovoka's message and the new life it promised spread across the Sierras into the desolated Indian communities of California, to the conquered tribes on reservations in the Pacific Northwest, the Southwest, on the Great Plains, and in the Indian Territory. Dejected and disillusioned in defeat, and

Performers of the Ghost Dance, a late nineteenth-century Indian evangelical religious movement particularly popular among the Plains tribes. (Smithsonian Institution, National Anthropological Archives)

threatened by the Americanization program, Native Americans were desperate for solace and hope. The Ghost Dance religion promised to provide both.

Native Americans eagerly sought word of the messiah. Indians from reservations all over the West traveled to Nevada to learn of the new dispensation. They, like apostles from other faiths, questioned the messiah about various features of the new faith, and his answers had the force of revealed word. Wovoka explained that the white race had been sent to punish Indians for their sins; their suffering under European and Anglo-American rule was sufficient atonement; and they could expect deliverance which Wovoka prophesied would occur in 1891.

Apostles returned to their reservation homes to introduce Wovoka's message of hope among their tribes. From the Canadian border south to Indian Territory and west to California, Ghost Dance celebrants joyously prepared for the promised cataclysm and restoration.

The Ghost Dance religion took an unexpected turn among the Sioux. Sioux holy men learned of Wovoka's message of hope and journeyed to Nevada to learn his new way. They returned to the Dakota Territory reservations converted and zealously committed to sharing the glad tidings. Many Sioux including Sitting Bull became devotees of the Ghost Dance religion because it provided a timely diversion from their desperate situation. Recently federal

478

officials had drastically reduced Sioux reservation lands to open tracts for homesteaders, and the Indians were attempting to support themselves on their diminished territory by farming and stock raising. However, a devastating drought seared their crops and dried up pasture forage and water, killing their livestock. They now had a greatly diminished territory to forage over for game, plants, and roots to sustain themselves, and their plight was compounded by approach of winter's cold. Thus Sioux leaders appealed to the federal government for succor to relieve a very real threat of mass starvation. Officials promised rations which were not delivered because Congress dallied.

Local holy men, riding on a peak of Ghost Dance religious fervor and embittered by the federal government's reduction of Sioux lands and dereliction in providing promised rations, altered Wovoka's doctrine. His teachings of peace and brotherly love were replaced by advocacy of strident activism and insurgency against their keepers. And the Ghost Dance cult became a secret resistance society, including a sanctification ceremony for warrior garments. The Ghost Dance shirt when blessed reputedly was capable of turning back enemy bullets.

In mid-November 1890 the situation became so threatening that agents on the Sioux reservations banned Ghost Dance rites. The Indians ignored the order and seemed so menacing that officials telegraphed for military intervention, stating that "Indians are dancing in the snow and are wild and crazy," and an uprising was imminent. The arrival of troops sharpened the Sioux determination to continue the Ghost Dance rites. Thereupon officials ordered the arrest of several tribal leaders, including Sitting Bull, who were accused of agitating and inciting the Indians to disregard federal orders. When Sitting Bull was slain by reservation police sent to arrest him, Indians were frightened, stunned, and angered, and many prepared to flee from the surveillance of agents and soldiers.[11]

Big Foot led several hundred refugees into the Bad Lands. Troopers of the Seventh Cavalry intercepted and surrounded the fugitives, marched them to Wounded Knee Creek, northeast of Pine Ridge Agency, and on December 29, 1890, moved in to search the Indians for arms. Several refused to submit, a fight broke out, and troops raked the encampment with rapid-firing Hotchkiss guns, killing 150 Indians. Another 50 received serious wounds, and perhaps as many as 100 Indians scattered over the countryside where they froze to death. Twenty-nine soldiers died in the exchange. An Indian who survived the Wounded Knee massacre has composed from his chilling recollections a Native American tragedy:

We followed down the dry gulch, and what we saw was terrible. Dead and wounded [Indian] women and children and little babies were scattered all along where they had been trying to run away. The soldiers had followed along the gulch, as they ran, and murdered them in there. Sometimes they were in heaps because they had huddled together, and some were scattered all along. Sometimes bunches of them had been killed and torn to pieces where the wagon guns hit them. I saw a little baby trying to suck its mother, but she was bloody and dead.

The tragedy at Wounded Knee. Sioux Ghost Dance communicants were massacred in 1890 by troops of the 7th U.S. Cavalry at Wounded Knee Creek, South Dakota. (Photo by G. Trager, Courtesy of Nebraska State Historical Society)

When we drove the soldiers back, they dug themselves in, and we were not enough people to drive them out from there. In the evening they marched off up Wounded Knee Creek, and then we saw all that they had done there.

Men and women and children were heaped and scattered all over the flat at the bottom of the little hill where the soldiers had their wagon-guns, and westward up the dry gulch all the way to the high ridge, the dead women and children and babies were scattered. . . .

This is the way it was: . . . The women and children ran into the gulch and up the west, dropping all the time, for the soldiers shot them as they ran. There were only about a hundred warriors and there were nearly five hundred soldiers. The warriors rushed to where they had piled their guns and knives. They fought soldiers with

480

only their hands until they got their guns. . . . It was a good winter day when all this happened. The sun was shining. But after the soldiers marched away from their dirty work, a heavy snow began to fall. The wind came up in the night. There was a big blizzard, and it grew very cold. The snow drifted deep in the crooked gulch, and it was one long grave of butchered women and children and babies, who had never done any harm and were only trying to run away.[12]

Wovoka's followers performed the Ghost Dance ritual and waited for respite from their reservation ordeal and the restoration, but to their dismay agents, teachers, misionaries, and plows remained. However, before their disillusionment was complete, a new way to deliverance came out of the Southwest.

The Peyote Cult

The new way was the peyote cult, a holy rite which centered on the sacramental use of the peyote button. Peyote is a turnip-shaped fruit of the spineless *Lophophora williamsii,* a cactus which grows in northern Mexico and, less profusely, in the far southwestern United States. The peyote fruit, called the button, cut and dried, was chewed or made into tea which produced "great elevation of spirit and a feeling of good will toward all mankind."[13]

Recent research has found that peyote contains a mild, non-habit-forming halucinogenic element which produces visions and dreams in "technicolor." In some places peyote is locally called mescal, a term also applied to the yield of the large agave or century plant, and beans from a leguminous shrub. Indians who ate these beans were called "mescal eaters"; mescal reportedly produced the same kind of hallucinations as peyote.

Mexican tribes and several Apache bands from the southwestern United States had used peyote for centuries. Comanches learned of peyote in their raids into northern Mexico in prereservation times. They were primarily responsible for introducing peyote among the tribes of the Indian Territory. Even during the Ghost Dance fervor, peyote cult cells flourished among the Comanches. Gradually the cult spread to the Kiowas, Cheyennes, Arapahoes, and other Comanche neighbors. Following the collapse of the Ghost Dance movement, the peyote cult spread rapidly throughout the Indian communities of the West.

Initially the peyote rite was used to produce a mild hallucinatory state, a simple exercise of flight from the daily ennui of reservation life to a satisfying level of quiet, peace, and freedom. Ingesting peyote produced dreams and visions and caused a gastrointestinal reaction and vomiting, a symbolic cleansing for the worshipers, somewhat like the practice of the southeastern tribesmen who as a prelude to worship took the "black drink" or sacred *cussena* to purge themselves of evil and become worthy of the blessings of the Great Holy Force Above.

As the peyote cult spread across the reservations of the West, Native Americans expanded its doctrine and practice. Thus a peyote cult worship service came to include, besides ingesting peyote, individual and group singing, praying, drumming, meditating, performing mystical rites, and personal and group dedication to the 'Peyote Road," the ethical code whereby each follower was required to be temperate, truthful, upright, devoted to family, and to hold a high estimation of self and abstain from corrupting and destructive practices including use of alcohol.

The Bureau of Indian Affairs regarded the peyote religion, like other Indian ways,. as a threat to the Americanization program and banned it on the reservations. Federal agents claimed that the peyote cult had to be

prohibited for the same sociological reasons as we have led the Government strongly but tactfully to modify Indian dance. As is well known, exercises which the Indians consider of a religious nature are made the occasion of taking the drug. These meetings are held as often as once a week and invariably last throughout the night. The time occupied in going to these meetings, the demoralizing effects of all-night seances, and consequent nervous languor and exhaustion, very considerably encroach upon the time that should normally be devoted to work. Furthermore, the effects of the drug in making the Indian contented with his present attainments seriously interfere with his progress by cutting off from him the possibility of healthful aspiration.[14]

States and territories with Indian populations also forbade use of peyote. Oklahoma Territory, formed from the western half of Indian Territory in 1890, attempted to deprive its populous Indian communities of this worship alternative by banning the peyote cult in 1898. The United States Department of Agriculture cooperated in the suppression of the cult by forbidding importation of peyote into the United States. Each year federal agents on the Mexican border purchased and destroyed the visible supply of peyote. Nonetheless, sufficient amounts of this cactus fruit filtered through to the western reservations to maintain the worship.

Through the years Indian holy men increasingly integrated new elements into their forms of worship so that by 1900 the peyote religion had become a mixture of Native American and Christian concepts and rituals. Thus taking peyote became a sacrament of communion in which the worshipers substituted peyote for bread and wine. Eventually the peyote cult was organized as the Native American Church. And the dominant Anglo-American society, by suppressing it and forcing it underground, assured its longevity. Predictably the Native American Church increased its appeal and following, and survives with considerable force today.

The nineteenth century had been a particularly destructive period for Native Americans. However, Indians had to endure one additional ordeal—allotment in severalty—before the century closed. Although it was inconceivable that anything could exceed the trauma of the Indians' reservation experience, partitioning the reservations and assigning the Indians homesteads did just that.

Notes

1. Helen Hunt Jackson, *A Century of Dishonor* (New York, 1881); reprinted (Williamstown, Mass., 1973).
2. Francis Paul Prucha, *American Indian Policy in Crisis: Christian Reformers and the Indian, 1865–1900* (Norman, Okla., 1976), p. 321; and Lonnie E. Underhill and Daniel F. Littlefield, Jr. (eds.), *Hamlin Garland's Observations on the American Indian, 1895–1905* (Tucson, Ariz., 1976), p. 175.
3. Underhill and Littlefield, *Hamlin Garland's Observations*, p. 175.
4. Prucha, *American Indian Policy*, p. 212.
5. Herbert Welsh, "The Meaning of the Dakota Outbreak, "*Scribner's Magazine* 9 (April 1891), pp. 43–45.
6. Kenneth Kay, "Gunga Din, Danny Dever, and the U.S. Cavalry," *Army* 27 (April 1977), pp. 48–49.
7. See Arrell Morgan Gibson, "Frontier Medicine Show," *American West* 4 (February 1967), pp. 33–39, 74–79, for a discussion of the use of Native Americans as public entertainers.
8. *Report of the Commissioner of Indian Affairs for 1890*, pp. lvii, lix; and Prucha, *American Indian Policy*, p. 320.
9. James Mooney, *The Ghost Dance Religion and the Sioux Outbreak of 1890* (Washington, D.C., 1893), pp. 711–16.
10. See *Ibid.* for the definitive study of the Ghost Dance religion.
11. Prucha, *American Indian Policy*, p. 361.
12. Jack D. Forbes (ed.), *The Indian in America's Past* (Englewood Cliffs, N.J., 1964), p. 50.
13. *Report of the Commisioner of Indian Affairs for 1909*, p. 10.
14. *Report of the Commisioner of Indian Affairs for 1911*, p. 35.

Selected Sources

Studies of the reservation experience which include treatment of strategies of evasion are Francis Paul Prucha (ed.), *Americanizing the American Indians: Writings by the "Friends of the Indian," 1880–1900* (Cambridge, Mass., 1973), and *American Indian Policy in Crisis: Christian Reformers and the Indian, 1865–1900* (Norman, Okla., 1976); Loring B. Priest, *Uncle Sam's Stepchildren: The Reformation of the United States Indian Policy, 1865–1887* (New York, 1969); Jennings C. Wise, *The Red Man in the New World Drama: A Politico-Legal Study with a Pageantry of American Indian History*, edited with an Introduction by Vine Deloria, Jr. (New York, 1971); Robert W. Mardock, *The Reformers and the Indian* (Columbia, Mo., 1971); Henry E. Fritz, *The Movement for Indian Assimilation, 1860–1890* (Philadelphia, 1963); and S. Lyman Tyler, *A History of Indian Policy* (Washington, D.C., 1973).

Specific tribal response to reservation life is found in William T. Hagan, *United States-Comanche Relations: The Reservation Years* (New Haven, Conn., 1976); Donald J. Berthrong, *The Cheyenne and Arapaho Ordeal: Reservation and Agency Life in the Indian Territory, 1875–1907* (Norman, Okla., 1976); James A. Clifton, *The Prairie People: Continuity and Change in Potawatomi Indian Culture, 1665–1965* (Lawrence, Kans., 1977); and Lonnie E. Underhill and Daniel F. Littlefield,

Jr. (eds.), *Hamlin Garland's Observations on the American Indian, 1895–1905* (Tucson, Ariz., 1976).

Retrospective and regenerative responses by Native Americans to their reservation plight are discussed in Nancy O. Lurie, "The World's Oldest On-Going Protest Demonstration: North American Indian Drinking Patterns," *Pacific Historical Quarterly* 40 (August 1971), pp. 311–32; William T. Hagan, "Indian Policy After the Civil War: The Reservation Experience," *Indiana Historical Society Lectures, 1970–1971* (Indianapolis, 1971); Charles S. Brant, "Indian-White Relations in Southwestern Oklahoma," *Chronicles of Oklahoma* 37 (Winter 1959–1960), pp. 433–439; Clyde B. Dollar, "Renaissance on the Reservation," *American West* 11 (January 1974), pp. 6–9, 58–62; Chunilal Roy, "Indian Peyotists and Alcohol," *American Journal of Psychiatry* 103 (March 1973), pp. 329–30; Weston LaBarre, "Primitive Psychotheraphy in Native American Cultures: Peyotism and Confession," *Journal of Abnormal and Social Psychology* 42 (1947), pp. 294–309, and *The Peyote Cult* (New York, 1969); J. S. Slotkin, *The Peyote Religion: A Study in Indian-White Relations* (Glencoe, Ill., 1956); David F. Aberle, *The Peyote Religion Among the Navajo* (New York, 1966); Donald N. Brown, "The Ghost Dance Religion among the Oklahoma Cheyenne," *Chronicles of Oklahoma* 30 (Winter, 1952–1953), pp. 408–16; Paul D. Bailey, *Wovoka, The Indian Messiah* (Los Angeles, 1957); David F. Aberle, "The Prophet Dance and Reactions to White Contact," *Southwestern Journal of Anthropology* 15 (Spring 1959), pp. 74–83; James Mooney, *The Ghost Dance Religion and the Sioux Outbreak of 1890* (Washington, D.C., 1893); Carol Hampton, "The Sacrament of the Native American Church: Peyote," MA Thesis, University of Oklahoma (Norman, Okla., 1973); Weston La Barre, *The Ghost Dance: The Origins of Religion* (New York, 1970); and William K. Powers, *Oglala Religion* (Lincoln, Neb., 1975).

An analysis of the pan-Indian effect of the regenerative responses appears in Hazel W. Hertzberg, *The Search for an Indian Identity: Modern Pan-Indian Movements* (Syracuse, N.Y., 1971). Exile to another country as a strategy of evasion is discussed in detail in Arrell Morgan Gibson, *The Kickapoos: Lords of the Middle Border* (Norman, Okla., 1963).

CHAPTER 19

FINAL DIVESTMENT
OF THE INDIAN
ESTATE

We did not think of the great open plains, the beautiful rolling hills, and winding streams with tangled growth, as "wild." Only to the white man was nature a "wilderness" and to him was the land "infested" with "wild" animals and "savage" people. To us it was tame. Earth was bountiful and we were surrounded with the blessings of the Great Mystery.

Luther Standing Bear (Sioux) on loss of tribal estate, 1902

Progressive diminution of tribal lands and exile of Indians to remote western wilderness regions had very well accommodated national goals and citizen land needs for the first half of the nineteenth century. However, after the Civil War, the nation's citizens populated the western frontier with unexpected, unsurpassed rapidity; they established new territories in the trans-Mississippi region and there remained no wilderness into which to exile Native Americans. Thus the national army conquered the Indian nations that resisted and federal officials compressed all tribes on reservations. But as we have seen, even these were reduced to make lands available to the tide of settlers flowing across the American West. Even reservations were a part of the ultimate aboriginal territorial compression process in that federal officials regarded them as temporary abodes for Native Americans, ostensibly training grounds for achieving Americanization and assimilation, including destruction of Indian life-style, to be replaced by the Anglo-American life-style which would require substantially less land for each Indian's survival.

In the last quarter of the nineteenth century, unfulfilled land desires of Anglo-American home seekers were in the process of forcing the federal government to make reservations, the last remaining tribal estates, available for settlement. At this juncture a group of reformers, known to history as "Friends of the Indian," fortuitously came forth with a plan conceived for the good of Native Americans which would meet their needs and also satisfy settler demands—allotment in severalty, terminating tribal ownership of land by partitioning reservations and assigning each Indian a 160-acre allotment in fee simple or outright ownership. "Friends of the Indian" argued that an Indian's ownership of a patch of land would accomplish that much-desired

Chapter Opening Artifact: Detail of "Mimbres," a watercolor by Tony Da. (Courtesy Heard Museum and Abrams Photo/Graphics)

486

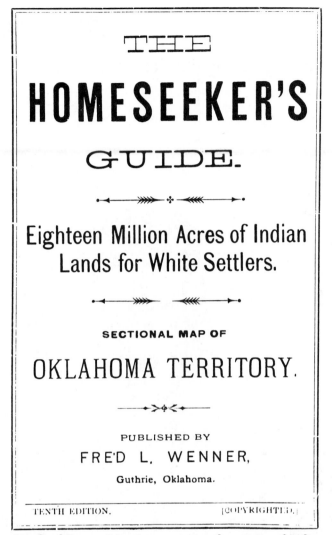

THE

HOMESEEKER'S

GUIDE.

Eighteen Million Acres of Indian
Lands for White Settlers.

SECTIONAL MAP OF

OKLAHOMA TERRITORY.

PUBLISHED BY

FRED L. WENNER,

Guthrie, Oklahoma.

TENTH EDITION.   [COPYRIGHTED.]

Sample of Boomer Literature promoting the opening of Indian
Territory to settlers. (University of Oklahoma Library)

transformation to a mainstream American, and settlers could homestead the
surplus reservation land. Their ideas were put into practice in the form of
allotment in severalty, the ultimate in the reduction and appropriation of the
tribal estate. It was carried out under the General Allotment Act, popularly
called the Dawes Act, adopted in 1887.

The effect of this progressive diminution of the tribal lands is illustrated
by the Comanche experience. During much of the nineteenth century their
Great Plains territory, extending from the Arkansas River to the Rio Grande,
comprised a domain of nearly 300 million acres. Anglo-American expansion
and rulings by the federal government in the postwar era produced a rapid

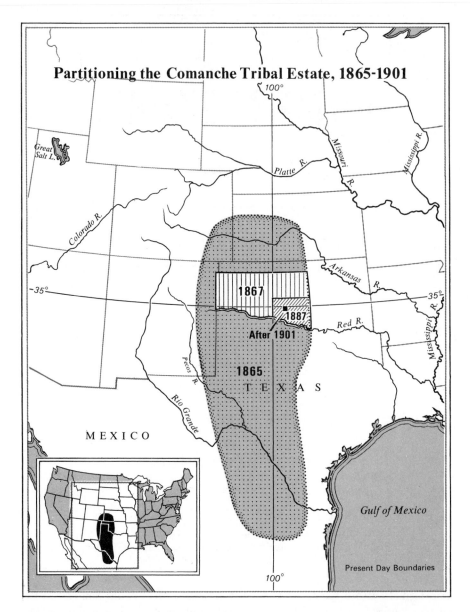

Partitioning the Comanche Tribal Estate, 1865-1901

reduction of their territory. The Treaty of the Little Arkansas (1865) compressed the Comanches into a territory that extended from 98 degrees to 103 degrees longitude, flanked by the Cimarron and Red rivers. A nation numbering less than 5,000, they still retained a range of nearly 30 million acres. But so swift was post–Civil War Anglo-American expansion that in less than two years federal officials forced the Comanches to submit to the Medicine Lodge Treaty by which they ceded most of their land to the United States and were assigned a reservation in the southwestern part Indian Territory of about 3 million acres. Thus in the decade of the 1860s the Comanche tribe's territory was reduced 100-fold. Around 1900 application of the General Allotment Act to the Comanches reduced their diminished tribal estate to a patchwork of individual holdings. Thereafter each Comanche was restricted to a 160-acre homestead. This dramatic territorial reduction among Comanches and other Indians, with accompanying change from strength to weakness, from affluence to poverty, from fredom to dependence and repression, from a grandly infinite world to a miserly finite terrestrial parcel, is the subject of this chapter.

GENESIS OF ALLOTMENT

Federal officials regarded reservations as the halfway house to Native American assimilation, controlled environments for accomplishing the detribalization process, and thus their expected existence was to be brief. In an age of intense individualism and limited patience, there was a growing public conclusion that the federal government's Americanization experiment had failed, that Indians were as single-mindedly committed as ever to old ways. Clearly their strategies of evasion had strengthened tribalism.

During the 1880s, Helen Hunt Jackson and other critics of Indian policy were demanding that reservations be abolished. Therefore, federal officials admitted failure and began to search for a graceful way to terminate the "national ghettos," the "ethnic slums." Destroying reservations because Indians were not proceeding along the road to civilization as the reformers desired was a naive, simplistic approach. In their attempts to transform and Americanize the aboriginal peoples of the nation, public and private groups for a century had applied education and Christian missions with no appreciable effect. Therefore, federal officials decided to add private landownership through allotment in severalty to education and Christian missions, creating a trilogy of transformation. Hopefully, fee-simple private landownership would so individualize Indians that they would Americanize themselves. Thus national leaders made the decision to abolish reservations and require Native Americans to submit to allotment in severalty.

Experiments with Allotment in Severalty

From colonial times Americans had been concerned that the Indian landholding system differed from theirs. Because most national leaders believed that the assimilation of Native Americans into the Anglo-American community was inevitable and because this required compliance with established norms, they worked to replace tribal communal ownership of land with fee-simple private ownership through allotment in severalty. The first allotment law was adopted in 1633 by the Massachusetts General Court (legislature). The statute permitted colonial leaders to assign Indians small individual tracts for their maintenance and to develop a sense of private ownership. Colonial attempts at allotment in severalty had little enduring effect upon Native Americans.

Early in the nation's life, leaders stressed to Indians the benefits of abandoning communal ownership and taking land in private fee-simple ownership, compatible with the established Anglo-American system of land tenure. They regarded this step as basic to the desired transformation which would lead to assimilation. Secretary of War Henry Knox was an early advocate of private land tenure by Indians. He maintained that fee-simple landownership provided Indians with a foundation for developing "love of exclusive property." President Thomas Jefferson also urged Indians to replace communal ownership of land with fee-simple tenure, to transform them into the Anglo-American yeoman-farmer model which he cherished. Indians generally ignored these entreaties. However, several land cession treaties, including an agreement with the Cherokees in 1817, contained an allotment in severalty clause and a few Cherokees accepted fee-simple tenure. Through the years Congress passed laws providing for allotment in severalty for certain tribal remnants. Thus an 1839 law allotted the Brotherton Indians in Wisconsin and granted them citizenship.

The Choctaw and Creek removal treaties contained clauses permitting allotment in severalty for tribal citizens as an alternative to removal to Indian Territory. Many Indians attempted unsuccessfully to live on allotments in Alabama and Mississippi under repressive state laws, public ostracism, and predictable white settler exploitation, but eventually they gave up and joined their tribes in the Indian Territory.

The Manypenny treaties concluded in 1853–1854 with the tribes of the northern half of the Indian Territory provided for partitioning the reservations into allotments for the resident tribes. Allotment in severalty brought no visible benefits to these Indians. Soon most of them were stripped of their lands by Anglo-American neighbors.

The Pacific Northwest tribes were an allotment anomaly in the antebellum period. Following their conquest by federal and militia armies in 1855, the Spokanes, Snakes, Umatillas, Palouses, and Yakimas were assigned reservations. However, many refused to go to their reservations, preferring to squat upon public lands in the Northwest wilderness, forming isolated pockets of settlement. Over one half of each tribe shunned the reservation set aside for it. An 1875 law permitted Indian squatters to validate their claims on the public domain under the federal homestead law. Large numbers of Indians absent from the reservations were assumed to reduce the need by the tribes for all the reservation area assigned, with the result that many were proportionately reduced, the surplus land made available to settlers. Many Indians taking homesteads lost out to white adversaries as the Northwest interior began to fill with settlers following railroad construction there. Many Indians did not understand the rules for proving up a homestead in order to obtain title to it; most of them could not raise the money to pay the filing costs. As a result Indian homesteads were taken for debt, legal fees, and other devices used so successfully in Alabama and Mississippi fifty years earlier.

In an attempt to move Indians in the direction of personal, private fee-simple ownership, Congress applied the aforementioned 1875 law to all Indians. The Indian Homestead Act extended the land benefits of the 1862 statute to persons who were willing to give up tribal status, although they were to retain their share of tribal funds. The intent of the measure was to encourage Indians to terminate their tribal association and to expedite their eligibility for United States citizenship.

Few Indians applied for land under the amended homestead law. To this point allotment in severalty had been carried out on a tribal or individual basis, and it had not met with the success its advocates expected. Increasingly the view developed that only a general allotment law applying to all tribes, to all Indians, would accomplish the desired change in Native American land tenure. A group of well-meaning but misguided reformers called "Friends of the Indian" took up this cause.

Friends of the Indian

Advocates of Indian welfare were few in the early postwar period; best-known private citizens urging Indian reform were Henry B. Whipple, the Episcopal bishop of Minnesota, John Beeson, the pamphleteer, and Helen Hunt Jackson, the pioneer muckraker. There were also a few officials in the federal government who attempted to soften bureaucratic indifference, including Captain Richard H. Pratt, founder of Carlisle as the model training center for Americanizing Indians, who became the foremost educator of Native Americans, and Carl Schurz, secretary of the interior from 1877 to 1881, who attempted to cleanse and reform the bureaucracy which administered the cooped-up Indians. The quasi-official Board of Indian Commissioners for the most part also worked for Indian service reform and justice.

While these pioneer reformers were genuinely concerned about justice for the Native Americans, they were still ethnocentric. To them, Indianness—tribal language, values, religion, societal models, communal ownership of land, the aboriginal life-style—was anathema. Their goal was to lift Indians from pagan depravity and transform and assimilate them into the Anglo-American mainstream. Because in their view reservations thwarted Americanization and abetted tribalism, they should be abolished and replaced with allotment in severalty—at once.

Countering these pioneer Indian welfare advocates was a coterie led by Thomas A. Bland and Alfred B. Meacham who agreed that Indians should be transformed and reservations abolished, but they urged that change in aboriginal life-style should take place gradually, at a pace set by the Indians. Bland and Meacham insisted that Indians be permitted to exercise self-determination, that they be consulted as to what was best for them.

An incident on the Nebraska frontier in 1879—the Standing Bear decision—precipitated the fusion of individual reformers into political action groups which eventually persuaded Congress to adopt a general allotment law. Thomas A. Tibbles, a reporter for the Omaha *Herald,* had rallied a small group of Nebraskans, including a lawyer, to work for justice among the Poncas. They eventually won the writ of habeas corpus in federal district court for Standing Bear and his Ponca followers who were held for unlawful flight by military authorities for return to their much-despised Indian territory reservation. Sensing the *cause célèbre* possibilities of this action, Tibbles with Bright Eyes, a young Ponca Indian woman, his wife, went east and lectured in public halls from Boston to Baltimore on the deplorable state of Indians on reservations, focusing on Standing Bear and the Poncas, the appropriation of their Dakota Territory homeland and their exile to a small reservation in the Indian Territory. Tibbles stirred and Bright Eyes dazzled attentive audiences; Standing Bear became the symbol of injustice to Native Americans.

Their message touched a particularly responsive public chord among New Englanders. Helen Hunt Jackson of Boston, an enthusiastic member of their audiences, became the most outspoken writer for the cause of Indian reform, especially for allotment in severalty. Her books, *Century of Dishonor* and *Ramona,* were widely read, touched many people, and provoked public support which resulted in the General Allotment Act.

Other New Englanders formed investigatory and action committees. It has been said that they "approached the problem in a spirit of moral urgency which was suggestive of the abolitionist movement." One advocate commented that "it is fitting that Massachusetts, foremost in putting an end to the servitude of the black men, should now be foremost in putting an end to this worse servitude of the red men." Thus the reformers' creed became Indians "must have privileges and citizenship, protection of law, and individual land patents, the same as Anglo-Americans." These "Friends of the Indian" groups formed to improve the lot of Indians held to the view that private fee-simple ownership of reservation land was a *sine qua non* for both Indian assimilation and citizenship. Reformers pointed to the abolitionist crusade as the model for action to achieve for Indians the rights of the thirteenth, fourteenth, and fifteenth amendments to the Constitution which ostensibly had elevated blacks into the American mainstream.[1]

In 1879 a committee of Boston business and civic leaders established the Indian Protective Committee, one of the first action groups formed to promote Native American welfare. This group's goals were to protect Indian title to reservation lands by halting further reduction for the purpose of opening lands for homesteaders, to promote passage of a general allotment law, and to extend civil and political rights to Indians.

During 1882 in Philadelphia, Henry B. Pancoast and Herbert Welsh founded another Native American reform group, the Indian Rights Association. They established chapters of the association in cities throughout the United States, sent their agents all over the West inspecting reservations, investigating conditions, and collecting evidence of agent malfeasance and mistreatment and exploitation of Indians, and published and distributed great numbers of pamphlets on Indian affairs to rally public support for Indian reform legislation, primarily allotment in severalty and citizenship. Credo of the Indian Rights Association was to secure "civilization of . . . Indians . . . and to prepare the way for their absorption into the common life" of the American nation.[2]

Churchwomen in Philadelphia founded another "Friends of the Indian" organization in 1883, the Women's National Indian Association. Within three years the association had established 83 branches in cities across the nation. Its staff published a monthly periodical, *The Indian's Friend,* circulated petitions for presentation to the Congress and the President protesting Indian mistreatment, urging reform of the Indian service, and demanding that the federal government honor all treaty obligations to the tribes with "scrupulous fidelity." The association also pressed Congress to increase schools for Indians and improve quality of instruction, allot each Indian a 160-acre homestead in fee simple, and extend to all Indians American citizenship.

The National Indian Defense Association, another organization promoting Native American welfare, was formed in 1885 by Thomas A. Bland, editor of *Council Fire,* a journal devoted to Indian affairs. This group took issue with reformers who urged rapid Americanization of Indians, rushing them into allotment in severalty and citizenship. Members of the Indian Defense Association favored ultimate assimilation, but they sought to protect Indian culture, permitting moderate Americanization at a pace desired by Indians rather than that expected by white reformers. Although Bland's group had little effect upon the "Friends of the Indian" reform movement, its stress on aboriginal self-determination anticipated the Native Americans' great quest of the 1970s.

Albert A. Smiley, Quaker philanthropist and member of the Board of Indian Commissioners, owned a resort hotel on scenic Lake Mohonk. Beginning in 1883, he invited "Friends of the Indian" to this New York retreat to discuss and formulate solutions to Indian problems which were to be transmitted to appropriate officials in the national government. For several years representatives of "Friends of the Indian" groups, members of the Board of Indian Commissioners, and reform-minded congressmen and other government officials gathered at Lake Mohonk for the semiannual sessions hosted by Smiley. Their deliberations produced several substantive alterations in federal Indian policy including eradication of reservations through allotment in severalty.

Guest rosters of the Lake Mohonk conferences glittered with luminaries from the nation's business and professional community. Dominating the sessions through the years were Lyman Abbott, Herbert Welsh, Charles Painter, Henry L. Dawes, William Strong, and Merrill E. Gates. Abbott, a Congregational clergyman, editor, reformer, and popular orator, frequently served as principal speaker at the conferences. Not a gradualist in Indian reform, Abbott expected drastic change to be accomplished at once. He stressed the evils of the reservation system and worked for Indian advancement through expanded educational opportunities and prompt assimilation.

Welsh, a Philadelphian, founder of the Indian Rights Association and its executive secretary, was a leading figure at Lake Mohonk. He claimed that he decided to devote his life to Indian reform after an extended tour of the western reservations. At the Lake Mohonk conferences Welsh stressed the need for reform laws and sound administration of these laws. A strong advocate of allotment in severalty, he emphasized that "Indian tenure of land, full protection of the law and citizenship [were the] three necessary foundation stones for Indian civilization." Painter, a lobbyist for the Indian Rights Association in Washington, traveled widely in the West, investigating conditions on reservations which he regularly reported to Lake Mohonk delegates. Painter urged abolition of reservations, allotment in severalty, and citizenship for Indians.[3]

Henry L. Dawes, United States senator from Massachusetts and chairman of the Senate Committee on Indian Affairs, was the principal advocate of allotment and citizenship for Indians in the Congress. He worked closely with Indian reform groups and participated in several Lake Mohonk conferences. Other public officials attending the Lake Mohonk conferences included William Strong, United States Supreme Court justice. Strong supported allotment in severalty and was particularly interested in the constitutional aspects of Indian citizenship.

Merrill E. Gates, college president, first at Rutgers then Amherst, and a member of the Board of Indian Commissioners, frequently presided over Lake Mohonk sessions. He stressed the need for Christian society to accept Indians and, like most "Friends of the Indian," was scornful of aboriginal culture, particularly native religion. He claimed that "the tribal system paralyzes at once the desire for property and the family life that ennobles that desire," and he characterized reservations as "debasing." Gates's stirring oratory on Indian reform to the Lake Mohonk delegates frequently revealed the materialism of the period:

We have, to begin with, the absolute need of awakening in the savage Indian broader desires and ampler wants. To bring him out of savagery into citizenship we must make the Indian more intelligently selfish before we can make him unselfishly intelligent. We need to awaken in him wants. In his dull savagery he must be touched by the wings of the divine angel of discontent. Then he begins to look forward, to reach out. The desire for property of his own may become an intense educating force. The wish for a home of his own awakens him to new efforts. Discontent with the teepee and the starving rations of the Indian camp in winter is needed to get the Indian out of the blanket and into trousers—and trousers with pockets in them, and with a pocket that aches to be filled with dollars.[4]

"Friends of the Indian," through their Lake Mohonk conferences, speeches, writings, and organization publications, mobilized public opinion on the "Indian problem" to the point that during the 1880s a greater number of citizens became interested in Indian affairs than ever before in American history. Through public discussion they had applied such devastating criticism to reservation policy that its replacement was but a matter of time. Reformers' solution of the "Indian problem" was threefold: (1) destroy tribalism and reservations by individualizing Indians on allotments; (2) confer citizenship upon all Indians; and (3) educate Indian youth to assure continuation of the reforms. "Friends of the Indian" gospel was strongly Darwinian, individualistic, blindly Christian, ultra-patriotic, and uncompromisingly ethnocentric. Their simplistic view was that destroying reservations would deliver Indians from paternalistic control by the federal bureaucracy. Their plan to educate, Christianize, and civilize Indians began with allotment in severalty which, they firmly believed, would engender among Indians the desired adoration for private property.

The General Allotment Act

Beginning in the late 1870s liquidating the last vestiges of tribal lands, the reservations, received increasing support. Much of it came from a land-hungry public. The Department of the Interior, through its General Land Office, faced increasing pressure from home seekers, and the only fit land remaining was that on Indian reservations. In the debates on the issue of the final liquidation of the Indian estate it became clear that most westerners scorned their Indian neighbors and regularly urged the federal government to move them to some other territory or state so that their reservation land could be settled. But they eventually became convinced that they could not have all of the acres embraced in the reservations, so they reluctantly settled for a portion. However, their "pressure upon reservations was so strong that a realistic outlook forced recognition of the necessity for surrender of some Indian land in return for undisputed title to the rest." Therefore, humanitarians and land-grabbers and many Indian agents united to urge the policy of allotment in severalty.[5]

The Indian bureaucracy came to accept allotment as desirable because, with a smaller area to roam over, Indians would be more manageable. One agent commented,

As long as Indians live in villages they will retain many of their old and injurious habits. Frequent feasts, heathen ceremonies and dances, constant visiting—these will continue as long as people live together in close neighborhoods and villages. I trust that before another year is ended they will generally be located upon individual land or farms. From that date will begin their real and permanent progress.

Another agent admitted that with allotment "in many ways the Indians will be wronged and cheated, but such a condition has got to be met sometime, and why not commence at once instead of putting off the evil day?"[6]

Of all the reservation partitioning proposals submitted the most attractive one to congressmen was that of Senator Richard Coke of Texas. The Coke bill provided for the division of reservations into 160-acre homestead allotments, title to be held in trust by the federal government for 25 years. However, allotment would not proceed unless two thirds of the adult male members of a tribe voted approval, an application of self-determination for Indians advocated by Bland and Meacham and the National Indian Defense

Association. This measure met wide public opposition because it was claimed that Indians, given a choice, would delay allotment indefinitely to preserve common ownership. One authority has commented, "The difficulty of the Coke bill stemmed from the fact that it was framed to favor the interests of the Indian rather than of the Western landgrabber." Painter, the Indian Rights Association lobbyist, explained to Lake Mohonk reformers that this measure delayed settler access to reservation land and he predicted, correctly, that the Coke bill would never pass "unless reform legislation could be identified with the interests of white citizens."[7]

During the late 1880s there emerged an allotment-in-severalty proposal in the Congress called the Dawes bill, after Senator Dawes, who proposed it, which became the General Allotment Act. It sought to meet the fault of the Coke proposal by striking Indian self-determination and making allotment of reservations mandatory at the discretion of the President. Tribal spokesmen had denounced each allotment proposal; they were outraged at the Dawes bill. Native American leaders explained that reservations were bad enough, but allotment would be impossible. The Seneca council's resolution opposing allotment stated that under their communal land system all tribal members were protected and provided for; "no Indian, however improvident and thriftless, can be deprived of a resort to the soil for his support and that of his family. There is always land for him to cultivate free of tax, rent or purchase price." Several Sioux leaders including Sitting Bull protested the Dawes proposal by visiting tribes on reservations in the northern Rocky Mountains and Great Plains and urging resistance to allotment. The Five Civilized Tribes maintained permanent delegations in Washington to lobby against bills not in the tribal interest. These lobbyists spent much time trying to turn back allotment proposals.[8]

As tribal protests to allotment spread over the Indian nations and reservations, Commissioner of Indian Affairs J. D. C. Atkins became alarmed. Fearing that tribal activists might re-create a Standing Bear-type spectacle and agitate before eastern audiences against allotment in severalty, he directed agents to forbid Indians to leave their reservations and to arrest and detain the recalcitrant ones. This order only increased Indian antagonism.

When Chief Jake of the Caddoes and Lone Wolf of the Kiowas attempted to escape to Washington to protest adoption of the Dawes proposal, their agent enforced Commissioner Atkins' order by arresting and detaining them. However, they escaped to the Creek nation where supporters raised money for their train fare to Washington. Congress had approved the Dawes proposal before they arrived, but they still protested, expressing their views to any official or journalist in Washington who would listen. Returning to Indian Territory, Lone Wolf called a council of southwestern Indian Territory tribes to protest the General Allotment Act, and appealed to the Five Civilized Tribes for support. Thereupon the Creeks convened a pan-Indian council attended by 57 representatives from 19 tribes. In the course of the council proceedings, Tawaconie Jim, a Wichita delegate, protested, "The government treats us as if we had no rights." The intertribal council adopted a resolution urging the President to halt enforcement of the General Allotment Act, but to no avail.[9]

Native Americans were joined by non-Indians who also opposed the General Allotment Act. Lewis Henry Morgan, James Mooney, and other pioneer anthropologists generally objected to partitioning reservations and rapid assimilating as unsound and impossible to achieve in the short time expected by the reformers. The Bureau of Indian Affairs and the Congress deliberately ignored "expert guidance with respect to the sociological needs of the red race" which was available at the time. The "ethnological experts were to be found, not in the Bureau of Indian Affairs, but in the Smithsonian Institution. However, their superior knowledge was bitterly resented by the politically appointed clerks in charge of Indian affairs." The experts on Native American culture "were jealously excluded from consideration by the committees of Congress charged with passing on the policies and measures framed in the Bureau of Indian Affairs. 'Impractical dreamers' they were called."[10]

However, not all members of the Bureau of American Ethnology opposed allotment. Alice Fletcher, a specialist on the Omaha tribe, was a strong advocate of this change in Indian landholding. She was largely responsible for persuading the Omaha tribe to accept partitioning of communal lands. John W. Powell, director of the Bureau of American Ethnology, also favored allotment in severalty. "No measure could be devised more efficient for the ultimate civilization of the Indians of this country" he wrote, "than one by which they could successfully and rapidly obtain lands in severalty."[11]

Surprisingly, some doubt to efficacy of allotment, even opposition to it, developed within the government. President Grover Cleveland commented that allotment in severalty appeared to him to be just another way for settlers to obtain Indian land—the "hunger and thirst of the white man for the Indian's land is almost equal to his hunger and thirst after righteousness." United States Senator Henry M. Teller warned prophetically that within 40 years Indians would be separated from their titles to allotment homesteads, and they would "curse the hand that was raised professedly in their defense." And the minority report prepared by the House Committee on Indian Affairs for the General Allotment Act stated, "However much we may differ from the humanitarians who are riding this hobby, we are certain that they will agree with us in the proposition that it does not make a farmer out of an Indian to give him a quarter section of land. . . . the real aim of this bill is to get at the Indian lands and open them to settlement. . . . If this were done in the name of greed, it would be bad enough; but to do it in the name of humanity and under the cloak of an ardent desire to promote the Indian's welfare by making him like ourselves, whether he will or not, is infinitely worse."[12]

The General Allotment Act, approved in 1887, authorized the President to direct the survey of each reservation, the preparation of tribal rolls, and the assignment of an allotment of 160 acres to each family head, 80 acres to a single person over 18 and orphans under 18, and 40 acres each to other single persons under 18. Allottees were expected to select their homesteads, but if they failed to do so government agents were to select the allotments. The federal government was to hold each allotment title in trust for 25 years. Allotments were to be tax-exempt for the period of the trust. The law also conferred citizenship upon each allottee. Exempted from allotment were the Five Civilized Tribes, the Osages, the Seneca nation of New York, and the Miami, Peoria, Sac, and Fox tribes of Indian Territory. Objections by these tribes to the General Allotment Act were derived from several concerns including the fear that land grants made to private companies in early national times as well as more recent railroad land grants would be validated if their communally held lands were allotted. Surplus tribal lands, those acres remaining on reservations after each Indian had received an allotment, were placed in the public domain of the United States and opened to settlement. Homeseeker pressure was so intense on the federal government that no part of the original reservations were set aside for unborn Indian children, although shrewd tribal leaders delayed consummation of allotment to permit all known expectant mothers to deliver.

Congress made many changes in the General Allotment Act, largely in response to public demand. A law in 1890 equalized allotment roughly on the basis of its earning capacity. Rather than setting the size of all allotments at 160 acres as reformers had proposed, the statute prescribed agricultural allotments of 80 acres each and grazing homesteads at 160 acres each. Subsequently this section of the tribal land division program came to vary with the tribe; most Indians received a basic 160-acre allotment although some were considerably larger. After their exemption was removed, Choctaws and Chickasaws received allotments averaging 320 acres. Some were smaller— Pimas received 10-acre allotments within irrigable areas and 10-acre allotments of non-irrigable land in the adjacent desert. The Mexican Kickapoos, held as prisoners of war on a small reservation in the Indian Territory, were awarded allotments of only 80 acres each when all of their aboriginal neighbors were being assigned 160-acre allotments. This discrimination was punitive; they had for years made war on settlements in southern Texas before they were forced to move from Coahuila, Mexico, to the Indian Territory; and it was also meant to assure that there would be some surplus land for homeseekers. An 1891 statute provided for the appointment of three commissioners to investigate the tribes of southern California, many of them former Mission Indians, who reportedly were landless and poverty-stricken. The commissioners were to select reservations for each band, settle the members thereon, and prepare allotments.

One of the most important changes in the General Allotment Act came in 1893 when Congress made the Five Civilized Tribes and Osages subject to the allotment process. In 1906 Congress approved the Burke Act. Its purpose was to end blanket conferring of citizenship on Indians at the time of assignment of allotments. It deferred citizenship for allottees until the expiration of the 25-year trust period. In addition the Burke Act delegated to the secretary of the interior discretionary authority to remove restrictions on allotments. This law did not apply to the Indian Territory tribes.

From time to time Congress also approved legislation removing restrictions on allotments for particular tribes or factions thereof. A 1903 law removed restrictions from some of the allotted lands held by members of the Five Civilized Tribes. Then when Oklahoma became a state in 1907, local political and business leaders urged Congress to remove restrictions on allotments in the state in order to make additional land available for purchase and to increase the tax base. Congress responded the next year by adopting a law which lifted restrictions on allotments held by thousands of mixed bloods and freedmen. Under exemptions to the General Allotment Act trust requirement provided by this law, called by reformers the "Crime of 1908," it is estimated that 90 percent of the allottees disposed of a portion or all of their lands. This statute also ended supervision of probating estates of the Five Civilized Tribes by the secretary of the interior and transferred that function to county courts, which opened productive channels for even grosser malfeasance and prostitution of public trust.

Proceeds from sale of surplus lands were to be held in trust by the federal government and dispensed for "Indian benefit," interpreted by the Bureau of Indian Affairs to be for education and civilization. This placed additional funds in the hands of Congress to manipulate as that body chose. Most federal agents were derelict in appraising surplus land. For example, the acres remaining after allotment on the Sioux reservations were taken by the federal government for distribution to settlers, reimbursing the tribes an average of 25 cents an acre when the market value of this land ranged from 3 to 10 dollars an acre.

Following allotment the former reservations and the allotted Indians came under territorial and state law and jurisdiction. Thereafter Native Americans had to cope with 3 layers of jurisdiction—tribal (which they observed although federal officials denied that it existed), state, and federal. Inevitable legal conflicts grew out of questions of Indian marriage and family relations, property titles, probate practices, and law and order.

Federal officials enforced the General Allotment Act with unusual speed and alacrity. Examination of the official reports inevitably gives the impression that this law was for the benefit of the home seeker, opening land for him to settle upon, rather than for the Indian, providing him a final landed birthright. Commissioner of Indian Affairs Morgan stated that the General Allotment Act clearly demonstrated that the "settled policy of the government is to break up the reservations, destroy tribal relations, settle Indians on their own homesteads, incorporate them into the national life, and deal with them not as nations or tribes or bands, but as individual citizens." And Secretary of the Interior John W. Noble crowed that he had been responsible for opening "to settlement more Indian reservations than all his predecessors combined."[13]

The General Allotment Act and related legislation were enlarged by administrative rulings which clarified the basic measure and expedited its en-forcement. Thus when federal agents met difficulty in preparing tribal rolls because they found Indian names difficult to spell, the Commissioner of In-dian Affairs issued an order directing that all Indians be renamed. Unless allottees had been to school, they had a given first name but no last name. When agents asked chiefs for the names of their people, many deliberately delayed reporting until all mothers known to be expecting had delivered, thus assuring homesteads for as many newborn as possible. And even in defeat, as allotment in severalty surely was for most Indians, many Native Americans had the last laugh when the allotting agents studiously recorded names of dogs and horses in the village reported on tribal rolls as bona fide allottees. Federal officials and congressmen did not appreciate this brand of Indian humor. Difficulty of using the Indian naming system and making it compatible with the Anglo-American system based on a father's surname, led to several attempts to rename Indians. Hamlin Garland, a staunch defender of aboriginal culture and life-style, favored this change primarily because Indians had no choice but to accept allotments, and he believed that it would protect their property rights. He said that the need for this change was pointed out to him by Chester Poe Cornelius, an Oneida Indian and attorney, who told him "lawyers will always be concerned largely with Indian lands, in-heritance, and titles. The agency rolls do not show family relationships. Each man and woman has an individual name and there is certain to be much liti-gation." Thus Garland worked with federal officials for several years in an unsuccessful attempt to rename Indians.[14]

Liquidating the Indian Estate

Federal officials found that negotiating allotment contracts with the Indian nations, a step they regarded as essential protection against future litigation, and preparing tribal rolls, were difficult, patience-wracking tasks. Home seekers' insistent demands that they complete the process quickly in order to open the surplus lands and their political pressure on the Congress caused federal officials to resort to intimidation, chicanery, and assorted injustices on Indians in order to complete allotment. Many Indians refused even to con-sider accepting allotments and various methods, many of them devious, were used to bring the recalcitrants to terms.

On some reservations the tribal agent was commissioned to supervise the allotment process. On others, federal commissions were appointed for this pur-pose; the principal ones were the Jerome Commission and the Dawes Com-mission. The Jerome Commission, named for its chairman, David H. Jerome, former governor of Michigan, was to negotiate allotment contracts with the tribes in the Indian Territory who lived west of the Five Civilized nations. It sometimes was called the Cherokee Commission from one of its first assign-ments—to negotiate with the Cherokee nation for sale of the Outlet. Asso-ciate members of the Jerome Commission were Alfred M. Wilson and Warren

G. Sayre. The other allotment supervisory group was the Dawes Commission. In 1893 Congress removed the Five Civilized Tribes' exemption to the General Allotment Act; in that same year Henry L. Dawes retired from the United States Senate and President Grover Cleveland appointed him to chair the group assigned the task of liquidating the lands of the Five Civilized Tribes, which came to be called the Dawes Commission. Meredith Kidd and Archibald S. McKennon were associate members of the Dawes Commission.

Methods used by allotting agents and commissions to overcome tribal resistance to partitioning Indian nations and reservations varied. Most were intimidative and deceitful. Three examples will be presented.

The Yankton Sioux determinedly resisted allotment in severalty. Finally their agent forced them to cooperate by persuading the secretary of war to station two companies of troops from Fort Randall in their reservation. The agent explained that when dealing with Indians, if conciliation failed, then "prompt, decisive action becomes necessary. There must be no yielding to Indian whims nor compromise to gratify Indian caprice, at the sacrifice of law and good government."[15]

The second example concerns the Mexican Kickapoos. Fresh from exile in Mexico and restive under their status as prisoners of war, the Kickapoos smarted in defeat on their Deep Fork Reservation in central Indian Territory. In 1890 the Cherokee Commission members began pressing Kickapoo leaders for an allotment contract. They made four attempts with no success. Each time Kickapoo leaders refused to discuss allotment. The fifth time they were accompanied by John T. Hill, an intermarried Creek and an acquaintance of many Kickapoos because he frequently grazed cattle on their reservation. Hill explained to tribal leaders that he had just learned that the Kickapoos would not have to submit to allotment but would be permitted to retain their lands in common, and that they were to receive accumulated annuity funds held in trust for them by federal officials. In order to obtain the funds and to avoid allotment and thus retain their lands in common, the Kickapoos would have to send two of their leaders to Washington with Hill to sign a contract.

The Kickapoo council assented and chose headmen Ockquanocasey and Keeshocum to accompany Hill to Washington. En route the Kickapoo spokesmen were surprised that Cherokee Commission members were on their train. And when they reached Washington, Hill took them to Secretary of the Interior John W. Noble's office where Cherokee Commission members were present. Ockquanocasey and Keeshocum were uneasy and refused to sign the paper Secretary Noble tendered to them. Thereupon Hill took the Indians on a Potomac excursion in a "big boat" to soothe them. Next day Hill again tried to persuade them to sign the contract; he swore to them that it provided for retaining their lands in common and a substantial money payment. Ockquanocasey and Keeshocum continued suspicious but after hours of intense pressure and finally bullying from Hill, including a threat that soldiers were coming to take them to the Potomac to throw then into the "Big Water," they signed. When Ockquanocasey and Keeshocum returned to Indian Territory, allotting officers were busily partitioning their reservation and they realized that Hill had lied to them; that he had been in the employ of the Cherokee Commission and the contract they had signed in Noble's office provided for the allotment of their reservation and the sale of surplus lands. A final insult to Kickapoos was Hill's payment of $5,172 "from a grateful United States for his Kickapoo success, characterized by the Indian Rights Association as a 'palpable fraud.'" This sum was to be deducted from the total $64,650 which the Kickapoos would receive for the nearly 200,000 acres of their reservation which was declared surplus. Neighboring tribes, including Potawatomis, had received $1.50 an acre for their surplus lands, but Kickapoos received only about thirty cents an acre. And while few tribes in the Indian Territory had to submit to allotments of less than 160 acres, several receiving twice or more this amount, the Kickapoos received only 80 acres each. The injustice was compounded by the fact that their reservation had enough land for each member of the tribe to receive the customary 160-acre allotments with a surplus remaining for settlers.[16]

The third illustration of public pressure on Indians to submit to allotment is the experience of the Five Civilized Tribes and their relations with the Dawes Commission. After they were stripped of their exemption from the General Allotment Act in 1893, leaders of these populous Indian communities had adamantly refused to meet with the Dawes Commission to discuss allotment of their communally owned lands. Therefore Congress in 1896 delegated to the Dawes Commission authority to prepare rolls unilaterally and proceed with allotment. Thereupon tribal resistance began to cave. In 1897 the Choctaws and Chickasaws concluded the Atoka Agreement, a contract providing for total allocation of their lands to tribal citizens with no surplus for home seekers. The other tribes persisted in delay so Congress in 1898 passed the Curtis Act which abolished tribal governments, required the citizens of the abolished Indian nations to submit to allotment, instituted civil government for the Indian Territory, and provided a guide for statehood. This statute forced the other tribes to capitulate: the Seminoles signed their allotment contract in 1898, the Creeks in 1901, and the Cherokees in 1902.

Cheating, criminal collusion, and chicanery of every description corrupted the allotting process. Home seekers, town developers, lawyers, all manner of boomers and promoters and hangers-on lurked about the Indian nations, a predacious wolf pack lusting for the last parcels of tribal land. And in several ways at various stages in the allotment process they scored. One access to Indian land in the allotting process was through the tribal rolls. Non-Indians got on the tribal rolls and thereby became eligible for allotments of land by marriage to Indians, by adoption into the tribes, and by claiming Indian descent. Allotment contracts concluded with the Five Civilized Tribes provided a fourth access. Cherokees, Choctaws, Seminoles, Creeks, and Chickasaws had been slaveholders before the Civil War. Reconstruction Treaties required these tribes to confer tribal citizenship upon their former slaves. Tribal citizenship prerogatives included sharing in use of the tribal domain. The tribes' allotment contracts stipulated allotments to these former slaves. Thousands of blacks from Texas, Louisiana, Arkansas, and Mississippi swarmed across Indian Territory claiming descent from former slaves of the Indians, joining additional thousand of whites claiming a sufficient tincture of Indian blood to merit enrollment. The Dawes Commission prepared to enroll over 400,000 persons claiming to be of Chickasaw, Choctaw, Seminole, Creek, or Cherokee descent, or former slaves of these tribes. Indian leaders refused to permit wholesale, unchallenged enrollment. They formed tribal citizenship commissions which examined all applicants' qualifications and rejected 75 percent of the claimants. The Dawes Commission finally enrolled the names of 101,000 persons deemed eligible for allotments on the domains of the Five Civilized Tribes.

The Last Indian Rebellion

Mandated allotment in severalty forced a revolution in life-style on Native Americans. A few Indians, perhaps, welcomed it. Many accepted it as they had most recent changes as another denial of self-determination, an ordeal inflicted upon them by the federal government which they were powerless to prevent. However, some resisted and attempted to escape it. The greatest and boldest defiance arose among the Five Civilized Tribes. Resistance factions appeared in the Cherokee, Creek, Seminole, Choctaw, and Chickasaw nations. Cherokee activists reconstituted an ancient tribal society, the Keetoowah. Led by Red Bird Smith, it became their agency of resistance. The Choctaws, Chickasaws, and Seminoles also formed groups to protest and resist enforcement of the General Allotment Act. However, Creeks mounted the most threatening resistance. Chitto Harjo (Crazy Snake), an intelligent, eloquent full blood who was ardently devoted to the legacy of Opothleyaholo in his commitment to preserve and transmit cherished traditional Muscogee customs, led the resistance movement. His followers were called Snakes. Harjo reestablished traditional tribal government, and assuming the headship of a revitalized Creek nation, he insisted that treaties with the United States granting to the Creeks their lands in the Indian Territory in perpetuity, and the right to hold these lands in common, remained in effect, and that no law of Congress could override those stipulations. In 1901 Harjo led what came to be called the Snake Uprising. The council for this de facto Indian government adopted laws which were declared to be binding on all tribal citizens; the legislation included a ban on Creeks accepting allotments. Harjo's "lighthorse" arrested and whipped persons who accepted allotments. The insurgents created widespread unrest and indecision among the Creeks, stalled the land partitioning process, and caused allotting officials to appeal for succor. Posses of federal marshals and columns of cavalry surged over the Creek nation arresting and jailing Snakes and so completely smothering Harjo's resistance movement that allotting officials were able to resume their work.

However, the Snakes' spirit of overt resistance spread to the other Indian

Chitto Harjo (1846–1912), Creek leader. (Courtesy the Oklahoma Historical Society)

nations. Choctaw insurgents became so threatening that federal officials used force to disperse them. And Keetoowah members in the Cherokee nation harassed allotting officials until their leaders were arrested and jailed. Eventually federal marshals and troops in the domains of the Five Nations ended all threat of overt resistance.

Thereupon, antiallotment partisans resorted to passive resistance. First, they refused to accept allotments. But, in compliance with the law, government agents selected homesteads for them. However, private ownership of land was so unthinkable to the protesters that they refused to live on designated allotments; for years they camped on school, council, and church grounds. As late as 1912, 2,000 Cherokees persisted in their refusal to live on assigned allotments. Their lands lay unused or were occupied by squatters. The fabulously rich Cushing oil pool lay under lands forcibly allotted to 80 Snakes (before oil was found there). No enticement could lure them onto their government-assigned properties; they even refused royalty checks from the petroleum bonanza on their allotments tendered to them by federal agents.

Finally, many antiallotment Cherokees, Creeks, Choctaws, and Chickasaws saw the futility of resistance, overt or covert. Led by Eufaula Harjo and Red Bird Smith, they formed the Four Mothers Society, committing themselves through collective action to seek alternatives. They raised modest sums from pitifully poor partisans to send delegations to Washington to protest their treatment by the federal government and to urge that they be permitted to return to their cherished tribal customs, including communal ownership of land. Their eventual strategy, based on reluctant acknowledgment of inevitability of loss of the right to hold their lands communally, was to plead with Congress to remove restrictions on sale of their allotments to permit them to dispose of their properties, place the proceeds in a common fund, and purchase land in Mexico where the members had been assured that the Mexican government would permit them to live as they wished, including holding their lands in common. Jacob Jackson, a college-educated full-blood Choctaw and principal advocate of emigration, appeared before a congressional committee and delivered an eloquent, moving appeal for approval of the plan which would permit voluntary exile to Mexico.

Surely a race of people, desiring to preserve the integrity of that race, who love it by reason of its traditions and their common ancestors and blood, who are proud of the fact that they belong to it may be permitted to protect themselves, if in no other way by emigration. Our educated people inform us that the white man came to this country to avoid conditions which to him were not as bad as the present conditions are to us; that he went across the great ocean and sought new homes in order to avoid things which to him were distasteful and wrong. All we ask is that we may be permitted to exercise the same privilege. We do not ask any aid from the Government of the United States in so doing. We do ask that we may be permitted, in a proper way, by protecting our own, to dispose of that which the Government says is ours, and which has been given us over our protest against the distribution, to the end that another home may be furnished, and another nation established.

Jackson continued that his plan would please the white man.

He does not want the Indian any more than we want him, and by carrying out this plan he will get that which he wants—the Indian land. We will leave and trouble him no longer. [Allotment in severalty was completely unacceptable to his partisans; his proposal was] just. . . . There is no remedy for us except removal . . . we believe that the Great Father of all men created the Indian to fill a proper place in this world. That as an Indian he had certain rights, among which is a right to exist as a race, and that in the protection of that right, it our belief that we are fulfilling the purpose of the Divine Creator of mankind.

It is reported that the senators ridiculed Jackson's appeal. Clearly, the federal government as guardian of the national image would not permit the embarrassing spectacle of Indians, for whom it served as trustee and guardian, to flee to another nation. Congress soon removed restrictions on sale of allotted land for many of these tribes, not so much for Indian benefit as for Anglo-American (agricultural, lumbering, mining, oil, railroad, and municipal, county, and state government) benefit. And ironically Indians were not permitted to leave the United States. Rather they were forced to remain and endure additional exploitation and torment at the hands of intruder hordes flooding the partitioned Indian nations.[17]

Despoiling Allotments

The General Allotment Act was in effect from 1887 to 1934. It liquidated all of the reservations and nations of the 67 tribes of the Indian Territory, the lands of the northern Kickapoos and Potawatomis in Kansas, the Sioux in Nebraska and North and South Dakota, northern Cheyennes and Arapahoes in Wyoming, the Gros Ventres and Blackfeet in Montana, Jicarilla Apaches in New Mexico, Mohaves of the lower Colorado River region, several Pacific Northwest tribes including the Yakimas, Nez Percés, and Spokanes, and certain Pima bands in the desert Southwest. This statute nearly completed the divestment of tribal territories, a process initiated by the pioneers of European empires over 300 years before. The Anglo-American nation, succeeding to their dominion over North America, became the most proficient in appropriating tribal lands, virtually erasing Indian title to lands on the continent. Thus the Native American estate within the present limits of the United States in 1500 consisted of nearly 3 billion acres; it had been successively reduced by conquest, seizure, treaty, and statute, until by 1887, the year final divestment of tribal lands began through application of the General Allotment Act, the surviving tribes retained only about 150 million acres; when the General Allotment Act was repealed in 1934 this had declined to about 48 million acres, much of it desert.

The General Allotment Act's safeguards to protect and preserve the Native Americans' last remaining landed birthright failed most Indians. The Anglo-American settler had an insatiable appetite for Indian land. Even as federal officials prepared for allotment, settlers demanded and received a share in that in final drastic partitioning of tribal estates Indians surrendered the surplus lands for homesteading. And we have seen that non-Indians also shared in allotment through marriage, adoption, and claim of Indian or freedman descent which provided inclusion on tribal rolls for sharing in the distribution of land. And those denied access to the tribal estate through homesteading the surplus or receiving an allotment inventively contrived alternatives. Their success is confirmed by the record of continuing divestment. When Congress repealed the General Allotment Act in 1934, Indians were in possession of less than one third of their original allotted lands.

Leasing was one way that non-Indians appropriated use of allotments. Many Indians were so completely disillusioned and for cultural reasons were so determined to ignore the reality of allotment that they leased their lands to stockraisers, farmers, lumbermen, miners, and oil producers, and were content to collect an annual pittance in rental which they subsisted upon. After lumbermen lessees had stripped allotments of timber, miner lessees had scarred allotments with mine tailings and strip pits, and oil men lessees had milked the allotments' subterranean pools of petroleum and polluted surfaces with greasy sumps from derelict wells, they abandoned their leases. Farmers and ranchers held onto leased allotments for longer periods, but they customarily overgrazed and one-cropped Indian lands into a state of eroded ruin. At the conclusion of allotment in severalty in the 1930s, scientists from the Bureau of Indian Affairs and Soil Conservation Service found that all allotments had been eroded, more than half of them classed as "critically" or "severely eroded."

Although in its original form the General Allotment Act contained safeguards for Indian ownership of allotted land, most of the law's protective features were rather quickly repealed. Even in the beginning when the 25 year trust period applied to all allotments, which was the principal deterrent to separating Indians from their land, non-Indians got control of allotments by marriage to allottees, gaining at least a shared right to the land during the lifetime of the Indian spouse and, often at the death of the allottee, complete title. Also heirship land, estates of deceased allottees, could be purchased by non-Indians.

Business and political interests in the states and territories containing allotted Indian land applied great pressure upon federal officials to remove restrictions on allotments in order to make the Indian land immediately available for purchase and the ever-cooperative national legislature began, soon after 1900, to lift restrictions on individual allotments as well as selected groups within a tribe, and at times an entire tribe. The Burke Act, passed in 1906, delegated discretionary authority to the secretary of the interior to remove restrictions on individual allottees. Thus the suspicion expressed in the Dawes Act Minority Report was confirmed—truly the General Allotment Act's "real aim [was] to get at the Indians' lands and open them to settlement."[18]

This statute created a large landless class among the Indians. Erstwhile owners of all of the North American continent shortly were so divested that many possessed not even a fragment of it. Wherever there were allotted Indian lands, there occurred sudden and decisive expropriation. Three instances will serve to illustrate. One occurred in far northern Minnesota on the former White Earth Reservation. Indians had been allotted homesteads containing thick stands of white pine timber. In 1906 Congress adopted legislation removing restrictions on allotments held by the White Earth mixed bloods. Powerful lumbering interests quickly purchased these timber-rich allotments at shamefully low prices.

The Sisseton Sioux of South Dakota lived on a reservation containing nearly 1 million acres of fertile land, fine pasture, some timber, and good water, certainly sufficient resources to make this 2,000-member tribe if not affluent at least self-supporting. Then the federal government partitioned their reservation. Tribal members received about 300,000 acres of their reservation in allotments; the remainder was declared surplus and homesteaded. Then laws by Congress and rulings by the secretary of the interior progressively reduced restrictions on allotments and permitted transfer of title to outsiders. By 1909 two thirds of the Sisseton Sioux allotted land had passed to non-Indians. Tribal population steadily increased through the years reaching 3,000 in 1940. Few moved elsewhere; most lived in increasing destitution on an ever-diminishing land base.

The third and worst example occurred in the Indian Territory. Indians there received especially close attention from grafters and despoilers because their allotments contained, besides rich farming and grazing tracts, dense forests, rich lead and zinc deposits, thick coal seams, and the most extensive petroleum deposits then known in the world.

Most of the non-Indian citizens and leaders in the new state of Oklahoma carried the Anglo-American frontier mentality of their fathers and grandfathers from Kentucky, Tennessee, Mississippi, Alabama, Louisiana, Texas, Arkansas, Missouri, and Kansas. They were racist, ethnocentric, and contemptuous of Indians and indifferent to their plight. Private and public expectations were that Congress would quickly remove restrictions on Indian lands—private to open access to allotment riches, and public to place tax-exempt Indian allotments into the state revenue pool. Congress responded with several remedial laws; the most notorious statute, called "the crime of 1908" by reformers, removed all restrictions on freedmen and intermarried and adopted citizens' allotments and reduced partial to total restrictions on mixed bloods' allotments. Thus nearly 13 million acres went on the market, and the tidings were "received with almost universal rejoicing as a charter of opportunity to the state. Muskogee as the metropolis [of the old Indian Territory section of the new state] planned a whole week's celebration with special entertainment to excursionists from all parts of the United States, and speeches by Governor Haskell and members of the Oklahoma delegation in Congress."[19]

This statute also transferred Indian guardian and probate matters from the secretary of the interior to county courts, largely staffed with incompetent and corrupt judges. Thus county judges controlled all restricted allotments in their respective counties. All adult Indians and 60,000 children holding restricted allotments were declared incompetent to manage their personal affairs; each was deemed to require a guardian to manage each property. As could be expected, a lucrative traffic in sale of guardian appointments followed. At stake were trust properties with rich agricultural, grazing, timber, coal, lead, zinc, and oil resources valued at well over a billion dollars. Attorneys also had a field day in that county judges who appointed them to handle Indian estate matters permitted then to charge a 50 percent contingency fee. Attorneys and guardians could not own restricted allotments, but they were able to control the proceeds from agricultural and grazing leases and lumber, coal, lead, zinc, and oil royalties. Bitter competition developed among aspiring guardians and attorneys for control of Indian estates. A Creek allottee holding a rich petroleum tract was kidnapped by a presumptive guardian and hidden from competitors; eventually the Indian was spirited off to England where he was held a virtual prisoner for 6 months. Forgery, theft, malfeasance, embezzlement, prodigious violation of trust, kidnapping, perjury, and homicide were common occurrences in the guardian-attorney contest for control of Indian property. In those rare cases where an honest judge or county attorney attempted to protect Indians and prosecute derelict guardians, white juries consistently voted to acquit.

Federal agents provided scarcely any protection. They continued to work among the tribes in the new state, ostensibly to protect Indians from exploitation, and to guide them in their progression into the new order. However, most found the temptation for wealth from speculative schemes connected with Indian estates too great. Justice Department investigations repeatedly revealed violation of public trust by members of the Indian bureaucracy.

Sadly for Indians, interest by "Friends of the Indian" in their welfare faded soon after adoption of the General Allotment Act. Thereafter, other than the Board of Indian Commissioners which conducted an occasional investigation of allotment fraud, almost the only reform group maintaining genuine interest was the Indian Rights Association. However, their revelations of abuse and violation of public trust were generally ignored by state and federal prosecutors.

Only one defender of Indian interests came forth in this grim postallotment era. She was Kate Barnard, the Commissioner of Charities and Corrections for the new state of Oklahoma. She was a sincere and dedicated crusader, and her sensitivity to human needs made her incorruptible. Soon after her election to public office in 1907 she discovered what she termed hideous exploitation of Indian children by guardians in her investigation of a report that three "wild" children lived in the hills of eastern Oklahoma.

She found three small Indians sleeping in the hollow of an old tree, drinking from a stream, and securing food from neighboring farmhouses. No one knew to whom they belonged and it was six weeks before her assistant was able to locate their guardian. She found then that their parents were dead, that they owned valuable oil land, and that the guardian had been collecting their royalties and charging them exorbitant prices for their education and support [which they did not receive.]

The same guardian had 51 Indian children under his guardianship. Another guardian sought to gain control of a group of 161 children whose allotments were on valuable tracts of timber.[20]

Vested interests in the new state controlled the malleable legislature. They objected to Ms. Barnard's "meddling," and that body adopted laws severely crippling her means to intervene on behalf of Indian orphans. Her appeal for legal assistance to investigate and prosecute exploiters finally passed the legislature after she made dramatic and embarrassing revelations, but Governor Lee Cruce, himself married to an Indian woman, vetoed the bill. And Ms. Barnard had little success in winning juries to render verdicts for Indian orphans in the county courts because judges, prosecuting attorneys, and white juries exonerated those whom she accused of abusing and exploiting Indian youth.

The chilling irony of allotment in severalty was that, conceived for Indians' benefit, particularly to assure them protected titles to homesteads, in practice it made most Indians landless. Certainly it did not produce the millenium of Indian transformation and better conditions envisioned by "Friends of the Indian." A few reservations—Cherokee in North Carolina; Seminole in Florida; Alabama and Coushatta in Texas; Seneca in New York; Sac and Fox in Iowa; several Ute bands in Colorado; Pueblo and Mescalero Apache in New Mexico; Zuñi, Hopi, and Navajo in Arizona and New Mexico; Maricopa, Papago, and some Pima lands in Arizona; Tule River, Hoopa, and Yurok in California; Yuma in the Colorado River region; and lands in Alaska—escaped the partitioning process. In the twentieth century Indian proprietors of these lands found their status generally better than that of allotted Indians. While few reservation Indians prospered, sustained by their communal land base, they did escape the grinding poverty and cultural dislocation, the psychic disorientation endured by so many allotted Indians, made landless by designing non-Indians. Curiously, reservations, regarded as prisons during the nineteenth century, became havens in the twentieth. Native Americans could venture from their reservation homes into the white man's world comforted and supported by the assurance that they had a place to return to to find some of their cultural roots.

Public interest in Indian welfare ran its course after adoption of the General Allotment Act, and Indians faded into the nation's shadows. For the first three decades of the twentieth century, the general public was occasionally reminded of their presence by their performances in Wild West shows and in the emerging cinema, which recreated the frontier epic, casting the Indian as a threat to fulfillment of the American Dream, the prototype of evil. The Indian's fate in the first third of the twentieth century is the subject of Chapter Twenty.

Notes

1. Henry E. Frtz, *The Movement for Indian Assimilation, 1860–1890* (Philadelphia, 1963), p. 197.
2. Francis Paul Prucha, *American Indian Policy in Crisis: Christian Reformers and the Indian, 1865–1900* (Norman, Okla., 1976), p. 139.
3. Francis Paul Prucha (ed.), *Americanizing the American Indian: Writings by the "Friends of the Indian," 1880–1900* (Cambridge, Mass., 1973), p. 98.
4. Prucha, *American Indian Policy*, pp. 51–53; and Prucha, *Americanizing*

the American Indian, p. 334.

5. Loring B. Priest, *Uncle Sam's Stepchildren: The Reformation of the United States Indian Policy, 1865–1887* (New York, 1969), p. 232; and Angie Debo, *A History of the Indians of the United States* (Norman, Okla., 1970), p. 252.

6. *Report of the Commissioner of Indian Affairs for 1877*, pp. 75–76; and Priest, *Uncle Sam's Stepchildren*, p. 235.

7. Fritz, *Movement for Indian Assimilation*, pp. 210–11.

8. D. S. Otis, *The Dawes Act and the Allotment of Indian Land*, edited with an Introduction by Francis Paul Prucha (Norman, Okla., 1973), p. 43.

9. Debo, *History of the Indians*, p. 254.

10. Jennings C. Wise, *The Red Man in the New World Drama: A Politico-Legal Study with a Pageantry of American Indian History*, edited with an Introduction by Vine Deloria, Jr. (New York, 1971), p. 301.

11. Otis, *The Dawes Act*, p. 38.

12. William T. Hagan, *American Indians* (Chicago, 1961), pp. 141–42; and D'Arcy McNickle, *Native American Tribalism: Indian Survivals and Renewals* (New York, 1973), p. 82.

13. Priest, *Uncle Sam's Stepchildren*, p. 251.

14. Lonnie E. Underhill and Daniel F. Littlefield, Jr. (eds.), *Hamlin Garland's Observations on the American Indian, 1895–1905* (Tucson, Ariz., 1976), p. 31.

15. Otis, *The Dawes Act*, p. 96.

16. Arrell Morgan Gibson, *The Kickapoos: Lords of the Middle Border* (Norman, Okla., 1963), p. 302.

17. Angie Debo, *And Still the Waters Run* (Princeton, N.J., 1940), pp. 59–60.

18. McNickle, *Native American Tribalism*, p. 82.

19. Debo, *And Still the Waters Run*, p. 180.

20. *Ibid.*, p. 185.

Selected Sources

Ideological foundations for partitioning the Indian reservations and origins of the General Allotment Act are found in Francis Paul Prucha (ed.), *Americanizing the American Indians: Writings by the "Friends of the Indian," 1880–1900* (Cambridge, Mass., 1973), and *American Indian Policy in Crisis: Christian Reformers and the Indian, 1865–1900* (Norman, Okla., 1976); Loring B. Priest, *Uncle Sam's Stepchildren: The Reformation of the United States Indian Policy, 1865–1887* (New York, 1969); Robert W. Mardock, *The Reformers and the Indian* (Columbia, Mo., 1971); and Henry E. Fritz, *The Movement for Indian Assimilation, 1860–1890* (Philadelphia, 1963).

Studies of the General Allotment Act in operation include D. S. Otis, *The Dawes Act and the Allotment of Indian Lands*, edited with an Introduction by Francis Paul Prucha (Norman, Okla., 1973); Jennings C. Wise, *The Red Man in the New World Drama: A Politico-Legal Study with a Pageantry of American Indian History*, edited with an Introduction by Vine Deloria, Jr. (New York, 1971); and J. P. Kinney, *A Continent Lost—A Civilization Won* (Baltimore, 1937).

Indian experience with allotment in severalty is detailed in Edward Everett Dale, *The Indians of the Southwest: A Century of Development Under the United States* (Norman, Okla., 1949); Donald J. Berthrong, *The Cheyenne and Arapaho Ordeal: Reservation and Agency Life in the Indian Territory, 1875–1907* (Norman, Okla.,

1976); William T. Hagan, *United States-Comanche Relations: The Reservation Years* (New Haven, Conn., 1976); Imre Sutton, *Indian Land Tenure* (New York, 1975); Wilcomb E. Washburn, *Red Man's Land, White Man's Law* (New York, 1971), and *The American Indian and the United States: A Documentary History,* 4 vols. (New York, 1973); Henry E. Fritz, "The Board of Indian Commissioners and Ethnocentric Reform, 1878–1893," *Indian White Relations* (Washington, D.C., 1976); William T. Hagan, "Private Property, the Indian's Door to Civilization," *Ethnohistory* 3 (Spring 1956), pp. 126–37; and Herman J. Deutsch, "Indian and White in the Inland Empire: The Contest for the Land, 1880–1912," *Pacific Northwest Quarterly* 47 (April 1956), pp. 44–51.

Despoiling allotments is traced in Angie Debo, *And Still the Waters Run* (Princeton, N.J., 1940); and Arrell Morgan Gibson, *The Kickapoos: Lords of the Middle Border* (Norman, Okla., 1963). Also see Harold M. Hyman (ed.), *The Assault on Tribalism: The General Allotment Act (Dawes Act) of 1887* (Philadelphia, 1975); and Imre Sutton, *Indian Land Tenure: Bibliographical Essays and a Guide to the Literature* (New York, 1975).

CHAPTER 20

NATIVE AMERICANS
IN THE TWENTIETH
CENTURY
1900–1945

The Secretary of the Interior stands before one of the candidates and says:—
"Joseph T. Cook, what was your Indian name?"
"Tunkansapa," answers the Indian.
"Tunkansapa, I hand you a bow and arrow. Take this bow and shoot the
arrow." The Indian does so.
"Tunkansapa, you have shot your last arrow. That means you are no longer to
live the life of an Indian. You are from this day forward to live the life of the
white man. But you may keep that arrow. It will be to you a symbol of your
noble race and the pride you feel that you come from the first of all Americans."
Addressing Tunkansapa by his white name. "Joseph T. Cook, take in your
hands this plough." Cook does so. "This act means that you have chosen to
live the life of the white man. The white man lives by work. From the earth
we must all get our living, and the earth will not yield unless man pours upon
it the sweat of his brow." . . . The Secretary now takes up the American flag.
He and the Indian hold it together. "I give into your hands the flag of your
country. This is the only flag you will ever have. It is the flag of free men, the
flag of a hundred million free men and women, of whom you are now one."

The Ritual Admission of Indians to citizenship, 1916

In the early years of the twentieth century, Anglo-Americans held a variety of
attitudes about Indians. Some people regarded dispossessed Indians festering
in grinding poverty, declining tribal health, and rising mortality rate with
apathy, others with indifference or disinterest, and some, particularly in the
West, with glowering resentment. Only a small group, centering on the Indian
Rights Association, maintained sympathetic, concerned, and supportive attitudes toward Indians. The public view toward Native Americans changed
somewhat during the 1920s as reformers again paid some attention to Indians. The reform movement gained momentum during the 1930s, then
expired on the eve of World War II as the nation turned to the compelling
concerns of national security and international involvement. Meanwhile, in

Chapter Opening Artifact: Seed jar by Anita Lowden from the Acoma Pueblo, 1967
(Maxwell Museum of Anthropology)

the Indian community there was emerging a national Native American leadership which was striving for Indian-conceived solutions to the enlarging social, political, and economic injustices endured by Native Americans.

THE VANISHING AMERICAN

Briefly during the final decade of the nineteenth century, Native Americans had been at center stage of national concerns. Powerful citizens marshaled as "Friends of the Indian" and "Christian Reformers" had gained for suffering Indians, constrained on repressive reservations, what they believed was the millenium for the cause of better conditions for them. Through allotment in severalty the Indian as a landowner would surely accomplish that transformation process which would make him a worthy subject for full assimilation into the societal mainstream. However, this hope quickly became a mocking disappointment. It failed because of the inability of many Indians to cope with the alternative life-style the new order required; because of Indian intransigence; because of callousness and greed of Anglo-Americans who dispossessed over half of the allotted Indians of their land before the reform program had been in effect for twenty years; and because of nonproductive public attitudes.

Public View and Practice Toward Indians

At least four nonproductive attitudes toward Indians found voice and following in the period 1900–1930. One held by many citizens, derived from an unrealistic view, perhaps depraved hope, and based on ignorance rather than fact, contended that the "Indian problem" was about to be resolved by the steady decline in aboriginal population to the point that Indians would vanish as an ethnic entity. Figures from a recent census showed from an estimated 1,500,000 at Contact, the Indian population had declined to 250,000. Excessively high death rates, particularly infant mortality and loss of mothers at childbirth, shockingly low life expectancy because of poverty and degradation induced by their government-imposed life-style, plus the move of an estimated 60,000 Indians into the societal mainstream, corroborated the view that the Indian was a vanishing American. Rather than express regret or some sense of national shame over this apparent trend, most citizens felt relief. However, even while the "vanishing American" view was most current, the Indian population decline had halted and a steady increase soon provided an expanding Native American demographic base so that by 1970 the aboriginal population of the United States had returned nearly to its original level.

Another nonproductive attitude that worked against a better life for Indians was pervasive inertia that followed the zealous crusade for allotment in severalty. The reform spirit spent itself soon after adoption of the Dawes Act. Rapid decline in public interest in Indian welfare was shown by the decline in membership and contributions to reform organizations. Many leaders and most rank-and-file members of Indian reform groups considered their work completed by 1900 although their interest and oversight were still needed just as much to assist Indians in adjusting to the new conditions. Reformers' interest in the Indian waned, and they turned to other matters.

Congress, rarely a bold formulator of public opinion but for the most part a follower of civic will, reflected this trend of growing disinterest in support of better conditions for Indians. On several occasions after application of the General Allotment Act, national legislators nearly refused to appropriate funds for support of Indian education, money which in most cases belonged to the tribes and was only held in trust by the federal government, as a manifestation of the growing determination to "resist special concessions to red men." This rapid cooling of zeal has been characteristic of Anglo-American reform movements—a spate of private and public indignation at abuse, evil, injustice, a corpus of corrective laws, inevitably followed by decline of advocate interest, permitting no essential continuing attention and oversight, and generally defeating the reform because those or that which the reform legislation was designed to regulate and control soon find ways to evade or manipulate the reform. Today's reforms inevitably become the subjects of tomorrow's reforms. Thus allotment in severalty did not produce the ultimate in prosperity and transformation touted by reformers.[1]

Attitudes of citizens of western states with large Indian populations, continuing the early frontier prejudice, were by and large nonproductive. Westerners wanted lands and the timber, minerals, and farming and grazing resources they contained. And they spared no effort to possess them. Most Anglo-Americans refused to accept Indians as fellow citizens or to permit them to enter the mainstream of society which "Friends of the Indian" had advocated. Native Americans generally were denied basic constitutional rights, including the vote, and were subjected to discrimination when they attempted to express citizenship.

Public officials, who should have been better informed, also reflected an unrealistic attitude toward Indians. Interior Department personnel, responsible for managing Indian affairs, who could be expected to be sufficiently informed to fulfill their administrative function, all too frequently manifested complete lack of essential understanding of ethnic matters. But perhaps the crowning ignorance of the age on the true state of Native Americans in the United States was expressed by Secretary of State Robert Lansing to the British government in 1913 in connection with British-American claims arbitration proceedings. The British government, on behalf of Cayuga Indians in Canada, was seeking compensation for the Cayugas because the state of New York, in violation of the treaty concluding the War of 1812, had seized their lands and disposed of them as state property. Lansing, in his defense of treatment accorded Native Americans by the United States and the state of New York, declared,

Under that system the Indians residing within the United States are so far in-
dependent that they live under their own customs and not under the laws of the
United States; that their rights upon the lands they inhabit or hunt are secured to
them by boundaries defined in amicable treaties between the United States and
themselves; and that whenever those boundaries are varied it is also by amicable
and voluntary treaties, by which they receive from the United States ample com-
pensation for every right they have to the lands ceded by them.

The United States had terminated the treaty process with Indian nations in
1871, and Native Americans had been subjected to detribalization since
the 1870s![2]

Exploitation Continuum

The twentieth century brought Indians no respite from private and public
exploitation and abuse. Greedy non-Indians continued to prey upon allotments and tribal resources. And for the most part, federal and state laws and
court decisions denied Indians full citizenship and equal protection and
forced them to accept a patently unfair, discriminatory dispensation of justice.
In no instance were territorial and state laws and court decisions in the Indians' favor; occasionally Congress passed a statute which was modestly
protective of Indian rights, and now and then a federal tribunal would render
a decision in favor of Indians. However, for nearly three decades of the new
century, the federal government as primary trustee for Native American
rights and property was basically indifferent to its charge.

The period from 1900 to 1934 was a time of continued divestment of Indian
title to allotted lands. Most divestment was by state action, particularly in
Oklahoma, the old Indian Territory, where local politicians in league with
corrupt county judges shamelessly desecrated public trust, cruelly abused
Indian wards, and extorted their property, largely land, with impunity. However, one instance of huge land appropriation occurred at the highest level.
Two days before he left the presidency, Theodore Roosevelt, in the name of
conservation, issued eight executive orders directing that 2,500,000 acres of
timbered reservation land be transferred to the national forests. Subsequently
these lands were restored to the Indian tribes, less to serve justice and more
to serve conservation: as forest lands they were more easily exploitable
under Indian tenure than under federal conservation management.

Private and public interests in states with large Indian populations con
tinued to voice demands that federal officials further relax protective restrictions on Indian property. Private groups sought to gain access to Indian
allotments to exploit them for personal profit; public groups in the states
sought to bring tax-exempt Indian lands under state jurisdiction to increase
state revenues. Robert L. Owen, mixed-blood Cherokee and one of the first
United States senators from the new state of Oklahoma, openly admitted that
he had worked to remove restrictions on allotments while Oklahoma was still
the Indian Territory, and he claimed that he had been instrumental in per-

suading Congress to pass laws granting citizenship to Indians of the Five Civilized Tribes, thus ending federal supervision over most of the restricted allotments in the Indian Territory. During each legislative session, congressmen introduced bills to remove all restrictions on allotments, as they put it, "to set Indians free," and to continue the abuse-ridden system of permitting county courts through guardians to control property of minor and adult Indians with restricted allotments, meanwhile defending the system of wholesale, fraudulent divestment of Indian property in the face of shocking cumulative record of malfeasance, corruption, and abuse of public trust in handling Indian properties.

The pattern of plundering Indian estates, so efficiently applied to the lands of the Five Civilized Tribes, was extended to other tribes across the West. The Burke Act of 1906 had delegated discretionary authority to the secretary of the interior to remove restrictions on sale of allotments. Over the years various secretaries of the interior had exercised this function on an individual basis so that between 1906 and 1917 they had declared nearly 10,000 Indians competent and had issued them patents or deeds to their allotments. Franklin K. Lane, Secretary of the Interior from 1913 to 1920, an early advocate of Termination, as the policy of concluding federal oversight of Indian properties was called, was determined to end federal guardianship for as many Indians as possible. Termination became especially popular in the 1950s, but early in the century Lane reportedly went at issuing "competency clearance" and removing restrictions on allotments "with a vengeance." In 1917 he appointed a competency commission; its members traveled to settlements of allotted Indians and made a house-to-house canvas to determine the competency of aboriginal householders, meaning their ability to cope in a white man's world. Competency commission members reportedly spent less than fifteen minutes interviewing each Indian. During Lane's three-year program (1917–1920), which he called "blanket competency," he issued over 20,000 patents to allottees, discontinuing federal guardianship of their lands. Most of those Indians released from federal supervision soon lost their land to local Anglo-American bankers, businessmen, farmers, and stockmen. The outcry against Lane's easy competency and the accompanying rapid loss of Indian land led federal officials in 1920 to return to a more deliberate, individual process for determining competency.

Besides wholesale appropriation of Native American allotments by non-Indians, federal officials continued the process of allotting tribal reservations in spite of compelling evidence that doing so did little to promote Indian welfare. Each reservation allotted became a new area of opportunity for divestment of individual Indian title. The northern Cheyenne reservation was the last communally owned tract to be allotted; it was plotted in 1930–1931.

Indians lost control of their lands under other guises as well. A widely used ploy for appropriating choice tracts of reservation land was the mining claim. Federal law permitted citizens to enter public lands and occupy plots believed to contain minerals. While several Indian reservations escaped allotment in severalty, largely because they were located in remote regions or were mostly desert and mountain and of little value for Anglo-American enterprises, tribal title to these lands was uncertain, particularly if the reservation had been assigned to the tribe by executive order. Several high officials had ruled that reservations of this class were public land, the Indians only temporary tenants. During the 1880s, whites exercised mineral-claim entry rights on the Colville Reservation, created by executive order, in eastern Washington, displacing many resident Indians. This intrusion continued into the 1890s, with squatters taking possession of scattered sites for farms and ranches and diverting much of the available water from the Indian settlements. Anglo-Americans also used the mining claim as a cover for occupying the executive-order reservation of the Papago tribe of Arizona. In 1917 intruders entered the Papago reservation and filed mineral claims on the scattered springs of the reservation and thus controlled the peripheral grazing lands. Finally, after much tribal protest, Congress enacted a statute in 1955 that established Papago ownership of any minerals found on their reservation.

One of the most flagrant threats to Indian property involved lands belonging to the Pueblo Indians on the Rio Grande and its tributaries in New Mexico. By the Treaty of Guadalupe-Hidalgo in 1848, concluding the Mexican War, the United States obtained New Mexico, Arizona, and California. All Mexican nationals in the ceded territory could become citizens of the United States if they chose. Because Pueblo Indians had been Mexican nationals, they became citizens of the United States; thus the federal laws prohibiting entry on Indian land did not apply to Pueblo property. Through the years Anglo-Americans and Spanish-Americans settled on Pueblo lands, until soon after the beginning of the twentieth century, they numbered over 12,000. Then in 1913 the federal courts held that Pueblo lands were a part of the Indian Country; the Pueblo communities were domestic dependent nations under the protection of the United States and thus could not dispose of their lands without authorization of the federal government. Settlers on Pueblo lands faced expulsion. Most of them were voters and thus attracted the interest of New Mexico politicians who sought to protect the settlers' interests in the Pueblo lands. In 1922 congressmen from New Mexico submitted land relief legislation in the form of the Bursum Bill. It favored the settlers by forcing the burden of proof on Pueblo Indian communities to prove ownership of their lands. Their failure to establish proof would vest title in the intruders. The Pueblo lands issue was to become the *cause célèbre* for resumption of Indian reform.

In the new century Indian civil rights suffered no less than Indian property rights. One of the greatest setbacks to Indian prerogative was the case of *Lone Wolf* v. *Hitchcock* in 1902. Kiowa leader Lone Wolf attempted to prevent Secretary of the Interior Ethan Allen Hitchcock from taking tribal land and converting it to public use. The nation's highest tribunal denied Lone Wolf's contention by ruling that Congress had plenary power to dispose of Indian property. The decision read, in part, "The power exists to abrogate the provision of an Indian treaty. . . . When, therefore treaties were entered into between the United States and a tribe of Indians, it was never doubted that the power to abrogate existed within Congress." Federal officials interpreted this to mean that "such Indian lands as it saw fit to take might be appropriated and the owners left to obtain such redress as Congress might be willing to make."[3]

As trustees of tribal funds, federal officials continued to deny Native Americans self-determination or a voice in the disbursement of these assets. Thus officials in the Bureau of Indian Affairs contracted with church organizations to provide Indian education through sectarian schools, committing tribal trust funds for this purpose without consulting Indian owners. Tribal leaders objected to this unilateral appropriation of tribal property, and the United States Supreme Court in 1905 ruled that the Bureau of Indian Affairs as principal trustee for Indian property was within its rights.

Federal courts also took a generally limited, restricted view on individual Indian rights. Foundation for this stance was the *Elk* v. *Wilkins* decision, rendered in 1884. John Elk, a Sioux, had left the reservation and was gainfully employed in Omaha, Nebraska. Claiming that he was no longer a member of the Sioux tribe but under United States jurisdiction and thereby a citizen, he presented himself to vote in a local election. When he was refused a ballot, he filed suit in federal court claiming that his rights as a citizen had been denied. On appeal the United States Supreme Court ruled that one could not by personal initiative make himself a citizen, with the accompanying rights and privileges, without the consent and cooperation of the government; therefore, the lower court decision upholding denial of ballot was sustained.

But while Indians in the early twentieth century were generally losing their attempts to achieve protection by laws of Congress and decisions of federal courts, they occasionally triumphed. The prodigal plundering of oil-royalty-rich Osages by unscrupulous Oklahoma citizens became so odious nationally that Congress could no longer ignore the evil and in 1925 passed a law providing for joint supervision of Osage properties by federal agents and the corrupt county courts and guardians. This measure checked some of the more extravagant, glaring instances of state-accredited larceny. Also in this age of public indifference to the Indians' plight, federal courts occasionally ruled on the Indians' side. In 1904, federal courts reaffirmed Yakima tribal fishing rights in Pacific Northwest streams which had been stipulated by earlier treaties, and Blackfeet tribal water rights were confirmed in the *Winters* v. *United States* decision in 1906. In the Southwest, Indians occasionally received some protection from federal courts. Congress had granted right-of-way lands to the Santa Fe Railway across the Hulapai Reservation in Arizona. Tribal leaders subsequently attempted to recover the land issued to the railroad by right of Indian title. Lower courts held against the Indians, but the United States Supreme Court in 1925 ruled in favor of the Hulapai tribe and nearly half a million acres were eventually restored to the Hulapai tribe.

But it was under the local courts and citizens in the states that the Indians suffered the most. All over the West the federal government had abolished tribal governments, and Indians increasingly became subject to state, territorial, and federal laws and courts. As allottees, Indians were expected to take their place in the dominant society; in practice they endured discrimination. A double standard called selective enforcement was applied to Indians. Like blacks in the South, Native Americans regularly faced vigilante action, the citizen-mobs generally performing their ghoulish acts with impunity. An exception was the aftermath of a double execution in the Seminole nation. Jules Laird, a white tenant, had settled with his family in the Seminole nation on Lincoln McKeisey's allotment. In 1898, while Laird was in the nearby settlement purchasing supplies, his house was robbed and his wife raped and slain. Laird's seven-year-old son was a witness to the crime. A vigilante pack of tenant neighbors captured 7 young Seminole male suspects, chained the prisoners together, and marched them before Laird's young son. When the boy was unable to identify his mother's killers, the vigilantes withheld food and water from the chained prisoners and beat them to force admissions of guilt. The vigilantes were coached in extracting confessions from the prisoners by United States Deputy Marshal Nelson Jones. Finally one of the Indian suspects, Palmer Sampson, broke under the physical and mental torment and confessed. After more torture he named Lincoln McGeisey, son of the Lairds' landlord, as his accomplice. Thereupon the white mob, 300 strong, dragged the 2 Indian youths to a nearby Baptist church, and chained them to a blackjack tree on the church grounds. The vigilantes piled tinder-dry brush about the boys' feet then ignited the pyre; their fires burned for half a day until only smoldering ashes and charred bones remained. Soon after the executions, Kinder Harjo, a Seminole, confessed to the crime. Seminole leaders demanded that local officials investigate the vigilante action but they refused, which led them to appeal to officials in the United States Department of Justice. A federal attorney eventually filed charges against Jones and 10 vigilantes. The court sentenced Deputy Jones to 21 years in federal prison; 10 vigilantes received lesser terms.

Native Americans also endured some political exploitation in the early twentieth century. Although westerners were not prepared to welcome the Indian as a fellow citizen and voter, a number of Indians were rallied for the presidential election of 1916. Secretary of the Interior Lane assiduously organized the many federal employees in his department to support President Wilson. He also anticipated the prospects of Native American voter support. Politicians had largely ignored them until this time as an electoral force, but many under the General Allotment Act qualified for citizenship, and Lane reasoned that a step in fulfillment of their citizenship would be voting. An examination of the Indian population statistics of North and South Dakota, Wyoming, Montana, Oklahoma, Arizona, and New Mexico revealed enough potential voters to determine the electoral vote of these states. In May 1916 he visited the Yankton Sioux Reservation in South Dakota where he extended full citizenship to 150 Indians.

Native American Initiatives

Indians on allotments and on reservations continued in the twentieth century to seek ways to cope with the new order. Some sought to achieve competency through education in order to protect their allotments and to find a place in the white society by mastering a craft or a profession.

Graduates of Haskell, Carlisle, Hampton, and the government schools at Santa Fe, Albuquerque, and Phoenix acquired special vocational skills which prepared them for productive employment. The industrial expansion during World War I created jobs for Native Americans, many of them graduates of Indian vocational institutions.

Each year after 1900 the number of Indian children attending school increased. Most Indian learners enrolled in Indian schools, but under pressure from officials in the Bureau of Indian Affairs, an increasing number attended public schools, so that by 1931 out of a total of 75,000 Indian students, more than half attended public schools. Native Americans preferred Indian schools and attended them whenever they had a choice. In the public schools they often drifted in a dominant Anglo-American student body and suffered discrimination which hampered their academic progress. In the all-Indian institutions their ethnic identity was not a handicap or a source of scorn.

In the early twentieth century, Indian schools also became more attractive. First, school administrators were moving away from the nineteenth-century Bureau of Indian Affairs position of eradicating all sign of Indian culture and began to permit instruction in it. Commissioner of Indian Affairs Francis Leupp commented in 1905,

I like the Indian for what is Indian in him. . . . Let us not make the mistake, in the process of absorbing him, of washing out whatever is distinctly Indian. Our aboriginal brother brings, as his contribution to the common store of character, a good deal of which is desirable, and which only needs to be developed along the right line. Our proper work is improvement, not transformation.

And in 1916 Commissioner of Indian Affairs Cato Sells said the bureau should have "taken into account those abilities of the Indian student with which he is peculiarly endowed and have come down to him as a racial heritage; his religion, art, deftness of hand, his sensitive artistic temperament." Thus, with official sanction, educators at Haskell in 1908 permitted Indian students to present an exhibit titled "The Indian, His Capabilities and Achievements, His Arts, Music, Customs, and Religion." There followed formation of the Department of Native Indian Arts at Carlisle, and by 1912 freshman students were learning about famous Indian leaders while seniors were studying "Sociology Applied to the Indian Race" and "Native Industries."[4]

Another primary reason why Indian students preferred Indian schools was the rise of strong, nationally recognized athletic programs at Haskell, Carlisle, and Hampton. Jim Thorpe, the Potawatomi-Sac and Fox Indian, whose legendary feats in baseball, football, and track won him recognition as the world's greatest athlete, had quickened Native American interest in competi-

Jim Thorpe, famous backfield football star of the Carlisle School. He was named the greatest football star of the half-century in the Associated Press Midcentury poll in 1950. (Wide World Photos, Inc.)

tive athletics. Indian school programs came to include varsity competition in baseball, basketball, football, and track. And Native American athletes at Carlisle and Haskell regularly received national recognition for outstanding performance. Those recognized as All-American football players included John Levi, Louis Weller, Buster Charles, and Pete Hauser. Indians of all ages on allotments, reservations, and in towns and cities all across the United States found a source of ethnic pride in the widely reported exploits of young Indian athletes.

By 1910 it was estimated that 10 percent of the Indian population had achieved some measure of economic and social success. However, most Native

Americans hovered between acceptance and rejection of the new order, hesitantly holding to the old customs but considering a change in life-style. Some Indians withdrew to their allotments or reservations, seeking refuge from the maelstrom of change in Indian customs and religion, or in alcohol. And an increasing number of Indians turned to the peyote cult which was flowering into the Native American Church.

In the reservation era, the peyote cult had succeeded the Ghost Dance as the new hope of Native Americans. Worshipers used the fruit of the peyote cactus as a sacrament in their service; it was believed to transmit power to the worshiper and bring "internal peace and harmony rather than competition and conflict." Peyote cult practice stressed personal rehabilitation and integration from following the Peyote Road, a strict code of behavior requiring strength of character, integrity, and honor in interpersonal relations, a high level of personal performance and achievement, abstinence from alcohol—the bane of so many Indians in those trying times—and emphasis on self-reliance, self-support, and economic independence, in short, responsible living.[5]

Local, state, and federal authorities, even some tribal leaders, scorned the peyote cult's mysticism and power endowment, denounced its use as a pernicious diversion, and attempted to suppress it. They were supported by missionaries who, finding the cult a powerful threat to their attempts to convert Indians to Christianity, denounced peyote as a harmful, debasing, sinful, habit-forming drug. Peyote exclusionists were so determined to crush the cult that, besides harassing Native American followers, they lashed out at the cult's few Anglo-American defenders. Thus James Mooney, an anthropologist and advocate of the Indian's right to freedom of worship, including use of peyote, was prohibited by a federal order from conducting anthropological research on the Kiowa reservation.

Federal officials attempted to eradicate peyote from Indian communities by including it with alcohol among those items forbidden on Indian reservations. And officials in the Department of Agriculture assisted Bureau of Indian Affairs agents by banning the importation of peyote from Mexico, the principal source. But these measures failed because sufficient peyote reached Indian users. Finally in 1922 the commissioner of Indian affairs informed Congress that "legislation is urgently needed to control the growing and harmful habit among the Indians of using peyote." Thus at the urging of Congressman Carl Hayden of Arizona, the United States House of Representatives regularly adopted resolutions banning use of peyote, but each time the bills failed in the Senate.[6]

State action against peyotists began in Oklahoma, the former Indian Territory, where the cult had been born among the Comanches and Delawares. In 1898 the territorial legislature adopted a statute forbidding possession and use of the exotic cactus fruit. By 1923 the legislatures of North Dakota, South Dakota, Montana, Utah, Kansas, Nevada, and Colorado had adopted similar laws. Opposition to use of peyote came from Indians, too, particularly practitioners of traditional Indian religion, who viewed the cult as heresy. By 1940 the peyote cult has been banned on the Navajo Reservation, on the White Mountain Apache Reservation, and on the lands of Taos Pueblo by action of tribal councils.

These suppressive efforts had the predictable effect of abetting the peyote cult. James Mooney and several Oklahoma peyote cult members took steps to protect the nativistic religion. First, in 1908, as a result of intense lobbying by the old Quahada Comanche war chief Quanah Parker, a confirmed peyotist, the Oklahoma legislature repealed the 1898 statute banning use of peyote. Next the peyotists sought to obtain a state charter which would provide the cult a legal status and, hopefully, guard it against threatening state and federal rules and laws. In 1918, after a series of intertribal conferences, peyote leaders applied for and received from the state of Oklahoma a charter authorizing the peyote cult to function as the Native American Church.

This elevated status for peyotists sanctioned by state action provoked strong opposition across the nation among Christian religious bodies, which in turn caused members of the Native American Church to seek a national charter, claiming that the use of peyote in their worship was sacramental like the Christian eucharistic use of bread and wine. Peyotists added that their worship was a valid exercise of the constitutional right of freedom of religion. Slowness of federal officials to respond to the peyotists' appeal for a national charter led them to launch an evangelical drive in Indian communities throughout the West for more members and thus increased strength. Many of the converts were young Indians, including large numbers of graduates of Carlisle, Haskell, Hampton, Chilocco, and other Indian schools. By 1930 it was estimated that at least half the nation's Indian population were Native American Church members.

As Native American Church evangelists carried their message of hope for distressed Indians northward, substantial portions of the tribes in Nebraska, North Dakota, South Dakota, Wisconsin, Minnesota, Montana, and Colorado committed themselves to the demanding discipline of the Peyote Road. Winnebago converts exercised considerable influence on the sect's practices, particularly the inclusion of Christian elements. By the late 1920s, the Native American Church, functioning as a composite of Indian and Christian practices including a sacramental life centering on use of peyote, the ultimate power source, required no appreciable written doctrine, theology, or tenets. The worship practice varied widely from one congregation to the next, but the purpose was universally acknowledged: to promote personal reconstruction and betterment, preserve Indianness, and provide awareness among all Native Americans of their ethnic affinity. Thus the Native American Church became a powerful force in an emerging pan-Indian movement. With the appointment of John Collier, a strong advocate of self-determination for Native Americans, as commissioner of Indian affairs in 1933, the bureau no longer attempted to eradicate the Native American Church.

Other Indian initiatives of the early twentieth century included emergence of an articulate Native American secular leadership committed to pan-Indian interests and welfare. From the 10 percent or so of Indians who had achieved some measure of success and joined the middle class came the secular Indian leaders who fashioned reform goals and programs. They included Dr. Carlos Montezuma, Apache physician; Henry Roe Cloud, Winnebago teacher and tribal leader; Thomas L. Sloan, Omaha lawyer; Arthur C. Parker, Seneca anthropologist; Dr. Charles Eastman, Sioux physician, and his brother the Reverend John Eastman; Laura Cornelius, Oneida social reformer; John M. Oskisson, Cherokee author; Gertrude Bonnin, Sioux writer and musician; and the Reverend Sherman Coolidge, an Arapaho. Called "Red Progressives," this Indian cadre accepted education and hard work and adapted their attitudes, values, and habits to those of the larger American society. They established a national secular pan-Indian movement.[7]

In 1911, with encouragement from Professor Fayette McKenzie, sociologist at Ohio State University, leaders of eighteen tribes, including Montezuma, Roe Cloud, Sloan, Parker, the Eastman brothers, Cornelius, Oskisson, Bonnin, and Coolidge, met at Columbus, Ohio on October 12, Columbus Day, and founded the Society of American Indians. During the formative deliberations the Indian delegates demonstrated a "strong sense of pride in being Indian"; the proceedings were full of "references to the virtues of the Indian past," their orations a "mix of nostalgia . . . for aboriginal life and progress." However, most of the delegates conscientiously attempted to deemphasize tribalism and to stress pan-Indianness. Some delegates insisted that "racial and tribal identity were complimentary," but most were willing to permit racial identity to replace tribal identity. They applied evolutionary doctrine to Indians and "viewed 'the race' as in the process of working itself up the evolutionary ladder." Society of American Indian members placed strong emphasis upon education as the means to advance and achieve primary goals of ethnic improvement. The organization's bylaws committed the society to promote advance in "enlightenment which leaves him as a free man to develop according to the natural laws of social evolution," to preserve the Indian race's history and "emulate its distinguishing virtues," to obtain citizenship for Indians and "the rights thereof," and to investigate Indian problems and "obtain remedies." The Society of American Indians stressed Native American self-reliance, self-help, and initiative as the foundations for Indian betterment, the already well-established expectations of the Peyote Road, and it regularly denounced the Bureau of Indian Affairs for its failure to assist Indians to achieve these virtues.

Subsequent meetings of the Society of American Indians produced proposals for Indian improvement. Gertrude Bonnin, educated at Earlham College and the New England Conservatory of Music, a regular contributor to *Harper's Magazine* and *Century Magazine*, advocated establishing "social betterment stations," similar to settlement houses among the urban poor, in allotted Indian settlements and on reservations. The first station opened at Fort Duchesne, Utah, among the Utes with Ms. Bonnin in charge. She stressed Indian home improvement. Cornelius, the Oneida, submitted a plan to convert reservations into "self-governing industrial villages" along the lines of Mormon settlements. Society of American Indian members agreed that in keeping with the evolutionary principle, vocational-industrial development for Indians should match their respective stages of development and readiness.[8]

Society of American Indian officials established the organization's headquarters in Washington where they could maintain surveillance over laws and administrative rulings pertaining to Indians. The society published a quarterly journal beginning in 1913, the *Society of American Indians Magazine* edited by Parker; in 1916 its name was changed to *American Indian Magazine*. This publication attempted to popularize Indian reform plans including self-governing industrial villages and social betterment stations on reservations, provided information on public affairs of concern to Indians, and stressed a curious blend of Indian nationalism and Indian commitment to American patriotism; its editor advocated use of the flag salute and singing of the *"Star Spangled Banner"* by Indians at public gatherings. The *American Indian Magazine* also pressed for national recognition of Native Americans by observing an annual American Indian Day, to be held on June 22, the time of the "moon of the first fruits." Only New York, Connecticut, and Wisconsin observed American Indian Day. The Society of American Indians was part of the strong wave of social fraternalism in American society during the early twentieth century. Thus to promote pan-Indianism it sponsored the Descendants of American Aborigines, modeled after the Daughters of the American Revolution, and the Grand Council of American Indians, its symbols the American eagle and a lighted torch, bearing some resemblance to the Odd-Fellows Lodge.

Member insurgency and the issue of peyotism weakened the impact of the Society of American Indians on public opinion and reform policy. Carlos Montezuma became the most divisive force in the organization. A zealous advocate of public education and rapid assimilation for Indians, the Apache physician scorned the Society of American Indian's advocacy of the evolutionary process, and he opposed Indian schools for teaching Native American crafts, dances, traditions, and attempting to preserve and transmit Indian culture. And Montezuma was the most persistent and bitter Indian critic of the Bureau of Indian Affairs; he blamed it for the sad plight of Indians, and he demanded its immediate abolition. His vituperative ranting alienated the membership which he subsequently accused of being in surreptitious league with the Bureau of Indian Affairs. He denounced American Indian Day as a "farce and worst kind of fad." He warned, "It will not help the Indians, but the Indians will be used as tools for interested parties. To the Indian it is a laughing mockery because he does not enjoy freedom, but is a ward and is handicapped by the Indian Bureau." Montezuma established *Wassaja*, a monthly publication to disseminate his fury against the Bureau of Indian Affairs and what he rated as "innocuous programs" of the Society of American

Carlos Montezuma, 1867–1923. (Courtesy the Arizona Historical Society)

Indians. During the 1915 Society of American Indians conference at Lawrence, Kansas, he delivered his most bitter public attack on the Bureau of Indian Affairs in a polemic titled "Let my People Go." "The iron hand of the Indian Bureau has us in charge," he thundered. "The slimy clutches of horrid greed and selfish interests are gripping the Indian's property. Little by little the Indian's land and everything else is fading into a dim and unknown realm."[9]

Peyotism also came to the fore at the Lawrence meeting. Representatives of 25 tribes from the old Indian Territory, South Dakota, Montana, Kansas, Nebraska, and Minnesota heard peyote advocates complain of increasing pressure and harrassment from federal officials and missionaries and overt interference with worship services. They urged that the delegates join them in a formal protest against what they claimed was an unconstitutional invasion of their right to freedom of religion. However, the majority of delegates refused to support the peyotists and shortly the Society of American Indians went on record as favoring federal legislation to outlaw the use of peyote.

Thus Montezuma's attacks on Society of American Indian programs for improving conditions among Indians and the withdrawal of peyotists weakened the organization. Its leaders persisted in maintaining its life in the post–World War I era by taking up the self-determination theme which President

Woodrow Wilson advocated for the peoples of the world and applying it to themselves. Their stress was on cultural pluralism in American society and the claim that the United States was a "nation of nations." Indian leaders also attempted to convert the Society of American Indians into a national political pressure organization but they failed because Indians "did not possess the power or the willingness to act together as a significant pressure group. A substantial number of Indians lacked the right to vote."[10]

As the Society of American Indians became increasingly moribund, "Red Progressives" created new groups to carry on the cause of Indian reform. In 1926 they formed the National Council of American Indians. Bonnin as president attempted to rally Indian voters but met with only minimal success, largely in Oklahoma and South Dakota. This organization advocated a federal ban on the peyote religion and the Native American Church, it took a moderate stand on the Bureau of Indian Affairs, and its officers cooperated with the General Federation of Women's Clubs to agitate for Indian reform during the late 1920s. However, continuing factionalism robbed the National Council of American Indians of essential vigor and membership strength to succeed as an alternative force in Indian rehabilitation. Yet, with all their differences, the "Red Progressives" kept alive the spark of interest to reform the national government's policy for Native Americans. They provided an indispensable continuum of hope during the 1920s which enlarged during the 1930s into the most comprehensive Indian policy reform in the nation's history.

THE INDIAN MAGNA CHARTA

In 1934 Congress approved the Wheeler-Howard Bill (Indian Reorganization Act) hailed by its advocates as the Indian Magna Charta. Its adoption marked the climax of a bitter contest waged throughout the 1920s between Indian protectors and reformers—led by John Collier and Gertrude Bonnin—and obscurantists and exploiters of Indians—led by Albert B. Fall and Charles H. Burke. The reformers had been able to reduce some of the immense power of the exploiters, which centered in an insensitive Congress and an uncaring bureaucracy, during the 1920s wringing from a reluctant national administration a few modest improvements in Native American welfare. Then in 1934 they won their signal victory through passage of the Indian Reorganization Act, their cause riding on the momentum of the New Deal commitment to transform the nation.

The Antagonists

During the early 1920s Secretary of the Interior Albert B. Fall was principal spokesman for the obscurantist element. The former senator from New Mexico was a staunch advocate of the business community's unhindered access to mineral and petroleum resources on reservations. Fall's choice for Commissioner of Indian Affairs was Charles H. Burke, former congressman from South Dakota and author of the Burke Act which chilled Native American citizenship hopes and emasculated the trust features of allotment in severalty by making access to restricted allotments a matter of administrative discretion. The New York *Times* described Burke as a "rugged individualist" with a "frontiersman's" attitude toward Indians. Hubert Work, Fall's successor in 1923, was as honest as Fall was corrupt but just as ethnocentric. Along with Christian missionaries he sought to stamp out Indian culture, particularly native religion and the peyote cult. He bent to reformers' demands only after they applied great pressure upon him.

Fall, Burke, and Work had strong support from the Indian bureau which at the time had over 200 employees in Washington and 5,000 field workers (teachers, vocational instructors, and general agents), a high ratio of personnel to the 250,000 Indians living on reservations. The move for reform of Indian policy threatened their jobs, and they closed ranks behind their administrative superiors.

More and more, public opinion was formed by mass-circulation national periodicals and newspapers. Shrewd obscurantists resorted to magazine and newspaper interviews to justify their positions. The *Saturday Evening Post, School Life,* and *Good Housekeeping* regularly carried articles antagonistic to the emerging Indian reform movement. In addition, the obscurantists were backed by several church publications including the *Missionary Review,* which carried articles written by missionaries working among the Indian tribes. They called Indians "pagan worshippers" in desperate need of Christianity and described the difficult task they faced in attempting to overthrow native religion and the peyote cult.

Obscurantists were particularly concerned with Indian dances which they thought showed Indian recalcitrance, defiance, and ethnic corruption. Those who defended ethnic pluralism and the Indians' right to worship as they chose, including dancing, were denounced as "anti-American, and subversive . . . agents of Moscow." It was charged that they encouraged the persistence of "Indian paganism" and heathen cults which were "horrible, sadistic, and obscene." Further, they were accused of attempting to "weaken and discredit the United States government. Edith M. Dabb, national director of YWCA work among Indian girls, joined the Native American detractors, charging that native dances were a waste of time and that "sentimentalists who dwell on the beauties of the quaint and primitive world do well to remember that primitive beauty is frequently found in close company with primitive cruelty and primitive ugliness." During an inspection of New Mexico pueblos in 1926 Commissioner Burke publicly excoriated the residents as "half animals" because of "their pagan religion," and he ordered several Indian leaders jailed "for violating the Bureau's religious crimes code."[11]

Secretary Work in 1924 inveighed against "gross sexual immorality" which he claimed "accompanies many of the native dances." He denied that the

Bureau of Indian Affairs was trying "to prohibit Indian dances, either as a secular or religious ceremony, or as an amusement." However, he expressed the hope "that the Indians may be reasoned away from practices attached to some of them which the public never sees, cannot censor and would not approve, but which tend to destroy the higher instincts that should be safeguarded in any people."[12]

The obscurantists were countered by "Red Progressives," who held tenaciously to the cause of improvement of Indian status, and a growing corps of white reformers. Their leader was John Collier, a social worker who for years had labored to improve living conditions for immigrants in eastern cities. From his work Collier gained a respect for differing cultures. He also had studied the writings of George Willard Schultz, Ernest Seton Thompson, and Hamlin Garland which gave him perspective on Native American life. Garland's writings in particular inspired Collier's lasting commitment to protect Indianness, improve Native American status, and promote ethnic pluralism. Near the turn of the century, Garland lived for several years among the Indians on western reservations. He became fascinated with Native American culture; he regarded Indianness as a vital resource which enriched national life, and he applied his literary talents to arouse the public to protect it. He advocated preserving distinctive Indians arts and crafts by encouraging elders to teach tribal youth silversmithing, weaving, and carving in stone, bone, and clay. Above all, he urged federal officials to prevent "missionaries from regulating the amusements and daily lives of the natives."[13]

Garland concluded that while reservations were bad for Indians, partitioning reservations and assigning individual allotments was worse. He contended that individualizing the land and separating Indians on isolated allotments demoralized them. However, because the federal government was determined to proceed with allotment, he urged agents to settle Indians in clusters of extended families to ease "transition from their old life to the new" and to "lessen rather than add to the weight of their suffering." Garland insisted that settling Indians in family clusters was desirable because the Native American was a "sociable animal. . . . a villager, never a solitary. He dreads solitude." One of the most terrifying punishments was to "exile an offender from the group." He explained, "It is this gregariousness of habit, this love of kind, and this deep-seated fear of loneliness," which in part accounted for the near universal Indian resistance to allotment in severalty. Garland urged that allotments be so arranged as to permit the Indians to "live as the French peasants do, in villages and farm their outlying lands."[14]

Steeped in utopian hopes for Indian betterment and supported by many "Red Progressives" and the General Federation of Women's Clubs, Collier in 1923 formed the American Indian Defense Association as the agency to effectuate what he regarded as the essentials for Indian policy reform—citizenship, termination of allotment, improved education and health services, reestablishment of tribal governments, reinstitution of Native American self-determination, and permitting Indians to retain their religion and other native ways. Thus AIDA differed from the late nineteenth-century "Friends of the Indian" reform organizations in that it stressed cultural pluralism and self-determination and sought to apply social science methodology to the solution of the Indians' problems. The Indian Rights Association, one of the few surviving nineteenth-century reform groups, supported the AIDA goal of protecting Indian property. Otherwise it remained committed to its historic position of eradication of Indianness and thorough Americanization. AIDA membership included, besides Indian leaders, social scientists and reformers and many authors, artists, and poets.

The reformers, like their obscurantist adversaries, used publications to carry their message to the public. The New York *Times* consistently supported their viewpoint. *Survey, Current History Magazine, The Nation, Forum,* and *Sunset Magazine* carried articles by Collier, Schultz, Mary Austin, and other reformers denouncing federal Indian policy and urging substantive changes in the management of Native Americans. The Indian Rights Association, supported by a grant from John D. Rockefeller, published the monthly *Indian Truth*. And AIDA published *American Indian Life;* Collier served as its editor for seven years. Often the articles by reformers were muckraking exposés. The most dramatic disclosure was published in 1924 as a pamphet by the Indian Rights Association titled *Oklahoma's Poor Rich Indians: An Orgy of Graft and Exploitation of the Five Civilized Tribes—Legalized Robbery.* Gertrude Bonnin, a "Red Progressive" employed by the General Federation of Women's Clubs, Charles H. Fabens of AIDA, and Matthew K. Kniffen of the Indian Rights Association collaborated to expose the rapacious handling of allotted Indians by Oklahoma lawyers, judges, guardians, bankers, and public officials. Their findings confirmed Kate Barnard's claim of a local ring of private and public parties robbing and defrauding Indians with impunity.

Reformers' Triumph

Action by Secretary Fall precipitated open conflict between obscurantists and reformers. First, with strong support from the Indian Rights Association and many missionaries, he issued order forbidding Indians to perform dances and ceremonials. Next, in response to demands from oil interests that rich petroleum reserves on Indian reservations be opened to them, Fall ruled that because executive-order reservations—those set aside by presidential order—were only "temporarily withdrawn" from the public domain, they were available to developers under terms of the General Leasing Act of 1920. His order opened 22 million acres of reservation lands to drillers. And, third, as a former senator from New Mexico, he sensed a partisan benefit to be derived from the 12,000 New Mexican squatters who faced expulsion from Pueblo Indian lands. Thus, in 1921 New Mexico Senator Holm O. Bursum introduced a bill in Congress which virtually confirmed squatter rights to the contested Pueblo Indian lands by placing the burden of proof of title on the Pueblo governments. Failure to establish convincing proof of ownership automatically vested title in the settler claimants.

Reformers countered Fall's actions in various ways. The Indian Rights Association supported Fall's no-dance order but strongly opposed his ruling on executive-order reservations and on the Pueblo lands issue. The American Indian Defense Association prepared to contest Fall on all three issues. Executive Secretary Collier maintained that Fall's no-dance order "represents an interference with the constitutional right of the Indians to religious freedom." He insisted that the secret ceremonials were not immoral or indecent but on the contrary, "beautiful and moving rituals of a deeply religious character." Fall called his critics "propagandists" and members of the ever-supportive House Committee on Indian Affairs charged that the reformer attacks were "insidious, untruthful, and malicious."[15]

The Bursum Bill, like the Standing Bear decision, stirred a wider public interest in Indian welfare. Through AIDA Collier mobilized reform support from the General Federation of Women's Clubs, he counseled tribal leaders to form the All-Pueblo Council as an Indian protective association, and he fused the colony of artists and writers at Santa Fe and Taos, in the very heart of the Pueblo country, into a committed support group. They provided funds to enable delegations of Indians to travel to Washington to protest the Bursum Bill before federal officials and congressional committees; they wrote newspaper and magazine articles denouncing the Bursum Bill; they made public appearances across the nation on behalf of the Pueblo land interest; and they wrote many letters and petitions on behalf of the cause of protecting Indian title to Pueblo lands. One petition composed in 1922 contained signatures of Mary Austin, Witter Bynner, John Collier, Alice Corbin, Zane Grey, Robert Henri, Gustave Baumann, Ernest L. Blumenschein, D. H. Lawrence, Burt G. Phillips, Carl Sandburg, J. H. Sharp, John Slocum, Mabel Dodge (Luhan), Walter Ufer, Carlos Vierra, William Allen White, Vachel Lindsay, and Edgar Lee Masters.

AIDA-mobilized collective action brought a storm of public pressure to bear upon the Congress to defeat the Bursum Bill. In its place Congress adopted legislation which reinvested the Pueblos with title to their lands and in effect placed burden of contest and proof on the squatters. The statute created the Pueblo Land Board to determine ownership of the disputed lands. In those rulings made in favor of settlers, the board compensated the Pueblo tribal governments by cash settlement.

The reformers won another victory in 1923 when Albert Fall, the single-minded champion and principal spokesman for the obscurantists, was forced to resign from his strategic position as Secretary of the Interior. Soon after his resignation a ruling from the United States attorney general's office set aside Fall's order permitting petroleum and mineral leases on executive-order reservations. Then in 1926 Congress passed a law placing executive-order reservations on an equal basis with treaty reservations.

While for the moment reformers did not gain relaxation of the federal ban on Indian dances and ceremonials, they did achieve several additional benefits for Indians. The Osage Guardianship Act of 1925 forced Oklahoma district court judges to share appointment of guardians for Indian property with federal agents. Pressure from the American Indian Defense Association and Indian Rights Association forced a slowdown by federal officials on lifting restrictions on allotted lands.

Next to turning back the threat of appropriation of Pueblo lands, the reformers' most substantial achievement for Indian welfare during the 1920s was conferral of citizenship. Through the years federal officials had regarded Indians as citizens of their respective tribes. Token United States citizenship had been extended to selected Native Americans before 1887. During the 1830s, removal treaty provisions granted citizenship to limited numbers of allotted Indians in Mississippi, Alabama, and certain other states, primarily to eliminate objections to the dissolution of eastern Indian nations and their control of territory within states. In 1853, citizenship had been promised those Indians who accepted allotments following negotiation of treaties which dissolved the northern half of the Indian Territory. The General Allotment Act of 1887 extended United States citizenship to allotted Indians. An act of 1901 conferred citizenship upon all Native Americans in the Indian Territory. The Burke Act of 1906 delayed conferral of citizenship for certain allotted Indians, and the following year an act conferred citizenship upon all Indians in Oklahoma (the former Indian Territory) not covered by the 1901 statute. The dilemma of citizenship and restricted status of allottees was resolved in *United States* v. *Nice* in 1916 when the Supreme Court ruled that citizenship was not incompatible with tribal existence or continued guardianship. The justices agreed that the federal government could confer citizenship on Native Americans without removing those restrictions which Congress had adopted to protect them.

Native American participation in World War I widened United States citizenship for Indians. Many hundreds of young Indian males crossed into Canada and enlisted in the Canadian army before 1917. After the American declaration of war over 15,000 Indians enlisted and served on active duty. For this response to the war effort, Congress in 1919 adopted a law which extended United States citizenship to Indians who were not yet citizens and who had served in the Allied armed forces. And finally in 1924 Congress passed a law which provided that all noncitizen Indians born within the nation's territorial limits were citizens of the United States. Following adoption of this law the New York *Times* commented, "If there are cynics among the Indians, they may receive the news of their new citizenship with wry smiles. The white race, having robbed them of a continent, and having sought to deprive them of freedom of action, freedom of social custom, and freedom of worship, now at last gives them the same legal basis as their conquerors."[16]

However, for most Indians this grant of citizenship was an empty gesture because of the states' latitude of power and action over voting and other rights of citizenship and the obscurantist attitudes of persons in the states toward Indians. Even in 1938, seven states still refused to permit Indians to vote. Ten years later only New Mexico and Arizona denied Indians suffrage; in 1948 these two states relented, and thereafter, United States citizenship began to take on a meaning of some consequence for Native Americans.

Reform Commissions of the 1920s

Modest improvements in Indian welfare won by reformers from their limited victories over the obscurantists produced a momentum which inevitably pressed for additional reforms. Hubert Work, Fall's successor as Secretary of the Interior, responded to an enlarging public pressure and formed several citizen and professional study groups to examine the Indian problem.

First, in 1923, Work appointed the Committee of One Hundred "to review and advise on Indian policy." Members included civic leaders Bernard Baruch, William Jennings Bryan, General John J. Pershing, Mark Sullivan, and William Allen White; several reformers led by John Collier; "Red Progressives" from the Society of American Indians including Henry Roe Cloud, Sherman Coolidge, Thomas D. Sloan, and Arthur C. Parker; and anthropologists Frederick W. Hodge, Alfred L. Kroeber, Warren K. Moorehead, and Clark Wissler. The Committee of One Hundred met on Work's call in Washington and from its 2 days of deliberations came both recriminations and constructive recommendations. Obscurantists on the panel, led by Bryan, denounced Indians as "a race of primitive, untutored, nature-worshippers." Bryan was particularly impatient with Indians who resisted the federal government's Americanization program. He would "shove the Christian religion down the throat of every Indian." Reformers urged Work to improve Indian schools, place more Indians in public schools, provide scholarship aid for college education to train Indian leaders, expand health care, and establish a special tribunal to settle tribal claims against the United States. The committee also recommended that Work order a scientific study of peyote to determine whether its use was detrimental to Indian health and morals. Work's Committee of One Hundred took no stand on Indian citizenship. Collier as spokesman for the activist AIDA rated the committee's accomplishments as "innocuous." Because of congressional indifference the committee's recommendations served only as a foundation for succeeding groups assigned the task of seeking improvements in Native American management.[17]

Next, Work called on the Board of Indian Commissioners to study the Indian problem. Their report, completed in 1926, yielded no new information and no suggested solutions. It did recommend that Work engage a disinterested, nongovernmental organization with a professional staff to undertake an objective field study of conditions among the Indian tribes. The commissioners held the view that the findings of such a panel, with its recommendations for change in Indian policy, if published and widely distributed, would so impress the public that the lethargic Congress might be stirred to act on legislative essentials to accomplish the required changes in policy toward Indians.

Work requested W. F. Willoughby, director of the Institute for Government Research, a privately endowed organization subsequently called the Brookings Institution, to sponsor a survey of conditions among the Indian tribes. Willoughby obtained a grant from John D. Rockefeller, Jr., to finance the study and appointed Lewis Meriam to direct it. Meriam, a social scientist, selected a staff of 9 experts in education, health, economics, and Indian affairs—Ray A. Brown, Henry Roe Cloud, Edward Everett Dale, Emma Duke, Herbert R. Edwards, Fayette McKenzie, Mary Louise Mark, W. Carson Ryan, Jr., and William J. Spillman. Beginning in 1926 the group spent 7 months in the field investigating Indian communities throughout the United States. Their findings submitted in 1928, titled *The Problem of Indian Administration* and popularly known as the Meriam Report, described in detail what the members designated "deplorable conditions" in virtually every Native American settlement in the United States. They found shockingly high mortality rates among Indians of all ages. The general mortality rate among Indians was 25.9 per 1,000, twice the Anglo-American rate, while infant mortality rates for whites (70.8 per 1,000) and for blacks (114.1 per 1,000) were considerably below the Indian infant mortality rate of 190.7 per 1,000. Leading death causes among Indians, according to the Meriam Report, were measles and respiratory diseases, particularly pneumonia and tuberculosis; in Arizona alone the tuberculosis death rate among Indians was 17 times the national average. In addition, the Meriam staff found an abnormally high prevalence of trachoma among Indians. Their report pointed to the pitifully low annual medical expenditures authorized by Congress for Indians—$756,000. Of this only $200,000 was available for field treatment, amounting to about 50 cents per Indian per year. Meriam staff researchers found that Indian children were placed in unsanitary classrooms and dormitories at government schools and fed a daily 11-cent ration which rarely included milk or fresh vegetables. Stark Indian poverty explained widespread malnutrition; nearly half of the Native American population lived on a per capita income of from $100 to $200 per year, compared to a national average of nearly $1,350. The Meriam Report concluded that the federal government's allotment in severalty and Americanization programs were failures. It recommended increased appropriations for Indian health and education, that allotment cease, and that Indians be provided more effective protection in the tenure of their landed property, that education programs train leaders capable of directing tribal political and business interests, that Indians form cooperatives, and that Congress create a loan fund to provide capital for tribal business enterprises. And their report offered as an alternative to assimilation the hope that Indians could be "fitted to live within the dominant society without being obliterated by it."[18]

The Meriam staff did not include agricultural and irrigation specialists, so Work requested that government engineers make an additional survey to complete the study of Indian resources. In 1927 Porter Preston, of the Bureau of Reclamation, and C. A. Engle, of the Bureau of Indian Affairs, studied irrigation and agriculture among the western tribes. Their findings, published in 1928 as the Preston-Engle Report, recommended abandonment of several Indian irrigation projects because they either were too costly or were of little value to Indian agriculture, and assignment of remaining projects to the Bureau of Reclamation.

Congress also investigated the condition of the Indian tribes. In 1928 the Senate approved a resolution offered by William H. King, senator from Utah, that the Senate Committee on Indian Affairs study the Indian problem. The committee began its work in November 1928, conducting hearings in Washington and at various points across the nation. Because it duplicated the ground covered by the 4 previous studies and reiterated much of their content, the most impressive feature of Congress' ongoing study of Native Americans was the size of its final published report—23,069 printed pages. Even with 5 published studies to guide it, Congress remained unwilling to take steps to achieve substantive reform in management of Indian affairs.

In 1929 President Herbert Hoover appointed Ray L. Wilbur as Secretary of the Interior and Charles Rhoads as Commissioner of Indian Affairs. Both men accepted the findings of the 5 studies of conditions among the Indian tribes made during the 1920s, particularly the Meriam Report recommendations. In those areas where they could effect improvements through administrative action, for example, education, they promptly took what corrective steps the limited financial resources provided by a reluctant Congress would permit. However, most of the reforms required congressional action. Wilbur and Rhoads spent much time drafting proposals to establish Indian leadership and business management training programs, procedures for tribal incorporation, authority for creating cooperatives, and appropriations to establish loan funds for capitalizing Native American enterprises. They also urged congressional action on long-standing claims of tribes against the United States. Rhoads estimated that the United States Court of Claims docket was so crowded that Indians would have to wait a century for tribal claims to receive a hearing. Therefore, he proposed that Congress create a special tribunal to handle Indian claims. Several bills were introduced by the few friends of the Indian in Congress, including one in 1929 by Congressman Scott Leavitt, to create the Court of Indian Claims. However, on this and other reform bills a generally indifferent Congress took no action. Besides a continuing disinterest on the part of most congressmen, the Great Depression was creating broader national concerns which absorbed their attention. Ironically, out of the most devastating economic disaster in history came a comprehensive national rehabilitation program which included, finally, immense gains for Indians.

The Indian and the New Deal

The election of 1932 brought Franklin Delano Roosevelt to the presidency and the New Deal to the nation. Roosevelt's New Deal was a vast relief program to succor the millions of Americans who were suffering from the devastating, impoverishing effects of the Great Depression and to rehabilitate the nation's faltering economy. Roosevelt appointed Harold L. Ickes Secretary of the Interior and John Collier Commissioner of Indian Affairs. Ickes shared Collier's deep sympathy for Indian plight and consistently supported the former American Indian Defense Association official in his stance that because Native Americans also suffered from the national economic disaster, they too merited relief and reform attention. Thus Ickes and Collier shaped a New Deal for Indians which included emergency measures to curb widespread destitution among Indians (in 1933 Indian per capita income was $81) including issuance of emergency rations and application of federally funded work programs to reduce widespread unemployment among Native Americans.

Thus, Indians were employed to improve reservation lands by applying to eroded and deforested areas restorative conservation practices. Much of this work was coordinated by the Emergency Conservation Work (ECW) agency, its designation later changed to the Indian CCC. Agents gathered Indian families in conservation camps. The men worked at reforestation and soil restoration by constructing terraces and check dams to halt water erosion, and planting shelterbelts of trees to check wind erosion. They built roads in the western wilderness and guarded timbered areas against forest fires. Native workmen also constructed dams for water impoundment, dug wells, and reseeded ranges. The Indian CCC camps included schools where government teachers provided basic education of reading, writing, and arithmetic to Indian adults and children. They also provided vocational education and taught agriculture, forestry, and animal husbandry. As early as 1934, over 25,000 Native Americans were employed in Indian CCC work; federal agents established 72 camps in 15 western states to service the Indian workers and their families.

The Ickes-Collier New Deal for Indians also included substantive reforms to improve Native American status. Some improvements could come only from laws passed by Congress, but many important changes were the results of executive orders by the President, Ickes, or Collier as appropriate. The Board of Indian Commissioners, created in 1869 as an advisory group on management of Native Americans and a symbol of the old order, was abolished by executive order in 1933. Next, Ickes ordered an end to the sale of allotments and urged that no additional fee patents be issued. Then Collier officially terminated the long-standing federal program of Americanization for Indians. Both Ickes and Collier pushed to increase the number of Indians employed in the Bureau of Indian Affairs. In 1934 of the 5,325 classified positions in the bureau, only 1,785 were held by Indians. Collier also issued an order to bureau field workers forbidding them to interfere with Indian religious life. He directed that the "cultural history of Indians is in all respects to be considered equal to that of any non-Indian group. And it is desirable that Indians be bilingual. . . . The Indian arts are to be prized, nourished, and honored."[19]

Most Indian boarding schools had received a negative rating from Meriam commission members. Collier transferred many Indian children from boarding schools to community day schools. His plan was that the community day schools would also serve as centers for adult Indians. Several of the boarding schools were assigned special functions, including serving as orphanages. Collier also de-emphasized "big-time football" at Haskell, Chilocco, and other boarding schools. Besides protecting tribal religion, Collier abolished the bureau requirement that Indian students at government boarding schools attend Christian worship service. He also persuaded Congress to discontinue appropriations to suppress traffic in peyote. Missionaries raged at Collier and denounced him for what they called returning Indians to "degrading tribalism." On several occasions he was summoned before the House Committee on Indian Affairs to answer charges of "atheism, Communism, and sedition."[20]

At Collier's urging, Congress in 1934 approved the Johnson-O'Malley Act which permitted the federal government to contract with states and territories to provide educational, medical, and social welfare services for Indians. Well before 1900 federal funds had been allotted to certain states to pay the tuition for Indian youths in public schools. This statute updated and expanded the process of making federal grants to states for services to Indians.

Then in 1934 Congress approved the Indian Reorganization Act, also known as the Wheeler-Howard Act from its sponsors, in the House Edgar Howard of Nebraska and in the Senate Burton K. Wheeler of Montana. Collier and other administrative officials contributed to the measure but Felix Cohen, attorney and foremost authority on Indian law, drafted most of it. Broadly, the proposal would promote cultural pluralism by guaranteeing to Indians rights to traditional religion and life-style free of government interference; provide for "creative self-determination" as Collier described it; substantially improve Indian education and access to health services; produce tribal leaders; encourage formation of business corporations for managing tribal property; establish revolving funds to provide capital for Indian enterprises; and end allotment in severalty. In many respects it attempted to fulfill the recommendations of the Meriam study and the aborted reforms proposed by former Commissioner of Indian Affairs Charles Rhoads.

Collier sent drafts of the bill to bureau superintendents, tribal councils, and tribal leaders for their reactions. He convened regional conferences at centers of Indian population from Oklahoma and South Dakota to Oregon and California where federal officials and Indians met and discussed the proposal, marking the first time ever that federal officials seriously solicited the Indian viewpoint on proposed legislation.

Many missionaries, some politicians, and several Indians opposed the Wheeler-Howard proposal. Christian clergy working among the Indians charged that the proposal, if enacted, would permit use of federal funds to support "alien" religions and social practices among the Indians. Some western congressmen opposed it because it would end the easy access to Indian lands which many of their constituents wished to continue. And a surprising number of Indians opposed the measure for personal, petty, or doctrinal reasons. Collier's suggestion that allotted Indians place their lands in a common pool and share these lands with the improvident who had lost their homesteads alarmed many Indians who had retained their allotments and had become Americanized to the point that they had shed old values of obligatory sharing. They feared that in the new order created by the proposed Indian Reorganization Act they would lose their allotments.

The doctrinal antagonism toward Collier and the proposed Indian Reorganization Act came from the American Indian Federation. Its president, Joseph Bruner, a Creek Indian from Oklahoma, charged that the measure was "conceived and sponsored by the American Civil Liberties Union, a Communistic organization with headquarters in New York City." He said the proposal was "a dangerous Christ-mocking, Communistic aiding, subversive set-up." Bruner further denounced Collier's efforts as "red" and an "un-American attempt to force Indians back to the blanket." Thomas L. Sloan, former president of the Society of American Indians and Delos K. Lone Wolf, a national peyote-cult leader, also opposed the Wheeler-Howard proposal and worked to defeat it. One writer has claimed that Bruner and the American Indian Federation "in ideology and activities . . . resembled white extremist right-wing groups, within which it developed close ties. Cordial federation relations with the German-American Bund were thought to be legitimized through the German government's bizarre declaration that the Sioux, and presumably by extension, all Indians, were in fact Aryans."[21]

Nonetheless, Congress approved the Wheeler-Howard proposal. It confirmed Collier's ruling on cultural pluralism and protected Indians in their right to freedom of religion and life-style. It reestablished tribal government but permitted alternatives of new models better calculated to cope with the new order. Thus the tribes were permitted to function under governments of their choosing guided by written constitutions, although customary usages also were permitted. In effect the act extended "home rule" to the tribes, their constitutions serving much like charters for municipal governments. Reformulated tribal governments could conduct elections, create courts with jurisdiction over local offenses, and perform other local governmental functions.

The act ended allotment in severalty. Any remaining surplus lands were to be restored to tribal ownership, and sale to non-Indians of allotted land was drastically curtailed. The secretary of the interior was to receive an annual appropriation of $2 million to buy land for Indians to recover portions of tribal estates. Tribal business committees were permitted to form chartered Indian corporations and draw from a $10 million revolving loan fund for capital to finance tribal businesses. The law provided funds to support Indian students in vocational schools and colleges. It also promoted bilingual education—instruction in the tribal language, Spanish, and English. And Indians were to receive preference in civil service appointments in the Bureau of Indian Affairs. The law stipulated that its provisions would apply to a tribe

"Eagle Dancer," a painting by Woody Crumbo, a Creek-Potawatomi Indian, 1946. (Courtesy Koshare Indian Museum/Harold G. Finke)

only after its members had voted to accept it. Advocates of the General Allotment Act of 1887 hailed it as the ultimate in the progress of individualism and marked the occasion as "Indian Emancipation Day." Collier and other advocates hailed passage of the Indian Reorganization Act in 1934 as the ultimate in collectivist reform and the occasion as "Indian Independence Day."

In subsequent tribal referenda on the Indian Reorganization Act, 189 tribes accepted it and 77 rejected it. Several subsequently approved it. Under its auspices, 135 Indian communities drafted tribal constitutions.

The Indian Reorganization Act did not apply to Indians in Oklahoma and Alaska. In 1936 Congress applied certain of its provisions to the Alaskan natives and passed the Oklahoma Indian Welfare Act. In effect it adapted portions of the Indian Reorganization Act to the "tribeless Indians" of Oklahoma, so called because all their lands had been liquidated by allotment. This statute permitted them to form corporations and to draw capital from a special revolving loan fund of $2 million for their projects.

The Indian New Deal did not accomplish the millenium for Indians that Collier expected. But he was a utopian reformer, a zealot, impatient in his expectations to achieve perfection for Native Americans. And he was impatient with problems of faulty administration of measures conceived for better conditions for Indians. The Johnson-O'Malley Act, which he hoped would improve the quality of Indian education, was a disappointment. To his chagrin Collier found that state education officials were far more interested in the additional funds than in Indian pupils. Mishandling of federal funds by state officials became "notorious," and the education they provided Indian youths in the public schools was "inferior."[22]

Collier was also distressed with the workings of certain features of the Indian Reorganization Act, particularly those designed to reactivate Indian self-determination. Many tribes found the majority-rule provisions of the act difficult to carry out. That which is "taken for granted in Anglo-Saxon governing bodies, was at first a divisive rather than a unifying principle in Indian groups, where action is customarily delayed until all people are in agreement, or at least until the dissidents agree to stand aside." In earlier times dissenting factions could secede and go elsewhere, but by the 1930s there was no place to go. Thus dissidents remained and became a continuing source of divisiveness. In addition, Indians had become so accustomed to having decisions made for them by federal officials that "they were reluctant to act on their own in exercising the new powers."[23]

But on the positive side, Collier's emphasis on self-determination eventually became a compelling force in aboriginal renaissance. And his stress on respect for Indian culture renewed pride in Indianness. Repeal of the General Allotment Act and the end of allotment in severalty brought immense benefit to Indians. And federal loans enabled them to buy back land; from 1934 to 1947 the Indian land base increased by nearly 4 million acres. Federal loans under the Indian Reorganization Act also provided Indians with capital to buy livestock, equipment, seeds, and enabled them to use land that they had formerly leased to others. Thus in the period 1934–1947, Indian-owned livestock increased from 171,000 head to 361,000, and total agricultural income grew from $1,850,000 to $50 million for the same period. Indians also gained experience in tribal leadership and developed assertiveness in promoting tribal welfare.

Above all, the Indian New Deal, particularly the Indian Reorganization Act, seriously attempted to "restore the wreckage of a hundred years." Its drastic turnabout character was tantamount to admitting that "federal control of Indian life had been a destructive and self-defeating device, not a solution" to the "Indian problem." However, the cause of improving Indian status faced new threats as the nation's attention after 1941 was diverted from reform to the all-engrossing concerns of World War II and its troubled aftermath. The fate of Native American status and welfare since 1945 is the subject of Chapter Twenty-One.[24]

Notes

1. Loring B. Priest, *Uncle Sam's Stepchildren: The Reformation of United States Indian Policy, 1865–1887* (New York, 1969), p. 250.
2. Jennings C. Wise, *The Red Man in the New World Drama: A Politico-Legal Study with a Pageantry of American Indian History,* edited with an introduction by Vine Deloria, Jr. (New York, 1971), p. 314.
3. *Ibid.,* p. 308.
4. *Reports of the Commissioner of Indian Affairs for 1905 and for 1916.*
5. David F. Aberle, *The Peyote Religion Among the Navajo* (Chicago, 1966), pp. 14–15.
6. *Report of the Commissioner of Indian Affairs for 1920,* p. 20.
7. Hazel Hertzberg, *The Search for an American Indian Identity: Modern Pan-Indian Movements* (Syracuse, N.Y., 1971), p. 31.
8. *Ibid.,* p. 138.
9. *Ibid.,* p. 142.
10. *Ibid.,* pp. 179, 199.
11. Jack D. Forbes (ed.), *The Indian in America's Past* (Englewood Cliffs, N.J., 1964), p. 117.
12. "Our American Indians," *Saturday Evening Post* (May 1924), pp. 92–94.
13. Lonnie E. Underhill and Daniel F. Littlefield, Jr. (eds.), *Hamlin Gar-*land's Observations on the American Indian (Tucson, Ariz., 1976), p. 48.
14. *Ibid.,* p. 46.
15. Hertzberg, *Search for an American Indian Identity,* p. 202.
16. New York *Times,* July 7, 1924.
17. *The Nation,* December 1923, p. 735.
18. *The Problem of Indian Administration* (Baltimore, 1928); see also D'Arcy McNickle, *Native American Tribalism: Indian Survivals and Renewals* (New York, 1973), p. 92.
19. *Report of the Commissioner of Indian Affairs for 1934,* p. 90.
20. Angie Debo, *A History of the Indians of the United States* (Norman, Okla., 1970), p. 292.
21. S. Lyman Tyler, *A History of Indian Policy* (Washington, D.C., 1973), p. 142; and Hertzberg, *Search for an American Indian Identity,* p. 289.
22. See Margaret Szasz, *Education and the American Indian: The Road to Self-Determination, 1928–1973* (Albuquerque, N.M., 1974).
23. McNickle, *Native American Tribalism,* p. 95.
24. Harold E. Fey and D'Arcy McNickle, *Indians and Other Americans: Two Ways of Life Meet* (New York, 1959), p. 109.

Selected Sources

A fresh and exceedingly useful guide to literature pertaining to the American Indians including their status in the twentieth century is Francis P. Prucha, *A Bibliographical Guide to the History of Indian-White Relations in the United States* (Chicago, 1977). The most useful study of the Indian in the early twentieth century is Hazel Hertzberg, *The Search for an American Indian Identity: Modern Pan-Indian Movements* (Syracuse, N.Y. 1971). Also see G. E. E. Lindquist, *The Red Man in the United States* (New York, 1923); Jennings C. Wise, *The Red Man in the New World Drama: A Politico-Legal Study with a Pageantry of American Indian History*, edited with an introduction by Vine Deloria, Jr. (New York, 1971); Angie Debo, *A History of the Indians of the United States* (Norman, Okla., 1970); and Harold E. Fey and D'Arcy McNickle, *Indians and Other Americans: Two Ways of Life Meet* (New York, 1959).

The prelude to the Indian New Deal is discussed in John Collier, *From Every Zenith* (Denver, 1963); and by the same author, *Indians of the Americas* (New York, 1947); Angie Debo, *And Still the Waters Run* (Princeton, N.J., 1940); Herbert O. Brayer, *Pueblo Land Grants of the Rio Abajo* (Albuquerque, N.M., 1938); Lawrence Kelly, *The Navajo Indians and Federal Indian Policy, 1900–1935* (Tucson, Ariz., 1968); and Randolph Downes, "A Crusade for Indian Reform, 1922–1934, *Mississippi Valley Historical Review* 32 (December 1945), pp. 331–54.

Improvement of Indian status during the 1920s is traced in R. Alton Lee, "Indian Citizenship and the Fourteenth Amendment," *South Dakota History* 4 (Spring 1974), pp. 196–221; Felix S. Cohen, *Handbook of Federal Indian Law* (Washington, D.C., 1942), reprinted (Albuquerque, N.M., n.d.); John Collier and Ira Moskowitz, *American Indian Ceremonial Dances* (New York, 1972); Gary Stein, "The Indian Citizenship Act of 1924," *New Mexico Historical Review* 47 (July 1972), pp. 257–74; Robert Gessner, *Massacre: A Survey of Today's American Indian* (New York, 1931); Turbesé Lummis Fiske and Keith Lummis, *Charles F. Lummis: The Man and His West* (Norman, Okla., 1975); John Collier, "Do Indians Have Rights of Conscience?" *Christian Century* 42 (March 12, 1925), pp. 346–49; and *The Problem of Indian Administration* (Baltimore, 1928).

Sources on Indian policy reform and the New Deal and the Indian include Donald L. Parman, "The Indian and the Civilian Conservation Corps," *Pacific Historical Quarterly* 40 (February 1971), pp. 39–56, and *The Navajos and the New Deal* (New Haven, Conn., 1976); Kenneth R. Philp, *John Collier's Crusade for Indian Reform, 1920–1954* (Tucson, Ariz., 1977); Wilcomb Washburn, *Red Man's Land, White Man's Law* (New York, 1971); Margaret Szasz, *Education and the American Indian: The Road to Self-Determination, 1928–1973* (Albuquerque, N.M., 1974); Peter M. Wright, "John Collier and the Oklahoma Indian Welfare Act of 1936," *Chronicles of Oklahoma* 50 (Autumn 1972), pp. 347–71; William Zimmerman, "The Role of the Bureau of Indian Affairs Since 1933," *Annals of the American Academy of Political and Social Science* 102 (May 1957), pp. 31–40; "Tribal Self-Government and the Indian Reorganization Act of 1934," *Michigan Law Review* 70 (April 1972), pp. 955–86; Jay B. Nash (ed.), *The New Day for the Indians: A Survey of the Working of the Indian Reorganization Act of 1934* (New York, 1938); and William H. Kelly (ed.), *Indian Affairs and the Indian Reorganization Act: The Twenty-Year Record* (Tucson, Ariz., 1954).

CHAPTER 21

NATIVE AMERICANS
IN THE TWENTIETH
CENTURY
1945 TO THE PRESENT

The Native American Movement represents the awakening of the Native American people and the revival of Americanist principles. It is the spiritual descendant of the earlier movements for unity organized by Tecumseh ... Po-pe ... Wovoka and other great leaders. The movement seeks to realize justice for Native Americans and all other peoples who suffer from discrimination. It does not draw any color line or exclude anyone. All persons who seek to advance the cause of true Amerindians and of American unity are welcome.... All who struggle for justice and freedom are brothers.... Every person in the United States and in the Americas who has a drop of Native American ancestry is a member of the Movement if he stands for freedom and justice.

Creed of the National Indian Youth Conference, 1963

Although many Native Americans did benefit from educational improvements, the availability of capital funds for tribal enterprises, the restoration of tribal government, and the legalizing of tribal culture including religion, the full potential of the Indian Reorganization Act of 1934 was never realized. Bureaucratic inertia and hostility toward the reforms by entrenched federal employees who had direct contact with Indians on the western reservations and who were responsible for carrying out the statute's transforming provisions managed to reduce its potential impact. Another deterrent to fulfillment of the goals of the Indian Reorganization Act was the nation's involvement in World War II which necessarily turned public and private attention from internal to external concerns.

As in World War I, Native Americans strongly supported the nation's war effort; over 25,000 Indians served on active duty with the United States armed forces, and additional thousands were employed in war-related industries. Then, in the post–World War II era, when application of the Indian Reorganization Act could seriously be resumed, a powerful bloc in the Congress began to urge that the federal government "liberate" Indians from national oversight, that it break up reservations and liquidate tribal governments, only recently restored by the Indian Reorganization Act, and that it stop "coddling" Native Americans.

Chapter Opening Artifact: Menominee carved wood heddle for loom beadwork. (Courtesy Milwaukee Public Museum)

DEMISE OF INDIAN REFORM

In the early postwar years a huge public debt from heavy wartime expenditures stirred wide concern and inevitably led Congress to an economy-in-government course. Congressional committees examined all functions supported by federal funds. Expenditures for improvement of Indian welfare were readily challenged, and several legislators began to agitate that Congress end the federal government's relation with the Indian tribes. Their demands evolved into a policy which came to be called Termination.

Origins of Termination

What Termination-bent congressmen were seeking to accomplish was to conclude federal responsibility for Native Americans: end federal treaty obligations to the Indian tribes, settle all outstanding claims of the tribes against the United States, conclude all treaty-assigned special concessions to tribes, liquidate trust funds, wipe out reservations as anomalous political enclaves within the states, and eradicate tribal governments which the Indian Reorganization Act had only recently restored. This proposed policy of Termination would apply to most tribes with the exception of Indian communities in several of the original states. Battered and scattered by colonial wars, by the time of American independence only remnants of the original tribes—Penobscot, Passamaquoddy, Pamunkey—survived. After 1776 most of these tribal fragments, from New England to Virginia, were presumably absorbed by the original states and thus had no treaty relationship or ward status with the United States.

For Native Americans under federal wardship, law and custom had established their respective tribes as quasi-sovereign entities. Through the years, several states had attempted to establish local jurisdiction over tribes and their lands, but federal court decisions, particularly *Worcester* v. *Georgia* (1832), had exempted Indian tribes from state jurisdiction.

Assimilation—that is, the absorption of Indians into the dominant society erasing tribal culture and status and enabling the federal government to terminate its special relation with the Indian tribes—was an early goal of Henry Knox and Thomas Jefferson. Most federal Indian policy during the nineteenth century was directed to that end, although the general public's attitudes made its consummation impossible. President Andrew Jackson's forced exile and segregation of the eastern tribes in the western wilderness delayed the assimilation process and complicated its achievement, although federal action terminated several tribes in the nineteenth century. After the Treaty of Dancing Rabbit Creek (1830), those Choctaws who elected not to relocate in the Indian Territory were stripped of their federal relationship and assigned to Mississippi state jurisdiction. Following liquidation of the northern portion of the Indian Territory (1853–1854), federal officials terminated Indians from several tribes in Kansas Territory; subsequently they terminated

Cherokees who lived in North Carolina. A primary goal of the General Allotment Act (1887) was to liquidate tribal estates, abolish tribal governments, and place Indian allottees in a position where they could be individualized and thus terminated from federal direction and protection.

The corollary citizenship acts passed between 1887 and 1924 were attempts to terminate Indians and transfer them from federal to state jurisdiction. Certainly that portion of the Burke Act (1906) which empowered the secretary of the interior to declare allottees competent to manage their affairs was intended, besides gaining for non-Indians easier access to restricted allotments, to terminate Native American allottees. This was particularly the case during the "forced patent" period (1917–1921) when farcical competency hearings drastically increased the number of Indians separated from the federal relationship.

Increasingly the federal government had delegated functions in Indian affairs to the states, each as a gesture in the direction of eventual termination. This transfer occurred quite early in Indian education and was formalized by the Johnson-O'Malley Act (1934) which, besides education, permitted federal officials to contract with state governments for provision of welfare and health services to Indians. And many of the features of the Indian Reorganization Act were conceived to enable the federal government eventually to reduce its oversight of the tribes and to terminate certain functions. Another step in concluding federal relations with Indians was the Social Security Act (1935), in which Congress delegated social services to the states. The statute provided aid for families with dependent children, for the blind, and for permanently disabled persons. The program was to be administered through the states for all persons, including Indians both on and off reservations. And through the years, either by federal delegation or state assumption, state laws regulated sanitation, quarantine, inheritance, health, education, and general law-and-order matters on many Indian reservations. The secretary of the interior applied state law to determine the descent and distribution of individually owned Indian property as well as restricted allotments except in the cases of the Five Civilized Tribes and the Osages. Under the Assimilative Crimes Act of 1948 offenses committed on reservations not covered under a specific federal statute and punishable under state law were to be tried in federal courts in accordance with the appropriate state laws. Certain offenses committed by one Indian against another, however, could be tried under tribal law.

A major step toward ending the federal relationship with the Indian tribes was taken by Congress in 1946 when it created the Indian Claims Commission. The federal government is immune from suit except by permission; thus in 1855 Congress established the Court of Claims to adjudicate actions against the United States. However, an act of 1863 prohibited the court from considering any claim growing out of treaties with foreign nations or Indian tribes. Thus a tribe had to obtain a special act of Congress in order to bring suit against the United States for damages, and doing so proved extremely difficult. Even if a tribe received congressional approval to bring suit against the United States, the Court of Claims' docket had become so encumbered that it might have to wait years, perhaps a century, for a hearing. During his tenure as Commissioner of Indian Affairs, Charles Rhoads recommended formation of a special tribunal to hear Indian claims, and beginning in 1929 several bills to this end were introduced in the Congress. Not until 1946, however, was legislation adopted establishing the Indian Claims Commission. Its function was to adjudicate all valid claims of the tribes against the United States. Awards of the commission were to equalize or offset "unconscionable negotiations" by government agents with tribal leaders for land and other Indian properties. In addition, the awards were to make restitution for misuse of tribal trust funds, loss of hunting and fishing rights, improper appropriation of tribal minerals and timber, and any other unbecoming actions perpetrated by the Anglo-American nation against Indian communities.

In 1947 a comprehensive study of the national government for ways to remove waste, duplication, and inefficiency, and to reduce public expenditures strongly recommended ending the federal government's relationship with the Indian tribes. Former President Herbert Hoover headed the special study commission which examined all phases of the national government. Its report anticipated Termination in its recommendation that

pending discontinuance of all specialized Indian activity on the part of the federal government, the Bureau of Indian Affairs be transferred ... to a new department for social security, education, and Indian affairs. ... When the trust status of Indian lands has ended, thus permitting their taxation, and surplus Indian families have established themselves off the reservations, special aid to the state and local governments for Indian programs should end. The Indians will have been integrated, economically and politically, as well as culturally. [The commission recommended] that essential federal services to Indians be turned over to the states as the federal government closes out its responsibilities to the Indian people.[1]

Supported by the Hoover Commission report recommendations on Termination, congressional leaders in 1947 requested that the Bureau of Indian Affairs list those tribes best prepared to dispense with federal services. They planned to use the selected tribes as the pilot group for Termination. Shortly, Commissioner of Indian Affairs Dillon S. Myer established a special staff to prepare all tribes for Termination.

Indian Reactions

By the mid-1940s Indian leaders realized that the nation was not interested in Indian welfare, that bureaucratic inertia and hostility to the Indian Reorganization Act were weakening its potential benefits, and that tribal treaty rights were in jeopardy. In an attempt to safeguard Native American interests, tribal leaders and prominent Indian professional men and women met at Denver in 1944 and formed the National Congress of American Indians. The organization was committed to informing the public of the continuing prob-

549

lems of Indians, to protecting Native American treaty rights and guarding tribal land and resources, preserving Indian culture, and retaining the advances made under the Indian Reorganization Act and pressing for the act's fulfillment. The National Congress of American Indians became a strong lobby force working with the Indian Rights Association to protect Native American interests before Congress. For years it directed most of its attention to defeating the Termination policy.

Termination

Unprecedented industrial and urban expansion after 1945 placed great pressure on the nation to provide natural resources and space to match the demands of its drastically increasing population and industrial establishment. Surviving Indian reservations held promise of partial solutions, for they were rich in minerals, energy, timber, and water, and development space for the nation's sprawling cities. Coexisting with postwar resource and space needs was a growing public resentment toward Indians derived from what the obscurantists claimed was "coddling" of Native Americans under the Indian Reorganization Act. Thus there arose a demand in the Congress to "liberate" Indians from control by the Bureau of Indian Affairs, break up the remaining reservations, abolish tribal governments, only recently restored by the Indian Reorganization Act, and terminate all federal responsibility for Indian welfare.

Several persons were involved in working out details of the policy of Termination. Commissioner Myer was a principal. As director of the War Relocation Authority during World War II Myer had managed over 100,000 Japanese-Americans held in prison camps across the nation. Myer characterized reservations as prison camps; he favored "liberating" the Native Americans from reservations by terminating federal health services, education, and other benefits provided by the Indian Reorganization Act. He believed that providing Indians with these services and protecting their property from "white predators" were "discriminate over-privileges."[2]

Termination advocates in Congress were led by Arthur Watkins, senator from Utah and chairman of the Senate Interior Subcommittee on Indian Affairs, and E. Y. Berry, congressman from South Dakota and member of the House Indian Affairs Committee. Watkins was determined to move Indians into the "mainstream," freeing the federal government of its responsibility to them.

Using the Hoover Commission report and other studies of the Indian tribes as foundations for action, Congress began putting together the Termination program in 1952. House Resolution 698 directed the staff of the Bureau of Indian Affairs to report on the ability of Indians to manage their affairs, to determine, as recommended by the Hoover Commission report, those functions for Indians that could be transferred either to another federal agency or to the states.

Myer reported that federal relations with Indians in California, Michigan,

Kansas, and New York could be discontinued at once, and that for several years federal agents had been preparing Indians in Oregon, Washington, Wisconsin, Utah, Idaho, Colorado, and Louisiana for termination. Thereupon the House Committee on Indian Affairs urged that legislation be adopted concluding the trust status of Indian allottees, and that all Indians be required to take up all duties, obligations, and privileges of free citizens. Thus in 1953 Congress adopted House Concurrent Resolution 108 which stated that tribes in California, Florida, New York, and Texas, as well as the Flatheads in Montana, Klamaths in Oregon, Menominees in Wisconsin, Potawatomis in Kansas and Nebraska, and those Chippewas on the Turtle Mountain Reservation in North Dakota, should be terminated from their federal relationship. The resolution further stated that once appropriate legislation had been adopted, members of these tribes were expected to assume the rights and privileges of American citizenship and all Bureau of Indian Affairs services for them were to cease.

Congress subsequently adopted a series of laws implementing the policy of Termination. One law transferred Indian medical and health services from the Bureau of Indian Affairs to the United States Public Health Service. Another authorized officials in the states of California, Minnesota, Nebraska, Oregon, and Wisconsin to exercise general civil and criminal jurisdiction over Indians on reservations within their state boundaries. State jurisdiction over Indians had been increasing since passage of the Assimilative Crimes Act of 1948. Michigan, North Carolina, and Florida had assumed civil and criminal jurisdiction over local reservation Indians without federal authorization, and certain counties in Washington, Nevada, and Idaho had applied local law to Native Americans.

In 1954 Termination applied to specific tribes began when the Alabama and Coushatta tribes of Texas (the state of Texas took over their reservation in trust), the California rancheria and reservation tribes, the Klamath tribe and scattered bands of Indians in Oregon, the Menominee tribe of Wisconsin, the Ottawa, Wyandot, and Peoria tribes of Oklahoma, and Paiute tribe and the Uintah and Ouray Ute mixed bloods in Utah were severed from the federal relationship. Legislation in 1959 terminated the Catawba Indians of South Carolina, and, in 1962, the Ponca tribe of Nebraska. Thus between 1954 and 1962 Congress stripped 61 tribes, groups, bands, and communities and rancherías of federal services and protection.

The Seminoles of Florida were marked for Termination even though "only one-fifth of the tribe spoke English and most of them were so poor they didn't own a pair of shoes. Somehow the subcommittee felt that if they simply tried a little harder they would come through the experience unscathed."[3]

One phase of the Termination program was relocation, the process by which federal agents transferred Indian families from rural allotments and reservations to urban centers and provided the émigrés with vocational training and assistance in finding housing and employment. For half a century, particularly during World Wars I and II, many Indians by their own initiative and resources had moved to the cities to work in war industries. Through the years Indians educated academically, vocationally, or professionally were also making their way in the cities. The recent phenomenal increase in Indian population put great pressure upon the limited reservation land. As recommended by the Hoover Commission report, relocation as the means to encourage surplus Indian population to move to the cities to establish a new life of urban employment was made a part of the Termination program in 1952 when the Bureau of Indian Affairs established the Voluntary Relocation Program, later called the Employment Assistance Program. It provided Indians vocational training, travel money, moving expenses, and assistance in finding jobs and housing, in addition to one year of medical care and a month's subsistence allowance. In 1957 the Bureau of Indian Affairs' Adult Vocational Training Program improved Indian education by providing exceedingly valuable vocational and academic education to produce marketable skills among relocated Indian workers. Denver, Phoenix, Albuquerque, San Francisco, Dallas, Los Angeles, Oklahoma City, Tulsa, and Chicago have been the principal centers of relocated Indian settlements. By 1960 more than 35,000 Indians had been relocated; about 30 percent returned to the reservations.

Termination, except for relocation, had generally negative effects upon all tribes separated from federal oversight; the policy created almost total chaos and destitution among the Menominees and Klamaths. Both tribes lived on reservations containing valuable timber tracts. The Menominees had prospered for years from their tribally owned commercial forest industry which provided employment for Indian workers and profits for the tribe. The Klamaths lived on a 1 million-acre reservation in Oregon; their timber was valued at $120 million. Federal officials pressured both tribes to approve Termination by warning tribal leaders that funds owed the tribes from federal settlements (the Menominees were to receive $8 million) would be withheld until they voted affirmatively. Neither tribe was permitted to vote on the specific Termination statute affecting it, only to approve Termination in principle. Thus the Menominees had been assured that under Termination their hunting and fishing rights would be preserved, but their Termination statute made no mention of this. Upon conclusion of their federal relationship their former reservation lands were incorporated as a county in Wisconsin, and they became subject to the state's game and fish laws. Almost overnight several millions of dollars in tribal assets "disappeared in the rush to transform the reservation into a self-supporting county of Wisconsin." A factor pushing for approval of Termination in both tribes was the influence of urban Indians, those who had moved from the reservations to the cities but maintained a political and economic interest in tribal affairs on the reservation. Most of them favored Termination which would convert tribal assets to cash for per capita distribution. The Klamath tribe numbered slightly over 2,000 persons; the per capita share at liquidation of tribal assets was to be $50,000 for each man, woman, and child on the tribal roll.[4]

Senator Arthur Watkins. (Wide World Photos Inc.)

Senator Watkins as the leading advocate of Termination searched out every possible way to destroy the Indian-federal relationship. With Congressman Berry he formed a joint subcommittee on Indian affairs to survey tribal readiness. He directed the secretary of the interior to review all treaties and laws to find ways by which the United States could release itself from responsibility to Indians, and he urged him to open tribal lands to the public. Thus by 1957 the secretary had authorized sale of 2,500,000 acres, generally prime tracts containing minerals, timber, oil, coal, and water sites, to private interests. He also removed restrictions on 1,600,000 acres of allotted land which subsequently was sold to non-Indians. Many Indians claimed that they sold their lands because they were unable to obtain loans to purchase livestock, equipment, seed, and other essentials although an $8 million loan fund languished in the federal treasury, reserved for capital loans to Indians, while Senator Watkins so overpowered the Bureau of Indian Affairs staff that they ignored valid Indian applications for capital loans.

During the late 1950s Termination lost its force as a policy for rapidly assimilating Native Americans. First, in 1958 the zealous terminationist Watkins lost his bid for reelection to the United States Senate. Second, Indians, individually and in groups, particularly through the National Congress of

American Indians, launched strong countermoves to defeat Termination. Most Indians opposed Termination and regarded the policy a threat to their lands, their special legal status, and their survival as Indians. The doleful experiences of the Klamaths and Menominees under Termination, briefly affluent and then pauperized, became grim object lessons for those tribes still to be terminated. And third, officials from states which had initially supported Termination were having second thoughts. Very soon Texans were demanding that their state government get out of the "Indian business." Governors and even some congressmen began to criticize Termination as an ill-advised policy, prematurely and precipitously applied without regard to the human cost. Some critics charged that the overriding motivation of Termination advocates was to gain control of Indian land for constituents. They accused its supporters of deliberately, callously denying Indians capital loans from funds appropriated for their benefit and owed them under the law when other farmers and stock raisers as well as business people, even foreign governments, were regularly receiving generous loans from the federal government; the purpose of this denial was said to be to force destitute Indians to sell their allotted lands in order to survive.

Mounting antagonism toward Termination led Secretary of the Interior Fred A. Seaton to rule in 1958 that thereafter no Indian community would be separated from its federal relationship without its consent. Further, he promised that federal Indian policy would concentrate on providing Native Americans with improved health services and education and assistance in economic development. However, in Congress Termination remained a continuing threat throughout the 1960s. Thus, when the Corps of Army Engineers prepared to build Kinzua Dam which would flood a part of the Seneca Reservation in western New York, officials, prompted by the Congress, told Seneca leaders that the federal government would pay damages to the tribe only if the Senecas prepared a Termination plan. And for years Colville Indians in eastern Washington had sought restoration of their lands appropriated by federal action during allotment. They were supported in their plea by Commissioner of Indian Affairs Philleo Nash. Congress agreed to restore the land only if the Colville Indians submitted a plan of Termination. Nash was removed from office because, it was charged, he supported the Indians and opposed Termination imposed by Congress. Studies made during the 1960s to determine the effect of Termination on Indians indicate that it "has led to extreme social disorganization" among the Klamaths, and "fear of Termination has poisoned every aspect of Indian affairs," and accounts in part for the rage of Indian activists in the 1970s.[5]

Curiously, recent response by many of the states to Termination has been to attempt to reverse state jurisdiction and responsibility for Indians. Thus following termination of tribes in California, state officials applied education, welfare, and law-and-order programs to Indians as it did for other state residents. But during the 1960s state officials began to have second thoughts about accepting this added social responsibility. They joined Indian leaders in agitating for restoration of Johnson-O'Malley funds and authority to place Indian children in federal boarding schools. California politicians began to urge that resident Indians have the same federal aid which Native Americans received in other states. In 1953 Nebraska assumed civil and criminal jurisdiction over local Indian reservations. A law adopted by the Nebraska legislature in 1969 attempted to relieve the state of responsibility for law and order on the Omaha and Winnebago reservations, largely because of unanticipated costs in management. The secretary of the interior accepted return to federal control of the Omaha Reservation only.

Thus Termination maintained an ambivalent course throughout the 1960s. Tribal leaders denounced it, study groups pointed to it as the major cause of Indian malaise, and some politicians argued against it, but Termination maintained a covert administrative life until 1970. Its greatest contribution to Indian welfare was that it eventually produced such an intensively negative public reaction that it brought about policy changes which promised fulfillment of Indian Reorganization Act goals of ethnic restoration.

NATIVE AMERICANS IN THE NEW ORDER

Antagonism to Termination eventually attracted public attention and, during the 1960s, generated a serious search by national leaders for alternative ways to improve Indian status and welfare. This decade was also a time of increasing Indian insurgency, first serious activism, then militancy. Urban Indians were principally responsible for precipitating ethnic consciousness and articulating demands for social and economic improvement. For the first half of the twentieth century most Indians lived on allotments, in rural settlements, and on reservations, and as a group were isolated from the nation's centers of activity. Urbanization changed this. The trickle of city-bound Indians, increased by relocation, appreciably swelled after World War II, adding substantially to the urban Indian population. Thus, by the close of the decade of the 1960s, when the Indian population numbered about 1 million, one third lived in cities, concentrating in Seattle, San Francisco, Los Angeles, Chicago, Phoenix, Denver, Minneapolis, and Albuquerque. Many were educated, keenly aware and embittered at the exploitation and deprivation their people had endured for centuries at the hands of a succession of imperial nations. Rather than permitting non-Indians to act on their behalf, urban Indians sought an independent course. And their activist efforts inevitably took on an increasingly strident tone.

At the same time, reservation Indians also became sensitized to action for ethnic betterment, but their activism was more measured and restrained. Urban and reservation Indians occasionally joined forces in a serious push for improvement in education and health, for justice and equal protection, and for economic development to reduce endemic poverty through better employment opportunities, land restoration, and Indian management of tribal resources. All ethnic strivings for improvement were based on the theme of self-determination. Paradoxically, the tempo of Indian stridency increased in proportion to growing government response to Indian demands for economic and social justice, culminating in militant outbreaks of the early 1970s.

The Native American Condition

As politicians began to heed Native Americans and their problems, the decade of the 1960s, like the 1920s, became a time of investigation and study of conditions among Indians by commissions, task forces, congressional committees, and individual specialists. Their findings yielded data which embarrassed the nation, led President Lyndon Johnson to call Indians "forgotten Americans," and eventually produced corrective action by the Congress.

Soon after his inauguration, President John F. Kennedy pledged to Indians that self-determination, protection of tribal lands, remedial justice, and respect for ethnic heritage would be paramount concerns of his administration. And in 1961 Secretary of the Interior Stewart Udall appointed a task force on Indian affairs, chaired by W. W. Keeler, principal chief of the Cherokee nation. Like the Meriam Commission 35 years earlier, this investigatory group visited Indian settlements, interviewed Indians, and inspected conditions on reservations. The task force report claimed that emphasis by Bureau of Indian Affairs officials on Termination rather than development of tribal resources had "impaired Indian morale and produced a hostile or apathetic response" to federal programs. It added that federal policy should be so framed that it would assist Indians

to advance socially, economically, and politically to the point where special services for this group of Americans are no longer justified. Then Termination can be achieved with maximum benefit for all concerned.... Indians can retain their tribal identities and much of their culture while working toward a greater adjustment and, for the further enrichment of our society, it is in our best interests to encourage them to do so.

Keeler's group recommended that Indians should assume greater control over reservation matters, develop reservation resources, and attract industrial firms to provide employment. The task force concluded that self-determination, "development rather than Termination," and Indian cooperation and participation were essential for future federal policy.[6]

In 1961 two additional studies of Indians were released. One was conducted by the Commission on Rights, Liberties, and Responsibilities of the American Indian, headed by William Brophy and sponsored by the Fund for the Republic. The report was largely a survey of the cumulative effects of Termination upon the Indian tribes, and it pointed to new directions for the federal government in developing a more constructive Indian policy which stressed self-determination. The second study, by the United States Commission on Civil Rights, was concerned with the status of Indians regarding discrimination in employment of Indians, lack of equality before the law, and other

Taos Pueblo, 1979. (Elizabeth Hamlin/Stock, Boston)

manifestations of prejudice and differential treatment of Indians attempting to make it in the "mainstream."[7]

A comprehensive study of Indian education, the Coleman Report, was released in 1966. It surveyed education as dominated by the Bureau of Indian Affairs which had attempted to transform Indians into the image of Anglo-Americans but had failed, in the process creating many dysfunctional, marginal persons. In addition, it exposed the trials of Indians in public schools and the corrupt diversion by school administrators of Johnson-O'Malley funds earmarked for their benefit. The report concluded that "American Indians experience more stigma and self-hatred than any other ethnic group." Also in 1966 a White House Task Force on Indian Health surveyed medical and sanitation conditions on reservations. Its findings on health care for Indians were so horrendous that the results were never released to the public.[8]

And in 1969 at presidential request, Alvin Josephy, Jr., author, editor, and authority on Indian history, made an extensive study of federal Indian policy. Josephy recommended action at the highest level to allay fears among the Indians of Termination. In addition, he urged that functions of the Bureau of Indian Affairs be transferred to the office of the President for more prompt and direct attention to Indian matters.

Congressional investigations during the 1960s included work by a Senate special subcommittee on Indian education. Chaired initially by Robert Kennedy, later by his brother Edward, this tribunal held hearings on western reservations, in urban Indian settlements, and in Washington on the question of the quality of Indian education. After two years of hearings, staff studies, and field investigations, the subcommittee released a seven-volume report. It concluded that the Bureau of Indian Affairs–managed educational system was "hopelessly inadequate" and "unable to lift Indians from a self-perpetuating poverty cycle." Senator Edward Kennedy noted, "The root of the trouble appears to be that the white man, in his benevolence, has sought to make Indian children over in his own image." Federal efforts to educate Indians "have been marked by near total failure, haunted by prejudice and ignorance." A major step in the direction of a solution, in the view of the Senate subcommittee, would be applying self-determination to education— permit school boards composed of Indians to formulate curriculum and school policy.[9]

This rash of investigations of condition among the Indians led Wendell Chino, governor of the Mescalero Apaches, to complain, "We Indians have been studied to death by task forces." However, because the findings of these studies were released and published, they were useful in stirring wide interest in the Indian plight. The surveys revealed that unwholesome conditions among Native Americans, exposed by the Meriam Commission, continued— neglect of Indian students in public schools and diversion of funds meant for Indian benefit to other purposes, resumption of Americanization in the schools, persistence of Bureau of Indian Affairs marginal schools, and an Indian student dropout rate of 50 percent. An estimated 10,000 Indians had received vocational training that bore little relevance to the job market. The studies revealed that both on reservations and in the cities poverty was the common condition among Indians. During the 1960s, unemployment among Indians averaged 40 percent, and among the Oglala Sioux at Pine Ridge Reservation the rate was 75 percent for much of each year and 95 percent in winter. Surveys made during the 1960s revealed that in 1968 more than half of all white families had incomes of $5,893 and non-whites netted $3,161. Indian families received about $1,500. Housing for Indians was rated substandard both on reservations and in cities; 63,000 reservation families lived in dilapidated dwellings without plumbing; in cities most Indians lived in crowded ghettoes. On 22 percent of the reservations scientists found that water was contaminated and 70 percent of the water for household use on all reservations had to be hauled one mile or more. Poverty, crowded households, and unsanitary conditions bred shockingly high rates of disease among Native Americans. Their frequency of infection from hepatitis was 8 times greater than among other population groups. They were 3 times as likely to die of pneumonia and influenza as non-Indians, and Indian infant mortality, tuberculosis, and alcoholism rates were the highest in the nation. These lugubrious conditions gave Native Americans a life expectancy of only 44 years compared to nearly 70 years for the white component of the nation's population. Incidence of suicide for Indians was found to be 6 times greater than for any other population group in American society. These grim revelations from the studies of the 1960s smote the national conscience and stirred politicians to adopt corrective programs which will be discussed subsequently. They also fed an escalating ethnic consciousness and generated Native American activism as Indians sought themselves to accomplish improvements of their condition.[10]

Native American Activism

Lack of progress in policy reform, deceit of federal officials, and tremendous pressure for Termination had destroyed the traditional patience among Indians. And the increasing number of urban Indians, their rising ethnic consciousness, their crushed expectations at improving their condition, and their frequent witness to black and Mexican-American activism helped precipitate their own insurgency. Urban Indians in the ghettos became increasingly alienated and hostile, feeling much like "immigrants in their own country." While the Bureau of Indian Affairs provided at least minimal services for Indians on reservations, it had virtually no program of assistance for urban Indians other than getting them relocated. The Department of Labor maintained job centers for Indians and the Department of Health, Education, and Welfare provided limited health services but, for the most part during much of the 1960s, urban Indians remained an abandoned, neglected, suffering minority in the nation's swelling cities, responsive recruits for an emerging cadre of Indian activist leaders.

Indian activism began at the University of Chicago in 1961 when Sol Tax, an anthropologist, convened the American Indian Chicago Conference which resolved itself into the American Indian Charter Convention. Nearly 500 Indians representing 67 tribes attended this conference. The stated purpose of the meeting was "to review past policies and to formulate new ones." Among other actions the group adopted the Declaration of Indian Purpose which articulated Indian goals and expectations with strong emphasis upon self-determination and urged "Indian involvement in the decision-making process for all programs that would affect them."[11]

The Chicago conference was also seminal for the cause of Indian activism. Older tribal politicians, most of them active in the National Congress of American Indians, had dominated the Indian response to public policy from the close of World War II through the 1950s; they controlled the Chicago conference. Many young Indian delegates felt excluded and, instead of following custom and silently deferring to age, they attempted to assert themselves. Thwarted by the professional tribal politicians, they began to form a separate organization to accomplish their goals of improvement of Indian life. From Chicago the young activists proceeded to Gallup, New Mexico, where, during the late summer, they completed formation of the National Indian Youth Conference, committed to the mobilization of "Red Power," to articulate the discontent of urban Indians, to defend Indian rights, and to establish a pattern of moderate radicalism to draw public attention to the Native American condition and support for reform. Many NIYC leaders were well educated, confident, proud of their Indianness and "ethnic uniqueness," and sensitized to the plight of Indians; they included Clyde Warrior, a Ponca from Oklahoma, and Melvin Thom, a Paiute from Nevada. NIYC founders denounced and ridiculed those Indians who submitted to establishment policy and protocol, calling them Uncle Tomahawk, Apple Indian, Middle-Class Indian, and Indian Bureau Indian, adopted the slogan "For a Greater Indian America," and published a newspaper called *ABC: Americans Before Columbus*.

The National Indian Youth Conference action program, borrowing from the civil rights movement, sponsored demonstrations to protest deprivation of Indian rights. Its members participated in the American Indian Capital Conference on Poverty in 1963 to agitate for inclusion of Indians in the Economic Opportunity Act. And the following year the NIYC supported the Pacific Northwest tribes by staging "fish-ins" to protest state action against local tribes. Many of the Pacific Northwest tribes had lived for centuries by fishing. Their fishing rights were set forth in treaties with the United States, confirmed by federal court decisions and by a law of Congress in 1954 specifically exempting these Indian communities from state jurisdiction as to exercise of fishing rights. However, state courts, particularly in Washington, countered these exemptions. State game rangers harassed Indian fishermen, seized their boats and equipment, and arrested them for violating state laws. NIYC-sponsored "fish-ins" mustered over 100 Indians from a score of tribes to protest this state suppression of Indian rights.

Other Indian activist groups of the 1960s included the Indian Land Rights Association, formed to seek restoration of sequestered tribal lands, and the American Indian Civil Rights Council, created by Sioux leaders for the benefit of all Indians. Alaskan native peoples, caught up in the decade's rising ethnic consciousness and confronted by serious threats to their tribal lands and resources by expanding timber, mineral, and petroleum interests, also united in protective associations. The Alaskan Native Brotherhood and Alaskan Native Sisterhood, founded in 1912, had stressed Native American acculturation and rights, but of necessity had become increasingly protectionist of the aboriginal interest. Then in 1966 native peoples in the nation's northernmost state formed the Alaskan Federation of Natives to strengthen their position in the contest for control of Alaskan lands and resources. Throughout the 1960s, the National Congress of American Indians remained the principal organization for advancing general Indian interests. As it became increasingly involved in urban Indian problems, tribal leaders on reservations formed the National Tribal Chairman's Association to protect their position and interest. All these groups were a significant force in the formulation of new policy, programs, and general improvement of the Indian condition, a hallmark of the 1960s.

Urban eskimo youths in Fairbanks, Alaska. (Ellis Herwig/Stock, Boston)

Corrective Programs for Native Americans

Presidents John F. Kennedy, Lyndon B. Johnson, and Richard M. Nixon provided crucial leadership for the Congress to adopt social reform laws which mitigated poverty and afforded opportunity for improvement of the lives of poor whites in Appalachia, blacks in ghettos, Mexican-Americans in barrios and, finally, Indians on reservations and in cities. Authoritative surveys by all measures of economic status ranked Indians the lowest, as a group enduring the most social deprivation. All three chief executives stressed self-determination and development of individual skills and reservation resources as ultimate goals of new Indian policy. Kennedy urged "lifting Indian living standards." Both Johnson and Nixon presented special messages on Indian affairs to Congress in their appeals for support of Indian programs. Johnson's speech in 1969 stressed "partnership, not paternalism" to serve as the guideline for federal relations with the tribes; he placed emphasis on Indian self-help, and "respect for Indian culture." President Nixon in his special message on Indian affairs to Congress in 1970 rejected "forced Termination" as harmful and committed the United States government "to strengthen the Indian's sense of autonomy without threatening his sense of community."[12]

One of the first relief measures of the decade for improving the Indians' standard of living came in the Public Housing Act of 1961, which assisted Indians in improving their homes. Federal funds, advanced in the form of loans, enabled Indians through "mutual self-help"—donating land and labor for construction—to obtain new dwellings. First construction of Indian homes under this program began on the San Carlos Apache Reservation and by 1963, 31 tribes were participating.

Also during 1961 Indian tribes became eligible for employment assistance under the Area Redevelopment Act. The Economic Development Administration was authorized to make grants to communities in areas of chronic economic distress and unemployment, including Indian reservations. Tribes could apply for grants to construct public buildings including community halls, tribal headquarters, and structures to attract industry to reservations. Tribes were permitted to contribute land and services in lieu of cash as matching funds.

Scattered federal efforts to cope with poverty came to focus on a series of national conferences. One, the Capital Conference on Indian Poverty held in Washington in 1964, was sponsored by the Council on Indian Affairs, a coalition of Indian-support groups including the Indian Rights Association and several religious bodies. Indian delegates reported on the extent of poverty in each tribe. Warrior and Thom for the NIYC and LaDonna Harris, Comanche leader, urged federal officials to include Indians in the antipoverty programs then under consideration in Congress. Their efforts were successful. The Economic Opportunity Act, adopted in 1964, created the Office of Economic Opportunity (OEO) to administer comprehensive antipoverty programs. The act permitted Indian communities to be sponsoring agencies, to develop community programs on reservations, and to employ Indians in these programs.

As sponsoring agencies the tribal governments could receive federal funds for Head Start (early childhood education to develop language and social skills), Upward Bound (to encourage students to complete secondary education and continue into college), Vista (volunteers serving Indian communities to work on projects developed by tribal leaders), and Indian Community Action programs (to bring technical services and financial assistance to the reservations to initiate worthwhile projects employing Indians). Tribes were encouraged to formulate plans for local improvements and then contract with the federal government to operate the projects on an advance of federal funds. The Economic Opportunity Act transferred decision making to the community. As under the Indian Reorganization Act, Indian tribes were recognized as local governments eligible to receive OEO funds.

Programs providing additional assistance to Indians included the State and Local Fiscal Assistance Act (1972) establishing revenue sharing between the federal and state and local governments. The act included those Indian tribes having a recognized governing body performing substantial governmental functions. In 1974 Congress enacted the Indian Financing Act. It consolidated several loan funds and increased the principal amount available for approved Indian business projects. In 1974 the Housing and Community Development Act set aside $15 million each year for two years for construction of Indian housing. And the Indian Self-Determination Act in 1975 permitted Indian tribes to participate in all social welfare programs and services conducted by the federal government. Tribal leaders were allowed to establish priorities and goals in projects for Indian employment and for social services free of federal domination. By this statute the tribal governing body became the sole authority for the tribe in regard to Indian self-determination matters. It set forth the procedures for contracting for Bureau of Indian Affairs programs and services including education. Thus tribes could formulate plans to restructure Bureau of Indian Affairs programs and influence the way programs function. And the statute contained a denial of Termination: "Congress declares its commitment to the maintenance of the federal government's unique relationship with and responsibility to the Indian people."

Congress also gave considerable attention to Indian education, regarding it as the ultimate means of accomplishing permanent Native American improvement. The Manpower Development and Training Act (1962) provided vocational facilities and programs for preparing Indians for the labor market in semiskilled and skilled assignments. The Economic Opportunity Act extended educational opportunity for Indian students from kindergarten to college. Then in 1972 Congress passed the Indian Education Act which established innovative and compensatory educational programs for Indian students. The Indian Self-Determination Act contained an education section providing assistance to Indian students and schools and required increased Indian management of their schools. Indian school boards had managed educational instruction among the Navajos, Pimas, and Sac and Fox of Iowa during the 1960s. This practice increased after adoption of the Indian Self-Determination Act. Federal law required teachers of Indian students to be trained to instruct students in their native languages as well as in English. By 1970, 70 percent of the Indian student body attended public schools; Congress provided "impact aid" as a subsidy to public schools with Indian student enrollment but required that these funds be used for the benefit of Indian children. The number of scholarships for Indian students in higher education also increased substantially.

Private support for Indian education and social welfare also increased during the 1960s and 1970s and comprises an important resource for developing Indian leaders and professionals (law, medicine, teaching, engineering). Since 1970 the Ford Foundation has allocated over $17 million for Indian education, technical assistance, and support of Indian art. The grants have underwritten scholarship support of Indian students, bilingual education, remedial reading programs, mobile libraries for reservation readers, technical assistance to Alaskan natives, livestock improvement, and training of Indian lawyers. Ford Foundation funds also have provided engineering assistance for water resource projects in the Southwest, training of Indians in journalism and publishing, and theater, painting and dance, and production of a documentary film on Indian rights.

To protect these hard-won advances in Indian welfare and to guard against political backlash, President Johnson in 1969 created the National Council on Indian Opportunity in the office of the Vice-President, composed of 7 cabinet members, 8 Indian representatives, and a professional staff. President Nixon retained the NCIO and increased its powers of Indian program oversight. In 1971, NCIO, the Office of Economic Opportunity, and departments of Health, Education, and Welfare and Housing and Urban Development joined with the Department of Labor to create a Model Urban Indian Center Program to provide essential services to Indians living in cities including employment counseling and placement, housing, vocational training, and support for Indian cultural and heritage programs. To assure continuing fair treatment and fulfillment of federal commitments to Indians, the President created in 1975 the American Indian Policy Review Commission to analyze the Indians' "unique relation" with the federal government.

These corrective programs for Indians have produced considerable economic improvement. The Economic Development Administration of the Commerce Department and the Office of Economic Opportunity have provided capital funds for several Indian-operated enterprises. The Laguna Pueblo Indians are quarrying rock on their land and selling it to construction companies. Navajos operate sawmills and transistor, camera, and instrument factories on their reservation. White Mountain Apaches in Arizona and Mescalero Apaches in New Mexico maintain recreation and ski resorts on their reservations. By 1970 non-Indian industrialists had established over 100 plants on Indian reservations providing employment for over 10,000 Indians, including an electronics plant on the Florida Seminole reservation, a furniture factory for the North Carolina Cherokees, electronic components and food processing plants for New Mexico Indians, diamond processing and a yarn mill for the Arizona tribes, a plywood factory for Idaho Indians, a bearing factory in North Dakota, and precision gears manufacturing plant for Wisconsin Indians. In 1970 the Indian family median income had increased to nearly $6,000, a fivefold increase in a decade. However, this remarkable advance in relieving Indian poverty and improving tribal health and education was not matched in the realm of Indian civil rights.

Quest for Justice

During the 1960s the civil rights status of all ethnic groups in the American community, including Indians, was in the public spotlight. In 1961 the United States Commission on Civil Rights scrutinized Indians as United States citizens to determine how they fared in voting, education, employment, housing, and justice. The commission report stated,

If American Indians are a minority, they are a minority with a difference. [They faced problems] common to all minorities—jobs, homes, and public places are not as accessible to them as to others. Poverty and deprivation are common. Social acceptance is not the rule. In addition, Indians seem to suffer more than occasional mistreatment by the instruments of law and order on and off the reservations. . . . Indians differ from other minority groups in three principal ways: (1) They have a strong tendency to preserve their separate cultures and identities. . . . While this drive by itself is not unique—other minority groups live in separate quarters and not always unwillingly—it has elements of form and substance peculiar to Indians alone; (2) They are a quasi-sovereign people, enjoying treaty rights with the Federal Government, land set aside for their exclusive use, and Federal laws applicable only to them; (3) And Indians bear a quasi-dependent relationship to the Federal Government. [The] Indian has a three-faceted legal personality: (1) He is a tribal member with cultural, social, economic, religious, and political ties to tribal life; (2) A "ward" of the Federal Government; (3) A citizen with most of the same rights and privileges possessed by other citizens. And when an Indian severs tribal ties and asserts his rights as a citizen, and tries to make his way in the white man's world, frequently he discovers that in addition to the three facets of his legal personality . . . he is socially a member of a racial minority. [His attempt at assimilation] may meet resistance almost as determined as that faced by the Negro.[13]

Commission investigators found Indian complaints of unequal treatment in the administration of justice valid. Law and order were not adequately maintained on reservations and in states in which jurisdiction has been ceded. In addition, they found outright ill-treatment of Indians by police and courts in towns near large reservations. Indian neighborhoods sometimes were denied adequate police and fire protection by local authorities. Also the commission report disclosed a differential in justice in many states. Thus in Arizona the Indian complaint was of a "pattern of severe sentences for all including traffic violators." Indians in South Dakota claimed that they were treated unfairly by the courts, pointing to a 34 percent inmate population at the state penitentiary while Indians comprised only 5 percent of the state's population.[14]

The commission found reservation housing generally bad. And urban Indians faced the same kinds of discrimination which confronted other minorities. Indian opportunities for employment seemed to be as restricted as they were for blacks. Some state agencies were reluctant to hire qualified Indians. The commission found that Indians generally were free to register and to vote although they concluded that a high illiteracy rate among older Indians and their preoccupation with tribal affairs kept Indian registration well below the national average.

Mild improvement in Indian status occurred after the Civil Rights Commission released its report; on several occasions state courts supported their civil rights. In 1964 the California Supreme Court overruled lower court convictions of several Native American Church members on charges of vio-

A reservation Indian family. (Karen Rosenthal/Stock, Boston)

lating state narcotic laws. The high court declared that the constitutional freedom of religion applied to Indians observing aboriginal rituals, including sacramental use of peyote.

Indians also made some progress in voting rights. Although citizens since 1924, many had been restricted by state law in their attempts to vote. The Arizona Supreme Court in 1948 annulled that state's restriction on Indian voting, Maine lifted its ban on Indian voting in 1954, and New Mexico took similar action in 1962. Thus, in the Southwest particularly, Indians became a potential political force; Navajo nation voters hold the balance of electoral power in New Mexico, Arizona, and Utah. In 1970 the federal government changed the system for selecting leaders of the governments of the Five Civilized Tribes. Since 1906 these tribal chief executives had been appointed by the President. After 1970 tribal citizens were permitted to elect their principal chiefs, or governors as they are called by the Chickasaws and Seminoles.

In 1968 Congress passed the Indian Civil Rights Act which provides Native Americans free exercise of religion, speech, press, right of assembly and petition, protection against taking property without just compensation, and other constitutional guarantees. In addition, it requires tribal consent before a state can assume civil and criminal jurisdiction over Indian reservations within its borders.

In spite of recent corrective federal legislation, Indians in the 1970s were suffering remnants of the same discrimination and social suppression revealed by the Civil Rights Commission investigation in 1961, demonstrating the ability of the local white majority to evade or ignore the will of national law. Reported instances of persistent bias include an insulting sign found in a South Dakota general store near the Pine Ridge Reservation: "No Dogs or Indians Allowed." And recent studies show that the arrest rate for Indians in towns near reservations averaged 30 times the rate for whites and 6 times that for blacks. Indian spokesmen claim that Native Americans are frequently harassed by police and that they are subject to selective law enforcement and preventive detention (arrest before an offense is committed). Indians are picked up on the common charges of vagrancy, drunkenness, or loitering and jailed without counsel.

There is also evidence that Indians still suffer at the hands of vigilante outbreaks. James Hatmaker, a twenty-four-year-old Cherokee, was severely beaten by Ku Klux Klansmen at Homestead, Florida, in 1971. Hatmaker claimed that law-enforcement officers were present at the Klan rally and that they refused to intercede. The following year in Gordon, Nebraska, vigilantes beat Raymond Yellow Thunder to death. Local authorities ruled his death was caused by suicide. Over 1,000 Sioux from the Pine Ridge Reservation protested what they called "callous and indifferent" handling of Yellow Thunder's death. Their demonstrations attracted national attention and forced an autopsy and change of verdict of cause of death to manslaughter, and arrest and conviction in Nebraska courts of 2 of Yellow Thunder's killers. After studying the proceedings Nebraska Governor J. J. Exon declared that there was "no doubt that some Indians . . . are very badly treated in this state."[15]

And a survey of conditions among Indians in 6 western Oklahoma counties by the Oklahoma Human Rights Commission in 1977 revealed that area law-enforcement officers arrested and jailed Indians under conditions and circumstances where whites were not bothered, especially for public drunkenness. More force was commonly used in arresting Indians than whites, and racial bias against Indians was frequently voiced by law officers. The survey charged that the public educational system functioned in ways which had the effect of driving Indian youth out of the system because it attempted to force Indians into a mold that was incompatible with their culture. School administrators were unresponsive to the concerns of Indian parents and denied them any meaningful input into decision making. School curricula did not contain balanced accounts of the role and history of the Plains Indians in the state and that region, and Indians were ignored in planning and implementing programs by federally funded agencies. Employers, public and private, did not hire Indians on the same basis as they did whites. And legal assistance was seldom available and often inadequate when it was available.

These sketches show that the application of corrective programs and civil rights guarantees for Indians have been uneven; in some Indian communities they have hardly been applied at all. This lag between the law's intent and the opportunities the measures open up to Indians and the denial of these opportunities explain in part the shift of Indian response from mild radicalism and activism in the 1960s to virulent militancy during the early 1970s.

Native American Militancy

Henry Fritz has cogently observed that "because of the egocentric nature of men, political democracy has seldom been humanitarian in its motivation. [It] has always best served the interests of powerful groups, and has neglected weak minorities. This perhaps was the most important reason why a policy intent upon the acculturation [of Indians in the 1890s] had not reduced significantly the number of those living apart from Anglo-American society at the middle of the twentieth century." By the 1960s many Indians demonstrated an awareness of the accuracy of his assessment, and they were developing the position that their hope for social improvement was not in surrogate action by reformers but from direct political action, even radicalism, by themselves. To offset their limited numbers as a minority in the Anglo-American mass, increasingly they applied the strategies of organization, demonstration, and occasional violence.[16]

As the Indian urban population grew, its discontent mounted, and Native American action became increasingly aggressive. Urban Indians particularly were restive over failure of officials to fulfill the promises of corrective federal programs. Moreover, while they had made some progress in their rise from abject poverty, the rate of improvement did not satisfy them. And although many social welfare benefits for Indians were to be provided by the Departments of Health, Education, and Welfare, and Housing and Urban Development and the Department of Labor, the Bureau of Indian Affairs continued to maintain substantial direction over Indian programs. Officials in that agency still defined Indian policies and programs and applied them to the tribes, and "still behaved bureaucratically as if they, and they alone, knew what was best for Indians." Thus the Bureau of Indian Affairs became the focus of activist rage as Indians sought to end what they called "colonial rule" by the federal government. Those officials in charge of bureau programs, the secretary of the interior and the commissioner of Indian affairs, were often controversial personalities which added to the Indians' disenchantment. Walter Hickel, President Nixon's Secretary of the Interior, particularly was a *persona non grata* because of his claim that the federal government "overprotected" Indians, and their belief that he was uncommitted to carrying out the corrective legislation reforms Congress had directed.[17]

Indian activism of the 1960s which grew into militancy during the 1970s was fed by several newspapers, magazines, and journals devoted to subjects of Indian interest. Also certain best-selling, polemical books popularized the Indian cause, particularly Dee Brown's *Bury My Heart at Wounded Knee* and *Custer Died for Your Sins* by Vine Deloria, Jr.

Additional organizations, formed by off-reservation and urban Indians, including American Indians United, the Indian Task Force, United Native Americans, Coalition of American Indian Citizens, Native American Students, the Iroquois League, and American Indian Movement, joined the National Congress of American Indians and the National Indian Youth Conference to press the Native American cause. The American Indian Movement became the most militant of these organizations. Founded in 1968 in Minneapolis by two Chippewas—Dennis Banks and George Mitchell, later joined by Clyde Bellecourt, also a Chippewa—AIM's original purpose was to assist Indians moving from upper Midwest reservations to the cities, particularly to protect them from selective law enforcement. All groups supported restoration of those Indian lands illegally taken by the federal government, serious application of the Indian civil rights law and social welfare law, and ouster of Secretary Hickel, accused by activist leaders of being a terminationist.

The period of greatest insurgency, 1969 to 1973, varied in response from political demonstration to radical action including seizure of land and buildings, destruction of property, and even occasional armed resistance to established authority. All across the nation Indian militants occupied public property to protest discrimination and exploitation: the federal building in Littleton, Colorado, camping in a restricted area atop Mount Rushmore, attempted occupation of Ellis Island, assertion of treaty-guaranteed fishing rights on the Puyallup River in Washington, and occupation of several military reservations including Fort Lawton in Puget Sound and the Coast Guard station on Lake Michigan near Milwaukee, acts symbolizing recovery of property and rights taken from their ancestors by Anglo-Americans.

One of the most dramatic actions by Native Americans was their occupation of Alcatraz, a twelve-acre island in San Francisco Bay and site of a federal penitentiary. In 1963 federal officials discontinued its use as a penal institution, and the following year they declared it surplus property. Indians attempted to occupy Alcatraz in 1964, filing claim to the land under federal law, but they were ejected. Activists returned to Alcatraz in November 1969, claiming their right to the island under the Fort Laramie Treaty of 1868, which permitted any male Indian over 18 whose tribe was a party to the treaty to file for a homestead on government land. Indian spokesmen on Alcatraz declared that their action was in protest over the failure of Bureau of Indian Affairs officials to apply laws intended for improvement of conditions among Indians and their inability to "deal practically" with Indian welfare. The Alcatraz occupation drew wide public attention, and resulting support lasted several years. Then in 1971, when federal officials found that public interest in Indian causes had waned, they quietly removed the demonstrators from the island.

Other actions by militants included the Broken Treaties Caravan to Washington in 1972. During a 6-day demonstration insurgents occupied the Bureau of Indian Affairs building and destroyed large quantities of public property and records. The most daring and provocative action by Indian militants occurred in 1973 in South Dakota where armed Indians, led by AIM members, symbolically occupied the village of Wounded Knee, site of the dreadful massacres of Sioux men, women, and children by the Seventh Cavalry in 1890, and defied a long siege by federal and state forces. Their principal purpose was to dramatize maladministration and mistreatment of Indians over the centuries. It has been said that Wounded Knee II in all its seeming irrationalism "celebrated separatism instead of integration, political activism instead of dignified acquiescence, repudiation of white goals and values, and rejection of existing tribal organizations."[18]

After Wounded Knee II, Indian militancy took on additional dimensions. In 1977 activists presented a resolution to the International Human Rights

Indian activists on "The Longest Walk" in Washington, D.C., July 15, 1978 (Arthur Grace/Sygma)

Conference in Geneva, Switzerland, calling upon the United Nations to investigate their charge that the United States had "imposed" on Indians "conditions that suppress or destroy their cultures," and urged that the General Assembly recognize Indian tribes "as nations with territories, governments, and the ability to enter into relations with other states."[19]

While some Indian leaders were striving for international recognition of Indian rights, others were seeking to recover tribal lands, to expand tribal capital reserves, and to apply prudent management to the development of Indian resources. Their efforts, matched with the slowly unfolding corrective federal programs, produced continuing improvement in Indian status and welfare during the 1970s.

Indian Entrepreneurship

In the 1970s many Indian leaders placed increasing emphasis on Indian self-help, developing potential in human and natural resources. Indian human resources were expanded by ever-enlarging numbers of young Native Americans entering colleges and universities to study business administration, engineering, law, teaching, and medicine, certainly for personal enhancement but also to prepare them for leadership and service to their tribal communities. And to derive maximum benefit from the natural resources of the reservations, tribal leaders more and more shifted from traditional surrogate development (leases to Anglo-American business interests, the Indian proprietors receiving in most cases only a small royalty from exploitation of their mineral, energy, timber, grazing, and water resources; most of the development jobs were filled by non-Indians) to tribal management. Tribal leaders continued to permit some outside capital and management to tap reservation resources, but they applied closer scrutiny to operations and required employment of more Indian workers.

However, the tribes provided increased amounts of capital and management to reservation resource exploitation. Twenty-three western tribes formed the Council of Energy Resource Tribes (CERT), headed by Peter McDonald, tribal chairman of the Navajo nation. CERT represented two thirds of the Indian population, the member reservations spread over ten western states from North Dakota to Washington and south to Oklahoma, New Mexico, and Arizona. CERT studies revealed that the reservations contain rich stores of several strategic minerals (about 80 percent of the nation's uranium), petroleum, coal (one third of the nation's low-sulphur, strippable coal; in southern Montana alone on the Crow and northern Cheyenne reservations lie at least 5 percent of this reserve), water, and timber. The organization serves as a cartel to enable member tribes to guard and manage these natural resources and to curb exploitation by outsiders. Their action represents a substantial application of self-determination, using as its model the Organization of Petroleum Exporting Countries (OPEC) to control prices and assure maximum benefits for Indians. CERT is committed to derive as much future benefit as

Navajo worker in Window Rock, Arizona. (Jim McHugh/Sygma)

possible for the tribes, acknowledging a keen awareness that, except for water, timber, and rangeland, these resources are nonrenewable. Therefore, they plan to use earnings as capital to develop projects of permanent benefit to the tribes—job-producing industries, agricultural and stock-raising improvements, and water development for irrigation—all to expand employment opportunities for Indians and to reduce poverty.

Additional capital resources for tribal entrepreneurial ventures include awards by the Indian Claims Commission. Many recipient tribes, after per capita distribution of a portion of the award, reserve the rest of the funds for improving health facilities, housing, and education, creating tribal cultural centers, and establishing businesses which provide income for the tribes and employment for tribal workers. Recent awards by the Indian Claims Commission include $16 million to the Seminoles of Florida, $4,500,000 to the Pawnees of Oklahoma, and nearly $2 million to the Otos and Missouris of Oklahoma. Most of these settlements are compensation for tribal lands taken by Federal officials in "unconscionable negotiations" in the last century.

Many Indians prefer land to money, but until the 1970s federal officials refused to consider this alternative except in isolated cases of restoring small tracts which had been reserved for schools and other tribal purposes. Thus the Havasupai tribe has been awarded trust title to 185,000 acres and permanent use rights to another 95,000 acres in the Grand Canyon. Also, following appeals by Yakima Indians of Washington and Warm Springs Indians of Oregon, who had petitioned for return of lands "wrongfully taken," Congress acted in their favor.

The most celebrated return of Indian land was the return of Blue Lake, a 48,000-acre tract of alpine lake and timberland in northern New Mexico, to Taos Pueblo. Blue Lake was the nature shrine for Taos Indians, home of tribal deities and source of life. In 1906 federal officials persuaded Taos leaders to permit annexation of the Blue Lake tract into Carson National Forest under the guise of protecting the area from white encroachment. The Forest Service proceeded to develop Blue Lake as a recreation area for fishermen, hunters, hikers, and the general public, and virtually excluded Taos Indians from using it as a religious shrine. Predictably the American tourist public desecrated Blue Lake with noise and trash. Through the years Taos leaders pleaded with federal officials to restore Blue Lake, all to no avail. In 1965 the Indian Claims Commission awarded Taos Pueblo a cash settlement for Blue Lake which tribal leaders refused. Congressmen friendly to the cause regularly attempted to win approval of legislation restoring Blue Lake to Taos Pueblo, but New Mexico politicians, led by Senator Clinton Anderson, determined to retain it as a tourist attraction, successfully opposed restoration. However, in 1971, with support from President Nixon, Congress restored Blue Lake to Taos Pueblo.

Another advance for material resources of native peoples came in 1971 when Congress approved the Alaska Native Claims Settlement Act. By its terms, members of the Alaska Federation of Natives were assigned title to 40 million acres in the state and allocated $1 billion, the land and funds to be distributed among corporations formed from the Native American communities. The legislation required that the assets derived from this settlement be "entirely Native controlled."

Resources in the form of access to federal programs are being restored to terminated Indians. Congress in 1973 returned the Menominees to federal trust status, repealing Termination for them. And in 1978 Congress restored four Oklahoma tribes—Modocs, Wyandots, Peorias, and Ottawas—to trust status.

Indians in several eastern seaboard states, never under federal trust status, are attempting to improve their economic position by seeking access to federal programs. Several are also attempting to recover tribal land taken by the states. Thus in 1976 a federal court decision ruled that the Passamaquoddy and Penobscot tribes in Maine are entitled to the same protection and assistance that federal law provides other Indians. Until this decision was handed down, Maine was considered responsible for the 4,000 Indians within its borders. These Indians will receive federal benefits in housing, education, health care, and other services. In addition, both tribes have filed suit in federal court against the state of Maine for return of nearly 10 million acres which they claim was taken illegally. The Wampanoags of Massachusetts are seeking to recover 16,000 acres in the Cape Cod resort area. Their claim was rejected by a federal court in 1978 because, the tribunal ruled, Wampanoags did not comprise a legal tribe when the suit was filed two years previously, and therefore were not entitled to pursue their claim.

Native Americans Today

One of the most striking aspects of Indian life in recent times, besides successful application of self-determination and gradual ascent from poverty, has been a phenomenal increase in population. At the time of discovery around 1500 the Native American population of present-day United States numbered perhaps 1,500,000. Exploitation, epidemics of new, killer diseases, and general malaise from life as subject peoples caused the Indian population to decline to the point where some tribes virtually disappeared. Native Americans numbered only about 250,000 in 1890. By 1960 this figure had more than doubled; in the succeeding decade it increased to nearly 800,000, and by 1978 almost 1 million.

Most of the nation's Indians are concentrated in the trans-Mississippi West. Oklahoma, the old Indian Territory, leads in Indian population with 100,000, followed by Arizona with 96,000; California, 92,000; New Mexico, 73,000; Washington, 34,000; South Dakota, 33,000; and Alaska with 17,000. In 1970 over half the nation's Indians lived in urban areas, the remainder on allotments and on 267 reservations, varying from tiny California rancherías containing only a few acres to the giant 14 million-acre Navajo reservation sprawling over portions of Arizona, New Mexico, and Utah. Although most Indians are concentrated in the trans-Mississippi West, the nineteenth-century Indian removal program did not completely remove them from the eastern United States. There are Cherokees in North Carolina, Seminoles in Florida, Creeks in Alabama, Georgia, and Florida, Choctaws in Mississippi, Houmas in Louisiana, Lumbees in North Carolina, and Rappahannocks, Chickahominys, and Pamunkeys in Virginia. In 1968 the Eastern Cherokees, Choctaws, Creeks, and Seminoles formed the United Southeastern Tribes of American Indians

(USET) to protect tribal interests and to prevent federal welfare and economic and educational programs from being turned over to state and local governments. Other eastern tribal remnants include survivors of the old Iroquois Confederation in northern New York, several Algonkian and Siouian tribes in Wisconsin and Michigan, the Penobscot and Passamaquoddy tribes in Maine, Shinnecocks on Long Island, and Narragansetts in Rhode Island.

Native Americans have interacted with Anglo-Americans for centuries. Their contributions to national culture have been substantial, certainly proportionately greater than their numbers would imply. The effects of the Indian presence in the Anglo-American community, Native American influence on national development, and their cultural legacy are treated in the concluding chapter.

Notes

1. *The Hoover Commission Report on Organization of the Executive Branch of the Government* (New York, 1949), pp. 267, 473.
2. Jack D. Forbes (ed.), *The Indian in America's Past* (Englewood Cliffs, N.J., 1964), p. 120.
3. Jennings C. Wise, *The Red Man in the New World Drama: A Politico-Legal Study with a Pageantry of American Indian History*, edited with an introduction by Vine Deloria, Jr. (New York, 1951), p. 368.
4. Alvin M. Josephy, "Toward Freedom: The American Indian in the Twentieth Century," *Indiana Historical Society Lectures, 1970–1971* (Indianapolis, 1971), pp. 55–56.
5. D'Arcy McNickle, *Native American Tribalism: Indian Survivals and Renewals* (New York, 1973), p. 107–108.
6. Forbes, *The Indian in America's Past*, p. 128.
7. See William A. Brophy and Sophie D. Aberle (comps.), *The Indian: America's Unfinished Business: Report of the Commission on the Rights, Liberties, and Responsibilities of the American Indian* (Norman, Okla., 1966); and *Justice: 1961 United States Commission on Civil Rights Report*, Book 5 (Washington, D.C., 1961), and *Civil Rights: Excerpts from the 1961 United States Commission on Civil Rights Report* (Washington, D.C., 1961).
8. See James S. Coleman et al. *Equality and Educational Opportunity* (Washington, D.C., 1966).
9. Oklahoma City *Times*, February 14, 1968, and *Daily Oklahoman*, February 1, 1970.
10. *Daily Oklahoman*, February 1, 1970.
11. Hazel Hertzberg, *The Search for an American Indian Identity: Modern Pan-Indian Movements* (Syracuse, N.Y., 1971), p. 292.
12. McNickle, *Native American Tribalism*, pp. 124–25.
13. *Justice*, Book 5, pp. 115–16.
14. *Ibid.*, p. 125.
15. Norman, Okla. *Transcript*, January 23, 1973.
16. Henry E. Fritz, *The Movement for Indian Assimilation, 1860–1890* (Philadelphia, 1963), p. 221.
17. Josephy, "Toward Freedom," p. 62.
18. Wilcomb E. Washburn, *The Indian in America* (New York, 1975), p. 250.
19. Norman Okla. *Transcript*, October 25, 1977.

General studies of the American Indian with material on the period since 1945 include Wilcomb E. Washburn, *The Indian in America* (New York, 1975); Edward E. Dale, *The Indians of the Southwest: A Century of Development Under the United States* (Norman, Okla., 1971); Angie Debo, *A History of the Indians of the United States* (Norman, Okla., 1970); Hazel Hertzberg, *The Search for an American Indian Identity: Modern Pan-Indian Movements* (Syracuse, N.Y., 1971); D'Arcy McNickle, *Native American Tribalism: Indian Survivals and Renewals* (New York, 1973; and Alvin M. Josephy, "Toward Freedom: The American Indian in the Twentieth Century," *Indiana Historical Society Lectures, 1970–1971* (Indianapolis, 1971).

Indian-federal relations for the period after 1945 are discussed in Gary Orfield, *A Study of the Termination Policy* (Denver, 1965); Joan Ablon, "American Indian Relocation: Problems of Dependency and Management," *Phylon* 24 (Winter 1965), pp. 362–71; Margaret Szasz, *Education and the American Indian: The Road to Self-Determination, 1928–1973* (Albuquerque, N.M., 1974); and Alan L. Sorkin, *American Indians and Federal Aid* (Washington, D.C., 1973).

Published reports of studies of the Indian tribes made during this period include: *The Hoover Commission Report on Organization of the Executive Branch of the Government* (New York, 1949); William A. Brophy and Sophie D. Aberle (comps.), *The Indian: America's Unfinished Business: Report of the Commission on the Rights, Liberties, and Responsibilities of the American Indian* (Norman, Okla., 1966); *Justice: 1961 United States Commission on Civil Rights Report,* Book 5 Washington, D.C., 1961); *Civil Rights: Excerpts from the 1961 United States Commission on Civil Rights Report* (Washington, D.C., 1961); James S. Coleman et al., *Equality and Educational Opportunity* (Washington, D.C., 1966); *Report of the April 26, 1977, Hearing on Indian Civil Rights Issues in Northwest Oklahoma* (Oklahoma City, 1977); and *Final Report of the American Indian Policy Review Commission,* 2 vols. (Washington, D.C. 1977).

The topic of the Indian and the Constitution is treated in Ralph A. Barney, "Legal Problems Peculiar to Indian Claims Litigation," *Ethnohistory* 2 (Fall 1955), pp. 314–24; Warren H. Cohen and Philip J. Mause, "The Indian: The Forgotten Minority," *Harvard Law Review* 81 (June 1968), pp. 1824–25; Warren Weston, "Freedom of Religion and the American Indian," *Rocky Mountain Social Science Journal* 2 (March 1965), pp. 1–6; and Jerry Muskrat, "The Constitution and the American Indian: Past and Prologue," *Hastings Constitutional Law Quarterly* 3 (Summer 1976), pp. 657–77.

Descriptive and polemical works on Indian activism include Rupert Costo, "Alcatraz," *Indian Historian* 3 (Winter 1970), pp. 4–12; Stan Steiner, *The New Indians* (New York, 1968); Edgar S. Cahn (ed.), *Our Brother's Keeper: The Indian in White America* (Washington, D.C., 1969); Alvin M. Josephy, Jr., *Red Power: The American Indian's Fight for Freedom* (New York, 1971); Dee Brown, *Bury My Heart at Wounded Knee: An Indian History of the American West* (New York, 1971); Sar A. Levitan and Barbara Hetrick, *Big Brother's Indian Programs—With Reservations* (New York, 1971); Vine Deloria, Jr. *Custer Died for Your Sins: An Indian Manifesto* (New York, 1969), and *God Is Red* (New York, 1973), *Of Utmost Good Faith* (San Francisco, 1971), and *We Talk, You Listen: New Tribes, New Turf* (New York, 1970).

CHAPTER 22

THE INDIAN LEGACY

Corn swaying in the rhythm of the wind—
Graceful ballerinas,
Emerging at the edge of the forest.
All dip and dance;
Wind tunnels through the long silken hair.
Golden teeth-seeds.
Trees chatter nervously
Awakening sky in fright,
Pointing at woodman.
A mighty thud! Blow leaves deep scar;
He strikes again. . . .
Corn mourns golden tears,
Bows, praying for fallen brother.
Jay mocks the greedy beast
who has doomed majestic brother,
His life home.
The forest, damp and silent,
Mourning for lost Oak.

"Death in the Woods," by Little Bird (Santo Domingo-Laguna), 1969

♥

The melancholy five-century record of European and Anglo-American relations with Indians confirms that the latter benefited very little from this imperial patronage; they gave much more than they received in the way of positive benefit. Ignoring the immutable law that "acculturation proceeds in both directions," the American nation has historically refused to acknowledge any cultural debt to Indians. Thus, "as Rome hid its debt to the Etruscans," the United States has persistently denied its Indian inheritance.[1]

Only recently has there begun to be a fair assessment of the Indian contribution. Indian know-how and technology enabled Europeans to succeed in the American wilderness. Compassionate Indians rescued starving colonists and taught them methods of subsisting and surviving in the new land. Pioneers coped with the primeval wilderness largely by emulating Indian life-

Chapter Opening: Water color painting, "Osage Straight Dancer," by Carl Woodring, 1957. (Courtesy Museum of the American Indian, Heye Foundation)

style. Many eastern tribes enclosed their towns with log palisade walls, a defensive style copied by colonists. Indians blazed the trails that became the national highways.

Indian hunters revolutionized European economies with the fur trade. Their annual harvest of hides and pelts flowed into the channels of world commerce and drastically altered clothing fashion and design. Perhaps their greatest influence on world commercial affairs has been in providing basic plants for food, fiber, and tobacco production. Indians were keenly skilled in the techniques of domesticating plants and developed over 100 useful species which

Selected Indian Contributions

Cash Crops	Food Crops		Drugs	
Cotton	Corn	Pumpkin	Datura	Bloodroot
Tobacco	Tomato	Melon	Ipecac	Snakeroot
Hemp	Potato	Pepper	Jalap	Peyote
	Squash	Peanut	Cascara	Ilex Cassine
	Bean		Dogwood	

Words	Idiomatic Phrases	Architectural Forms
Hominy	Go on the warpath	Sibley tent
Toboggan	Bury the hatchet	Quonset hut
Moccasin	Run the gauntlet	Wigwam geodesic dome
Succotash		Pueblo module
Tobacco		

Europeans adopted and dispersed around the world. Indian tobacco provided for European planters an immediate cash crop, and native cotton and other fiber plants yielded additional materials for textiles and rope.

The Indian contribution of important food plants was even greater. Their nursery of over 100 plants, particularly corn, gained greater commercial importance and have been used by more of the world's population than from food plants discovered at the other three centers of plant domestication— Near East, Southeast Asia, and North Africa. Indian-developed plants widened the world's subsistence base and provided the means for nations to support drastically increased populations. Indian corn and potatoes rank with rice and wheat as the most important staples. And it is estimated that slightly over half of America's farm products are grown from plants developed by Indians.

The healing arts also were substantially advanced by the Native American contribution. Indians discovered more than 200 useful drug-yielding plants which are listed in the United States *Pharmacopoeia*. Contemporary interest in camping, nature study, and woodcraft are largely responses to the Indian legacy of wilderness living. Military officers trained ranger units in Indian tactics for combat in World War II and applied Alaskan native experience to troop survival training.

Americans have appropriated thousands of Indian words to enrich their language. And the Indian influence on place-names of the United States is immense; many mountains, rivers, counties, cities, and 27 states carry Indian names. New England alone has 5,000 Indian place-names and California 200. Indians also provided a manual sign language which today is used in part for mute communication. Architects have freely drawn upon Indian building design to create fresh models.

The Indian influence on Anglo-American forms of government likewise has been substantial. European explorers and colonists came from a milieu where divine right of kings was in vogue, their nations' governments were becoming increasingly centralized, society was stratified into rigid classes, position and recognition generally were determined by heredity and class position, tyranny flourished and general self-determination was unknown. Explorers and colonists found the Indian nations, except for the Natchez, to be primitive democracies where personal freedom and rights of the individual were paramount. Indian society was generally classless, status and rank were based on ability and performance. Native American governments were models of decentralization, local self-rule, and voluntary confederation.

While most colonists came to scorn Indians and sought to destroy them, they emulated their techniques for coping in the New World wilderness and copied their democratic procedures and models. The most widely used model was the Iroquois Confederation, a limited government based on tradition or common law which could be called an unwritten constitution, a decentralized confederation with male and female suffrage, and provision for initiative, referendum, and recall. Benjamin Franklin acknowledged that the Iroquois Confederation served as the model for the Albany Plan of Union, eventually for the government organized under the Articles of Confederation and the local autonomy and guarantees of states' rights found in the federal system established for the American nation in 1789.

Indian forms of government also influenced European philosophers' doctrine of natural rights. Columbus and other early explorers carried favorable accounts of the Indians and their way of life to Europe. They were struck by the Indians' hospitality, graciousness, personal freedom, and natural way of living.

For centuries there had circulated in Europe the myth of a golden age of natural man. As life became more complex, as Europeans found it more difficult to deal with the social, political, and technological changes occurring about them, many yearned for the simplicity and innocence of the legendary primal era which had been free of "corruptions of civilization."

French essayist Michel de Montaigne, intrigued by explorers' descriptions of American Indian life, began to popularize the view that finally Europeans had found the legendary natural man; he was the Indian and by Montaigne's edification he became the noble savage. European philosophers, increasingly restive under the divine right despotisms and vexed with the growing complexity of their times, liked Montaigne's theories. In England, John Locke posited a state of nature where men lived in natural equality under a system of natural law. In France, Montesquieu, Voltaire, and Rousseau each regarded the Indian nations as democracies, free of the complications of Europe and its despotisms, where human freedom was cherished. These European philosophers found in the Indian a child of nature, the source of individual sovereign authority. Rousseau in *Discourse on Inequality* (1755) praised Indians for their passion for freedom and equality.

Thus the Indian experience in limited government and self-determination provided the foundation for the natural rights doctrine of the age of Enlightenment. Revolutionists claimed that the freedom of the Indian and the doctrine of natural rights was a heritage to which all people were entitled. Indians as noble savages, in a sense, became a source of exploitation, in that revolutionists and philosophers used them and their freedom-steeped institutions to develop the doctrine which would destroy the orthodoxy and despotism of the old order. The Native American contribution to the ideology of revolution for the United States, France, and Spain's New World colonies was profound. Thomas Jefferson in the Declaration of Independence applied the Enlightenment natural rights doctrine, writing that persons "are endowed by their creator with certain inalienable rights" and governments derive "their just powers from the consent of the governed."

Felix Cohen, late international authority on Indian law and polity, has stated that "American democracy, freedom and tolerance are more American than European and have deep aboriginal roots in our land." The Indian example of self-determination and local sovereignty "undoubtedly played a strong role in helping to give the colonists new sets of values that contributed to turning them from Europeans into freedom loving Americans." And it is out of a rich Indian democratic tradition that the distinctive political ideals of American life emerged including the practice of treating leaders "as servants of the people instead of as their masters," and the "insistence that the community must respect the diversity of men and the diversity of their dreams."[2]

Native Americans have contributed to literature both as a popular subject for fiction and nonfiction and as producers of literature. The Indian has captivated the interest of authors from earliest discovery times. Their writings have produced stereotypes of the Indian as a noble savage and as the bloodthirsty spawn of Satan. The vicissitudes of the Indian as a literary figure have varied over the years from praise to scorn. But whether writers have used them as love or hate symbols, Indians have fascinated the literatti, generating thousands of books, hundreds of poems, and scores of plays.

In the Enlightenment tradition, French novelist and dramatist François René Chateaubriand turned the noble savage image to fiction and produced an idealized view of the New World wilderness and the Indian in *Atala* (1801), The use of this theme spread to England then to the United States. Charles Brockden Brown, "father of the American novel," produced the first American novel to contain an Indian theme—*Edgar Huntly* (1801). Thereafter John Heckewelder, Washington Irving, George Catlin, Henry R. Schoolcraft,

Thomas L. McKenney, Lewis Henry Morgan, and Francis Parkman idealized the Indian in nonfiction. Verse on the Indian by poets Philip Freneau, Walt Whitman, John Greenleaf Whittier, William Cullen Bryant, and Henry Wadsworth Longfellow contributed to the "vogue of the Indian" in literature. Best-known fiction author of the period before the Civil War was James Fenimore Cooper. His Indian-frontier writings were bestsellers over a longer period than those of any American writer until the rise of Samuel Clemens (Mark Twain) in the 1870s. In an age of limited book production, by 1820 5 novels on Indian themes had been published; 15 appeared during the 1830s, and 39 novels during the 1840s. Between 1825 and 1860, 50 of the 190 plays published were on the Indian. Best known was John Augustus Stone's *Metamora, or King Phillip, Last of the Wampanoags*, which played to large audiences in the eastern United States for 20 years. Ranking next in public appeal was J. N. Barker's *Pocahontas, the Indian Princess*.

Many of these works were in the noble savage tradition and romanticized Indians and their life-style. Thus *Old Hicks Guide* (1848) introduces the reader to "Peaceful Valley" set in the Southwest. Cast in the theme of primitivism, it articulates "the decadent impulse to go back to nature," a characteristic "peculiar to the over-civilized" who seek "the original harmony with nature enjoyed by virtuous savages" who are guided by the "intuitive ethics of the wilderness." Indians are portrayed as "children of the ancient mother nature."[3]

Not all works published in this period were favorable to the Indian. Robert Montgomery Bird's *Nick of the Woods* (1837) has been rated as the "most memorable attempt" to destroy the image of the Indian as a noble savage. It presented Indians in the "maddened frontiersman's" viewpoint. Rather than an innocent child of nature, Bird characterized the Native American as a wild beast to be "exterminated." *Nick of the Woods,* one of the best sellers of the day, went through 25 editions.

The most damaging class of literature for the Indian image, however, was the captivity narrative. Clearly the hundreds of published memoirs of white captives who escaped or were liberated from their Indian captors were more than ego-serving sagas, sharing terror-filled ordeals with the reading public. More often each served a public purpose. Puritan accounts consistently denigrated Native Americans as "devils incarnate." Puritan religious leaders believed that captivity narratives were valuable for moral and religious instruction, and they encouraged their publication, writing several themselves. In their hands "Indian captivity became the symbolic equivalent of a journey into hell." On the other hand captivity accounts written during the era of national expansion (1820–1848) were tailored to the needs of the age, justifying territorial acquisition much like the ideology of Manifest Destiny. The Indian nations were obstacles to expansion, and writers of captivity accounts assured the reading public that Native Americans were "degenerates and therefore without right to the lands they inhabited." Moreover, it appeared

Will Rogers, Cherokee populist philosopher and entertainer. (Courtesy the Oklahoma Historical Society)

N. Scott Momaday, the Kiowa-Cherokee Pulitzer Prize winning author. (Copyright 1979 by Jim Kalett)

that many Americans in the antebellum age did not "want to read favorable accounts of a culture they were destroying." Clearly the utility of the captivity narratives extended beyond that of providing recreational reading. Throughout the nineteenth century they were applied to teach the young "reading, writing, history, and moral behavior ... and to perpetuate conventional attitudes, among them the conviction of white superiority."[4]

Literary interest in the Indian faded after 1860, a move that can be explained in part by increased preoccupation with blacks. Popularization of burlesque melodramas which ridiculed the Indian, including *Revamped Metamora or the Last of the Pollywogs* by John Brougham, was also responsible. Beadle and Adams Company publication of dime novels vulgarized

Native Americans. In 1860 this firm published *Malaeska,* the first of many scores of diatribes on the Indian, each in an edition of half a million copies. And postbellum popularity of evolution, particularly its doctrine of the struggle for survival, presumed to place the Indian in the role of an "inferior man." All these combined to consign the older literary image of the Indian to oblivion. Thereafter most historians ignored the Indians' role in national development, referring to them briefly by such epithets as "wild man," "viperous brood," "wild beasts in the path of civilization," "red peril," and "savage." Several writers categorically denied that the Indian provided any contribution to Anglo-American culture. Since 1960 the Indian has returned to literary "vogue." One of the leading sources on Indians, their culture, and their place in history is the Civilization of the American Indian series, published by the University of Oklahoma Press and presently numbering over 150 volumes.

Just as Indians have been the subject of literature, they have produced literature themselves. Elias Boudinot (Cherokee), John Rollin Ridge (Cherokee), and Alexander Posey (Creek) were prominent nineteenth-century writers. Twentieth-century Indian authors include Will Rogers (Cherokee), Lynn Riggs (Cherokee), John Oskisson (Cherokee), Vine DeLoria, Jr. (Sioux), Natachee Scott Momaday (Cherokee), Black Elk through John Neihardt (Sioux), Charles Eastman (Sioux), Gertrude Bonnin (Sioux), Emerson Blackhorse (Navajo), Alonzo Lopez (Papago), Juanita Platero (Navajo), and Siyowin Miller (Navajo). The best-known twentieth-century Indian writer is N. Scott Momaday (Kiowa-Cherokee) who was awarded the Pulitzer Prize in fiction in 1969 for his novel *House Made of Dawn.* Musician Jack Frederick Kilpatrick (Cherokee) has composed the ballet *Raven Mocker,* the opera *Blessed Wilderness,* and the lyrical suite *Autumn Love.*

The Indian contribution to the arts other than literature includes bone and ivory carving, etching, ceramics, weaving, and painting. Pueblo pottery and Navajo blankets, rugs, and jewelry, baskets by the Papagos and other southwestern tribes, and paintings by a growing corps of Native American artists long valued by private collectors, are increasingly popular items for display in museums.

Five of the major names in international ballet are of Indian descent, most of them Osage. Yvonne Chouteau at the age of fourteen was the youngest American ever accepted for the Company of Ballet Russe de Monte Carlo. She was a member of this famous group for 14 years and served 8 years as the acclaimed ballerina. Maria Tallchief at one time was the ranking ballerina in the United States; her sister Marjorie Tallchief was noted for her career with the Paris Ballet Company. And Rozella Hightower and Moscelyne Larkin were ballerinas with European groups including the Ballet Russe de Monte Carlo.

Although Western people have been reluctant to acknowledge the Indian legacy, they have widely appropriated Indian culture to enrich their way of life, particularly in government, borrowing models to fashion freedom-insuring institutions. Ironically, at the same time they have carried on a campaign to destroy Indians and to eradicate their culture, particularly their religion which was regarded as discourse with the Devil. As we have seen, in spite of centuries of effort by governments, missionaries, bureaucrats, and teachers, Indian culture has maintained a remarkable resiliency, continuity, and mystical determination to survive. For example, of the estimated 300 different Indian languages spoken at the time of discovery by tribes in that portion of the New World that became the United States, at least half survive and are in current use. Indians maintain separate social and political orders today by adhering to ancient kinship systems and lines of descent including clans and moieties, retain their traditional ways of naming, and marriage and family forms, and observe their festivals, ceremonials, dances, and religion.

Despairing of eradicating Indianness and destroying Indian culture, and

Maria Martinez, the potter of San Ildefonso Pueblo. (Courtesy Los Alamos Scientific Laboratory)

Harrison Begay's painting, "Navaho Weavers." (Philbrook Art Center)

suddenly desperate for new ways to resolve private and public malaise, Americans are showing an unexpected respect for Indian ways, particularly religion. John Collier claimed that Indians

had what the world had lost. They have it now. What the world has lost, the world must have again lest it die.... We have lost the way, and the power to live is dead. What . . . is this power to live? It is the ancient, lost reverence and passion for human personality, joined with the ancient lost reverence and passion for the earth and its web of life.[5]

Even the federal government, so long committed to destroying Indianness, is finally becoming its protector. In the beginning of national life, federal policy regarded the Indian tribes as sovereign nations in a state of "guardianship" to the federal government. In the nineteenth century the federal government adopted "a second approach which viewed the tribes as impediments to 'progress' (i.e. assimilation of individual Indians into white society)." Presently the federal government "views the tribes as positive vehicles necessary to insure the integrity of Indian culture."[6]

The judiciary, too, has become a protector of Indian culture, its decisions on aboriginal questions explaining to the public what Indian culture means to the greater society. In the landmark *People* v. *Woody* decision (1964), in which the California Supreme Court extended the constitutional right of freedom of religion to Indians, the justices stated:

In a mass society, which presses at every point toward conformity, the protection, of a self-expression, however unique, of the individual and the group becomes ever more important. The varying currents of the subcultures that flow into the mainstream of our national life give it depth and breadth. We preserve a greater value than an ancient tradition when we protect the rights of the Indians.[7]

There seems to be increasing acceptance of the belief that Native Americans might possess a "superior truth," derived from their nature-based religion, a transcendent wisdom which might provide a remedy for society's ills, particularly to counter its materialism. This was acknowledged in 1972 in Los Angeles when 3,000 theologians and biblical scholars convened in the American Academy of Religion Congress. They concluded that "the American Indian, whose culture was almost destroyed by the white man" who brought Christianity to "save him from his barbarism, may all the time have held the key to the survival of his conqueror and the foreign culture." This the theologians concluded because Indian religion "provided in its concept of the wholeness of man with nature a forgotten key to a viable theology for modern man." To a surprised world they stated "Indian religion must take its rightful place as one of the great religious traditions. . . . Indian religion has few new concepts and forms of faith, but offers fresh approaches to long held beliefs." These include the "importance of sacrifice, mutilation and suffering as a means to establish affinity with supernatural powers, and how these parallel the Christian crucifixion concept; the symbolism of rituals, which often are very intricate and meaningful." The Native American concept of "wholeness . . . in the Indian's view of himself and nature" must be regained by the greater society. The theologians concluded that the "calculated, methodical, cynical destruction of the native cultures and peoples found here was a global crime and the most notable vandalism of all history."[8]

Clearly, Native American contributions to national life are substantial. Besides exotic ways of life enriching the Anglo-American culture, the Indian's respect for nature has provided a compelling example for Anglo-Americans to emulate, inspiring the timely conservation, ecology, and save-the-earth movements. The Indian persistence in defeat, courageous stance in seemingly insurmountable adversity and toward awesome public suppression and persecution, preyed on the national conscience and eventually softened its prejudice. And Indian presence, as an unlike people in the Anglo-American community has, in recent times, tempered the nation's long-standing ethnocentrism and cultural monism and contributed to an emerging cultural pluralism.

Notes

1. Virgil J. Vogel, *The Indian in American History* (Chicago, 1968), p. 8.
2. Lucy Kramer Cohen (ed.), *The Legal Conscience: Selected Papers of Felix S. Cohen* (New Haven, Conn., 1960), pp. 315–27.
3. Henry Nash Smith, *Virgin Land: The American West as Symbol and Myth* (New York, 1950), p. 79.
4. James Levernier and Hennig Cohen (eds.), *The Indians and their Captives* (Westport, Conn., 1977), contains an analysis of this genre's use in national expansion.
5. Jack D. Forbes (ed.), *The Indian in America's Past* (Englewood Cliffs, N.J., 1964), pp. 31–32.
6. Michael Morgan Gibson, "Indian Policy and State Jurisdiction," *Environmental Protection Agency Position Paper* (1978), p. 7.
7. Jerry Muskrat, "The Constitution and the American Indian: Past and Prologue," *Hastings Constitutional Law Quarterly* 3 (Summer 1976), p. 677.
8. *Oklahoma Journal*, September 4, 1972.

Selected Sources

Indian contributions to Anglo-American culture and their treatment by writers is the subject Virgil J. Vogel, *The Indian in American History* (Chicago, 1968).

Interpretative works on the Indian as a literary figure and philosophical subject include Bernard W. Sheehan, "Paradise and the Noble Savage in Jeffersonian Thought," *William and Mary Quarterly* 26 (July 1969), pp. 327–359; Roy Harvey Pierce, *The Savages of America: A Story of the Indian and the Idea of Civilization* (Baltimore, 1953); Henry Nash Smith, *Virgin Land: The American West as Symbol and Myth* (New York, 1950); Wilcomb E. Washburn (ed.), *The Indian and the White Man* (New York, 1964); and Richard Slotkin, *Regeneration Through Violence: The Mythology of the American Frontier, 1600–1860* (Middletown, Conn., 1973).

Native American writers are discussed in Natachee Scott Momaday, *American Indian Authors* (1972).

GLOSSARY

Ababinili Omnipotent creative-directive force for the Southeastern tribes.

ABC: Americans Before Columbus Newspaper published by the National Indian Youth Conference.

Adena Earliest of Eastern moundbuilder cultures to develop, around 800 B.C.; concentrated in the Ohio River Valley.

Alaskan Federation of Natives Formed by Native Americans in Alaska in 1966 to guard their economic, political, and social interests.

Alaskan Native Brotherhood; Alaskan Native Sisterhood Founded by Alaskan aborigines in 1912 with missionary assistance to protect individual and group rights.

Algonkian A language family embracing many tribes, including Shawnees, Kickapoos, Delawares, Cheyennes, and Potawatomis.

American Indian Chicago Conference Conference in 1961, held on campus of University of Chicago where Indian leaders formulated new goals, including stress on self-determination.

American Indian Defense Association Founded in 1923 by John Collier to improve Indian status.

American Indian Federation Organization of Indian leaders opposed to the Indian Reorganization Act.

American Indian Movement (AIM) The most violently active of the contemporary Indian protest groups.

Americanization The primary goal of federal officials before 1934 to transform Indians, shorn of their native culture, into hybrid Americans.

Anasazi Most brilliant culture to develop in the Southwest during the Golden Age of Prehistory; located in the San Juan drainage of the Four Corners area. The people were preeminent as basket makers, construction engineers, and farmers.

Archaic Age Prehistoric era from the close of Pleistocene, around 8,000 B.C., to about 1200 B.C., characterized by intensive exploitation of the natural environment by the American Indian ancestors.

Archeomagnetism Method for dating ceramic pieces containing oxides of iron.

Artifact Material object made by people —a tool, weapon, vase.

Assimilation Acceptance and absorption of one social group by another.

Athapascan A language family embracing Apaches and Navajos.

Atlatl Prehistoric spear thrower made from stick about two feet long with a weight for balance and whip action.

Avuncular Under the matrilineal system, the mother's brothers are responsible for upbringing of her male children; their father cares for his sisters' children.

Beringia The natural causeway bridging Asia and North America during the Pleistocene Age.

Bidarka The light, waterproof, highly-maneuverable two-man Aleut hunting boat.

Black Drink Extract from the *cussena* plant, used as a ceremonial purgative to cleanse the worshiper and prepare him for the Busk ritual.

Blue Laws Statutes regulating personal behavior.

Bosch loopers Runners of the woods,

Dutch traders living much like the French *coureurs de bois.*

Bosque Redondo A site on the Pecos River in eastern New Mexico where Union troops concentrated the Mescalero Apaches and Navajos during the Civil War.

Burke Act 1906, deferred citizenship for Indians, promised by the General Allotment Act, 1887.

Busk The Green Corn Festival, an annual renewal rite celebrated by the Southeastern tribes.

Caddoan A language family embracing Wichitas, Caddoes, and Pawnees.

Calumet Highly ornamented flat pipe stem fitted with a stone elbow pipe, which tribal leaders smoked ceremonially.

Carbon 14 Dating Method for assigning a life date to an item by measuring the amount of Carbon 14 isotope present.

Cascade Man Sometimes called Old Cordilleran culture, 9,000 B.C. to 5,000 B.C.; Paleo-Indians residing in the Pacific Northwest.

Citizenship Act Approved by Congress in 1924, a statute extending United States citizenship to all Indians.

Clan A cluster of related families claiming a common ancestor.

Clovis Man Paleo-Indians present 15,000 B.C. to 11,000 B.C. They hunted the megafauna, and were identified by their distinctive projectile point, the Clovis, 3–6 inches long and fluted with channels cut on either side of the projectile face.

Cochise People Paleo-Indian pioneers in southern Arizona about 10,000 B.C. who developed a culture based on gathering and processing seeds and grains.

Columbian Mammoth Extinct elephantlike creature with huge tusks, weighing an average of six tons and standing nearly fourteen feet high.

Comancheros Spanish-American traders from the Rio Grande settlements who trafficked with the Southern Plains tribes.

Committee of One Hundred Formed in 1923 by Secretary of the Interior Hubert Work to review Indian policy and recommend reforms.

Communal Ownership The Indian tribes universally practiced common ownership of land. Title was vested in the tribe rather than the individual.

Composite Tribe Within a tribe, a change in culture and readaptation as characterized by the Plains tribes.

Corpus Juris Body of law.

Coup Count Record of a Plains warrior's feats of bravery.

Coureurs de Bois Independent French traders who lived more or less permanently with the Indians.

Creation Account Tradition held by most tribes of a common creation by a supernatural entity.

Cultural Monism The major group's expectation that unlike groups conform to a predetermined common pattern of culture.

Cultural Pluralism The majority group in a society respecting unlike lifeways and permitting their exercise.

Dawes Act The General Allotment Act of 1887, named for its author, United States Senator Henry L. Dawes of Massachusetts.

Death Cult A preoccupation of the Adena, Hopewell, and Mississippian cultures that placed national attention on funerary matters and after-life status.

Deganawidah Mythical folk-hero of the Iroquois.

Dendrochronology Determination of approximate dates of past events and periods of time by studying tree rings in wood present in the prehistoric site.

Desert Culture A life mode developed in the Utah portion of the Great Basin, about 10,000 B.C., based on gathering and processing seeds.

Dreamer Religion Established by the Shahaptian prophet Smohalla, stressed resistance to Americanization by Indians and meditation or dreaming to find "the way."

Economy The collective material pursuits of a people by which they sustain themselves.

Encomienda A system devised by the Spanish crown to convert Indians to Iberian civilization.

Eschatology The part of a religion that treats death, judgment, and future state of the soul.

Esperanto An artificial language, created in 1887, and offered as an international language.

Ethnocentrism The belief that one's own ethnic group and culture are superior to all others.

Ethnology Branch of anthropology concerned with the study of racial and ethnic groups in their origins, characteristics, distribution, and cultures.

Exogamy Marriage practice of requiring the bride and groom to be from different clans.

Exotic Milieu The environment of the Pleistocene Age, before 8,000 B.C.

Fee Simple Ownership Private ownership of land, largely based on the traditional English common-law practice of land tenure.

Friends of the Indian Well-intentioned, but generally misguided philanthropists and social reformers who, during the late nineteenth century, attempted to Americanize the Indian through allotment in severalty.

Folsom Man Paleo-Indians, 11,000 B.C. to somewhat after 8,000 B.C., who subsisted largely on the primordial bison. Identified by their distinctive projectile points, about 2 inches long and fluted like the Clovis.

Force Policy Favored by the military in the postwar era over the "Peace Policy" as the surest way to accomplish Americanization of the Indian.

General Allotment Act Enacted in 1887 to provide for partitioning reservations and assigning each resident Indian an allotment of land, a homestead generally of 160 acres in fee simple.

General Court The legislative body of Massachusetts Bay Colony, which adopted many laws attempting to regulate Indian life.

Geology Science that treats the origin and structure of the earth.

Ghost Dance Religion Founded by Tavibo and Wovoka during the later nineteenth century, stressing peace and special worship, which included dancing to receive the reward of restoration of cherished tribal ways.

Glottochronology A method of determining the age of a culture from the characteristics of its language.

Great American Desert The nineteenth-century popular view, fed by explorers, that the land west of Missouri was a veritable desert.

Guerrilla Warfare Military operations, generally of a nuisance raid type, carried out by irregular partisan military units.

Hand-to-Mouth Existence The practice of subsisting from day to day, largely by hunting and gathering, with no attempt to establish a surplus.

Hohokam High agrarian culture established in the Salt and Gila river valleys of southern Arizona. Emphasized village living, with singular irrigation works.

Hodesaunee Iroquois League of the Five Nations.

Hopewell Second of the moundbuilder cultures to develop, 200 B.C. to 500 A.D.; found in Ohio and lower Mississippi River valleys.

Hydrologic Cycle The flow of moisture from the ocean as water vapor to land where it precipitates and then drains back to the sea, where the process is repeated.

Indian New Deal The group of reform laws, including the Indian Reorganization Act, adopted by Congress during the 1930s to improve Native American status.

Indian Reorganization Act Also called the Wheeler-Howard Act and Indian Magna Carta, formulated largely by John Collier, Commissioner of Indian Affairs. Adopted in 1934, it concluded the federal government's Americanization program and permitted cultural pluralism for Indians.

Indian Rights Association Founded in 1882 by the Society of Friends (Quakers), this organization has worked for improvement in the Native American life.

Indio Capace A class of Indians regarded as sufficiently civilized by Spanish standards to function in Spanish colonial society.

Infantilism Morbid adult dependence.

Institution A principle, custom, or system that forms part of a society's culture; often a system to control individuals for the group's benefit.

Iroquoian A language family embracing the Cherokees, Mohawks, Senecas, Wyandots, and others.

Isolate Ability of certain Indian communities, isolated from the local and Mexican cultural streams, to develop a separate, satisfying existence.

Johnson O'Malley Act A part of the Indian New Deal; established to provide supplementary funds to local school districts for improvement of Indian education.

Katchina A small wooden colorfully decorated effigy or icon figure representing a tribal deity.

Lingua Franca Diplomatic language or jargon and trade patois of a region.

Linguistics The scientific study of languages.

Llano A Paleo-Indian hunting culture associated with the Clovis.

Manifest Destiny The national view during the nineteenth century that it was the American mission to expand to natural territorial limits.

Manitou Omnipotent creative-directive force for the Algonkians.

Mano The hand-held grinding stone used on the metate to process seeds and grains.

Mastodon Extinct elephant-like creature with large tusks, weighing an average of six tons and standing nearly fourteen feet high.

Matriarchate A community ruled by women, as was the case for the Iroquois Confederation.

Matrilineal Family form which is mother-centered; descent and property devolve through the female line.

Matrilocal Requirement that married couple reside with the wife's mother's clan.

Medicine An individual Indian's power derived from a supernatural source.

Megafauna The huge extinct creatures of the Pleistocene Age: the columbian mammoth, mastodon, and primordial bison.

Mercantilism The prevailing economic doctrine during the imperial age of Indian history, which stressed for each European nation self-sufficiency and the need for overseas colonies.

Meriam Commission During 1926 this group studied Indian problems and made a formal report to Congress recommending reforms.

Messianic Tradition The periodic appearance of Indian prophets.

Mestizo Mixed-blood Indian and European.

Metate Flat milling stone for processing seeds and grains.

Meteorology The science of atmospheric phenomenon; the study of weather of a particular place.

Migration Epic Tradition held by most tribes that their ancestors migrated from the West.

Millenial Doctrine Revealed teachings that stress the imminence of the earth's transformation, the prophet's return, and the judgment.

Mississippian The last of the Eastern moundbuilder cultures, 500 A.D. to 1250 A.D., concentrated in the Mississippi Valley.

Mogollon Desert dwellers of western New Mexico and eastern Arizona in the Archaic period. They were the first Native Americans in the present United States to adopt farming and pottery making.

Moiety A cluster of clans comprising a division, often one-half, of a tribe.

Monogamy Practice of having one spouse at a time.

Monogenesis View that American Indians were connected with known human sources in Europe, Asia, and Africa; from a common ancestor.

Moundbuilders People of the Adena, Hopewell, and Mississippian cultures who erected large structures as religious shrines, burial chambers, and residence sites.

Muskhogean A language family embracing the Natchez, Choctaws, Chickasaws, Creeks, and Seminoles.

National Completeness View held by leaders in the first third of the nineteenth century that the nation, having established settlements to the western border of Missouri, was complete in its land needs.

National Congress of American Indians Organization of tribal leaders formed during the 1940s and a continuing spokespiece for many Indians.

National Indian Defense Association Formed by Thomas A. Bland, 1885, a pioneer effort at protecting Indianness and promoting cultural pluralism.

National Indian Youth Conference Formed in 1961 by tribal youth to provide them a voice in policy reform.

Native American Church Chartered denomination, largely Indian in membership, and centering on sacramental use of peyote.

Nativism Practice by a people of returning to hallowed past lifestyles.

Naval Stores Forest products used in ship construction, including timbers, masts, pitch, and turpentine.

Neophyte Novice member of a religious order.

Obsidian Hydration Method for determining age of a tool or weapon made from volcanic glass by examining its water absorption rate.

Okipa Mandan religious rite including reenactment of folk drama centering on Mandan creation and maturation.

Orenda Omnipotent creative-directive force of the Iroquois.

Paleo-Indian A Native American of the Pre-Columbian Age; i.e., a Stone Age person.

Paleontology Science that treats ancient life forms.

Pan-Indian Association of Indians for a common cause without regard for tribal affiliation.

Particularism A characteristic of most Indian governments; local supremacy; autonomy of the town over the nation.

Patayan Agricultural peoples of the Prehistoric Age who resided in the Colorado River drainage, descendants of the Cochise People.

Patriarchate A community ruled by men.

Patrilineal Family form which is father-centered; descent and property devolve through the male line.

Patrilocal Requirement that married couple reside with the husband's father's clan or people.

Patroon Dutch landed proprietor in New Netherland.

Peace Policy Formulated by President Ulysses S. Grant, applying a pacific approach to speed the Americanization of Indians. Terminated in 1877.

Permit Holder A licensed non-Indian residing in Indian Territory during the postwar era.

Peyote Turnip-shaped fruit of *Lophophora williamsii* cactus, used in Indian worship as a sacrament.

Pharmacopoeia Collection of standard formulas and methods for the preparation of medicines.

Phonetics The system of sounds of a language.

Plano Sometimes called Plainview, a hunting-gathering culture, 7500 B.C. to 4500 B.C. which bridged the Paleo and Archaic periods of prehistory.

Pleistocene Age Pre-8000 B.C., when much of the Northern Hemisphere was covered with a thick ice cap.

Polyandry Plural marriage; wife with more than one husband.

Polygamy Plural marriage; more than one spouse.

Polygenesis View that American Indians were the result of a separate, local creation.

Polygyny Plural marriage; husband with more than one wife.

Polity The constitutional-political form by which a people is governed.

Polynesian Brown-skinned people of Polynesia, of Malay stock stemming from a Caucasian strain of Asia.

Polytheistic Belief in and worship of multiple deities.

Potlatch Public sharing of one's goods.

Pre-Columbian Age Term used by prehistorians to designate the time in America before the European advent.

Pre-Projectile Point Stage Period before 25,000 years ago, when ancestors of the American Indian used undifferentiated pieces of wood and stone for weapons and tools.

Primordial Bison An extant bison, twice as large as the modern American bison or buffalo.

Promyshlenniki Russian fur traders in North America.

Reconstruction Process fashioned by federal officials whereby the Confederate Indian nations reestablished their wardship relationship with the United States.

Red Power Mobilization of the collective ethnic consciousness and pride in Indianness to benefit Native Americans.

Red Progressives Educated Native Americans who, during the early twentieth century, attempted to reform Indian policy and improve Indian status.

Regula The rules and regulations set by clerics for Indians at the Spanish missions.

Relocation Federal policy formulated after 1950, which sought to transfer Indians from rural and reservation areas to urban areas.

Repartimiento An annual levy on the Indians for labor and produce, collected by Spanish officials.

Requerimiento The royal decree read by conquistadors to tribes informing them of their duty to the crown.

Restoration The common promise of Indian messiahs; the return of old, hallowed ways.

Retribalization The fusing of several tribal remnants with a new tribal name.

Riparian People Indians living near a river bank and practicing irrigation.

Sachem Iroquois chieftain.

Sandia Man Traces found in Sandia Mountain caves near Albuquerque indicating pioneer effort in technological advance by Indian ancestors, including Sandia point, a large stone spear point.

Savanna Relatively level land covered with low vegetation, largely coarse grass.

Sedentary A condition where a people abandon migratory hunting and gathering and establish a permanent residence site, generally to take up agriculture.

Self-Determination The quest of modern Indians—to have a voice in formulating the policies that direct their lives.

Sewan Small shells that Indians fashioned into wampum belts.

Shaker Religion Founded by the Puget Sound Indian, Squsachtum; included symbolic brushing off of sins which led to name "Shakers."

Shaman The priest and healer among certain tribes.

Siouian Language family embracing many tribes, including the Osages, Poncas, Kanzas, Santees, and Tetons.

Society of American Indians Organization formed in 1911 by Native American leaders to reform Indian status from the Indian viewpoint.

Sodality Social and functional grouping.

Spiro Westernmost extension of the Mississippian moundbuilder culture, situated in the Arkansas and Poteau river valleys of eastern Oklahoma, site of rich archeological sites.

Squaw Man Intermarried non-Indian, by tribal law eligible for all tribal benefits, including use of tribal land.

Staple A basic food; i.e. corn, buffalo meat, fish, acorns.

Stratigraphy The order and relative position of the strata of the earth's crust.

Sun Dance Sioux and other Plains tribes observed this annual renewal rite, which included warrior self-torture to edify the nation's spiritual state.

Swanneken Indian name for Dutch colonists.

Syllabary A list or table of syllables, or a list of characters representing syllables.

Taboos Restrictions or bans founded on custom or social convention.

Taovayas Wichita and Caddo tribesmen who served as middle men for French traders in the Southwest.

Technology The ability of a people to produce material things.

Termination A federal Indian policy followed during the 1950s which sought to conclude the national government's relationship with the Indian tribes.

Theocracy State dominated by religious authorities; state functions as an arm of the religious establishment.

Travertine Mineralized layers on cave floors formed by water dripping from cave ceilings.

Triblet A small grouping of Native Americans, generally composed of several families or villages, characteristic of many of the California Indian communities.

Tsa-La-Ghi Contemporary Cherokee folk drama.

Uto-Aztecan A language family embracing the Paiutes, Shoshones, and Comanches.

Values Beliefs, standards, and moral precepts.

Wakan Omnipotent creative-directive force of the Sioux.

Walloons French-speaking Calvinists from the Low Countries who settled in New Netherland.

Wampum Belts Red, white, and black shell belts used by Native Americans to communicate peace, war, and other international messages.

Wardship Status of each Indian under federal jurisdiction; each Indian after 1871 became a ward of the United States.

Woodland A stage in prehistoric Indian cultural evolution, characteristic of the Eastern tribes on the eve of the European advent when the Native Americans reached the ultimate adaptation to their environment.

Yasak Tribute, 10 percent of value, levied by Russian imperial government on the fur trade.

INDEX

14 15